REGIONALISM AND MODERN EUROPE

Also available from Bloomsbury:

WRITING THE HISTORY OF NATIONALISM,
edited by Stefan Berger and Eric Storm

NATIONALISM IN MODERN EUROPE: POLITICS, IDENTITY,
AND BELONGING SINCE THE FRENCH REVOLUTION
by Derek Hastings

HISTORIES OF NATIONALISM IN IRELAND AND GERMANY: A
COMPARATIVE STUDY FROM 1800 TO 1932
by Shane Nagle

REGIONALISM AND MODERN EUROPE

IDENTITY CONSTRUCTION AND MOVEMENTS FROM 1890 TO THE PRESENT DAY

Edited by
Xosé M. Núñez Seixas and Eric Storm

BLOOMSBURY ACADEMIC
LONDON • NEW YORK • OXFORD • NEW DELHI • SYDNEY

BLOOMSBURY ACADEMIC
Bloomsbury Publishing Plc
50 Bedford Square, London, WC1B 3DP, UK
1385 Broadway, New York, NY 10018, USA

BLOOMSBURY, BLOOMSBURY ACADEMIC and the Diana logo are trademarks
of Bloomsbury Publishing Plc

First published in Great Britain 2019

Copyright © Xosé M. Núñez Seixas, Eric Storm and Contributors, 2019

Xosé M. Núñez Seixas and Eric Storm have asserted their right under the Copyright, Designs
and Patents Act, 1988, to be identified as Editors of this work.

Cover design by Toby Way
Cover image © Bibliothèque nationale de France, département Estampes et photographie, El-13

All rights reserved. No part of this publication may be reproduced or
transmitted in any form or by any means, electronic or mechanical,
including photocopying, recording, or any information storage or retrieval
system, without prior permission in writing from the publishers.

Bloomsbury Publishing Plc does not have any control over, or responsibility for, any third-party
websites referred to or in this book. All internet addresses given in this book were correct at the
time of going to press. The author and publisher regret any inconvenience caused if addresses
have changed or sites have ceased to exist, but can accept no responsibility for any such changes.

A catalogue record for this book is available from the British Library.

A catalog record for this book is available from the Library of Congress.

ISBN: HB: 978-1-4742-7520-0
PB: 978-1-4742-7519-4
ePDF: 978-1-4742-7521-7
eBook: 978-1-4742-7522-4

Typeset by Newgen KnowledgeWorks Pvt. Ltd., Chennai, India
Printed and bound in Great Britain

To find out more about our authors and books visit www.bloomsbury.com
and sign up for our newsletters.

CONTENTS

List of Figures   vii
List of Maps   viii
List of Contributors   ix

1. **Introduction: Region, Nation and History**   1
   Xosé M. Núñez Seixas and Eric Storm

2. **Language and Regionalism**   25
   Johannes Kabatek

3. **Regionalism and Folklore**   43
   David Hopkin

4. **Nature: From Protecting Regional Landscapes to Regionalist Self-Assertion in the Age of the Global Environment**   65
   Jan-Henrik Meyer

5. **Regional Foods**   83
   Kolleen M. Guy

6. **Tourism and the Construction of Regional Identities**   99
   Eric Storm

7. **Fascism and Regionalism**   119
   Xosé M. Núñez Seixas

8. **Communism and Regionalism**   135
   Susan Smith-Peter

9. **Democracy and Regionalism in Western Europe**   151
   Daniele Petrosino

10. **Regionalism and Its Diverse Framings in German-Speaking Europe across the Long Twentieth Century**   169
    Jeremy DeWaal

Contents

11 Scandinavia: Regionalism in the Shadow of Strong States 193
   Peter Stadius

12 Regionalism in the Low Countries 213
   Joep Leerssen

13 Regionalism in South-Western Europe: France, Spain, Italy and Portugal 233
   Xosé M. Núñez Seixas and Fernando Molina

14 Borderlands, Provinces, Regionalisms and Culture
   in East-Central Europe 251
   Irina Livezeanu and Petru Negură

15 Regionalism in Russia 271
   Mark Bassin and Mikhail Suslov

16 Baltic and Polish Regionalism(s): Concepts, Dimensions and Trajectories 291
   Jörg Hackmann

17 Regionalism in South-Eastern Europe 307
   Tchavdar Marinov

18 The Emergence of Conjoined Nationalisms and Regionalisms
   in the British Isles 323
   James Kennedy

19 Conclusion: Overcoming Methodological Regionalism 343
   Xosé M. Núñez Seixas and Eric Storm

Index 355

FIGURES

6.1	Poster Parador de Gredos.	106
6.2	Amsterdam metropolitan area map.	112
7.1	Valencia, 26 April 1939. Women wearing the regional dress salute the Francoist troops.	126
7.2	Madrid, 27 October 1940. The Reichsführer SS Heinrich Himmler visits a folklore performance during his stay in Madrid.	127
10.1	Map of approximated German dialect groupings (1894).	171
10.2	Map of the federal states and provinces of Prussia in the Weimar Republic in 1925.	177
10.3	*Heimat* journal publication in the territories of West Germany (including the Saarland, excluding West Berlin) in the long twentieth century.	178
10.4	Observations of the expellee 'Day of *Heimat*' in Berlin 1955.	182
11.1	Dala Horse, New York World Fair, 1939.	197
11.2	Travel in Swedish Finland.	205
12.1	The linguistic landscape of the Low Countries.	214
17.1	Campaign poster of the Istrian Democratic Assembly from 2016.	312

MAPS

1	Regions in Northern Europe	xii
2	Regions in Southern Europe	xiii
3	Regions in Eastern Europe	xiv

CONTRIBUTORS

Mark Bassin is Baltic Sea Professor of the History of Ideas, in the Center for Baltic and East European Studies at Södertörn University in Stockholm. His research focuses on problems of space, ideology and identity in Russia and Germany. His most recent monograph is *The Gumilev Mystique: Biopolitics, Eurasianism and the Construction of Community in Modern Russia* (2016), and he has co-edited the collections *Between Europe and Asia: The Origins, Theories, and Legacies of Russian Eurasianism* (2015), *Eurasia 2.0: Russian Geopolitics in the Age of New Media* (2016) and *The Politics of Eurasianism* (2017).

Jeremy DeWaal is a postdoctoral fellow at the Friedrich-Alexander-University Erlangen-Nuremberg (after January 2019, lecturer in History at the University of Exeter) and is a scholar of modern German history. His book manuscript, entitled *Geographies of Renewal: Heimat and Democratization in Postwar West Germany*, examines a turn to local and regional sites of Heimat in the aftermath of the Second World War as sites of imagined life after death, federalism and alternative sources of European and democratic identification.

Kolleen M. Guy is associate professor of history at the University of Texas at San Antonio. She has published on regional foods and identity and is the author of the award-winning book *When Champagne Became French: Wine and the Making of French Identity, 1820–1920* (2003; paperback 2007).

Jörg Hackmann is Alfred Doeblin Professor of East European History at the University of Szczecin, Poland, and is also associated with the University of Greifswald, Germany. He has been a visiting scholar at several universities in the Baltic Sea region, as well as the University of Chicago. His research focuses on spatial conceptualizations, collective memory and civil society in Central and Eastern Europe.

David Hopkin is professor of European social history at the University of Oxford where his specialist field is oral culture, including the valorization of oral culture by regionalists in Lorraine, Brittany, the Basque Country and Flanders. He is also on the Council of the Folklore Society. His study of folk songs and tales as sources for social history – *Voices of the People in Nineteenth Century France* (2012) – won that society's Katharine Briggs prize. He has also co-edited the collections *Folklore and Nationalism in Europe during the Long Nineteenth Century* (2012) and *Rhythms of Revolt: European Traditions and Memories of Social Conflict in Oral Culture* (2018).

Contributors

Johannes Kabatek is a professor of Ibero-Romance linguistics at the University of Zurich (Switzerland). His areas of research include synchronic and diachronic aspects of the evolution of the Romance languages. For more information, see http://www.rose.uzh.ch/de/seminar/personen/kabatek.html.

James Kennedy is senior lecturer in sociology at the University of Edinburgh. He is author of *Liberal Nationalisms: Empire, State and Civil Society in Scotland and Quebec*, which was awarded the Canadian Sociology Association's John Porter Prize. His current research, with Liliana Riga, explores the role of American policymakers in the twentieth-century post-war settlements which shaped East-Central Europe.

Joep Leerssen is chair of modern European literature at the University of Amsterdam, and a member of the Royal Netherlands Academy of Arts and Sciences. A comparatist and cultural historian, he has extensively written on Irish cultural history, imagology, transnational diffusion of nationalist ideas and cultural nationalism in Europe. His most recent publications are *National Thought in Europe* (2006) and (ed.) *Encyclopedia of Romantic Nationalism in Europe* (Amsterdam, 2018 University Press, 2 vols).

Irina Livezeanu is associate professor of East-Central European history at the University of Pittsburgh. She is especially interested in cultural history, intellectuals, nationalism and regionalism. Her first book published by Cornell University Press was entitled *Cultural Politics in Greater Romania: Regionalism, Nation Building, and Ethnic Struggle, 1918–1930* (1995, 2nd updated edition 2000).

Tchavdar Marinov is adjunct lecturer at the Plovdiv University. His research interests include the construction of national ideologies and historiographies, as well as the invention of national cultural heritage in the Balkans. He is the author of *La question macédonienne de 1944 à nos jours: Communisme et nationalisme dans les Balkans* (2010) and *Nos ancêtres les Thraces: Usages idéologiques de l'Antiquité en Europe du Sud-Est* (2016), and has also co-edited three collective volumes on modern and contemporary Balkan history and heritage policies.

Jan-Henrik Meyer is an associate professor at the University of Copenhagen and an associate researcher at the Centre for Contemporary History, Potsdam. He specializes in European history, environmental history, the history of social movements and international organizations.

Fernando Molina is a tenured research fellow in modern history at the University of the Basque Country. His main research interests are Spanish nationalism, nation-building and political violence. He has published articles in *Nations and Nationalism*, *Ethnic and Racial Studies*, *European History Quarterly* and *Journal of Contemporary History*, and co-edited *ETA's Terrorist Campaign: From Violence to Politics, 1968–2015* (2017).

Xosé M. Núñez Seixas is full professor of modern history at the University of Santiago de Compostela, and has also taught at the Ludwig-Maximilian University of Munich (2012–2017). He has authored or co-authored more than a dozen books on nationalist movements, national and regional identities, the history of migration and the cultural and social history of war in the twentieth century. His latest books are *Die spanische Blaue Division an der Ostfront (1941–1945)* (2016) as well as (ed.) *Metaphors of Spain* (2017) and *War Veterans and the World After 1945* (Routledge, 2018).

Petru Negură is associate professor at the Free International University of Moldova and researcher at the Centre for Studies in Sociology and Social Psychology in Chisinau. He received his PhD in sociology from the École des Hautes Études en Sciences Sociales (Paris). He authored the monograph *Ni héros, ni traîtres: Les écrivains moldaves face au pouvoir soviétique sous Staline* (2009), re-edited in Romanian translation in 2014 (2014).

Daniele Petrosino is associate professor of sociology at the Department of Political Sciences of the Aldo Moro University of Bari. He specializes in ethnonationalism, ethnic relations and migration, with particular attention to the problems of identity and recognition. His last co-edited book is *Buonanotte Mezzogiorno* (2016).

Susan Smith-Peter is associate professor of history at the College of Staten Island/City University of New York. She is the author of *Imagining Russian Regions: Subnational Identity and Civil Society in Nineteenth-Century Russia* (2018) and has published widely on regions and regionalism.

Peter Stadius is a historian, professor in Nordic Studies and research director at the Centre for Nordic Studies at the University of Helsinki. His research focus includes the north as a macro region and the mental mapping of north and south in an European perspective.

Eric Storm is associate professor of European history at Leiden University. His research interests include Spanish history and the construction of regional and national identities in Western Europe. He is the author of *The Culture of Regionalism: Art, Architecture and International Exhibitions in France, Germany and Spain, 1890–1940* (2010), as well as co-editor of *Region and State in Nineteenth-Century Europe: Nation-Building, Regional Identities and Separatism* (2012) and *Writing the History of Nationalism* (2019).

Mikhail Suslov is an assistant professor at the Department of Cross-Cultural and Regional Studies, University of Copenhagen. He studies Russian history of ideas and ideologies with a special focus on right-wing political and geopolitical imagination. His most recent publications include '"Russian World" Concept: Post-Soviet Geopolitical Ideology and the Logic of "Spheres of Influence"', *Geopolitics* (2018) and 'Bigger Is Better: Continent Eurasia in Russian Geopolitical Imagination', in *Russland und/als Eurasien: Kulturelle Konfigurationen*, ed. Ch. Engel and B. Menzel (2018).

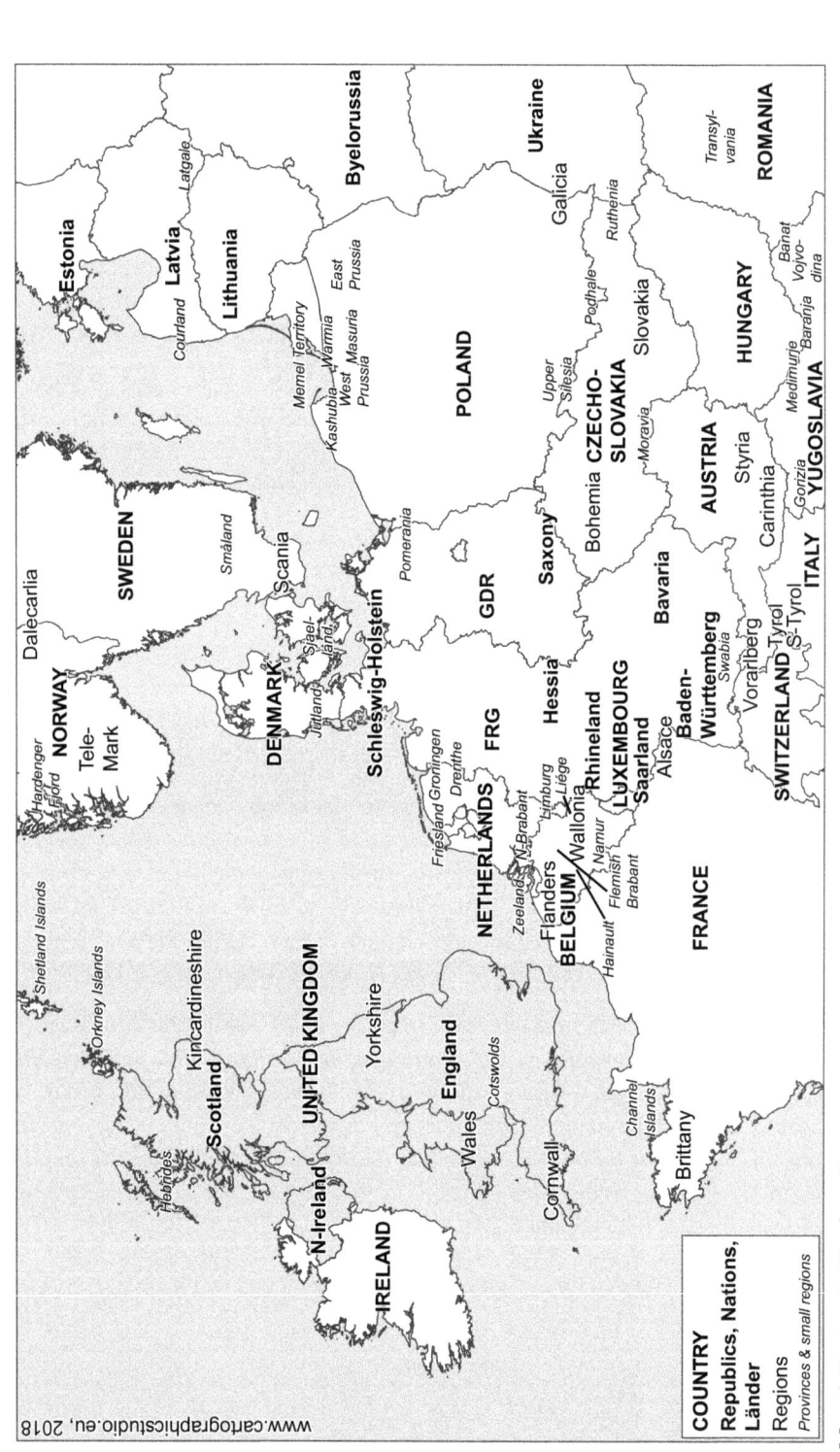

Map 1 Regions in Northern Europe.

Map 2 Regions in Southern Europe.

Map 3 Regions in Eastern Europe.

CHAPTER 1
INTRODUCTION: REGION, NATION AND HISTORY
Xosé M. Núñez Seixas and Eric Storm

On 13 October 2017, Jean-Claude Juncker, the president of the European Commission, criticized the attempt of the Catalan regional government to secede from Spain by saying, 'I would not like a European Union [. . .] that consists of 98 states', adding, 'It's already difficult with 28 [member states]', but 'with 98 it would be impossible'.[1] Obviously, there were legal obstacles as well to accepting the actions of the separatists, since the Catalan referendum on independence, held less than two weeks before, had been declared illegal by the Spanish Constitutional Court and its turnout amounted to barely 43 per cent of the regional electorate. Nevertheless, it is quite ironic that Juncker should oppose a territory much larger than his native Luxembourg becoming a new nation state: the state of Luxembourg actually consists of less than half of the original duchy of the same name, has only about half a million inhabitants and only became an independent sovereign state in 1890 by dynastic coincidence. Catalonia, on the other hand, is a prosperous region with approximately 7.5 million inhabitants and would be a middle-sized state comparable to Austria or Finland.

Luxembourg is therefore considered a nation state, although its size is very limited and it does not have a very unified national culture. Its official languages are German, French and Luxembourgish, which is a Franconian language also spoken in neighbouring areas of Germany, France and Belgium. Catalonia, on the other hand, remains for the moment a region (autonomous community) of Spain, since the attempt to proclaim an independent republic ended in failure. Although, officially, the region is bilingual, and Spanish remains the mother tongue of over half of its inhabitants, Catalan is the primary language of education; Catalan culture is thriving and about half of the electorate consistently votes for nationalist parties. Several scholars therefore argue that Catalonia – like Scotland, Quebec or Kurdistan – is a nation without a state.[2]

However, in this case the picture is also more complicated, since the Catalan language and culture does not exclusively belong to Catalonia; the language is spoken in a much wider area from the Roussillon region, on the French side of the Pyrenees, to Guardamar in the south-east of Spain, while also including the Balearic Islands. Catalan is even the official language of the independent principality of Andorra. Although some inhabitants of the other Catalan-speaking areas within Spain sympathize with the attempt of the regional government in Barcelona to create an independent state, most of them are satisfied with the considerable level of autonomy that their regions have and do not feel any inclination to join the Catalan nationalists. In the region of Valencia, there is even a clear tendency to distinguish its own version of the Catalan language as Valencian.

In Roussillon, the Catalan cultural heritage is only celebrated by a limited number of associations which can be subsumed under the label of cultural regionalism. Cultural regionalism is combined with forms of political regionalism in the Balearic Islands and in the Autonomous Community of Valencia (which includes the provinces of Valencia, Alicante and Castellón). Although many inhabitants of the Autonomous Community of Catalonia define themselves as nationalists, others would prefer the label of regionalists, while a considerable part of the population even prioritizes their belonging to the Spanish nation over any regional feelings. In the case of Andorra, Catalan is the only official language of the state, but, in practice, many inhabitants speak Spanish, French, Galician or Portuguese, the latter two because of a large group of immigrants from Galicia and Portugal.

Therefore, the distinction between region and (nation) state is rather arbitrary and the result of historical contingency, as is the distinction between regional and national identities. Catalan culture (and ethnicity) can form the basis for regional identities in Valencia, the Balearic Islands and Roussillon, but also of national identities in Andorra and the territory of Catalonia. There is consequently no clearly defined Catalan people that slowly became aware of its shared history and heritage, while developing the wish to create its own independent nation state. One could even argue that a Catalan national identity is largely the product of the autonomous status of Catalonia.

In *Regionalism in Modern Europe*, we try to disentangle some of these complexities and provide them with a historical background, covering the period from the late nineteenth century until the present. Distinguished specialists from various disciplines examine the process of regional identity construction and regional movements – both of a cultural and political nature – in all parts of the continent. Before explaining the objectives and structure of the volume in more detail, we will first discuss the historiographical debate on regionalism and regional identity construction and provide some definitions.[3]

The historiographical debate (1970s–2017)

The general shift in the historical analysis of territorial identities, nationalism and ethnicity that has taken place in social sciences since the late 1980s has led historians from structuralism to postmodernism and from privileging the study of the 'social preconditions' where nationalism emerges and develops (as was common in the 1970s and 1980s) to researching the cultural processes of territorial identity-building, as well as their reception and reproduction by individuals. This development has also affected the study of regionalism. A parallel phenomenon that has helped focus research on subnational identities was the increasing necessity to study the dynamics of nation-building from below, by adopting a micro-historical outlook that owed much to new directions in historiography from the late 1970s, which emphasized the role of individuals and communities in shaping their own destiny. This approach uncovered multiple hybrid identities and national imaginaries perceived through the mirror of local and subnational realities. Contrary to the assertions of some classic approaches to nation-building (beginning with Eugen Weber's *Peasants into Frenchmen*, 1976), it revealed that becoming national did not necessarily mean ceasing to be local or giving up one's hometown pride.[4]

The basic questions in current research on nationalism may also be applied to regions, regional identities and regionalism. First, the chicken-and-egg question: What came first, the regions or the regional identity? Moreover, are regions given pre-existing entities, or are they rather a construct of regionalist doctrines and movements? Why are some regions successfully constructed or even invented while others are not? Are regional identities complementary or opposed to national identities? These questions could be broadened by relativizing the term 'regionalism' and including other territorial dimensions within it. Is localism a complementary phenomenon to regionalism, or is it more compatible with state nationalism, which tends to enhance local (and urban) identities, seeing them as less threatening?

Any attempt at an exhaustive compilation is doomed to failure, given the huge amount of literature dealing with particular territorial units across the Old Continent. However, some remarks can be made about the terminology used. *Regionalism* was an extremely diffuse concept at the start of the twentieth century. The term was coined at the end of the nineteenth century and applied principally to the French situation – although, in the 1880s, the term was also being used in public debates in Spain.[5] In 1911, the founder of the Fédération Régionaliste Française, Jean Charles-Brun, stated that the term 'regionalism' was successful precisely because of its lack of precision. By that time, 'regionalism' meant everything that questioned the 'excesses' of state centralism, from the revival of substate folk cultures, local and provincial architecture and arts, the organization of local fairs or the demand for administrative decentralization, up to the more ambitious political goals of the early Breton or Basque nationalist groupings.[6] This broad category, although centred more on the demands of national movements of East-Central and Western Europe, was taken up again by the French historian Charles Seignobos, who used the label 'autonomism' to differentiate political demands for self-government from cultural claims.[7]

Regionalism and, to some extent, *localism* have played a highly ambiguous role in European history. Regional identities helped fashion the national states that arose in the nineteenth century.[8] Yet, the resilience of some territorial identities forged during the pre-modern period also contributed to the emergence of several substate nationalisms opposed to the existence of a single nation identified with the territory of the state and advocating self-determination for their specific territories. In fact, regionalist forerunners have generally preceded, but also accompanied, the emergence of substate nationalisms. The many examples of this, from Catalonia to Brittany, make good case studies in the ambiguous processes of region- and nation-building.

A clear definition of *what a region is* seems as complex and elusive as defining what a *nation* is. Geographers, economists, political and social scientists have considered regions to be economic entities, historical territories, frontier areas and geographical units bounded by natural features, but they can also be regarded as a form of collective identity, as an imagined community. A region can be described as a smaller territorial part of a bigger whole, either with administratively defined borders or linked to emotionally defined spatial categories that may act as links between the individual and collective sentiments of belonging, such as *Heimat, paese, terruño* and *kraj*. These may be considered an extension of the landscape and characteristics of the space that defines everyday experiences.[9] The region – or any form of local demarcation – is not a pre-existing entity, or a 'natural' alternative to the nation state. The contents of a region, its territorial limits and its inclusive or exclusive character cannot be defined objectively unless the objects of study are 'physical' regions defined by landscape and nature. In fact, the region is a constructed identity, dependent on social agency. Its members never come into personal contact with all others, and, as such, the region is a putative group, constructed upon the performative utterance of those who claim its existence or believe in it. Similarly, the region can be both a cultural construct and the result of public policy or of a region-building effort carried out by institutions and intellectuals. The question is, To what extent can *region-builders* be identified with *nation-builders*? To focus a research agenda on the local sphere and the region does not imply embracing a new '*regio*-primordialism'; it instead involves determining whether that sphere of identification has been more or less successful in relation to others.

To what extent is it possible to analytically differentiate regionalism from nationalism? Most authors rarely identify any differences between them, basically because *regionalism* has been given little attention in the 'classic' nationalism studies.[10] The term 'regional nationalism' has been also coined to refer to substate nationalist movements, going all the way from the Czech movement in the nineteenth century to the Sardinian one in the twentieth century. It is a commonly used term among historians and political scientists, and some use regionalism and minority nationalism quite interchangeably.[11] 'Regionalist' is used by most francophone authors to refer to ethnonationalist movements in Europe, *particularly* in Western Europe. Some scholars, primarily political scientists, have argued that regionalism has three characteristics in common with minority nationalisms: 1) the shaping of a territorially-bound collective identity; 2) the development of a cultural, economic or political centre/periphery conflict with the state; and 3) the existence of social mobilization and/or political organizations of a territorial (i.e. *regional*) character. Thus, regionalism and minority nationalism could be considered as two parallel products resulting from the existence of both an ethno-territorial conflict and social mobilization, with diffuse lines of demarcation.[12] These lines tend to be flexible and subject to change, although two common underlying elements are *ethnic* mobilization – understanding ethnicity broadly as a social construction of differences based on some malleable combination of primordial elements – and a demand for the territory of interest to be considered a political unit.

Is one to assume that regionalism always serves as the first expression of an ideology that may develop further, into a minority or substate nationalism? Or can regionalism also be seen as a very different phenomenon, intrinsically linked to state nationalism?

Introduction

Some classical definitions of nationalism presupposed that an increase in social communication and a weakening of substate identities were necessary preconditions for nation-building. Regional identities were therefore implicitly perceived as pre-modern vestiges and opposed to national identities.[13] The *modern* form of collective identity, which was also linked to the legitimacy of power, was to be the nation, which was to become the subject of sovereignty; the regions would remain only as areas of traditional culture, rural values and so on. This perspective permeated historical research on the topic until the early 1990s, holding that the survival of mesoterritorial or medium-range identities and of any form of regional claims during the modern period should be seen as a symptom of weak nation-building and a possible forerunner of minority nationalism.

Similar positions resulted from some of the debates during the 1980s and early 1990s regarding Italian and Belgian historiographies of nation- and state-building in the modern period. All of them claimed that their countries had experienced weak nationalization, expressed as an inverted mirror in the survival of subnational loyalties. Subnational, and particularly regional, assertiveness was regarded as a symptom of weak nation-building and unfulfilled state modernization. This assumption has also decisively influenced French and Spanish academic research on the national question. In the Spanish case, for instance, historical studies of Basque, Catalan or Galician nationalism has led historians in other Spanish regions to highlight any form of regional affirmation and/or local claim for autonomy by applying the same explanatory scheme to all cases. Something similar happened to France in the 1970s: the model applied to Brittany seemed to be valid for many other territories. Regionalism was seen as a forerunner of minority nationalism and, regardless of ideology, all possible predecessors (including federal republicans, monarchists, cultural folklorists, etc.) were lumped into a sort of catch-all movement that would surely result in the emergence of a new substate nationalism. Perhaps only British historians, who were very aware of the exceptional nature of the national question on their island(s), regarded the concept of unity in diversity as a natural outcome of an imperial state. The survival of a post-imperial identity, now reduced to its insular core, would still allow for the integration of different nations into a common polity, in much the same way as the Austro-Hungarian or the Ottoman empires had managed to maintain regional and territorial diversity within their borders before the First World War. Here, the alternative concept of territorial *loyalty* has been recently proposed as a polyvalent concept, which makes it possible for historians to apprehend the complexity of territorial belongings and their mutations over time.[14]

Recent research, however, has undermined the classical assertion of region-building as an opposite to nation-building. Some scholars have even theorized that nation-building may also imply building regional or local identities, to the point that the former may depend heavily on the latter, or vice versa. Collective identities, and territorial loyalties, may be regarded as a series of overlapping and complementary concentric spheres – like the layers of an onion – that result from dynamic historical processes,[15] as do all forms of collective identity. In many cases, nationalist movements, 'nationalizing' states and long-established nation states that carried out nation-building policies also reaffirmed local and regional identities in order to strengthen the roots of national identity among the population. Moreover, this phenomenon occurred in diverse currents and varieties of nationalism, as can be seen, for example, in nineteenth-century Germany or in the Soviet Union under Stalin. Promoting regional symbols and patterns of identity was regarded as a way of promoting *national* identities at the grass-roots level. The case of Germany demonstrated this: love for the *Heimat* implied love for the *Vaterland,* as the *Heimat* – a concept also invented at the end of the nineteenth century – could be extended to a local, classless national community.[16] From the Social Democrats to the Nazis, many social and political actors played the regionalism and *Heimat* card, and continued to use similar packaging of local identity images to give support to divergent worldviews.[17]

This was not always the case with other European nation states. In the French case, the increasing concern with the cult of 'local memories' expressed by small-towns librarians, antiquarians, historians and 'middling provincials' was not able to supersede the big debates – Monarchy versus Republic – that affected French political life during the nineteenth century. Still, local nostalgia was often linked with a preference for the social models that were identified with the past.[18] During the Third Republic, on the other hand, regional identification was stimulated from above, especially through education, where the local and regional sphere were encompassed within the larger whole of the nation.[19] In fact, although some forms of regional identity can come into conflict with the national identity, this does not always happen. Regional identities can be sustained by a more or less invented historical tradition, or they may be founded on common cultural traits, fostered by the prior existence of collective political institutions and the production of symbolic frames of meaning that help members of the *region* to identify themselves as members of a community.[20]

The relationships between empire-, nation- and region-building are not fixed but are subject to constant change over time.[21] However, not all forms of collective identity have a similar political dimension, and not all expressions of subnational identity are infused with present-day political consequences, such as the claim for self-determination, which is exclusive to the realm of nationalism and may turn into open separatism. The same could be said regarding the sensitive aspects of territorial identity; not all sentiments of belonging possess the same level of emotional appeal. The nation is invested with sacredness and strong affective ties, while this is not always the case with subnational identities, although it could be argued that, in dying for the nation, many soldiers also died for the tangible and familiar meanings of the homeland, associated with the places they had experienced. This gave common people concrete reasons to fight: to defend their homes and families as an expression of their nation.[22]

Much new material has been written since the beginning of the twenty-first century concerning the cultural dynamics of region-building, the invention of regions and the place of subnational identities in Europe.[23] Although regionalism as a specific domain of political history has become less visible, there have been some innovative contributions to the reassessment of the transversal influence of regionalist programs within some national traditions of political thought.[24] Regionalism has become a field of study in itself, but the lines of demarcation with the study of nationalism, on the one hand, and of local identities, on the other, are not always clear. Moreover, they will remain so, given that identification processes, forms of territorial loyalty and ways of imagining territory vary throughout Europe and can change over time within a given nation state, territory and area. The very fact that all forms of subnational identity are intertwined has paradoxically contributed to increasing confusion about how to establish differences, how to conceptualize them properly for analytical purposes and how to compare them.[25]

Therefore, the lack of authentic cross-European or multiple case-comparative studies is problematic. Comparisons between Eastern and Western Europe, or between Southern and Northern Europe, are still quite unusual in the field of nationalism studies; they are even scarcer in the field of subnational identities. Some comparisons have been made between regions divided by a border in order to understand how subnational identities have evolved differently over time in East and Central European 'frontier cities' or in regions belonging to different states, such as Flanders or Catalonia.[26] Although few truly comparative studies are available so far,[27] comparisons have been made between different forms of subnational identity in two or more territories within one nation state or polity. Perhaps as a result of this, much of what was commonly stated about the 'differences' in the historical evolution of Eastern and West European subnational identities has reflected the prevailing paradigms of the aprioristic dichotomy between 'Eastern' (ethnic) and 'Western' (civic) types of nationalism.[28] It has occasionally given rise to an inverted typology – hence the very specific East European concept of *Landespatriotismus*, initially translated as 'patriotism of the land' or 'loyalty to the land' where one lives, has sometimes been defined as an implicitly good, supra-ethnic and territorial regionalism based on love of one's territory, and was considered to be opposed by the 'nationalizing' tendencies in the territories of the Austro-Hungarian and Tsarist Empires. Therefore, regionalism in the Central European context was understood as a form of supra-ethnic territorial loyalty similar to the *Landespatriotismus*, which was devoid of ethnic content and could thus be shared by linguistically or ethnically diverse segments of the population.[29] However, this definition could not be applied in Western Europe. In any case, methodological regionalism continues to dominate the field and most historians have restricted themselves to analysing just one region, and normally their own.

On definitions

Regionalism in Modern Europe is firmly situated within more recent historiographical trends: most chapters will start in the late nineteenth century when regionalism became a mass movement in many parts of Europe and when many regional identities began to be defined more closely.[30] Moreover, we will not only deal with regions where a strong regional movement began to claim political autonomy or even independence but also with those regions where expressions of regional identity largely remained within the cultural sphere. So how exactly could we define regions and regionalism? Some authors have put forward the thesis that regions are solely political-administrative entities. Every territorial community that does not meet this definition would fall into the category of mere *ethnies* (a term invented by Anthony Smith). However, defining a *region* as a territory embodied with political-administrative institutions is too reductionist. The term 'region' existed before the vindication of decentralization, and may be independent of the demand for political decentralization and the claim of possessing representative or administrative institutions that span the region.[31] The 'region' may be merely a cultural or ethnocultural concept, imbued with a religious character, possessing relatively shifting territorial limits; this concentric sphere of territorial identification does not necessarily have to be defined in ethnic terms. A broader definition of regionalism could include *the culture that upholds and therefore shapes in the public sphere the existence of a region as an imagined community*. This community may or may not make political claims but is located somewhere between the nation (subject of sovereignty and territorially broader) and the local sphere (the space of human experience and daily interaction).

If a certain regionalism demands political-administrative decentralization, we could classify it as a *political regionalism* or even as a *regionalist movement*. There are certainly many regionalisms, or local/mesoterritorial claims, which we shall define as *cultural regionalism*, where political aims do not occupy the centre of their agenda, and the main channel of expression is cultural (be it historiographic, folklore-based, etc.).[32] However, they do advocate the existence of an historical, ethnocultural or simply 'functional' territorial entity that is integrated within a greater national narrative. An alternative label to describe this cultural regionalism would be the term 'regionalized nationalism', which was coined by Anne-Marie Thiesse for the French case (*nationalisme régionalisé*).[33] In the first case, the claim of some form of self-government and/or decentralization is central to the regionalist agenda. In the second case, that of cultural regionalism, the political agenda generally emphasizes the strength of the 'greater' nation by fostering local, provincial or regional layers of identification. Here, the nationalism of the *petite patrie*, *Heimat* and *rodina* may be compared with the nationalism of the 'most Portuguese village' (*povo mais português*) of Portugal.[34] However, even in this last case, the images, discourses and distinctive arguments which were used to define the subnational *Heimat*, and originally intended before 1890 to emphasize their peculiar contribution to national glory, may generate potential mid- and long-term territorial conflicts of loyalty with the nation over time. These discourses can be based on history, culture, language or dialects, folklore, the creation of landscape images and so on. Although these arguments were initially conceived as parts of a broader narrative, their autonomous development may be subject to reinterpretation by new actors.[35] Everything depends on who takes up the task of reinterpreting those cultural materials, with which ideological tenets they are combined, and within which political cultures they are embedded.

The critical issue, therefore, is *who* the regionalists are, and *why* they are waving the territorial flag? The particular interests of the actors can lead to very different consequences. The more such mobilization succeeds in gaining social acceptance, the more regionalism will be re-fostered as a self-propelling strategic argument for political mobilization. Some recent twentieth-century examples include the Northern League in Italy, whose invention of the 'Padanian nation' relies not on a 'strong' nationalist narrative but rather on 'light' secessionist rhetoric, and the short-lived resurgence of Moravian regionalism in Czech lands during the 1990s.[36]

A crucial difference between nationalism and regionalism is the demand for political sovereignty. Regionalists do not claim their defined territory to be the subject of collective political rights. They may ask for decentralization, self-government, political autonomy and federalism in variegated forms, but they do not consider their territory to be sovereign. However, there were cases of greater complexity. Some examples of cultural regionalism that gained impetus as a reaction to a centrifugal substate ethnonationalism have evolved into their own separate substate nationalisms, as illustrated by the Walloon movement: since its birth in the nineteenth century, it has largely developed as a response to Flemish nationalism.[37]

On several occasions, regionalist claims were cloaked with an 'ethnonationalist' rhetoric and vice versa; Catalan nationalists before 1918, and even Czech and Irish nationalists before 1914, often presented themselves in more ambiguous terms. This was a question of strategy that would lead some movements to be 'association-seeking' rather than independence-seeking. In this respect, 'separatism' is not necessarily a criterion for establishing a typological divide between regionalists and nationalists, since independence may move on or off the agenda of the political elites of a nationalist movement depending on the international circumstances and the political opportunity structure. Within a nationalist movement, one tendency may be hegemonic over another, while pro-autonomy and pro-independence currents can vary over time within more or less diffuse lines of demarcation.[38]

This divergence of political strategies concerning the level of self-government to be attained by a substate nation reflected the coexistence of different worldviews within nationalist movements, but it did not always imply a break with the existing polities they belonged to. In Spain, this was the case for conservative Catalanism, a 'regenerationist' substate nationalism with an imperial project for the whole of the nation state, aiming at an Iberian federation including Portugal. Certainly, at different moments the short-term political strategies developed by regionalist and nationalist movements may seem similar; Catalan moderate nationalists in the 1910s and 1920s may be compared to the Sardinian regionalists of 1918–1922 as far as their home-rule claims within a polycentric state were concerned. However, the theoretical basis of Catalan 'moderate' nationalism was different from that of the Sardinians: they considered their territory to be a nation, which had then the right to decide over its incorporation into a greater unit. Sardinian regionalists never came to define Sardinia as a nation but as a peripheral region of the Italian nation.[39] The inverse phenomenon was the multiplication of regionalist movements from above since the implementation of political decentralization throughout Spain in the early 1980s. Many presented themselves as new 'nationalisms', although they did not fall into this category from an ideological point of view.[40]

Another fundamental difference relates to the degree of discursive articulation, the density of the frames of meaning and the cultural and historic narratives. The regionalists' discourses as well as their repertory of images concerning the mythical past, the specificity of their culture and the collective awareness of 'regionhood' were much weaker and less articulated than those of (substate) nationalists.[41] This is in part due to the contradiction involved in claiming that a territory represents a *specific difference* based on a mixture of organic, historic and cultural arguments, while maintaining its compatibility and ultimate *subordination* to a wider, concentric identity that is considered hierarchically superior. Regionalist narratives are always expected to be tributary to a broader national narrative with which they are to merge. However, regionalists are constantly confronted with a long-term contradiction: how to combine an emphasis on the *specific difference* of a territory with the ultimate subordination to a wider sphere of identification. In contrast, national(ist) narratives are autonomous and mostly self-referential, though obviously not less performative than regional(ist) narratives. There are cases throughout Europe that illustrate how one process of region-building turned into full-blown nation-building while another did not, how regional and national identities are shifting and are sometimes contradictory over time and also how different social actors constructed different concepts of the *region* that partially evolved into independent national narratives.[42]

The nation also creates the region. With the advent and consolidation of the modern nation as the supreme principle upon which to base the territorial legitimacy of power, other territorial loyalties of different extent and nature, which had coexisted as political bodies within the organic order of the early modern composite monarchies, had to be restructured and subjected to a new hierarchy. The emergence of the nation at the end of the eighteenth century transformed those territories into subordinate entities.[43] It was at this moment when the term 'region' began to spread in France and Spain and steadily replace the more archaic term of 'province'; it was also then that the concept became increasingly associated with the vindication of present-day political rights. Hence, local and regional elites, particularly those who had enjoyed a certain degree of institutional power before 1800, resorted in their political and cultural discourse to the nostalgia of a better past, when the borders between territorial hierarchies were more diluted. This became more evident where the breakdown of the Ancien Régime had been radical, as in France. The appeal to local identity necessarily included nostalgia for pre-liberal times.

However, radical republicans who embraced federalism at different moments of the nineteenth and twentieth centuries were strongly influenced by regionalist tenets, from the Occitan *Félibrige rouge* to some Italian groups influenced by Carlo Cattaneo's theories, as well as Galician and Catalan regional federalists. They tended to endorse with historical and cultural arguments the legitimacy of the territorial units they want to become subjects of a federation. This introduced a left-wing variant in regionalist discourse that also found stronger continuity during the first decades of the twentieth century.[44] Moreover, in spite of their self-proclaimed internationalism, even socialists and communists were confronted with the issue of subnational identities and the challenge of how to cope with them in order to win adherents for the revolutionary cause. Just the coming of the Second World War and the radical upheaval of state borders brought about by the end of the conflict, as well as the subsequent Cold War period, seemed to 'freeze' the relevance of subnational belongings for three decades. However, the internal development of the European Union, as well as the impact of decolonization on new generations of regional activists gave rise to the so-called 'revolt of the regions', which ran parallel to the development of new social movements, May 1968 and the emergence of new paradigms of left-wing regional discourses. The break-up of the Soviet empire, as well as of Yugoslavia and Czechoslovakia after the fall of communism, meant a new wave of interest for subnational identities and their amazing capacity of resilience, also demonstrated at the beginning of the twenty-first century. The evolution of regional identities was certainly flanked by the advance of globalization, but did not vanish as a result its advance, as many had predicted.

Structure of the book

Regionalism in Modern Europe aims to provide an overview of the rise and development of regionalism in Europe from the late nineteenth century until the present. One of its objectives is to overcome the traditional case-study approach, which has been dominant among historians thus far. This has led to a methodological regionalism by which the rise of regionalism is primarily explained by internal factors and by focusing on domestic actors. Regionalism clearly was a transnational phenomenon and we should study it as such, although at this stage this is still quite difficult. It will be clear especially in the geographical chapters that historiographical traditions throughout the continent are still quite different; as a result, many authors differ from each other in some of their approaches. Nevertheless, by discussing a preliminary version of all chapters during a workshop at Leiden University in November 2016,[45] we tried to ensure the coherence of the volume, and, as a result, we decided that all chapters will have a comparative approach.

The volume consists of both thematic and geographical chapters. A first group of five chapters deals with cultural aspects of regionalism and discusses the role of language, folklore, nature, food and tourism. All explore the entire long twentieth century and basically cover the whole continent, although it is obvious that in line with the specific expertise of each of the authors, some periods and some parts of Europe receive more attention than others. A second group of three chapters examines the interaction between the ideologies of fascism, communism and democracy with regionalism and are somewhat more limited in their geographical and chronological scope, which is obviously a result of their focus on those countries and regimes that most thoroughly adopted these ideologies. Finally, there is a cluster of nine geographical chapters that generally deal with a number of neighbouring countries following the rise and evolution of regionalism from about 1890 until the present. These chapters deal respectively with the German lands, Scandinavia, the Low Countries, Southwestern Europe, East-Central Europe, the Baltic Area, Russia, Southeast Europe and the British Isles.

The cultural part starts with language: in Chapter 2, Johannes Kabatek explains that the mother tongue is very important for collective identification processes but that linguistic identities are not given. Sometimes, there is a clear tendency towards universalization, such as the Jacobins, who, during the French Revolution, tried to impose French upon the entire population. During the Romantic era, there was a trend towards particularism by placing emphasis on language diversity. Mass communication and education generally led to the standardization of languages, but it also led to regional counter movements that promoted the use of local dialects and languages. After the First World War, some of these regional languages became national languages, whereas others remained in a subordinate position. Although structural differences were not decisive in this process, it was more difficult to relegate very distant language such as Welsh, Basque, Estonian or Albanian to a status of mere dialects. A new wave of globalization, from the 1970s onwards, led to a revival of regional languages and sentiments. Some cases, such as the 'normalization' of Catalan, were influential examples for other regional movements. Support also came from the European Bureau for Lesser Used Languages (1982–2010) and the Universal Declaration of Linguistic Rights (1996). Immigrants sometimes also adopt regional languages or create hybrid mixed languages of their own, such as the German-Turkish *Kietzdeutsch*. The revival of some regional languages was a success; in the case of Welsh and Basque, urban neo-speakers now outnumber those for whom either language is their mother tongue.

In Chapter 3, David Hopkin discusses the role of folklore. He explains how the interest in folklore grew rapidly during the Romantic era but that the collectors of tales, legends and songs connected them primarily to the nation. Only towards the end of the nineteenth century did it become more common to inventorize folklore by region, whereby historical regions were preferred over artificial administrative units. In general, the regions were presented as an organic but subordinate part of the national whole. Some regions, such as the Gaelic-speaking West of Ireland or Karelia in Finland, were regarded as 'relic areas', whose ancient traditions could form a source of inspiration for the regeneration of the entire nation. Folklorists often tried to protect the authentic cultural traditions against encroachment from the state, urban modernity and commercial interests. During the twentieth century, large-scale projects to map the spatial distribution of folkloric traditions became popular, but were finally abandoned after it became clear that their borders generally did not overlap and that many customs were actually highly transnational. Folklorists also created repertoires of regional folk songs and dances that could be used at festive occasions. Revivalism was largely an urban phenomenon and often started among rural migrants in the larger cities. Sometimes, this led to curious results: the omnipresent drum and pipe band at today's Breton festivals were invented in Paris and only spread to the region after 1945. Folk festivals, where one could dress up and sing folk songs, became quite popular during the second half of the twentieth century. Whilst before the Second World War, folklore generally was associated with the political right, the folk revival in the post-war period was more left-leaning and even found inspiration in Marxism and anti-colonial movements, while autonomists and separatist ambitions were voiced more openly.

Jan-Henrik Meyer examines in Chapter 4 how the relationship between nature and regionalism evolved during the long twentieth century. Not only did the region's cultural heritage have to be protected, but the same was true with its natural patrimony. As a consequence, many of the early regionalist movements began to make inventories of their region's natural highlights, in order to render them accessible to visitors and, if required, to protect them against the levelling forces of modernity. During the first half of the twentieth century, efforts to protect the natural environment were mostly stimulated by urban intellectuals and governmental agencies. The local population, who often had a more utilitarian attitude towards nature, sometimes opposed protective measures, such as the creation of national parks. In the communist bloc, nature in theory did not fall prey to capitalist exploitation; however, the new socialist economy did not regard ecological motives very highly, while frequent environmental disasters eroded the local and regional support for the communist regimes. In Western Europe, new regional ecological movements arose in the 1970s, often to protest against a specific threat such as the building of a nuclear power plant or a specific form of pollution. More recently, the protection of characteristic landscapes can clash with attempts to combat climate change by introducing windmills or new power lines.

Chapter 5 deals with the rise of regional foods that, according to Kolleen Guy, largely emerged as a consequence of the globalization of food markets towards the end of the nineteenth century. Mechanical refrigeration, combined with trains and steamships, made the transport of agricultural products and regional specialities over longer distances possible and profitable. Although there were considerable differences in food habits across Europe before the twentieth century, which were largely determined by climate, agricultural traditions and the use of microbial cultures to preserve food, in general people ate whatever was available. Only among the rich, who travelled and could afford to consume luxury items from abroad, there was some awareness of geographical differences and regional specialities. The globalization of the food market led to the rise of the large-scale commercialization of food production, particularly in Northern Europe. In Southern Europe, there was more support for the protection of regional food production and many products came to be seen as part of the cultural patrimony of the nation. External factors also had a large impact; emigrants often remained heavily attached to their regional foodways, thus creating new export markets for regional products. But there was also a growing international demand for 'authentic' products, such as chateaux wines, and this constituted an important stimulus to market products as connected with a specific *terroir*. The earliest attempts to protect regional food products date from the late nineteenth century, but this task has nowadays been largely taken over by the European Union.

The impact of tourism on regional identities is shown by Eric Storm in Chapter 6. Since the Romantic era, rural areas were regarded as the heartland of the nation. However, they only became accessible to a growing number of tourists by the development of secondary railways and the introduction of bicycles and automobiles later on. The demand from tourists for characteristic products was met by inventing regional dishes and new folkloric festivals. Many hotels, restaurants and second homes were built in neo-vernacular styles, therefore making many regions more 'typical' than they had ever been. After 1945, mass tourism focused more on the beaches of the Mediterranean and a vogue for modernist buildings now converted many sleepy fisher villages into modern bathing resorts. However, this tendency towards more uniformity was countered after about 1970 by a growing interest in cultural heritage, which has even led recently to the transformation of old industrial complexes into regional tourist attractions. Roots or 'homesick' tourism of migrants to the regions where they or their ancestors had been born has also stimulated the protection of regional heritage. All in all, tourism had a considerable impact on the regional identities of most European regions; existing differences were highlighted largely for commercial reasons, while new ones were created.

The ideological part starts with Chapter 7 in which Xosé M. Núñez Seixas shows how regionalism was strongly promoted under fascist regimes, such as those of Mussolini, Hitler and Franco. Some attention is also paid to Vichy France and Salazar's Portugal. The author makes clear that the first priority of all fascist and para-fascist dictators was to create a strong state; separatist tendencies or even pleas for regional devolution were, therefore, anathema. There was no clear fascist idea on regions and regional cultures, and no clear distinction was drawn between the local and the regional. However, in practice, all fascist regimes tried to increase the attachment of the population to the homeland by promoting regional folklore, customs, dialects and sometimes even the instrumental use of regional languages and/or dialects. The strong interest in the past also stimulated the study and revival of local and regional history, traditions and folklore, while natural heritage was protected. Regionalist images also pervaded exhibitions, publicity and commercial culture. Although regional attachment was unmistakably subordinate to national loyalty, fascist respect for subnational plurality also made it possible for some regionalist cultures to survive the regimes and resurface after the transition to democracy.

Chapter 8 deals with communism, both in the Soviet Union and Eastern Europe. The Soviet Union was set up as a federation of a dozen Soviet Republics, some of which were further subdivided into autonomous republics and even autonomous regions. Regional economic councils were set up to help coordinate economic planning, while regional studies flourished. Nevertheless, in the early 1930s, regional studies was one of the first victims of the Stalinist purges and in 1932, the regional economic councils were abolished as well. The Soviet Union became an even more strongly centralized state. This centralist model was also imposed on Eastern Europe, and the break with Tito's Yugoslavia was at least in part related to his plans to take federalism seriously. Tito subsequently turned to economic regionalism; local and regional workers' councils formed the heart of the political and economic organization of the Yugoslav federation. Attempts to reform communism in Poland, Hungary and Czechoslovakia often involved measures of economic regionalism. Even in the Soviet Union, the regional economic councils were reintroduced for a short time in the late 1950s. Economic decentralization went further in Yugoslavia but did not help the country to overcome the crisis and stagnation of the 1970s. In the end, the entire system collapsed in a very short period after the Fall of the Berlin Wall in 1989.

Regionalism in the democratic states of Western Europe is discussed in Chapter 9 by Daniele Petrosino. Regional identity construction took already place in the nineteenth century and in various European countries there were movements that advocated regional autonomy before 1945. In the immediate post-war period, a few regions were created, for instance, in Italy, but they did not have much practical implications. The process of regionalization only began in earnest in the 1970s. The establishment of new administrative regions created new opportunities for the articulation of local and regional interests, thus increasing political pluralism. From the late 1980s, the growing global competition between regions and the development of regional policies by the European Community enhanced the political and economic role of regions, while richer regions such as Catalonia, Bavaria and Northern Italy increasingly complained about the redistribution mechanisms that transferred part of their wealth to less-developed parts of the country. These tendencies seem to have become even more pronounced after the financial crisis of 2008. Traditional nation-wide ideological parties seem to lose ground to regional parties who claim to more directly represent the wishes of the population, while the wish to secede even became acute in Scotland and Catalonia.

Jeremy DeWaal initiates the geographical part with Chapter 10 on the German-speaking parts of Europe. He makes clear that the use of the term *Heimat* to denote a rootedness in a local or regional homeland was the product of the Romantic era. The regionalist *Heimat* movement became a mass phenomenon only after German unification in 1871. In general, regionalism defended a unity in diversity nationalism and this was also true in the German-speaking parts of Switzerland and the Austrian half of the Dual Monarchy. The attachment to the region seemed to have increased under the Weimar Republic; the number of regionalist publications grew enormously and *Heimatkunde* became a school subject. Although the Nazis paid lip service to the regionalist ideals, they in fact subordinated everything regional to the nation and to their plans for territorial expansion. Just as in 1918, after the end of the Second World War, separatist fantasies did not enjoy much resonance. However, in the uncertain circumstances after the defeat, the *Heimat* idea reached new heights. This would only change in the 1960s, when particularly the more internal and backward-looking aspects, added to the expellee demand for their right to *Heimat*, irritated many of the younger generation. Nevertheless, from the 1970s onwards, regionalism made a comeback and now also became associated with increasing protests against environmental pollution, technocratic (re-)construction projects and excessive centralization.

Chapter 11 focuses on regionalism in Scandinavia. Peter Stadius explains that political regionalism is not very important in the Nordic countries, although regional identities did play a crucial role. Karelia in Finland, Dalecarlia in Sweden and Telemark in Norway were perceived as national heartlands, as idyllic rural regions where the authentic traditions of the fatherland were still alive. An added advantage was that Karelia seemed to be untainted of Sweden influences, whereas Dalecarlia had played a vital historical role in the resistance against the 'occupation' of Sweden by the Danish kings in the late medieval period. Border regions such as Scania, the Torne Valley Region and the Åland Islands also developed a strong sense of regional identity, partly for linguistic and historical reasons. More complicated was the regional identity of the Swedish-speaking minority in Finland. It continues to have a very strong institutional and cultural infrastructure, but does not have a unified territory. From the 1960s onwards, the Sami also created their own transnational border region in the Arctic North. A final fascinating case is the transborder region of Öresund that came into existence when in 2000 a new bridge connected Sjælland in Denmark and Scania in Sweden, and which presents itself as a dynamic, modern Euro region.

Regionalism in the Low Countries is explored by Joep Leerssen in Chapter 12. The strong decentralized nature of the political system in the early modern period and the rather arbitrary division between the Netherlands, Belgium and Luxembourg after 1830 led to strong particularist feelings in almost all provinces. Within the Netherlands, Frisia, which had its own language and traditions, was seen as a kind of national heartland and separatism never made any headway. Particularist feelings also led to manifold expressions of cultural regionalism in two other peripheral regions, which, moreover, were Catholic instead of Protestant: Brabant and Limburg. Whereas in the Netherlands religion caused division, in Belgium, language was the main dividing mechanism. During the twentieth century, Flemish regionalism developed into full-blown nationalism, while as a compromise solution from 1962 onwards the country was administratively split up along linguistic lines. As a reaction, a Walloon movement also developed, which could be seen as a kind of Belgian 'rump nationalism'. Luxembourg forms a fascinating case of a provincial movement whose cultural explorations became – through geopolitical developments and dynastic accident – the basis of a new national imagined community.

Xosé M. Núñez Seixas and Fernando Molina examine the development of regionalism in South-western Europe – France, Spain, Italy and Portugal – in Chapter 13. In France, during the late nineteenth and early twentieth centuries, nation-building was accompanied by region-building but did not lead to political decentralization. In Italy, urban identities were generally stronger than regional ones and it was mainly the economic imbalance between the different parts of the country that led to regionalist feelings in the South and Sardinia. Regions did not have an important role in Portugal, where larger municipalities built strong local identities, but peripheral islands, such as the Azores, voiced claims for decentralization. In Spain, the rise of nationalist movements in Catalonia, the Basque Country and, later on, Galicia complicated the picture, although cultural regionalism continued to flourish in all parts of the country. Regionalism never became monopolized by one ideology, but there was a clear shift towards the political right during the interwar period. Because of the fascist appropriation of regional folklore and traditions, regionalism received a setback in the post-war period. However, from the 1960s onwards, economic efficiency and the Europe of the regions, on the one hand, and a new left-wing interest in 'internal decolonization', on the other, provoked a comeback. First in Italy after 1947, and then since the 1970s, political decentralization was pursued in all four countries, with Spain, partially driven by the strong nationalist movements in its periphery, taking the most drastic measures.

The focus shifts to the eastern parts of the continent in Chapter 14, written by Irina Livezeanu end Petru Negura, which analyses the developments in the regions that are located in Romania and Moldova. The shifting state borders and nation-building policies largely determined the context in which region-building activities could be deployed. Although many attempts were made to weaken or disrupt existing (regional) allegiances in order to strengthen the attachment to the new nation states, the memories of smaller provincial or regional administrative units did not disappear and often were invoked to express discontent with the growing intervention from a centralized state, be it from Bucharest in Romania, from Kiev or Moscow in Moldova or from Chisinau in Transnistria. How exactly these tensions worked out during the long twentieth century is explained in detailed sections on Transylvania, Banat and Bessarabia/Moldova.

Russia and the Soviet Union, and their way of dealing with regional differences, are discussed by Mark Bassin and Mikhail Suslov in Chapter 15. They assert that because of the vast extension of the Tsarist Empire and its fluctuating borders, which were difficult to protect, centralism has been a defining feature of the Russian state since early modern times, regardless of the actual regime that was in power. Local and provincial authorities did not have much autonomy and unless the central state was in disarray – which was the case around 1917 and in the 1990s – expressions of regionalism from below were strictly monitored or even suppressed. Nevertheless, a progressive, federalist tradition emerged that pleaded for reconnecting with the ancient 'democratic' traditions of the former provinces, while there were also more conservative back-to-land regionalists. The example of Siberia, which is described in more detail, shows that the regionalist movement was dominated by ethnic Russians. They presented Siberia as a kind of Russian heartland. While complaints about excessive centralism and colonial exploitation were voiced regularly, demands for political autonomy or even secession only flared up briefly during the Civil War and after the collapse of the Soviet Union.

Chapter 16 on regionalism in the Baltic states and Poland is written by Jörg Hackmann. The first to develop a sense of regional identity were the Baltic Germans in the Tsarist Empire. During the late nineteenth century, regional or national movements also developed among Lithuanians (both those residing in the Russian and the German Empire), Latvians and Estonians and in various Polish areas within the German and Austrian Empire. At the end of the First World War, Poland, Estonia, Latvia and Lithuania became independent nation states where regional differences were frowned upon as remainders of imperial rule. The main exceptions were Upper Silesia and the Kashubian region within Poland, where expressions of cultural regionalism were tolerated as long as they remained subordinate to a larger Polish identity. Obviously, the communist era that began in 1945 was not very favourable to any form of regionalism, although the Estonian and Latvian song festivals continued to exist, while within Poland the Kashubs retook their activities in favour of their own language, folklore and culture after the death of Stalin. In the late 1980s, Gorbachev's perestroika brought new freedom, which first expressed itself in environmental protests in Estonia and Latvia. Soon the so-called Singing Revolution led to the independence of the three Baltic states. The presence of large numbers of Russians – which generally was seen as problematic by the new authorities – prevented the development of strong regionalist movements within Estonia, Latvia and Lithuania. This was different in Poland where regionalism gained strength from the 1980s onwards in the Kashubian region, Upper Silesia and in the territory of former East Prussia.

South-eastern Europe, which is a more neutral term than the Balkans, is discussed in Chapter 17 by Tchavdar Marinov. It provides a broad geographical overview of the various regional movements and focuses on the most significant examples. Within Croatia the regions with the most active regionalist movements were Dalmatia and Istria, which both had been part of the Venetian empire; recently, Istria has even secured a semi-autonomous status. Vojvodina is an interesting case, because it is largely a new, twentieth-century invention, and the current regionalist movement is multi-ethnic and uses the six official languages of the region. Other idiosyncratic cases are those of Montenegro, Bosnia and Macedonia; their regional identities became more pronounced because of the rise of rivalling nationalist groups, such as Serbs, Croats and Bulgarians, and in the 1990s, they all became nation states themselves. The chapter ends with some short reflections on regionalism in Romania – where the case of Transylvania shows some interesting parallels with Vojvodina – and Greece. In the end, the legacies and influence of Austro-Hungary, the Ottoman Empire, communism and the European Union led to various surprising outcomes, some areas became part of homogenized nation states, other regions cherished their distinct cultural traditions, while a few exceptions developed strong regional identities and eventually became fully-fledged nation states.

Finally, the somewhat exceptional situation of the British Isles is explained in Chapter 18 by James Kennedy. First of all, the United Kingdom is a composite monarchy that has never been transformed into a centralized nation state as is the case in most Western European countries. Moreover, the constituent parts are called nations, although only Ireland became an independent nation state. Irish, Welsh and Scottish movements that wanted to strengthen their cultural identity and protect or increase their political autonomy are called nationalist, although most of their members wanted to remain within the union. The strong rivalry between the four nations impeded the development of strong regional identities within them; with the exception of Northern Ireland. Nevertheless, the situation in each of the four constituent parts was very different; Scotland still had a lot of institutions that functioned largely independent of London, while Wales had been formally incorporated into England. Northern Ireland, although it came into being because its Protestant majority fiercely opposed Irish Home Rule, was the first to receive its own parliament in 1921. Nevertheless, expressions of cultural regionalism in both literature and folklore could be found in regions such as Cornwall, Yorkshire and so on. Both the partial dismantling of the welfare state and the heavy industries in the 1980s, which were mostly located in peripheral parts of the United Kingdom, increased the appeal of nationalist parties in Scotland and, to a lesser extent, Wales. In the late 1990s, referenda on devolution were held in Scotland and Wales, while the Troubles in Northern Ireland were brought to an end in 1998 with the Good Friday Agreements. Partly instigated by the European Union, counties and regions also received more competences, which particularly led to the strengthening of metropolitan regions, such as Greater London.

The volume ends with Chapter 19, in which the editors Xosé-M. Núñez Seixas and Eric Storm draw some preliminary conclusions, based on the broad overview offered in the rest of the chapters, on the rise and evolution of regionalism in Europe during the long twentieth century. What patterns, turning points, similarities and differences can be observed between the different parts of Europe? What influence did the various cultural and ideological factors have? They also suggest that further research is needed about the interaction between localism, regionalism, nationalism and imperialism, while it would be worthwhile to compare the situation within the different parts of Europe with the development of regionalism in the rest of the world.

Leiden and Santiago de Compostela, December 2017

Notes

1. 'Juncker: "If we allow Catalonia to separate, others will do the same"', *El País* (13 October 2017), https://elpais.com/elpais/2017/10/13/inenglish/1507907261_402876.html.
2. See Michael Keating, *Nations against the State: The New Politics of Nationalism in Quebec, Catalona and Scotland* (Basinstoke: Palgrave Macmillan, 1996); and Montserrat Guibernau, *Nations without States: Political Communities in a Global Age* (Cambridge: Polity, 1999).
3. These parts are largely based on Xosé M. Núñez Seixas, 'Historiographical Approaches to Sub-national Identities in Europe: A Reappraisal and Some Suggestions', in *Region and State in Nineteenth-Century Europe: Nation-Building, Regional Identities and Separatism*, ed. Joost Augusteijn and Eric Storm (Basingstoke: Palgrave Macmillan, 2012), 13–36.
4. Eugen Weber, *Peasants into Frenchmen: The Modernization of Rural France 1870–1914* (Stanford: Stanford University Press, 1976). See also Miguel Cabo and Fernando Molina, 'The Long and Winding Road of Nationalization: Eugen Weber's *Peasants into Frenchmen* in Modern European History (1976–2006)', *European History Quarterly* 39 (2009): 264–86; and Eric Storm, 'The Spatial Turn and the History of Nationalism: Nationalism between Regionalism and Transnational Approaches', in *Writing the History of Nationalism*, ed. Stefan Berger and Eric Storm (London: Bloomsbury, 2019).
5. Anne-Marie Thiesse, 'L'invention du régionalisme à la Belle Époque', *Le Mouvement Social* 160 (1992): 11–32.
6. Jean Charles-Brun, Appendix: 'Le mot régionalisme', *Le régionalisme* (Paris: Bloud, 1911). See also Julian Wright, 'Charles-Brun et l'idée du régionalisme: réalisme et conciliation', in *Le Régionalisme*, ed. Jean Charles-Brun, Mireille Meyer and Julian Wright (Paris: Éditions du CTHS, 2004), 45–60.
7. See Charles Seignobos, *Les aspirations autonomistes en Europe (Albanie, Alsace-Lorraine, Catalogne, Finlande, Îles Grecques, Irlande, Mácedoine, Pologne, Serbo-Croatie)* (Paris: Alcan, 1913).
8. For a good sampling of case studies, see Heinz-Gerhard Haupt, Stuart J. Woolf and Michael Müller, eds, *Regional and National Identities in Europe in the XIXth and XXth Centuries* (The Hague, London and Boston: Kluwer, 1998); Philipp Ther and Holm Sundhaussen, eds, *Regionale Bewegungen und Regionalismen in europäischen Zwischenräumen seit der Mitte des 19. Jahrhunderts* (Marburg a. Lahn: Herder-Institut, 2003); Rolf Petri, ed., *Regione e storia regionale in Europa: Antitesi o metafora della nazione?*, monographic issue of *Memoria e Ricerca* (2006): 22; and Xosé M. Núñez Seixas, ed., *La construcción de la identidad regional en Europa y España (siglos XIX y XX)*, monographic issue of *Ayer* 64 (2006): 11–231; as well as Peter Haslinger, ed., *Regionale und nationale Identitäten. Wechselwirkungen und Spannungsfelder im Zeitalter moderner Staatlichkeit* (Würzburg: Ergon, 2000); Gerhard Brunn, ed., *Region und Regionsbildung in Europa. Konzeptionen der Forschung und empirische Befunde* (Baden-Baden: Nomos, 1996); Laurence Cole, ed., *Different Paths to the Nation: Regional and National*

Identities in Central Europe and Italy, 1830–70 (Basingstoke: Palgrave Macmillan, 2007); and Joost Augusteijn and Eric Storm, eds, *Region and State in Nineteenth-Century Europe: Nation-Building, Regional Identities and Separatism* (Basingstoke: Palgrave Macmillan, 2012).

9. See R. Petri, 'Nostalgia e *Heimat*. Emozione, tempo e spazio nella construzione dell'identità', in *Nostalgia. Memoria e passaggi tra le sponde dell'Adriatico*, ed. R. Petri (Rome and Venice: Edizioni di Storia e Letteratura, 2010), 15–45.

10. This tendency continues to be evident in the last two decades: see, e.g., Umut Özkirimli, *Contemporary Debates on Nationalism: A Critical Engagement*, 3rd ed. (Basingstoke: Palgrave Macmillan, 2017); and John Breuilly, ed., *The Oxford Handbook of the History of Nationalism* (Oxford: Oxford University Press, 2013).

11. Michael Keating, *The New Regionalism in Western Europe. Territorial Restructuring and Political Change* (Cheltenham-Northampton: Edward Elgar, 1998); and Michael Keating, 'Regionalism, Peripheral Nationalism, and the State in Western Europe: A Political Model', *Canadian Review of Studies in Nationalism* 18 (1991): 117–29. See also C. Levi, ed., *Italian Regionalism: History, Identity and Politics* (Oxford and Washington: Berg, 1996); and Frans Schrijvers, *Regionalism after Regionalization: Spain, France and the United Kingdom* (Amsterdam: Amsterdam University Press, 2006).

12. See Luis Moreno, *The Federalization of Spain* (London: Routledge, 2001), 9–31. Likewise, Lieven de Winter and Huri Tursan, eds, *Regionalist Parties in Western Europe* (London: Routledge, 1998); Lieven De Winter, Margarita Gómez-Reino and Peter Lynch, eds, *Autonomist Parties in Europe: Identity Politics and the Revival of the Territorial Cleavage* (Barcelona: ICPS, 2006), 2 vols; as well as a more conventional view by Daniel-L. Seiler, *Les partis autonomistes*, 2nd ed. (Paris: Presses Universitaires de France, 1994).

13. Beginning with Karl W. Deutsch, *Nationalism and Social Communication* (Cambridge, MA: Harvard University Press, 1953).

14. Gabriele Turi and Simoneta Soldani, eds, *Fare gli italiani: scuola e cultura nell'Italia contemporanea* (Bologna: Il Mulino, 1993); Kas Deprez and Louis Vos, eds, *Nationalism in Belgium: Shifting Identities, 1780–1995* (Basingstoke: Palgrave Macmillan, 1998); Keith Robbins, *Nineteenth-Century Britain: England, Scotland and Wales: The Making of a Nation* (Oxford: Oxford University Press, 1989); and Jana Osterkamp and Martin Schulze-Wessel, eds, *Exploring Loyalty* (Göttingen: Vandenhoeck & Ruprecht, 2017).

15. Anthony D. Smith, *National Identity* (London: Penguin, 1991), 1–43.

16. Celia Applegate, *A Nation of Provincials: The German Idea of Heimat* (Berkeley: University of California Press, 1990); Alon Confino, *The Nation as a Local Metaphor. Württemberg, Imperial Germany, and National Memory, 1971–1918* (Chapel Hill: University of North Carolina Press, 1997); Abigail Green, *Fatherlands: State-Building and Nationhood in Nineteenth-Century Germany* (Cambridge: Cambridge University Press, 2001); Georg Kunz, *Verortete Geschichte. Regionales Geschichtsbewusstsein in den deutschen historischen Vereinen des 19. Jahrhunderts* (Göttingen: Vandenhoeck & Ruprecht, 2000); Siegfried Weichlein, *Nation und Region. Integrationsprozesse im Bismarckreich* (Düsseldorf: Droste, 2004); and Michael B. Klein, *Zwischen Reich und Region: Identitätsstrukturen im Deutschen Kaiserreich (1871–1918)* (Stuttgart: Steiner, 2005).

17. Alon Confino, *Germany as a Culture of Remembrance: Promises and Limits of Writing History* (Chapel Hill: University of North Carolina Press, 2006). See also chapters by Núñez Seixas, DeWaal and Petrosino.

18. Stéphane Gerson, *The Pride of Place: Local Memories and Political Culture in Nineteenth-Century France* (Ithaca; London: Cornell University Press, 2003).

19. Anne-Marie Thiesse, *Ils apprenaient la France. L'exaltation des régions dans le discours patriotique* (Paris: Maison des Sciences de l'Homme, 1997).
20. Anssi Paasi, 'Bounded Spaces in the Mobile World: Deconstructing "Regional Identity"', *Tijdschrift voor Economische en Sociale Geografie* 93 (2002): 137–48.
21. Alexei Miller and Stefan Berger, eds, *Nationalizing Empires* (Budapest: Central European University Press, 2015); Josep M. Fradera, *La nación imperial (1750–1918). Derechos, representación y ciudadanía en los imperios de Gran Bretaña, Francia, España y Estados Unidos* (Barcelona: Edhasa, 2015); and James Kennedy, *Liberal Nationalisms. Empire, State and Civil Society in Scotland and Quebec* (Montreal: McGill-Queen's University Press, 2013).
22. Benjamin Ziemann, *War Experiences in Rural Germany, 1914–1923* (Oxford; New York: Berg, 2007); Alexander Watson, *Enduring the Great War: Combat, Morale and Collapse in the German and British Armies, 1914–1918* (Cambridge: Cambridge University Press, 2008); and Sven-Olliver Müller, *Die Nation als Waffe und Vorstellung: Nationalismus in Deutschland und Großbritannien im Ersten Weltkrieg* (Göttingen: Vandenhoeck & Ruprecht, 2002).
23. See some recent overviews in Celia Applegate, 'A Europe of Regions: Reflections on the Historiography of Subnational Places in Modern Times', *American Historical Review* 104 (1999): 1157–82; Eric Storm, 'Regionalism in History, 1890–1945: The Cultural Approach', *European History Quarterly* 33 (2003): 251–65; Andreas Fahrmeir and H. S. Jones, 'Space and Belonging in Modern Europe: Citizenship(s) in Localities, Regions, and States', *European Review of History/Revue Européenne d'Histoire* 15 (2008): 243–53; and Rolf Petri, 'Il risorgere delle regioni nel contesto dell'integrazione europea. Sviluppi recenti e prospettiva storica', in *L'intelletuale militante. Scritti per Mario Isnenghi*, ed. G. Albanese et al. (Portogruaro: Nuova Dimensione, 2007), 365–88.
24. Julian Wright, *The Regionalist Movement in France: Jean Charles-Brun and French Political Thought* (Oxford: Clarendon, 2003).
25. Heinz-Gerhard Haupt and Charlotte Tacke, 'Die Kultur des Nationalen: Sozial- und kulturgeschichtliche Ansätze bei der Erforschung des europäischen Nationalismus im 19. und 20. Jahrhundert', in *Kulturgeschichte Heute*, ed. W. Hardtwig and H.-U. Wehler (Göttingen: Vandenhoeck & Ruprecht, 1996), 255–83.
26. Timothy Baycroft, *Culture, Identity and Nationalism: French Flanders in the Nineteenth and Twentieth Centuries* (London and Woodbridge: Boydell & Brewer, 2004); Peter Sahlins, *Boundaries: The Making of France and Spain in the Pyrenees* (Berkeley: University of California Press, 1989); and Nicolas Berjoan, *L'identité du Roussillon: Penser un pays catalan à l'âge des nations, 1780–2000* (Canet: Trabucaire, 2014). On East-Central European 'frontier cities' and borders, see Kimmo Katajala and Maria Lahteenmarkt, eds, *Imagined, Negotiated, Remembered: Constructing European Borders and Borderlands* (Münster: LIT Verlag, 2012); as well as Katarzyna Stoklosa and Gerhard Besier, eds, *European Border Regions in Comparison: Overcoming Nationalistic Aspects of Re-Nationalization* (London: Routledge, 2014).
27. Exceptions are Eric Storm, *The Culture of Regionalism: Art, Architecture and International Exhibitions in France, Germany and Spain, 1890–1939* (Manchester: Manchester University Press, 2010); Augusteijn and Storm, eds, *Region and State*; Keating, *The New Regionalism in Western Europe*; and Michael Keating, *Rescaling the European State: The Making of Territory and the Rise of the Meso* (Oxford: Oxford University Press, 2013).
28. See Ulrike von Hirschhausen and Jörn Leonhardt, 'Europäische Nationalismen im Ost-West Vergleich: Von der Typologie zur Differenzbestimmung', in *Nationalismen in Europe: West- und Osteuropa im Vergleich*, ed. Ulrike von Hirschhausen and Jörn Leonhardt

(Göttingen: Vandenhoeck & Ruprecht, 2001), 11–45; Xosé M. Núñez Seixas, 'Nations and Territorial Identities in Europe: Transnational Reflections', *European History Quarterly* 40, no. 4 (2010): 669–84.

29. See Miroslav Hroch, 'De l'ethnicité à la nation. Un chemin oublié vers la modernité', *Anthropologie et Société* 19, no. 3 (1995): 71–86; and Ulrike von Hirschhausen, *Die Grenzen der Gemeinsamkeit: Deutsche, Letten, Russen und Juden in Riga, 1860–1914* (Göttingen: Vandenhoeck & Ruprecht, 2006).

30. Eric Storm, 'The Birth of Regionalism and the Crisis of Reason: France, Germany and Spain', in *Region and State*, ed. Augusteijn and Storm, 36–57.

31. Rolf Petri, 'Heimat/Piccole patrie. Nation und Region im deutschen und im italienischen Sprachraum', *Geschichte und Region/Storia e Regione* 12 (2003): 191–212.

32. On the changing relations between nationalism and culture, see Joep Leerssen, *National Thought in Europe: A Cultural History* (Amsterdam: Amsterdam University Press, 2006).

33. Anne-Marie Thiesse, 'Centralismo estatal y nacionalismo regionalizado. Las paradojas del caso francés', *Ayer* 64 (2006): 33–64.

34. See José M. Sobral, 'O Norte, o Sul, a raça, a naçâo – Representaçôes da identidade nacional portuguesa (séculos XIX-XX)', *Análise Social* 171 (2004): 255–84; Daniel Melo, 'Regionalismo, sociedad civil y Estado en el Portugal del siglo XX', *Hispania Nova. Revista de Historia Contemporánea* 7 (2007); as well as Daniel Melo, 'Out of Sight, Close to the Heart: Regionalist Voluntary Associations in the Portuguese Empire', *e-Journal of Portuguese History* 5, no. 1 (2007). For the Dutch case see Frank H. Löwik, 'De Twentse Beweging. Strijd voor modersproake en eigenheid' (Ph.D. thesis, Rijksuniversiteit Groningen, 2003).

35. Partha Chatterjee, 'Whose Imagined Community?', in *The Nation and Its Fragments: Colonial and Postcolonial Histories*, ed. Partha Chatterjee (Princeton, NJ: Princeton University Press, 1993), 3–14.

36. Robert Luft, 'Die Grenzen des Regionalismus: das Beispiel Mähren im 19. und 20. Jahrhundert', in *Regionale Bewegungen und Regionalismen*, ed. Ther and Sundhaussen, 63–85; and Margarita Gómez-Reino, *Ethnicity and Nationalism in Italian Politics: Inventing the Padania: Lega Nord and the Northern Question* (Aldershot: Ashgate, 2002).

37. Maarten van Ginderachter, *Le chant du coq. Nation et nationalisme en Wallonie depuis 1880* (Gent: Academia Press, 2005).

38. See Miroslav Hroch, *In the National Interest. Demands and Goals of European National Movements of the Nineteenth Century: A Comparative Perspective* (Prague: Faculty of Arts Charles University, 2000); Henry E. Hale, *The Foundations of Ethnic Politics: Separatism of States and Nations in Eurasia and the World* (New York: Cambridge University Press, 2008); G. Stevenson, *Parallel Paths: The Development of Nationalism in Ireland and Quebec* (Montreal: McGill-Queen's University Press, 2006); and Kennedy, *Liberal Nationalisms*.

39. Enric Ucelay-Da Cal, *El imperialismo catalán. Prat de la Riba, Cambó, D'Ors y la conquista moral de España* (Barcelona: Edhasa, 2003); and Gianfranco Contu, 'La questione nazionale sarda tra autonomismo e independentismo', in *L'Europa delle diversità. Identità e culture alle soglie del terzo millennio*, ed. Michele Pinna (Milan: Franco Angeli, 1993), 97–119.

40. See Xosé M. Núñez Seixas, 'Regions, Nations and Nationalities: On the Process of Territorial Identity-Building during Spain's Democratic Transition and Consolidation', in *Spanish and Latin American Transitions to Democracy*, ed. Carlos H. Waisman and Raanan Rein (Brighton and Portland: Sussex University Press, 2005), 55–79.

41. See Peter Haslinger and Klaus Holz, 'Selbstbild und Territorium. Dimensionen von Identität und Alterität', in *Regionale und nationale Identitäten*, ed. Haslinger, 15–38.

42. Josep M. Fradera, *Cultura nacional en una sociedad dividida. Patriotismo y cultura en Cataluña, 1833-1868* (Madrid: Marcial Pons, 2003); Sören Brinkmann, *Der Stolz der Provinzen. Regionalbewußtsein und Nationalstaatsbau im Spanien des 19. Jahrhunderts* (Bern and Frankfurt a. M.: Peter Lang, 2005); Carlos Forcadell and M. Cruz Romeo, eds, *Provincia y nación. Los territorios del liberalismo* (Zaragoza: Institución Fernando el Católico, 2006); and Luis Castells, ed., *Del territorio a la nación. Identidades territoriales y construcción nacional* (Madrid: Biblioteca Nueva, 2006).
43. Maiken Umbach, 'Nation and Region', in *What Is a Nation? Europe 1789-1914*, ed. Tim Baycroft and Mark Hewitson (Oxford: Oxford University Press, 2006), 63-80.
44. See, e.g., Julian Wright and H. S. Jones, eds, *Pluralism and the Idea of the Republic in France* (Basingstoke: Palgrave Macmillan, 2012), 179-97; Pere Gabriel, *El catalanisme i la cultura federal* (Reus: Fundació Josep Recasens, 2007); and Manuel Chust, ed., *Federalismo y cuestión federal en España* (Castellón: Universitat Jaume I, 2004).
45. The workshop was funded by the Leiden University Institute for History, the Leiden University Fund and the Chair of Modern European History of Ludwig-Maximilians-University Munich, for which we are very grateful. Formatting and editing of the manuscript was also possible thanks to the financial support of the research group *Hispona* (University of Santiago de Compostela).

CHAPTER 2
LANGUAGE AND REGIONALISM
Johannes Kabatek

Introduction

It would be difficult, if not impossible, to describe regionalism without reference to language or linguistic variety. Most of the European regionalist movements in the last 150 years are at least partly constructed on linguistic grounds, and in the majority of the chapters of this book, language as a factor is more or less present when describing the evolution of regionalism in different areas of Europe. In this chapter, some of the situations that are treated more comprehensively in other chapters will be focused upon in order to show, from a linguistic point of view, the significance of language in regionalist debates and in order to demonstrate that linguistic regionalism can be described with reference to a series of parallelisms and antagonisms which help to structure the particular facts. If we try to analyse the differences between European regional language situations and the varying importance of language in regionalism, we must go back in history and identify the factors and moments when these differences emerged. It is difficult to say how deeply rooted the present situation is, but we can identify some factors which during the last 150 years have had a decisive impact. This chapter will not offer a comprehensive overview on the relationship between regionalism and language since the nineteenth century; it will rather, with reference to certain exemplary moments and situations in the past, illustrate some factors which played a role in this relationship. Owing to the author's background, focus will be mainly placed on situations in Western Europe.

Regionalism is strongly linked to questions of linguistic identity or identity construction. However, the importance of language for defining regions is not uniform, neither in the different regions nor over time. Moreover, even if some dominant tendencies like 'globalization' or 'new regionalisms' can be identified in a certain period, this does not exclude their presence in other periods as well. This means that the chronological scheme chosen for this chapter is a relative one, with some prototypical facts which, in a broader context, should be further specified.

Language universalism and particularism

'Language' is not an unambiguous term. English distinguishes between the bare noun *language* and *a language*, with a determiner. The founder of modern linguistics, the Swiss scholar Ferdinand de Saussure,[1] used a distinction given in the French language to separate terminologically *langage*, *langue* and *parole*: language as a universal, a social and an individual phenomenon. Language in the sense of *langage* is the main characteristic of humans as opposed to other primates; but language never exists as such in a purely universal manner: we always speak *a language,* and we do it with individual variation.[2] There is a general tension between linguistic convergence and divergence: speakers accommodate to others in order to be understood or in order to be integrated socially. However, speakers also search for differentiation and create and enhance individual and social boundaries. Both tendencies display the aim of communicating with others without linguistic limits, on the one hand, and the aim of marking a particular linguistic identity, on the other.

In early childhood, the so-called 'first language' or L1 is usually acquired in a natural environment, and very early speech perception and speech production is marked by this 'mother tongue'.[3] The identification with the group of L1-speakers is probably an evolutionary advantage linked to the evolution of language as such: babies recognize their peer group and distinguish its most human characteristic, the language of the group, from languages of other groups. The mother tongue is the one where fundamental syntactic, phonetic and prosodic patterns are acquired; all other languages and varieties are, according to most theories of language acquisition, learned secondarily, as 'L2', in a different way, departing from the L1 structures.

However, even if the L1 has a fundamental importance for our linguistic biography, other languages and varieties are acquired later during the life of an individual and contribute to what we can call his or her 'linguistic biography'. During their life, individuals learn to move, according to the actual situation, between different languages and varieties, but they will always be marked by their mother tongue. This means that in actual linguistic behaviour, two tendencies can be identified, tendencies we can describe as behavioural vectors: a 'stemming' vector, which indicates the linguistic origin of the speakers, and a 'heading' vector, which indicates the actual social objective the group(s) speakers are aiming to integrate by the way they speak. The interplay of origin, biographical evolution and actual communicative objective generates what we may call the *linguistic identity* of an individual.[4]

Since there is no human without language, linguistic identity is by definition a universal fact. Linguistic identity, as identity in general, is a construct, and it allows for collective constructions which may stress a regional identity as well as an identity linked to a larger communicative range. And both are neither exclusive nor stable or 'given'. This is where regionalism and universalism foster their potential for becoming political movements of conviction and choice, even if protagonists frequently use the 'givenness' of the one or the other tendency as an argument.

As inherent tendencies, both universalism and particularism are universal and omnipresent, but there are phases and regions where one or the other tendency dominates, generally with shifts from one to another pole as a reaction to the previous period.[5] For modern European linguistic thought, the prototypical movements for the two extreme positions of linguistic universalism and particularism can be seen in the French Revolution and in Romanticism.

The fundamental principle of the French Revolution was to achieve the equality of all people by uniformization and universalization.[6] The Jacobins were faced with a country with enormous social and regional differences and they saw uniformization as a main goal. After a first phase of translation of writings with revolutionary thought into regional languages and dialects, the opposite policy was proposed: as all areas of social organization, language was also affected by uniformization and universalization. Regions and their linguistic variety were seen as representing the Ancien Régime, hindering the spread of revolutionary doctrine over the country. The French language, a renewed and purified French (a language which corresponds to the principles, according to its defenders, of nature and analogy), was considered to be the adequate instrument for wiping out social differences. Dialects and sociolects should be destroyed, and the nation should be built on a society without variation.

The anchoring of universalism in the history of the French Revolution has led to a tendency towards a certain political connotation of regionalism with right-wing ideology. In the second half of the nineteenth century, John Stuart Mill regarded linguistic diversity within a nation as a problem for achieving freedom and a liberal society and preferred the tendency towards uniformization. Peter Kraus even argues, '(D)uring a long period of time, lasting far into the twentieth century, this preference remained a standard ideological orientation for liberal nationalists, who tended to adopt the approach *one people, one state*.'[7] Marxism and Marxist regimes often adopted linguistic uniformism due to the same tradition. This does not mean that there is a necessary link between universalism and particularism and a certain political orientation, but rather that universalism is a kind of default ideology in left-wing thinking, and that 'progressive' left-wing regionalism often needs further justification. However, maybe more important than these traditional tendencies are the current contexts, and regionalism is often just ideologically opposed to the dominating ideology in the superposed entity. In some cases, universalism was also the dominant paradigm of authoritarian and rightist central governments.

The opposite movement to universalism is the particularist thought which can be found prototypically in German idealism and Romanticism. Philosophers such as Herder, Hamann, Fichte, August and Wilhelm Schlegel, or the linguists Bernardi or Wilhelm von Humboldt, focused on language diversity as the base for the definition of nations, denying the possibility of reducing mankind to one universal language. For Herder, the particular language of the human being (not language on a universal level) was the prerequisite of human autonomy, identity and freedom.

Both movements highlight different aspects of human language, and both offer arguments that have remained part of nationalist and regionalist discourse until the present.

Universalism and particularism are two intimately related and mutually conditioned phenomena, and we will not find one without the other. For regionalist movements, this means that they are related to movements of universalization and that they have to be discussed together with their universalizing counterparts. Shortly after the French Revolution, particularist movements spread all over Europe and in the New World. Wherever the revolutionary ideal of mass education in the dominant language was realized in areas with local language diversity, resistance was articulated and the local languages and dialects were defended: dialect dictionaries such as Schmeller's work on Bavarian or local language movements and cultural renaissances such as the Catalan *Renaixença* or the Galician *Rexurdimento* were nineteenth-century answers to the tendency of unification in a 'roof' language or variety. Similarly, when more than a hundred years later the tendency of globalization is becoming manifest after the intensification of mass communication and global mobility over recent decades, 'new regionalisms'[8] react against this unifying tendency postulating counter-reactions and stressing regional identity as opposed to global anonymity.

Region and language in Europe from the nineteenth century until the Second World War

The nineteenth century can be regarded as the century of the 'birth of regionalism' in the modern sense.[9] Language was a crucial factor in many of the regionalist movements all over Europe. The European history of language standardization has undergone a series of evolutionary steps,[10] in which vernacular languages emancipated in the medieval period and became written languages, but only a reduced number of languages underwent 'Ausbau'-processes of elaboration.[11] At the beginning of modernity, book printing and standardization were further processes which created asymmetries between languages selected for written elaboration, literature and prestigious uses and others with more restricted local functions. In areas of coexistence between standardized languages of wider communicative range and local languages or varieties, a diglossic coexistence between a written, prestigious standard language and a spoken local idiom is frequent, sometimes with restricted written usage of the local language.[12] There seems to be a linear evolution of the large-scale standard language becoming more and more important and spreading horizontally from centres to peripheries, and vertically from written to spoken use and from upper to lower social strata. This apparently linear evolution, catalysed by the ideology of the Enlightenment and the principle of linguistic *égalité*, was a fertile ground for the establishment of regional countermovements, which profited from the potential of regional diversity and constructed regional identities defined as alternative models to larger units and national roof languages. Some further external factors helped to foster these movements, basically the economic decline of peripheries in the process of industrialization, sometimes accompanied by massive emigration due to poverty or immigration which made the local linguistic particularities visible.

I should clarify at this point that we call these movements 'regional', even if some of them define themselves as 'national': the use of both terms is not always clearly differentiated and varies regionally. I will use 'national' for political and cultural constructions on a state level and 'regional' for regional constructions on a hierarchically inferior level: regions as parts of states or as entities within nations.[13] This does not prevent regionalist movements from evolving and becoming nationalist, postulating the establishment of an entity equal to the formerly superior one, as in the case of the Catalan movement until present.

Since linguistic regionalism in the nineteenth century is a movement defending the 'losers' of expansion processes from the medieval period against the 'winners', one of the most frequent metaphors used in the emancipation discourse is the rebirth, the Renaissance of languages which aims at repairing the historically given asymmetry between A-languages and B-languages in the diglossia. We find, in different regions, the Catalan *Renaixença*, the Galician *Rexurdimento*, the *Renaissance Provençale*, the Gaelic revival (*Athbheochan na Gaeilge*) and the *Renaschientscha Rumantscha*. All of these movements coincide in that they claim, to different degrees and with different contexts, the existence of some glorious past of the languages and the aim of recovering their lost importance. They all looked for delimitation of a differentiated language space and the consolidation of the local language as a dignified instrument for written usage. Poetry was generally the most important instrument for this dignification at the beginning of the process, and in poems and manifestos, the importance of the mother tongue was praised:[14] as a basic instrument of identification, the link between the ancestors and the present, and the symbol of community and home. A well-known example is Bonaventura Aribau's *Oda a la Pàtria*, published in 1833, which is considered as the foundational document of Catalan regionalism. A considerable part of the text is dedicated to the Catalan language; it states, among others, the following:

En llemosí sonà lo meu primer vagit	My first infant wail was in Catalan
quan del mugró matern la dolça llet bevia;	when I sucked the sweet milk from my mother's nipple;
en llemosí al Senyor pregava cada dia	I prayed to God in Catalan each day
e càntics llemosins somiava cada nit.	and dreamed Catalan songs every night.
Si, quan me trobe sol, parl' amb mon esperit,	When I find myself alone, I talk with my soul,
en llemosí li parl' que llengua altra no sent,	it speaks Catalan, it knows no other tongue,
e ma boca llavors, no sap mentir ni ment,	and then my mouth does not lie, or know how to lie,
puix surten mes raons del centre de mon pit.	and my words well up from the centre of my breast.[15]

Apart from poetry, other manifestations of these 'rebirth' movements are collections of folk songs, phrase books and oral literature, lexicological studies and dictionaries, grammars and other linguistic works elaborated frequently by members of the local elites and often in a frame of the dominant language.

Although nineteenth-century regionalist movements had many things in common, they also differed substantially in several aspects, and principally the following:

- the degree to which they are rather conservative or rather emancipatory
- their degree of support in the population
- the degree to which there is a substance and a tradition for the construction of a local identity
- their economic background
- their respective frame of reference which gives them more support or less

In their evolution until the First World War, when the old orders in Europe were destroyed and the whole continent was newly organized, these heterogeneities prepared the ground for a diversity in evolution: while some of the nineteenth-century regional languages grew into national movements and became part of political emancipation processes and national languages of new political units (such as in the case of the Baltic states and their languages, in Ireland or in Czechoslovakia), other regional languages or dialects were not successful in combining a cultural process with political support (such as the aforementioned Catalan) or even remained in their regional, subordinate position without strong attempts to change it (like in Bavaria or in Asturias).

In general, this is more a sociopolitical than a linguistic matter. If we look at the objective linguistic distance between languages, we can state that this seems not to be a central criterion for regional languages or varieties to become emancipated. It could be argued that the reason for the distinction between 'regional dialects' and 'regional languages' lies in the objective linguistic distance and that 'real languages' tend to emancipation whereas dialects tend to remain as such. This is, however, difficult to maintain since structural distance is not an objective criterion that would allow linguists to distinguish between languages and dialects and the survival of regional varieties does not seem to depend on their structure, as we can see if we compare different regional languages in the same political context such as the regional languages in Spain. However, language distance is a factor which might play a role in regionalist movements: whereas in communities where the regional language is closely related to the language of the state, speakers might choose the strategy of speaking the local language in order to stress their local identity even in communication with speakers who only know the state language, this is not possible in situations with typologically very distant languages due to the impossibility of mutual understanding.

If structural distance is not a sufficient criterion for the distinction between a dialect and a language, other criteria must be relevant. A classical distinction in twentieth-century language sociology is the one presented by Heinz Kloss between *Abstand* languages (languages by distance) and *Ausbau* languages (languages by elaboration). An *Abstand* language is a language which, due to its obvious structural difference, may not be subsumed as a dialect to the neighbouring languages, even if it is only spoken and not elaborated as a 'language of distance'.[16] Breton, Welsh, Albanian, Estonian or Basque are examples of *Abstand* languages: it is impossible to subsume them as dialects under the roof of French, English, Serbian, Russian or Spanish/French.

The second type, in turn, is not determined by inherent structural properties of the language: there must, of course, be some difference with regards to other languages or varieties in order to 'elaborate' a dialect as a different language. But the objective distance is not the most important criterion: It suffices to have a difference considered by a group of speakers as such and to have a name, an *adiectivum proprium*, for the identification of that difference.[17] *Ausbau* or language elaboration is a process which, according to Kloss, can be measured in two dimensions: on the one hand, the 'level' of the texts ('popular prose' – 'elaborated prose' – 'scientific prose') and, on the other hand, the thematic scope of texts (local issues – cultural referents – scientific referents).

Language

The process of elaboration goes from popular texts with local referents (V-E) to more developed texts and may eventually achieve the level of scientific prose (F-N).

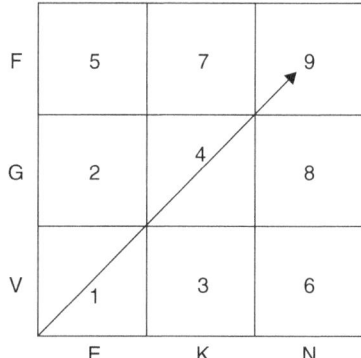

Kloss's scheme had originally been conceived for the description of Germanic minority languages but has then been applied in a more general way to language development processes. Several aspects of Kloss's scheme have been criticized: first, the distinction between both types of languages is of a different kind and an *Abstand* language can also be more or less developed (which can make an important difference). Second, the scheme only takes into account the mere existence of text types but not the respective degree of social diffusion and acceptance. It is, however, useful for a first rough distinction of languages and varieties. In the case of European regional varieties, the degree of *Ausbau* is an interesting measure which enables the differentiation of situations like those of German or Italian dialects, which generally do not go beyond the level of popular poetry or popular prose, and regional languages which underwent processes of development and achieved, in some cases like Catalan, Basque or Galician, the level of scientific prose due to conscious language planning processes. Even in regions where no political emancipation process and no linguistic *Ausbau* took place at the beginning of the twentieth century, it can be said that the second half of the nineteenth century contributed strongly to the creation of a regional identity and to the shaping of regional differences that set the arguments for future movements, which postulated regional language rights or political autonomy linked to linguistically defined areas.

An interesting example of the difference between nineteenth-century Europe and the newly emerging European order after the First World War is the Habsburg monarchy.[18] Until 1914, there were two radically different, geographically separated models of linguistic organization within the empire: on the West of the river Leitha, multilingualism was the rule and a liberal coexistence of languages and varieties was part of everyday linguistic practices; on the other side, in the Hungarian zone, a hierarchical language situation which echoed the principles of the French revolution was maintained. Both language situations had different legal bases and if we compare the constitution of Cisleithania from 1867, they recognized all customarily spoken languages at school, in official contexts and in public life, whereas the Transleithanian national law of 1868 gave clear priority to Hungarian in an 'indivisible and united

Hungarian nation', even if in some regions other languages such as Croatian or Romanian were allowed. Some of the regional languages and their territories served then as a base for newly emerging national units in the new century, as Haslinger asserts: 'Under the conditions of the Austrian political and constitutional system, cultural regionalism of linguistic communities became closely connected with national programmes as well, because in national discourse, some crown lands served as core regions for a future national statehood (Bohemia for Czechs, Galicia for Poles, Carniola for Slovenes or Transylvania for Romanians).'[19] The case of the Austro-Hungarian Monarchy shows that regional movements can emerge under the roof of unitary structures as well as in more pluralistically organized societies. However, in long-term views, monolingual tendencies and ignorance towards regions seem generally to have converging and diverging effects at the same time, and some of the important European regional movements derive their strength from the reference to previous oppression and impossibility of regional development, sometimes transferring the monolingual pattern of the nation state to the new regional framework.

The basis for the definition of regional territories is frequently linguistic, although there are not always clear linguistic borders. Languages seem to stem from a certain territory, and territoriality is often associated with two correlates: clearly distinguishable limits and stability, as if language was anchored or rooted in the territory. This is, of course, fallacious, and it leads to debate. Obviously, when we speak about the language of a certain territory, we refer to the speakers and not to the 'land'. The territory itself does not speak, and referring to language territories is in fact using a metonymy.

Moving again back to history, the interwar period is characterized by two antagonist tendencies. The first one consists in establishing former regions as new political units, as in the case of Czechoslovakia, the Baltic countries and Ireland. Also in the post-revolutionary Soviet Union, the former tendency towards Russification is replaced by a pluralist acceptance of language diversity after the tenth congress of the Russian Communisty Party in 1921. Russian, however, served as lingua franca and as a language for science and for the central government. The other tendency marks the Stalinist Soviet Union from 1938 onwards, when the universal knowledge of Russian (alongside with the introduction of the Cyrillic spelling system for regional languages) became a principal goal of Soviet language policy.[20]

Tendencies towards monolingualization can also be found in the Balkans and, within a completely different political context, in Spain, where the two dictatorships of Primo de Rivera (1923–1930) and Franco (1939–1975) contrast with the pro-regional Second Republic (1931–1936/1939) and the co-officialization of regional languages in democratic times. A similar contrast can be found in the case of minorities in Germany: whereas the Weimar Constitution promoted the protection of the mother tongue and between 1924 and 1939, the Organization of National Minorities in Germany (Verband der nationalen Minderheiten in Deutschland) defended the language rights of the Sorabic, Frisian, Danish, Polish and Lithuanian minorities, organizations of this kind and the official use of minority languages were prohibited later by the Nazis.[21]

Globalization and 'new regionalism' in Europe

After the Second World War and the political reshaping of the world with the end of the colonial age, economic networks began to overwrite political alliances and in the Western world, English became more and more dominant as an international lingua franca. Globalization began to emerge, and the metaphor of the 'global village' insinuated a global dialect as its correlate. The Jacobine dream of linguistic universalism was apparently about to be fulfilled, with universal English instead of universal French. However, if it is true that universalism and particularism are mutually conditioned, it was expectable that countermovements would emerge. Obviously since the last third of the twentieth century, this is what happened: cultural and regional factors reappeared and regionalist movements were reactivated or newly created throughout the world. The movements towards democratization and social changes in the 1960s might have played a further role. Furthermore, local factors such as certain political events must be added and are responsible for different moments of emergence of the 'new regionalisms' in different European regions from the 1970s onwards.

The relationship between the newly awakened emphasis on local identity and globalization was highlighted by scholars from different disciplines from the early 1970s onwards. Thus, the sociolinguist Joshua Fishman anticipated that globalization would be activating the need of particular identities,[22] and similar observations were made by sociologists, economists and historians.[23]

Linguistically, new regionalism has several facets, all having in common the focus on linguistic diversity of a certain territory as opposed to others. In some areas, new regionalism includes nationalist tendencies and aims at building up separate cultural and political entities, such as in Flanders and the Basque Country, in others, such as Bavaria or Sardinia, it rather defends a regional identity considered as compatible with a superposed national identity, even though also in the latter cases, some sectors of the regionalist movement defended or still defend political independence. It is important to insist on the constructional character of new (as well as of traditional) regionalism without therewith denying the existence of 'real' bases and differences. However, a continuum can be identified between the prototypical poles of a rather homogeneous region with its traditionally recognized own language and support for regionalist movements among a broad majority and newly constructed or awakened regional identities with few differential linguistic facts and low support among the population. In between, there are regions where the local variety is considered as different but its use is rather limited to informal oral communication or for ludic written uses, or where the local variety is considered to be a different language by some local activists, but this status is doubted by linguists and by parts of the population.

Clearly, little support for linguistic difference must not be confounded with the lack of regional identity. In some regions, the identity is built on other factors, such as geographic or economic, and language plays a secondary role. Close to the pole of a strong regional movement anchored in history is a case like Catalonia, where the regional language is the most important factor upon which the local identity is built and where regionalism has meanwhile shifted to a broad nationalist independence movement.[24] At the other extreme, we find cases such as local languages and varieties which after having almost died out are being revitalized or where local linguistic identities with very little historical anchoring are constructed on a rather weak basement. The latter phenomenon must be explained by a discursive transversality from one situation to another: throughout Europe, we find situations where regional identity strongly built on language contributes to social, political or economic advantages, and neighbouring regions with lesser linguistic differences adopt the strategies from 'stronger' regions. This can be observed, for instance, in Aragón, adopting elements of the Catalan discourse; in Upper Brittany with the discourse on Gallo adopted partly from lower Brittanie's discourse on Breton;[25] or with Cornish and Welsh or with Ulster Scots and Irish.

Transversality includes the adoption of sociolinguistic terminology, which then may enter into legislation or public debate. An example is the distinction between corpus planning and status planning: corpus planning refers to the planning of orthography, lexicon and grammatical forms, while status planning refers to the planning of the functions a language will have in society. Catalan sociolinguistics adopted this difference in the 1960s partly and introduced a distinction between language *normalization* (a term originally also used for corpus planning) and language *normativization*, the latter referring to corpus planning whereas the former refers to status planning and the 'making normal' of a language. This is, of course, a political and not descriptive term, since it implies the necessity to elevate a language on the level of other languages (generally the level of the state languages in contact with the regional language), and it has been adopted by other communities in order to consider the emancipation of the local idiom as a kind of naturally foreseen destiny which restores normality to the language.

This transversality of discourse on language diversity also is mirrored in institutional organization and in legal initiatives. On an international level, the Catalan Law of Linguistic Normalization (first edition 1983) served as a model for several other initiatives of language legislation in Europe and beyond; its influence can be traced even to cases in America like the Mexican General Law of Linguistic Rights for the Indigenous Peoples from 2003. The European Bureau for Lesser-Used Languages operated from 1982 onwards, organizing meetings and fostering communication among language activists within the European Union. It closed due to lack of economic support in 2010. In 1992, the Council of Europe adopted the *European Charter for Regional or Minority Languages*, prepared under the influence of representatives of the regions. In this charter, a number of fundamental linguistic rights for regional languages are postulated, such as the recognition and the protection of regional languages, their promotion on all levels of spoken and written usage as well as their institutional anchoring in administration, education and media. The charter has been criticized for its being limited to territorial languages and thus excluding languages of immigrant communities, while crucial European countries like France have never ratified it since they consider it unconstitutional. However, the charter is an important reference for what should be considered to be the minimum status regional languages should be allowed to attain. Together with UNESCO's Universal Declaration of Linguistic Rights (approved following a Catalan initiative in Barcelona in 1996), it serves as an important argumentative background for regional language emancipation.

If we want to consider the emergence and evolution of new linguistic regionalism in the second half of the twentieth century, a good example to look at is Wales. Since the nineteenth century, the number of Welsh speakers decreased. In 1960, a 'turning point in the history of the language'[26] can be fixed, when the flooding of the monolingual Welsh village Trewerin served as a starting point for a regionalist political movement in which the language was seen as a symbol for local resistance against governmental arbitrariness.

One of the most immediate and simple expressions of local emancipation can be seen in the phenomenon of writing autochthonous names on traffic signs and wiping out the denominations in the dominant language; this is a very widespread tendency and can be observed in very different regions. In recent years, the study of so-called linguistic landscapes[27] aims at systematizing this kind of linguistic visibility. In Wales (as in many other European areas), this visible protest has led to the officialization of bilingual street signs from the 1970s onwards. Several political initiatives (First Welsh Language Act 1967, Second Welsh Language Act 1993, Government of Wales Act 1998) led to more and more emancipation of the language. In 1991, the census data indicated that the number of speakers had grown for the first time in the century, and the 2001 census with 20.5 per cent of Welsh-speaking people showed a further increase. This, however, can also be due to changes in attitude and statistical data on language use must be treated cautiously. The growth is due to so-called new speakers or neo-speakers, a 'recurrent figure in urban linguistic activists' movement'.[28] In some regions such as the Spanish Basque Country, where they are known as *euskaldun berriak*, neo-speakers outnumber 'traditional' L1-speakers of Basque.[29] They are persons with the national dominant language as mother tongue, who decide to use the regional language 'regularly and as consistently as possible for daily communicative purposes'.[30]

Neo-speakers such as those in Wales can be found in different communities. In language revival movements, urban neo-speakers might be the leaders of regional language emancipation.[31] The fact that neo-speakers have shifted from one language to another has several inner-linguistic consequences: the new language of neo-speakers is – even if they grew up in a region where this language is commonly spoken – an L2, and they acquire it with all the consequences of an L2-acquisition process (interference from the L1, limited knowledge of forms, hypercorrections, etc.). The decision to shift to the regional language entails an enormous linguistic and social effort, which is reflected in attitudes of neo-speakers towards regional languages. Neo-speakers generally show a strong inclination towards purism and are frequently criticized by native speakers since they may have a strong accent and their linguistic behaviour might be strongly marked by the presence of the dominant language. In Wales and in other areas, such as the Basque Country, neo-speakers are probably decisive for the survival of the regional language, a language phonetically different from the autochthonous dialects and influenced by the dominant language at all levels of linguistic structuring.

The case of Wales also allows for illustrating new methods that were introduced in the last years in order to measure and to predict language shift (the individual loss of a language in favour of another one) and language maintenance. Mathematicians, statistical physicists and sociolinguists have tried to construct models that enable the measurement of the future development of regional languages. In 2003, Daniel M. Abrams and Steven H. Strogatz presented a paper in *Nature* with a simple model for calculating language death[32] or language survival. Two of the situations they put into the model were Welsh in Monmouthshire (c, in the graph below) and Welsh in all of Wales (d, in the graph below). The authors 'demonstrated' how, in comparing both situations, it can be shown how the increase of a supposed parameter *status* (s) slows down the rate of language loss and helps to maintain the language. The model is claimed to be able to predict future evolutions.

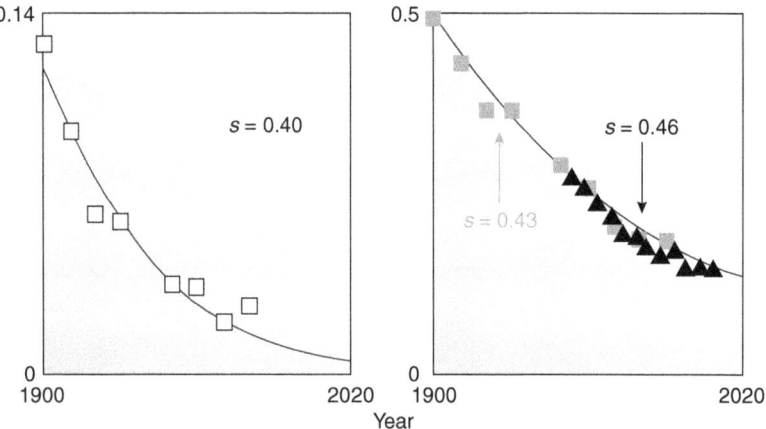

This has been criticized as simplistic and circular,[33] and in the last years models have increasingly improved and linguists and mathematicians have collaborated in order to refine the prediction techniques. However, it appears that the multifactorial phenomenon of language is not easily to be reducible to a few calculable numbers, and the prediction of future evolutions seems to be a rather uncertain task.

Migration and regions

The end of the Cold War and the opening of the Iron Curtain opened the way for massive inner-European migration, mainly from East to West, and reshaped the political landscape in several areas of the continent. Former republics of the Soviet Union became independent states and regional languages or dialects became official national languages there as in former Yugoslavia or former Czechoslovakia. Western German regions received massive inner-German migrants from the former German Democratic Republic and Russian migrants with German origin.[34] Already since the 1960s, migrants from southern Europe, North Africa and Turkey had moved to the richer states in central and northern Europe, as well as migrants from former colonies did to Britain, France, Belgium or the Netherlands.

On the one hand, this massive presence of speakers with different linguistic origins had an impact on dialect-levelling since the communicative culture in the receiving countries partly favoured switching to the standard language when talking to people from abroad. However, if we consider a vertical stratification in European regions, where the regional language tends to more likely be used in lower rather than in upper classes and migrants tend to enter lower levels of the social pyramid, migrants are frequently confronted with regional languages and dialects, adapting to the local varieties rather than adopting the standard in first generation contact. This means that migrants are not automatically factors of levelling or a 'danger' for the local languages. Situations such as the German-speaking part of Switzerland or Catalonia, where migrants often adopted the regional language, show that much depends on the prestige of the local language or variety and on educational policies above all in early childhood.

The traditional integration scheme of migrants is that the first generation acquires partial competence in the language of the receiving country, the second generation is bilingual and the third generation has the local language as the dominant one. In recent times, criticism against this traditional scheme of unidirectional acculturation and linguistic assimilation has been formulated and a more dialogic process of mutual approaching is preferred. However, as Mahendran argues, '[L]earning the language is totemic in integration debates' and the 'use of the dominant national language is viewed as pivotal'[35] for migrants. Between full linguistic integration and maintenance of the original language (two tendencies which by no way are mutually exclusive), numerous linguistic possibilities of merge and combination are possible, all of them with identitarian values or at least side effects.

Above all in the second generation, but according to the situation also in the third, code-switching is a frequent phenomenon within families and with peers. However, in some areas, where migrants were (and partly still are) concentrated in urban or suburban areas with high numbers of others of the same origin, code-switching between the contact languages may become a more general habit and hybrid mixed lects phonetically marked by the original language, like German-Turkish *Kiezdeutsch*, may emerge.[36] These hybrid mixtures can be associated with certain urban neighbourhoods and be 'regionalized'. There are also tendencies that the hybrid forms influence traditional speakers and that they can become part of humoristic imitation within and without the groups of migrants. Comedians are sometimes interesting indicators of language use and identity construction. Cases like the second-generation Bavarian Django Asül show how migrants break up the traditional scheme where dialect use serves as an indicator for local origin.[37]

Conclusion

Between their individual identity and their common, universal identity as part of mankind, humans create social units of different extension, degree of binding and stability. Language, in its local, regional and national forms, mirrors and shapes these units. The traditional unit of local linguistic identity in settlement societies is the dialect;

together with standardization, nation-building led to the creation of national languages. The last 150 years in Europe are marked by the strengthening of an intermediate entity, regional languages or regional forms of dialectal *koinés*. These entities may assume identity functions formerly associated with dialects, and they may be considered as attractive alternatives to the more aseptic and anonymous national standards. In principle, several language forms of different ranges may coexist in a more or less stable way, but European history shows that regional actors may link the construction of a regional linguistic identity to political emancipation, with acceptance or inhibition from the side of the larger national units. As we have seen, the interplay of the different levels should be considered in its systemic interaction and not be limited to isolated aspects. This allows for a better understanding of the processes, but it still remains impossible to make clear predictions about the following evolutions.

The twenty-first century came up with some unpredictable changes and with economic as well as ecological problems which had, in part, not been foreseeable. Climate changes affect the globe with variable regional impact; globalization and European integration, which seemed to be unidirectional and irreversible processes, are challenged from the left and from a newly emerging extreme right; populism reduces postmodern constructivism into an emotion-based post-factual view of the world and induces political disorder. It is hard to predict what the role of regional languages and language varieties will be within this new panorama, but regional identity in Europe counts on a historical background which serves as a fertile ground for newly emerging regionalisms, and the dynamics of European societies will always create needs or interests for fostering the importance of regional units dialectically opposed to smaller and larger ones. In this general sense, regional linguistic differences will keep on offering one of the potential scenarios for establishing contrasting discourses in Europe's future. However, as we have seen, there are phases of dominance of regionalist movements, and if we look at some concrete developments and their strength and impact in recent years, it is quite possible that a new wave of regionalism, including linguistic aspects, will characterize the next decades.

Notes

1. Ferdinand de Saussure, *Cours de Linguistique Générale*, ed. Tullio de Mauro (Paris: Payot, 1972, 1st ed., 1916).
2. Eugenio Coseriu, 'Linguistic Competence: What Is It Really?', The Presidential Address of the Modern Humanities Research Association, *Modern Language Review* 80, no. 4 (1985): 25-35.
3. Birgit Mampe, Angela D. Friederici, Anne Christophe and Kathleen Wermke, 'Newborns' Cry Melody Is Shaped by Their Native Language', *Current Biology* 19, no. 23 (2009): 1994-97.
4. See Michael Silverstein, 'Indexical Order and the Dialectics of Sociolinguistic Life', *Language & Communication* 23 (2003): 193-229; and Mary Bucholtz and Kira Hall, 'Locating Identity in Language', in *Language and Identities*, ed. Carmen Llamas and Dominic Watt (Edinburgh: Edinburgh University Press, 2010), 18-28.
5. Georg Bossong, *Sprachwissenschaft und Sprachphilosophie in der Romania: Von den Anfängen bis August Wilhelm Schlegel* (Tübingen: Narr, 1990); and Eugenio Coseriu,

Geschichte der Sprachphilosophie: Band 2: Von Herder bis Humboldt, ed. Jörn Albrecht (Tübingen: Narr, 2015).

6. Brigitte Schlieben-Lange, *Idéologie, révolution et uniformité de la langue* (Sprimont: Mardaga, 1996).
7. Peter A. Kraus, *A Union of Diversity: Language, Identity and Polity-Building in Europe* (Cambridge: Cambridge University Press, 2008), 86.
8. See Michael Keating, *The New Regionalism in Western Europe: Territorial Restructuring and Political Change* (Cheltenham; Northampton, MA: Edward Elgar, 2000).
9. See Joost Augusteijn and Eric Storm, eds, *Region and State in Nineteenth-Century Europe: Nation-Building, Regional Identities and Separatism* (Basingstoke: Palgrave Macmillan, 2012).
10. Peter Auer, 'Europe's Sociolinguistic Unity, or, A Typology of European Dialect/Standard Constellations', in *Perspectives on Variation: Sociolinguistic, Historical, Comparative*, ed. Nicole Delbecque, Johan van der Auwera and Dirk Geeraerts (Berlin: Mouton de Gruyter, 2005), 7–42.
11. Heinz Kloss, '"Abstand Languages" and "Ausbau Languages"', *Anthropological Linguistics* 9, no. 7 (1967): 9–41.
12. Johannes Kabatek, 'Diglossia', in *The Oxford Guide to the Romance Languages*, ed. Adam Ledgeway and Martin Maiden (Oxford: Oxford University Press, 2016), 624–33.
13. See also the introduction to this volume.
14. See Ricco Valär, *Weder Italiener noch Deutsche! Die rätoromanische Heimatbewegung 1863–1938* (Baden: Verlag hier + jetzt, 2013).
15. Source of the English translation: https://antigone1984.com/2012/11/20/homage-to-catalonia/.
16. Peter Koch and Wulf Oesterreicher, *Gesprochene Sprache in der Romania: Französisch, Italienisch, Spanisch* (Berlin: De Gruyter, 2013).
17. Johannes Kabatek and Brigitte Schlieben-Lange, 'Zu Notwendigkeit und theoretischem Status der Sprachkategorisierungsforschung', *Sociolinguistica* 14 (2000) [2001]: 115–20.
18. Hans Goebl, 'Die Sprachensituation in der Donaumonarchie', in *Sprachen in Europa. Sprachsituation und Sprachpolitik in europäischen Ländern*, ed. Ingeborg Ohnheiser, Manfred Kienpointner and Helmut Kalb (Innsbruck: Institut für Sprachwissenschaft, 1999); Peter Haslinger, 'How to Run a Multilingual Society: Statehood, Administration and Regional Dynamics in Austria-Hungary, 1867–1914', in *Region and State*, ed. Augusteijn and Storm, 111–28; and Tamara Scheer, 'Habsburg Languages at War: "The Linguistic Confusion at the Tower of Babel Couldn't Have Been Much Worse"', in *Languages and the First World War: Communicating in a Transnational War*, ed. Julian Walker and Christophe Declercq (Basingstoke: Palgrave Macmillan, 2016), 62–78.
19. Haslinger, 'How to Run', 123.
20. See Gary C. Fouse, *The Languages of the Former Soviet Republics: Their History and Development* (Lanham, MD: University Press of America, 2000).
21. See Ferdinand Knabe, *Sprachliche Minderheiten und nationale Schule in Preussen zwischen 1871 und 1933: Eine bildungspolitische Analyze* (Münster: Waxmann, 2000). See also the chapter by DeWaal and Núñez Seixas.
22. Joshua A. Fishman, *Language and Nationalism* (Rowley: Newbury House, 1973).
23. See Anne Judge, *Linguistic Policies and the Survival of Regional Languages in France and Britain* (Houndmills: Palgrave Macmillan, 2007); and Mario Telò, ed., *European Union and New Regionalism: Competing Regionalism and Global Governance in a Post-Hegemonic Era* (London: Routledge, 2014).

24. Johannes Kabatek and Mónica Castillo Lluch, eds, *Las lenguas de España. Política lingüística, sociología del lenguaje e ideología desde la Transición hasta la actualidad* (Frankfurt a.M./Madrid: Vervuert/Iberoamericana, 2006).
25. Hans-Ingo Radatz, 'Französisch, Bretonisch und ... Gallo – Ist die Bretagne dreisprachig?', in *Kulturkontakt und Sprachkonflikt in der Romania*, ed. Dieter Kattenbusch (Vienna: Braumüller, 1997), 163–89.
26. Judge, *Linguistic Policies*, 165.
27. Rodrigue Landry and Richard Y. Bourhis, 'Linguistic Landscape and Ethnolinguistic Vitality: An Empirical Study', *Journal of Language and Social Psychology* 6 (1997): 23–49; and Roert Blackwood, Elizabeth Lanza and Hirut Woldemariam, eds, *Negotiating and Contesting Identities in Linguistic Landscapes* (London: Bloomsbury, 2016).
28. Johannes Kabatek and Claus D. Pusch, 'Language Contact in Southwestern Europe', in *The Languages and Linguistics of Europe. A Comprehensive Guide*, ed. Johan van der Auwera and Bernd Kortmann (Berlin/New York: Mouton de Gruyter, 2011), 393–408. See also Johannes Kabatek, *Die Sprecher als Linguisten. Interferenz- und Sprachwandelphänomene dargestellt am Galicischen der Gegenwart* (Tübingen: Niemeyer 1996).
29. Xabier Aizpurua Telleria and Jon Aizpurua Espin, 'The Sociolinguistic Situation in the Basque Country According to the 2001 Sociolinguistic Survey', *International Journal for the Sociology of Language* 174 (2001): 39–54.
30. Kabatek/Pusch, 'Language Contact', 402.
31. See Kabatek, *Die Sprecher*, for Galician cases.
32. Daniel M. Abrams and Steven H. Strogatz, 'Modelling the Dynamics of Language Death', *Nature* 424 (2003): 900. See also David Crystal, *Language Death* (Cambridge: Cambridge University Press, 2000).
33. See Johannes Kabatek and Lucía Loureiro Porto, 'Mathematical Models Meet Linguistic Data and Vice-Versa', *International Journal of the Sociology of Language* 221 (2013): 1–10; as well as Johannes Kabatek, 'Modelos matemáticos e substitución lingüística', *Estudos de Lingüística Galega* 4 (2012): 27–43.
34. See Heinz Fassmann and Rainer Münz, *Migration in Europa. Historische Entwicklung, aktuelle Trends und politische Reaktionen* (Frankfurt a. M./New York: Campus, 1996), 365; and Klaus J. Bade, Pieter Emmer, Leo Lucassen and Jochen Oltmer, eds, *The Encyclopedia of Migration and Minorities in Europe: From the 17th Century to the Present* (Cambridge: Cambridge University Press, 2011).
35. Kesi Mahendran, '"A Two-Way Process of Accommodation": Public Perceptions of Integration along the Migration-Mobility Continuum', in *The Discourses and Politics of Migration in Europe*, ed. Umut Korkut (New York: Palgrave Macmillan, 2013), 109–31 (here, 124 and 130).
36. See, e.g., Uwe Hinrichs, *Multi Kulti Deutsch: wie Migration die deutsche Sprache verändert* (München: Beck, 2013).
37. See chapter by DeWaal.

Further reading

Auer, Peter, and Jürgen E. Schmidt, eds, *Language and Space: An International Handbook of Linguistic Variation* (Berlin: Mouton de Gruyter, 2016).

Chambers, Jack, and Natalie Schilling, eds, *Handbook of Language Variation and Change (second edition)* (Oxford: Wiley-Blackwell, 2013).

Evans, Betsy E., Erica J. Benson and James Stanford, eds, *Language Regard: Methods, Variation and Change* (Cambridge: Cambridge University Press, 2018).

Evans, David, ed., *Language, Identity and Symbolic Culture* (London: Bloomsbury, 2018).

Hinskens, Frans, ed., *Language Variation – European Perspectives* (Amsterdam/Philadelphia: J. Benjamins, 2011).

Kortmann, Bernd, ed., *The Languages and Linguistics of Europe: A Comprehensive Guide*, 2 vols (Berlin: De Gruyter Mouton, 2011).

Kraus, Peter A., *A Union of Diversity. Language, Identity and Polity-Building in Europe* (Cambridge: Cambridge University Press, 2008).

Moore, Emma, and Chris Montgomery, eds, *Language and a Sense of Place: Studies in Language and Region* (Cambridge: Cambridge University Press, 2015).

CHAPTER 3
REGIONALISM AND FOLKLORE
David Hopkin

Introduction: Origins and definitions of folklore studies

According to the American Folklore Society, '[f]olklore is the traditional art, literature, knowledge, and practice that is disseminated largely through oral communication and behavioural example'.[1] The term embraces genres of oral literature such as folk tales, folk songs, legends, proverbs and riddles, but it also extends to practices such as traditional drama, dance and costume. It is not unusual to encounter terms such as folk medicine, folk religion and folk belief . . . and one can also include other traditional aspects of everyday life such as food, vernacular architecture and handicrafts, if they 'are generally maintained without benefit of formal instruction or institutional direction'.[2]

Over the course of the twentieth century, scholars have sometimes distinguished between oral lore and belief – that is folklore – and the more material aspects of tradition which are termed either 'ethnography', 'ethnology' or 'folk life'. In Finland and Estonia, for instance, the two subjects have their own university chairs, departments and journals.[3] The shift from folklore studies towards ethnology can be seen in other countries, for example, in Lamberto Lorio's Museo di Etnografia Italiana founded in 1906 in Florence and the French Musée des arts et traditions populaires founded in 1937.[4] Their instigators criticized folklorists as amateurs who cherry-picked the most digestible elements of tradition and failed to contextualize oral culture within other aspects of folk life. Ethnography often has closer ties to state institutions, compared with the local participatory enthusiasm which characterizes folklore studies.[5] However, in practice the fields overlap, as do their practitioners and their publics.

If 'man is [. . .] a storytelling animal' then folklore has existed throughout human history,[6] but the separate study of folklore is a more recent innovation. The term itself was only coined in 1846 by the English antiquarian and admirer of the Grimm brothers, William Thoms, as a replacement for the phrase 'popular antiquities'.[7] Early modern antiquarians had already engaged in activities that look like folkloric research, such as recording superstitions, calendar customs and historical legends associated with landscape features,[8] but consistent scholarly attention to oral culture can be dated to the ballad revival of the late eighteenth and early nineteenth centuries, exemplified by James Macpherson's *Fragments of Ancient Poetry, collected in the Highlands of Scotland* (1760) and Johann Gottfried Herder's *Volkslieder* (1778/1779).[9] Interest grew in the Romantic period and beyond, in part because of the influence of the brothers Jacob and Wilhelm Grimm, who largely initiated the fashion for recording folk tales.[10] However, the emergence of folklore as a fully fledged scholarly activity, with the panoply of national and international societies, learned journals and international conferences, is almost contemporaneous with the start of the 'long twentieth century' covered in this volume.

Folklore societies were set up Britain in 1878 (The Folklore Society), in Denmark in 1883 (Folkemindesamfundet), in France in 1885 (Société des traditions populaires) and in Switzerland in 1896 (der Schweizerischen Gesellschaft für Volkskunde). Journals soon followed: the Italian journal *Archivio per lo studio delle tradizioni popolari* first appeared in 1882, the Dutch journal *Volkskunde* in 1888 and the Jewish folklore journal *Mitteilungen der Gesellschaft für Jüdische Volkskunde* in 1898.[11] The first official university position in folklore was given to Moltke Moe at Christiana (now Oslo) University in 1886; the next was awarded to Kaarle Krohn at Helsinki in 1898.[12] The first international congress took place in Paris in 1889; the second in London in 1891. It is possible that, as an academic subject, folklore may not survive the long twentieth century, for it has disappeared or been subsumed in many universities that were once leading research centres.

The rise of the region as folklore's default geography

Given that folklore, according to the definition cited above, relies on face-to-face communication and directly observed performance, one might imagine that its territorial frame is necessarily local. However, it is inherent in the concept 'tradition' that the elements of lore – such as a riddle or a proverb – have been repeated, and these iterations spread not just through time but also space. Establishing the geographical and temporal limits of a tradition has been one of the concerns of academic folklore, though in works meant for popular consumption both are often taken for granted. In the first half of the nineteenth century, romantic writers usually took the nation as their given frame of reference. Herder's influential *Volkslieder* was republished in 1807 as *Stimmen der Völker in Liedern* (Voices of Peoples [or Nations] in Song), and many of the song collectors that followed referred, implicitly or explicitly, to a nation, albeit sometimes one which had yet to establish full territorial sovereignty. Claude Fauriel's *Chants populaires de la Grèce moderne* (1824–1825) was an influential trendsetter.[13] Although the Grimms were willing to identify the regional origins of their stories, the first generation of folk tale collectors they inspired tended to invoke the national in their titles, for instance, Georg von Gaal's *Mährchen der Magyaren* (Folk Tales of the Hungarians, 1822), Peter Asbjørnsen's and Jørgen Moe's *Norske Folkeeventyr* (Norwegian Folk Tales, 1841–1844) and Alexander Afanasyev's *Narodnye russkie rkazki* (Russian Folk Tales, 1855–1867). Of course, neither Hungary nor Norway were independent states then, but this romantic 'cultivation of culture' helped develop a national consciousness in the book-buying public.[14]

Hence, in histories of the long nineteenth century, folklore is often depicted as a handmaiden of nationalism, particularly in new nations.[15] Folk tales were to be the basis for a revived national literature, folk songs the basis for a revived national music, and the two would come together in national dramas staged at new national theatres such as The National Theatre of Norway (founded in 1899) or the Abbey Theatre in Dublin (founded in 1904). In histories of the long twentieth century, the connection between folklore and militant nationalism turned more sinister, due to the dominance of German *Volkskunde* and its ready collaboration with National Socialism.[16]

The 'phantoms of romantic nationalism' are difficult to exorcise from folklore.[17] Yet in Western Europe, which will be focus of this chapter, the region or province soon emerged as the more appropriate framework within which to collect and publish popular traditions. The earliest collections of folk tales in France, such as Emmanuel Cosquin's *Contes populaires de Lorraine* (1876), Paul Sébillot's three volumes of *Contes populaires de la Haute-Bretagne* (1880–1882) and Jean François Bladé's three volumes of *Contes populaires de la Gascogne* (1886) all lay claim to a province. The same was true of folk song collectors in Italy, starting with Costantino Nigra's influential *Canti popolari del Piemonte*, first published in the *Rivista Contemporanea* from 1858 to 1862. It is perhaps worth noting, given the otherwise apparent weakness of regionalism in Italy, that Italian folklorists almost invariably use such provincial titles. Given Imperial Germany's federal constitution, it is perhaps less surprising that the German association concerned with folklore, the Verband der Vereine für Volkskunde founded in 1904, had a federal organization. Yet the same was also true of the more unitary Spanish monarchy where El Folk-Lore Español was made up of regional societies in Andalusia, Castile, Galicia, Extremadura and the Basque Country.[18]

The name of the Folklore Society in London placed no territorial limits on its intellectual jurisdiction, and the 'anthropological' interpretation of folklore which its leading figures promoted was aligned to Britain's role as an imperial power, because it relied on the comparison of European data with that supplied by administrators and missionaries in the colonies.[19] Nonetheless, one of the Society's first initiatives, after the success of the 1891 Congress, was to sponsor a series of County Folklore volumes covering the United Kingdom.[20] This unfinished project was revived in a more commercial guise in the 1970s by the publisher Batsford, demonstrating that there remained a public appetite for folklore when it was regionally packaged.

Such book series, which are fairly common in this field, can reaffirm the nation and the region simultaneously because they present the latter as a building block of the collective culture and identity of the former. This idea is explicit, for example, in the general introduction to the series of legend books, the *Deutscher Sagenschatz* edited by Paul Zaunert, which ran to fifteen volumes between 1917 and 1944, and which opened, provocatively given that the German army was then occupying Flanders, with *Vlämische Sagen, Legenden und Volksmärchen*.[21] It is explicit also in the introduction to Paul Delarue's catalogue of tale types, *Le Conte populaire français* (1957), just as it is implicit in the series of folk tale books he edited in the 1950s, *Contes merveilleux des provinces de France*. The publisher Gallimard would resurrect the project in the 1970s and 1980s with its series of *Récits et contes* organized by province. The same logic is still at work in Stefaan Top's more recent collection, *Op verhaal komen* (2004–2008), a legend collection with a volume dedicated to each Flemish region (though not the French-speaking provinces of Belgium).

Throughout the twentieth century, the region has remained folklore's preferred geography in most West European countries. National folklore societies used the region as their primary organizing principle both in collecting and cataloguing traditions. The Belgian Commission nationale de la vieille chanson populaire, for example, sponsored its members to produce regional publications such as Lambrecht Lambrechts's *Limburgsche liederen* (1936–1937), Albert Libiez's *Chansons populaires de l'ancien Hainaut* (1939), Theophiel Pieters's *Oude Kempische liederen* (1951) and Roger Pinon's *Chansons populaires de la Flandre wallonne* (1965). Even when the national framework provides the first order of organization, as in the national tale and legend type catalogues published by the Folklore Fellows (an international organization with a Finnish base), the region usually provides the internal second order.

Few folklorists offer an intellectual justification for this allegiance to the region, and beyond the title they seldom attempt to demonstrate that the recorded tales and songs were the exclusive cultural property of – or express something particular about – the region. One might argue that their regional remit was purely practical: it was hard enough to record the songs of Limburg or Hainaut, for a single collector to extend his or her search to the entirety of Belgium would have been impossible. However, practicalities are not really the issue, as the reference to historical, as opposed to actual administrative units in these titles makes clear. There is, in terms of local government, no such place as Walloon Flanders or the Campine, but Pieters's and Pinon's aim in using these names was to imply that they had a reality as cultural, if not political regions.

Of the French folk tale collections mentioned above, one was made entirely in a single locality, the other two extended their range to include a second village. Rather than *Contes populaires de Lorraine*, what were recorded were the tales told in Montiers-sur-Saulx, a commune which, when Cosquin was active, was home to a little over a thousand inhabitants. Why, then, ascribe the contents to 'Lorraine' as a whole? At the time Cosquin was writing, the province of Lorraine had not formally existed for nearly a hundred years: administratively speaking, Montiers was a commune of the department of the Meuse. Cosquin was an arch-royalist and may have baulked at invoking a revolutionary territorial unit such as the department, but his contemporary Paul Sébillot, a committed Republican, likewise eschewed departmental titles, ascribing his tales to Upper Brittany (rather than the hamlet of Isle de Saint-Cast where he had actually recorded the bulk of them, which was in the department of the Côtes-du-Nord).

In both cases, the titles inferred that there existed distinct cultural regions called 'Lorraine' and 'Upper Brittany'. But, in fact, both of these authors knew that there was little that was particularly Lorrainer or Breton about the tales they published. Cosquin provided notes to all eighty-four texts to show that the same tale had been recorded elsewhere across the Eurasian landmass. His theory was that the tales had mostly originated in India and been diffused from there along routes of war, trade, migration and religious evangelism. This diffusionist model was extremely influential in the early years of academic folklore, yet its logic undermined claims to cultural difference, whether national or regional.[22]

Folk songs, because of their reliance on rhyme, are not quite so universal in their distribution; nonetheless, almost all the folk songs that Libiez collected in Hainaut and Pinon in Walloon Flanders could also have been heard in the other French-speaking regions of Belgium as well as France, Quebec and the Suisse Romande, a point that both authors indeed made themselves. As the scholarly apparatus of folklore grew, claims to national or regional cultural exceptionalism weakened. The process of cataloguing folklore iterations according to internationally accepted criteria really took off with the folk-tale classification system, initiated by the Finn Antti Aarne in 1910. All of the many national folk-tale catalogues apply this system so in a matter of minutes one can establish that there is really no such thing as a Lorrainer tale, or even a French tale. Type indexes for songs tend to be limited to single language areas, but from the time of Herder on it was clear that plots reoccur in the ballad repertoire of many nations: the story of the Dutch 'Heer Halewijn' is essentially the same as the Anglo-Scots 'Outlandish Knight', and there are parallels in French, German, Polish, Hungarian, Danish, Italian, Portuguese and other song traditions.[23] That folklore, which is highly local in its form of transmission, but eminently transnational in its content, should have alighted on the region as its proper perspective for study and presentation, requires some explanation.

Realizing the region through folklore

Some academic folklorists have attempted to establish the reality of cultural regions and mark their boundaries. The Swedish folklorist Carl von Sydow borrowed the term 'ecotype' from the natural sciences to illustrate that, while a folk tale like *Cinderella* might be all but universal in its distribution, there were distinct national and regional variations in how it was told; whether its hero was male or female, for example. A particular variant was preferred in a particular cultural zone because the story (or any other element of tradition) had been adapted to that milieu.[24] Thus cultural differentiation, undermined by diffusionist models, was rediscovered at the level of the 'variant'.

Such ecotypes can be revealed through mapping. Already in the 1880s and 1890s the Spanish folklorist Antonio Machado y Álvarez and his French correspondent Paul Sébillot had urged the use of cartography in order to establish the spatial distribution of traditions. At the time, folklore collecting was simply too haphazard for reliable maps, but in the wake of the interwar dialect atlases, cartography did become a recognized folklore methodology. There exist underused atlases of German, Austrian, Swiss, Polish, Swedish, Finnish, Dutch and Yugoslavian folk cultures.[25] Since the 1980s, folklore cartography has fallen into disrepute, partly because it was associated with racialist attempts to establish ethnic boundaries in the 1930s, but also because the maps themselves did not cohere. Cultural regions defined through the use of a particular technology (such as a type of plough) did not necessarily overlap with cultural regions defined by observation of particular festivities. Perhaps the death knell was J. J. Voskuil's bestselling satirical novel series *Het Bureau* (1996–2000) about the Dutch centre for folklore studies, the Meertens Instituut, and its attempts, among other things, to map whether farmers buried the placentas of horses or hung them in trees.[26] Traditions, Voskuil had concluded in his day job as an ethnologist, were simply too fluid to be represented in a static form like a map with its implied claims to long-term continuity.

In the late twentieth century, in common with other social scientists, academic folklorists have turned their attention away from collectivities towards the individual. They have become less interested in establishing the genealogies of traditions and instead concentrate on how they were adapted and used in the moments when they were performed.[27] Delimiting traditions is no longer fashionable. But academics make up a rather small subset among folklore writers and practitioners, and among the wider public the region remains much the preferred space. It is part of the habitus of popular folklorists, their publishers and their consumers. Folklorists do not need to explain their choice because their public already expects it. If one browses the shelves dedicated to the local region in a bookshop in Cork, Barcelona or Aarhus, one anticipates books on the folklore of Munster, Catalonia or Jutland.

Default regionalism does not mean that folklore is necessarily hostile to nationalism. As Chris Manias has shown, the scholars responsible for establishing the sciences of human culture such as archaeology, anthropology and folklore had relatively little truck with ideas of racial purity and national segregation but rather understood modern nations as the product of historical interactions between many peoples and cultures whose distinct contributions were still visible in regional particularities.[28] The nation was a garden of many blooms, each region contributing, through its costumes and its dances, a particular burst of colour. In 1860, Jules Champfleury published his *Chansons populaires des provinces de France* in which each province was represented by a selection of songs brought together for the enjoyment of the nation as a whole. This proved to be a very popular model. Ernest Closson's 1905 *Chansons populaires des provinces belges* was a direct imitation. The same logic underwrote the Community Singing Movement in interwar Britain[29] and the 'Singing Together' programmes made by the BBC for use in schools from 1939 to 2001.[30] Entire generations of Britons grew up with a song repertoire that included representatives from the Scottish Highlands ('The Skye Boat Song'), Wales ('Men of Harlech') and Cornwall ('Trelawney'). The fact that all three songs relate moments of regional resistance to the hegemonic English centre in no way detracted from their appeal; rather, it demonstrated that historical resistance could be co-opted into a single narrative of national coming together.

A more idiosyncratic method for harmonizing the regional and the national in folklore was the adoption of a particular region as a metonym or an archetype for the national whole. Linguistic purity can explain this substitution, which is one of the reasons that the Gaeltacht, the Irish-speaking west of the Ireland, was (and is) frequently described as the 'most Irish' of regions, whose cultural distinctiveness could serve as a reservoir to revitalize the entire nation.[31] Anglophone Ascendancy Irish writers, such as Lady Augusta Gregory and John Millington Synge, journeyed west, in particular to the Aran Islands, to learn Gaelic, record folklore and find inspiration for a modern but distinctively national literature. The first play put on at the Abbey Theatre in 1904 is exemplary in this regard. *Cathleen Ní Houlihan*, ascribed to William Butler Yeats but mostly written by Lady Gregory, draws on the pair's folklore collecting in the west of

Ireland. The eponymous Cathleen is a folkloric/literary personification of Ireland as a poor old woman, who nonetheless inspires the play's hero, a Mayo peasant, to embrace martyrdom for the national cause.[32] In 1893, another Ascendancy Protestant, Douglas Hyde, founded the Gaelic League which aimed to 'de-anglicize Ireland' by drawing on the material he and others had collected in the Gaeltacht. The League ran classes in Gaelic and encouraged singing, folk dancing and folklore collecting. It was also, although not by design, a nursery for physical force nationalists.[33] The Irish Free State took up many of the League's objectives after independence, for instance, making Irish a compulsory subject in public schools. The oral autobiography of a Gaelic-speaking islander, the storyteller Peig Sayers from Great Blasket, recorded by another Anglophone and folklore-minded visitor, Molly O'Kennedy, became the set text on the curriculum. The intention was to reconnect the urban, anglicized centres of Ireland – the 'people' as a political entity – with their Gaelic heritage – the 'people' as bearers of a distinct cultural tradition.

In a similar manner, the Zuiderzee region in the Netherlands, Dalarna in Sweden and Hardangerfjord in Norway have been treated by folklorists as 'relic areas' (the term comes from dialectology, but indirectly from the natural sciences), which still practised distinctive national customs and manners, whereas urbanized areas had become more cosmopolitan. Henrik Ibsen himself had been sponsored by the Norwegian government to collect folklore in Hardanger in 1862, and some of what he heard made its way into his later plays.[34] The promotion of such relic areas was most visible in the presentation of folk cultures at world fairs and international expositions, such as the Hindeloopen room (from a town on the coast of the Zuiderzee) which formed part of the Dutch contribution at the 1878 Paris Exposition Universelle.[35] Open-air museums, including Skansen in Sweden, developed directly from these enormously popular ethnographic recreations.[36] Such assemblies of regional vernacular building styles in turn inspired the formation of 'national romantic' architectural styles.[37] This is perhaps most visible in the Nordic countries, but simultaneously in Hungary the Fiatalok group of architects looked to the vernacular building of Transylvania, another 'relic area', to develop their new national style.[38]

The most striking example of the region as archetype of the nation must be Karelianism, a cultural movement in nineteenth- and early-twentieth-century Finland, which saw Finnish writers, artists and composers travel to Archangel Karelia to witness for themselves performances of the rune songs that, a generation before, had been noted down by the song collector Elias Lönnrot and reassembled into the Finnish national epic, the *Kalevala* (1835).[39] The peculiarity of the Karelian case is that, though its language is related to Finnish, the region lies outside the boundaries of both the historic Duchy and the modern sovereign state of Finland: it remains a province of Russia. As Pertti Anttonen has argued, the value of an external relic area to the successful Finnish nationalist movement was that, while Karelia showed Finns what they had been, the nation state could emphasize its own modernity in contradistinction. Karelia was the national past, a heritage worthy of recording but as a base on which to develop a modern national culture and a trajectory towards the future, which Karelia itself could not enjoy.[40]

However, folkloric regionalism cannot always be subsumed into narratives of nation-building. To quote another attempt to define the field of folklore, folklorists are not just orientated towards the informal but also 'the marginal (in relation to the centres of power and privilege)'.[41] This is a predilection rather than an obligatory position, but it is quite pronounced, and it often puts folklorists at the forefront of attempts to promote the region and to defend it against the overpowering state. Hence, folklorists have often been active in regionalist politics.

Folklore and the politics of regionalism

This political engagement can take many forms, ranging from limited attempts to protect distinct cultural heritages to more radical campaigns for regional autonomy or even separatism. In the first half of the period, such regionalist activism was more often, though not exclusively, the tool of the conservative right, intent on preserving rural social hierarchies and religious identities from the threat posed by national and class-based politics. Since the Second World War, however, regionalism has developed a left-wing, anti-imperialist discourse. But in both cases, defence of folk culture has provided a justification for alternative political arrangements, as well as the material through which to voice and disseminate a regionalist message.

As folklore is concerned with tradition, its attention is necessarily turned towards the past, and this was especially marked in the generations of folklorists before the Second World War who tended to exaggerate the age and immutability of traditions. One could argue that, in many European countries, the region was also becoming a thing of the past, overtaken by the centripetal forces of nation-state building. This seemed particularly evident in countries where historic regions had been deprived of all administrative functions, such as France, Italy and Sweden. Nation-building was the opposite of folklore in that it relied on 'formal instruction or institutional direction' through national bureaucracies and national curricula in education, and national disciplining institutions such as the army and the police. The informality and anonymity of folklore can give the impression that it is a more natural culture expression, the organic issue of a particular environment. Hence, the appeal of 'ecotype', 'relic area' and other metaphors from the natural sciences to folklorists.[42] Modern and, in particular, urban culture was just the opposite, fabricated and often the work of a single named author. Increasingly, the sources of urban popular culture were heterogeneous and often foreign: think of jazz. It was commercial and ephemeral, brought to 'the people' rather than made by 'the people'. But elite national culture was just as alien and relied on schools as a method of inculcation. Both threatened the specific culture of the regions, whose protection therefore became a spur to political activism.

Folkloric regionalism often denies its own political nature. Nostalgia for a regional past was perceived as an escape from the strident howls of interest-group politics that bedevilled the modern – that is to say the national – public sphere of parliamentary parties, newspapers, leagues and trade unions. The region, usually depicted as a rural hinterland, appeared untarnished by the blight of ideological division which characterized national politics. The region could be presented as a place free from class conflict (itself seen by many conservatives as a product of industrial modernity and unhealthy cosmopolitanism). Through folklore, two definitions of 'the people' – as a social class opposed to the elites and as a social whole bound by shared traditions that included elites – could be reunited. Many of the folklorists already mentioned, including Sébillot, Cosquin, Machado, Yeats, Lady Gregory and Hyde, initially recorded folklore from their servants: through folklore, elites could connect with other social classes.[43] Thus, although folkloric texts contained many bitter statements of social antagonism, edited for public consumption they appeared more as a dialogue that bonded the different members of a single community. This downplaying of class conflict was easier to imagine in the countryside, and therefore the region, where direct relations pertained between employer and employee, than in the *anomie* of the factory and the city.

The region was a retreat from the pressures of modernity, literally so in the case of Dalarna which was, and is, one of the prime locations for summer holidaying by urban Swedes. Because folklore dealt with collective custom and ritual – quite literally 'Singing Together' – it could be used to emphasize the ties that bind, the communal and traditional *Gemeinschaft*. Through folkloric practices, such as regional costuming, social differences could be elided. Participating as part of a choir or a dance generated a sense of *communitas*, a feeling of collective well-being. Those who had been divided by the processes of modernization and nation-building could be reunited through folklore and the region.

Of course, the rejection of ideology (and class conflict) is itself an ideological position. Marxist historians have been withering in their critique of the conservative mythologies of 'merrie England' which underlay the first English folk-song revival of the early twentieth century.[44] One could make a case that, within the United Kingdom, this search for 'Englishness' was itself a kind of regionalism.

Despite appearances, however, the folkloric region was not a politics-free zone. One cannot fail to notice that folklorists were most visibly active in those regions whose cultural identity was in dispute or whose relationship to the state was most strained. Examples include Andalusia, Galicia, Catalonia and the Basque Country in Spain; Alsace, Lorraine and Brittany in France; Sicily and the Val d'Aosta in Italy; Flanders in Belgium. Regions whose relationship to the political centre was uncontested, such as the Picardy in France, were less frequently visited. Regionalist activism and folklore collecting expanded in parallel.

This is not to say that folklorists have taken a unified position on political regionalism. Costantino Nigra, the collector of Piedmontese songs, was also a diplomat and Cavour's lieutenant during the years of Italian Unification. Sent by Cavour on behalf of the new Italian state to take control of the South in 1861 from its conqueror Garibaldi, Nigra wrote to his mentor 'for heaven's sake stand out against the regional system or we are lost'.[45] Being a regional folklorist did not necessarily entail being a political regionalist. But Nigra was relatively unusual: on the whole folklorists' sympathies are with the small against the large, and thus with the region rather than the state. But even folklorists who were committed regionalists held a great variety of views about the politics of regionalism.

There are many folklorists for whom affection for a specific region is the wellspring of all they do. Félix Arnaudin, for example, dedicated his entire life to recording the dialect and songs, the tools and even the fauna and flora of his native Landes de Gascogne. Yet, he refused to participate in regionalist associations such as the Escòla Gaston Febus (the Gascon Félibrige, founded in 1896). A reluctance to collaborate was certainly part of Arnaudin's personality, but this rejection was also an intellectual position: he lamented the cultural and environmental destruction of the Landes of his youth, but he considered its passing inevitable and irreversible.[46] On the other hand, Arnaudin's rough contemporary Louis Pinck, who collected thousands of songs in Germanophone Lorraine, was so committed to defending the culture of his native region that he would involve himself in autonomist politics. Pinck, a Catholic priest, was a vocal critic of the secular and Republican French state. He considered it an existential threat to the identity of Germanophone Lorrainers who for him were defined by their language and their faith, both expressed in their songs. Language and faith were bound together because the truth of religious sentiments could only be imprinted on the heart in one's mother tongue. Pinck's many critics believed his overt regionalism was a cover for German nationalism, but while it is the case that he had been more comfortable within the pre-1918 borders of the Reich, he could be equally vituperative in his attacks on the German state, if it threatened his region's cultural specificity.[47]

In both these cases the folklorist was concerned only with their home region. Antonio Machado y Álvarez and his Portuguese counterpart Teófilo Braga (briefly the second president of the Portuguese Republic in 1915) also did much to record the folklore of their native provinces – Andalusia and the Azores, respectively – but their commitment to regionalism extended beyond local patriotism. They were federalists and republicans, who saw the strengthening of the region as a mechanism to realize democracy within a diverse state. They saw decentralization as necessary not just to protect traditional culture but also to revitalize the economy and society.[48] An equivalent in France might be Charles Beauquier, a folklorist who also served as the Radical Socialist deputy of the Doubs between 1880 and 1914. Fiercely anticlerical, Beauquier was certainly not wedded to all forms of traditionalism. As a folklorist he restricted himself to the province of Franche-Comté, but as the president of the Fédération régionaliste française he argued against fetishizing historical regions in favour of a more modern form of decentralization based around economically determined regions.[49]

Brittany provides a rather more direct example of the marriage of folklore and political regionalism. A historic province, Brittany nonetheless lacked an extensive written literature in Breton: oral tradition, therefore, had to provide the evidence of cultural distinctiveness and regional-cum-national consciousness. Hersart de la Villemarqué was already using folklore in this manner in his *Barzaz Breiz*, the first substantial publication of Breton ballads made in 1838,[50] but Breton patriotism did not really translate into overt regionalist political action until the formation of the Union régionaliste brétonne in 1898. One of its first co-presidents was Anatole Le

Braz, who taught French and Celtic literature at the University of Rennes but who was also the busiest folklorist in Brittany in the last decade of the nineteenth and first decade of the twentieth century. His vice president was Charles Le Goffic, a less reliable but nonetheless prolific folklorist. The Union's secretary was François Taldir Jaffrenou, a Breton poet who also edited folk songs for use in schools. He would be one of the people who broke away from the Union to form the more radical Fédération régionaliste de Bretagne in 1911, taking with him François Vallée, linguist and folk-song collector; Jean Choleau, economist and folk-song collector; Maurice Duhamel, composer and folk-song collector; Léon Le Berre, journalist and folk-tale collector; and Yves Le Diberder, bookseller and folk-tale collector. Duhamel would go on to secede from the *Fédération* to form a militant Breton autonomist party in the interwar period.[51] For some Breton folklorists, regionalism meant working with the French state, for others it meant opposing it utterly.

Regionalists and the uses of folklore

Just as folklore is 'coded' regional, so regionalism is 'coded' folkloric. For some of these Breton regionalist activists, such as Le Braz, Duhamel and Le Diberder, folklore collecting was a core element of their professional lives. But the same was not true for Choleau, Vallée and Le Berre: for them, folklore collecting was very much a sideline, their major contribution to regionalist activism was in other fields. Nonetheless, as regionalists they felt it was an appropriate thing for them to engage in. Their regionalist agenda was not set by folklore, but it was not divorced from it either.

This becomes quickly apparent if one consults any regionalist publication. From the 1890s onwards, new journals appeared that articulated a clear regionalist cultural or political agenda, succeeding early-nineteenth-century provincial antiquarian and learned society journals which eschewed overt political campaigning. Examples from France include *Lémouzi* founded and edited by the journalist and folklorist Johannès Plantadis from 1893 to 1922; the *Revue du Nivernais*, founded in 1895 by Achille Millien, a poet but also the most successful collector, in numerical terms, of folk tales and songs in nineteenth-century France; and the *Le pays lorrain*, which was founded and edited by the folk-song and tale collector Charles Sadoul from 1904 to his death in 1930.[52]

Not surprisingly, given the interests of their editors, all these journals gave a lot of space to folklore. However that was also true of regionalist journals that were not edited by folklorists, such as the *Annales de Bretagne*, which was founded in 1886 as house journal of the Faculté des Arts of Rennes University. It had (and continues to have) articles on regional history and literature, but in its early years it gave over many pages to folkloric material, particularly songs and tales. These articles normally consisted of texts alone without interpretation, and their presence alongside more academic content was never really explained. It was simply assumed that this is what readers wanted in a scholarly journal dedicated to their region.

This practice, of inserting bald folkloric texts, is common in regionalist journals. The Auvergne region was particularly fecund in regionalist publications in the twentieth century, and they covered a variety of different publics: *L'Auvergne littéraire, artistique et historique*, founded in 1924, was an overtly regionalist journal that supported campaigns for decentralization and was aimed primarily at local literati such as university lecturers and teachers; *La Montagne d'Auvergne: revue illustrée, littéraire, artistique, touristique, sportive* (1912–1913) was not intended for a local market at all but was an attempt to direct the growing number of motorized tourists to places of interest, including regional cuisine, handicrafts and sites associated with legends, whereas *L'Écho d'Auvergne* was a Parisian journal aimed at Auvergnats resident in the capital. In all three, folk tales and folk songs simply appear without comment: although the readership was different, it was axiomatic that a journal dedicated to a region should contain folklore.

Folklore did not only appear in this 'undigested' form. It was part of the agenda espoused by journals like *Le pays lorrain* to encourage a regional high culture which could compete with metropolitan literature, music and art. However, it was not enough for that literature and art to be from Lorraine, Auvergne, Flanders, it had to be for Lorrainers, Auvergnats, Flemings ... and it should be authentically about them. Therefore it should draw its inspiration from their cultural expression, that is their folklore. Hence, *Le pays lorrain* was enthusiastic about the *dayâge*, a local game which involved verbal exchanges between groups of boys and young men outside a house, and groups of women inside a house: the boys started by proposing a sale; the women proposed a counter-sale and so the game continued until it either descended into insults or the boys were invited in to start courting more formally. As both speakers remained anonymous, the exchange created plenty of opportunities to deliver scandalous messages or to make political points. Thus, it provided an excellent plot device which was regularly utilized by regionalist writers in their contributions to *Le pays lorrain*.[53]

Regionalism and revivalism

Reviving literature was only one of the uses that regionalists envisaged for folklore. Regionalist journals also covered the revival of folkloric practices: the song festivals, the dance festivals, the *eisteddfodau*, the *jeux floraux*, the parades in traditional costume. For instance, most French regionalist journals covered the Fêtes Régionalistes de Bourges of 1911, organized by the sculptor and regionalist fanatic Jean Baffier, who led events with his musical troupe, Les gâs du berri, playing traditional dance tunes of the region. Les gâs du berri, founded in 1888, are still going strong.[54] They continue to demonstrate that folklore in the long twentieth century was not something just to be recorded, but something to be revived, practised and lived.

Regionalist publications were crucial in this process of revival. In 1903, Johannés Plantadis, editor of *Lémouzi* and a contributor to lots of other Limousin papers, started a campaign to revive the folk craft of lacemaking in the Tulle region. Despite the fact that there had been no local lace industry for the previous hundred years, he reported that at various social events of that year the great ladies of the region had, out of Limousin patriotism, started wearing local lace 'barbes'. Aristocratic women's patronage of handicrafts was widespread across Europe in the decades before the First World War and was envisaged as a mechanism to overcome growing class divisions in the countryside.[55] Plantadis urged the authorities to get behind this project and invest money in lace teaching in Tulle. The campaign was successful: the prefect of the Creuse was won over, a local lace industry was briefly revived, activist women really started wearing local lace to regionalist events and, of course, all of this success was reported in the regionalist press which log-rolled the whole enterprise, with the bizarre consequence that invalid soldiers in Tulle were taught lacemaking during the First World War.[56]

The effort put into such revivalism demonstrates that folklore really mattered to regionalists. After all, it could be hard work. Most of the leadership of the militant Féderation régionaliste bretonne were not native Breton speakers, any more than Hyde, Yeats, Synge and Lady Gregory were native Irish speakers. They had to learn the language whose defence and propagation was one of the primary motivations for their political action.[57] Maurice Duhamel and Yves Le Diberder also learnt to play traditional, and almost moribund, musical instruments such as the small pipes, the *biniou coz*. They thus paved the way for the resurrection of the Breton bagpipe in the twentieth century. This revival really took off not in Brittany itself but among the Bretons of Paris. The *bagad*, the drum and pipe band, which is now the ubiquitous accompaniment of any public festivity in Brittany, only arrived there after the Second World War, having already been a feature of interwar Saint-Denis, a suburb of Paris with a large Breton population.[58]

Regionalist events are almost always accompanied by costume, dances, song and other displays of what is perceived as regional folk culture. One's commitment to a region cannot just be a matter of words: it has to be performed. Although this dressing up, *tout ce folklor'* in the French colloquial usage of the term, can make regionalists an object of public mockery, one advantage is that it brings regionalist political activists into contact with a wider public which, while it might possess a sense of local patriotism or an interest in local custom, was not yet committed to regionalist politics. Singing and dancing together might be a weak bond but a bond nonetheless, and one which could be mobilized for propaganda purposes.

The most spectacular occasions for singing and dancing are folk festivals. Popular choral societies and song festivals have a long history and, in the nineteenth century, they were important vehicles for the development of a mass participatory national culture.[59] Yet even in this period, the region as a constitutive element in the make-up of the nation was on display. At the first Laulupidu, the Estonian National Song Festival held in 1869 and an important moment in the Estonian national awakening, many of the fifty-one participating teams dressed in their regional costume. The nation was exhibited to the nation in all its local variety, visual as well as aural.[60]

The regional character is more pronounced in those festivals that label themselves 'folk'. The origins of such events can be traced to before the First World War, such as Basque *fêtes folkloriques* held at Saint-Jean-de-Luz in 1897 and the Stratford-upon-Avon Festival of Folk Song and Dance in 1909. There was a quickening of the pace in the interwar period with, for instance, the foundation of the Morris Ring in 1934 and the first International Folk Dance Festival, organized by the English Folk Dance and Song Society in London in 1935.⁶¹ But the real heyday of this kind of musical and costumed revivalism came after the Second World War and the establishment of annual folk festivals, such as that held in Sidmouth every year from 1955, Newport Folk Festival (since 1959), the Finnish Kaustinnen Folk Festival (since 1968) and the Festival Interceltique de Lorient (every year since 1971).

An interesting political shift can be observed in the post-war folk revival and its festival culture. Despite the numerous examples of radical and socialist folklorists, there is a tendency, before 1945, to think of folklore as an ideological tool of the traditionalist right, and one can see how the valorization of a rural inclusive culture could serve those opposed to radical working-class politics.⁶² However, the post-war revival appeared more left-leaning. Ewan MacColl and Bert Lloyd, who were prominent in English folk circles, and Hamish Henderson, a Scot who initiated the Edinburgh People's Festival Ceilidh, were all members of the Communist Party.⁶³ One explanation is that post-war regionalism learnt its rhetoric from anti-colonial and broadly Marxist movements. The Scottish folk singer Dick Gaughan famously claimed that 'the first colony of the British Empire was in fact England'.⁶⁴ Opposition to imperialism and capitalism could fuel not just separatist movements within the four nations of the United Kingdom, but even English regionalism. No doubt, just as with the generalizations about the pre-1939 period, such a characterization of post-war revivalism as leftist does not do justice to the variety of political positions adopted by folklorists. The absence of a substantive literature on the period, outside Anglophone countries, makes this point difficult to pursue. However, it does confirm folklorists' reputation as *frondeurs* at heart. Folk songs could vocalize collective resistance to imperial and other forms of oppressive power.⁶⁵ Folk clubs and folk festivals were important venues in the 1960s and 1970s in the articulation of autonomist and separatist political ambitions.⁶⁶

Performing the region

Festive folklore illustrates some of the paradoxes of twentieth-century regionalism. The culture on display was largely rural, but the organization and audience were largely urban. Folklore, by definition, should be acquired without 'formal instruction or institutional direction', but revivalism relies on formal organizations and their ability to train and mobilize. It is no accident that the *Bagad* developed among the Breton diaspora of Paris, for this is where the capacity to run classes, organize marches and print flyers existed. Urban institutionalization in the form of the society Kenvreuriezh ar Viniaouerien from 1932 preserved the skills of bagpipe playing which the informality of Breton village traditions had condemned to extinction.

The point of such revivalism was not just to imbue provincials, albeit displaced, with a sense of their own cultural traditions, but to valorize those traditions by performing them to others. The rapid urbanization of the late nineteenth and early twentieth centuries saw a massive transfer of rural inhabitants into new urban settings, such Bretons and Auvergnats in Paris. One of the prime aim of folklorists, such as the François Cadic, vicar of the Breton parish of Paris, was to ensure that his fellow countrymen were not acculturated by their immersion in the noise and vice of the big city, but remained steadfast Catholic Bretons. Religious practices alone were not enough: song and, in particular, dance were methods of reaffirming links to 'the old country'.[67]

However, even in the absence of committed activists with regionalist agendas, migrants created a market for regional traditions. In the first half of the twentieth century, folklorists travelled to the mountains of the Auvergne to record shepherds performing *bourrées*, but this traditional dance could also be observed in the dance halls of Saint-Etienne, Lyon and Paris.[68] Auvergnat dance nights were occasions for people from the region to meet up and most importantly to court. Couple formation is an overlooked component to regionalism in the twentieth century. At home in the countryside, rural dwellers tend to marry people from their own village or a limited number of adjacent villages. In the cities, the geographic pool became larger, but was restricted to people from one region: Bretons in Paris largely married other Bretons.[69] This effect is well known to demographers, but the degree to which such couples and their offspring provided the market for regionalist folklore, and politics, has not been explored.

However, you did not have to be Auvergnat to dance a *bourrée*. A dance could be taken up by commercial and, indeed, high culture, where it was used as an aural marker of rurality in general.[70] When the Musée des arts et traditions populaires organized a field trip to the remote corners of the Haute-Loire in 1946, the musicologists would always ask, '[A]nd where did you learn this *bourrée*?' To which the answer was often 'from the radio' or 'from a record'.[71] The shepherds were learning their own regional culture from the cities. Since the Second World War, and the spread of folk clubs, the *bourrée* has become a standard across France. Indeed, in international folk-dance festivals, the *bourrée* often represents 'France' generally as much as the Auvergne specifically.[72] And yet Auvergnats, both in the region and among the diaspora, both rural and urban, continue to learn and perform the *bourrée* as an expression of a regional identity.

Displays of regional specificity can be performed by both insiders and outsiders to the local community, but in either case they are intended to parade cultural distinctions. The most obvious beneficiary of these displays has been the tourist market. Regional identity is performed for visitors so that they can authentically experience what it means to be somewhere different. Perhaps the visitor will be able to join in, as at a Breton *fest noz*, and temporarily be absorbed into a alternative, seemingly more intense community than the one left at home.[73] This link between regional tourism and regional folkloric display goes back to the beginning of mechanized travel, but it really developed with excursion tourism – that is, with the bicycle and then the car, the defining technologies of the 'long twentieth century'.[74]

Folklorists were important to this tourist economy. They supplied the stories which explained why you visit this castle (haunted by a white lady), this gorge (from which lovers leapt), this inn (used by a smuggling gang). They could be more directly involved too: Paul Sébillot, the leading figure in French folklore circles in the late nineteenth and early twentieth centuries, did most of his fieldwork in the village of Saint-Cast on the north Breton coast. He was also an artist and encouraged other artists to visit the region.

One of these was Alfred Marinier, a watercolourist, who not only set up his studio there but bought land to turn into holiday villas. His son-in-law wrote tourist pamphlets for the local railway company which promoted Saint-Cast as a tourist destination. Saint-Cast, a fishing village when Sébillot visited in the 1880s, is now almost entirely given over to the tourism industry and is one of the prime destinations on Brittany's Côte d'Emeraude. This title, applied to the coast west of Saint-Malo, and which is now ubiquitous on tourist literature, was invented by the folklorist Eugène Herpin in 1894. Because tourist literature is often ephemeral, its role in establishing a corpus of narratives and beliefs about places and regions is easy to overlook, but it is important.[75]

Are the folk regionalists?

The production of identity – cultural and political – is a key element of revivalism. But in the period before revivalism, folklore collectors seldom asked their informants whether they told a story in a particular way or participated in a particular custom because they perceived it to be part of their regional culture. Did Lorrainers playing the *dâyage* think of the game as something specific to them *qua* Lorrainers? Did mountaineers dancing the *bourrée* feel themselves more Auvergnat? Did they recognize others as members of a regional community because of their knowledge of distinctive traditions (or as outsiders because of their ignorance)? As we have seen, it was folklorists who ascribed a regional label to folk songs and tales; there is little indication that singers and storytellers understood their repertoires as expressive of a regional identity. In most studies of nation-building from the ground up, it is assumed that pre-existing loyalties seldom extended beyond the village, the parish or the immediate locality. The parish or commune existed as an institution that legally bound inhabitants into a single entity; practices associated with the ritual year (Lenten dances, rogations, Maypoles, Saint-John's bonfires) involved the inhabitants of one village. Thus the culture which we now label as 'folkloric' largely gave expression to a village community, rather than a regional one. Neighbouring villagers were rivals who needed to be excluded.

Yet there were occasions, even before regionalist campaigning reached the countryside in the long twentieth century, when some sort of regional identity that extended well beyond the village appears to have been mobilized. Peasant revolts in the early modern period often took a whole province as their field of action. In nineteenth-century rural autobiographies, one can occasionally observe an awareness of demarcations between a regional 'us' and 'them', indicated by changes in dialect, costume and song. And even in the absence of clear-cut cultural distinctions, one can still find articulations of a regional identity. An anthropologist working in the village of Elmdon on the Essex/Cambridgeshire border 'heard an Elmdon mother, distressed at the thought of her daughter marrying a man living as far away as Chelmsford [the county town], console herself with the thought that "anyhow, he is an Essex man".[76] What value she attached to this fact is difficult to know, but it meant something. It may be that folklore collections provide an archive through which to investigate these popular expressions of regional identity.

Conclusion

In Western Europe, the region has become folklore's preferred operational space, even though the collecting zone of a single folklorist was usually more localized and the lore itself much more widely dispersed than a single region. Nor is there much evidence that folklorists' informants – tradition bearers in the disciplinary jargon – understood their own performances as expressions of a distinct regional identity. Yet, folklorists' use of regional demarcators in their titles clearly appears natural not only to them but also to their public; hence, few deem it necessary to offer an intellectual rationale for their choice.

The relationship of folklore to regionalism emerged at the beginning of the long twentieth century, as they were parallel responses to state modernizing projects and the development of class politics. Both could become forms of escapism, a retreat into ruralist visions of immutable traditions and unthreatening social relations. This is not to deny the cultural and intellectual achievements of both tendencies, only to point out that they shared an appreciation of the small, the local, and the domestic.

Although folklore was sometimes mobilized in support of more militant forms of regionalist politics, it could also become the raw material of 'banal regionalism'. For most of us, locals and visitors alike, the region is enacted through folk manifestations, such as music festivals, costumed dolls and local delicacies. The folklorized region becomes a safe space as regional differences are reduced to a map of speciality cakes exhibited on a tea towel sold in a National Trust cafe. But banality has its own power: in these forms, the region has become a ubiquitous and uncontroversial geography.

But contained in the wealth of material collected by folklorists are opportunities for historians to look again at what defines a region and what constitutes a regional identity. Distinct cultural regions are hard to detect, but that does not mean that there are no regional differences in 'traditional art, literature, knowledge, and practice', which interact with other geographical, political and administrative definitions of the region. By and large, we do not know what it meant to nineteenth-century villagers to wear what we call 'regional costume', to learn regional dances and to maintain regional styles of architecture. However, given that they involved cost and effort, it is plausible that they considered them of some importance. Before discarding the region as yet another form of 'invented tradition', it would be worth investigating what folkloric traditions meant to those who practiced them.

Notes

1. http://www.afsnet.org/?page=whatisfolklore, last access on 27 March 2017.
2. U.S. Congress, American Folklife Preservation Act, Law 94–201, 2 January 1976.
3. See Matti Räsänen, *Pioneers: The History of Finnish Ethnology* (Helsinki: Studia Fennica, 1992).
4. Sandra Puccini, *L'itala gente dalle molte vite: Lamberto Loria e la Mostra di Etnografia italiana del 1911* (Rome: Meltemi, 2005); and Daniel Sherman, ' "Peoples Ethnographic": Objects, Museums, and the Colonial Inheritance of French Ethnology', *French Historical Studies* 27, no. 3 (2004): 669–703.

5. In Russia, ethnography received state support: Roland Cvetkovski and Alexis Hofmeister, eds, *An Empire of Others: Creating Ethnographic Knowledge in Imperial Russia and the USSR* (Budapest: CEU Press, 2014).
6. Alasdaire MacIntyre, *After Virtue* (London: Bloomsbury, [1981] 2011), 250.
7. Jonathan Roper, 'Thoms and the Unachieved "Folk-Lore of England"', *Folklore* 118, no. 2 (2007): 203–16.
8. Alexandra Walsham, 'Recording Superstition in Early Modern Britain: The Origins of Folklore', *Past & Present* 199, Supplement 3 (2008): 178–206.
9. William Wilson, 'Herder, Folklore and Romantic Nationalism', *Journal of Popular Culture* 6, no. 4 (1973): 819–35; and Renate Schellenberg, 'The Impact of Ossian: Johann Gottfried Herder's Literary Legacy', in *The Voice of the People: Writing the European Folk Revival, 1760–1914*, ed. Matthew Campbell and Michael Perraudin (London: Anthem, 2013), 9–20.
10. See Tom Shippey, 'A Revolution Reconsidered: Mythography and Mythology in the Nineteenth Century', in *The Shadow Walkers: Jacob Grimm's Mythology of the Monstrous*, ed. Tom Shippey (Turnhout: Brepols, 2006), 1–28.
11. See Jean Baumgarten and Céline Trautmann-Waller, eds, *Rabbins et savants au village: L'Étude des traditions populaires juives, XIXe–XXe siècles* (Paris: CNRS, 2014).
12. Dag Strömback, ed., *Leading Folklorists of the North* (Oslo: Universitetsforlaget, 1971).
13. Fañch Postic, ed., *La Bretagne et la littérature orale en Europe* (Brest: CRBC, 1999).
14. Marte Hvam Hult, *Framing a National Narrative: The Legend Collection of Peter Christen Asbjørnsen* (Detroit: Wayne State University Press, 2003). See also Terry Gunnell, 'Daisies Rise to Become Oaks: The Politics of Early Folktale Collection in Northern Europe', *Folklore* 121 (2010): 12–37. The phrase 'cultivation of culture' was coined by Joep Leerssen, 'Nationalism and the Cultivation of Culture', *Nations and Nationalism* 12, no. 4 (2006): 559–78.
15. Tim Baycroft and David Hopkin, eds, *Folklore and Nationalism in Europe during the Long Nineteenth-Century* (Leiden: Brill, 2012). See also Michael Herzfeld, *Ours Once More: Folklore, Ideology, and the Making of Modern Greece* (New York: Pella, 1986).
16. James Dow and Hannjost Lixfeld, eds, *The Nazification of an Academic Discipline: Folklore in the Third Reich* (Bloomington: Indiana University Press, 1994).
17. Roger D. Abrahams, 'Phantoms of Romantic Nationalism in Folkloristics', *Journal of American Folklore* 106 (1993): 3–37.
18. Mercedes Gómez García-Plata, *Le Folklore d'Antonio Machado y Álvarez: un cadre scientifique transnational au service d'un projet national (objet, méthode, discours et enjeux)* (Paris: Les Carnets de Berose, forthcoming).
19. Chris Gosden and Chris Wingfield, 'An Imperialist Folklore? Establishing the Folk-lore Society in London', in *Folklore and Nationalism*, ed. Baycroft and Hopkin, 255–74.
20. Stephen Miller, 'The County Folk-Lore Series (Volumes 1–7) of the Folk-Lore Society', *Folklore* 124, no. 3 (2013): 327–44.
21. Hermann Bausinger, *Volkskunde ou l'ethnologie allemande* (Paris: MSH, 1993), 66–67.
22. See Giuseppe Cocchiara, *The History of Folklore in Europe* (Philadelphia, PA: ISHI, 1981), chap. 17.
23. William Entwistle, *European Balladry* (Oxford: Clarendon Press, 1939), 84–85.
24. Carl W. von Sydow, 'Geography and Folk-Tale Oicotypes', *Béaloidas* 4 (1934): 344–55. See also David Hopkin, 'The Ecotype, or a Modest Proposal to Reconnect Cultural and Social

History', in *Exploring Cultural History: Essays in Honour of Peter Burke*, ed. Melissa Calaressu, Filippo de Vivo and Joan-Pau Rubiés (Farnham: Ashgate, 2010), 31–54.

25. Robert Wildhaber, 'Folk Atlas Mapping', in *Folklore and Folklife: An Introduction*, ed. R. M. Dorson (Chicago, IL: Chicago University Press, 1982), 479–96.

26. Gerard Rooijakkers and Peter Meurkens, 'Struggling with the European Atlas. Voskuil's Portrait of European Ethnology', *Ethnologia Europaea* 30 (2000): 75–95.

27. Américo Paredes and Richard Bauman, eds, *Toward New Perspectives in Folklore* (Austin: Texas University Press, 1972).

28. Chris Manias, *Race, Science, and the Nation: Reconstructing the Ancient Past in Britain, France and Germany* (Abingdon: Routledge, 2013).

29. Dave Russell, 'Abiding Memories: The Community Singing Movement and English Social Life in the 1920s', *Popular Music* 27, no. 1 (2008): 117–33.

30. Gordon Cox, *Living Music in Schools 1923–1999. Studies in the History of Music Education in England* (Aldershot: Ashgate, 2002).

31. Martin Ryle, *Journeys in Ireland: Literary Travels, Rural Landscapes, Cultural Relations* (Aldershot: Ashgate, 1999).

32. Deborah Fleming, *'A Man Who Does Not Exist': The Irish Peasant in the Work of W.B. Yeats and J.M. Synge* (Ann Arbor: Michigan University Press, 1995).

33. John Hutchinson, *The Dynamics of Cultural Nationalism: The Gaelic Revival and the Creation of the Irish Nation State* (London: Allen & Unwin, 1987); and Diarmuid Ó Giolláin, *Locating Irish Folklore: Tradition, Modernity, Identity* (Cork: Cork University Press, 2000).

34. Per Schelde Jacobsen and Barbara Fass Leavy, *Ibsen's Forsaken Merman: Folklore in the Later Plays* (New York: New York University Press, 1988).

35. Adriaan de Jong and Mette Skougaard, 'The Hindeloopen and the Amager Rooms. Two Examples of an Historical Museum Phenomenon', *Journal of the History of Collections* 5, no. 2 (1993): 165–78.

36. Daniel Degroff, 'Artur Hazelius and the Ethnographic Display of the Scandinavian Peasantry: A Study in Context and Appropriation', *European Review of History* 19, no. 2 (2012): 229–48.

37. Peter Blundell Jones, 'Ideas of Folk and Nation in Nineteenth and Twentieth Century European Architecture', in *Folklore and Nationalism*, ed. Baycroft and Hopkin, 69–98.

38. David Crowley, 'The Uses of Peasant Design in Austria-Hungary in the Late Nineteenth and Early Twentieth Centuries', *Studies in the Decorative Arts* 2, no. 2 (1995): 2–28.

39. William A. Wilson, *Folklore and Nationalism in Modern Finland* (Bloomington: Indiana University Press, 1976).

40. Pertti Anttonen, *Tradition through Modernity: Postmodernism and the Nation-State in Folklore Scholarship* (Helsinki: Studia Fennica, 2005).

41. Elliott Oring, ed., *Folk Groups and Folklore Genres: An Introduction* (Logan: Utah State University Press, 1986), 17–18.

42. Valdimar Hafstein, 'Biological Metaphors in Folklore Scholarship: An Essay in the History of Ideas', *Arv: Nordic Yearbook of Folklore* 57 (2001): 7–32.

43. Lawrence P. Morris, '"Aristocracies of Thought": Social Class in the Early Folklore of Yeats and Hyde', *Irish Studies Review* 18, no. 3 (2010): 299–313; and David Hopkin, 'Intimacies and Intimations: Storytelling between Servants and Masters in Nineteenth-Century France', *Journal of Social History* 51, no. 3 (2018): 557–91.

44. Dave Harker, *Fakesong: The Manufacture of British Folk Song, 1700 to the Present Day* (Milton Keynes: Open University Press, 1985); and Georgina Boyes, *The Imagined Village: Culture, Ideology and the English Folk Revival* (Manchester: Manchester University Press, 1993). But see also David Gregory, 'Fakesong in an Imagined Village? A Critique of the Harker-Boyes Thesis', *Canadian Folk Music* 43, no. 3 (2011): 18–26.

45. Quoted by Stefano Cavazza, 'Regionalism in Italy: A Critique', in *Region and State in Nineteenth-Century Europe: Nation-Building, Regional Identities and Separatism*, ed. Joost Augusteijn and Eric Storm (Basingstoke: Palgrave Macmillan, 2012), 74.

46. Guy Latry, 'Introduction: Arnaudin à la lettre', in Félix Arnaudin, *Correspondance*, ed. Guy Latry, Oeuvres complètes de Félix Arnaudin 5 (Bordeaux/Mont-de-Marsan: Confluences, 1999).

47. Laurent Mayer, *Culture populaire en Lorraine francique: coutumes, croyances et traditions* (Strasbourg: SALDE, 2000).

48. Enrique Baltanás, 'Folk-lore, política y literatura popular en el siglo XIX (cartas inéditas de A. Machado y Álvarez a Teófilo Braga)', *Estudos de Literatura Oral* 7–8 (2001–2002).

49. Julian Wright, *The Regionalist Movement in France, 1890–1914: Jean Charles-Brun and French Political Thought* (Oxford: Oxford University Press, 2003).

50. Nelly Blanchard, *Barzaz-Breiz: Une fiction pour s'inventer* (Rennes: Presses Universitaires de Rennes, 2006).

51. Sharif Gemie, *Brittany 1750–1950: The Invisible Nation* (Cardiff: University of Wales Press, 2007), chaps 7–8.

52. David Hopkin, 'Identity in a Divided Province: The Folklorists of Lorraine, 1860–1960', *French Historical Studies* 23, no. 4 (2000): 639–82.

53. David Hopkin, 'Love Riddles, Couple Formation, and Local Identity in Eastern France', *Journal of Family History* 28, no. 3 (2003): 339–63. See also Anne-Marie Thiesse, *Écrire la France: le mouvement littéraire régionaliste de langue française entre la Belle Époque et la Libération* (Paris: Presses Universitaires de France, 1991).

54. Neil McWilliam, *Monumental Intolerance: Jean Baffier: A Nationalist Sculptor in Fin-de-Siècle France* (University Park: Pennsylvania State University Press, 2000).

55. See Stana Nenadic and Sally Tuckett, 'Artisans and Aristocrats in Nineteenth-Century Scotland', *Scottish Historical Review* 95, no. 2 (2016): 203–29.

56. This story can be pieced together from the material in the Archives départementales de la Corrèze, 11 F 'Fonds Plantadis'.

57. Jean-Yves Guiomar, 'Régionalisme, fédéralisme et minorités nationales en France entre 1919 et 1939', *Le Mouvement social* 70 (1970): 89–108; and Michel Oiry, 'Yves Le Diberder: Un lettré au service de la tradition orale', *Ar Men* 141 (2004): 38–44.

58. Armel Morgant and Jean-Michel Roignant, *Bagad: vers une nouvelle tradition* (Spézet: Coop Breizh, 2005).

59. Krisztina Lajosi and Andreas Stynen, eds, *Choral Societies and Nationalism in Europe* (Leiden: Brill, 2015).

60. Karsten Brüggemann and Andres Kasekamp, '"Singing Oneself into a Nation"? Estonian Song Festivals as Rituals of Political Mobilisation', *Nations and Nationalism* 20 (2014): 259–276.

61. Georgina Boyes, '"Potencies of the Earth": Rolf Gardiner and the English Folk Dane Revival', in *Rolf Gardiner: Folk, Nature and Culture in Interwar Britain*, ed. Matthew Jefferies and Mike Tyldesley (Farnham: Ashgate, 2011); and Frank Howe, 'The International (European) Folk Dance Festival', *Journal of the English Folk Dance and Song Society* 2 (1935): 1–16.

62. See Christian Faure, *Le projet culturel de Vichy. Folklore et révolution nationale* (Lyon: Presses Universitaires de Lyon, 1989).
63. Michael Brocken, *The British Folk Revival, 1944–2002* (Aldershot: Ashgate, 2003); and Pino Mereu and Owen Dudley Edwards, eds, *At Hame Wi' Freedom: Essays on Hamish Henderson and the Scottish Folk Revival* (Ochtertyre: Grace Note, 2012).
64. Dick Gaughan, *Handful of Earth* (1981), writing in the sleeve notes about the song 'World Turned Upside Down' by Leon Rosselson. The statement has been much quoted.
65. This trend can also be seen in France: Jonathan Briggs, *Sounds French: Globalization, Cultural Communities, and Pop Music in France, 1958–1980* (Oxford: Oxford University Press, 2015), chap. 4.
66. May McCann, 'Music and Politics in Ireland: The Specificity of the Folk Revival in Belfast', *British Journal of Ethnomusicology* 4, no. 1 (1995): 51–75. Although the role of folk music in Ireland may be particular, the use of folk song as a badge of identity and a mobilizer of collective emotions is common among separatist movements: The Occitan song 'Se Canta', a product of the folk revival, is uniformly sung at Languedocian activist gatherings, and is the formal anthem of the semi-autonomous Occitan valleys in Spain; the folk 'Song of the Reapers' has, in an adapted form, become the anthem of the Catalan nation as imagined by Catalan activists: Josep Massot i Muntaner, Salvador Pueyo and Oriol Martorell, *Els Segadors: Himne nacional de Catalunya* (Barcelona: Abadia de Montserrat, 1993).
67. Fañch Postic, ed., *François Cadic: Un collecteur vannetais, 'recteur' des Bretons de Paris* (Brest: CRBC, 2012).
68. Marianne Bröcker, 'A French Minority in Paris', in *Manifold Identities: Studies in Music and Minorities*, ed. Ursula Hemetek *et al* (Amersham: Cambridge Scholars Press, 2004), 129–61.
69. Leslie Page Moch, *The Pariahs of Yesterday: Breton Migrants in Paris* (Durham, NC: Duke University Press, 2012).
70. Hence an Auvergnat *bourrée* features in the Cornish regionalist opera 'The Logan Rock' by Inglis Gundry (premiered 1956).
71. Didier Perre and Marie-Barbara Le Gonidec, eds, *Chansons et contes de Haute-Loire. L'enquête phonographique de 1946* (Paris: CTHS-AMT, 2013).
72. E.g. at the 'Festival of National Dances' held at the Albert Hall in London in March 1955. See Violet Alford, 'A Jubilee Symposium', *Folk Music Journal* 2, no. 2 (1971): 79–101.
73. Desi Wilkinson, 'Celtitude, Professionalism and the Fest Noz in Traditional Music in Brittany', in *Celtic Modern: Music at the Global Fringe*, ed. Martin Stokes and Philip V. Bohlman (Lanham: Scarecrow Press, 2003): 219–56.
74. See also the chapter by Storm.
75. See also Patrick Young, *Enacting Brittany; Tourism and Culture in Provincial France, 1871–1939* (Farnham: Ashgate, 2012).
76. Jean Robin, *Elmdon: Continuity and Change in a North-West Essex Village, 1861–1964* (Cambridge: Cambridge University Press, 1980), xii.

Further reading

Baycroft, Tim, and David Hopkin, eds, *Folklore and Nationalism in Europe during the Long Nineteenth-Century* (Leiden: Brill, 2012).

Regionalism and Modern Europe

Bendix, Regina, *In Search of Authenticity: The Formation of Folklore Studies* (Madison: Wisconsin University Press, 1997).

Brock, Peter, *Folk Cultures and Little Peoples: Aspects of National Awakening in East Central Europe* (Boulder, CO: East European Quarterly, 1992).

Campbell, Matthew, and Michael Perraudin, eds, *The Voice of the People: Writing the European Folk Revival, 1760–1914* (London: Anthem, 2013).

Cocchiara, Giuseppe, *The History of Folklore in Europe* (Philadelphia: ISHI, 1981).

Cvetkovski, Roland, and Alexis Hofmeister, eds, *An Empire of Others: Creating Ethnographic Knowledge in Imperial Russia and the USSR* (Budapest: CEU Press, 2014).

Thiesse, Anne-Marie, *Écrire la France: le mouvement littéraire régionaliste de langue française entre la Belle Époque et la Libération* (Paris: Presses Universitaires de France, 1991).

CHAPTER 4
NATURE: FROM PROTECTING REGIONAL LANDSCAPES TO REGIONALIST SELF-ASSERTION IN THE AGE OF THE GLOBAL ENVIRONMENT

Jan-Henrik Meyer

In the autumn of 2015, Horst Seehofer, the prime minister of Bavaria, hurried to defend his region's natural beauty against the onslaught of what is now frequently described as eco-modernization.[1] New high-voltage power lines intended to transport wind power from northern Germany to consumers and industry in Germany's thriving south threatened to despoil Bavarian landscapes. Seehofer's party, Bavaria's powerful regionalist conservative party, the Christian Social Union (CSU), successfully pushed at the national level for the defence of what they presented as 'Bavarian interests'. In order to avoid the visual impact on the Bavarian landscape, the power lines were to be buried in the ground. Not only did this come at a much higher cost to national taxpayers and consumers, but it would also lead to major delays. Ironically, by tearing up the ground, it also threatened to inflict much greater damage to ecosystems than the conventional method of erecting pylons. Some power lines were to be re-routed so that they would not cross Bavaria; others were to be postponed or cancelled, thus endangering Germany's energy transition and the security of electricity supply in Bavaria itself after the closure of the last nuclear power plants in 2022. Who stood to benefit, apart from the Bavarian Christian Social Union (CSU), was the – albeit privatized – regional utility operating a new gas-fired power plant in Bavaria; it would fill the void in electricity supply that was partially created by the delays in the power grid as a result of CSU policy.[2]

This episode demonstrates multiple aspects of the continued relevance of nature in regionalism. First, it shows that nature is deeply *political*: it is linked to economic interests as well as ideas and perceptions and is, thus, frequently controversial. At various levels, political actors, notably governments and party leaders, seek to define which environmental concerns they consider most important – natural beauty or the fight against climate change. However, political actors do not act in a vacuum: societal actors, such as social movements, interest groups and the media are each providing their own definitions and framings of what constitutes valuable nature, worthy of protection. This interplay of different actors circumscribes political leaders' options. In Bavaria, as elsewhere, protests against the power lines had started locally and invoked local and regional identities.[3] What was specific in Bavaria was that Bavarian premier Seehofer rallied to their cause when the CSU feared that the conflict over the power lines would strengthen the vote for opposition parties. This would be a worst-case scenario for the CSU in a state with a strong regional identity, where the regionalist party has been in government without interruption since the 1950s.

Second, traditional perceptions of what constitutes home and regional *identities* matter with regard to both nature and the region. Emotional aspects, such as the attachment to place and natural beauty, often go hand in hand with aversions to landscape change and continue to be important to environmental politics. In some cases, visible and tangible local concerns override the more complex scientific insights into ecological links or global climate change.[4] However, identity and science are not necessarily contradictory, but in modern environmentalism have frequently been mutually reinforcing.[5]

Finally, nature is a relevant concern at various political and geographical levels. As the episode above illustrates, more often than not there have been conflicts between local and regional concerns with natural beauty and land uses, national policy priorities, such as Germany's energy transition, and global issues, notably the battle against climate change. At each of these levels and also across them, conflicts about nature are not simply conflicts of identity:[6] throughout history, conflicts over land use have important economic and distributional consequences.[7]

This chapter seeks to provide a historical overview from the late nineteenth century onwards of the relations between 'nature' and 'regionalism' in Europe, focusing on the role of identity constructions – as core ideas related to nature and the region – and movements – as crucial actors relating to both nature and the region. While region and regionalism have been defined in the introduction to this volume, this chapter will start with a brief definition of 'nature', drawing on the insights of environmental history. I will comment on the – very fragmented – state of the art on regionalism and nature. Subsequently, the chapter will present its overview in a chronological fashion, covering four periods and following the major political divides and changes in the politics of nature: a phase of incipient nature protection until the First World War; the interwar years, characterized by the emergence of new nation states and nationalisms, democracy and dictatorship; and the post-war period, in which Europe was divided and nature protection was fully established. The final period is marked by the new environmentalism and environmental movements of the 1970s which coincided with new regionalist mobilization in many countries.[8]

Defining nature

Defining nature is not as straightforward as it may seem. Nature is conventionally understood to describe the material world around us, including living creatures, most prominently plants and animals, and dead matter, such as rocks or sand. Nature includes combinations of the two, such as rivers, wetlands, forests or entire landscapes. Definitions and perceptions of nature have changed over time and often carried strong normative connotations and political implications.[9]

Since the nineteenth century, as a response to the large-scale interventions into nature brought about by industrialization, nature was no longer treated as a given but increasingly deemed in need of conservation and protection. On both sides of the Atlantic, citizens – including scientists[10] – founded associations and lobbied the state to protect nature. In American nature conservation (and in the national park movement[11]), preserving 'wilderness' – as 'pure' nature unencumbered by human intervention – has been the central ideal.[12] By contrast, in Europe, the continuous imprint of humans on the landscape has been all-pervasive, and, indeed, protecting man-made landscapes – primarily for aesthetic and nostalgic reasons – played a crucial role in nature protection in Europe at the end of the nineteenth century and continues to be a dominant concern in many countries.[13]

The issue of acceptable uses of nature has been an important touchstone in nature protection. Since the late nineteenth century, the ideal of nature 'preservation' implied non-intervention or restitution to its supposedly natural state, and therefore the limitation of human uses. At the same time, humans have always appreciated and 'protected' nature for its uses in forestry, hunting, fishing or tourism. In the twentieth century, contemporaries defined such a utilitarian approach as 'conservation' of nature and the 'wise use' of 'natural resources'.[14] The present-day buzzword of sustainability is rooted in conservationist traditions dating back to eighteenth-century scientific forestry.[15]

The massive growth of science in the post-war period and the advance of ecology and the earth sciences changed perceptions of nature. Instead of nineteenth-century views of nature as an inventory of geographies and species, nature was increasingly perceived as complex, interrelated and globally connected ecological systems. Scientific observation also made visible the damage to nature wrought by novel kinds of human intervention, such as the mass use of chemicals.[16] This in turn led to the rise of the more comprehensive concept 'environment' that all but replaced 'nature' in the political realm. The environment as a political concept included not only traditional nature protection issues but also newer concerns regarding pollution.[17] Since the 1970s, also at the level of popular movements, traditional nature protection concerns have increasingly been subsumed under the new, more comprehensive environmentalism.[18] With the growing importance of political ecology, scientific expertise was increasingly considered the only legitimate criterion for judging environmental problems.[19]

These varying conceptions of nature (aesthetic vs. scientific, preservation vs. conservation, nature vs. environment) can only be distinguished analytically. In everyday practice, they are inseparably intertwined. At the same time, nature is not only viewed in scientific, aesthetic and utilitarian terms. Since the late nineteenth century, both nationalists and regionalists have projected political meaning onto certain spaces and their nature and used nature as markers of identity.

The state of the art on regionalism and nature is extremely dispersed; only very few publications combine both issues, and if so, they treat regional issues more broadly, including, for instance, regional development and regional planning.[20] Nature and the region are usually discussed in separate literatures: on the one hand, there is a substantial and differentiated literature on regionalism, reflecting the renewed interest notably in the politics of regionalism since at least the 1990s.[21] However, this literature has been interested primarily in political, ideological or organizational aspects, as well as issues of culture and identity.[22]

On the other hand, most publications dealing with nature as a point of reference for territorial attachment primarily focus on nationalism. Explicit references to regionalism and regional attachment are sparse, even though many researchers rely on regional-level case studies. The relatively few publications that explicitly address both aspects highlight the ambiguous relation between regionalism and nationalism. While most regionalists chose to present regional nature as representative of both the region and the nation, regionalists less sentimentally attached to the nation sought to define regional nature in opposition to the nation.[23] This chapter is based on mining a wide range of publications for what can be learned about how regionalism and nature connected, which actors were involved in the construction of these connections and the consequences of their actions.

Nature and the region until the First World War

Throughout Europe, the final decades of the nineteenth and early decades of the twentieth century were characterized not only by an upsurge of nationalism but also by growing associational life, first among the middle classes, but increasingly also among the working classes, often in separate organizations.[24] While these associations frequently favoured and reinforced national(ist) sentiments, most of them were locally and regionally organized and dealt with local concerns. Among these associations, we find the forerunners of today's environmental groups: organizations that sought to protect nature, most importantly birds and landscapes. While women had – by nineteenth-century standards – an unusually strong role in bird protection groups such as the Royal Society for the Protection of Birds or the Deutscher Bund für Vogelschutz, which were also less socially exclusive, the protection of landscapes was the preserve of associations dominated by men.

The appreciation of the beauty of landscapes is not an altogether new phenomenon during the late nineteenth century; its original ideas can be traced back at least to eighteenth and early nineteenth-century traditions, to Romanticism, notably in landscape painting but also in landscape descriptions as part of travelogues.[25] What changed in the late nineteenth century, however, was the specifically nostalgic view and urge to preserve pristine and seemingly perennial traditional landscapes in the face of accelerating societal, economic and technological change. Rapid economic development in the late nineteenth century not only left an imprint on cities, which expanded enormously and suffered from increasing air and water pollution; the countryside was equally affected by the construction of infrastructures, such as railways, canals or dams and resource extraction. Founded across Europe during the two decades before 1914, nature protection associations' names and primary objectives differed to some extent, but their goals were similar. At the time, the protection of the natural and cultural heritage was considered one single concern. This is well illustrated by their names, such as Pro Montibus et Silvis founded in Italy in 1892, the National Trust for Places of Historic Interest or Natural Beauty established in the United Kingdom in 1895, the Société Nationale pour la Protection des Sites et des Monuments founded in Belgium in 1897, the Société pour la Protection des Paysages de France established in 1901 or the Bund Heimatschutz (Federation of homeland protection) established at the national level in 1905 in Germany, with similar groups emerging simultaneously in Switzerland and the Austro-Hungarian empire.[26]

The German *Heimat* protection movement is a prototypical example of regionalism in nature protection. Even more so than the French usage of *pays* or *petite patrie*, which designated a space between the local and the region in the face of Paris centralism,[27] the notion of *Heimat* lent itself to a broad range of interpretations: it could be used to signify attachment to places called 'home' at the local, regional or even national level. What made this movement so attractive was exactly this ambiguity which allowed combining all these levels of attachment at the same time.[28] Across national borders many of these groups shared views critical of capitalist modernity and its consequences, and had a strong sense of aesthetics. Protectionists tended to deplore change in the landscape as loss – of both culture and nature. For example, Ernst Rudorff, the founder of the German *Heimat* protection movement, criticized economically driven agricultural reform, resulting in the simplification of traditional cultural landscapes, such as the cutting of hedgerows or the straightening of rivers. This implied both a loss of beauty and also a loss of nature and its variety, a phenomenon we would describe as biodiversity today.[29]

Despite the rhetoric of preservation and anti-materialism, *Heimat* protection groups did not universally reject all economic uses. Many of these groups emerging from below and within the regions accepted tourism as a suitable form of 'using' *Heimat* landscapes and beneficial for the health and recreation of the nearby city dwellers. This issue was relevant right from the start, because when *Heimat* protection emerged at the turn of the twentieth century, it was often faced with already existing associations: Alpine and tourist clubs, or 'beautification' societies. These organizations promoted the appreciation of landscapes and natural beauty, and tourism. For instance, already in 1869, in the romantic German Rhineland, locals had founded the Beautification Society for the Siebengebirge, a scenic mountain range near Bonn. Its activities were dedicated to facilitating hiking by setting up footpaths and other infrastructures for visitors. A similar association in the nearby Eiffel region promoted the nature of the more remote and 'backward' region for hiking and tourism, as did numerous such societies elsewhere in Europe. In Croatia, at that time a region of the Austro-Hungarian Empire, citizens founded a Society for the Beautification of the Plitvice Lakes and their Environments in 1893 in order to promote both tourism and the protection of the lakes, which are today a UNESCO site. Often these associations brought together educated and well-to-do citizens from the national or regional capital and people from the region.[30]

Such a broad societal base proved important, as nature protection often conflicted with other land uses. In the 1880s, when one of the most scenic parts of the Siebengebirge was threatened by mining activities, the beautification association mobilized substantial support within the region to put pressure on Prussian officials to approve of lotteries, which provided the means to purchase and close the quarries. Additional grants from cities and the regional authority provided money for additional land acquisitions for a nature park. As a consequence, the official dedication of the beautification society shifted from the recreational purposes more strongly towards the protection of the Siebengebirge landscape.[31] The protection of scenic rocks from quarrying was also an issue in Brittany, where Parisian artists, architects and lawyers had started the initiative, establishing a Syndicat Artistique pour la Protection des Sites Pittoresques de Ploumanach in 1901. However, they only won the battle against the mine in alliance with the regional authorities and regional tourism advocacy groups (*syndicats d'initiative*), highlighting the importance of natural monuments for regional identity and benefits of landscape protection for attracting tourists to Brittany. Again, the state acquired land and enacted a law on site protection in 1906.[32]

Reconciling local and regional identities (and interests) with national identities proved important in old and new nation states. In some states such as Germany, presenting regional nature as both regional and national at the same time contributed to the process of national integration. However, this was more difficult within the multi-ethnic empires of Eastern and Central Europe, such as Austria-Hungary, that included regions that increasingly considered themselves nations. National conflicts over natural spaces, for example, the Slovenian Alps or the Tatra mountains, had already begun during the last decades of the Austro-Hungarian empire, when German-speaking and Slovene-speaking Alpinists or Hungarians and Slovaks in parliament in Budapest claimed sovereignty over the same mountain ranges.[33]

At the same time, invoking national significance proved an important tool in the defence of natural beauty. This was also reflected in one of the guiding concepts in turn-of-the century nature protection in Europe, namely the focus on 'natural monuments'. Natural monuments transferred and extended the older objective of caring for cultural heritage to natural sights. Aesthetically appealing peaks, ancient trees or other features of the landscape required protection as part of both local-regional and national heritage.

Botanist Hugo Conwentz, the Prussian state commissioner for natural monument preservation was the main advocate of this idea. While his critics derided his ambition to collect large numbers of small-scale sites as 'Conwentz'-ional nature protection, Conwentz was one of the central figures at the First Congress on the International Protection of Landscapes in 1909, where his ideas were discussed and spread. The conference brought together a strange international alliance of nature-protecting and regionally oriented nationalists; this network did not survive the First World War.[34] The idea of natural monuments, by contrast, continued to serve as a point of reference for some time, in France and Italy,[35] but also in Central Europe, in Slovenia, then a region of the new Kingdom of the Serbs, Croats and Slovenes, or in the new state of Czechoslovakia, while the leading Russian scientist in the field rejected it as unsuitable for the situation in Russia.[36]

However, a different model of nature protection at a larger scale slowly gained ground, which was less embedded in regional identity and agency but sought to protect nature for its own sake and often against the local people, and also for the glory of the nation. The American model of the national park became an important point of reference among the promoters of nature protection and was controversially discussed in national and regional parliaments in Europe in the decade before the First World War. Conwentz had maintained that setting aside land at a large scale, and the American 'wilderness' ideal, was incompatible with the situation in densely populated Europe. Nevertheless, Sweden and Switzerland moved towards establishing national parks in remote parts of their countries, as did late-tsarist Russia in 1916, with the founding of its first strictly protected *zapovednik* near Lake Baikal.[37] The Swiss national park in the Alps, established in 1914, subsequently became the central point of reference for nature protection both at the national and at the regional levels in Europe.[38]

Interwar years

The First World War led to growing nationalism and national confrontation in Europe and put an end to the multi-ethnic empires in Central and Eastern Europe. However, the redrawing of borders produced new regional and/or minority problems, since many of the new nation states were effectively multi-ethnic states also.

In this context, establishing national parks seemed an effective instrument for national integration. Drawing on pre-war proposals, in 1922–1923, newly fascist Italy established two sizable national parks: the Gran Paradiso Park in the Alps and the Abruzzo National Park, both former royal hunting reserves. A third park, the Stelvio National Park, was added during the Mussolini dictatorship in 1935. It was situated in the Alto Adige/South Tyrol, the German-speaking region ceded by Austria after the First World War. The arrangements for the park were designed to serve tourist interests. However, by establishing the park, the fascist regime sought to strengthen the Italian control of the region. Its fascist origins continue to make the national park unpopular among many German speakers in the region, who continue to see it as an imposition from Rome. This has fuelled to demands among regional politicians to abolish the park altogether since the 1990s.[39]

National conflicts over natural spaces which had started during the Austro-Hungarian Empire continued in Central Europe. In interwar Czechoslovakia, German- and Czech-speaking advocates of nature protection continued to operate their linguistically (and often also regionally) separate *Heimat* – beautification – and scientific societies dating back to the Austro-Hungarian Empire. Only slowly, in the late 1930s, did they start to cooperate for the sake of protecting nature in multi-ethnic Czechoslovakia.[40]

Nature protection in the more peripheral Slovak part of the state was dominated by Czechs from the Prague centre. Despite the fact that a Carpathian tourist society had existed since the 1870s, when Slovakia was part of the Kingdom of Hungary,[41] Czechs argued that there was a lack of beautification societies in Slovakia. Thus, Czech associations extended their activities eastward in order to integrate the Slovak region into the new compound nation. They greatly appreciated Slovakia's 'unspoilt' nature, its remote and scenic mountain ranges and beautiful natural monuments that the region contributed to the new nation state. However, the Czech societies projected their values and practices in nature and natural monuments protection onto the region, without much concern for or involvement of local people.[42]

At the same time, nature protection occasionally also served to defuse national tensions. As part of an agreement on the border between Czechoslovakia and Poland, in 1924, a joint cross-regional Tatra mountain national park had been planned, to promote tourism and protect nature. It failed to materialize due to political opposition and because local landowners refused to sell their land. However, a cross-border park between Poland and Czechoslovakia, the Pieniny National Park, was indeed established, one of the six national parks the Polish state established in the interwar years.[43]

Even more so than before, in the interwar years, *Heimat*, Alpine and tourist clubs contributed to branding regions and their specific natural features as embodiments of the nation, in both the new nations – such as Czechoslovakia – but also the older ones. For Switzerland, the Alps became their national heartland; for Scotland, the Highlands served this purpose, as did the Cotswolds for England.[44] Similar ideas about regional landscapes epitomizing the nation and contributing to national pride informed the complex programme of landscape architecture and propaganda that the Nazi regime undertook in the 1930s and 1940s when constructing the German highway network. The measures were intended to integrate the Autobahn into the natural landscape. Some of the new roads were designed to allow drivers impressive vistas on great natural monuments in the different regions of the German landscape. The transalpine Austrian Großglockner road built in the 1930s served similar purposes, including funnelling tourists into the Alps.[45]

The arrival of mass tourism in the interwar years reinforced older alliances and forged new ones between nature protection and the advocates of tourism. Tourism was considered an 'acceptable' use of the landscape and legitimated intervention, such as bans on billboards and protection of natural monuments, characteristic of the region (as in Brittany), as well as access to land for hikers and the upgrading of urban and rural landscapes to enhance their aesthetic appeal not only in interwar but also in post-war Ireland. The branding of regional natures for tourism catered – again – to aesthetic and cultural ideals of a premodern 'authentic', variegated and regionally specific landscape, devoid of present-day interventions, homogenizing impacts and the horrors of commercialism.[46]

The post-war period

Started by the German attack on Poland, the Second World War did not only lead to an unprecedented destruction of people, cities, infrastructures and nature; it was also accompanied and followed by civil wars and by the expulsion of millions of people from their ancestral regions. After the war, new national borders were imposed, and Europe was divided into two societal and economic systems and political regimes, which confronted each other in a Cold War.[47]

On both sides of the systems divide, in the 1950s and 1960s, efforts at reconstructing the destroyed economies took precedence over the care of nature. Nevertheless, frequently at the regional level, protests arose against measures designed to further economic development, such as dam-building for electricity generation. In post-war Bavaria and Austria, regional opposition was more successful in preventing small-scale works that strongly impacted on scenic nature relevant for tourism than in preventing larger dams that promised to produce substantial amounts of electricity, and were projected by politically well-connected state-owned utilities. Protests were somewhat stronger in Bavaria with its strong sense of regional identity.[48]

At the same time, efforts to heal the wounds of the war and to integrate people back into the national community created a new appreciation for notions of home and nature. In divided Germany, the notion of *Heimat* was revived on both sides of the Iron Curtain. *Heimat* movies were highly successful in capitalist West Germany. They showed beautiful, often Alpine landscapes and catered to nostalgic sentiments in a country inhabited by millions who had lost their home in the East. Among these expellees, foresters from East Prussia tried to preserve and recreate the pristine nature and culture of their former home region to help the expellees to maintain their regional identity, which they viewed as serving the nation, too. For the regional association of the former East Prussians, they organized a hunting exhibition in 1953 that led to the establishment of a regional museum presenting the culture and nature – including the characteristic moose and amber jewellery – of the lost Prussian province in the south-eastern corner of the Baltic Sea.[49]

By contrast, the German Democratic Republic (GDR) presented itself as the socialist home, a place without capitalist exploitation of man and nature. However, the GDR also abolished the regional level of government in 1952 in favour of administrative districts which cut across traditional regions. The older *Heimat* and nature protection movements were integrated into the relatively generously funded but state-controlled Cultural League, which encompassed the protection of both culture and nature, including nature reserves. Despite state control of civil society, GDR authorities were not able to totally change identity constructions and entirely prevent alternative views and spaces; indeed, to some extent, the state tolerated them. Traditions proved resilient, too:[50] in the 1950s, the GDR Cultural League continued to promote the same idealized imageries of pre-modern bucolic landscapes and nature just as the *Heimat* movement had done in the early twentieth century.[51] The continued appreciation of pre-modern cultural landscapes was widely shared at the time across the Iron Curtain, for example, in France or in Slovakia.[52]

By the 1970s and 1980s, the clearly apparent environmental side effects of the socialist economy eroded the credibility of the claim that a socialist home would be a better one. The legitimacy of the socialist regime was undermined by official secrecy on environmental information in the face of visible environmental disasters. Thus, local and regional environmental initiatives contributed strongly to political opposition in the 1980s.[53]

On the other side of the Iron Curtain, for instance, expellees from the German-speaking parts of Czechoslovakia decried the lack of care of the natural and cultural landscape by the new Czech inhabitants. They criticized the lack of appropriate land use, the decline of buildings and monuments and – in later decades – increasing pollution. The Germans compared this unfavourably with their own previous care of these regions, and similar to the message underlying the East Prussian hunting exhibition, these arguments served their ongoing claim to their former home regions. However, since the 1960s, the Czechs had also critically discussed that the new inhabitants had not been able to forge a sense of regional identity in the newly settled areas.[54]

Regionalism and Modern Europe

On both sides of the iron curtain, the post-war period saw a rise in national parks, which – in line with the American model – catered to growing tourism. The Tatra National Park established by the Slovak regional authorities within Czechoslovakia in 1949 and on the Polish side in 1954, and the Plitvice and Triglav National Parks in Yugoslav Croatia and Slovenia in 1949 and 1961 all combined tourist access with nature conservation.[55] From the 1950s, in Western Europe, regional governments started setting up nature parks and reserves to provide recreational opportunities in the region. In the late 1960s, regional actors in France and Germany who lobbied for the establishment of national parks also hoped to attract tourists to the remote and marginal areas of the Cévennes or the Bavarian forest, where parks were established during the European Conservation Year in 1970.[56] Setting aside land for parks thus served regional self-assertion, too, by fostering regional identities and livelihoods in economically marginal areas.[57]

In practice, the distinctions between national parks and regional or nature parks were often blurred. Whereas in Italy rules restricting access and uses of nature in regional nature parks were as strict as those in national parks,[58] the French national park of the Cévennes was explicitly devoted to protecting cultural landscapes, rather than 'wilderness'.[59] French regional nature parks explicitly drew on the German model of the *Naturschutzpark*.[60] Promoted by a private association (Verein Naturschutzpark), founded in 1909 to acquire land for preservation, the objective of the *Naturschutzpark* was to protect man-made nature, such as the nostalgically preserved pre-modern agricultural landscapes and characteristic buildings of the Lüneburg Heath, for tourism and regional recreation. Led by a charismatic entrepreneur from Hamburg, the association advanced an ambitious programme of parks in 1956, of which sixty-two were realized until 1980.[61]

New environmentalism and new regional self-assertion since the 1970s

The arrival of the new environmentalism of the 1970s coincided with broader societal mobilization and a revival of regionalism, as part of a more general reassertion of societal and democratic participation in Western Europe in the wake of 1968. Local environmental groups and citizen action groups devoted to local and regional environmental concerns, such as pollution, waste and also the protection of local and regional nature, now perceived in more scientific terms as ecosystems or habitats, mushroomed mostly across the Western half of the continent, with more limited room for environmental activism under conditions of state socialism in Eastern Europe. Interestingly enough, like the spread of nature conservation and natural monuments ideas throughout Europe before 1914, these phenomena were often transnationally connected and, in a number of cases, sought to overcome national borders.

The main point of reference for this new alliance among environmentalists and regionalists in the 1970s was the protest against the massive extension of a military camp on the Larzac plateau in the Massif Central in the deep south of France. The government plan created a classic 'locally unwanted land-use' (so-called 'LULU') problem; converting land from pasture to military uses threatened the livelihoods of local farmers, who used the land to graze their sheep and produce the famous Roquefort cheese. The local farmers' protest was soon reinforced by that of young left-wingers and draft-dodgers who were attracted by the grass-roots activities that they nostalgically viewed as a peasant revolution: during the Vietnam War, many Marxist and regionalist youths admired Mao and Hồ Chi Minh. Protest was framed not only as the class struggle of local peasants but also as an anti-military, anti-nuclear weapons and an ecological protest defending traditional farming practices and landscapes. Last but not least, it constituted regional self-assertion in order to maintain the rural way of life against the centralized and modernizing French state, epitomized by metropolitan Paris. Larzac committees sprang up throughout France and abroad, and young people came to the Larzac to do voluntary work and study activism, thus bringing back with them what they saw, in terms of ideas and protest tactics.[62]

Apart from other protests against military sites in France, the non-violent protest in the Larzac became the model for protest against nuclear power, notably in France and Germany in the 1970s. The conflict about nuclear power was a strong mobilizing force in environmentalism in both countries. In Germany, it eventually led to the foundation of a Green political party, which still has its strongholds in the regions where nuclear facilities had been planned, such as in the rural county of Lüchow-Dannenberg, where the Gorleben nuclear waste site was to be located.[63]

Due to their need for ample cooling water, nuclear power plants have usually been sited along major rivers or the sea. For safety reasons, according to international rules, reactors could only be placed in areas with low population densities. In the 1970s, many countries in Europe responded to the oil crisis by reinforcing their efforts of building nuclear power plants. Regional planners considered the plants a core input into regional policies dedicated to overcoming 'backwardness' and industrializing rural regions. In the eyes of the Swiss, French and West German planners, the upper Rhine valley fulfilled all these requirements. French reactor plans at Fessenheim in the Alsace were initially intercepted by an occupation of the construction site. This model was copied on the German side in the village of Wyhl in Baden, where vintners resented any change in land use. They feared that their grapes would not ripen, due to the mist produced by the cooling towers, and resented the planned industrialization of their region, in a similar way as the Larzac farmers. As with the Larzac, the vintners' protest was reinforced by left-wing students from nearby Freiburg and further afield; connections were soon established and the anti-nuclear protests were framed as regionalist protests at the same time – against the government planners and utilities in the city of Stuttgart, the historical capital of the other part of the compound state of Baden-Württemberg. Traditional inter-regional animosities and centre-periphery relations, aggravated by condescending behaviour by the state government, also fueled the conflict. Such regionalism was common at other rural nuclear plant sites, such as in Brokdorf, where the protesters celebrated – and possibly invented – the tradition of the free 'farmers of the marsh'. Transnational protest also occurred elsewhere, such as the Danish-Swedish protest against the nuclear power plant Barsebäck, and the Dutch-German protests against the Kalkar fast breeder. However, the protests in Wyhl and Fessenheim were specific in their transnational regionalism.[64]

Protesters framed their protest as a revival of traditional cultures of resistance, harking back to the peasants' war in the 1500s. Most importantly, they celebrated the local Allemannian dialect, which provided a shared means of communication and identity across the national border, connecting the Alsace, Baden and the neighbouring Swiss cantons. The dialect was used for protest songs created by regional singer-songwriters, on posters and on the pirate radio station Radio Verte Fessenheim. Regional activists even created a name for their transnational region – the *Dreyeckland* (triangle country), a play on words on the German administrative term *Dreiländereck*, that is, the corner where three countries meet.[65]

Nuclear power was of course not the only issue of controversy during this period. Tourism continued to create conflicts over the scale of tourism and its compatibility with landscape and nature conservation, and traditional ways of life in the region. In the 1980s and 1990s this led to public protest e.g. on the Balearic Island of Formentera.[66] However, as the example in the introduction to this chapter demonstrates, regionalism and regional interests were not always necessarily in support of the increasingly expert and science-based environmentalism. Conflicts about land use, for example, have arisen not only about high-voltage power lines but also on wind turbines and dams, whose purpose is to provide green energy in the face of climate change. Furthermore, in recent years, vocal protests against plans of setting aside land for national parks have frequently invoked regional identities along with regional economic interests.[67] Here, regionalism served to lay claim to local democratic credentials, in the face of what some regional actors – including hunters and foresters – criticized as the authoritarian imposition of environmental policies – such as the imposition of 'wilderness' ideals in national parks, or bans on bird hunting in rural France – on people in the periphery, by central governments and international norm setters, such as the European Union.[68]

Conclusions

All in all, how can we characterize the relationship between regionalism and nature? And how did this change over time? Nature protection and nationalism emerged almost simultaneously in the nineteenth century, along with a first wave of regionalism in many countries. The mostly middle-class associations emerging in the late nineteenth century sought to protect nature from the uses and forces of capitalism and modernization. Nostalgic attachment to a quickly changing rural world and aesthetic ideals informed nature protection, which at the time included landscapes, cultural and natural monuments of home. In many cases, this involved a complex relation between the national and the regional levels – integrating the regional in the national and vice-versa, and highlighting distinctions, where national attachment was yet unclear, as in Austria-Hungary. Material interests – notably in tourism – were important motivations for branding nature in regional terms, highlighting specific beauty and traditions.

Nature protection and regionalism from above played an important role during the twentieth century, as societies and political actors from the political centre imposed their vision on the supposedly pristine nature of peripheral regions, as exemplified by the Czech beautification societies' outreach into the natural spaces of rural Slovakia. Similarly, the imposition of national park rules brought about conflicts over land use, where regionalist arguments and identities have increasingly been invoked against nature protection, such as in Alto Adige/South Tyrol.

A new regionalism from below since the 1970s demanded democratic participation in the periphery and at the subnational level. Its rise coincided with the emergence of the new environmentalism that thought about nature at a global scale. Both joined forces across national borders in the 1970s in the struggle against nuclear power. However, in recent years, critics of wind power or power lines within the region have started to mobilize more conservative older aesthetic traditions of conservation, protecting the supposedly eternal landscapes of home. Regionalist conceptions of nature have thus worked against modern environmentalism with its focus on global issues such as climate change. This has made the traditional, mutually supportive connection between regionalism and nature protection more fragile, notably in those cases where regionalism is allied with right-wing or populist movements that tend to be more critical of environmentalism.

Notes

1. Martin Bemmann, Birgit Metzger and Roderich von Detten, eds, *Ökologische Modernisierung. Zur Geschichte und Gegenwart eines Konzepts in Umweltpolitik und Sozialwissenschaften* (Frankfurt: Campus, 2014).
2. Ludger Fittkau, 'Diskussion on SuedLink. Die Kabel kommen unter die Erde', *Deutschlandfunk* 5 December 2015; dpa, 'Energie-Gipfel im Kanzleramt: Seehofer: Sämtliche "Monstertrassen" in Bayern vom Tisch', *Münchner Merkur* 2 July 2015; and Susanne Lettenbauer, 'Kampf gegen Stromtrassen. Warum Bayern die Energiepolitik blockiert', *Deutschlandfunk* 11 June 2015. On German energy transition: Morris, Craig and Arne Jungjohann, *Energy Democracy: Germany's Energiewende to Renewables* (Basingstoke: Palgrave Macmillan, 2016).
3. Stine Marg, 'Heimat. Die Reaktivierung eines Kampfbegriffs', in *Bürgerproteste in Zeiten der Energiewende. Lokale Konflikte um Windkraft, Stromtrassen und Fracking*, ed. Christoph Hoeft, Sören Messinger-Zimmer and Julia Zilles (Bielefeld: Transcript, 2017), 221–34; and Olaf Kühne and Florian Weber, 'Conflicts and Negotiation Processes in the Course of Power Grid Extension in Germany', *Landscape Research* 43, no. 4 (2018): 529–41.
4. Olaf Kühne, Heidi Megerle and Florian Weber, eds, *Landschaftsästhetik und Landschaftswandel* (Wiesbaden: Springer, 2017).
5. E.g. in bird protection: Jan-Henrik Meyer, 'Saving Migrants. A Transnational Network supporting Supranational Bird Protection Policy in the 1970s', in *Transnational Networks in Regional Integration: Governing Europe 1945–83*, ed. Wolfram Kaiser, Brigitte Leucht and Michael Gehler (Basingstoke: Palgrave Macmillan, 2010), 176–98, 182–90.
6. Ludger Gailing, *Kulturlandschaftspolitik: Die gesellschaftliche Konstituierung von Kulturlandschaft durch Institutionen und Governance* (Detmold: Rohn, 2014).
7. David Blackbourn, *The Conquest of Nature: Water, Landscape, and the Making of Modern Germany* (New York: Norton, 2007), 7.
8. Paul Goossens, 'Belgium: The End started in 1968', *Bulletin of German Historical Institute Washington DC Supplement* 6 (2009): 191–94. This chapter benefited from the thoughtful feedback

by the editors. Furthermore, I would like to express my gratitude to Luigi Piccioni and Ute Hasenöhrl for their careful reading and recommendations and to the Center for Contemporary History in Potsdam, where I was a fellow while writing this chapter, and notably its very helpful and friendly library service. This article has benefited from my work within the project HoNESt – History of Nuclear Energy and Society (2015–19). This project has received funding from the Euratom research and training programme 2014–2018 under grant agreement No. 662268.

9. Donald Worster, *Nature's Economy: A History of Ecological Ideas* (Cambridge: Cambridge University Press, [1977] 1994).

10. Jan-Henrik Meyer, 'From Nature to Environment: International Organizations and Environmental Protection before Stockholm', in *International Organizations and Environmental Protection. Conservation and Globalization in the Twentieth Century*, ed. Wolfram Kaiser and Jan-Henrik Meyer (New York: Berghahn, 2017), 31–73, 36–39.

11. Bernhard Gissibl, Sabine Höhler and Patrick Kupper, 'Introduction: Towards a Global History of National Parks', in *Civilizing Nature: National Parks in Global Historical Perspective*, ed. Bernhard Gissibl, Sabine Höhler and Patrick Kupper (New York: Berghahn, 2012), 1–27.

12. For a critique: William Cronon, 'The Trouble with Wilderness, or, Getting Back to the Wrong Nature', *Environmental History* 1, no. 1 (1996): 7–55.

13. Charles-François Mathis, *In Nature We Trust: Les paysages anglais à l'ère industrielle* (Paris: PUPS, 2010); and Giorgio Osti, 'Nature Protection Organisations in Italy: From Elitist Fervour to Confluence with Environmentalism', in *Protecting Nature: Organizations and Networks in Europe and the USA*, ed. C. S. A. van Koppen and William T. Markham (Cheltenham: Edward Elgar, 2008), 117–39.

14. For the terminological distinction between conservation and preservation see Richard White, 'American Environmental History: The Development of a New Historical Field', *Pacific Historical Review* 54, no. 3 (1985): 297–335.

15. Paul Warde, 'The Invention of Sustainability', *Modern Intellectual History* 8, no. 1 (2011): 153–70; and Elke Seefried, 'Rethinking Progress. On the Origin of the Modern Sustainability Discourse, 1970–2000'. *Journal of Modern European History* 13, no. 3 (2015): 377–400.

16. Jacob Darwin Hamblin, *Arming Mother Nature. The Birth of Catastrophic Environmentalism* (Oxford: Oxford University Press, 2013).

17. Jens Ivo Engels, 'Modern Environmentalism', in *The Turning Points of Environmental History*, ed. Frank Uekötter (Pittsburgh: University of Pittsburgh Press, 2010), 119–31.

18. C. S. A. van Koppen and William T. Markham, 'Nature Protection in Western Environmentalism. A Comparative Analysis', in *Protecting Nature: Organizations and Networks in Europe and the USA*, ed. C. S. A. van Koppen and William T. Markham (Cheltenham: Edward Elgar, 2008), 263–85.

19. Engels, 'Modern Environmentalism'.

20. Kerstin Kretschmer and Norman Fuchsloch, eds, *Wahrnehmung, Bewusstsein, Identifikation. Umweltprobleme und Umweltschutz als Triebfedern regionaler Entwicklung* (Freiberg: Technische Universität Bergakademie Freiberg, 2003); Monika Gibas and Rüdiger Haufe, eds, *Mythen der Mitte. Regionen als nationale Wertezentren. Konstruktionsprozesse und Sinnstiftungskonzepte im 19. und 20. Jahrhundert* (Weimar: Verlag der Bauhaus Universität Weimar, 2005); and Gailing, *Kulturlandschaftspolitik*.

21. Detlef Schmiechen-Ackermann and Thomas Schaarschmidt, 'Regionen als Bezugsgröße in Diktaturen und Demokratien', *Comparativ* 13, no. 1 (2003): 7–16, 7; and John Newhouse, 'Europe's Rising Regionalism', *Foreign Affairs* 76, no. 1 (1997), https://www.foreignaffairs.com/articles/europe/1997-01-01/europes-rising-regionalism, last access on 25 July 2018.

22. E.g. Thomas Schaarschmidt, *Regionalkultur und Diktatur. Sächsische Heimatbewegung und Heimat-Propaganda im Dritten Reich und der SBZ/DDR* (Köln: Böhlau, 2004).

23. E.g. William H. Rollins, *A Greener Vision of Home: Cultural Politics and Environmental Reform in the German Heimatschutz Movement, 1904–1918* (Ann Arbor: University of Michigan Press, 1997); Thomas Lekan, *Imagining the Nation in Nature: Landscape Preservation and German Identity, 1885–1945* (Cambridge, MA: Harvard University Press, 2003); and Willi Oberkrome, *'Deutsche Heimat'. Nationale Konzeption und regionale Praxis von Naturschutz, Landschaftsgestaltung und Kulturpolitik in Westfalen-Lippe und Thüringen (1900–1960)* (Paderborn: Schöningh, 2004).

24. Ute Hasenöhrl, 'Nature Conservation and the German Labour Movement: The Touristenverein Die Naturfreunde as a Bridge between Social and Environmental History', in *Common Ground: Integrating the Social and Environmental in History*, ed. Geneviève Massard-Guilbaud and Steven Mosley (Newcastle upon Tyne: Cambridge Scholars, 2011), 125–49, 126–28; and Stefan Bargheer, *Moral Entanglements: The Emergence and Transformation of Bird Conservation in Great Britain and Germany, 1790–2010* (Chicago: PhD thesis, University of Chicago, 2011), 152.

25. Claude Reichler, 'Wahrgenommene Landschaft: Gelehrte, Schriftsteller und Künstler', in *Geschichte der Landschaft in der Schweiz. Von der Eiszeit bis zur Gegenwart*, ed. Jon Mathieu, Norman Backhaus, Katja Hürlimann and Matthias Bürgi (Zürich: Orell Füssli Verlag, 2016), 119–36; and François Walter, *Les figures paysagères de la nation: territoire et paysage en Europe (16e–20e siècle)* (Paris: Ecole des hautes études en sciences sociales, 2004).

26. Luigi Piccioni, 'The Rise of European Environmentalism. A Cosmopolitan Wave 1865–1914', *Ekonomska i ekohistorija* 10, no. 10 (2014): 7–15, 9–11; and Simon Bundi, 'Landschaft bewahren. Natur- und Heimatschutz', in *Geschichte der Landschaft in der Schweiz. Von der Eiszeit bis zur Gegenwart*, ed. Jon Mathieu, Norman Backhaus, Katja Hürlimann and Matthias Bürgi (Zürich: Orell Füssli Verlag, 2016), 206–18, 206, 211.

27. Danny Trom, 'Natur und nationale Identität. Der Streit um den Schutz der "Natur" um die Jahrhundertwende in Deutschland und Frankreich', in *Nation und Emotion. Deutschland und Frankreich im Vergleich im 19. und 20. Jahrhundert*, ed. Etienne Francois, Hannes Siegrist and Jakob Vogel (Göttingen: Vandenhoeck & Rupprecht, 1995), 147–67, 149–52.

28. Thomas Lekan, 'The Nature of Home: Landscape Preservation and Local Identities', in *Localism, Landscape, and the Ambiguities of Place: German-Speaking Central Europe, 1860–1930*, ed. David Blackbourn and James N. Retallack (Toronto: University of Toronto Press, 2007), 165–92, 173.

29. William Rollins, 'Heimat, Modernity and Nation in the Early Heimatschutz Movement', in *Heimat, Nation, Fatherland: The German Sense of Belonging*, ed. Jost Hermand and James Steakley (New York: Peter Lang, 1996), 87–112, 88–90.

30. Lekan, 'The Nature of Home', 173–76; and Ivan Brlicand and Anita Busljeta Tonkovic, 'The Origins and Development of the Plitvice Lakes National Park', in *Environmentalism in Central and Southeastern Europe*, ed. Hrvoje Petric and Ivana Zebec Silj (London: Lexington Books, 2017), 175–95, 178.

31. Lekan, 'The Nature of Home', 176–77.

32. Patrick Young, 'A Tasteful Patrimony? Landscape Preservation and Tourism in the Sites and Monuments Campaign, 1900–1935', *French Historical Studies* 32, no. 3 (2009): 447–77, 462–65.

33. Carolin Firouzeh Roeder, 'Slovenia's Triglav National Park. From Imperial Borderland to National Ethnoscape', in *Civilizing Nature: National Parks in Global Historical Perspective*,

ed. Bernhard Gissibl, Sabine Höhler and Patrick Kupper (New York: Berghahn, 2012), 240–50, 240–44; and Roman Holec, 'Man and Nature in Central Europe during the "Long" Nineteenth Century from the Slovak Point of View', in *Environmentalism in Central and Southeastern Europe*, ed. Hrvoje Petric and Ivana Zebec Silj (London: Lexington Books, 2017), 135–55, 148.

34. Charles-François Mathis, 'Le premier congrès international pour la protection des paysages: quelle convergence européenne?', Paper presented at the conference 'The Environment and European Public Sphere. Perception, Actors, Policies', 18 October 2017 (Paris: 2017).

35. Luigi Piccioni, 'Nature Preservation and Protection in Nineteenth- and Twentieth-Century Italy, 1880–1950', in *Nature and History in Modern Italy*, ed. Marco Armiero and Marcus Hall (Athens: Ohio University Press, 2010), 251–67, 255, 259.

36. Katarina Polajnar Horvat, Ales Smrekar and Matija Zorn, 'Environmental Thought in Slovenia', in *Environmentalism in Central and Southeastern Europe*, ed. Hrvoje Petric and Ivana Zebec Silj (London: Lexington Books, 2017), 21–33, 22; Jana Pinosova, 'Die Naturschutzbewegung in der Tschechoslowakei 1918–1938', in *Umweltgeschichte(n). Ostmitteleuropa von der Industrialisierung bis zum Postsozialismus*, ed. Horst Förster, Julia Herzberg and Martin Zückert (Göttingen: Vandenhoeck & Ruprecht, 2013), 275–97, 275; and Paul R. Josephson, Aleh Cherp, Dmitry Efremenko, Nicolai Dronin and Ruen Mnatsakanian, *An Environmental History of Russia* (Cambridge: Cambridge University Press, 2013), 57.

37. Eve Conant, 'Look Inside Russia's Wildest Nature Reserves – Now Turning 100', *National Geographic*: 10 January 2017 (2017), https://news.nationalgeographic.com/2017/01/russia-nature-reserves-year-ecology/, last access on 25 July 2018; and Natalia Danilina, 'The Zapovedniks of Russia', *George Right Forum* 18, no. 1 (2001): 48–55.

38. Patrick Kupper, 'Translating Yellowstone: Early European National Parks, Weltnaturschutz and the Swiss Model', in *Civilizing Nature: National Parks in Global Historical Perspective*, ed. Bernhard Gissibl, Sabine Höhler and Patrick Kupper (New York: Berghahn, 2012), 123–39.

39. Luigi Piccioni, 'Protecting the Alps. Italian Protected Areas in the Alpine Range, 1911–1991', in *Environmentalism in Central and Southeastern Europe*, ed. Hrvoje Petric and Ivana Zebec Silj (London: Lexington Books, 2017), 157–74, 162–63, 168; and Wilko Graf von Hardenberg, 'Nützen oder Schützen? Naturverwaltung im Alpenraum im 20. Jahrhundert', *Bohemia* 54, no. 1 (2014): 41–55, 48–49.

40. Pinosova, 'Die Naturschutzbewegung', 290–93.

41. Holec, 'Man and Nature in Central Europe', 149.

42. Pinosova, 'Die Naturschutzbewegung', 290–93.

43. Bianca Hoenig, 'Durch den Menschen für den Menschen schützen. Naturschutz und Tourismus im Tatranationalpark nach 1949 in transfergeschichtlicher Perspektive', in *Umweltgeschichte(n). Ostmitteleuropa von der Industrialisierung bis zum Postsozialismus*, ed. Horst Förster, Julia Herzberg and Martin Zückert (Göttingen: Vandenhoeck & Ruprecht, 2013), 299–316, 306; and Bianca Hoenig, 'Kleinod und Ressource: Die polnische Naturschutzbewegung und die Tatra', *Bohemia* 54, no. 1 (2014): 56–73, 65.

44. Catherine Brace, 'Looking Back: The Cotswolds and English National Identity, c. 1890–1950', *Journal of Historical Geography* 25, no. 4 (1999): 502–16; Oliver Zimmer, 'In Search of Natural Identity: Alpine Landscape and the Reconstruction of the Swiss Nation', *Comparative Studies in Society and History* 40, no. 4 (1998): 637–65; Hayden Lorimer, 'Ways of Seeing the Scottish Highlands: Marginality, Authenticity and the Curious Case of the Hebridean Blackhouse', *Journal of Historical Geography* 25, no. 4 (1999): 517–33.

45. Axel Zutz, 'Harmonising Environmentalism and Modernity: Landscape Advocates and Scenic Embedding in Germany, c. 1920–1950', *National Identities* 16, no. 3 (2014): 269–81, 274–76; and Hardenberg, 'Nützen oder Schützen?', 48.

46. Young, 'A Tasteful Patrimony?', 471–77; and Eric G. E. Zuelow, *Making Ireland Irish: Tourism and National Identity since the Irish Civil War* (Syracuse, NY: Syracuse University Press, 2008), 178–82. See also the chapter by Storm.

47. Keith Lowe, *Savage Continent. Europe in the Aftermath of World War II* (London: Viking, 2012).

48. Ute Hasenöhrl, '"Weisse Kohle" oder "Ausbeutung der Natur"? Konflikte um die Nutzung der Wasserkraft im (Vor-)Alpenraum am Beispiel Bayrisch-Östereichischer Grenzflüsse', *Bohemia* 54, no. 1 (2014): 119–41, 123–28; and Ute Hasenöhrl, *Zivilgesellschaft und Protest. Eine Geschichte der Naturschutz- und Umweltbewegung in Bayern 1945–1980* (Göttingen: Vandenhoeck & Ruprecht, 2011), 124–62.

49. Albrecht Stein von Kamienski, 'Loeffke, Ernst Ludwig Hans', in *Altpreußische Biographie, Vol. 5.1*, ed. Klaus Bürger (Marburg/Lahn Elwert, 2000), 1637. On Heimat films and the integration of refugees: Alina Laura Tiews, *Fluchtpunkt Film. Integrationen von Flüchtlingen und Vertriebenen durch den deutschen Nachkriegsfilm 1945–1990*. Berlin: be.bra wissenschaft verlag, 2017, 86–126.

50. Astrid Mignon Kirchhof, '"Der freie Mensch fordert keine Freiheiten, er lebt einfach"', *Geschichte und Gesellschaft* 41, no. 1 (2015): 71–106; and Jan Palmowski, 'Building an East German Nation: The Construction of a Socialist Heimat, 1945–1961', *Central European History* 37, no. 3 (2004): 365–99.

51. Jens Jäger, 'Heimat', *Docupedia-Zeitgeschichte*: Version: 1.0, 09.11.2017, http://dx.doi.org/10.14765/zzf.dok.2.1113.v1, last access on 25 July 2018.

52. Martin Zückert, 'Auf dem Weg zu einer sozialistischen Landschaft? Der Wandel der Berglandschaft in den slowakischen Karpaten', *Bohemia* 54, no. 1 (2014): 23–40, 38; and Karine-Larissa Basset, 'L'invention des parcs nationaux français entre modernisation et décolonisation: la quête d'une singularité', in *Une protection de l'environnement à la française, XIXe–XXe siècles*, ed. Jean-François Mouhot and Charles-François Mathis (Seyssel: Editions Champ Vallon, 2013), 170–81, 172–73.

53. Frank Uekötter, 'Ökologische Verflechtungen. Umrisse einer grünen Zeitgeschichte', in *Geteilte Geschichte. Ost- und Westdeutschland 1970–2000*, ed. Frank Bösch (Bonn: Bundeszentrale für Politische Bildung, 2015), 117–52.

54. Eagle Glassheim, 'Unsettled Landscapes: Czech and German Conceptions of Social and Ecological Decline in the Postwar Czechoslovak Borderlands', *Journal of Contemporary History* 50, no. 2 (2015): 318–36.

55. Brlic and Tonkovic, 'The Origins and Development', 176; Roeder, 'Slovenia's Triglav National Park', 249; Hoenig, 'Kleinod und Ressource', 56–73, 68; and Hoenig, 'Durch den Menschen für den Menschen schützen', 306.

56. Jens Ivo Engels, *Naturpolitik in der Bundesrepublik. Ideenwelt und politische Verhaltensstile in Naturschutz und Umweltbewegung 1950–1980* (Paderborn: Schöningh, 2006), 237–51; Hasenöhrl, *Zivilgesellschaft und Protest*, 235–54.

57. Basset, 'L'invention des parcs nationaux français', 172; Hasenöhrl, *Zivilgesellschaft und Protest*, 235–54.

58. Piccioni, 'Protecting the Alps', 165–68; Harald Engler and Ute Hasenöhrl, 'Erholungsplanung und Nutzungskonflikte im Ost-West-Vergleich. Das Rheinland und Brandenburg in den 1950er bis 1970er Jahren', *Geschichte im Westen* 32, no. 1 (2017): 165–98.

59. Basset, 'L'invention des parcs nationaux français'.
60. Nacima Baron-Yellès and Romain Lajarge, 'Essai sur la genèse idéologique et institutionnelle des parcs naturels régionaux français', in *Une protection de l'environnement à la française, XIXe–XXe siècles*, ed. Jean-François Mouhot and Charles-François Mathis (Seyssel: Editions Champ Vallon, 2013), 182–96, 190.
61. Engler and Hasenöhrl, 'Erholungsplanung und Nutzungskonflikte', 172.
62. Robert Gildea and Andrew Tompkins, 'The Transnational in the Local: The Larzac Plateau as a Site of Transnational Activism since 1970', *Journal of Contemporary History* 50, no. 3 (2015): 581–605; and Michael Bess, *The Light Green Society. Ecology and Technological Modernity in France, 1960-2000*. (Chicago: University of Chicago Press, 2003).
63. Stephen Milder, *Greening Democracy. The Anti-Nuclear Movement and Political Environmentalism in West Germany and Beyond, 1968-1983* (Cambridge: Cambridge University Press, 2017).
64. Andrew Tompkins, *Better Active than Radioactive! Anti-nuclear Protests in 1970s France and West Germany* (Oxford: Oxford University Press, 2016), 119; and Engels, *Naturpolitik in der Bundesrepublik*, 344–78.
65. Andrew Tompkins, 'Grassroots Transnationalism(s): Franco-German Opposition to Nuclear Energy in the 1970s', *Contemporary European History* 25, no. 1 (2016): 117–42, 132; and Tompkins, *Better Active than Radioactive!*, 119–20.
66. Maximilian Laun, *Tourism and the Limits to Growth. The Protest Movement on the Island of Formentera 1975-1995* (Free University Berlin, 2016); Maxilimilian Laun, '¡Camping No!' Un momento de gloria (Documentary Film, 2018) https://youtu.be/Keb4FkrjqzM. Last access 25 July 2018.
67. E.g. Hoenig, 'Kleinod und Ressource', 72; and Sophie Rohrmeier, 'Der Wald und die Wut. In Bayern soll ein Zehntel des Spessarts zum Nationalpark werden – und der Widerstand dagegen ist gewaltig. Woher kommt der Zorn', *Die Zeit* 17 March 2017.
68. Meyer, 'Saving Migrants', 192.

Further reading

Hasenöhrl, Ute, *Zivilgesellschaft und Protest. Eine Geschichte der Naturschutz- und Umweltbewegung in Bayern 1945-1980* (Göttingen: Vandenhoeck & Ruprecht, 2011).
Koranyi, James, and Tricia Cusack, 'The Making of Landscape in Modernity', Special issue of *National Identities* 16, no. 3 (2014): 191–287.
Lekan, Thomas, *Imagining the Nation in Nature: Landscape Preservation and German Identity, 1885-1945* (Cambridge, MA: Harvard University Press, 2003).
Milder, Stephen, *Greening Democracy. The Anti-Nuclear Movement and Political Environmentalism in West Germany and Beyond, 1968-1983* (Cambridge: Cambridge University Press, 2017).
Mouhot, Jean-François, and Charles-François Mathis, eds, *Une protection de l'environnement à la française, XIXe-XXe siècles* (Seyssel: Éditions Champ Vallon, 2013).
Petric, Hrvoje, and Ivana Zebec Silj, eds, *Environmentalism in Central and Southeastern Europe: Historical Perspectives* (London: Lexington Books, 2017).
Rollins, William H., *A Greener Vision of Home: Cultural Politics and Environmental Reform in the German Heimatschutz Movement, 1904-1918* (Ann Arbor: University of Michigan Press, 1997).
Tompkins, Andrew, *Better Active Than Radioactive! Anti-nuclear Protests in 1970s France and West Germany* (Oxford: Oxford University Press, 2016).

CHAPTER 5
REGIONAL FOODS
Kolleen M. Guy

The emergence of regional foods in Europe was directly tied to the globalization of food markets at the end of the nineteenth century. It was during this 'first globalization', as it has been called, that European regional foods with a distinct taste profile and identity emerged as commodities of national and international trade.[1] While agricultural commodities, such as coffee, sugar and tea, were a part of international trading networks for centuries, it was only at the end of the nineteenth century that staples (wheat, rice and wine) could be moved from continent to continent in large quantities at competitive prices. Many local or regional European specialties, such as bottled wines, fresh cheeses and hams, were fragile or highly perishable, making them unlikely candidates for long-distance travel over many weeks and countless miles. The combination of improved continental rail networks and the invention of mechanical refrigeration in the 1880s meant that producers could send formerly regional specialties quickly and safely to ever broader markets with less risk of spoilage or loss. With Lloyd's Register of Shipping recording 460 ships with refrigerating plants on board by 1902, regional food makers from across Europe had an abundant and safe pathway across land and ocean to move their products from farm to fork.

As food markets became global, agriculture became a central political and economic concern in Europe. Across the continent, farmers organized at the national level to contest what they saw as unfair trade practices as their products entered global trade networks and the flooding of European markets with cheaper commodities from abroad. Food manufacturers lobbied for cheaper shipping costs and protection of trademarks and trade secrets. Consumer groups, too, pressured governments over issues of food safety and purity. Most European countries responded with market interventions and protectionism. For regional food producers, new laws protecting agriculture as well as products with place-based names and 'local, loyal and constant' production methods marked the elevation of regional foods to a collective national patrimony. While some historians and economists have seen these measures as a first sign of a 'globalization backlash', others have noted that the new laws and institutions to regulate and protect agriculture that emerged in the early twentieth century were part of an 'internationalist spirit' that sought to create a transnational governance to cope with the effects of the new global market structure.[2] The Treaty of Madrid, for example, signed by Great Britain, France, Spain, Portugal, Switzerland, Tunisia and Brazil in April 1891 marked the first in a series of international regulations of food intended to protect 'regional marks' and 'collective marks'. The current European Union regulations to protect regional products through Protected Designation of Origin (PDO) and Protected Geographical Indication

Regionalism and Modern Europe

(PGI) are, in many ways, an extension of this internationalist spirit and collective vision of food as a cultural heritage. Whether we prefer to see these regulations as backlash or a new cooperation, the result of these exchanges was, as this chapter will argue, the globalization of regional foods and the advent of a regional food consciousness in Europe.

Regional foods and the *longue durée*

While many regional foods evoke an uninterrupted connection to the past, it would be difficult to speak of regional food profiles, as we understand them today, before the nineteenth century. One reason for this was the highly local nature of most food production and consumption until the agricultural revolution. Agricultural production was largely for auto-consumption or local exchange. Limited transport networks resulted in very few food items traveling substantial distances. The vast majority of people in Europe travelled no further. This meant that food provisioning was local or at best regional, providing very few opportunities for the majority of people to compare food or foodways. As scholars have noted, 'The "local" product, if consumed only at a local level, is devoid of geographical identity'.[3] The vast majority of Europeans ate what was readily available locally and seasonally through foraging, fishing, hunting and farming.

This does not mean that local or regional food remained unchanged over time. The adaptation of new crops, particularly as part of the Columbian Exchange, shifted regional cultivation patterns and culinary preferences. It would be hard to imagine Italian regional cuisine without the tomato or Swiss foodways without the potato. Both of these South and Central American nightshade crops diversified the European diet and shaped regional food preferences. Take, for example, *Solanuma tuberosum*, as it was named by the Swiss botanist Gaspard Bauhin. The humble potato was cultivated in Austria, Belgium, Holland, France, Switzerland, England, Germany, Portugal and Ireland by 1600. Adaptation was slowed, however, by prejudice and fear of nightshades, which included in their number several poisonous or deadly plants (i.e. belladonna, mandrake, henbane) associated with witchcraft and magic. Sicilians, for example, used potato tubers like voodoo dolls to cast death spells against enemies. In other places, such as Franche Comte and Burgundy, cultivation of potatoes was prohibited because it was feared that the plant brought disease. Feared and reviled, the potato seemed unlikely to become the second-most common starch, after wheat, at the base of European regional cuisines.

Planting potatoes, however, proved to be a highly effective means of offsetting one of the most persistent shapers of regional food and foodways before the nineteenth century – hunger and dearth. At the base of most European regional foods and cuisines was a staple crop, wheat, potatoes or, to a lesser extent, maize (corn), barley, rye and millet, that served as a bulwark against hunger. These were shaped into generic dishes or beverages that cut across cultural and geographic boundaries of Europe and were given a local variation or taste. Porridge (potage or gruel), for example, can be found throughout

Europe in varied regional 'styles' depending on the thickener (faro, rye, barley, oats, animal blood, etc.). Similarly, bread can be found in endless varieties, reflecting crop availability, religious strictures and taste preferences. Ground raw grains or roots, a quantity of fresh water and the microorganisms to induce fermentation could produce many bread variations within regions, let alone between them.

Securing supplies of staple crops such as these was a concern of not only the consumer populations, or 'masses', but also the centralized states well into the modern period. The maintenance of order was predicated on a social contract between state and society. At the heart of that contract was a stable supply of the staple crop, particularly in the lean winter months. Urban populations, in particular, were vulnerable to shortages and price instability. One need look no further than the revolutionary disruption of continental Europe in 1789 to attest to the destabilizing power of urban shortages and market fluctuations of a nation's staple food. It was a historic lesson so thoroughly understood that after the Second World War the French state charged the French National Center for Coordination of Studies and Research on Food and Nutrition (CNERNA) to take stock of innovations and methods in bread baking to assure a baseline of quality for the nation's bread supply.[4]

Some of the generic food types that we see throughout Europe were a result of the ever-present threat of hunger induced by natural disasters or man-made events. The peasantry of Europe, even in grain-producing areas, for example, could plant potatoes as a defense against famine. Despite early reticence, peasants found that the potato had the advantage of being easily hidden underground away from tax collectors or, more importantly, invading armies during times of war. The result was that during nearly every military conflict after 1560, including both world wars, the amount of acreage planted in potatoes across Europe increased. In some places, like Belgium and Russia, potatoes replaced grain as the principle staple, particularly for the poorer classes. While many foods of hunger, such as nettles and acorns, were gradually abandoned, these staple crops endured serving as the foundation for emerging local and regional cuisines in the nineteenth century.

While the decline of feudalism and the rise of cities redirected European agriculture away from subsistence and towards a market orientation, the environment continued 'to dictate a whole range of agricultural choices from the type of grain that could be grown to the kind of livestock that could be raised.'[5] What this means is that even as science and technology further transformed European agriculture in the eighteenth and nineteenth centuries, regional food patterns and traditions followed outlines dictated by nature. The Mediterranean regions, for example, were suited for olive groves, vineyards, wheat production, lamb and goat herds, as well as almonds, figs and even oranges. This environmental advantage was reflected in cooking techniques (e.g. oil in cooking rather than butter) and diet (wheat bread and pastas instead of potatoes). Northern latitudes largely abandoned vines for fear of frosts and took advantage of the availability of grains such as barley and rye to develop varieties of beers and spirits. Similarly, cooler climates were suited for dairy production, beef, ham preservation, apples and potato cultivation. The far northern regions, such as Norway and Iceland, consumed less grains and starch and much higher quantities of dairy and fish. Global climate change acceleration in the twentieth century may have slowly shifted these patterns in ways that scholars are only beginning to map and study.

One of the most overlooked environmental factors in the emergence of regional foods and cuisines over the *longue durée* is the role of microorganisms. Across Europe, people harnessed the power of microorganisms to make new foods. Cheese, yogurt, wine, beer, bread, ham, spirits – all of these are a result of the manipulation of naturally occurring microbial food cultures. Microbial food cultures are locally unique and mutate when moved beyond their microhabitat. This is because these microbial food cultures are a result of a mixed population of living microprobes that could come from elements as diverse as the water, the soil flora, the gut bacteria of animals or even the skin flora of the person preparing the food. In nature, microbial food cultures (made up of yeasts, molds and bacteria) are directly tied to local or regional environments and, thus, the foods that they produce retain that tie.

Europeans harnessed these microbes mainly to preserve food (through formation of inhibitory metabolites) often combining them with a decrease of water activity (by drying or use of salt). Yet, we also know that the microbial food cultures at the basis of many of these regional products could improve the organoleptic quality of food – the taste, texture, smell and visual appeal. Taste preferences surely mattered. While their senses might have encouraged use of cultures based on yeasts, moulds and bacteria, they had no way of knowing that these same cultures could improve food safety by inhibiting pathogens or toxic compounds and improving the overall nutritional value. It was only in 1665 that Robert Hooke in England and Antoni van Leeuwenhoek in the Netherlands first observed and described microorganisms in food. Another 200 years would pass before scientists, such as Louis Pasteur and Emil Christian Hansen, would prove the functioning of microbes in fermentation and begin to isolate specific cultures. It would take yet another 100 years (into the 1970s) before the production of the first industrial, concentrated cultures. Even today, our understanding of the role of microbial food cultures to regional foods and taste profiles continues to evolve.

These were the broad patterns over the *longue durée* that shaped food production and preferences in Europe. We should not assume, however, that this meant the existence of regional food specialties as we know them today. Bread or beer or wine fermented with the wild yeast spores floating around a locale, for example, could produce vastly different results from season to season, let alone from year to year. Europeans today, with their reliance on commercial or cultured yeasts, are not eating the bread of their forefathers. Before the nineteenth century, most Europeans relied on the science of nature when it came to fermentation and preservation and ate what was available on their farm or in the markets, depending, of course, on a family's means. In times of dearth, people ate whatever they could find or face starvation. Moreover, the advent of the Anthropocene era, when man-made changes began to impact the climate and environment, altered microorganisms and, thus, the foods that they produced in ways that we are only beginning to examine. To the extent that a 'regional cuisine' emerged, it was predicated on habits, traditions and techniques over the *longue durée* that were determined as much by environmental and economic necessity as taste preferences. Regional foods took on meaning and a place-based identity in the sphere of exchange. We should never lose sight of the fact that the vast majority of Europeans struggled to produce enough cheese or ham or yogurt to feed their family or community. Having enough to eat along with a variety of foods within reach both physically and economically remained a primary challenge. The relatively recent period surrounding the Second World War was a potent European-wide reminder of the specter of hunger.

European markets for regional foods

The one group that did have enough to eat and a variety to choose from across time was the European ruling classes. Whether it was the leaders of the Third Reich or the Russian court under the tsars, we see a demand for regionally based luxury food items. Evidence suggests that among this group there was a long-standing consciousness of place and its impact on foods, particularly wines. Historian Jean-Marie Fritz dates this consciousness to the Crusades. He suggested that consciousness of place came from not only the flow of new foods into Europe but also from the experience of travel for trade and military purposes. It was the Crusades, he argues, that first acquainted Europeans with the products of the Middle East but also products of a shared heritage whose variety and refinement offered a contrast to what was available on European markets. European travellers noted that shared grape varietals or wine-making techniques did not produce identical wine tastes. It was this contrast that contributed to the consciousness of what was unique about wines from a distinct territory or space. Emerging vernacular languages gave expression to that experience.[6] Nascent regional food consciousness was a result of these exchanges bringing culinary customs, cooking practices or food products into sharper focus as a result of 'contact with different systems and cultures'. Food's geographic identity was created through a process of dislocation of people or products whether through peaceful market exchange or military conquest.

Historians have noted growing emphasis on regional diversity in texts (menus, travel writing, recipes, shipping manifests, etc.) as early as the seventeenth century. Wine connoisseurship, in particular, emerged among the ruling classes who could choose among wines from across Europe. Although here, again, it should be noted, the preferences for wines associated with regional production areas do not map neatly on today's regional wine maps. Spoilage for wines shipped across distances remained a problem and hampered provisioning areas. It is not surprising to see among the emerging food literature a large number of treatises designed to assist merchants and buyers on remedying or correcting wine that had gone bad in transport or storage. These limitations on transport and constraints on the retention of quality in storage no doubt contributed to the planting of vineyards along transport routes, particularly rivers, and in new areas of European settlement. Environmental factors as much as market challenges determined these patterns. As the author and soil scientist Olivier de Serres noted in his seminal *Théâtre d'Agriculture* (1600), 'If you are not in a place where you can sell your wine, what would you do with a great vineyard?'[7] By the seventeenth century, Europeans were planting vineyards and introducing European grape varietals around the globe as they extended European colonization. Spanish missionaries planted vines throughout Latin America. The eastern seaboard of North America saw English settlers adapting grape varietals to wine production. The Dutch government assisted settlers in the Cape Colony to plant vineyards, laying the foundation for the South African wine industry.

Dislocation and exchange of people and products brought greater consciousness of unique geographic bound food traits and traditions in the eighteenth century. By this period, we see commercial guides listing products that originated in a discreet area of villages and hamlets under a nascent 'collective trademark' based on the name of a locality or the largest commercial center. The famous *jambon de Bayonne*, for example, is found under that place-based name in the 1767 bulletin *Gazetin du comestible*.[8] Travel writers also commented on the regional varieties of wines and their qualities. British travellers, particularly young well-off Englishmen on the Grand Tour, wrote about the variety of wines and vineyards and created a taste profile for regional wines. Men of science, too, not only provided detailed commentaries on grape varietals and vinification techniques but also offered useful comparisons across regions. The academician and botanist Peter Simon Pallas, for example, visiting Crimea in 1794, provided one of the first full descriptions of Crimean viniculture with comparisons to wines and techniques in Hungary, Greece and Cyprus. It is also in this same period that we see the publication of cookery books in France and Italy with texts that provide descriptions of the eating habits of people in various provinces. The culinary arts, as practiced in aristocratic courts, was widely documented and we can speak of an emerging 'national' cooking style of the elite courts that included specific wine, cheese and meat accompaniments from villages, towns and regions with a recognized distinction for both taste and quality.[9]

By the time that King Louis XVI made the ill-fated decision to interrupt his flight from revolutionary Paris to stop in the town of Sainte-Menehould to dine on the region's renowned pig's trotters, there was a discernable link between culinary specialty products and place among Europe's notables.[10] The economic, social, cultural and political changes that would end the French King's gastronomic outing (along with his reign) produced a discernable shift in agriculture and food markets that profited those notables who owned land well into the next century. Among this land-owning class profiting from technological advances that produced higher yields, brought new land into cultivation and improved transport to market, we see a growing interest in local products and their qualities. This interest can be seen in dramatic increase in discussion of regional foods not only in gastronomic texts, like the oft-quoted works of French gastronome Brillat-Savarin, but also in the volumes of administrative reports, technical works, specialty agricultural journals and state-generated statistics on production and markets.[11] We see, for example, the emergence of municipal food production instructional manuals and recipe collections, in Milan, Naples, Turin and throughout Tuscany.[12] Both new and old centralized states showed interest in measuring production of regional fermented and distilled beverages to generate tax revenues. What all of these documents suggest is that by at least the mid-nineteenth century, not only consumers and producers but also states had a growing consciousness of the value and potential of regional foods and cuisines.

Nationalizing regional foods for the global market

After the mid-nineteenth century, we might say that what bound Europeans to regional foods was not 'cords of necessity', to paraphrase Pascal, but 'cords of imagination'. The agricultural and industrial revolutions increased the availability of all food stuffs, eliminated subsistence farming, and reoriented local or regional food economies towards national and international markets. Chemical and mineral fertilizers renewed the soil and assured greater productivity. Mechanization of reapers and tractors innovated the use of labour. New preservation techniques, such as pasteurization, along with canning, made food safer and provisioning more secure. Industrial manufacturing created new artificial products, such as margarine, to replace the traditional 'natural' product, such as butter, with their shorter shelf-lives. All of these cut the 'cords of necessity' that had given rise to regional food patterns in Europe.

The Nordic countries are one area of Europe where we can see the dramatic shifts in patterns of consumption that came with urbanization, industrialization, democratization and growing agricultural links within Europe and to the larger global economy. Fresh food – fruits, vegetables and meats – became widely available outside of the short Nordic growing seasons in the late nineteenth and early twentieth centuries. Roasts, minced meats, pork cutlets and even steaks became popular alongside of the traditional preserved meats and fish. New leavened breads diversified the variety of breads available in Norway, Sweden and Denmark. And the milk industry, a traditional mainstay of the Nordic diet, was radically transformed by the direct sales of milk to new factories where butter and cheeses were mass produced for global markets. Cheese specialists were brought in from Switzerland as well as towns such as Gouda, Edam and Leiden to produce domestic versions of popular Dutch and Swiss cheeses. New cheeses, such as Norwegian Jarlsberg, were created as well for export. This was also an era of particularly abundant herring catches, bringing down prices and increasing the place of herring in the 'traditional' Nordic meal.

These large-scale shifts in agricultural production and consumption meant the invention of new regional food traditions and, in some cases, the increase in existing regional food consumption. The 'cords of imagination' remained remarkably enduring. Demographic increases and agricultural efficiency pushed populations off the land and into cities and even across oceans. These former rural dwellers brought with them an attachment to regional foods as part of a shared memory and as tokens of belonging to a community. Special occasions and rites of passage, even in rapidly changing foodscapes like those of the Nordic countries, meant the continued consumption of special regional dishes and products.[13] Areas of mass immigration also saw a renewed attachment to regional foods. Italians, who made up the largest group of immigrants to the United States between 1880 and 1921, for example, retained their regional food preferences and style of eating despite tremendous pressures to change and assimilate. Since the majority of these immigrants were from the Mezzogiorno, they created demand and a profitable market for imported specialties from areas such as Sicily, Calabria and Abruzzi. Where imports remained prohibitively expensive (such as cheeses), a domestic production developed to supply the demand for Italian-style products.[14] And French chefs, transplanted to cities around the globe, brought with them versions of the simple soups, daubes and *pot-au-feux* of their childhoods in the French countryside to generations of restaurant diners who never set foot in France.

We should not be surprised by the endurance of regional food preferences. Taste is a rather conservative sense. Societies and communities raise individuals with relatively fixed and stable understandings of what is edible or desirable and the absence of that familiarity can produce a strong longing or nostalgia. Indeed, the word 'nostalgia' was coined by a Swiss doctor to explain the physical reaction of soldiers far from home when they were served a regional or local soup or porridge. Leaving one place and residing in another – whether it is a new town or a city across the ocean – can strengthen attachments and lead to a search to recover or reconstruct the tastes and smells of 'home'.[15] This may explain, in part, why consumption of regionally specific fermented beverages remained fairly constant throughout Europe well into the twentieth century. Cereal consumption, as the base of regional or local stables such as porridges and breads, peaked in France, England, Germany and Italy not in the preindustrial period but at the end of the nineteenth century. We see similar attachment to food stuffs that formed the basis of regional cuisines, such as the potato in Germany, well into the twentieth century.[16] Even when fruits or vegetables from the new colonial empires of the late nineteenth century were introduced into European culinary repertoires, they tended to be assimilated into existing recipes or 'naturalized', such as the case of curries in England, into a national dish.[17]

The absorption of new food products or 'exotic' ingredients, however, could not help but raise issues about 'authenticity' and the boundaries of region. Gastronomic texts and the emergence of regional recipe books by the late nineteenth century contributed to reshaping the bonds between the local, the regional and the national. Taste professionals praised the merits of not only products but also the regional dishes and culinary traditions that showcased these delights. Regional cuisines transformed local products into 'symbols of historical continuity and shared memory as well as tokens of community'.[18] The second half of the nineteenth century saw the appearance of not only regional recipe collections and lists of products but also a new consumption of the local through tourism. Culinary specialties joined other representations of the local in guidebooks and tours, a trend that would be amplified by the advent of automobile tourism in the twentieth century. This new prominence of regional cuisine, whether through texts or tours, meant that the boundaries of the 'region' required a codification in definition in culinary rather than administrative terms. Gastronomic associations and writers, hotel and restaurant owners, and regional food producers and trade organizations had an interest in linking specialty dishes to place through a historical narrative that said little about the 'cords of necessity' and much more about the 'cords of imagination'.[19]

When these 'cords of imagination' combined with the 'invented traditions' of nation states, regional foods and cuisines came to represent more than taste preferences or local traditions. Food could represent the nation itself. As food scholar Amy Trubeck has pointed out, both food and nations are material things that are tied to the earth, the natural world and geographic locales. This has become so powerful in the modern era that 'foods have become associated with cuisines and places with nations to such an extent that one does not perceive any difference between them.'[20] Regional foods became subsumed in the 'national cuisines' that emerged around the nation state and the rise of a sense of national belonging in the nineteenth and twentieth centuries. So, it is common to read about food as a patriotic symbol in newspapers like the 1850 version of the *Illustrated London News*. The paper states definitively that '[p]lum pudding is a national symbol. It does not represent a class or a caste but the whole of the English nation.' Kent pudding pies or a Yorkshire pudding recipe might still mark historic regional variations, but it was the act of consuming a pudding, particularly at Christmas, that marked a true English man or woman.[21] The French were just as direct in linking the geographic space of the nation with food. Popular images and maps of the state of France 'were shaped by compilations of regional culinary specialties' indicating the status of local food products 'in both the popular imagination and symbolic representations of national identity.'[22] For countries like Belgium whose national unification was a product of the nineteenth century, the emergence of a distinctive national cuisine composed of local and regional specialties was nascent on the eve of the First World War. It would only be after the war that these regional specialties were elevated to national treasures.[23]

Europe as moveable feast

The investiture of regional foods, foodways and products with the cultural capital of the nation was a result of both dislocation of people and products. Dislocation took many forms. English pudding, for example, was associated not only with 'Englishness' but also the Christmas holiday at 'home' in the British Isles. Throughout the British colonies in the southern hemisphere, puddings with their heavy lacing of sugar, treacle, suet and spices retained a central place on the Christmas menu despite the fact that the holiday fell in the hot summer months, when preparing and eating such a dish was completely out of sync with the season and weather. Consumption linked the colony to the British crown and the English narrative, not to the realities of an Australian summer and a more complex history. Likewise, in France, an entire tourist industry grew up around visits to rural regions. 'Regional movements', writes one scholar, 'sponsored celebrations in which local culinary specialties were served up against a backdrop of parades, colorful costumes, lectures in patois, and traditional folk songs and dances'.[24] And when foreigners showed up to make a pilgrimage to what they believed was the 'birth place' of a particular regional food, local officials and regional producers eagerly responded by preserving, promoting or even, in some cases, inventing customs and traditions that conformed to this external vision of the region. Such was the fate of camembert cheese when the American Dr. Joseph Knirim arrived in the village of Vimoutiers in March 1926 in search of the tomb of Marie Harel who, he believed, was the creator of the 'véritable Norman Camembert'. The result was the creation of a mythology about the cheese and its place in a larger French narrative about the nation.[25] Similarly, in Belgium, we see a concerted state effort to promote a vision of a harmonious and varied Belgian cuisine at the Universal Exposition in Brussels of 1910. This was an effort that was intended to promote a patriotic vision for the consumption of both those inside and outside the country.[26]

Dislocation meant that the region was both marketed according to internal notions of what was 'authentic' and customary and, at the same time, in response to external responses to the region and regional foods. While the consumer market for undifferentiated, inexpensive or 'generic' foods and wines from Europe expanded, there was also a growing interest in regional specialty items with links to historic areas of production and specialized production techniques. These products were promoted transnationally as 'authentic' and consumers, particularly the expanding middle class, came to associate them with a quality not to be found in mass-produced food. We can see this most clearly in worldwide demand for estate or *chateaux* wines where emphasis was placed on the rural, provincial roots of taste and quality. Bottled wines from Europe often stressed this linkage with place through the use of both the *chateau* label and the place-based wine name. The European *chateau* came to be seen as representative of something solid and permanent linked to an 'Old World' past while local and regional names – Bordeaux, Champagne, Montepulciano, Porto – came to denote a unique place-based wine style and taste, often summarized with the French word *terroir*. As food and wines were increasingly sold as generic commodities, connection to European villages, towns and regions represented consistent, reliable quality in the eyes of consumers and emerged as the key to wine-marketing strategies. The success for winemakers was evident in not only the increase in global sales but also the popularity of wine cellar tours and the increase in travel guides recommending vineyard visits as an essential part of the tourist itinerary. Cheeses, hams and other European regional specialty items adopted this same place-based marketing strategy in the twentieth century.

The success of European regional products as part of a worldwide popular culture of ingestion was not without its challenges. European place-based products built up reputations that new producers – in Europe and abroad – hoped to imitate or emulate. Champagne, for example, was historically a place-based sparkling wine grown and produced in villages and cities in France that fell in the region of the same name. By the twentieth century, however, regional producers found themselves competing with sparkling wines labeled 'champagne' originating in areas from Crimea to California. These products often had little in common with the regional French wine and put at risk the prized reputation of the original regional product.[27] It is perhaps not surprising to see European regional producers and their governments leading international discussion of the limits of commercial property rights, the meaning of fraudulent production and the desirability of protecting collective trademarks in agriculture. Beginning with the international accords signed in Madrid in 1891, there was a near-continuous effort to work out the legal protocols for determining when a once regional product (such as *eau de Cologne*) was widely accepted as a generic and when the place of origin and the name attached to the product retained its meaning (such as Bordeaux or Porto). The Madrid agreement, like many of the subsequent conferences and accords, left much of the work of defining the parameters of what constituted an 'authentic' regional product to the country of origin. The process of determining what was 'local, loyal, and constant' production required not only a definition of the product but also a mapping of the parameters of a region, whose boundaries were rarely rigidly defined historically. These definitions would form the basis of the legal structure for protection of regional foods and wines as a cultural patrimony. With the founding of the European Economic Community, we see clear international cooperation on preserving regional food heritage and a coherent body of laws protecting regional products emerge, beginning in 1992 and extended by the European Union in 2012, with PDO and PGI.

Regional foods: Towards the twenty-first century

Interest in protecting regional food products coincided with a major shift in world agricultural production that had a profound impact on Europe. The twentieth century saw a remarkable increase in agricultural production around the world. Increasingly, continental Europe was supplied with staple crops from Asia, Africa and South America, a trend that continues to this day. Reduced freight rates and improved technology, which were so essential to globalizing European regional specialties, played a key role in making this abundant flow of global goods into Europe possible. At the same time, growing demand for European products at home and abroad came with a new industrial organization of European agriculture. Large firms and vertical integration in the food sector was most pronounced in northern Europe but can be seen across the continent throughout the twentieth century.[28] In France, for example, regional producers of the famous Roquefort cheese consolidated their interests to take advantage of new distribution opportunities. The Société des Caves Réunies de Roquefort was able to standardize production and control quality while taking advantage of preferential rates of refrigerated train wagons to move their cheese on scale to new markets throughout Europe and the Americas. These changes transformed the village of Roquefort into a 'factory town' and the surrounding dairy farms into one link in the integrated production of cheese.[29] The Roquefort cheese industry was just one of many local and regional food stories where we see the 'the division between agriculture, trade and industry that characterized earlier periods declining in importance, while new forms of integrated firms appearing, especially in the highly commercialized sector of the international food trade'.[30]

What did this mean for regional food production? South European countries have, generally, shown a political and cultural resistance to the mechanization and standardization of the food system that comes from integration. By contrast, North European countries have proven more open to production on scale and the agri-food commodity chain. This has meant much stronger popular and governmental support for protection of regional food production through protective legislation, tariffs and subsidies in the south. Indeed, South European countries have generally approached their regional food products as a central part of a cultural patrimony. This has meant not only the continued survival and even revival of regional specialty products but also an unprecedented opportunity for European producers of recognized products to improve their lives by gaining advantage in markets. One analysis of the distribution of registered regional products in Europe at the turn of the twenty-first century shows a clear concentration of protected regional food designations in Southern Europe. 'Between them', writes one group of scholars, 'France, Italy, Portugal, Greece, and Spain account for more than 75 percent of registered, regionally designated products.'[31] Attachment to regional foods in the south can be attributed to both cultural and structural factors that have tended to elevate rural life and regional foods to status as national treasures. Here, consumers tend to link region of origin with tradition and quality. And popular consumer movements, such as the hundreds of Slow Food Convivia across Europe, have assured that the history and traditions of regional foods are both recognized and protected. Place matters in food consumption.

This emphasis on place has taken on even greater importance as Europeans have questioned both the health value and the ethics of the capitalist industrial agri-food system of the post-Second World War period. It is important to note that not all European countries participated in the capitalist marketing of regional foods and cuisines in the twentieth century. During the Soviet era, communist regimes brought nutrition, food production and food consumption under the direction of the state in the name of the socialist state-building project. Regional foods or dishes were often integrated or subsumed into a new national cuisine and food culture that emphasized the health values of foods along with the need for inclusivity and accessibility. This was a new 'authentic' people's cuisine that stood in opposition to the bourgeois products of capitalist economies. This 'authentic' cuisine placed emphasis on a few key ingredients and simplified cooking techniques more than regional diversity. Nonetheless, even within 'Soviet Cuisine', there remained clearly identifiable regional dishes and the use of specialized ingredients from identifiable regions that could be obtained through private markets and trade.[32] An inclusive, communist-era cuisine was further re-enforced through communal dining in public cafeterias and workers canteens (*stolovaya*). Communal dining on the national fare promised a utopia at the table that would bring the nation together as a family to taste the abundance of the new workers state. Collectivization and the reorganization of agriculture, however, often produced a much less edible cuisine based on shortages and rationing.[33] Citizens supplemented their diets and satisfied culinary preferences through personal gardens, home-made dairy products using 'peasant methods', as well as wild foods, such as honey, herbs mushrooms or berries, picked from forests and meadows.[34] In this way, even in countries without a market orientation, there continued to be a thriving culture (and informal economy) of local foods and regional cuisines that produced a parallel belief in the value of the connection between food and place.

Conclusion

In Luisa Passerini's personal reflections on the generation of 1968 in Europe, she writes that for all the efforts of that generation to think and eat outside of their own place-bound culture, there was an undeniable 'pleasure in returning' to the 'comfort of finding simpler and less threatening food than you're forced to eat when traveling'.[35] Food remains a tie that binds. In this way, we should not overemphasize a north-south divide in the embracing of European Union schemes to protect regional foods or a capitalist-communist divide in valuing 'authenticity' bound with place. As the example of Soviet-era consumption suggests, registered regional products in capitalist markets is only one measure of attachment to regional foods. The hunger of two world wars, the shifting boundaries and barriers of the Cold War and multiple nationalists' conflicts in the twentieth century has only heightened European sensitivity to the meaning of place and an attachment to the taste of 'home'. Much of that attachment involves an occluding of the varied political meanings that regionalism and regional foods have taken on in the twentieth century. We see this, for example, in a nostalgia for Georgian foods from the Soviet Union in a post-Soviet Russia without the taint of the most infamous Georgian, Josef Stalin, and his love of those same dishes.[36] Likewise, some of the most popular cookbooks in West Germany in the 1950s and 1960s were reprints of 'traditional' cookbooks of the 1920s and 1930s. Some of these cookbooks had clear links to the Third Reich with its promotion of the *eintöpfe*, a dish to be made of 'native' German foods that was designed to diminish a dependence on imports and promote a healthy racial body. The post-war cookbooks, too, continued to include regional dishes and foods from the now 'lost' German lands in Poland and Czechoslovakia as part of a German regional culinary heritage. The German *Heimat* as a culinary entity could continue without the taint of Nazi politics.[37] All of this suggests that the region in Europe, as a culinary entity or place of food tradition, remains as deeply rooted as it is enduring.

Notes

1. See Suzanne Berger, *Notre Première Mondialisation: Leçons d'un échec oublie* (Paris: Seuil, 2003).
2. See Alexander Nützenadel, 'A Green International? Food Markets and Transnational Politics, c. 1850–1914', in *Food and Globalization: Consumption, Markets, and Politics in the Modern World*, ed. Alexander Nützenadel and Frank Trentmann (New York: Berg, 2008), 154–55.
3. Alberto Capatti and Massimo Montinari, *Italian Cuisine: A Cultural History* (New York: Columbia University Press, 2003), xiv.
4. Steven Laurence Kaplan, *Good Bread Is Back: A Contemporary History of French Bread* (Durham, NC: Duke University Press, 2006), 16.
5. Michel Morineau, 'Growing without Knowing Why: Production, Demographics, and Diet', in *Food: A Culinary History*, ed. Jean-Louis Flandrin and Massimo Montanari (New York: Columbia University Press, 1999), 377.

6. Jean-Marie Fritz, 'La carte des vins dans la France médiévale ou l'invention du *terroir*', *Papilles* 9 (1995): 11–22.
7. Roger Dion, 'Querelle des anciens et des modernes sur les facteurs de la qualité du vin', *Annales de Géographie* 61, no. 328 (1952): 418.
8. Laurence Bérard and Philippe Marchenay, 'Le Sens de la durée: Ancrage historique des "produits de terroir" et protection géographique', in *Histoire et identités alimentaires en Europe*, ed. Martin Bruegel and Bruno Laurioux (Paris: Hachette, 2002), 27–29.
9. See Jean-Louis Flandrin, 'Dietary Choices and Culinary Techniques, 1500–1800', in *Food*, ed. Flandrin and Montanari, 403–17.
10. Timothy Tackett, *When the King Took Flight* (Cambridge, MA: Harvard University Press, 2003), chapter 3.
11. Laurence Bérard and Philippe Marchenay, 'Le Sens de la durée: Ancrage historique des "produits de terroir" et protection géographique', in *Histoire*, ed. Bruegel and Laurioux, 28–31.
12. Alberto Capatti and Massimo Montinari, *Italian Cuisine: A Cultural History* (New York: Columbia University Press, 2003), 23–30.
13. Henry Notaker, 'Nordic Countries', in *Encyclopedia of Food and Culture*, volume 2, ed. Solomon H. Katz (New York: Scribner's, 2003), 558–67.
14. See Harvey Levenstein, 'The American Response to Italian Food, 1880–1930', *Food & Foodways* (1985): 1–23.
15. Svetlana Boym, *The Future of Nostalgia* (New York: Basic Books, 2001).
16. Hans Jurgen Teuteberg and Jean-Louis Flandrin, 'The Transformation of the European Diet', in *Food*, ed. Flandrin and Montanari, 442–45.
17. See, e.g., Lauren Janes, *Colonial Foods in Interwar Paris: A Taste of Empire* (London: Bloomsbury, 2016) or Lizzie Collingham, *Curry: A Tale of Cooks and Conquerors* (Oxford: Oxford University Press, 2007).
18. Julia Csergo, 'The Emergence of Regional Cuisines', in *Food*, ed. Flandrin and Montanari, 505.
19. See, e.g., Philip Whalen, '"Insofar as the Ruby Wine Seduces Them": Cultural Strategies for Selling Wine in Inter-war Burgundy', *Contemporary European History* 18, no. 1 (2009): 67–98.
20. Amy Trubeck, 'The Idea of National Cuisines', in *Encyclopedia*, volume 2, ed. Katz, 550.
21. Laura Mason, 'Les puddings et l'identité anglaise', in *Histoire*, ed. Bruegel and Laurioux, 169–81.
22. Csergo, 'The Emergence', 504.
23. Peter Scholliers, 'L'invention d'une cuisine belge: Restaurants et sentiments nationaux dans un jeune état, 1830–1930', in *Histoire*, ed. Bruegel and Laurioux, 151–68.
24. Csergo, 'The Emergence', 511.
25. Pierre Boisard, *Camembert: A National Myth* (Berkeley and Los Angeles: University of California Press, 2003).
26. Scholliers, 'L'invention d'une cuisine belge', 164.
27. Kolleen M. Guy, *When Champagne Became French: Wine and the Making of a National Identity* (Baltimore, MD: Johns Hopkins University Press, 2003).
28. Susan Freidberg, *French Beans and Food Scares: Culture and Commerce in an Anxious Age* (London: Oxford University Press, 2004).
29. Sylvie Vabre, *Le sacre du roquefort: L'Emergence d'une industrie agroalimentaire* (Tours: Presses universitaires François-Rabelais de Tours, 2015), 478–82.

30. Alexander Nützenadel, 'A Green International? Food Markets and Transnational Politics, c. 1850–1914', in *Food and Globalization: Consumption, Markets, and Politics in the Modern World*, ed. Alexander Nützenadel and Frank Trentmann (New York: Berg, 2008), 158.
31. Nicholas Parrott, Natashia Wilson and Jonathan Murdoch, 'Spatializing Quality: Regional Protection and Alternative Geography of Food', *European Urban and Regional Studies* 9, no. 3 (2002): 241–61.
32. See Anya von Bremzen, *Mastering the Art of Soviet Cooking: A Memoir of Food and Longing* (New York: Random House, 2013).
33. Mauricio Borrero, 'Food and the Politics of Scarcity in Urban Soviet Russia, 1917–1941', in *Food Nations: Selling Taste in Consumer Society*, ed. Warren Belasco and Philip Scranton (New York: Routledge, 2002), 258–76.
34. Melissa L. Caldwell, 'Gardening for the State: Cultivating Bionational Citizens in Postsocialist Russia', in *Ethical Eating in the Postsocialist and Socialist World*, ed. Yuson Jung, Jakob A. Klein and Melissa L. Caldwell (Berkeley and Los Angeles: University of California Press, 2014), 188–98.
35. Luisa Passerini, *Autoiography of a Generation: Italy, 1968* (London: Wesleyan University Press, 1996), 161.
36. von Bremzen, *Mastering the Art*.
37. Alice Weinreb, 'The Tastes of Home: Cooking the Lost Heimat in West German in the 1950s and 1960s', *German Studies Review* 34, no. 2 (2011): 345–64.

Further reading

Barrero, Mauricio, 'Food and the Politics of Scarcity in Urban Soviet Russia, 1917–1941', in *Food Nations: Selling Taste in Consumer Society*, ed. Warren Belasco and Philip Scranton (New York: Routledge, 2002), 258–76.

Bruegel, Martin, and Bruno Laurioux, *Histoire et identités alimentaires en Europe* (Paris: Hachette, 2002).

Capatti, Alberto, and Massimo Montinari, *Italian Cuisine: A Cultural History* (New York: Columbia University Press, 2003).

Flandrin, Jean-Louis, and Massimo Montanari, eds, *Food: A Culinary History* (New York: Columbia University Press, 1999).

Friedberg, Susan, *French Beans and Food Scares: Culture and Commerce in an Anxious Age* (London: Oxford University Press, 2004).

Guy, Kolleen, *When Champagne Became French: Wine and the Making of a National Identity* (Baltimore, MD: Johns Hopkins University Press, 2003).

Jung, Yuson, Jakob A. Klein, and Melissa L. Caldwell, eds, *Ethical Eating in the Postsocialist and Socialist World* (Berkeley and Los Angeles: University of California Press, 2014).

Nützenadel, Alexander, and Frank Trentmann, *Food and Globalization: Consumption, Markets, and Politics in the Modern World* (New York: Berg, 2008).

CHAPTER 6
TOURISM AND THE CONSTRUCTION OF REGIONAL IDENTITIES
Eric Storm

Tourism has grown enormously during the long twentieth century and it had and continues to have a profound and lasting impact on the process of regional identity construction throughout Europe. During the Belle Époque, vacations were still an elite affair, but it rapidly became a mass phenomenon and today, the tourism business is the largest service industry in the world. Tourism is also a highly competitive sector; entrepreneurs across Europe strive to find a profitable niche and retain or increase their market share. Tourists, however, are not a homogenous mass. Their economic capacities differ substantially; some stay in the tourist bubble, others choose to 'go native'; the entertainment and pleasures they seek vary immensely and foreign visitors might have different preferences than domestic tourists.

Obviously, the advent of tourism has major consequences for the socio-economic development of Europe, but it also has a vital impact on regions and their territorial identities. The way tourism affects the various parts of Europe depends on technological, socio-economic and political developments, such as the invention of the automobile, the introduction of paid holidays, the growth of commercial aviation, the expansion of the welfare state, governmental policies to stimulate or restrict leisure travel and questions of war and peace. However, more important for the impact of tourism on regional identities are cultural developments. Although tourists had many different preferences, a number of clear trends can be discerned. For instance, after sun bathing became fashionable, it occasioned a massive shift towards beach holidays. Other trends that had a strong influence on tourism were the fin-de-siècle interest in vernacular arts and crafts, the fascination with mass culture in the 1920s and 1930s, the modernization fervour of the post-war period and the growing appeal of cultural heritage in more recent decades. However, tourism does not only reflect major cultural trends, it magnifies them. Regions – just like resorts, cities and countries – have to stand out in a highly competitive market. Regions thus become a brand. This means that existing differences are emphasized, while new ones are created.

Tourism and rural heritage

During the Enlightenment, cultural life was inspired by Classical Antiquity and the Renaissance, while its contemporary centres were the courts and capital cities of

Western Europe. Tourists accordingly went to Italy – on the so-called Grand Tour – to visit the ruins, monuments and highlights of this shared European cultural heritage. The countryside, on the other hand, was not interesting and was perceived as backward. During the Romantic Era, this hierarchy was largely inverted. The backwardness and primitiveness of rural areas were reinterpreted in a positive light and the countryside began to be seen as the area where the vestiges of the nation's origins and its true culture or 'spirit' could still be found, whereas classicism, court life and urban civilization were slowly seen as artificial and inauthentic. Nevertheless, the countryside and its colourful costumes and traditions were primarily interpreted as representative of the nation, not of specific regional identities. This, for instance, is clearly visible in the folk tales that were collected by nationalist intellectuals like the Brothers Grimm and the attitude of painters specialized in rural themes,[1] such as Jean-François Millet, who primarily depicted the life of the peasants and a generic countryside, which generally was not recognizable as belonging to a specific region.[2]

Around 1900, as a consequence of the Second Industrial Revolution, secondary railway lines, bicycles, automobiles and buses made leisure trips to more remote areas easier to undertake. Everywhere in Europe, associations of excursionists sprang up and began organizing trips to the surrounding countryside. Boy scouts and other youth groups followed in their wake. All kinds of organizations stimulated domestic tourism, often with a clear nationalist undertone: citizens had a moral duty to get acquainted with the various regions of their fatherland. This message was already hammered home in many school manuals, such as *Le Tour de France par deux enfants* (1877).[3] People did not stop travelling to cities like Paris, Florence, Rome and London, but now also began to show interest in the natural and cultural patrimony of the countryside.

Excursions, however, did not always strengthen domestic unity. In East-Central Europe, tourism began to be organized along ethnic lines. German and Czech Bohemians, for instance, stimulated people to visit only the highlights of their 'own' heritage.[4] This also happened in some established nation states in Western Europe such as Spain. Thus, Barcelonese excursionist societies (re-)defined the monuments in the surrounding countryside as Catalan, while switching to Catalan as their main means of communication.[5] However, in general, it stimulated the inclusion of the region in the existing nation state, as happened, for instance, in Scotland, Brittany and Bavaria.[6] The construction of regional identities for touristic purposes was not only connected to domestic processes of nation formation or nation-building but was also strongly influenced by foreign travellers. To attract tourists from abroad, regions had to attract attention, and towards the end of the nineteenth century, this was primarily done by emphasizing their 'unique' rural and artisanal traditions.

This development can be analysed in condensed form at world fairs, which were major ephemeral tourist attractions drawing millions of visitors. At the 1867 Paris World Fair, the participating countries were invited not only to contribute machines and fine art to the gigantic central exhibition hall but also construct a national pavilion in a typical style to show their 'unique' culture and traditions. Most pavilions at this and successive exhibitions were copies of famous national monuments or were built in characteristic historical styles. However, North and East European countries, which probably had less impressive and recognizable monuments, increasingly used vernacular buildings to represent the nation. Thus, already in 1867 Sweden reconstructed the Dalecarlian peasant house in which Gustav Vasa found refuge before leading the Swedes in their 'War of Liberation' against the Danish king.[7]

At the 1873 world fair in Vienna, several peasant houses formed a kind of international village. Although regional differences were obvious – with, for instance, a Hungarian peasant house from Transylvania, cottages from Croatia and Galicia and an Alpine farmhouse from Vorarlberg – the primary goal of this section was to study traditional family homes as models for the future.[8] Ensembles with inhabited buildings, both in the form of a historical pastiche such as Old London (1884) or in the form of an ethnographic village, rapidly became a popular feature at later expositions, while the focus shifted from practical utility to instruction and amusement.[9]

Historical and ethnographic ensembles were institutionalized at the 1893 World Columbian Exposition in Chicago. The organizers decided to create a separate amusement sector where – among other attractions – more than a dozen ethnographic villages from all over the world could be visited. Europe was represented by a large German ethnographic village, two Irish villages and settlements from Lapland and Turkey. These picturesque re-creations appealed to all the senses; they were inhabited by natives who, dressed in traditional costumes, performed traditional dances and made crafts, while most of them also sold typical dishes and beverages. Most of these villages were commercial undertakings, although ethnologists were eager to lend a helping hand to make them as 'authentic' as possible.[10] Rather homogenous Irish, Tyrolean or Black Forest villages or representations of merry England continued to be popular attractions at world fairs until the 1930s.[11]

During the 1890s, nationalists also adopted the formula. The goal was no longer to represent the nation abroad, but to show the folkloric patrimony of the fatherland at home. The somewhat haphazard assembly of picturesque castles, town halls and farmhouses from various parts of the country was now replaced by a more systematic inventory of the nation's vernacular heritage. Thus, at the ambitious Czechoslavic Ethnographic Exhibition, which was held in Prague in 1895, activists reconstructed twenty-one vernacular buildings from across Bohemia, Moravia and Czech Silesia to underscore their claims that the Czechs were a nation in need of recognition. This also meant that the vernacular heritage of German-speaking Bohemians was deliberately ignored.[12] A similar ethnically inspired village could be found in Bucharest in 1906, when Romania organized a jubilee exhibition to celebrate the fortieth anniversary of Carol I's accession to the throne. The ethnographic village not only contained vernacular constructions from all parts of the country but also from ethnic Rumanians from Transylvania, the Banat, Bucovina and Macedonia.[13]

Ethnographic villages in East-Central Europe could also be more inclusive. This was the case when in 1896 the Hungarian half of the dual monarchy celebrated the arrival of the Magyars with a millennial exhibition. At the inevitable ethnographic village there were twenty-four rural buildings, among which were also vernacular constructions that represented Bulgarians, Slovaks, Rumanians and Danube Germans residing in Hungary. At the same time, however, ethnic minorities were strongly encouraged to adopt the 'superior' Hungarian language and culture.[14] Probably it was hoped that the recognition of their vernacular heritage would help all inhabitants to identify with the Hungarian state.

In Western and Southern Europe, ethnographic villages were generally less contested. Thus, the 1911 International Exposition in Rome, which commemorated the fiftieth anniversary of the Italian unification, contained an impressive ethnographic village that showed buildings from all parts of the country.[15] One of the most ambitious attempts to celebrate regional diversity at an exhibition was the Swiss Village. It consisted of fifty-six vernacular constructions representing all cantons and was assembled for the Swiss National Exhibition in Geneva in 1896 and then rebuilt at the Parisian world fair of 1900. The village contained chalets, shops, a bridge and a church and was inhabited by over 300 villagers. Moreover, it had a real lake, a creek, a waterfall and a forty-metre-high artificial mountain. Since it was wildly popular among visitors, the entrepreneurs enjoyed a considerable profit.[16] Even provincial exhibitions, for instance, in Lemberg/Lviv (1894), Dresden (1896), Leipzig (1897) and Nancy (1908), included an impressive ethnographic village, which presumably captured the spirit of the surrounding region.[17]

These ethnographic villages forced organizers to look for those buildings, costumes, crafts, songs, dances and dishes that were characteristic for a particular region. This meant that those elements that could not be found anywhere else had more chance to be selected as 'typical' than other more generic ones.[18] Moreover, they had to be recognizable and attractive to stand out at these enormous venues and convince visitors to spend precious time and money.

The curious results of this process can be illustrated by the case of the Hindeloopen room. Hindeloopen is a town on the Frisian coast in the Netherlands that had trading contacts with the Baltic and East Asia. During the seventeenth and eighteenth centuries, wealthy merchants acquired colonial wares such as china, while chintz from India became part of the traditional attire of their wives and daughters. Moreover, they decorated their interiors with colourful painted furniture, probably inspired by Scandinavian examples. Because these cosmopolitan upper-middle-class interiors were so unique and striking, they were perfect to attract attention at international exhibitions. A Hindeloopen room with lifelike mannequins in traditional costume was first shown in 1877 at the Frisian Historical Exhibition in Leeuwarden. This was an immense success and the next year it could be admired in the Dutch section at the Parisian world fair of 1878. In subsequent decades the attention shifted from the costumes to the interior as a whole, which came to be seen as the quintessence of Frisian folk heritage. As such, it could be used to show the regional diversity of the Dutch and even the German nation. Thus, in the 1890s entire rooms were bought by the German Museum for Traditional Costumes and Craft Products in Berlin and the Germanic National Museum in Nuremberg, where they were shown as a typical farm interior of one of the Germanic tribes.[19]

International exhibitions were closely interrelated with more permanent institutions and the growing tourism business. Thus, ethnographic museums – or specific ethnographic departments within larger national museums – were created in Berlin, Stockholm, Paris, Budapest and Prague, among others, in order to organize the ethnographic section at a major international exposition or to house the collection that had been brought together for such an occasion. Museum experts often played a leading role in the selection of exhibits. Ulrich Jahn, a staff member of the German Museum for Traditional Costumes and Craft Products, was the driving force behind the privately exploited German Village in Chicago, while Artur Hazelius, the director of the Nordic Museum in Stockholm, used the inspiration acquired at world fairs to found Skansen (1891), the first open-air museum, which displayed the vernacular heritage of the different regions of Sweden. Open-air museums were quickly copied in other parts of north and central Europe. At about the same time, all over Europe local museums were created to show the rich folklore and vernacular traditions of the surrounding areas.[20]

Remarkable, if not even outright eccentric, ancient furniture, decoration, costumes and buildings from a specific location thus became part of a regional heritage and had to be preserved.[21] In many countries, colourful vernacular traditions, houses and crafts of specific, remote regions were seen to embody the nation. Dalecarlia in Sweden, Telemark in Norway, Karelia in Finland, the Pusztas in Hungary and Podhale in Poland were often presented as a kind of heartland of the nation, where the country's traditional values were best preserved. Thus, national pavilions at world fairs were often inspired by vernacular constructions from these heartlands.[22] That foreign preferences played a crucial role is made clear in the case of Andalusia. During the first half of the nineteenth century, foreign travellers and artists, such as Washington Irving and Prosper Mérimée, had discovered the attractions of the Moorish remains and the flamenco music of the Andalusian gypsies. At the Parisian international exhibition of 1900 it would be a French company that mounted a vast *Andalusia at the Times of the Moors* exhibit, which included a replica of Seville's Giralda tower, donkeys and gypsy dancers.[23]

A new culture of regionalism

Towards the end of the nineteenth century, it had increasingly become common to represent regional identities at world fairs, in open-air museums and in all kinds of national, regional and local museums. No longer satisfied with making inventories of vernacular culture and protecting it, intellectuals and artists began to plea for reconnecting contemporary high culture – which they now condemned as academic, artificial and theatrical – with the authentic traditions of the fatherland. These could best be found in the countryside, where the true character of the nation was still alive. At the Parisian world fair of 1900 this was best exemplified by the Finnish pavilion. Several young, innovative painters, sculptors and architects had created a truly national *Gesamtkunstwerk* in which vernacular elements – mostly from Karelia – were harmoniously fused with fashionable Art Nouveau forms.[24]

Inspired by the British Arts and Crafts movement, everywhere in Europe artists tried to revive the decorative arts by reorienting them on vernacular traditions. Artists' colonies, such as Abramtsevo in Russia and Gödöllő in Hungary, played a leading role in bringing artists and craftsmen together and marketing their products abroad.[25] At the same time, architects looked for inspiration in vernacular buildings to develop a new style that would break with the dominant historicist and academic conventions. By using natural materials, existing artisanal techniques and integrating their constructions into the surrounding landscape, they hoped to create a more organic architecture that would reflect the local *Volksgeist* and be in consonance with the spirit of the times (*Zeitgeist*). During the first decades of the twentieth century, this neo-vernacular style became popular in Europe and was applied particularly to villas in suburbs and cottages in garden cities where the integration of buildings, gardens and landscape was especially relevant.[26]

The neo-vernacular style also gained headway in tourist areas, both in seaside and mountain resorts. In Poland, this style is even known as the *Zakopane* style, after the tourist town in the Podhale region at the foot of the Tatra Mountains.[27] All over Europe second homes were built in the different regional variants of this neo-vernacular style. In the French seaside resort Deauville, even the market and the train station were built in a neo-Normand style.[28] In order to attract more tourists and reconnect the population to native traditions, large cities also embarked upon ambitious schemes to transform the urban landscape. Thus, in Seville, the squalid, insanitary alleys of the old Jewish quarter were converted into an archetypical Andalusian neighbourhood, with cobbled streets, decorative tiles and cast-iron street lamps. New constructions in the Barrio de Santa Cruz were even more typical than the existing ones.[29] Meanwhile, Fritz Schumacher decreed that new municipal buildings in Hamburg should adopt a neo-Hanseatic style, while the architects of the Amsterdam School revived artisanal brick construction techniques in the Netherlands.[30] In Fascist Italy, cities such as Florence and Arezzo restored monuments, plazas and entire cityscapes in an idealized medieval or renaissance form, while adding characteristic towers and liberating old buildings from later additions. By reinventing popular 'medieval' festivals, the Tuscan character of these cities was further intensified.[31]

Vernacular heritage should not only be preserved, while inspiring contemporary cultural expressions, but was also used to attract visitors. Thus, towards the end of the nineteenth century, Leendert Spaander promoted his hotel in the Dutch fishing village of Volendam by having his daughters pose in traditional costume for painters, by printing postcards of the village's most traditional sights and by making publicity abroad.[32] In Brittany, the colourful local pilgrimages began to attract a growing number of visitors. Particularly in the tourist centres, old pilgrimages were revived and others were moved to the summer season while new folkloric feasts, such as the Festival of the Flowering Gorse in Pont-Aven and the Festival of Bleu Nets in Concarneau, were added to the calendar.[33]

Local, regional and national authorities also began to take action. Around 1900, the first tourist information centres began to provide maps, guides and leaflets. In the next few decades, this was followed by a growing number of regional and national tourist boards. This also meant that regions had to become identifiable. This could be done by including references to well-known tourist areas. Thus, in the nineteenth century, many hilly areas – for instance, in Saxony, Normandy and Luxemburg – became known as 'little Switzerlands'. Around the turn of the century, many coastal areas from the Black Sea to the Atlantic were named after the Italian Riviera,[34] and more individualizing designations such as Côte d'Azur or Costa Brava also gained currency.

Automobile clubs, national tourist associations and commercial enterprises became active in identifying regional highlights and making them accessible by erecting direction signs, marking foot paths and publishing road maps and guidebooks. This in part was meant to stimulate the inhabitants to get to know all the regions of the country. However, it also served to attract more foreign visitors. In both cases, the effect was that typical regional sights were put in the limelight. Thus, in 1904, the Touring Club de France began a campaign to identify the most important monuments and sites of the different parts of the country, while Michelin began to publish maps and its famous guide of cities, hotels and restaurants, giving stars to those that ought to be visited. The Danish Touring Club and the Ford factory in Copenhagen similarly stimulated trips to all beautiful parts of the country.[35] In the 1920s, the Spanish National Tourism Board even began its own chain of *paradores*, luxury hotels in ancient monuments in the more remote parts of the country (see Figure 6.1), where employees in traditional costume served regional dishes;[36] an example that was quickly followed by the Portuguese *pousadas*.

All these developments made many villages, cities and regions more characteristic than they had ever been. This was particularly true of those areas that were considered national heartlands or that attracted many tourists because of their specific charm. However, the heyday of this neo-vernacular trend did not last forever. Already before the First World War the first signs of its immanent decline could be detected. Traditional crafts and neo-vernacular buildings slowly prized themselves out of the market. Artisanal techniques could not compete with industrial mass production. Thus, in many countries ambitious plans were made for the reconstruction in a neo-vernacular style of the areas that were devastated during the war. However, in the end, the housing shortage and the post-war economic crisis made it impossible to adopt these plans. Standardization and the use of modern construction techniques – such as the use of concrete – became inevitable.[37]

Nevertheless, traditional craftsmanship and neo-vernacular architecture continued to be highly appreciated during the interwar period. Even many functionalist villas referred to local traditions. Architects in the Balkans, for instance, included protruding storeys and whitewashed walls that were inspired by local vernacular houses in their modernist designs.[38] At the Parisian world fair of 1937, an attempt was made to combine regional traditions with international modernity. France itself was represented by a large Regional Centre, with seventeen regional pavilions. All were built in an updated neo-vernacular style in which the use of steel and concrete was no longer proscribed. Inside, traditional arts and crafts were on display (see photo on the front cover). However, this was not a success. Some regional committees had difficulties finding traditional artisans, while vernacular forms made of concrete lost any pretence of authenticity.[39]

Figure 6.1 *Poster Parador de Gredos; Instituto de Turismo de España,* TURESPAÑA.

The rise of mass tourism in the late 1920s and 1930s would also undermine the prominent role of regionalist culture in the tourist areas. Mass tourism was stimulated explicitly by fascist dictatorships to win over the population. In Mussolini's Italy, *Dopolavoro* provided the masses with excursions and short holidays and this model was copied in Nazi Germany by *Kraft durch Freude* (Strength through Joy). Although these regimes celebrated the regional diversity of the country, their priorities were national unity and imperial expansion. Moreover, in order to make a holiday affordable to the masses, both fascist regimes had to be as efficient as possible. The massive four-kilometre-long Nazi holiday resort at Prora Bay, built of concrete and without any references to the region, was symbolic for the industrial functionalism that was deployed in order to let as many 'racially fit' Germans profit from it.[40]

Left-wing regimes also promoted mass tourism, but did not favour the culture of regionalism either. In 1922, the Soviet Union had been the first to introduce an annual vacation of two weeks for all workers. Regional tours that enabled the travellers to acquaint themselves with the history, landscape and social life of particular parts of the country – Crimea and the Caucasus being the most popular destinations – were more popular than organized trips to industrial enterprises or agricultural cooperatives. However, the goal of the excursions and holidays for workers and children was to convert them into exemplary soviet citizens. The progressive government that came to power in Spain in 1931 with the arrival of the Second Republic also preferred modern, urban culture over rural traditions and as a consequence many initiatives were undertaken to bring the countryside into contact with the nation's cultural highlights, such as paintings from the Prado Museum, plays from the Golden Age and films.[41] More conservative authoritarian governments, such as the Horthy dictatorship in Hungary or the Ulmanis regime in Latvia, on the other hand, strongly stimulated citizens to familiarize themselves with the vernacular culture and natural diversity of the countryside. The right-wing dictatorship in Portugal would continue this policy well into the 1960s and early 1970s.[42]

A fresh start

For most of Europe, the Second World War was a turning point. Tourism was disrupted and it took some years to return to pre-war levels, while the Cold War division of the continent hampered travel between East and West. The international exhibition tradition was interrupted as well and would only be revived in the 1990s. The main exception would be the Brussels world fair of 1958, which almost entirely ignored expressions of regionalist culture. Some aspects of the culture of regionalism had become suspect because they were now associated with the exalted nationalism and *Blut und Boden* (Blood and Soil) ideology of Nazi Germany. Thus, ethnographic villages with living inhabitants that supposedly represented the *Volksgeist* of the different regions or countries largely disappeared. Existing museums now focused on more matter-of-fact ethnographic displays, while at exhibitions the occasional artisan at work or folkloric shows were presented as relics from the past. This did not mean that ethnographic, local and open-air museums closed their doors but that they no longer pretended to show the quintessence of the nation.

Moreover, the Reconstruction era, which lasted into the 1960s, was very future-oriented and modernist solutions were preferred in both East and West. Most politicians, city planners and architects chose to rebuild cities and industrial areas in a functional way, provide space for modern means of transport and erect new modernist buildings. Many inhabitants, however, were in favour of restoring old buildings and retaining the historical character of their city and region. Probably the most extreme case was the old town of Warsaw, which was thoroughly reconstructed by taking eighteenth-century paintings – thus before the partitions of Poland – as the main source of inspiration.[43] Elsewhere in Poland, nationalist motives were important as well and particularly the areas in the West that had belonged to Germany should now be Polonized. However, because of the magnitude of the task only major monuments such as the ducal castle in Szczecin/Stettin, the former capital of Pomerania, were thoroughly cleansed of later 'Prussian' additions.[44] In the Federal Republic of Germany, only few municipal authorities, such as those of Nuremberg and Münster, decided to preserve the air of a historic city centre by reconstructing monumental buildings and largely retaining the existing street plan. New, generally quite austere buildings had to respect the traditionally used materials and proportions. However, this did not lead to the neo-vernacular pastiches which had been common in the decades before 1945.[45]

Tourism also underwent huge transformations. After a slow start in the late 1940s, it became a truly mass phenomenon. In 1952 France already received some 3 million foreign tourists. These numbers would increase rapidly, partly because of the introduction of tourist-class airfares and charter flights in the 1950s and rising living standards in the 1960s. The number of international visitors in Spain, for instance, increased from 4 million in 1959 to a spectacular 34 million in 1973.[46] The Soviet Union and the other countries from the Communist Block also opened themselves up hesitantly for Western tourists – mainly for economic reasons – with Yugoslavia clearly in the lead.[47] Package tours gained in popularity, but other collective forms of tourism also played a key role. Commercial organizations, such as Billy Butlin's holiday camps in Great Britain and the French Club Méditerranée, began to offer all-inclusive holidays in vacation villages. During the interwar period many trade unions, political movements and churches had organized excursions and holidays for their members and this type of social tourism continued to prosper after the war. Trips organized by party organizations were even the main form of leisure travel in the Soviet Union and Communist Eastern Europe.[48]

The old preference for monuments, museums and mountains in the interior also gave way to a more hedonistic enjoyment of sea, sand and sun at the beach. Although sunbathing had been introduced in the 1920s by tourists from Germany and other Nordic countries, it would only become the dominant form of vacationing in the 1950s. For reasons of expediency functionalist architecture became the norm for hotels and apartment buildings. High-rise concrete hotel accommodations turned sleepy villages, such as Torremolinos and Benidorm, into modern resorts. Travel agencies now sent more and more tourists on interchangeable holidays along the Mediterranean coast.

Folklore and regional character became a rather generic side dish – in the form of an excursion to a characteristic village, buying a typical artisanal product, taking a donkey ride or visiting a folkloric show – of holidays at the beach.[49] Thus, urban modernity – mass amusement enabled by new means of transport and modernist accommodations – again became the standard, but now in a massified, 'Fordist' form.

Nevertheless, traditional family life in the countryside continued to be appreciated. Life in small towns or a generic countryside was celebrated in movies and on television,[50] which now largely took over the role of world fairs as the main visual mass-medium. Tourism to the countryside was also stimulated, but now primarily for economic reasons. Ireland aimed to gain hard currency by stimulating former emigrants to return to their home country for a holiday. As part of this campaign, in 1958 the Tourist Board launched a Tidy Towns and Villages Competition in order to show the country as an attractive and sanitized destination with brightly painted houses and clean streets decorated with flowers.[51] Other governments also tried to stimulate tourism in the less developed parts of the country. Moreover, not everybody liked the new mass holidays at the beach and continued to make trips to the mountains, lakes, forests and picturesque villages of the interior. The growth of car ownership now made it easier to get off the beaten track. Especially from the 1970s onwards campsites and holiday homes – like the Swedish red cottage, the Russian dacha and the Yugoslav *vikendica* – mushroomed in the more attractive parts of the countryside. But contrary to what had happened in the interwar period, most of the campsites and holiday homes were fairly generic and did not emphasize the specific character of particular regions.[52]

The new cultural climate of the 1960s was not much in favour of the backward-looking regional movements. The younger generation was critical of the popularity of folkloric traditions such as costumes, songs and dance among regional associations, or their use in the tourism business, where authentic handicrafts were turned into mass-produced souvenirs. German ethnographers denounced this use of folklore outside of its original setting as 'Folklorismus'.[53] Nevertheless, the youth revolt also caused a renewed interest in ancient crafts, authentic traditions, spirituality and individual self-cultivation. Locally produced, natural products were appreciated and many (young) people preferred an alternative lifestyle, including a holiday in a nudist camp,[54] rural or ecotourism. At the same time, the anxiety over the levelling effects of modernization increased. Many ancient traditions, professions and landscapes were threatened with extinction and needed to be preserved. There were many local initiatives to preserve the highlights of their natural and cultural patrimony and new forms of tourism could be of help there. Thus, in the face of a rapid modernization, many traditional communities, such as the fishing villages in Scotland, began to market their traditional ways of life to attract tourists.[55]

Starting approximately in the 1970s the number of tourists visiting national parks, museums, archaeological sites, monuments and other heritage sites increased exponentially.[56] This tendency was reinforced by the creation in 1975 of the UNESCO List of World Heritage Sites. Although most cultural heritage sites that were proposed by national governments concerned individual monuments or cities, sometimes regions were nominated as well. Thus, medieval architectural remains of Aragon, Wales and Transylvania were included in the list between 1986 and in 1993. Sometimes a combination of cultural and natural regional heritage was admitted, such as the Orhid region in Yugoslavia (1979), Venice and its Lagoon (1987) and the Upper Harz Water Regal in Germany (1992).[57]

Although the new popularity of heritage preservation meant that characteristic sites were protected, this did not mean that they were made more typical than before as often had happened in the late nineteenth and early twentieth centuries. New, more rigorous restoration regulations impeded the removal of parts that did not fit an idealized image and the inclusion of new more typical elements. From the 1980s onwards, the postmodern addition of ultramodern structures that contrasted with the old preserved parts even became fashionable, thus in a sense including heritage as a fragment into contemporary, lived reality.[58]

Typical images and stereotypes that had been developed from the nineteenth century onwards were now also increasingly used for destination marketing. In the 1960s and 1970s countries like Great Britain, France, Italy and Spain began to decentralize their public administration, while the European Economic Community established the Structural Funds to strengthen the economy of less-developed regions. Many new regional authorities did not only compete to attract investors and economic activity, but also tourists.[59] Public relations departments and professional advertising agencies, often partially paid with European subsidies, emphasized the unique cultural heritage and natural beauty of each region. Local authorities, journalists, tour operators, museums and shopkeepers also identified regions with specific landscapes, events and even fictional heroes in order to attract more visitors. Thus, the Languedoc was marketed as the country of the Cathars, the heretics that had suffered terrible persecutions in the late Middle Ages, and Transylvania as the land of Dracula.[60] The Norwegian railways have a special Troll train to the Hardanger Fjord region; in Cornwall there are King Arthur Tours and, recently, La Mancha created a Ruta de Don Quijote.[61]

These government-related activities generally built on already-existing images and reputations. However, the notion of heritage was also extended to include defunct mines and industrial buildings. This also affected regional identities, and this is best exemplified by the Ruhr area in Germany. In the late 1980s, when mining and heavy industry were in clear decline, an ambitious programme of social, economic and ecological restructuring was adopted. One of its main goals was to attract tourists by creating a Route of Industrial Heritage.[62] The European Union financially supported the Ruhr project, but it also stimulated the development of new trans-border regions. The opening of Øresund Link in 2000, the tunnel-bridge between Copenhagen and Malmö that connected Denmark with Sweden, was accompanied by an effort to create a new Øresund region, consisting of both Sjælland and Skåne. It was branded as a creative hub by focusing on medical technology, leisure and quality of life.[63]

Tourism also contributed to create transnational regions of a very different nature. Genealogy or roots tourism of American and Australian emigrants returning to their native region in Europe gained importance in the 1950s and 1960s. It generally reinforced the regional and national identity of both returnees and hosts, who on some occasions organized 'homecoming' events, such as the Ireland at Home festival of 1954.[64] This type of roots or 'homesick' tourism received a boost after the fall of the Berlin Wall in 1989. Many East European Germans who had been expelled after the Second World War – or Transylvanian Saxons and Volga Germans who emigrated to the West in the 1980s and 1990s – could now more easily visit the areas where they had grown up. Many of them were not received with hostility as maybe could be expected. The inhabitants – many also expelled from other parts of East-Central Europe – were often eager to hear stories about the past. Former emigrants also played a stimulating role in the preservation of regional heritage. Moreover, social media now provide them with the means to create online regional communities.[65]

Over the last few decades, the impact of tourists on regional identities has become more pronounced as the tourism business continues to grow. Improved highways, low-cost airlines and high-speed trains now carry growing numbers of tourists to all parts of the continent. And although the Mediterranean beaches continue to attract the bulk of the tourists, cultural tourism is growing as well. The areas that profited most from these developments were attractive cities with a broad cultural offer, such as Paris, London, Barcelona, Amsterdam and Prague. Barcelona used the Olympic Games of 1992 for an ambitious programme of urban renovation turning a degraded industrial neighbourhood into the Olympic Village, while reconnecting the harbour in an elegant way with the city centre. International star architects such as Norman Forster and Santiago Calatrava added allure with an array of spectacular new buildings. The best conversion of an old degraded city into an attractive tourist destination is offered by the Basque town of Bilbao, where Frank Gehry's new Guggenheim museum, which opened its doors in 1997, formed the icing on the cake.[66] During the first decades of the twenty-first century, the amount of tourists in major European cities has grown so quickly that it is now even seen as problematic. As a response to the large tourist influx, in 2009 the Amsterdam Metropolitan Area began to market the surrounding areas of the city as Amsterdam Beach, Amsterdam Flowers, Old Holland and Castles and Gardens of Amsterdam (see Figure 6.2), thus promoting visits to the surrounding regions by selling them under the label of the city.[67]

Conclusion

Tourist demand had a crucial impact on the construction of regional identities. During the long twentieth century, tourism stimulated regions to distinguish themselves from others by underlining their most exceptional and spectacular aspects. Because of tourism's strong economic incentives – as part of the rise of consumer society – the regional identity of most parts of Europe became much more pronounced. Nonetheless, the actual importance and the role of tourism in each phase depended on developments of a cultural, economic, political or technological nature. Although since the Romantic era rural areas were seen as the heartland of the nation only towards the end of the nineteenth century, strongly encouraged by tourists and world fairs, regional identities

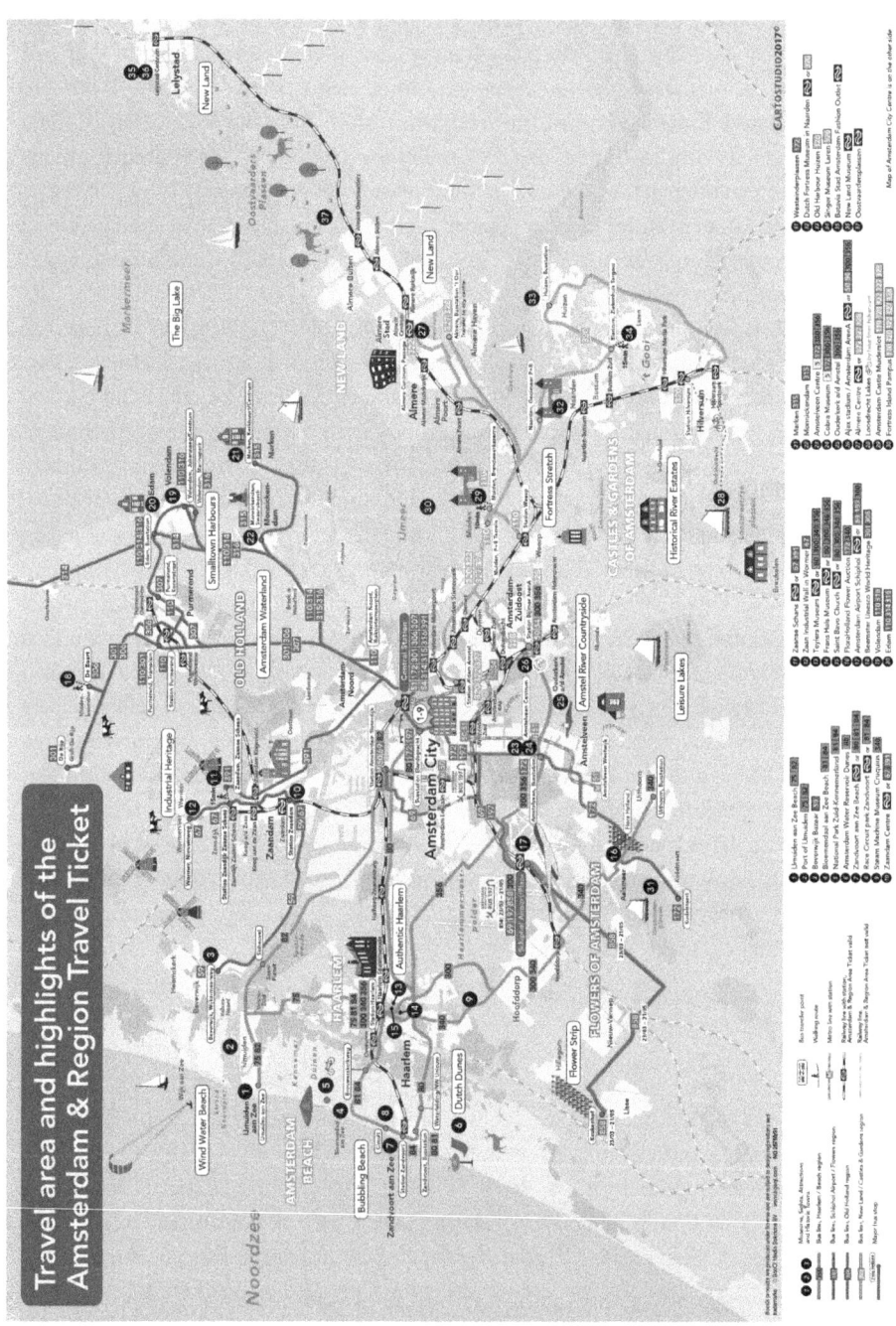

Figure 6.2 *Amsterdam Metropolitan Area Map; Amsterdam Marketing.*

became more narrowly defined. This tendency was reinforced during the early decades of the twentieth century when the culture of regionalism became extremely popular, filling tourist resorts with neo-vernacular villas and providing them with artisanal souvenirs and typical dishes.

The main watershed was the Second World War, which interrupted the tourism business for almost a decade. However, it was not the war itself that caused major changes but the ideological transformations that were related to its outcome. Before 1939, regions primarily positioned themselves in the tourist market by emphasizing tradition and favouring rural aspects; after 1945, modernity became fashionable and urban culture began to set the tone. However, this does not mean that the war was a sharp turning point; many new tendencies – such as sunbathing, paid holidays and modernist architecture – had been anticipated in the 1920s and 1930s, while older traditions continued in new forms. During the Reconstruction era, regions became more uniform – at least in the built environment – and this was especially true for the coastal areas where most tourists spent their holidays. Nevertheless, regional peculiarities remained a lucrative side-dish. In the 1970s, heritage preservation, cultural tourism and destination marketing again began to emphasize regional differences. Although new forms of tourism, such as roots tourism, rural tourism and visits to industrial heritage sites, further encouraged the construction and dissemination of regional identities, it seems that large cities profit most from the new vogue for cultural trips.

Tourism, obviously, did not have the same effect everywhere. Regions that already attracted a lot of tourists before the Second World War, such as Tyrol, Bavaria, Brittany, Andalusia and Tuscany, became more typified than before. Regions that became a major tourist destination after 1945, such as the Mediterranean coast, were more affected by the vogue for international modernity both in architecture and urban planning, although in the last few decades, typical buildings and folkloric traditions have made a strong comeback. Regions that were not very attractive for tourists until recently were barely affected. However, today, because of the considerable economic impact of tourism, entrepreneurs across Europe try to welcome visitors with their own regional specialities, dishes, beverages, festivals, typical buildings, natural patrimony and folkloric traditions. If they do not yet exist, they will have to be invented.

Notes

1. Anne-Marie Thiesse, *La création des identités nationales. Europe XVIIIe–XXe siècle* (Paris: Seuil, 1999).
2. Nina Lübbren, *Rural Artists' Colonies in Europe, 1870–1910* (Manchester: Manchester University Press, 2001).
3. Anne-Marie Thiesse, *Ils apprenaient la France. L'Exaltation des régions dans le discours patriotique* (Paris: Maison des Science de l'Homme, 1997).
4. Pieter Judson, '"Every German Visitor has a Volkish Obligation he must Fulfill": Nationalist Tourism in the Austrian Empire', in *Histories of Leisure*, ed. Rudy Koshar (Oxford: Berg,

2002), 147–68. See also Levente T. Szabó, 'Narrating "the People" and "Disciplining" the Folk: The Constitution of the Hungarian Ethnographic Discipline and Touristic Movements (1870–1900)', in *We, the People: Politics of National Peculiarity in Southeastern Europe*, ed. Diana Mishkova (Budapest: Central European University Press, 2016), 207–36.

5. Joan-Lluís Marfany, *La cultura del catalanisme. El nacionalisme català en els seus inicis* (Barcelona: Empúries, 1995).

6. Katherine Haldane Grenier, *Tourism and Identity in Scotland, 1770–1914: Creating Caledonia* (Aldershot: Ashgate, 2005); Patrick Young, *Enacting Brittany: Tourism and Culture in Provincial France* (Farnham: Ashgate, 2012); and Adam T. Rosenbaum, *Bavarian Tourism and the Modern World, 1800–1950* (Cambridge: Cambridge University Press, 2016).

7. Martin Wörner, *Vergnügung und Belehrung. Volkskultur auf den Weltausstellungen 1851–1900* (Münster: Waxmann, 1999), 49–57. See also Orvar Löfgren, 'Know Your Country: A Comparative Perspective on Tourism and Nation Building in Sweden', in *Being Elsewhere: Tourism, Consumer Culture and Identity in Modern Europe and North America*, ed. Shelley Baranowski and Ellen Furlough (Ann Arbor: University of Michigan Press, 2001), 137–54.

8. Matthew Rampley, 'Peasants in Vienna: Ethnographic Display and the 1873 World Fair', *Austrian History Yearbook* 42 (2011): 110–32.

9. Eric Storm, 'World Fairs and (Inter)national Exhibitions', in *Encyclopedia of Romantic Nationalism in Europe*, ed. Joep Leerssen (electronic version www.romanticnationalism.net, 2017).

10. Robert W. Rydell, *All the World a Fair: Visions of Empire at American International Expositions, 1876–1916* (Chicago: Chicago University Press, 1984); and Wörner, *Vergnügung und Belehrung*, 72–82.

11. Caroline R. Malloy, 'Exhibiting Ireland: Irish Villages, Pavilions, Cottages, and Castles at International Exhibitions, 1853–1939' (Dissertation, University of Wisconsin-Madison, 2013), 75–175; Jill Steward, 'Tourism in Late Imperial Austria: The Development of Tourist Cultures and Their Associated Images of Place', in *Being Elsewhere: Tourism, Consumer Culture and Identity in Modern Europe and North America*, ed. Shelley Baranowski and Ellen Furlough (Ann Arbor: University of Michigan Press, 2001), 108–37.

12. Marta Filipová, 'Peasants on Display: The Czechoslavic Ethnographic Exhibition of 1895', *Journal of Design History* 24, no. 1 (2011): 15–36.

13. Shona Kallestrup, 'Romanian "National Style" and the 1906 Bucharest Jubilee Exhibition', *Journal of Design History* 15, no. 3 (2002): 147–62.

14. Samuel D. Albert, 'The Nation for Itself: The 1896 Hungarian Millennium and the 1906 Romanian National General Exhibiton', in *Cultures of International Exhibitions 1840–1940: Great Exhibitions in the Margins*, ed. Marta Filipová (Farnham: Ashgate, 2015), 113–36. See also Alexander Vari, 'From Friends to Nature to Tourist-Soldiers: Nation Building and Tourism in Hungary, 1873–1914', in *Turizm: The Russian and East European Tourist under Capitalism and Socialism*, ed. Anne E. Gorsuch and Diane P. Koenker (Ithaca, NY: Cornell University Press, 2006), 64–82.

15. Todd Courtenay, 'The 1911 International Exposition in Rome: Architecture, Archaeology, and National Identity', *Journal of Historical Geography* 37 (2011): 440–59.

16. Sharon L. Hirsh, 'Swiss Art and National Identity at the Turn of the Twentieth Century', in *Art, Culture and National Identity in Fin-de-Siècle Europe*, ed. Michelle Facos and Sharon L. Hirsh (Cambridge: Cambridge University Press, 2002), 250–87; and Wörner, *Vergnügung und Belehrung*, 92–113.

17. Wörner, *Vergnügung und Belehrung*, 97–112.
18. Eric Storm, 'Overcoming Methodological Nationalism in Nationalism Studies: The Impact of Tourism on the Construction and Diffusion of National and Regional Identities', *History Compass* 12, no. 4 (2014): 361–73.
19. Adriaan de Jong and Mette Skougaard, 'The Hindeloopen and the Amager Rooms: Two Examples of an Historical Museum Phenomenon', *Journal of the History of Collections* 5, no. 2 (1993): 165–78; and Adriaan de Jong, *Die Dirigenten der Erinnerung. Musealisierung und Nationalisierung der Volkskultur in den Niederlanden 1815-1940* (Münster: Waxmann, 2007), 57–133.
20. Wörner, *Vergnügung und Belehrung*, 73–74, 237–46, 272 and 278–84.
21. Rudy Koshar, *Germany's Transient Pasts: Preservation and National Memory in the Twentieth Century* (Chapel Hill: University of North Carolina Press, 1998).
22. Bjarne Stocklund, 'The Role of International Exhibitions in the Construction of National Cultures in the 19th Century', *Ethnologia Europaea* 24, no. 1 (1994): 35–44.
23. Luis Méndez Rodríguez, *La imagen de Andalucía en el arte del siglo XIX* (Seville: Centro de Estudios Andaluces, 2008).
24. Barbara Miller Lane, *National Romanticism and Modern Architecture in Germany and the Scandinavian Countries* (Cambridge: Cambridge University Press, 2000).
25. Jeremy Howard, *Art Nouveau: International and National Styles in Europe* (Manchester: Manchester University Press, 1996).
26. François Loyer and Bernard Toulier, eds, *Le Regionalism, architecture et identité* (Paris: Éditions du Patrimoine, 2001); and Eric Storm, *The Culture of Regionalism: Art, Architecture and International Exhibitions in France, Germany and Spain, 1890-1939* (Manchester: Manchester University Press, 2010), 73–195.
27. David Crowley, 'Finding Poland in the Margins: The Case of the Zakopane Style', *Journal of Design History* 14, no. 2 (2001): 105–17.
28. Storm, *The Culture of Regionalism*, 152.
29. Eric Storm, 'A More Spanish Spain: The Influence of Tourism on the National Image', in *Metaphors of Spain: Representations of Spanish National Identity in the 20th Century*, ed. Javier Moreno Luzón and Xosé M. Núñez Seixas (New York; London: Berghahn, 2017), 239–60.
30. Storm, *The Culture of Regionalism*, 98–100; Nancy Stieber, *Housing Design and Society in Amsterdam: Reconfiguring Urban Order and Identity, 1900-1920* (Chicago: University of Chicago Press, 1998).
31. Medina Lasansky, *The Renaissance Perfected: Architecture, Spectacle and Tourism in Fascist Italy* (University Park: Pennsylvania State University Press, 2004).
32. Hans Kraan, *Dromen van Holland. Buitenlandse kunstenaars schilderen Holland 1800-1914* (Zwolle: Waanders, 2002), 333–43.
33. Young, *Enacting Brittany*, 76–92 and 171–215.
34. Dag Hundstad, 'A "Norwegian Riviera" in the Making: The Development of Coastal Tourism and the Recreation in Southern Norway in the Interwar Period', *Journal of Tourism History* 3, no. 2 (2011): 109–28.
35. Young, *Enacting Brittany*, 215–50; Stephen Harp, *Marketing Michelin: Advertising and Cultural Identity in Twentieth Century France* (Baltimore, MD: Johns Hopkins University Press, 2001); and Michael Frederik Wagner, 'The Rise of Autotourism in Danish Leisure, 1910–1970', *Journal of Tourism History* 5, no. 3 (2013): 265–85.

36. Storm, 'A More Spanish Spain'.
37. Storm, *The Culture of Regionalism*, 131, 111–14 and 144–53, respectively.
38. Tchavdar Marinov, 'The "Balkan House": Interpretations and Symbolic Appropriations of the Ottoman-Era Vernacular Architecture in the Balkans', in *Entangled Histories in the Balkans Vol 4. Concepts, Approaches and (Self-) Representations*, ed. Roumen Daskalov, Diana Mishkova, Tchavdar Marinov and Alexander Vezenkov (Leiden: Brill, 2017), 440–593.
39. Storm, *The Culture of Regionalism*, 219–47; and Shanny Peer, *France on Display: Peasants, Provincials and Folklore in the 1937 Paris World Fair* (Albany: SUNY Press, 1998).
40. Stefano Cavazza, *Piccole Patrie. Feste populari tra regione e nazione durante il fascismo* (Bologna: Mulino, 2003); Rudy Koshar, *German Travel Cultures* (Oxford: Berg, 2000), 115–61; and Hasso Spode, 'Fordism, Mass Tourism and the Third Reich: The "Strength through Joy" Seaside Resort as an Index Fossil', *Journal of Social History* 38, no. 1 (2004): 127–55.
41. Diane P. Koenker, *Club Red: Vacation Travel and the Soviet Dream* (Ithaca, NY: Cornell University Press, 2013); and Sandie Holguin, *Creating Spaniards: Culture and National Identity in Republican Spain* (Madison: University of Wisconsin Press, 2003).
42. Andrew Behrendt, 'Educating Apostles of the Homeland: Tourism and *Honismeret* in Interwar Hungary', *Hungarian Cultural Studies* 7 (2014), doi: 10.5195/ahea.2014.168; Aldis Purs, '"One Breath for Every Two Strides": The State's Attempt to Construct Tourism and Identity in Interwar Latvia', in *Turizm: The Russian and East European Tourist under Capitalism and Socialism*, ed. Anne E. Gorsuch and Diane P. Koenker (Ithaca, NY: Cornell University Press, 2006), 97–115; and Raphael Costa, 'The "Great Façade of Nationality": Some Considerations on Portuguese Tourism and the Multiple Meanings of Estado Novo Portugal in Travel Literature', *Journal of Tourism History* 5, no. 1 (2013): 50–72.
43. Duncan Light, Craig Young and Mariusz Czepczyński, 'Heritage Tourism in Central and Eastern Europe', in *Cultural Heritage and Tourism in the Developing World: A Regional Perspective*, ed. Dallen J. Timothy and Gyan P. Nyaupane (London: Routledge, 2009), 224–46.
44. Julia Roos, *Denkmalpflege und Wiederaufbau im Nachkriegspolen* (Hamburg: Diplomica, 2010).
45. Jeffry M. Diefendorf, *In the Wake of War: The Reconstruction of German Cities after World War II* (Oxford: Oxford University Press, 1993), 43–108.
46. Brian A. McKenzie, 'Creating a Tourist's Paradise: The Marshall Plan and France, 1848 to 1952', *Fench Politics, Culture & Society* (2003): 35–55; and Sasha D. Pack, *Tourism and Dictatorship: Europe's Peaceful Invasion of Franco's Spain* (Basingstoke: Palgrave Macmillan, 2006).
47. Adam T. Rosenbaum, 'Leisure Travel and Real Existing Socialism: New Research on Tourism in the Soviet Union and communist Eastern Europe', *Journal of Travel History* 7, nos. 1–2 (2015): 157–76; Duncan Light, '"A Medium of Revolutionary Propaganda": The State and Tourism Policy in the Romanian People's Republic, 1947–1965', *Journal of Tourism History* 5, no. 2 (2013): 185–200; and Anne E. Gorsuch, *All This Is Your World: Soviet Tourism at Home and Abroad* (Oxford: Oxford University Press, 2011).
48. Eric G. E. Zuelow, *A History of Modern Tourism* (Basingstoke: Palgrave Macmillan, 2016), 167–72; Ellen Furlough, 'Making Mass Vacations: Tourism and Consumer Culture in France, 1930s to 1970s', *Comparative Studies in History and Society* 40, no. 2 (1998): 247–86; and Koenker, *Club Red*.
49. Orvar Löfgren, *On Holiday: A History of Vacationing* (Berkeley: University of California Press, 1999), 155–209; and Pack, *Tourism and Dictatorship*.

50. Johannes von Moltke, *No Place Like Home: Locations of Heimat in German Cinema* (Berkeley: University of California Press, 2005); Anders Wilhelm Ålbert, 'Seacrow Island: Mediating Arcadian Space in the Folkhem Era and Beyond', in *Regional Aesthetics: Locating Swedish Media*, ed. Erik Hedling, Olof Hedling and Mats Jönsson (Stockholm: Mediehistoriskt Arkiv, 2010), 323–36.

51. Eric G. E. Zuelow, *Making Ireland Irish: Tourism and National Identity since the Irish Civil War* (Syracuse, NY: Syracuse University Press, 2009), 196–97.

52. Löfgren, *On Holiday*, 122–55; Dag Hunstad, 'A "Norwegian Riviera" in the Making: The Development of Coastal Tourism and Recreation in Southern Norway in the Interwar Period', *Journal of Tourism History* 3, no. 2 (2011): 117–27; Karin Taylor, 'My Own Vikendica: Holiday Cottages as Idyll and Investment', in *Yugoslavia's Sunny Side: A History of Tourism in Socialism (1950s–1980s)*, ed. Hannes Grandits and Karin Taylor (Budapest: Central European University Press, 2010), 171–210.

53. Venetia J. Newall, 'The Adaptation of Folklore and Tradition (Folklorismus)', *Folklore* 98, no. 2 (1987): 131–51.

54. Stephen L. Harp, 'The "Naked City" of Cap d'Agde: European Nudism and Tourism in Postwar France', in *Touring Beyond the Nation: A Transnational Approach to European Tourism History*, ed. Eric G. E. Zuelow (Farhnham: Ashgate, 2011), 37–59.

55. See, for a case study, Jane Nadel-Klein, *Fishing for Heritage. Modernity and Loss along the Scottish Coast* (Oxford: Berg, 2003).

56. Greg Richards, 'Production and Consumption of European Cultural Tourism', *Annals of Tourism Research* 23, no. 2 (1996): 261–83.

57. See whc.unesco.org/en/list/.

58. David Harvey, *The Condition of Postmodernity* (Oxford: Blackwell, 1989), 62–63 and 85–88.

59. Michael Keating, *The New Regionalism in Western Europe: Territorial Restructuring and Political Change* (Cheltenham: Edgar Elgar, 1998). See also chapter by Petrosino.

60. Emily McCaffrey, 'Imagining the Cathars in Late-Twentieth-Century Languedoc', *Contemporary European History* 11, no. 3 (2002): 409–27; and Duncan Light, *The Dracula Dilemma: Tourism, Identity and the State in Romania* (Farnham: Ashgate, 2012).

61. Newall, 'The Adaptation of Folklore', 137 and 144.

62. Gert-Jan Hospers, 'Industrial Heritage Tourism and Regional Restructuring in the European Union', *European Planning Studies* 10, no. 3 (2002): 397–404; and Sonja Ćopić e.o. 'Transformation of Industrial Heritage – an Example of Tourism Industry Development in the Ruhr Area (Germany)', *Geographica Pannonica* 18, no. 2 (2014): 43–50.

63. Gert-Jan Hospers, 'Borders, Bridges and Branding: The Transformation of the Øresund Region into an Imagined Space', *European Planning Studies* 14, no. 8 (2006): 1015–33. See also chapter by Stadius.

64. Zuelow, *Making Ireland Irish*, 124–35; Paul Basu, 'Roots Tourism as Return Movement: Semantics and the Scottish Diaspora', in *Emigrant Homecomings: The Return Movement of Emigrants, 1600–2000*, ed. M. Harper (Manchester: Manchester University Press, 2005), 131–51.

65. Sabine Marschall, ' "Homesick Tourism": Memory, Identity and (Be)longing', *Current Issues in Tourism* 18, no. 9 (2015): 876–92; Andrew Demshuk, 'Reinscribing *Schlesien* as *Śląsk*: Memory and Mythology in a Postwar German-Polish Borderland', *History & Memory* 24, no. 1 (2012): 39–86; and Monica Iorio and Andrea Corsale, 'Diaspora and Tourism: Transylvanian Saxons Visiting the Homeland', *Tourism Geographies* 15, no. 2 (2013): 198–232.

66. Storm, 'A More Spanish Spain', 254.
67. Boudewijn Bokdam, *Transforming Cities into Attractive Regions in a Sustainable Way: The Amsterdam Tourism Case* (Amsterdam: Amsterdam Marketing, 2014).

Further reading

Baranowski, Shelley, and Ellen Furlough, eds, *Being Elsewhere: Tourism, Consumer Culture and Identity in Modern Europe and North America* (Ann Arbor: University of Michigan Press, 2001).

Gorsuch, Anne E., and Diane P. Koenker, eds, *Turizm: The Russian and East European Tourist under Capitalism and Socialism* (Ithaca, NY: Cornell University Press, 2006).

Grandits, Hannes, and Karin Taylor, eds, *Yugoslavia's Sunny Side: A History of Tourism in Socialism (1950s–1980s)* (Budapest: Central European University Press, 2010).

Koenker, Diane P., *Club Red: Vacation Travel and the Soviet Dream* (Ithaca, NY: Cornell University Press, 2013).

Lasansky, Medina, *The Renaissance Perfected: Architecture, Spectacle and Tourism in Fascist Italy* (University Park: Pennsylvania State University Press, 2004).

Pack, Sasha D., *Tourism and Dictatorship: Europe's Peaceful Invasion of Franco's Spain* (Basingstoke: Palgrave Macmillan, 2006).

Wörner, Martin, *Vergnügung und Belehrung. Volkskultur auf den Weltausstellungen 1851–1900* (Münster: Waxmann, 1999).

Young, Patrick, *Enacting Brittany: Tourism and Culture in Provincial France* (Farnham: Ashgate, 2012).

Zuelow, Eric G. E., *Making Ireland Irish: Tourism and National Identity since the Irish Civil War* (Syracuse, NY: Syracuse University Press, 2009).

CHAPTER 7
FASCISM AND REGIONALISM
Xosé M. Núñez Seixas

Limited promotion of the region as the site of a distinctive type of identity politics was a characteristic feature of most fascist regimes. It involved remoulding the legacy of early modern composite states, like Germany and Spain, as well as newly formed states such as Romania and (to some extent) Italy, into a political and psychological mechanism for fixing subjects within seemingly immutable and authentic spatial contexts.

Comparative work on fascism has experienced a revival since the mid-1990s.[1] However, historians have rightly demanded that paradigms about the 'generic' nature of fascism be tested by comparing concrete political developments under different regimes. Fascist regionalism has rarely been the object of a comprehensive study within a single country,[2] and comparative analyses of the functions of regionalism in two or more fascist regimes are similarly few and far between.[3]

Historical research on fascism has underlined its intrinsically centralist nature. Thus, few historians of the Third Reich have challenged the premise that the Nazi regime aimed for the greatest possible degree of ideological homogenization. Nonetheless, strategic use of subnational identities and regional variation were never absent from policy implementation practices, as regional studies such as Broszat's project on Bavaria have shown. The 1990s saw a wave of important new studies on regionally based milieus and their interaction with the rise of National Socialism and radicalization, and some later work also argued that the Nazi *Gaue* were important administrative actors in National Socialism.[4] In the twenty-first century, studies on Italian fascism have underscored the relevance of regional settings in regime consolidation efforts during the 1920s, with particular attention given to regionalist cultural policies.[5]

In the historiography of Spain, the assumption that regional diversity and Francoism were diametrically opposed has remained unchallenged until recent times. Historians have emphasized how all areas of Francoist policymaking were informed by an aggressively unitary understanding of the Spanish nation state, which affected not only substate nationalist movements but also all forms of cultural regionalism. By extension, spatial imaginations focused on regional and substate levels are still regarded as sources of opposition to the Franco regime. However, large sectors of the population in the allegedly oppressed non-Castilian regions supported the Francoist rebels in 1936–1939. From the Basque-Navarrese Carlist militiamen to Catalan conservatives, regional elites often established themselves as the new local representatives of the Franco regime. The Francoist army also used regionalism as a tool for mobilizing popular support in non-Castilian-speaking regions of Spain, tapping into a flourishing discourse of regional and local pride among the provincial middle classes. Repression of vernacular languages lacked uniformity, and insurgent intellectuals presented the Civil War as a campaign to reconnect the nation to its authentic traditions. These were rooted in the countryside, the province, and in regional dialects and *mores*. This 'healthiest part' of the nation was to serve as a blueprint for reforming the sinful cities.[6]

Though they fiercely opposed substate nationalisms, Spanish fascists during the Second Republic (1931–1936) tended to de-emphasize race, language and ethnicity as markers of the Spanish nation, stressing instead the idea of a common destiny sustained by a 'mission' to build a new Empire. This belief also facilitated attempts by some Falangist intellectuals during the 1940s to develop a more 'Catalanized' view of Spain's history. They emphasized the Mediterranean contribution to Spanish culture and attempted to develop a form of fascist regionalism, albeit devoid of political aspirations.[7]

In terms of official ideology, the Hitler and Mussolini regimes were more closely related, while the Franco government, Vichy France and Salazar's Portugal were intimately allied with political Catholicism. However, in terms of state centralization dilemmas, Spain and, to some extent, Germany differed from Mussolini's Italy, which remained geographically disparate despite its totalitarian rhetoric. Piedmont lost dominance during the liberal era, whereas Rome's status as the capital had few foundations in *Realpolitik* but was propped up by near-mythological connections to the glories of the ancient Roman Empire.[8] In Italy, anti-centralist reactions before 1945 were comparatively weak and largely confined to Sicily, Sardinia and the border minorities of Gorizia and South Tyrol. In contrast, the Franco and Hitler regimes presented much more evenly balanced power relations between the central government and institutions, on the one hand, and the autonomous aspirations of individual regions, on the other.

Localism and regionalism were deliberately promoted to different degrees by the regimes of Hitler, Mussolini, Pétain and Franco because it suited their ideological agendas. Despite the many important differences in the value placed on the 'region' in all four countries, it seems clear that this strategy went beyond mere opportunism. Elites in Germany and Spain – and to a lesser extent in Italy and Portugal – shared a deep-seated suspicion of liberal, French-style centralization and bureaucratization. Against this, regional diversity was presented as the legacy of a pre-liberal, 'authentic' nation. At the same time, regionalism offered a form of 'blood and soil' politics that remained wedded to a realist sense of the political. As the locus of the newly defined *Volksgemeinschaft*, regionalism helped to give specific contours and a sense of historical continuity to the vague key concepts of fascist identity.[9] Fascist regimes also distrusted political Romanticism: recourse to the region and the locality allowed them to base their quest for spatially fixed identities on territorial divisions that were already defined as *political constructs*. This strategy also allowed for reconciliation of the ultra-conservative aspect of fascist ideology with its quest for modernization, which led fascist regimes to embark on massive projects within landscapes and constructed environments.[10] In the following pages, five aspects of fascist regionalism will be analysed: the implementation of regional and local administrations, the role of regional histories, the relevance of regional heritage, the role of languages and cultures and the translation of regional identities into visual cultures and exhibitions. This chapter will focus primarily on the most thoroughly examined cases of Germany and Spain, with some references to Italy, Vichy France and Salazar's Portugal.

Mapping territorial organization

As authoritarian nation states hijacked *Heimat* sentiments for their own purposes, these were emptied of all specific political content. Representations of place tended towards the generic, localism and revivalist practices were projected onto an external imperial dimension and inward-looking regionalism was generally avoided.[11] The vital role of *Heimat* in fascist constructions of nationhood does not necessarily challenge the notion of a centralized regime. However, the role of the intermediate tier between local and national identity, the region, is in fact a more revealing test case. Much depended on how a region was defined.

Francoism acknowledged Castile as the main source of Spanish identity, embodying the hegemony of Castilian culture, with its language and its Catholic interpretation of history. Similarly, the idea of Prussian hegemony was closely associated with Hitler's regime. In *Mein Kampf*, the Nazi leader proclaimed his desire to tear the 'mask of federalism' from the face of the German people, quash the harmful particularism that hostile foreign and Jewish influences had kept alive, and turn the Prussian capital of Berlin into the spiritual centre of the new *Germania*.[12] Certainly, many Fascists were hostile to any assertion of regional autonomy that might weaken loyalty to the state. Though they often attributed regional tensions to foreign conspiracies, Hitler conceded that this could not fully explain the strength of regional sentiments. Pride in one's own regional identity was to some extent an 'authentic' expression of German identity. Thus, Hitler saw dissociation of Berlin from the legacy of the Weimar Republic's centralist project as the cure for anti-Berlin sentiment in Bavaria.

In the Spanish case, fascists saw federalism and regional autonomy as the first steps towards national disintegration. This was partially because Spain lacked any stable tradition of functional federalism. Growing ethnonationalist aspirations in the metropolitan core of the old empire during the early twentieth century helped revive fin-de-siècle national frustrations: Catalans, Basques and, to some extent, Galicians looked as though they might follow the Cuban road to independence. Despite this, local identifications remained dear to the Spanish radical right as a way of reinforcing Spanish nationalism. This also applied to the Falangists: their leader, José Antonio Primo de Rivera, considered 'regional traditions' the most authentic way of feeling Spanish. Many of his followers took their cue from his spiritual understanding of the Spanish nation as a project of 'territorial coexistence united by a common enterprise', a common destiny. In their earliest political manifestos, Castilian fascist leaders even expressed the aim of local autonomy for Castilian municipalities, along with a certain sense of regional pride. They directed it against the supposed decadence of the Spanish soul, which was most acute in the towns, especially Madrid.[13]

Adolf Hitler also noted during the 1920s that popular sentiment in Bavaria was characterized by a hatred of all things Prussian. He was not altogether hostile to such sentiments. When the Nazis embarked upon their campaign to capitalize on regional identity politics in the German *Länder*, they took advantage of a political climate in which the political and economic crisis of the Weimar Republic had become associated with the notion of a central government. Many looked to devolution (and some even to separatism) as the solution. After he had seized power in early 1933, Hitler promised 'to do everything possible to preserve the historical building blocks of the nation'. Gottfried Feder stated that 'the composition of the German nation from various *Länder*, each of which is united by their tribal characteristics and history, necessitates the greatest possible independence for the federal states'. Although the *Länder* were abolished in January 1934, they were immediately reinstated. Ten *Reichstatthalter* (Imperial Governors) were stationed in the larger *Länder* as of April 1933 and appointed to 'supervise the observance of the policies of the Reich Chancellor'. Hitler then shifted his attention towards the district party leaders (Gauleiter) as paragons of devolution, although the limits of the *Gaue* did not coincide with previous territorial demarcations. Such moves were calculated to prevent the bureaucratization that characterized centralist state-building. Hitler's final vision of the Reich, articulated in 1941, envisaged that only the 'tools of leadership', such as control of the media, would be centralized. Even at subregional levels, Nazi cultural policy developed in close cooperation with existing organizations, especially those dedicated to celebrating customs, folklore and landscape preservation in their homeland, while also trying to channel their energies towards imperial expansion.[14]

Certainly, economic planning came increasingly under the aegis of the Nazi central state. However, the regions remained crucial as tools of economic development through local specialization and as vehicles for the marketing of products. Moreover, territorial expansion, especially in the east, led to a revival of ethnic regionalism. One of its chief proponents, Alfred Rosenberg, envisioned a Germany of tribes resurrected in a new context.

From the very first moment, the new fascist state in Italy willingly fostered both cultural regionalism and urban identities, while denying any political implications from these discourses. Benito Mussolini himself gave little attention to the regional question in his writings. He had inherited and reinterpreted the main tenets of nineteenth-century Risorgimento nationalism, but was more concerned with building a strong state than with redefining the internal articulation of the nation. Thus, Fascist party propaganda managed to display a certain degree of pragmatism in the peripheral regions during the early 1920s. The regime negotiated with regionalists in Sardinia and favoured the emergence of 'Sardo-fascism', a cultural hybridization with Sardinian myths and icons that emphasized the Mediterranean imperial dimension of Italian fascism.[15] Schoolchildren learned the history and folklore of their region, while municipalities devoted greater efforts to preserving their cultural heritage and re-enacted medieval traditions as a way of attracting tourists. State-sponsored local associations also promoted local folklore and limited literary cultivation of dialects.

This coexisted with the harsh homogenization policy imposed on the border regions of South Tyrol and Gorizia. After a first phase of tolerance, the Germanic and Slavic cultures there were systematically targeted as potential threats to national unity. These diverse ethnoterritorial dimensions led the regime to adopt an anti-regionalist stance in the early 1930s. Public use of dialects and languages distinct from Italian was banned and a more uniform national narrative was imposed in schools. This went hand in hand with embracing imperialism as the 'highest stage' of the national project inherited from the nineteenth-century *Risorgimento*.[16]

In Spain also, regionalized nationalism was vital to the establishment of the Francoist state, though often in contradictory ways. July 1936 initiated a period of uncertainty concerning the future distribution of territorial power within the new Spain. Carlist traditionalists had gone to war proclaiming their loyalty to the old territorial privileges (*Fueros*) of Navarre. In 1937, they still believed they would be able to create a new Spain based on regional home rule, which was founded on corporatist suffrage. However, the picture changed with the first administrative outlines of Franco's *New State* in mid-1937. All hope of restoring a regionalized Spain was swept away when Franco abolished the *Fueros* of Biscay and Guipúzcoa. The conquest of Catalonia in February 1939 served to reinforce this trend.

The provinces became the cornerstone of the francoist administration. Power was concentrated in the hands of the Civil Governors, who were also the provincial leaders of the FET de las JONS, the single party that had been formed through the merging of the fascist Falange with the traditionalist Carlists and other groupings. They became the key mediators between the state and the local authorities. The provinces remained crucial to the official Francoist view of Spain's plurality, and cultural institutions were usually organized along provincial lines. The Spanish provinces were reinforced by the survival of the old *Diputaciones*, the provincial institutions that coordinated funding and services for the municipalities. The insular councils in the Canary Islands and the limited survival of some *foral* privileges in Alava and Navarre, along with a later attempt (1958) at integrating the last colonial territories in Africa as 'provinces', added certain singularities to what seemed to be a fully provincialized Spain.

The regional past

Fascist obsession with the past has often been regarded as mere window dressing, to disguise radically 'modernizing' policies that would eventually dismantle traditional political bodies. Griffin has argued that the backward-looking orientation of fascists was not at odds with the movement's modernist credentials.[17] Rather, the myth of national rebirth, or *palingenetic fascism*, should be seen as a product of its utopian aspirations. This perspective captures how fascist regimes often made use of the past in highly innovative ways, and the specific contributions of regions to the historical development of the nation.

The Nazi view of history was hardly ever nostalgic. Rather, they invoked ideological paradigms such as 'inherited historical characteristics' to give specific shape to their policies, using two historical models. The first was academic *Volksgeschichte*. This new discipline used innovative structuralist and statistical methods to write a people's history 'from below' and contributed decisively to the formulation of Nazi racial policy.[18] Research into the alleged superiority of the Germanic race over adjacent tribes in neighbouring areas most openly served the Nazis' foreign political agenda. However, the Germanic or Arian race was not treated as a homogenous entity; the *Volksgeschichtler* themselves distinguished between the west, the north-east and the south-east. The trope of a Germany of tribes was extremely powerful within German *Volksgeschichte*. It usually identified several *Stämme* – the Nordic, the Falian, the Alpine and so forth – which in turn were divided into subgroups or *Schläge*.[19] Among the leading *Volksgeschichtler* in this development was Hermann Aubin, a pioneer of *Ostforschung* and editor of the multi-volume work *Der Raum Westfalen*.[20]

The second major strand of Nazi regional history emerged in connection with a largely affirmative political history of the Holy Roman Empire. The *Volksgeschichte* was less well funded than a high-political history of the German empires. Here, the very decentralized Holy Roman Empire was celebrated as something uniquely suited to the varied regions of the German nation. Such connections also shaped a broad historical culture. They figured to some extent in popular print culture, in the *Heimat* magazines and in Nazi schoolbooks. Some of the key offices that the Nazi state created in the regions derived their names from the polycentric traditions of the Old Empire. Invocations of Habsburg traditions were used to legitimate the *Anschluss* of Austria (1938) as a return to *grossdeutsch* imperial legacies.

Yet there was no unified historical narrative for the *new* Spain that the Francoist regime intended to create. Certainly, some of its main thematic axioms were shared by the Falangists, the Traditionalists, the Catholics and some conservative regionalists. They all took up a theme first coined by Spanish conservative historical writing of the nineteenth century, which identified distinctive 'Golden Ages' in Spanish history. Most notable among them were pre-Roman times, the medieval Reconquest from the Muslims, early modern Empire-building and overseas expansion. From the late nineteenth century on, local history was widely presented as complementary to this narrative. The varied kingdoms, lands and regions of Spain had been separate political entities in the past but had been integrated into a Spanish political community by virtue of their Catholic and dynastic loyalty.

The role of religion in Spanish history divided the supporters of the Franco regime early on. The Falangists tended to consider religion as subordinate to nation. Another contentious question concerned just how *Castilian* Spain was and had been. Francoist historiography contained a range of coexisting views on the role of Castile, Aragon, Catalonia and other regions in Spanish history.[21] In fact, Francoism led to a huge revival of local and regional history accompanied by flourishing new provincially based research institutes, from the Academia Alfonso X el Sabio in Murcia (1940) to the Instituto de Estudios Asturianos in Oviedo (1946). These institutions took up the task of researching local history, linking provincial traditions to their roots in the Middle Ages, recovering rural material culture and collecting folklore and costumes. Their activities gave rise to a plurality of narratives concerning the local and provincial past, aimed at rendering the master narrative of Spanish nationalist historiography more organic by showcasing the vigour of traditions in their respective lands.[22]

The results were often complex, even contradictory in the Spanish case, as demonstrated by the characteristic example of the fate of the Fernando el Católico Institute in Zaragoza (1943). Though intended to enhance the provincial identity of Zaragoza, it actually gave permanent emphasis and priority to the interests of Aragon. Meanwhile, Falangist newspaper articles insisted on the necessity of reconstructing Aragon's regional strength to place it at the disposal of the new Spain. Regional maps continued to illustrate Spanish primary school textbooks, yet were often ignored at administrative and political levels. During the final decades of Francoism, regionalists and ethnonationalists took up the project of exhuming dialects and languages. The Francoist-oriented Instituto de Estudios Asturianos, for example, produced some influential research on the 'Asturian language'. Its findings were subsequently mobilized in the 1970s under the auspices of the emergence of 'Asturian ethnonationalism', thereby subverting their official political purpose.[23]

Natural heritage

Another element of fascist regionalist policies was landscape preservation and development. The National Socialist state in Germany seemed content to allow existing regional infrastructures for homeland protection activism to remain as before. Such collaboration was useful to the regime, because the notion of *Heimat* reconciled the ideas of rootedness and place-based authenticity with progress and modernity. Most homeland protection leagues welcomed the new regime in 1933, and some of its advocates felt horrified later at the major landscape interventions perpetrated by the Nazi state.[24] Though some earlier *Heimat* practices continued to protect characteristic landscape features, such as the Westphalian banked hedgerows, the regime rejected the idea of mere 'homeland preservation' in favour of a developmental 'homeland policy', or *Heimatarbeit*.

The idea of regional characteristics in Nazi Germany incorporated a distinctive notion of progress. Even where the rural predominated, man-made regional landscapes were celebrated over the 'natural' ones. Significance stemmed from visible traces of human intervention, which documented the 'industrious nature of the Swabian tribe' and so forth. Accordingly, industrial landscapes were as integral to regional representations as agricultural ones. Dams, drainage projects and motorways did not necessarily obliterate the idea of the landscape as a marker of regional identity. Travel and tourism constituted another important driving force behind the Nazi cult of the region and the reinvention of subnational spaces. From Hitler youth leader guidebooks to commercial advertising, landscapes featured as attractions that invited travellers to explore and experience a region and its character.[25]

Here again, we find some parallels and many differences between Italy and Spain. Mussolini's regime crafted a cult of landscapes and urban medieval traditions, which was re-enacted to meet demand from foreign visitors. This reinvention of pre-modern traditions stemmed from the desire to return to 'authentic' practices via the new meanings ascribed to folklore. Urban and industrial modernity were largely absent from the overall picture.[26] Early Francoism also devoted some attention to propagating images of diverse Spanish landscapes that re-ruralized the regions.[27] The German idea of a *Volks und Kulturboden* had influenced the work of many forestry engineers in Spain during the 1920s, some of whom attempted to apply such ideas to the reforestation of abandoned areas.[28] Meanwhile, some Falangists sought to concentrate on symbols of industrial and urban modernity. Francoist propaganda during the 1940s popularized the idea of *terruño* and the re-folklorization of the province. Idyllic villages and snowy mountains were combined with representations of Catholic religiosity and traces of the Middle Ages. Regional religious sanctuaries such as Guadalupe in Extremadura and Covadonga in Asturias also occupied a privileged place in Francoist iconography. The regime continued to use regional stereotypes that had been constructed by ethnonationalist ethnographers before the Civil War, endowing them with new significance (Figure 7.1). Thus, stereotypical representations of the Basques as a hard-working people composed of shepherds, fishermen, sailors and peasant small-holders were transformed into archetypal Spaniards.[29]

Some parallels to the Nazi *Heimatarbeit* could be observed in Spain before 1945, when Francoist policies focused on the regions devastated by the Civil War. Many of

Figure 7.1 *Valencia, 26 April 1939. Women wearing the regional dress salute the Francoist troops (Arquivo Fotográfico Guerra Civil-Fondo Documental Mario Blanco Fuentes) (© 2018, Museu Reimóndez Portela/herdeiros de Mario Blanco Fuentes, E-36680 A Estrada, museo.aestrada.com/index.php/memoria-grafica-da-guerra-civil-espanola).*

Fascism

the cities and areas that had been severely damaged by air raids, battles and sieges, such as Teruel and Gernika, experienced state-led reconstruction programmes. While such policies were aimed at reconstructing landscapes, they also sought to re-shape them according to the new aesthetic and technical principles of the Francoist state.[30]

Regional cultures and languages

The inhabitants of the regions and their distinctive contemporary 'cultures' were central to regional identity construction in fascist regimes. Again, we find a dualism of traditional and modern tendencies that reflects the highly ambivalent and strategic approach to regionalism adopted by those regimes. In Nazi Germany, great effort went into reviving folk music and traditional handicrafts, and even to promoting dialects. Thus, *Niederdeutsch*, the dominant North German dialect, was integrated into National Socialist school instruction.[31] Dialect literature was also promoted and publicly showcased in annual poetry festivals. However, a distinction was made between Germanic dialects and related languages (including Danish in Schleswig-Holstein), which were treated with relative tolerance, and other (mostly Slav) languages (including Polish in East Prussia and Wendish in Bautzen) that were ruthlessly suppressed[32] (Figure 7.2).

Figure 7.2 *27 October 1940. The Reichsführer SS Heinrich Himmler visits a folklore performance during his stay in Madrid (© Hermes Pato, Archive EFE).*

In many instances, the promotion of traditional substate cultures was a continuation of earlier practices, but with some novel elements. First, substate cultures now formed part of a discourse of racial variety within Germany that was presented using the phraseology of 'modern' science. Second, regional cultures became part of the new cultural theatrics. Journals, brochures and exhibitions turned regional traditions into exhibits, and thus tools for a modern conception of identity politics.[33] Third, cultural regionalism was now massively integrated into official state propaganda and policy at the national level, as could be observed in the 1936 Olympic Games. Finally, regional culture was also on display in national venues, such as the numerous travelling exhibitions organized by the leisure organization Strength Through Joy (*Kraft durch Freude*).

Discussion of the authentic national essence and its expression in the regional sphere had also become radicalized in France during the interwar period. Folklore became an academic discipline and one more battlefield, increasingly dominated by scholars close to political Catholicism, in the fight to define the 'true' France. The new Vichy state to a large extent simply elaborated on their findings to build a new public image of French identity and disseminate it through public and cultural performances and exhibitions. These placed regionalism as the cornerstone for the survival of the nation and served as a common umbrella for fascists, traditionalists and conservative republicans, with the collaboration of some moderate *brétonnants* and political regionalists from Roussillon and Occitania. The Musée des Arts et Traditions Populaires, founded several years before, became the most visible symbol of this para-fascist appropriation of cultural regionalism.[34]

In Spain, folklore and material culture complemented the cult to the landscape, with heavily gendered connotations. During the early 1940s, the female section of the single party concentrated its efforts on collecting oral traditions, recovering local costumes and playing songs and music intended to express the most authentic Spanish 'soul'. They worked at this task successfully throughout the 1950s and 1960s, spreading 'banal regionalism' in Spain while representing Spanish culture abroad.[35]

A degree of modernity can be detected in this endeavour. The new Spanish nationalist music of the 1940s drew on local repertories of traditional songs and dances but also established a dialogue with the most important European trends of that time. This was reflected in the elaboration of new regional stereotypes in Spanish film. Some regional and local icons, such as the Andalusian gypsy, were endowed with new meanings, following the tradition launched by early Spanish 'traditionalist' cinema in the late 1920s. Francoist cinema in the 1940s is considered by experts to be a mixture of imperial fantasies and neo-folkloric regional images that became more regionalist and somewhat less Catholic in the 1950s.[36]

A similar phenomenon can be observed in Salazar's Portugal, beginning in the 1930s. The continuity of the pre-war Catholic concept of the local meant associating rural life with the national essence and tradition with peasant culture. Folklore was thus promoted as an accessory to imperial mystique and given expression in exhibitions (such as that devoted to the Colonial Empire in 1940), mass performances and political rallies. A prize was even established to exalt the nation's 'most Portuguese village'; the winners were generally located in the north, where Catholic tradition was best preserved.[37]

Francoist language policy was a particularly contentious field. Despite both scholarly and propagandistic interest in subnational languages during the 1940s, the role of languages other than Castilian Spanish in education and the public domain was disputed. Some Falangists warned against the evils of plurality, drawing a direct line from cultural diversity to separatism, while other voices advocated limited recognition of regional languages at the primary school level. They argued that tradition and religion had always been better maintained by peasants in their local languages. However, the former stance prevailed, and Francoist education laws forbade primary school instruction in vernacular languages until 1970. Though the legal framework that imposed Castilian was not monolithic and no general law prohibited the use of vernacular languages, a number of decrees imposed Castilian in shops, cemeteries or written statutes of associations. Even so, limited literary use of vernacular languages occurred in novels and poems and even official texts, during the early 1940s. As the Francoist elites became aware of the need to moderate the regime's image in the new Cold War context, cultural repression practices diminished in intensity. However, during the dictatorship non-Castilian languages never recovered the co-official status that some of them had enjoyed before 1939 in their respective territories. The regime was more tolerant with characters such as peasants and fishermen who used vernacular languages in publications or theatre plays, or linguistic crossovers intended to 'sponsor' non-Castilian languages. Since 1939, Francoist authorities promoted the Valencian dialect on the occasion of the *fallas*, for example, which celebrated regional pride and tradition, as a strategy to counteract any 'contagion' of neighbouring Catalan identity.[38]

Visual culture and regional marketing

Fascist regionalism was not just about preserving traditions: it was also about inventing distinctive regional identities for the future. Explicitly ideological imperatives, along with intertwined political and commercial modes of representation, strategic interests and ambivalent attitudes all fuelled this process. They shared the common denominator of spectacle, a fundamental notion that fascist regimes applied to fashioning their public image.

As seen in the case of Germany and Italy, the spectacularizing of aesthetics helped transform the spatial imagination that characterized fascist regimes. Hundreds of regional exhibitions took place, many of which featured surprisingly 'modernist' representations of regional motifs and mobilized a wide range of impressionist and expressionist techniques and moods. Second, under the auspices of Staffel für Bildende Kunst, established in 1942, an amazingly modernist collection of many thousands of Nazi works of art were created for envisioned post-war exhibitions.[39] Most works depicted specific regions and their inhabitants, with commercial visual representations often appearing markedly modernist and emphasizing the smooth transition between landscapes and productive forces.

Much less is known about the visual culture of the Franco regime, Vichy France and Salazar's Portugal, or the relation between Italian fascist aesthetics and regional cultures. In Spain, the hard years of autarky following the Civil War were characterized by the scarcity of regional fairs. Advertising at that time drew on a range of regional stereotypes and representations, though often avoiding mention of region names, and focused on the province or locality, which were cited as acceptable spatial references for former regional iconographies. However, tension between more traditional regional imaginaries and new attempts to shape the image of the provinces are evident in commercial publicity. Compared to German examples, Spanish designs were more reluctant to engage with modernist artistic tendencies. However, as early as the 1940s, regional and local representations permeated Francoist visual culture and served as the basis for the boom of images associated with the promotion of mass tourism from the early 1960s on.[40]

Conclusion

Fascist regimes utilized regionalism as a form of identity politics through a wide variety of avenues. By no means devoid of ambivalence, the strategy served many purposes: mobilizing popular support, promoting a particularly desirable vision of the state and nation, marketing and commerce. But did regionalism really matter in the realm of high politics?

The Nazis did not invent regionalism; to some extent they simply sustained pre-existing practices. However, regionalism contributed to the success of the Nazi regime in two ways. First, competition between regions contributed to the 'cumulative radicalization' associated with the workings of a polycratic government. Competition between the *Gaue* drove economic development.[41] Second, 'banal regionalism' gave the regime a harmless face that allowed many 'ordinary Germans' to identify with it. Translating ambitions for racial purity and world domination into seemingly innocuous everyday practices helped form the bedrock of popular support for Nazism. Qualities such as 'authenticity' and 'community' served as vehicles for this.

There were, of course, limits to fascist mobilization of regionalism. First, past inter-territorial tensions – moves towards separatism in the Weimar Republic, Sardinian and Sicilian regionalisms in Italy and the emergence and consolidation of substate nationalisms in Spain since 1898 – marked lines that could not be crossed. Separatism was often perceptually associated with social unrest and inward-looking regionalism regarded as a threat. Fascist nationalism featured a key imperialist penchant, so the region had to be put at the service of the empire.

Second, in the clearly established hierarchy of 'spheres of loyalty' from the individual to the nation, love of the *Heimat*, the *piccola patria* or the *terruño* and attachment to the region, *Land* or *Gau* always had to be subordinate to loyalty to the nation. However, attitudes towards this issue were far from uniform in the fascists ranks, and much depended on the perceived threat of ethnocultural diversity to state stability. The Nazi regime could 'afford' to be more regionalist. Italian fascism did not fear traditional regionalisms in 'the core' of Italy, but distrusted separatist tendencies in South Tyrol and, to a lesser extent, in Sardinia. In Spain, the strength of Basque and Catalan nationalisms fuelled the reluctance of sectors of the Francoist coalition to wholeheartedly embrace regionalism as a cultural practice. Such sceptics distinguished between a regionalized Spanish nationalism and regionalism *per se*, which they saw as a forerunner for separatism.

Third, there were also unintended consequences: fascist regimes failed to control all the meanings and political subtexts embedded in the regional identities they conjured up. This speaks to the importance of not denying that regionalism can be a valuable vehicle for democratization; regionalization in post-fascist Italy, Spain and Germany did not represent a break with the past. These processes demonstrate that regionalism can be used for different agendas: in all three countries, regionalism survived in some form under the dictators and resurfaced prominently in the restored democracies. This must not be regarded as some relic of an 'unmastered past'; rather, the regionalist cultures of the dictatorships paradoxically provided a vehicle for democratic reconstruction.

Fascist Italy, Nazi Germany and Francoist Spain show that, as an identity discourse, regionalism was compatible with authoritarian and totalitarian state-led nationalisms. Under the fascist (or para-fascist) regimes, regional or subnational imaginaries and iconography – and even the idea of regional and ethnographic pluralism to some extent – coexisted with centralized state-building and a highly emotive appeal to the nation as a superior community. Local and regional metaphors featured in various forms and stages of state nationalism, from liberal to communist and fascist[42]. Despite a hatred for separatism, fascist or quasi-fascist views of the state had a certain affinity towards the notion of regional diversity. The *idea* of regionalism could be invoked to combat the perceived dangers of Napoleonic-style state-building, with its liberalism, progressivism and bureaucratization. It could also infuse politics with desirable notes of populism, grass-root activism, social rootedness and ideological dynamism. If generic fascism was a form of 'palingenetic nationalism', placing the nation at the top of the hierarchy of values did not necessarily mean that the nation would be territorially and culturally homogenous. Fascists were not the only ones to consider the nation more authentic than the state and to define it through its spatial components rooted in tradition.

Fascist regimes invoked regionalism and localism, but unlike the French and Spanish Catholic right-wing attitudes of earlier years, this did not imply a rejection of political modernity *per se*. The Nazis always took pains to distance themselves from reactionary and Romantic visions of the *Heimat*. No other regime in Europe intervened so dramatically in the physical landscape, especially through 'modernist' dam building, as did the Franco regime. Consequently, the prominent role of regionalism in fascist identity politics must be understood as a form of *modern* anti-liberal spatial identity, which many fascists deliberately cultivated. This regionalism was marked by clear affinities with *Heimat* and *Volk* discourses, but it also offered something that these other movements did not: a more realist sense of the political, which prevented the notion of rootedness from sliding into the purely nostalgic or the purely other-worldly.

Notes

1. See Richard Bessel, *Fascist Italy and Nazi Germany. Comparisons and Contrasts* (Cambridge/New York: Cambridge University Press, 1996); R. Griffin, ed., *International Fascism: Theories, Causes, and the New Consensus* (London: Arnold, 1998); R. Griffin, *Modernism and Fascism: The Sense of a New Beginning Under Mussolini and Hitler* (Basingstoke: Palgrave Macmillan, 2007); Aristotle Kallis, *Fascist Ideology: Territory and Expansion in Italy and Germany, 1919-1945* (London: Routledge, 2000); and António Costa Pinto and Aristotle Kallis, eds, *Rethinking Fascism and Dictatorship in Europe* (Basingstoke: Palgrave Macmillan, 2014).
2. An exception for Germany is Claus-Christian W. Szejnmann and Maiken Umbach, eds, *Heimat, Region, and Empire: Spatial Identities Under National Socialism* (Basingstoke: Palgrave Macmillan, 2012).
3. See Xosé M. Núñez Seixas and Maiken Umbach, 'Hijacked Heimats. National Appropriations of Local and Regional Identities in Germany and Spain, 1930-1945', *European Review of History* 15, no. 3 (2008): 295-316.
4. See Martin Broszat, Elke Fröhlich and Falk Wiesemann, eds, *Bayern in der NS-Zeit: Soziale Lage und politisches Verhalten der Bevölkerung im Spiegel vertraulicher Berichte* (Munich/Vienna: Oldenbourg, 1977-1983, 6 vols); Wolfgang Jäger, *Bergarbeitermilieus und Parteien im Ruhrgebiet. Zum Wahlverhalten des katholischen Bergarbeitermilieus bis 1933* (Munich: Beck, 1996); Claus-Christian W. Szejnmann, *Nazism in Central Germany: The Brownshirts in Red Saxony* (Oxford/New York: Berghahn, 1999); Thomas Schaarschmidt, *Regionalkultur und Diktatur. Sächsische Heimatbewegung und Heimat-Propaganda im Dritten Reich und in der SBZ/DDR* (Cologne: Böhlau, 2004); Jeremy Noakes, 'Federalism in the Nazi State', in *German Federalism: Past, Present, Future*, ed. Maiken Umbach (Basingstoke: Palgrave Macmillan, 2002), 113-45; and J. John, Horst Möller and Thomas Schaarschmidt, eds, *Die NS-Gaue. Regionale Mittelinstanzen im zentralistischen "Führerstaat"?* (Munich: Oldenburg, 2007).
5. See Stefano Cavazza, *Piccole patrie. Feste popolari tra regione e nazione durante il fascism* (Bologna: Il Mulino, 2003); as well as Stefano Cavazza, 'El culto de la pequeña patria en Italia, entre centralización y nacionalismo. De la época liberal al fascismo', *Ayer* 64 (2006): 95-119.
6. See Xosé M. Núñez Seixas, *¡Fuera el invasor! Nacionalismos y movilización bélica durante la guerra civil española, 1936-1939* (Madrid: Marcial Pons, 2006).
7. See Ismael Saz, *España contra España. Los nacionalismos franquistas* (Madrid: Marcial Pons, 2002); as well as Xosé M. Núñez Seixas, 'La región y lo local en el primer franquismo', in *Imaginarios y representaciones de España durante el franquismo*, ed. Stéphane Michonneau and Xosé.M. Núñez Seixas (Madrid: Casa de Velázquez, 2014), 127-54.
8. David Laven, 'Italy', in *What Is a Nation? Europe 1789-1914*, ed. Timothy Baycroft and Michael Hewitson (Oxford: Oxford University Press, 2006), 255-71.
9. See Martina Steber, 'Regions and National Socialist Ideology: Reflections on Contained Plurality', in *Heimat, Region, and Empire*, ed. Szejnmann and Umbach, 25-42.
10. See Willi Oberkrome, *Deutsche Heimat: Nationale Konzeption und regionale Praxis von Naturschutz, Landschaftsgestaltung und Kulturpolitik in Westfalen-Lippe und Thüringen, 1900-1960* (Paderborn: Schöningh, 2006); and Thomas M. Lekan, *Imagining the Nation in Nature: Landscape Preservation and German Identitiy, 1885-1945* (Cambridge: Harvard University Press, 2004).
11. See the chapter by DeWaal.

12. Adolf Hitler, *Mein Kampf*, trans. James Murphy (London: Hurst and Blackett, 1942), 127–28.
13. See *Obras de José Antonio Primo de Rivera. Edición cronológica*, ed. Agustín del Río Cisneros (Madrid: Almena, 1971); Núñez Seixas, 'La región y lo local'; and Joan M. Thomàs, *José Antonio. Realidad y mito* (Barcelona: Debate, 2017).
14. See Ulrich von Hehl, 'Nationalsozialismus und Region', *Zeitschrift für Bayerische Landesgeschichte* 56, no. 1 (1993): 111–29; Willi Oberkrome, 'Gesundes Land, gesundes Volk. Deutsche Landschaftgestaltung und Heimatideologie in der ersten Hälfte des 20. Jahrhunderts', *Zeitschrift für Agrargeschichte und Agrarsoziologie* 53, no. 2 (2005): 26–40; Lekan, *Imagining the Nation*; Detlef Schmiechen-Ackermann, 'Milieus, Political Culture and Regional Traditions in Lower Saxony in Comparative Perspective', in *Heimat, Region, and Empire*, ed. Szejnmann and Umbach, 43–55; and the chapter by DeWaal.
15. Salvatore Cubeddu, ed., *Il Sardo-fascismo fra politica, cultura, economia* (Cagliari: Fondazione Sardinia, 1997).
16. See Sandro Fontana, ed., *Il fascismo e le autonomie local* (Bologna: Il Mulino, 1976); and Cavazza, *Piccole patrie*, 49–54, 125–37 and 198–217.
17. Griffin, *Modernism and Fascism*.
18. See Willi Oberkrome, *Volksgeschichte. Methodische Innovation und völkische Ideologisierung in der deutschen Geschichtswissenschaft, 1918–1945* (Göttingen: Vandenhoeck & Ruprecht, 1993).
19. Josef Nadler, *Das stammhafte Gefüge des deutschen Volkes* (Munich: Beckstein, 1934).
20. See Hermann Aubin and Eduard Schulte, eds, *Der Raum Westfalen*, II, 2. Teilband (Münster: Aschendorffsche Verlagsbuchhandlung, 1955 [1st ed. 1934]).
21. Saz, *España contra España*; a descriptive approach in Gustavo Alares, *Políticas del pasado en la España franquista, 1939–1964* (Madrid: Marcial Pons, 2017).
22. Miquel A. Marín Gelabert, *Los historiadores españoles en el franquismo, 1948–1975. La historia local al servicio de la patria* (Zaragoza: PUZ/Institución Fernando el Católico, 1995).
23. Jorge Uría González, *Cultura oficial e ideología en la Asturias franquista: El I.D.E.A.* (Oviedo: Universidad de Oviedo, 1984).
24. See Lekan, *Imagining the Nation*; and David Blackbourn, *The Conquest of Nature. Water, Landscape and the Making of Modern Germany* (London: Jonathan Cape Press, 2006).
25. See James D. Shand, 'The Reichsautobahn: Symbol of the Third Reich', *Journal of Contemporary History* 19, no. 2 (1984): 189–200; and Thomas Zeller, *Strasse, Bahn, Panorama: Verkehrswege und Landschaftsveränderung in Deutschland von 1930 bis 1990* (Frankfurt a. M.: Campus, 2002).
26. See Cavazza, *Piccole patrie*, 178–98.
27. See Angel Duarte, 'El catalán en su paisaje. Algunas notas sobre los usos del imaginario del paisaje catalán, y catalanista, en el primer franquismo', *Historia y Política* 14 (2005): 165–90.
28. Alberto Sabio Alcutén, 'Imágenes del monte público, "patriotismo forestal español" y resistencias campesinas, 1855–1930', *Ayer* 46 (2002): 123–54.
29. See Miriam Basilio, 'Genealogies for a New State: Painting and Propaganda in Franco's Spain, 1936–1940', *Discourse* 24, no. 3 (2002): 67–94; and Fernando Molina, 'Afinidades electivas. Franquismo e identidad vasca, 1936–1970', in *Imaginarios*, ed. Michonneau and Núñez Seixas, 155–75.
30. See, e.g., Stéphane Michonneau, *Fue ayer: Belchite. Un pueblo frente a la cuestión del pasado* (Zaragoza: PUZ, 2017).

31. Hermann Quistorf and Johannes Saß, *Hilfsbuch für den Unterricht im Plattdeutschen* (Hamburg: Meiner Hamburg, 1937).
32. See Reeta Toivanen, *Minderheitenrechte als Identitätsressource? Die Sorben in Deutschland und die Saamen in Finnland* (Hamburg: LIT Verlag, 2001).
33. Martina Steber, 'Fragiles Gleichgewicht: Die Kulturarbeit der Gaue zwischen Regionalismus und Zentralismus', in *Die NS-Gaue*, ed. John, Möller and Schaarschmidt, 141–58.
34. Christian Faure, *Le projet culturel de Vichy. Folklore et revolution nationale, 1940–1944* (Paris: CNRS, 1989).
35. Ana de la Asunción Criado, 'El folklore como instrumento político: los Coros y Danzas de la Sección Femenina', *Revista Historia Autónoma* 10 (2017): 183–96.
36. See Nancy Berthier and Jean-Claude Seguin, eds, *Cine, nación y nacionalidades en España* (Madrid: Casa de Velázquez, 2007).
37. See Daniel Melo, *Salazarismo e cultura popular (1933–1958)* (Lisbon: Imprensa de Ciências Sociais, 2001).
38. Gil Hernández i Martí, *Falles i franquisme a València* (Catarroja: Afers, 1996).
39. Gregory Maertz, 'The Invisible Museum: Unearthing the Lost Modernist Art of the Third Reich', *Modernism/modernity* 15, no. 1 (2008): 63–85.
40. See Alicia Fuentes Vega, *Bienvenido, Mr. Turismo. Cultura visual del boom en España* (Madrid: Cátedra, 2017).
41. Oliver Werner, 'Conceptions, Competences and Limits of German Regional Planning during the Four Year Plan, 1926–1940', in *Heimat, Region, and Empire*, ed. Szejnmann and Umbach, 166–82.
42. See Alon Confino, *Germany as a Culture of Remembrance: Promises and Limits of Writing History* (Chapel Hill: University of North Carolina Press, 2006).

Further reading

Cavazza, Stefano, *Piccole patrie. Feste popolari tra regione e nazione durante il fascismo*, 2nd ed. (Bologna: Il Mulino, 2003).
Faure, Christian, *Le projet culturel de Vichy. Folklore et revolution nationale, 1940–1944* (Paris: CNRS, 1989).
Michonneau, Stéphane, and Xosé M. Núñez Seixas, eds, *Imaginarios y representaciones de España durante el franquismo* (Madrid: Casa de Velázquez, 2014).
Núñez Seixas, Xosé M., and Maiken Umbach, 'Hijacked Heimats. National Appropriations of Local and Regional Identities in Germany and Spain, 1930–1945', *European Review of History* 15, no. 3 (2008): 295–316.
Oberkrome, Willi, *Volksgeschichte. Methodische Innovation und völkische Ideologisierung in der deutschen Geschichtswissenschaft, 1918–1945* (Göttingen: Vandenhoeck & Ruprecht, 1993).
Schaarschmidt, Thomas, *Regionalkultur und Diktatur. Sächsische Heimatbewegung und Heimat-Propaganda im Dritten Reich und in der SBZ/DDR* (Cologne: Böhlau, 2004).
Szejnmann, Claus-Christian W., and Maiken Umbach, eds, *Heimat, Region, and Empire: Spatial Identities under National Socialism* (Basingstoke: Palgrave Macmillan, 2012).

CHAPTER 8
COMMUNISM AND REGIONALISM
Susan Smith-Peter

Introduction

In the November Revolution in 1917, the Bolshevik Party, later renamed the Communist Party, took power of what would become the Soviet Union. In 1945, the Soviets were one of the main victors of the Second World War and they were eager to create a buffer zone between themselves and Germany, and so they turned Eastern Europe into a series of client states that later signed the Warsaw Pact. The hoped-for result of communism was that state control of the economy by a one-party state would be more productive than the vagaries of the market under capitalism and would, in time, lead to the spread of communism at capitalism's expense. In practice, the economies of the countries behind the Iron Curtain lagged behind the West, particularly after the information revolution of the 1970s. One of the major ways that communist states tried to reform their economies was to devolve powers to regions and factories, in hopes that nimble economic decisions could be made using local knowledge. However, a demand for economic regionalism became one of the only acceptable ways to express a covert nationalism within the communist system, particularly in the cases of the Soviet Union, Yugoslavia and Czechoslovakia, which had significant consequences.

This chapter looks at communist attempts to reform by devolving economic powers to the regions between 1945 and 1991 in Yugoslavia, Poland, Hungary, Czechoslovakia and the Soviet Union, some of which led to peripheral nationalism. It views as regions those parts of states that were not yet independent, such as Ukraine or Croatia, even if they later became so. Economic regionalism, or the devolving of powers to the regions, was an important part of the reform impulse within communism, and its failure to meaningfully stimulate the economy when implemented was one of the factors that led to disillusionment with and, later, the collapse of communism in Eastern Europe. In practice, economic regionalism led to conflicts between different groups that could not be mediated by a one-party state. Other chapters in this volume will deal with issues related to cultural regionalism in Eastern Europe and Russia.

Economic regionalism in the Soviet Union, 1917–1945

In the Soviet Union, there were two main institutions of economic regionalism. The first was the soviet, or local workers' council. Although it was co-opted by the Communist Party, at times the idea of the soviet was overlaid with local democratic aspirations connected to workers' control, rather than the control of the party/state. The second kind of institution was the *sovnarkhozy*, or regional economic councils. These councils coordinated economic plans with the centre while putting forward the needs of their regions. Stalin abolished them in 1932 but Nikita Khrushchev re-established them in the 1950s. In Eastern Europe, demands for more economic regionalism focused on requests to allow the establishment of their own versions of these two institutions. Even when they were allowed, it turned out they were failed solutions because different regions, and even groups within the same region, had different needs that, once articulated, could not easily be reconciled within the one-party state. This led to frustration and anger.

During the Civil War, which lasted from 1918 to 1920, some regions in Soviet Russia attempted to create autonomous regions or even independent countries but were militarily defeated by the Red Army. Both Siberia and the Russian North, on the shores of the White Sea, had a sense of regional identity stretching back to the seventeenth century and groups of regionalists who had defined themselves through scholarly organizations during the late nineteenth century. In 1865, in an early expression of political regionalism in Europe, a proclamation from Siberian regionalists was discovered that declared the need to create a United States of Siberia, to be federated with the United States of America. It had been written in 1863, when Siberian regionalists were disillusioned due to the Russian suppression of the Polish uprising of that year and the realization that the Great Reforms would not be extended to Siberia. This led them, at that moment, to imagine Siberia as potentially independent from Russia and to articulate the conditions under which this could happen.[1] The leading regionalists were arrested, tried and exiled away from Siberia to the Russian North.[2] During the Civil War, the regionalists in the Russian North and Siberia began by affiliating themselves with the Socialist Revolutionaries, a pro-peasant socialist party that had a large following. Over the course of the war, the regionalists ended up throwing their support behind the Whites, a conservative group of mainly former tsarist army officers that fought the Reds, or Bolsheviks.[3] This alienated most of the population of the regions. For example, when, in February 1920, there was a last-ditch attempt to stave off the Bolsheviks by declaring an independent state of the Russian North, no regionalists took part.[4] In addition, the Socialist Revolutionaries themselves failed to draw upon the rhetoric of regionalism to attract supporters. This mutual distancing made it easier for the Bolsheviks and the Red Army, capably led by Leon Trotsky, to defeat their opponents in both regions and elsewhere.

The Union of Soviet Socialist Republics (USSR) was a federation, created in 1922, and within each republic there was a state apparatus parallel to that of the party. A member of the titular nationality (Ukrainians in the Ukrainian Soviet Socialist Republic, for example) was usually the head of each apparatus, but often an ethnic Russian would be the second in command and in practice the person in charge. In addition, within the Russian Soviet Federated Socialist Republic, there were two main kinds of territorial divisions. The first consisted of republics of mostly ethnically non-Russian nationalities, along with an ethnic Russian core divided into regions (*oblasti*). The Soviets aimed at providing nationalities with the forms of nationhood while continuing to incorporate them into the larger Soviet state.⁵ Thus, there was an institutional basis for regionalism to develop into nationalism. The Baltic States, which were incorporated into the Soviet Union as a result of the Nazi-Soviet Pact, had been independent countries and retained a sense of nationalism.⁶

Vladimir Lenin, the leader of the Bolsheviks and the Soviet Union from 1917 to his death in 1924, wanted a regional history that focused on how the Bolsheviks came to power there. In a review, Lenin praised highly a history of the Bolshevik takeover of Tver province during the Civil War and the subsequent development of civilized life such as schools and a local press.⁷ This was part of his larger advocacy for historical works that chronicled the Bolshevik takeover of power, such as John Reed's *Ten Days That Shook the World*. In contrast, the emerging discipline of *kraevedenie* (regional studies), formed in the 1920s, focused on the study of the regional culture of the eighteenth and nineteenth centuries.⁸ During the golden age of regional studies in the 1920s, regional historians developed interdisciplinary approaches to such topics as life on the landed estates of the nobility, regional and provincial life, literature and art.⁹

Stalin moved against the cultural and economic bases of regionalism early on in his reign. Between the death of Lenin in 1924 and Stalin's defeat of his rivals by 1929, the Russian Academy of Sciences had been especially important for encouraging the growth of an interdisciplinary study of the regions that was very much in line with the newest European trends. However, one of Stalin's earliest moves was against the Academy of Sciences. In the 1930s, the 'academicians' affair' proved a harbinger of later Stalinist actions, as it involved a trial in which members of the academy were charged with various crimes and imprisoned or shot. Instead of a self-governing academy, it was reoriented to focus on the needs of industrialization.¹⁰ The leaders of what was called the 'old *kraevedenie*' were characterized as bourgeois and enemies of the people.¹¹ Instead of regionally based institutions and publications, the new focus was on industrialization and the history of the working class through Maxim Gorky's *History of Factories and Plants*. This organized the working class to collect oral history and thus come to a Stalinist-approved self-awareness. Factory workers established circles to study the history of their factories throughout the Soviet Union.¹² The question of the existence of regional culture was no longer something that could be asked, let alone answered.

Similarly, in 1932, Stalin abolished the regional economic councils known as *sovnarkhozy*. These had been an integral part of central planning since the revolution. On 15 December 1917, the Bolsheviks had established the Supreme Council of National Economy to control central and local agencies, industrial production, agriculture, finances and the military and to provide central planning. The *sovnarkhozy* administered the economic production of a region, which could be a small district area or a large one covering several provinces. They coordinated their activity with local soviets or workers' councils. By May 1918, there were *sovnarkhozy* in seven areas larger than provinces known as zones, in thirty-eight provinces and in sixty-nine districts.¹³

Economic regionalism, as practiced in the *sovnarkhozy*, meant making an argument that one's region should get more investment funds either due to its industrial or agrarian past; the former should be built upon, the latter overcome, regional planners would argue. At other times, such regionalism could advocate for a devolving of some decision-making authority to the regional or local level. In 1932, Stalin replaced *sovnarkhozy* with central ministries that directed particular industries from the centre but suffered from a lack of coordination at the local level, leading to inefficiencies and duplicated efforts.[14] Stalin chose an intensification of control rather than a regional coordination that might lead to the emergence of alternate centres of power.

During the 1930s, Stalin transformed the Soviet Union. He collectivized farming, establishing state control over agricultural production at the cost of millions of lives and a vibrant agrarian sector. The purges, which reached their height in 1937, led to the death of many military leaders, Old Bolsheviks, intellectuals and others caught up in a web of false accusations and show trials. This weakened the military in the years before the Second World War. Crash industrialization did allow for the Soviet Union to prepare for the coming clash with Nazi Germany. Despite the disorganization of Soviet forces when Hitler invaded the Soviet Union in 1941, by the end of the war, the Soviets had played the crucial role in defeating the Nazis and their sphere of influence in Eastern Europe was affirmed by the United States and the United Kingdom at the Yalta Conference.

The imposition of Soviet influence over Eastern Europe was achieved through local Communist Parties if possible but was imposed by force if necessary. Regional and national political and economic institutions were removed so that communist control would be more complete. Stalin oversaw the imposition of Soviet control over Poland, East Germany, Czechoslovakia, Hungary, Romania, Bulgaria, Albania and, for a time, Yugoslavia.

Economic regionalism and reform communism in Eastern Europe

In Yugoslavia, however, the leader, Josip Tito, had come to power on his own, without assistance from Stalin, and so had an independent power base. There was a similar situation in Albania. Tito had created a federative state, based on the Soviet model, to deal with the nationalities issue. He also had independent policies, including policies on how to deal with regions both politically and economically, and this was one of the reasons for the split between Stalin and Tito in 1948. As a result, Tito presented his more economically decentralized system as an alternative form of communism; since he became the leader of a non-aligned movement, this was particularly influential.

The differences in Stalin and Tito's political policies towards regions contributed to the split. Tito envisioned a Balkan federation led by himself, which Stalin saw as a threat to his hegemony. Tito worked with communist Bulgaria to create a federation that would deepen relations between countries and the regions within them. In 1947, the Yugoslavs and Bulgarians signed the Bled Agreement, which referred to a federation between the countries and a commitment to a new policy in Bulgaria towards its region, Pirin Macedonia.[15] In this, Tito was responding to pressure from members of the Communist Party of the People's Republic of Macedonia, which was a constituent part of Yugoslavia, who had argued that their control of their own Vardar region was too weak without a tie to Pirin Macedonia.[16] Stalin's subsequent attempt to control the nature of the Yugoslav-Bulgarian federation was one of the main factors contributing to the Stalin–Tito split, as Stalin demanded that any such federation consist of two equal units – Yugoslavia and Bulgaria – while Tito refused to give up the idea of a seven-unit federation in which each republic of Yugoslavia would have equal standing within the federation. Moscow rejected this and begun to shut off aid to Yugoslavia.[17] Tito was able to turn to the West for financial assistance, however, and Stalin's ferocious purges of East European communist parties that followed the split, with the stated intention of removing 'Titoists', only weakened the standing of the Soviets and the communist parties in the region.

The split allowed Tito to implement a broad-based policy of economic regionalism. The year 1950 was a turning point, as the continued Stalinist boycott emboldened him to try decentralization widely. The key institution was workers' councils, which were autonomous but led by communists and which oversaw the self-management of enterprises.[18] The councils were also integrated into the political system, as the councils elected representatives to one chamber of the federal parliament. Tito and others presented the workers' councils as a new model form of democracy that was collective, working class and locally based.[19] In 1952, local committees were introduced at the county or city level that could bargain for investment funds from the centre. This decentralization of control over industry was the most significant feature of the Yugoslav socialist experiment.[20] Thus, economic regionalism was at the very heart of reform communism. Stalin was absolutely opposed to such attempts, many of which echoed the workers' councils (soviets) and *sovnarkhozy* of the pre-Stalin Soviet era that he had weakened or abolished. The urge to economic regionalism can also be seen in other attempts to reform communism in the late 1950s.

After the death of Stalin in 1953, Poland and Hungary made demands that included more economic regionalism. In 1956, Poland saw calls for socialism with a Polish face, which was part of a nationalist resentment towards the Soviets/Russians that could not be publicly expressed. In September 1956, workers at a Warsaw car factory began forming workers' councils, which threatened communist control. In October of that year, a widespread crisis emerged that was contained only due to the Communist Party of Poland making considerable concessions to Polish nationalism, such as not attacking the Catholic Church in Poland and not thoroughly imposing collectivization.[21] The situation was different in Hungary.

In 1956, the Hungarian Revolution erupted, fuelled by nationalism. It began with nationalist demands, such as restoring the Kossuth coat of arms, the removal of Soviet troops from Hungary and open elections within a socialist system. It unfolded in a series of stages, but an integral part of the revolution was the creation of powerful regional councils that were sometimes called 'anti-Soviet soviets'. These councils sought to coordinate economic and political activity in their region.[22] In late 1956, the Greater

Budapest Workers' Council and several ministries put forth proposals for reform that called for giving more authority to enterprises and restricting the role of the centre to setting the annual budget and major national-level economic targets.[23] The councils exercised the real power in the country outside the capital. On 20 October 1956, the government abolished one-party rule and gave official recognition, as it stated, to 'the democratic organs of local autonomy which have been brought into existence by the revolution', and further stated that 'it relies on them and asks for their support'.[24] On 4 November 1956, 6,000 Soviet tanks invaded Hungary. The regional councils attempted to resist by creating an alternate government, but the forces arrayed against them were simply too overwhelming.[25]

Although the Soviet leader Nikita Khrushchev had agreed to the invasion of Hungary and the crushing of its experiment with regional councils in 1956, in the next year, he reintroduced in the Soviet Union those regional councils (*sovnarkhozy*) that Stalin had abolished earlier. Khrushchev disbanded the industry-based ministries that Stalin had established in place of the *sovnarkhozy*. There were to be 105 such regional councils, 70 of which would be in the Russian Soviet Federated Socialist Republic, while most other republics would have but one regional council each. The exceptions were Kazakhstan (nine regions), Ukraine (eleven) and Uzbekistan (four).[26] The regional councils did not coordinate with each other, and each demanded more funding for its own region, regardless of the needs of the whole. The all-union links of the ministries had been broken without anything to take its place. Gosplan, the central planning organization, had information but no executive power. Disorganization of production resulted. Once economic regionalism was instituted, there were no means by which the resulting conflicting demands of the regions could be mediated within the one-party state. The centre called the demands of the regions localism (*mestnichestvo*) and threatened officials with punishment, but this was a result of the system. It could not be curbed until the abolition of *sovnarkhozy* in 1965 and the reintroduction of industrial ministries, which were inefficient but could be controlled by Moscow.[27] Culturally, Khrushchev's reign (1953–1964), which was known as the Thaw due to its relatively wide-ranging reforms, also saw the emergence of Village Prose writers, who wrote approvingly of the rural past of Russia, sometimes including discussion of regional distinctiveness.[28]

While Khrushchev fell, replaced by the more conservative Leonid Brezhnev in 1965, the same 'reform' that ended *sovnarkhozy* also increased the powers of enterprise managers. This can be seen as a retreat from the possibly too democratic implications of the *sovnarkhozy*; giving the manager more powers did not really challenge central control of the economy and there would be fewer opportunities for regional power blocs to emerge. The 1965 reform sought to have managers set more targets for production, rather than have them set at the centre. The hope was that increased profits would encourage managers to respond more nimbly to the market, but as prices were still controlled by the state, it was difficult for a market feedback loop to get started. By 1970, most of the increased managerial powers given in 1965 had been taken back by the centre.[29] Some countries in Eastern Europe took up the technocratic spirit of the reform, giving more powers to managers to set goals and redistribute profits as they saw fit. Managers, it was hoped, would be able to make the system more efficient without changing its fundamental structure. This was not to be. Still, it is important to note that the local remained the level at which reform was seen as needing to take place.

The limits of economic regionalism

From 1953 to 1961, the Yugoslav economy grew more quickly than in other countries in the world, including in the bloc. Workers' councils and communal banks were able to respond to the market and to adjust production accordingly and to increase trade with Western countries. Some enterprises, however, were unable to produce for the market, as uneducated former partisans were their directors.[30] At the same time, however, the emphasis was on heavy industry, and the General Investment Fund, which distributed assistance to republics, tended to favour the least developed ones rather than the most.[31] Further decentralization led to demands for still more, and to increased resentment towards less-developed, generally southern, republics within the more developed northern ones.[32] This intensified ethnic resentments. There was also a tension between the micro level of economic development found in the workers' councils and the macro level of the General Investment Fund.[33] What was good for one factory was not necessarily good for the whole country, and the existing mechanisms were not always able to reconcile these differing interests.

The Reform of 1965 was a series of over thirty laws that set out to create a framework for market socialism and to help integrate Yugoslavia in the global economy. The Reform allowed for the creation of small businesses of between three and five employees, ended price controls and allowed enterprises to trade directly with the West.[34] While the Reform did stimulate growth in agriculture, it also led to the closure of more efficient banks, and the increase in wages took up most of the freed income of enterprises rather than leading to more investment. Some more farsighted enterprise managers did use the powers they received from the Reform to invest the money to improve the enterprise rather than dividing it up as bonuses for themselves and the workers.[35] At the same time, between 1963 and 1966, Yugoslavia entered Point No Point, as John Lampe termed it, when attempts to create a unified Yugoslav country and culture were reversed by continued decentralization to the republics and regions.[36] Local and regional interests continually demanded more investment funds, and regardless of the outcome, there were groups that lost or felt they should have received more. As long as the economy was growing, these feelings were more or less manageable.

Czechoslovakia was one of the countries in the Eastern Bloc that was influenced by the reforms of Yugoslavia as well as Poland in 1956.[37] In early January 1968, Alexander Dubcek became the new party secretary in Czechoslovakia and introduced a series of reforms that became known as the 'Prague Spring'. People began to talk about the need for more democracy, federalization and economic reform. Many saw a need to have an equal federation between the more economically advanced and industrialized Czech part of the country and the less developed and more agrarian Slovak part. Economic reform meant decentralization to the regional and local level, as we have seen before. In particular, it meant the introduction of workers' councils, on 1 July 1968. These were not under the control of the Communist Party and their composition and powers varied across the country.[38] They did not have long to develop, however. On 10 August 1968, draft statutes were published in Czechoslovakia that called for secret ballots in party elections, the separation of party and state offices and a deeper federalization of the party. Ten days later, the Soviets conducted a massive invasion, which succeeded militarily but not politically, as 'conservative' Czechoslovak communists failed to try to convince society of the need to end reforms. Soviet leader Leonid Brezhnev was forced to deal with Dubcek and the reformers rather than conservatives, and although most of the reforms were annulled, there was a state, although not party, federalization into Czech and Slovak halves on 28 October 1968.[39] The subsequent 'normalization' period encouraged Czechs and Slovaks to withdraw into private life, which worked while the economy did well. By 1977, however, what would be a long period of economic stagnation led to dissent, including the creation of Charter 77, which was based on a call for human rights rather than economic reform. The Soviet response to 1968 in Czechoslovakia stripped communism of its intellectual legitimacy. Force, not ideas, was its ultimate justification.

In Hungary, the party introduced the New Economic Mechanism (NEM) on 1 January 1968, which was marked both by the technocratic spirit of the Soviet reform of 1965 and also by the vision of the workers' councils in 1956 Hungary. Enterprises were to have more authority to set goals and were told to focus on increasing their profits. The centre was also to restrict its planning to major national economic objectives.[40] However, it retained a substantial amount of control over prices, making a focus on profits somewhat theoretical.[41] Even though one of the aims of the NEM had been to bring out into the open the conflicts between managers and central planners, there was no mechanism to adjudicate them once they became more visible, and so the only real option was to reimpose state control.[42] The reform was ended by 1972 due to pressure from the Soviet Union and the cooperation of a group within the Hungarian Communist Party. Another factor was that some Hungarian workers were dissatisfied with the social stratification that had resulted from the reform's decision to give managers a higher rate of pay if their enterprise did well; in addition, some workers moved to enterprises that paid higher salaries.[43] Although most aspects of the NEM ended in 1972, its effects continued to be felt in positive ways, particularly in the willingness to allow for market production in small-scale agricultural production and housing, cars and tourism for foreign currency. As a result, Hungary had a better food supply and consumer choice than other Eastern bloc countries, aside from Yugoslavia.[44]

The alternative socialist vision of Yugoslavia began to run into trouble in the 1970s. Economic regionalism was not enough as the Yugoslavs confronted the transition to information and service economies that began in the 1970s. This shift began in regions in the West, such as Silicon Valley, rather than in countries as a whole, and so the ability of regions to innovate or adapt to new economic systems was crucial. Communism in the

Soviet Union and Eastern Europe, despite a series of attempts, was not able to transition to new sectors such as transistor technology, telecom, robotics and pharmaceuticals, and also did not develop robust service economies. In Yugoslavia, a consumer society was created in which Yugoslavs did enjoy a much higher standard of living than other communist countries in the 1960s and 1970s. This did much to encourage a sense of being Yugoslav rather than Serb, Croatian, and so on.[45]

Unfortunately, the economic base was not capable of sustaining this in Yugoslavia other than through massive loans, paid off by yet new loans.[46] In 1974, the workers' councils in each factory were further subdivided into Basic Organizations of Associated Labour, which meant in practice that even a trained enterprise manager, who might be more likely to choose investing profits to improve the plant, might be swamped by a multitude of councils demanding different things.[47] In addition, Tito stepped back from the Reform. Liberal Serbs within the party had been calling to deepen the market orientation of the Reform and to create a modern Serbia and end the feeling that Yugoslavia was really a sort of Greater Serbia. Tragically, Tito and others purged the liberals in the Serbian Communist Party, a process that was complete by 1972.[48] This would have deeply negative effects in the future, but the short-term goal was to retain complete communist control over Yugoslavia. In 1979, the economy entered a prolonged period of crisis in Yugoslavia, with a 25 per cent decline in real earnings between that year and 1985, as well as a 1,000 per cent increase in inflation.[49] As the economy unravelled, people began to search for someone to blame.

In Poland, the independent labour union Solidarity showed the transformative power of bottom-up economic regionalism. Through Solidarity, economic regionalism, which reformists had hoped would transform communism, ended up destroying it over time. The lead up to Solidarity began in 1970, when workers in the Lenin shipyard in Gdansk went on strike and at least seventy-five strikers were killed.[50] The region around the Baltic ports, with Gdansk at its head, would be the centre of agitation for a transformation, and then for a replacement, of communist rule over the next two decades. In 1980, the Lenin shipyard in Gdansk again went on strike. The workers refused to consider demanding workers' councils, which they saw as too open to party control. Their demands included the recognition of free trade unions, pay raises, less censorship and the election of factory managers. Inter-factory strike committees helped to coordinate striking factories and became a sort of independent *sovnarkhoz* of the Baltic ports region. In September 1980, a meeting of these committees met in Gdansk and set up a national coordinating committee. It was named Solidarity. At first, the authorities attempted to deny Solidarity's claim to operate nationally by saying it was only a regional organization.[51] Solidarity, although it began in one region, sought to regenerate the nation, bringing in peasants as well as workers and arguing that Poland should become a 'self-managing republic' in which workers would manage the economy. The strength of Solidarity was such that the imposition of martial law in 1980–1981 and the widespread use of force only temporarily ended the crisis.[52] It also further delegitimized the regime.

In 1985, Mikhail Gorbachev came to power in the Soviet Union. He would push through reforms that would lead to the end of Soviet power in Eastern Europe and then the end of the Soviet Union itself. Gorbachev himself was an idealist who believed in the promise of communism and who was of the Khrushchev generation formed by the Thaw and the secret speech denouncing Stalin and his crimes. He was the first general secretary of the post-war generation and no longer felt an unquestioned need to control Eastern Europe in order to contain a possibly resurgent Germany in the future.

Instead, he promised reform that would lead to acceleration in growth and investment. This was particularly necessary, given that the Brezhnev era had been a time of stagnant growth. It is telling that many Russians refer to that era as the time of stagnation (*zastoi*). Gorbachev, in realizing this, sought to revitalize the economy through a restructuring (*perestroika*) of the system. Enterprises were given more authority over how to use their funds, which led, as was the case in Yugoslavia and elsewhere, to spending the money on increased wages rather than on investment in the plant.[53] Increased local control might mean more inefficiencies rather than less. At the same time, the system at the top was unwilling to allow for open discussion about the need for a market and market mechanisms. As a result, Gorbachev set about dismantling the system itself in order to carry out reforms.

One of the main ways that the system was challenged was through the policy of openness (*glasnost*), which originally was seen as a way to point out the flaws and inefficiencies of the system. In time, however, it began to undermine its fundamental legitimacy by seeing a flood of revelations attacking Lenin and Leninism as the basis of the state. In addition, *glasnost* allowed for the expression of nationalist sentiments, particularly in the Baltic republics. In 1988, a law allowing cooperatives did lead to the emergence of small-scale economic activity, but it was not enough to make up for the major decrease in state revenue that had resulted from an anti-alcohol campaign, as levies on vodka had formed one of the state's main sources of income for many years. Gorbachev's structural changes began to chip away at the foundation of the state rather than renovate it.[54]

End game

In 1989, Gorbachev made a fateful decision to no longer support the Soviet Union's satellite states in Eastern Europe. He even refused to use Soviet troops in order to prop up communist regimes when they were on the verge of being overthrown. This was part of a larger project of scaling back on spending (the Soviets had withdrawn from Afghanistan in 1989 as well). By that time, it was clear to the people in the various East European countries that capitalism had outproduced communism. Lacking mechanisms to deal with conflict other than the use of force, the various regimes collapsed rather quickly due to the effects of what at first seemed to be localized conflicts, such as a peace protest in Leipzig or the appeal of a pastor to his congregation to prevent officials from evicting him in Romania. Once large groups of people became involved in protests, official groups decided it would be better for them if the state were no longer communist. Other groups followed, and there was a collapse of communist legitimacy, in a process some have compared to a bank run.⁵⁵ In the case of Romania, the leadership was out of touch with reality, and so there was some bloodshed, while in other states the transition was smoother. If Gorbachev had been willing to use force, the outcome in the end may well have been the same, but the body count would have been higher. In Poland, Solidarity had created a parallel civil society that conceived itself as an alternative to the communist state. Despite their lack of interest in ruling, through a series of events that they themselves had not foreseen, the leaders of Solidarity became the new leaders of an independent Polish state. Poland was different in that there was an organized opposition; in most other East European countries, the opposition was unorganized and thus could not easily participate in the transfer of power. In some cases, former communists rebranded themselves as nationalists and continued to rule. Fundamentally, then, Gorbachev and failed economic policies were the sources of the collapse of communism in Eastern Europe.⁵⁶

In Yugoslavia, the Soviets had little to no influence and, fanned by nationalist political leaders, events unfolded in such a way as to precipitate a bloody war between ethnic communities that shocked the world in the early 1990s. The frustrations that found their outlet were not due to ancient ethnic conflicts, despite the statements of much of Western media, but rather due to the frustrations of a failed program of modernization that had led, by 1989, to an inflation of 2,000 per cent. In addition, unemployment was at 20 per cent and 60 per cent of workers lived in poverty.⁵⁷ Real income had declined by a third since 1979.⁵⁸

The three things that had held Yugoslavia together were Tito himself, the Yugoslav Communist Party and the federal army, but a resurgent Serbia was stronger. Tito died in 1980 and, in 1986, Slobodan Milosevic – the leader of the Serbian Communist Party – along with other institutions at the level of the Serbian republic, began to advocate for a Greater Serbia, which would mean the territorial expansion of Serbia into neighbouring republics and the end of Yugoslavia. Other non-Serb Communist Parties chose multiparty elections and market reforms and sought to contain Milosevic's powers, but the centre would not hold.

In 1989, there was a last attempt at economic reform from the centre that ended the divisions of workers' councils within factories that had hindered earlier reforms and stated that enterprises would have to declare bankruptcy if they could not pay their bills. And yet the whole system was itself bankrupt due to low production and high debt to the West. Price reforms led to extreme inflation. The reforms themselves were destroyed by a literal bank run, as republics could withdraw money from the central bank and did so in the fear that if they did not, there would be nothing left. Serbia finished it off with a withdrawal of 1.5 billion dinar.⁵⁹

The institutions that had held Yugoslavia together were themselves falling apart or turning to other goals. In January 1990, the Yugoslav Communist Party ceased to exist.⁶⁰ More advanced republics, particularly Slovenia, felt that they would be better off as independent states, and they were able to secede in 1991 and the Yugoslav army was not able to force them to return to the Yugoslav fold. Thereafter, the army, as 60 percent of the federal army's officer class was Serbian, shifted to serving the idea of Greater Serbia rather than Yugoslavia.⁶¹ The road to war now lay open.

Economic decentralization had been a feature of Yugoslavia's economy more consistently than in other East European countries, but it did not produce the hoped-for results. Focused particularly at the level of the individual factory or even a part of a factory, it generally led to a narrow self-interest rather than nimble economic decisions. Like other East European countries, Yugoslavia's economy was deeply troubled by the late 1980s and had not been able to make the transition to a service and information economy. When conflicts arose due to differing interests, the system was unable to mediate them, which was a long-range factor in the collapse of Yugoslavia.

Similarly in the Soviet Union, the most advanced republics, the Baltic States, as had Slovenia, led the way to the collapse of the Union itself. On 23 August 1989, about two million people in the three Baltic republics of Estonia, Latvia and Lithuania formed a 350-mile human chain to mark the fiftieth anniversary of the Nazi-Soviet Pact. This had led to the end of those countries' independent status and to their forcible incorporation into the USSR. In 1990, the countries each declared independence, which set off another metaphorical bank run.[62] Boris Yeltsin, the head of the Russian Soviet Federative Socialist Republic, itself a federation and the largest unit within the Soviet Union, joined the push towards independence. Gorbachev was willing to allow this. In 1989, Siberian miners struck for a sovereign Siberia, but Yeltsin was unwilling to allow further breakup of what soon became the Russian Federation.[63] On 31 December 1991, the Soviet Union ceased to exist.

Conclusion

In conclusion, attempts to reform communism by increasing powers to regions and factories were been stymied by a lack of conflict-resolution mechanisms. In time, the resulting economic weakness intensified conflict, which by 1989 and 1991 led to the collapse of the system rather than its reform. Economic regionalism, lacking a political means by which to mediate conflict it generated, was a source of weakness rather than strength in the Soviet sphere. Rather than leading the way to a radiant future, Soviet-style communism was a cul-de-sac that ultimately led a weakened Eastern Europe back to capitalism.

Notes

1. David Rainbow, 'Siberian Patriots: Participatory Autocracy and the Cohesion of the Russian Imperial State, 1858–1920' (Ph.D. dissertation, New York University, 2013), 57–60.
2. M. Shilovskii, *Sibirskoe oblastnichestvo v obshchestvenno-politicheskoi zhizni regiona* (Novosibirsk: 'Sova', 2008), 64.
3. Yanni Kotsonis, 'Arkhangel'sk, 1918: Regionalism and Populism in the Russian Civil War', *The Russian Review* 51, no. 4 (1992): 526–44; N. G. O. Pereira, *White Siberia: The Politics of Civil War* (Montreal: McGill-Queen's University Press, 1996); and Jonathan D. Smele,

Civil War in Siberia: The Anti-Bolshevik Government of Admiral Kolchak, 1918-1920 (Cambridge: Cambridge University Press, 1996).

4. Liudmila G. Novikova, 'A Province of a Non-Existent State: White Government in the Russian North and Political Power in the Russian Civil War, 1918–1920', *Revolutionary Russia* 18, no. 2 (2005): 134.

5. Terry Martin, *The Affirmative Action Empire: Nations and Nationalism in the Soviet Union* (Ithaca, NY: Cornell University Press, 2003).

6. Anatol Lieven, *The Baltic Revolution: Estonia, Latvia, Lithuania and the Path to Independence* (New Haven: Yale University Press, 1993).

7. A. I. Todorskii, *God s vintovkoi i plugom* (Ves'egonsk, Tver province, 1918); and Vladimir I. Lenin, 'Malen'kaia kartinka dlia vyiasneniia bol'shchikh voprosov', in *Polnoe sobranie sochinenii*, vol. 37 (Moscow: Gos. izd-vo polit. lit-ry, 1969), 407–11.

8. Emily D. Johnson, *How St. Petersburg Learned to Study Itself: The Russian Idea of* Kraevedenie (University Park, PA: Penn State University Press, 2006).

9. Susan Smith-Peter, 'How to Write a Region: Local and Regional Historiography', *Kritika: Explorations in Russian and Eurasian History* 5, no. 3 (2004): 527–42.

10. Loren R. Graham, *The Soviet Academy of Sciences and the Communist Party, 1927–1932* (Princeton, NJ: Princeton University Press, 1967).

11. 'Novyi etap v kraevedenii', *Sovetskoe kraevedenie*, 1–2 (1930): 22–24; and N. Rubinshtein, 'Bor'ba s klassovym vragom v kraevedcheskoi literatury i zadachi istorikov-marksistov', in *Protiv vreditel'stva v kraevedcheskoi literature*, ed. N. Rubinshtein and M. Zelenskii (Ivanovo-Voznesensk: n.p., 1931), 4–8.

12. David Brandenberger, *Propaganda State in Crisis: Soviet Ideology, Indoctrination, and Terror Under Stalin, 1927–1941* (New Haven: Yale University Press, 2011), 79; Nikolai Paialin, 'Istoriia Fabrik i Zavod,' *Rabsel'kor* 23–24 (1928): 24–25; and Nikolai Paialin, *Zavod imeni Lenina* (Moscow: Gos. sotsal'no-ekonomicheskoe izd-vo, 1933).

13. Alec Nove, *An Economic History of the USSR, 1917–1991* (London: Penguin, 1992), 45.

14. Nove, *Economic History*, 352.

15. R. J. Crampton, *Eastern Europe in the Twentieth Century – and After* (London: Routledge, 1997), 258.

16. John Lampe, *Yugoslavia as History: Twice There Was a Country* (Cambridge: Cambridge University Press, 1996), 243.

17. Crampton, *Eastern Europe*, 259.

18. Lampe, *Yugoslavia*, 250.

19. Crampton, *Eastern Europe*, 276.

20. Lampe, *Yugoslavia*, 252.

21. Crampton, *Eastern Europe*, 286–87.

22. Crampton, *Eastern Europe*, 297.

23. Nigel Swain, *Hungary: The Rise and Fall of Feasible Socialism* (London: Verso, 1992), 87.

24. Quoted in Crampton, *Eastern Europe*, 298.

25. Crampton, *Eastern Europe*, 300.

26. Nove, *Economic History*, 353.

27. Nove, *Economic History*, 368, 378.

28. Kathleen Parthé, *Russian Village Prose: The Radiant Past* (Princeton, NJ: Princeton University Press, 1992).
29. Nove, *Economic History*, 382–84.
30. Lampe, *Yugoslavia*, 276.
31. Lampe, *Yugoslavia*, 273–76.
32. Crampton, *Eastern Europe*, 310.
33. Crampton, *Eastern Europe*, 308.
34. Crampton, *Eastern Europe*, 309.
35. Lampe, *Yugoslavia*, 283.
36. Lampe, *Yugoslavia*, 279.
37. Crampton, *Eastern Europe*, 332.
38. Crampton, *Eastern Europe*, 331.
39. Crampton, *Eastern Europe*, 337.
40. Swain, *Hungary*, 99–100.
41. Swain, *Hungary*, 102.
42. Swain, *Hungary*, 108.
43. Mark Pittaway, *Eastern Europe 1939-2000* (London: Arnold, 2004), 77; and Swain, *Hungary*, 118.
44. Swain, *Hungary*, 108–9.
45. Patrick Hyder Patterson, *Bought and Sold: Living and Losing the Good Life in Socialist Yugoslavia* (Ithaca, NY: Cornell University Press, 2011).
46. Lampe, *Yugoslavia*, 293.
47. Lampe, *Yugoslavia*, 310.
48. Lampe, *Yugoslavia*, 303–4.
49. Lampe, *Yugoslavia*, 293.
50. Crampton, *Eastern Europe*, 359.
51. Crampton, *Eastern Europe*, 367–69.
52. Pittaway, *Eastern Europe*, 175–76.
53. Nove, *Economic History*, 405.
54. Nove, *Economic History*, 394–419.
55. Stephen Kotkin and Jan Gross, *Uncivil Society: 1989 and the Implosion of the Communist Establishment* (New York: Random House, 2009), *passim*.
56. Kotkin and Gross, *Uncivil Society*.
57. Ivan T. Berend, *Central and Eastern Europe, 1944-1993: Detour from the Periphery to the Periphery* (Cambridge: Cambridge University Press, 1996), 293.
58. Lampe, *Yugoslavia*, 326.
59. Lampe, *Yugoslavia*, 349.
60. Berend, *Central and Eastern*, 295–97; and Lampe, *Yugoslavia*, 337.
61. Berend, *Central and Eastern*, 298.
62. Kotkin and Gross, *Uncivil Society*, 135–36.
63. Kotkin and Gross, *Uncivil Society*, 141.

Further reading

Berend, Ivan T., *Central and Eastern Europe, 1944–1993: Detour from the Periphery to the Periphery* (Cambridge: Cambridge University Press, 1996).
Crampton, R. J., *Eastern Europe in the Twentieth Century – and After* (London: Routledge, 1997).
Kotkin, Stephen, and Jan Gross, *Uncivil Society: 1989 and the Implosion of the Communist Establishment* (New York: Random House, 2009).
Lampe, John, *Yugoslavia as History: Twice There Was a Country* (Cambridge: Cambridge University Press, 1996).
Nove, Alec, *An Economic History of the USSR, 1917–1991* (London: Penguin, 1992).
Palairet, Michael R., *The Balkan Economies c. 1800–1914: Evolution without Development* (Cambridge: Cambridge University Press, 1997).
Patterson, Patrick Hyder, *Bought and Sold: Living and Losing the Good Life in Socialist Yugoslavia* (Ithaca, NY: Cornell University Press, 2011).
Pittaway, Mark, *Eastern Europe 1939–2000* (London: Arnold, 2004).
Swain, Nigel, *Hungary: The Rise and Fall of Feasible Socialism* (London: Verso, 1992).

CHAPTER 9
DEMOCRACY AND REGIONALISM IN WESTERN EUROPE
Daniele Petrosino

Introduction

Europe today is a scene of contradictory political tensions. New or revitalized expressions of state nationalism claim the closure of borders to migrants and the restoration of national privileges. Additionally, substate nationalisms in Scotland and Catalonia, for example, are challenging the legitimacy of the existing states while defending the common European space and its institutions. In these scenarios, the main players are the states, which have lost some of their sovereignty; the regions, which have increasingly gained prominence; and the European Union, the representational nature of which is increasingly disputed.

Within this framework, regions have acquired greater prominence as a basic level of government and representation. However, regionally defined territories are not merely administrative units; in many countries, they also indicate some form of cultural identification. *Regionalism* thus refers to the processes involved in the construction of collective identities and the formulation of political demands focused on this territorial dimension. The similar concept of *regionalization* denotes the territorial decentralization of administrative functions, or even the creation of federated political units, in an institutional process implemented by states to accommodate national, cultural or simply territorial differences. Although regionalization and regionalism indicate two different phenomena, one feeds the other. Regionalization is also a formidable democratizing tool that has generated participation and pluralism even under communist regimes. Even so, it only fully realizes its participatory potential in democratic countries, at least as long as it comes into conflict with the states themselves.

This was not always the case. In most European countries, the regional dimension has been present since the nineteenth century, or even before. However, only in the second half of the twentieth century, regionalism became a crucial political-institutional current and a pillar of European democracies, serving as a conduit for political participation, cultural identification and business interests.

The versatility of the concept of region calls for analytical articulation to help us to unravel its complex story. We use the term to indicate substate territorial units and/or a subnational cultural identity. These units are located at a higher level than the local sphere and effectively fall into the group of imagined communities which Benedict Anderson spoke about. As such, their identity, institutions, political contours and dimensions must be constructed. In West European democracies, this multifaceted and complex process has both helped and hindered the building of nation states, sometimes even within the same state at the same time.

The creation and revitalization of cultural identities related to territories, which are not always identifiable with institutionally defined regions, was an important factor in the rooting of national identities themselves. Such territorial identities could be considered as components of nation state identities, because the relations between state and regions were regarded as concentric and their identities were perceived to have continuity. But regions have also been – and are – spaces where antagonistic, or at least competitive, demands against the nation state might manifest themselves.

The dialectic regarding territorial spaces are a fundamental dynamic of the political process. Its interpretation by historians and social scientists is closely related to the reference system in which it is situated. Within a framework defined by the nation state, which understood the nation state as the teleological end of the political process, the regional perspective has been considered either in exclusively functional terms – as an administrative subunit – or in antagonistic terms, as being opposed to the state-building process. Changes in academic perspectives have denatured the form of the nation state in recent decades, allowing us to see the subnational level as a reference space in a game of relationships. There, the forms of subordination and/or coordination between political units are established through negotiation and/or conflict among the actors.[1]

We can observe four phases in the development of regionalism. The first spanned from the mid-nineteenth century to the Second World War, the second from 1945 to the late 1960s, the third from the 1970s to the late 1990s and the fourth began with the twenty-first century. In the first phase, regionalism appeared as a prevalent cultural expression, which matured within nation states and sometimes became part of their structure, but with little political and institutional presence. The second phase, that of post-war reconstruction, features a relative absence (with some exceptions) of regionalist demands, accommodation of border issues and attempts to resolve territorial inequalities. The third phase is known as one of ethnonational revival, in which regionalist expressions assumed a predominantly antagonistic identity and character. At this point, regions emerge as central political, institutional and economic actors on the European stage. Finally, in the fourth phase we see the institutional consolidation of regions and the progressive disempowerment of European nation states, along with the repercussions of these dynamics. Each phase is articulated differently in the various West European countries but has experienced convergence in recent decades, thanks to the impetus given to regionalization by the European Union.

As we said earlier, regionalization involves an institutional framework that does not necessarily occur within democratic systems. However, regionalization does introduce an element of participation and representation that promotes democratic processes to the degree that it increases possibilities of mobilization, as it did in former socialist countries. Naturally, regionalization can have multiple expressions, but here we will give priority to its political manifestation, which is most prevalent in democratic systems. Accordingly, this chapter focuses on countries where regionalism is relevant as an important political and institutional process. We will not address European democratic states where regionalism is a minor issue – such as the Scandinavian countries, Greece or Portugal – and which are analysed in other chapters of this book.

Regionalism and substate identity before the Second World War

The presence of substate identities and how they were acknowledged played an important, though sometimes misunderstood, role in the rise of the great West European democracies.[2] In the first phase mentioned above, regional substate claims accompanied the debate on the institutional contours of the nation state from the very beginning. For the most part, regionalism was expressed early on in predominantly cultural terms and had little impact on the territorial organization of the state. In some cases, however, it represented a form of opposition to the typical centralization processes of nation-state building. This resistance was evident in the deliberations on state formation, which in several countries led to a dialectic between the choice for a federal model (decentralized state-building) or a strictly centralist one.

In some countries, reference to substate forms of identity accompanied national-identity-building processes and reinforced them with a sense of heritage. In the late nineteenth and early twentieth centuries especially, cultural regionalism acquired greater importance in most areas as new nation states attempted to encourage loyalty by promoting territorial identity ties. Though forms of political regionalism sporadically appeared, particularly in areas where rising (sub)national identities were present,[3] identification with the region usually did not substitute the loyalty to the nation state and did not compete with it. People could identify with both the region and the nation and regionalist culture was not necessarily backward looking; in many instances, it was surprisingly modern.

In post-revolutionary France, regionalism was considered an expression of resistance related to the privileges of the Ancien Régime and opposed to Jacobin centralism. Brittany provides an example of this with the conservative and elitist Union Régionaliste Bretonne, founded in 1898. However, it also became part of democratic discourse and expressed the demands of peripheral territories such as Provence. Federalist movements, such as Jean Charles-Brun's Fédération Régionaliste Française (founded in 1900), also contributed to the political debate of that time. Nonetheless, regionalism remained predominately a cultural expression – as it was typified in the Félibre movement at the end of the nineteenth century[4] – at least until the end of the First World War. In the broadly nationalist interwar climate, regionalism acquired some political importance and enjoyed limited electoral success, especially in Alsace.[5]

In the United Kingdom, subterritorialism was primarily expressed in subnational terms, but it did not constitute an alternative to the unitary state (except in Ireland, which can hardly be regarded as a 'region' of the United Kingdom). Anti-national regionalism was very weak and the plurality of British identity encompassed those of the nations belonging to it. Germany confronted territorial fragmentation by constructing a state identity rooted in local identities and by promoting the appreciation of traditions and heritage, as expressed in the concept of *Heimat*. In Spain, the first tensions emerged between Castilian centralism and other historic parts of the kingdom, which pushed for more decentralized solutions. The First Republic of 1873–1874 and the Second Republic of 1931–1939 proposed organizing the Spanish state in a heavily regionalized manner, but those initiatives failed and a clearly centralized monarchic state was favoured. However, political centralism left room for acknowledging local or regional roots, especially where there was folkloric interest, which promoted multiple identities among Spaniards.[6]

In Italy, we find the federalist sentiment that animated the Italian Risorgimento, expressed by intellectuals and politicians such as Carlo Cattaneo or Giuseppe Ferrari, alongside subregional upheavals that remained nonetheless within the orbit of the Italian state. In the period immediately following the First World War, the Sardinian movement became the mouthpiece of a territorial reality of the Italian state and also became a component of a search for mediation and connection with the nascent Fascist regime.[7] During this phase, forms of regional identification were generally elements of the nation-state identity-building process, which was seen as superordinate to the regional one. Region-building involved rooting national identity in local or regional cultural traditions that were much closer to the people. However, in some cases where regional identification had strong institutional and cultural markers – such as Sardinia, Scotland, Catalonia or the Basque Country – subnational questions emerged. The inherent ambivalence of the process is particularly evident in the interwar period, when some states experienced an accentuation of local identity roots and forced the nationalization of subnational minorities. The Italian state, for example, behaved differently with respect to its internal territories and borderlands such as South Tyrol.

Regionalism after the Second World War

After the end of the Second World War, institutional transformations and the consolidation of democratic political systems were affected by a twofold dynamic in which regionalism would not express its full potential until many years later.

First, the nation states of Europe had to face reconstruction and the challenge of overcoming differences among people within their borders. Cultural and linguistic differences had not completely disappeared, despite the nationalization efforts of previous decades. They persisted especially – but not exclusively – in border areas where situations remained unresolved. States also had deep economic and development imbalances that did not always coincide with cultural differences. Thus, state-building processes had to address both identity and socio-economic development issues.[8] Second, at that time the great non-communist states of continental Europe began a unification process. The first attempts at building a new political entity began in the 1950s with the existing states in Europe (West Germany, France, Benelux and Italy founded the ECSC in 1951 and the EEC in 1957) and culminated in the Schengen agreement for the abolition of borders (1985), the establishment of the European Union (1992) and the creation of a single market with a single currency (launched virtually in 1999 and physically in 2002).

These two initially separate processes tended towards convergence in subsequent years, as states advanced towards a different organization of powers, both downwards (regionalization) and upwards (supra-nationalization). During the European unification process, old tensions related to the formation of nation states re-emerged and new tensions surfaced. Immediately after the Second World War, the push towards regionalization was primarily fuelled by past conflicts. In the following decades, social, economic and political transformations created a centrifugal push that gave new life and strength to regionalization as a road to more responsive forms of governance.

At the centre of this process were the nation states of Europe and changes in their internal structure. Progressively, forms of democratic accommodation to territorial differences were introduced, governance underwent scalar and functional transformation and the democratic institutions of nation states were weakened in favour of supranational decision-making, which, however, offered no real possibilities of democratic control. The deeper European unification becomes, the greater the resistance in the form of a populist return to state nationalism.

The European states had to mend the socio-economic and political fabric that had been devastated by years of dictatorships and the Second World War. The three major issues to deal with were democratic reconstruction, economic reconstruction and the consolidation of geopolitical relations. In most states, minorities were basically pushed to the background as centralist vision and organization took hold, which corresponded to the emergence of the interventionist state. However, European states derive from the unification of peoples with diverse histories and cultures, along with territories of unequal characteristics and conditions. Such differences have not been completely overcome, despite efforts at nationalization and cultural homogenization.[9] They show up as subnational minorities within states or resulting from the definition of their boundaries, or in the tensions between profoundly heterogeneous territorial areas where the inhabitants have not developed their own conscious identity. In fact, issues concerning the relations among states remained unresolved until the end of Second World War and were difficult to accommodate. After long and arduous negotiation for the pacification of Europe, the peace agreements among states defined borders and acknowledged the rights of linguistic minorities, who should be assured of protection.

Meanwhile, all states faced territorial development imbalances, and solutions to the questions emerging from these divisions seem to fall along two temporally misaligned axes. The first involved activation of territorial development and social inclusion processes and the second concerned recognition of territorial peculiarities through political decentralization and/or administrative action. This was a top-down process in which the central governments defined the forms and limits of decentralization and determined territorial boundaries. In the years immediately following the Second World War, a strong need for reconstruction prevailed, which found its core in the states. Territorial decentralization responded primarily to the need to deal adequately with geopolitical pressures. Subterritorial arrangements in Europe presented profound differences due to the different institutional configurations of the states and the positions of some subnationalist movements during the war.[10] In many European countries, institutional systems did not begin moving towards recognizing some form of intermediate territorial government between the state and local levels until the late 1960s. The process of recognizing regional differences was most accentuated in Italy and Germany.

The 1947 Constitution of the Italian Republic provided a decentralized institutional structure that recognized regional territorial entities.[11] This regarded five special regions (*regioni autonome*) with distinct privileges: Aosta Valley, Trentino-Alto Adige, Sardinia, Sicily and Friuli Venezia Giulia.[12] The first four special regions were created in response to geopolitical configuration requirements and internal political tensions. Where pressures related to linguistic minorities and nationalist or independence movements had appeared, governing these border situations required flexible institutional instruments. In contrast, the Italian state intervened directly to resolve the country's main north–south territorial division. The other regions remained on paper until the 1970s, when the true season of Italian regionalism began.

Italy's regionalist bid also became an institutional model for other countries (i.e. Spain after 1975). It sought to dilute issues related to self-government in an institutional configuration that multiplied the actors by granting some institutional power to territorial entities (regions), regardless of their cultural or political claims. In this way, recognition of the rights of linguistic or subnational minorities was separated from recognition of forms of self-government. For a while at least, the political plan succeeded and centrifugal tensions diminished in most peripheral regions. Only in South Tyrol (the German-speaking part of the Trentino-Alto Adige region) did separatist forces continue to manifest themselves, at times even violently.[13]

In Germany, the complex history of the German state oriented it towards a federal structure that did not involve national minorities or self-government demands. With the split of East and West Germany immediately following the Second World War, the German institutional system was primarily motivated by the need to create counterweights in order to advance, which resulted in the Federal Republic of Germany in 1949. In contrast with the Italian scenario, the *Länder* were government entities encompassing regional identities that were not antagonistic to German identity.[14]

In the other European countries, a form of centralized government prevailed at the state level. Cultural and political imagination focused mainly on strengthening the national identity, even when national minorities were present. In France, the institutional model remained highly centralized, though regionalist groups assumed mainly cultural characteristics (such as the movements in territories where Occitan or *langue d'oc* is somewhat spoken). Nationalist forces lost much of their legitimacy before and during the Second World War, mainly because some substate-based movements supported the Nazis (such as in Brittany and Alsace). In the 1960s, regionalism began to acquire more politicized features in a new wave of social mobilization.[15] Regions were officially created in 1982 with the Law of Decentralization, but for the most part they function as merely administrative units. In Belgium, the Brussels region gained great importance during the post-war period, alongside the historical division between the Walloon and Flemish parts of the country. This sharp, persistent fracture did not translate into strong territorial decentralization until the first important state reform in 1970, partly because the Flemish movement had lost legitimacy due to its links with the German occupiers.[16] In the United Kingdom, with its long tradition of territorial autonomy, decentralizing pressures diminished in the post-war period.[17] The British system recognized the particular autonomy of Scotland, but territorial decentralization issues experienced a setback until the 1970s due to the weakness of the regional players and the ability of the Conservatives and Labour to win electoral victories. Subnational questions have since revived, primarily involving Scotland and Wales (which cannot, however, be considered simply regions, for they are component nations of the United Kingdom), and the Parliament of Scotland was re-established in 1998 with the Scotland Act.

Such diversity of institutional solutions corresponds to the cultures and political traditions in each country as well as the need to find solutions that accommodate multiple claims and unresolved border issues. The pacification of Europe involved the recognition of borders and linguistic minorities, who were granted some form of protection in the peace agreements. During the two decades immediately following the Second World War, therefore, a unitary vision of states prevailed in the general European framework. At the same time, post-war democracies were seeking to accommodate territorial tensions in ways that would reduce potentially disintegrative forces and overcome the armed conflicts that were still present.

Regionalism, regionalization and ethnonational revival

With the 1970s came the prodigious growth of movements that demanded cultural and political recognition of their national diversity and increased territorial powers, ranging from greater autonomy to sovereignty.[18] Without a doubt, the attention they received helped promote change in state institutions, and many European states gradually began implementing decentralizing institutional reforms or making territorial decentralization effective. Almost everywhere, this took the form of regionalization, which sometimes overlapped with subnationalism but usually constituted its antithesis.

Regionalization was the answer of central governments to territorial differences: it met the functional requirements of governance and the need to find levels of government that were closest to the distinct territorial environments. Of course, this process occurred for many reasons: multiplication of governmental levels created more posts in representative systems, the increasing complexity of governments pushed towards functional differentiation and the crisis of legitimacy of western democracies generated a new search for citizen proximity in representation. At the same time, creating administratively defined territories diluted rising or potential subnational claims within the broader spectrum of institutional representation. The Spanish case clearly illustrates this trend. Strong demand for self-government by the Catalan and the Basque movements after the transition to democracy in the late 1970s led the Spanish government to find an institutional design that would ensure a degree of autonomy for all substate entities.

This resulted in the Autonomous Communities that were established in the Constitution of 1978.

All West European countries, including the most centralized, experienced forms of territorial decentralization. A weak decentralization process even began in France, through which Corsica obtained in 1982 greater powers than the other regions of France. The new political-administrative units did not always have historical and cultural roots but did meet the need for territorial governance. Whether it met subnational demands or simply promoted regional levels of government, regionalization provided the institutional framework in which territorial political demands could be voiced. At times, this was accompanied by cultural markers or established identity-building processes; at others, it created opportunities to construct new territorial identities. The latter occurred in Italy with the invention of Padania, which established an institutional framework and the possibility for new political actors to take root in a territorial constituency.

There are conflicting hypotheses regarding the origins of this process: Did political demand produce subnational forms of regional decentralization, or did regional decentralization trigger subnational political demands? No single answer is possible since the two processes feed each other. In any case, the formation of substate political and institutional systems has opened a space for political actors at the substate level. It has allowed existing actors to continue or increase their presence and offered a chance for others to present themselves on the political scene. Consequently, regional parties and movements that operate within this territorial dimension have become increasingly relevant in the dynamics of regionalization and how it is transformed into a regionalist or substate claim.

Political pluralism is a unique characteristic of democratic regimes, and regionalization increases pluralism. It augments representation, as levels of governmental hierarchy proliferate, and complexity, as interests become established along territorial cleavage lines. Thus, the formation and articulation of regional political systems are very important elements in the forms that regionalism has taken in West European democracies. The characteristics of political representation decisively affect the transformation of state systems.[19] Particularly, the weight of parties with a heavily territorial electoral basis at the regional or state level is key to enhancing regionalist representation claims. We can identify situations in which no specific regional political system exists, but territorial representation is ensured by state parties without any regional specificity; in other situations, exclusively territorial parties are also present; and in still others, there are parties providing territorial representation and state parties that may have specific territorial branches.

A substate political system improves when all parties (including the statewide parties) organize themselves on a territorial basis (e.g. by transforming state parties into distinct regional parties, such as the Bavarian Christian Social Union (CSU) in Germany). Regional parties may have a minor presence on both the regional and state levels, a majority presence on the regional level but a minority presence on the state level, a majority presence on the regional level with power of determination on the state level or a majority presence on both the territorial and state levels. When analysing the various cases, regional political parties that represent a specific minority emerge as a powerful factor that can increase the possibility of institutional reform, especially those that can influence the state government because their support is indispensable.

Until the 1980s in Italy, ethnoterritorial parties were present in three regions: Sardinia, the Aosta Valley and Trentino-Alto Adige. In the first, the Sardinian Action Party (Partito Sardo d'Azione) has always been a minority party (just like other movements in the nationalist milieu), even in periods of greatest nationalist agitation, and regionalist demand is mainly expressed through state parties. Conversely, in South Tyrol (Alto Adige) and the Aosta Valley, ethnoterritorial parties represent the majority at the territorial level but have little power to influence national politics due to the small size of their regions and their electorates. However, they can negotiate specific measures for their regions and usually support the governmental majorities in parliament. In Sicily, at least until quite recently, potentially decentralizing forces have been completely absorbed by the state parties or their regional expressions. However, the most striking case of ethnoterritorialism in recent decades, the Lega Nord, exhibits surprisingly different dynamics. This party started as a federation of regional groups and quickly gained followers in all the northern regions. The Lega Nord has established itself as the majority party in some of them and participates as a major partner in coalition governments. From this position, it has succeeded in catalysing profound institutional changes.

In the United Kingdom, aside from the case of Northern Ireland, different dynamics operate in the two main territories where the ethnoterritorial question is present: Wales and Scotland. In Wales, Plaid Cymru has not succeeded in scoring electoral victories, nor does it have any weight within the national framework. In Scotland, the Scottish National Party (SNP) has increased its electoral base since the 1970s to become a majority party and a contender alongside state parties in the national elections. This has given the SNP quite a decisive role, even on the level of state policies.

In Spain, the great nationalist formations in Catalonia and the Basque Country were ideologically centrist (liberal and Christian-democratic). This allowed them to gain and maintain a large following as well as leadership in regional government. However, they did not always exert decisive influence on the central government, since the state-wide parties held the majority at the state level and were also present in all regions of Spain, while substate nationalist parties are also relevant in Galicia and the Canary Islands. Nationalist formations have strong bargaining power in regional political choices, especially when their votes are needed to sustain the political majority in government. Despite this influence, territorial parties do not seem to have sufficient weight to negotiate with Madrid about recognition of the right to vote on the desired level of self-government, as occurred with Scotland in the United Kingdom. Even the constitutional break produced by the Catalan Independence Referendum (October 2017) revealed the weak bargaining power of nationalist parties in dealing with the Madrid government.

In France, on the other hand, the only notable territorial expression of regionalism occurred in Corsica. Aside from its internal difficulties, the Corsican movement was an isolated force incapable of negotiating significant institutional changes until the twenty-first century, when it gained great electoral support. In Germany, the configuration of regionalism and regional political systems is linked to the form of federalism and the special role of the Bavarian CSU within the Christian Democratic Union (CDU). The CSU has influenced the general political decision-making process in West Germany but did not push for institutional reforms.[20] Since the reunification of Germany in 1990, the ponderous differences between East and West Germany have produced some changes in regional policy. Belgium represents perhaps the most interesting case.[21] The state federalization process largely resulted in the formation of regional political systems, with no party able to maintain representation across all regions. In the absence of a true territorial centre – as Brussels constitutes a region in itself but holds a minority position with respect to Flanders and Wallonia – survival of the state depends on finding ways to accommodate parties representing different linguistic groups and ideological orientations.

In most cases, ethnoregionalist/nationalist parties with majority positions were centrist parties, oriented not towards radicalization of conflicts but towards a gradual reformist approach aimed at diminishing the power of the central state in favour of regional self-government. The most radical parties have remained in a minority position.[22] The first outcomes for West European democratic states have been, in fact, to reduce and resolve armed conflicts and to avoid violent escalation of old and new territorial/subnational claims.

The new regionalism

Michael Keating identifies the late 1980s and 1990s as the time when new regionalism emerged.[23] It gained strength thanks to profound changes that affected the world and specifically Western Europe since the 1980s. Support for a neo-liberal model, which has generally been accepted even by the political left, and the emergence of supranational decision-making bodies serve as framework elements for new regionalism. Two crucial and complementary components of this are regional centrality in development and territorial economic competition and the advent of an institutional framework that favours the regionalization of political claims.

A superficial glance shows that regional parties became stronger and more able to exert significant pressure primarily in more developed areas or those with reasonable hopes of greater welfare and where the parties might control the resources of their territories. Transformations in regionalism and the re-emergence and strengthening of subnationalism must be placed in a broader framework of profound global change since the 1970s. Catalonia, the Basque Country, Flanders, northern Italy and Bavaria are certainly not poor regions, but the idea of their being 'exploited' by the poorer regions through state redistribution mechanisms has gradually gained consensus within them. This idea manifests itself within a framework of more liberal views on social relations and growing competition among territories. The combination of localism/territorialism and interregional competition makes the territory central to the political imagination and organization of interests. There are no longer individual entrepreneurs or classes but country, city or territorial systems all competing in a broader and more complex framework where the actors try to find room for a certain degree of sovereignty to strengthen their position.[24]

Beyond the great ideological differences, new state nationalisms and subnationalisms claim a territorial privilege whereby 'political' control of the territory becomes the instrument for ensuring the protection of the citizens who reside there and/or freeing themselves from ties to more backward regions that hinder their full development. As regional systems gain importance, they push towards accentuating claims to autonomy. At the same time, increasing pressure upon the middle classes and the impoverishment of the lower classes makes the territory a privileged place for defending their own interests. Confronted with the displacement of decision-making to remote locations (supranational organizations or multinational corporations) not subject to forms of democratic verification, territorial claims seek to bring decisions relevant to the well-being of individuals within a territorial framework of proximity, or at least to use the territory to ensure control of resources (economic, political, legal, etc.). A significant link exists between the promotion of a territory and the definition of collective identities. As the territorial system becomes a major element in economic competition, there are increased efforts to construct collective identities that help define the territorial brand.

A second important factor regarding the leading role of regionalism at the end of the twentieth century was its institutional and symbolic framework. If the regionalist movements, with their demand for autonomy, have boosted decentralization processes in the various European countries, the promotion of regional policies by the European Community and the European Union significantly accelerated this process and its strong symbolic legitimacy.[25] European regional policy began with the Single European Act of 1986, and the regions got on track to become major recognized actors in the European political community. They played a role in economic integration policies and became increasingly important actors in democratic participation and cultural pluralism.

Though territorial government has been a topic in the European debate since immediately after the Second World War, only with the 1992 Maastricht Treaty did the regions become key players in European Union policymaking. The establishment of the Committee of the Regions permanently institutionalized them as a third actor (alongside state governments and the European Commission) regarding European policies. Of course, the importance of the regions in the governance system should not be overestimated, because the European Union is made up of nation states.[26] However, in post-war Europe, the process of building an economically and politically unified Europe ran parallel to the institutional restructuring of the continental states. Since the 1970s, the states of the European Union have been in a rescaling process.[27] Areas of competence have progressively been subtracted from the nation states and added to the European institutions or devolved to substate institutions.[28]

It is also true, however, that the states maintain a central role; the powers devolved to the regions are relatively limited and vary considerably among the states. Anyway, increased assignation of power and decision-making capacity, as well as resources, to regional governments converted regional institutions into a significant level of government, giving them greater political leadership and a more central role in economic processes. The European framework has been a key to this process; it has provided room for the expression of political claims with a subterritorial foundation while engendering a regional political elite that is fairly autonomous with respect to the nation state. Though regionalist pressures are relatively independent of, and in some cases antagonistic to subnational protests, the regionalist push is generally stronger where subnational claims are present.

This regionalization process did not lead to the 'Europe of nations' desired by subnationalist movements, but it has produced and legitimized accentuated forms of decentralized power. It has also created a supranational framework for finding answers to some of the questions put to the subnationalists.[29] Alongside the leading issue of resource governance, European Union policies have also played a decisive role in legitimizing identity questions. Minority rights constitute a key subnational claim that is receiving increasing attention in the European Union, which exerts pressure on the states to recognize and ensure these rights.[30]

Recognition of cultural differences and redefined governance levels have created friction in and among many states. However, since states constitute the European Union, subnational claims cannot be fully recognized at the European level. The European Union is founded on states and not 'nations', peoples or regions. Thus, the European unification process has served as a powerful affirmation instrument for subnationalisms but also as a definitive barrier to their claims for statehood.

As the democratic process generated regionalization and the institutionalization of forms of regionalism in the old European Union countries, entry into the Union is itself a step in the transition to democracy for East European countries. The first of these was admitted to the European Union in 2004, after a lengthy application process. Once an application was accepted, the candidate states had to meet a compliance process involving institutional, economic and political requirements known as the Copenhagen criteria. These included institutional decentralization and respect for minority rights as two essential conditions. The eastward enlargement of the European Union had a twofold effect: it significantly modified the territorial balance among European regions while producing institutional transformation towards regionalization in the new member states. Introducing forms of regional decentralization aided their transition to democracy and European Union accession.

This process of regionalization, however, is grafted into different cultures, political traditions, ethnonational tensions and existing conflicts.[31] Communist political traditions, while acknowledging a certain type of national pluralism within the various states, forced regionalization into democratic centralism and highly centralized state organizations. Pressure from the European Union has mainly produced a functional reorganization with limited decentralization of powers. Regionalization to date has only produced mature regionalism in places where regional differences were already quite pronounced, such as Poland.[32] Even so, the push from above by the European Union has revitalized subnational claims. The tendency to associate regionalism with an ethnic identity dimension recalled a complex history of ethnic tensions, forced assimilation and population transfers in the not-so-distant past. This has made regionalization in Eastern Europe more difficult.[33]

Decentralization produces a dynamic of progressive negotiations regarding rights to self-government.[34] Radicalization of the sovereignty issue even among hitherto moderate political actors (as in the case of Catalonia and Scotland), attribution of competences to regions on the European level, the different geopolitical positions of the states (and overlapping blocs) and the availability of resources for self-government push the corresponding claims towards secession. Although subnationalist parties often emphasize the differences between their claims and those of a generic regionalism, the growing trend towards decentralization has also benefitted subnational movements by creating more favourable conditions for the devolution of power. In West European states, expressions of decentralization range from federalism or greater empowerment of subterritorial entities to secessionist claims.

The Italian case is emblematic. There, regional decentralization was initially applied only to special regions, which allowed for at least provisional resolution of outstanding issues. In the 1970s, implementation of a regionalist model began to weaken the central state and favoured a push towards increased decentralization, which has since taken entirely unexpected directions in the regions. In fact, Lombardy and Veneto convened an advisory referendum on 22 October 2017 regarding whether to demand a status similar to that of the special regions.

During its transition to democracy, Spain found inspiration in the Italian regionalist model. The institutional formula of giving autonomy to all regions attenuated the devolution of power to Catalonia and the Basque Country but ensured that those two regions and other *nationalities* such as Galicia had a framework that enabled political mobilization and even claims for self-determination. In the United Kingdom, devolution strengthened appeals for self-determination in Scotland and a similar impulse in Wales and Northern Ireland. Meanwhile, the Belgian federal structure facilitated the relegitimization of Flemish nationalism and furthered the devolution of powers.[35] In France, Corsica secured a limited autonomy that enhanced the appeal of Corsican nationalism. The accommodation inherent to the decentralization of powers has weakened the violent aspects of territorial protest but increased their potential, and their political radicalism in some cases.

The financial crisis that began in 2008 and increasing migration flows towards Europe have precipitated tensions that stretch the bonds among states. Subnationalist sentiments are jeopardizing current institutional configurations while defending the unitary European framework that makes their existence possible.[36] At the same time, backlash state nationalisms seek to maintain the nation states at the centre of the political scene. Many West European countries are now suffering the greatest threats to their unity since the Second World War. Scotland, Catalonia, South Tyrol and Veneto show increasing strain from secessionism, that most radical stage in the devolution of powers as it moves towards urging the discontinuation of a governmental relationship between the territory and the state in order to establish a new sovereign state.

Where regional decentralization is not a purely administrative organization of powers but a political level of representation that could be reinforced by grievances, the decentralizing process generates a demand for more power, sometimes even secession. This extreme request usually arises where territorial self-government coincides with historical antecedents relating to the national identity. Sometimes, though, it surges even in regions without such a past, such as those of northern Italy. Since the European Union is a conventional union and contemplates exit possibilities, it creates – at least theoretically – a situation favourable to this dynamic among its member states also. Here, we find a strident contradiction in European policy: substate entities have no possibility of remaining in the European Union and their respective nation states have the right to veto their admission. However, if a state leaves the European Union, the substate entities do not have the right to remain. This inevitably raises a question: Can democracy allow the expression of increased territorial representation without facing the possibility that the territorial configuration of the state can also be questioned?

Conclusion

The transformation of European political systems since the Second World War shows a gradual shift of political representation through functional/ideological parties to a representation based on territorial actors, among others. As traditional political systems slowly dissolve in the upsurge of new political actors, territorial parties have an apparent advantage because they claim to represent the people, as state-level 'populist' parties seek to do. What seems like a paradox is, in effect, a logical reallocation of forces in the political space. The Europeanization process led to regionalization/decentralization while reducing the cost for smaller political units, such as those that would eventually arise from a secession process. However, rules decided upon by the nation states inhibit this process. Reshaping representative systems has facilitated the growth of nation-state populism that opposes Europeanization.

Democracy and regional institutional frameworks are different matters, since one is concerned with citizen participation and the other with state organization. However, both affect political representation. Decentralization, whether federal or regional in form, enables the representation of territorial interests and converts the region into an actor on the main political scene. Regional attempts to gain greater competences and powers erode the nation state from the bottom up. Regions are a level of democratic participation closer to the citizens than the nation state. Similarly, the European Union has not yet ensured this participation. Why? The answer cannot be found in the past (though history is a useful tool) but in a new articulation of interests that privileges an organic vision of a world with competition/conflict among territorial systems. This is why the regional level is currently gaining greater importance in the political and organizational reshaping of democratic states in Western Europe.[37]

Notes

1. See the foundational study by Linda G. Basch, Nina Glick Schiller and Cristina Szanton Blanc, *Nations Unbound: Transnational Projects, Postcolonial Predicaments, and Deterritorialized Nation-States* (Basel: Gordon and Breach, 1994); as well as Andreas Wimmer and Nina Glick Schiller, 'Methodological Nationalism and Beyond: Nation–state Building, Migration and the Social Sciences', *Global Networks* 2, no. 4 (October 2002): 301; and Daniel Chernilo, *A Social Theory of the Nation-State the Political Forms of Modernity Beyond Methodological Nationalism* (London; New York: Routledge, 2007).
2. Celia Applegate, 'A Europe of Regions: Reflections on the Historiography of Subnational Places in Modern Times', *American Historical Review* 104, no. 4 (1999): 1157–82; and Heinz-Gerhard, Haupt, Michael G. Muller and Stuart. J. Woolf, *Regional and National Identities in Europe in the XIXth and XXth Centuries* (The Hague; Boston: Kluwer Law, 1998). See also the introduction by Núñez Seixas and Storm.
3. Joost Augusteijn and Eric Storm, *Region and State in Nineteenth-Century Europe: Nation-Building, Regional Identities and Separatism* (Basingstoke; New York: Palgrave Macmillan, 2012); and Eric Storm, *The Culture of Regionalism: Art, Architecture and International Exhibitions in France, Germany and Spain, 1890–1939* (Manchester: Manchester University Press, 2010). See also the chapter by Núñez Seixas and Molina.
4. Julian Wright, *The Regionalist Movement in France 1890–1914: Jean Charles-Brun and French Political Thought* (Oxford; New York: Clarendon Press, 2003).
5. Frans Joachim Schrijver, *Regionalism after Regionalisation: Spain, France and the United Kingdom* (Amsterdam: Amsterdam University Press, 2006).
6. See Kathryn Beresford, in Rolf Petri, ed., 'Regione e storia regionale in Europa. Antitesi o metafora della nazione?' *Memoria e ricerca*, no. 15 (2006): 118–21; Celia Applegate, *A Nation of Provincials: The German Idea of Heimat* (Berkeley: University of California Press, 1990); Xosé M. Núñez Seixas, 'The Region as *Essence* of the Fatherland: Regtionalist Variants of Spanish Nationalism (1840–1936)', *European History Quarterly* 31, no. 4 (2001): 483–518; and Ferran Archilés "'Hacer región es hacer patria". La región en el imaginario de la nación española de la Restauración', *Ayer* 64 (2006): 121–47. See also the chapters by Kennedy, DeWaal and Núñez Seixas and Molina.
7. See S. Cubeddu, ed., *Il Sardo-Fascismo fra politica, cultura, economia* (Cagliari: Fondazione Sardinia, 1997). See also the chapter by Núñez Seixas.
8. Stein Rokkan and Derek W. Urwin. *The Politics of Territorial Identity: Studies in European Regionalism* (London: Sage, 1982); and Stein Rokkan and Derek W. Urwin, *Economy, Territory, Identity: Politics of Western European Peripheries* (London: Sage, 1983).
9. Julius Weis Friend, *Stateless Nations: Western European Regional Nationalisms and the Old Nations* (New York: Palgrave Macmillan, 2012).
10. John Loughlin, *Subnational Democracy in the European Union: Challenges and Opportunities* (Oxford; New York: Oxford University Press, 2001).
11. Stelio Mangiameli, ed., *Italian Regionalism: Between Unitary Traditions and Federal Processes* (Cham: Springer International, 2014).
12. The fifth, Friuli Venezia Giulia, was only established on 31 January 1963 by Constitutional Law no. 1.
13. In Italy, the constitution of 1947 recognized three different levels of territorial government: *Comuni* (cities or towns), which were grouped into *Province*, which were

combined to form *Regioni*. Thus, Trentino Alto Adige has two provinces: Trento (Italian-speaking) and Bozen/Bolzano (German-speaking).

14. Maiken Umbach, ed., *German Federalism: Past, Present and Future* (Basingstoke: Palgrave Macmillan, 2002).
15. Anne-Marie Thiesse, 'Centralismo estatal y nacionalismo regionalizado. Las paradojas del caso francés', *Ayer* 64, no. 4 (2006): 33–64.
16. Theo Hermans and Louis Vos, *The Flemish Movement: A Documentary History, 1780–1990* (London; Atlantic Highlands, NJ: Athlone Press, 1992).
17. Alan Trench, ed., *Devolution and Power in the United Kingdom* (Manchester; New York: Manchester University Press, 2007); and Russell Deacon, *Devolution in the United Kingdom*, 2nd ed. (Edinburgh: Edinburgh University Press, 2012).
18. Literature about ethnic revival in Western Europe is endless; for a general overview see Friend, *Stateless Nations*.
19. Filippo Tronconi, *I partiti etnoregionalisti: La politica dell'identità territoriale in Europa occidentale* (Bologna: Il Mulino, 2011); Eve Hepburn, 'The Rise and Fall of a "Europe of the Regions"', *Regional & Federal Studies* 18, no. 5 (2008): 537–55; Eve Hepburn, ed., *New Challenges for Stateless Nationalist and Regionalist Parties* (London: Routledge, 2010); Lieven de Winter and Huri Türsan, *Regionalist Parties in Western Europe* (London: Routledge, 2003); Elias Anwen, *Minority Nationalist Parties and European Integration: A Comparative Study* (London: Routledge, 2009); and Wilfried Swenden and Bart Maddens, *Territorial Party Politics in Western Europe* (Houndmills, Basingstoke: Palgrave Macmillan, 2008).
20. Eve Hepburn and Dan Hough, 'Regionalist Parties and the Mobilization of Territorial Difference in Germany', *Government and Opposition* 47, no. 1 (2012): 74–96.
21. Kris Deschouwer, 'The Rise and Fall of the Belgian Regionalist Parties', *Regional & Federal Studies* 19, nos. 4–5 (2009): 559–77.
22. Saul Newman, 'Ideological Trends among Ethnoregional Parties in Post-industrial Democracies', *Nationalism and Ethnic Politics* 3, no. 1 (1997): 28–60.
23. Michael Keating, *The New Regionalism in Western Europe: Territorial Restructuring and Political Change* (Cheltenham: Edward Elgar, 2000); and Monika De Frantz, 'New Regionalism Top Down: Mobilizing National Minority Cultures', *Regional & Federal Studies* 18, no. 4 (2008): 403–27.
24. Andrew E. G. Jonas, 'Region and Place: Regionalism in Question', *Progress in Human Geography* 36, no. 2 (2012): 263–72; Andrew E. G. Jonas, 'City-Regionalism: Questions of Distribution and Politics', *Progress in Human Geography* 36, no. 6 (2012): 822–29; and Luigi Burroni, 'Competitive Regionalism and the Territorial Governance of Uncertainty', *Transfer: European Review of labor and Research* 20, no. 1 (2014): 83–97.
25. John Loughlin, '"The Europe of the Regions" and the Federalization of Europe', *Publius* 26, no. 4 (1996): 141–62; and Michael Keating, 'A Quarter Century of the Europe of the Regions', *Regional & Federal Studies* 18, no. 5 (2008): 629–35.
26. José M. Magone, *Regional Institutions and Governance in the European Union* (Westport: Praeger, 2003).
27. Christopher T. Harvie, *The Rise of Regional Europe* (London: Routledge, 1994); Michael Keating, 'Regions and regionalism in the European Community', *International Journal of Public Administration* 18, no. 10 (1995): 1491–1511; and Gordon MacLeod, 'Place, Politics and "Scale Dependence" Is Exploring the Structuration of Euro-Regionalism', *European Urban and Regional Studies* 6, no. 3 (1999): 231–53.

28. Liesbet Hooghe and Gary Marks, *Multi-Level Governance and European Integration*, Governance in Europe (Lanham, MD: Rowman & Littlefield, 2001).
29. John McGarry and Michael Keating, eds, *European Integration and the Nationalities Question* (London: Routledge, 2006).
30. Martin Kahanec, Anzelika Zaiceva and Klaus F. Zimmermann, 'Ethnic Minorities in the European Union: An Overview', discussion paper series // Forschungsinstitut zur Zukunft der Arbeit, No. 5397 (2010).
31. Michael Keating and James Hughes, eds, *The Regional Challenge in Central and Eastern Europe: Territorial Restructuring and European Integration* (Brussels: Peter Lang, 2003).
32. Melanie Tatur, ed., *The Making of Regions in Post-Socialist Europe – the Impact of Culture, Economic Structure and Institutions* (Wiesbaden: VS Verlag für Sozialwissenschaften, 2004).
33. François Bafoil, 'Regionalisation and Decentralisation in a Comparative Perspective: Eastern Europe and Poland', *Ministerstwo Rozwoju Regionalnego* (2010): 7.
34. Wilfried Swenden, *Federalism and Regionalism in Western Europe: A Comparative and Thematic Analysis* (Basingstoke; New York: Palgrave Macmillan, 2006).
35. Liesbet Hooghe, 'Belgium: From Regionalism to Federalism', *Regional Politics and Policy* 3, no. 1 (1993): 44–68.
36. Matthias Bieri, 'Separatism in the EU', *CSS Analyses in Security Policy* 160 (2014); and Roland Vaubel, 'Secession in the European Union', *Economic Affairs* 33, no. 3 (2013): 288–302.
37. Michael Keating, *Rescaling the European State: The Making of Territory and the Rise of the Meso* (Oxford: Oxford University Press, 2013).

Further reading

Augusteijn, Joost, and Eric Storm, eds, *Region and State in Nineteenth-Century Europe: Nation-Building, Regional Identities and Separatism* (Basingstoke; New York: Palgrave Macmillan, 2012).

Friend, Julius Weis, *Stateless Nations: Western European Regional Nationalisms and the Old Nations* (New York: Palgrave Macmillan, 2012).

Haupt, Heinz-Gerhard, Michael G. Muller and Stuart. J. Woolf, eds, *Regional and National Identities in Europe in the XIXth and XXth Centuries* (The Hague; Boston: Kluwer Law Intl, 1998).

Keating, Michael, *The New Regionalism in Western Europe: Territorial Restructuring and Political Change* (Cheltenham: Edward Elgar, 2000).

Keating, Michael, *Rescaling the European State: The Making of Territory and the Rise of the Meso* (Oxford: Oxford University Press, 2013).

Keating, Michael, and James Hughes, eds, *The Regional Challenge in Central and Eastern Europe: Territorial Restructuring and European Integration* (Brussels: Peter Lang, 2003).

Loughlin, John, *Subnational Democracy in the European Union: Challenges and Opportunities* (Oxford; New York: Oxford University Press, 2001).

Rokkan, Stein, and Derek W. Urwin, *Economy, Territory, Identity: Politics of Western European Peripheries* (London: Sage, 1983).

Swenden, Wilfried, *Federalism and Regionalism in Western Europe: A Comparative and Thematic Analysis* (Basingstoke; New York: Palgrave Macmillan, 2006).

CHAPTER 10
REGIONALISM AND ITS DIVERSE FRAMINGS IN GERMAN-SPEAKING EUROPE ACROSS THE LONG TWENTIETH CENTURY
Jeremy DeWaal

Introduction

In the 1950s, a German regionalist from the city of Lübeck, reflecting on the plight of German expellees, wrote on how being forced out of one's regional place of home was to be made into an 'only German', a term that sounded 'uncanny' to his ears. They must never, he argued, abandon the regionalist and federalist ideas.[1] The passage reflected a notion of Germanness as defined by regional diversity – an idea popularized by the *Heimat* movement around the turn of the century. The idea of *Heimat* referred to a sense of belonging and cultural uniqueness within local and regional places that could be extended abstractly to the nation at large. The concept proved central to German, Austrian and Swiss regionalisms, which promoted regional cultural particularities through *Heimat* books, *Heimat* journals, *Heimat* festivals and diverse *Heimat* traditions. While this chapter focuses primarily on regionalism in Germany, the question of ethnically mixed regions, contested borderlands, shifting national borders and violent struggle over who and what regions belonged to the nation render a broader purview of German-speaking Europe useful. At different times, millions of ethnic German regionalists lived either outside Germany or, particularly in the latter half of the century, within a German nation state but outside of regions from which they had been expelled. A broader purview on German-speaking Europe, meanwhile, allows for comparative consideration of examples from neighbouring Austria and Switzerland, which demonstrate both parallel and divergent developments.

The political framings of regionalism in German-speaking Europe were diverse. In Germany alone, this could be seen in the procession of regionalism through the different political systems across the century. Cultural regionalism found appeal among conservatives, liberals, and social democrats, as well as among urban and rural citizens, and particularly came to the fore at moments of crisis and change. Following its popularization in the Second Empire and its evolution in the interwar years, the Nazi regime appropriated key aspects of regionalism for propaganda while simultaneously displaying ambivalence towards the movement. After 1945, amid national defeat, mass dislocation and destruction, regional places of home emerged as sites of preoccupation. While the communist dictatorship in the east illustrated ambivalence towards regionalism, in the early Federal Republic, it came to the fore as a source of flexible identities that offered a site of engagement with federalism, democracy and ideas of European unification. Expellee desires for lost regions, meanwhile, became intertwined in Cold War conflict, partly informing later debates over the 'intrinsic' political meaning of regionalism.

Conceptions of the relationship between region and nation proved equally flexible and diverse. In theory, the relationship of region to nation could range from separatism on one end and to nationalist affirmation on the other and anywhere in between.[2] Limited examples of both separatism and unitary nationalism could be found in Germany and Austria, though notions of regionalism as dovetailing with nation-building proved dominant. This understanding, however, differed internally from the nationalist-affirming regionalism that dominated in the first half of the twentieth century to the post-war notion of regional *Heimat* as decentring, restraining and therein serving a new German national idea. Meanwhile, in Austria, different groups at varying times framed regionalism as strengthening loyalty to the Habsburg Empire, dovetailing with pan-German visions or cementing Austrian distinctiveness, the latter of which dominated after 1945.

The history of regionalism in Germany, Austria, Switzerland and other German-speaking areas were certainly not without their unique national inflections. National uniqueness could be found, among other places, in the role of German regionalism in imagining a post-war German federalism or in distancing the post-1945 Austrian national idea from a German one. At the same time, many of the underlying forces of the movement across the twentieth century had a broader European provenance with parallels in other national contexts.

Modernity, popular regionalism and the nation

In the mid-nineteenth century, the founder of German Folklore Studies, Wilhelm Heinrich Riehl, proclaimed that the uniqueness of German culture could be found in its regional cultural diversity that could only be discovered by wandering through its diverse landscapes.[3] By the end of the century, regionalism had emerged as a popular movement. The movement was certainly a modern phenomenon, though much diversity in regional cultural practices and dialects stemmed from century-long histories of territorial fragmentation. Looking as far back as the early medieval period, the settlement patterns of Germanic tribes or *Stämme* were reflected in important modern German dialect borders (Figure 10.1), while, throughout the early modern period, the Holy Roman Empire functioned as an 'incubator' that preserved territorial diversity.[4] The number of states would only be reduced first with the Napoleonic conquest, which forged sixteen expanded client states, followed by the German Confederation, consisting of thirty-nine states.

While earlier studies of nationalism assumed that nations overwrote 'pre-modern' regional identifications, scholars over the past several decades have shown that regional identities were not pre-modern at all, but rather a product of modernity that emerged

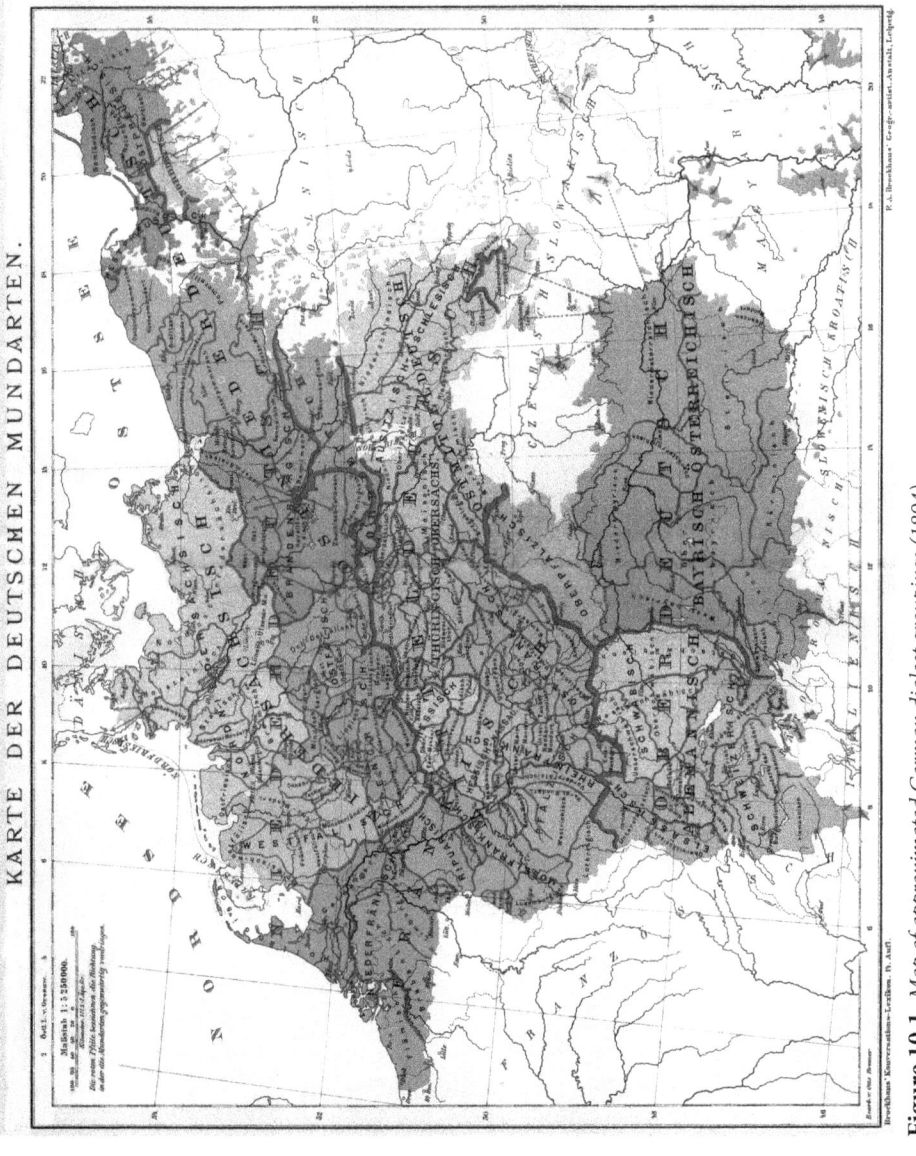

Figure 10.1 *Map of approximated German dialect groupings (1894).*
Source: Brockhaus' Konversationslexikon, *14th ed., vol. 5 (Leipzig: F.A. Brockhaus, 1894), p. 28a.*

hand in hand with nationalism. As David Blackbourn and James Retallack have further pointed out, local spaces were by no means more narrow-minded than national ones, nor did all modern dynamism come from the top.[5] The idea of *Heimat* as referring to rootedness in local and regional places was itself modern, with the word in previous centuries referring only to a legal right of settlement and inheritance.[6] The mindset of regionalism, like nationalism, relied on new ideas about selfhood, identity and space, the seeds of which emerged in Romanticism. The romantics were the first to evoke a notion of *Heimat* as about a subjective experience of space, with the binary of foreignness and the nearness of home representing a salient theme.[7] By mid-century, educated elites like Riehl took a growing interest in regional histories and cultural uniqueness, with the first regional *Heimat* and history journals emerging. Regional folklore studies, begun by educated elites, emerged as the scholarly arm of subsequent regionalist movements in Germany and throughout Europe.[8] While *Heimat* could also refer to domestic places of home, localities and, more abstractly, the nation at large, it emerged as a central concept evoked by regional cultural societies.

The forces of modernity, far from sweeping away focus on region, increased it exponentially. Filtering out the specific factors of modernization that 'triggered' regionalist movements is rendered problematic by the fact that they emerged fairly simultaneously throughout Western Europe while processes of modernization remained territorially uneven.[9] At the same time, the aggregate forces of modernization and urbanization proved crucial to sparking the modern regionalist movement by the end of the nineteenth century. In Germany, the decades from 1870 to 1914 saw not only the emergence of a new unified nation but also unprecedented levels of industrialization, urbanization and population movement that changed local and regional landscapes. During this period, the German population grew by over 58 per cent, while inner migration resulted in nearly half no longer living in the town of their birth by the turn of the century.[10] Urbanization during the Second Empire exploded, with the number of Germans living in cities rising from 36 per cent to 60 per cent.[11] Fast-paced industrial growth reshaped everyday life at an unprecedented rate, while technologies of communication and travel increased mobility and brought the outside into local and regional worlds like never before.

Rapid changes and the imperatives of nation-building both informed popular regionalism and interest in 'place-making'.[12] The regionalist movement encompassed a wide array of media, ranging from art, architecture, literature, music, protection of dialect and theatre to engagement in *Heimatschutz*, which focused on protecting environmental landscapes and cultural heritage sites. Regionalist activities thrived in new *Heimat* societies, regional history associations, singing and hiking groups, local 'beautification societies' and a range of *Heimat* journals and *Heimat* books aimed at a popular audience. While the educated middle class represented the backbone of the movement, it enjoyed both support from above and a relatively receptive audience from below. The actors who shaped ideas of region, moreover, included not only natives but also many from the outside.[13] Regionalist societies were rarely associated with a political party or interest group, emphasizing instead community cohesion over the social fracture churned up by processes of modernization. This appeal to regionalism to bridge across partisanships also had parallels in other national contexts.[14]

Despite the diversity of regional cultural practices that predated modern regionalism, modern regionalist movements did not simply 'discover' a defined regional substance just lurking beneath the surface.[15] Even the notion of what territorial spaces corresponded to a common region remained tremendously fluid and contested. Though often using the language of preservation, the birth of regionalism involved significant processes of invention and reinvention of tradition. Regionalists quickly co-opted and therein radically transformed pre-existing local practices, including agricultural events and city markets that were reinvented into celebrations of local and regional community. The Cannstatter festival, Bavarian Oktoberfest and the Bremer Freimarkt offered only a few examples of the phenomenon, invented or appropriated to bolster identification with Württemberg, Bavaria and Bremen, respectively. Sharpshooter festivals (*Schützenfeste*), once serving a functional defence purpose in centuries past, were often co-opted as celebrations of both regional and national communities. Appropriation of carnival as an expression of regional identity in the Rhineland represented a particularly salient case of how regionalists reinvented tradition. No longer the late medieval festival symbolizing the sinfulness of man to be overcome on Ash Wednesday, modern carnival in the Rhineland was reformulated as a positive celebration of local and regional identities.[16] Dialect became the primary language of such traditions, marshalled to underscore their function as pillars of regional identity.

Turn-of-the-century regionalists included diverse actors both urban and rural and from divergent political groups. Leading regionalists like Paul Schultze-Naumburg or Hermann Löns represented clear examples of nationalist conservative regionalism, often accompanied by anti-urbanism and scepticism of democracy. Among liberal groups, the participatory nature of regionalism and its contrast with the culture of elites both made it attractive. As Celia Applegate has pointed out in a study of the Palatinate, regionalism often included a 'democratization of public life' and a reaction against processes of centralization.[17] Regionalism also emerged as an important node of environmental protection in German-speaking Europe and in the regionalist movements of Western Europe more broadly.[18] Regionalism was not invariably ruralist, though anti-urbanism could certainly be found in a number of *Heimat* novels and artistic works.[19] Others perceived regionalism as compatible with both urban life and cosmopolitanism.[20] As Maiken Umbach and Bernd Hüppauf have pointed out, fostering regionalism and *Heimat* in urban architecture often represented not anti-modernism but rather a search for a 'vernacular modernism'.[21] Urbanites proved particularly prominent regionalists and, though sometimes indulging in romantic desires for the provinces, also viewed cities as sites of *Heimat*. As the Dresden musician Hugo Jüngst asked rhetorically in 1902, 'Do we love our Heimat less, because we grew up on the cobblestones of a large city?' Urbanites, he believed, held just as much to their regional cultural particularities as rural inhabitants and should feel equal rights to draw on *Heimat* in art.[22]

Among the forces that fuelled regionalism, the emergence of modern nation states proved crucial. Regionalists in the German Empire overwhelmingly emphasized regionalism as reinforcing the nation idea, while the *Heimat* concept, as Applegate points out, came to the fore as a mediator between the immediate spheres of local life and a broader national idea.[23] Such notions of national unity in regional diversity were not limited to Germany. They also played a role, at least to some degree, in national integration in Britain, Italy and France, among others.[24] The German Empire was unique perhaps only in the extent to which it relied on ideas of national unity as based on regional diversity – arguably outstripped in Europe only by neighbouring Switzerland, whose polyethnic cantons fundamentally relied on a strong idea of unity within regional diversity.[25] Meanwhile, within the multi-ethnic Austro-Hungarian Empire, most ethnic-Germans and some Austrians of other ethnicities saw regionalism and loyalty to the Empire as harmonious, while some non-ethnic German regionalisms in the Empire challenged loyalty to the state.[26]

Within Germany, ideas of nation as rooted in regional diversity were never entirely uncontested. Prior to national unification, early nationalists, such as Ernst Moritz Arndt, argued in his famous citation that the 'Fatherland' must be bigger than Swabia or the Rhineland, while Borussian historians often cast national unification as about transcending region. What could be seen from one perspective as regional-national harmony or *Heimat* as binding region and nation could from another be smeared as *Kleinstaaterei* (petty statism). Even in neighbouring Switzerland, critics of excessive decentralization criticized what they saw as a *Kantönligeist* (small canton spirit).[27] Yet, by the turn of the century, national unity and regional diversity in the German Empire were popularly seen as complimentary. The federalist structure of the state reinforced such understandings on the political level though it was dominated by Prussia, by far the largest state. Regional state-building that began prior to national unification continued in the Wilhelmine years. Such state-building in realms of education, infrastructure, as well as the promotion of regional festivals, museums and historical societies often promoted simultaneous identification with region and nation.[28] Harmonizing the two, however, did mean forgetting histories of conflict. Forgetting how states such as Württemberg sided with the Habsburg Empire in the Austro-Prussian war, as Alon Confino points out, proved a case in point.[29]

In national borderlands and ethnically mixed regions, the relation between region and nation became a particularly pressing question. Ethnic German border regions were often among the most vocal in emphasizing their region's Germanness, a trend visible in *Heimat* literature.[30] The notion of the Rhineland as a 'Watch on the Rhine' that protected the nation from French encroachment was a clear example. This phenomenon can be seen in other national contexts, as Bassin and Suslov point out for the case of Russia.[31] Ethnically mixed regions often proved surprisingly resilient. Though they often succumbed to the pressure of nationalist movements, historians have increasingly challenged the inevitability of the phenomenon.[32] In places like Bohemia, by the turn of the century, nationalization increasingly overtook multi-ethnic local and regional ideas – a phenomenon with parallels elsewhere in Europe.[33] In the ever-contested territory of Alsace, national struggle between France and Germany did much to shape the very notion of Alsace as a region. While outsiders sought to influence Alsatian ideas of region, Alsatians themselves used it to negotiate their position within the German Empire.[34] Meanwhile, regional tourism emerged as a nationalizing force in border regions.[35]

While growing nationalism brought border regions under increasing pressure, the outbreak of the First World War would represent an inflection point in twentieth-century regionalism more broadly. Though regionalists had generally not been militaristic in tone, they were forced to adapt to a wartime footing. While stopping many activities, *Heimat* enthusiasts channelled others into addressing sagging morale and keeping soldiers in the field connected to their *Heimat*.[36] The state, meanwhile, used *Heimat* tropes to mobilize regional energies.[37] A telling practice could be found in the creation of wooden sculptures of regional historical figures, with buyers of war loans each driving a nail into the sculpture – a process that covered the regionalist figure in a sheet of armour – symbolically linking the region and the nation in a common endeavour.[38] After the defeat of the First World War, largely seen as a moment of national humiliation in Germany and Austria, regionalism would continue to evolve through the tumultuous interwar years and the creation of new democratic states.

From democracy to dictatorship

Many of the challenges that faced the new infant democracies reshaped the regionalist movement. Weimar Germany had lost a number of its former regions, with the greatest losses to the east in Posen, West Prussian and Upper Silesia, as well as in Alsace-Lorraine and slivers of the Rhineland to the west and parts of Schleswig to the north. Meanwhile, the Rhineland was occupied by the allies, while the Saarland was placed under the League of Nations. Former German regions that became part of new nation states often found their national loyalties a matter of suspicion.[39] In the Alsace, French assimilation politics reduced the initial receptivity of many Alsatians to French rule, who used regionalism to defend, among other things, the use of German in schools.[40] Many ethnic Germans in regions transferred to Poland moved to Germany, while those who remained presented a notable problem for the new Polish state. Germans in Poland remained a diverse group whose attraction to German nationalism varied, fracturing particularly according to their previous belonging to the German, Austrian or Russian state.[41] Those who relocated to Germany developed new methods to promote their native regional cultures. 'City-sponsorships' (*Patenschaften*) – institutions that would gain more prominence after 1945 – emerged first in the Weimar Republic. Such sponsorships, like that of Mannheim for the Memelland in 1929 offered a common geographic centre for regional cultural preservation.[42]

Regionalism in Austria was similarly jolted by the collapse of the Habsburg Empire, territorial reconfiguration and the establishment of a new republic. The Austrian Republic was symbolically constituted by the declaration of accession of its regional states, while the loss of the Empire triggered a national identity crisis. The stability of regional identities in time of change made regionalism a clear asset, though the interwar years also saw shifting ideas of the relationship between region and nation. Struggle to accept visions of a small-state Austria informed an uptick in desires for unification with a greater Germany that could be found across multiple political groups.[43] This could particularly be seen in Tirol, whose southern half was ceded to Italy. While Tirolian regionalists had long viewed region, German ethnicity and Habsburg loyalties as harmonious, after 1918, Tirolian desires for unification with Germany grew exponentially.[44] Other Austrian regionalists promoted a distinct notion of Austrian national identity within a new federalist republic. Though the new Austrian republic maintained more centralist elements than neighbouring Germany, regional *Landeshauptmänner* (regional state presidents) played a significant role in the political administration.

While in arts and architecture, *Heimat* art partially gave way to new styles, the interwar years reveal tremendous growth in lay interest in regionalism in a number of fields. The political instability, social fracture and economic uncertainty that defined the interwar years fuelled popular desires for a more stable, cohesive and secure world within a familiar regional landscape. Publication of *Heimat* journals in Germany grew exponentially while *Heimatkunde* emerged as a school subject in a major way. Rather than advocating a narrow focus on the regional world, theorists of the subject often aimed to foster a broader sense of citizenship. While some advocates of the subject reflected a penchant for rural idealism, *Heimatkunde* found success in both urban and regional contexts and among both conservative and liberals.[45]

The political diversity of regionalism and its harmony with nation-building continued in the Weimar Republic. The federalist Weimar constitution reaffirmed the idea of Germany as a nation of diverse regions, declaring the German people to be a united group of regional *Stämme* (tribes). Improving the federalist system remained a tremendous preoccupation of reformers (Figure 10.2). Those like Hugo Preuß argued that national unity could only be preserved by emphasizing regional diversity through a balanced federalist system, with regions acting as critical sites of citizenship and political participation.[46] *Heimat* was also viewed as a site of unity above the fray of partisan conflicts that harangued the Republic.

Weimar regionalism was most influenced by the growth of nationalism, though minor separatist movements emerged in the early years, particularly along the western border where it enjoyed French support. Rhenish separatists attempted to declare an independent 'Rhenish Republic' in 1919 and again during the French occupation of the Ruhr in 1923, while groups of Upper Silesians, facing a plebiscite on their national belonging, indulged in separatist imaginings of an independent state. The Austrian state faced separatist challenges in the Vorarlberg which sought to unify with neighbouring Switzerland. Separatist movements, however, often struggled to gain traction, among other reasons because of their inability to marshal the same political promises of nation along with the vagueness of what constituted the region itself.[47] As the Weimar writer on the idea of *Heimat*, Kurt Stavenhagen noted while the constitution declared Germans to be a unified group of *Stämme*, no one knew precisely what or where they were – a reference to divergent imaginings of what places and groups constituted a regional people.[48] The growing convergence of regionalist and nationalist language proved more

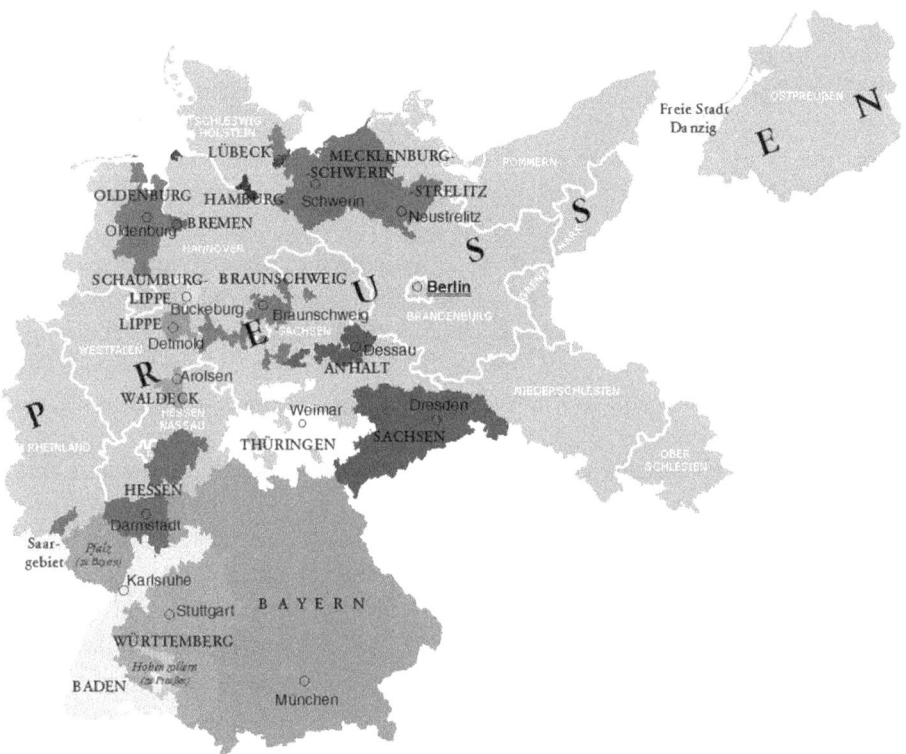

Figure 10.2 *Map of the federal states and provinces of Prussia in the Weimar Republic in 1925. Source: Wikimedia Commons.*

prominent, with many viewing the nation as under threat by the punitive Versailles settlement, economic disaster and foreign incursions and occupation.[49] Regionalists proved susceptible to the idea of an assertive nation as a source of redemption, while, as Peter Fritzsche has argued, many Weimar citizens confronted their challenges by projecting their fate onto the surface screen of the nation.[50]

The Nazi seizure of power in 1933 brought both change and strategic ideological appropriation of the language of regionalism. While at least one recent work has argued for a strong relationship between regionalism and Nazi ideology, much evidence points to the regime's ambivalent and divergent approach towards regionalism.[51] Nazi ideology, as Lutz Raphael points out, was in many realms not crisply defined, containing areas of plurality and contradiction, an observation that could be easily applied to its engagement with regionalism.[52] The divergent attitudes of the regime towards regionalism can be seen by moving beyond institutional analysis to the realm of cultural geography.[53] Though the regime selectively appropriated regionalism in propaganda, as one Nazi pedagogue insisted, they should only teach children history rooted in spaces of 'national destiny'. Historical views based on '*Heimat*', he argued, were the products of a 'liberal' world view that must be scrapped.[54] While publication of regional *Heimat* journals had exploded in the Weimar years, the regime drastically slashed them by around 40 per cent from 1933 to 1940 (Figure 10.3). Focus on regional *Heimatkunde* decreased significantly, with a parallel decline in publication of *Heimat* books.[55] Use of regionalism in propaganda did prove particularly attractive to Gauleiter seeking to consolidate their footing within the new regime.[56] As Núñez Seixas points out, the Nazi regime and other fascist regimes were skilled improvisers that were more than willing to appropriate regionalism when useful.[57] Though Hitler praised how technologies of movement would level regional cultural differences and declared they would rip federalism from the face of Germany, the Nazi state was hardly the most centralized dictatorship.[58] Nor did *Heimat* enthusiasts publicly resist attempts to forbid Jewish members from their societies or offer any open objection to destruction of sites of Jewish cultural heritage within the region. Little evidence, moreover, suggests that regionalist's support of Nazism was lower than that of German society at large.

Yet, the regime's ambivalent approach to regionalism was apparent in a number of areas, including in their 'coordination' of the regionalist Weimar-era journals. The *Rheinische Heimatblätter*, published in the Weimar years by a collection of *Heimat* societies, offers a telling example. After 1933, the largely antiquarian and unpolitical journal was removed from the control of *Heimat* societies, had the term *Heimat* removed from its title and was placed under the Kampfbund für deutsche Kultur. Non-political regional pieces

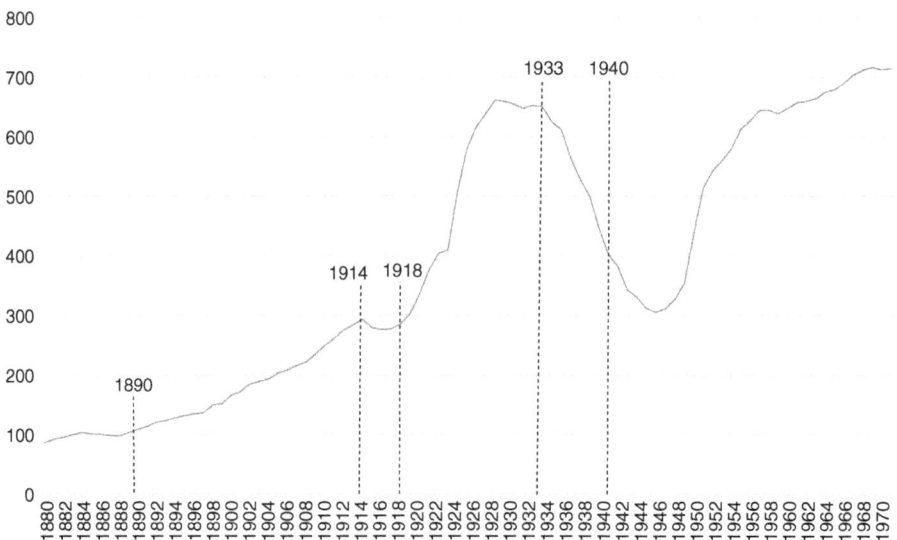

Figure 10.3 Heimat *journal publication in the territories of West Germany (including the Saarland, excluding West Berlin) in the long twentieth century. Numbers compiled from an analysis of Rudi Mechthold's index of Heimat journals. *These numbers are based on publications from established presses and do not include many of the ephemeral publications, often in self-publication, that frequently appeared in the early post-war years.*
Source: *Rudi Mechthold, ed.,* Landesgeschichtliche Zeitschriften 1800–2009: Ein Verzeichnis deutschsprachiger landesgeschichtlicher und heimatkundlicher Zeitschriften, Zeitungsbeilagen und Schriftenreihen *(Frankfurt: Vittorio Klostermann, 2011).*

were scaled back dramatically, with the new publication split approximately three ways between non-regional national propaganda, regional propaganda pieces and less overtly political regional articles. Several new themes became salient, including the military history of the Rhineland, the artificial nature of the western national border, ancient Germanic histories, denunciations of separatism and emphasis on regional economic output.[59] As one large-printed quotation in the journal maintained, '[w]ork is *Heimat*!'[60] Regionalism was to be stripped of its inwardness and funnelled into national expansion. In turn, the Nazis used the publication to declare that the Rhineland must 'radiate' German cultural influence across the western border, reject 'petty statism', embrace its 'war front legacy' and turn its focus to the plight of Germans in the east.[61] The theme of a national community of struggle, absent in the pre-1933 publication, saturated the periodical after the seizure of power.

Nazi propaganda in other regions illustrated a similar emphasis on eliminating regionalism's inward focus. As a propaganda book on Baden as a 'national borderland' maintained, 'we cannot think of our narrow Heimat Baden anymore without immediately thinking of the broader Empire.' The volume continued by emphasizing the crucial nature of regional labour in serving the nation.[62] In a speech on his own *Heimat* of Austria, Hitler argued for the irrelevance of a small space without it becoming part of a broader space.[63] Attempts to invert regionalism outward could also be seen in a 1937 work on Alemannic culture which emphasized how their regional culture extended into Switzerland, justifying future action in 'forcing the Swiss to their knees'.[64] The regime's visions of uprooting and resettling millions of Germans in the east illustrated perhaps the most patent disinterest in maintaining regional rootedness and likely informed its penchant for an abstract and generic regionalism in propaganda.[65]

The German declaration of war in 1939 altered the use of regionalism in propaganda, with greater emphasis on the cultural links between German regions and their newly conquered neighbours. In regionalist publications in the Rhineland, for example, the regime emphasized the cultural links with the Netherlands, Belgium, Alsace and Luxembourg, while holding a 'German-Flemish' cultural festival in the region.[66] As Joep Leersen demonstrates, the Nazis particularly engaged with Frisian and Flemish culture in the Low Countries to promote a notion of their Germanness.[67] After the annexation of Austria, while subverting the Austrian national idea, the regime reframed Austrian regions as German ones, keeping most historical regional territorial boundaries. At the same time, within Germany, the war deeply challenged citizen's connection to their *Heimat*, uprooting them to an unprecedented extent. As the anti-regime cleric Alfred Delp argued in a 1940 sermon on the *Heimat* concept, *Heimat* receded as they became a people on the road in 'war trips', 'work trips' and 'settlement trips'.[68] The homesickness of soldiers particularly became a problem while, as with other states, the need to funnel regional resources and sentiments into the war effort proved essential.[69] The regime's depiction of itself as the saviour of the *Heimat* proved increasingly difficult to reconcile with growing images of ravaged cities. Meanwhile, as recent work on mass evacuations have illustrated, the Nazi regime made little attempt to keep citizens near their local places of home – creating an unusual site of tension between citizens and the regime.⁷⁰ In the ruins of defeat, fears that 'Heimat was no more' emerged as a strong source of anxiety.

Redemptive regionalism in the aftermath

In 1947, a report from Cologne noted the astonishing 'wild-growing Heimat cultural activities' in the ruins. Amid the rubble, West Germans founded a surprising profusion of regional *Heimat* societies and publications, wrote a flood of dialect poetry reflecting on lost local worlds and held frequent *Heimat* evenings to cope with life in the ruins. Regionalists revived a range of *Heimat* traditions to much fanfare, while holding special regionalists events described as gathering energies for reconstruction.⁷¹ While Hanseatic *Heimat* enthusiasts on the northern coast noted how *Heimat* feeling exceeded that of times of 'blossom', others, including a regionalist in the south-west and a historian in Bavaria remarked how 'Heimat' reached greater heights amid collapse than in times of peace and how disaster triggered 'a new animation of Heimat thoughts'.⁷² Throughout the West, scores of ephemeral regional journals circulated, many published samizdat, replaced after 1949 by more firmly established successors. *Heimat* books, as historians of the press have remarked, also had an unusually high presence in the publications of the new Federal Republic.⁷³

This regional turn in the West after 1945 has been much neglected in the scholarship on German regionalism. While Celia Applegate and Jörg Arnold have pointed to the strong early post-war attraction to *Heimat* in the West, the stubborn myth of *Heimat* as taboo in the aftermath has persisted.⁷⁴ Yet, in examining thousands of sources on early post-war regionalism from a range of authors, places and media, we find not only numerous references to the *Heimat* idea reaching unprecedented heights but also virtually no reference to it as tainted.⁷⁵ This changed only in the 1960s, when a combination of generational, economic and political changes resulted in a contested turn against regionalism and *Heimat*. In the immediate post-war years, four primary factors informed the turn to regionalism. The first was the elimination of the nation state as an actor and resulting recourse to regional communities in reconstruction. *Heimat*, secondly, acted as a site of imagined protection, familiarity, and orientation at a time of uncertainty. The third was the need for flexible sources of identity and a site from which to rethink the national idea. While national identities proved burdened, regions offered alternative identities and a foundation from which to imagine a new federalist national idea. The fourth factor was the sheer extent of dislocation and destruction, with resulting fears of lost *Heimat* triggering a form of compensatory regionalism. While the physical built environment of *Heimat* had often been destroyed, many discussed how reviving non-material regional cultural practices could compensate. As one regionalist journal maintained, the inability to reconstruct the lost physical landscapes of *Heimat* made it all the more important to preserve regional cultural practices.⁷⁶

While West Germans could return home, revive regionalism and fashion new regional identities, this was impossible for German expellees from former eastern regions. Expellees engaged in regional cultural activities but only in a dispersed fashion outside their region. Meanwhile, in the Soviet Zone Germans had a clear attraction to regional cultural activities, though the occupiers and the East German state tapped down on independent *Heimat* activities. The resulting crack down deflated, but did not eliminate the regionalist movement. The new regime did eliminate the federal states and, over time, appropriated a new delocalized *Heimat* idea to promote identification with the state at large, while depicting the West as the imperialist abusers of the *Heimat* concept. Meanwhile, private ideas of *Heimat* in the dictatorship continued underneath the surface, while a host of regional cultural particularities could hardly be swept under the rug.[77]

While neither West nor East German regionalists abandoned German identities, the opposite was true in neighbouring Austria, where regionalists fundamentally abandoned previously contested notions of Austria's Germanness. The *Heimat* concept in post-war Austria, in turn, came to refer both to the nation and its regions, strictly separating the Austrian and German national ideas.[78] Although the federalist structures of the First Austrian Republic were largely restored in the Second Republic, Austrian regionalists enthusiastically embraced a small-state national idea after 1945. While the Austrian nation had gone from monarchy to republic and German dictatorship, in a new republic its historically continuous regions offered a stable cultural reference point.[79] Austrian federalism was less decentralized than in the Federal Republic while Austrian national identity was infinitely less burdened, making regional identities less essential as a site of alternative identification. Austrian regionalism also proved unique in the degree to which it politically revolved around tensions between the politically left metropolitan centre of Vienna and the conservative rural regions.

The most precarious and politicized ethnic German regionalists were unquestionably the millions of expellees from the east, whose regionalism continued without a region. While expellees in the German Democratic Republic (GDR) were forbidden to engage in regional cultural activities, expellees in the west founded a range of regional societies to preserve regional cultures and engage in politics. Meanwhile, former eastern regions became home to new Polish populations, many of whom had themselves been displaced from eastern Polish areas annexed by the Soviet Union. New Polish inhabitants, often having suffered greatly at the hands of Germans, sought to forge Polish narratives for new regions that erased German histories that went back to the Late Middle Ages. An odd alliance of Polish nationalists, communists and Catholic clergy cooperated in this process, though homesick tourism of German expellees later on triggered memories of their German history.[80] Expellees in West German cities sought to preserve eastern German regional cultures in cultural sponsorships (*Patenschaften*) taken up by West German cities for eastern counterparts. Such places also frequently served as sites for annual expellee reunions. A decade after the founding of the West German state, at least 296 such cultural sponsorship had been created.[81] Sudeten Germans particularly used the areas along the Czech border as a surrogate space for regionalist activities, unintentionally intensifying, as Yuliya Komska has demonstrated, the visibility of the iron curtain.[82] Annual *Heimat* meetings, including on the so-called expellee 'Day of

Heimat' offered a unique opportunity for regional cultural performances, often used to teach a new generation of children about eastern German cultures, combined with both private reunion and political speeches (Figure 10.4). The ability to preserve eastern regional cultures as lived cultures, however, proved a constant source of anxiety.

While expellees were unable to return to their native regions, regional *Heimat* offered West Germans a site of imagined new beginnings. While some scholarship has argued that post-war *Heimat* was about tending to a sense of regional victimhood,[83] it was also in many ways about a search for recovery. Throughout regionalist discourses, the words 'life-affirmation' and 'Heimat' were evoked in conjunction to a notable degree. As the author Wolfgang Borchert argued, for him and his fellow Hamburg locals, their *Heimat* represented 'more than a pile of stones', but rather their 'will to exist'.[84] A Badener regionalist similarly argued that, after the war, they could begin anew by 'holding together on the small bit of earth that is left to us, from the earth of the *Heimat*, in a small circle of the Badenese land and people'.[85]

In West Germany, regionalism became useful for imagining a decentralized federalist system. As one regionalists from the southwest argued, 'within the reach of the Heimat-like parliament', citizens found a comprehensible realm of democratic participation, while, by contrast, 'the germ of dictatorship' lied within the 'herd that has the ambition to be ever more numerous, ever more unitary, ever more powerful'.[86] Rather than assuming either a nationalist or separatist idea of region, West German regionalists after 1945 frequently argued for region as a force that restrained and therein served the nation. As the Badenese regionalist Max Picard argued, 'It is [. . .] possible that the

Figure 10.4 *Observations of the expellee 'Day of* Heimat' *in Berlin 1955.*
Source: Private Collection of the Bund der Vertriebenen, Bonn.

individual in Germany can find themselves when they take themselves out of the vague grandiose state and bring themselves into the concreteness of the small state'.[87] Few sought to toss German identity overboard and only a small minority argued for regional autonomy. The Swabian regionalist Otto Feger was among this group in arguing for an autonomous 'Swabian-Alemannic democracy'. He proved more representative, however, in arguing that regional traditions of 'democracy' and western orientations could aide democratization and European unity.[88]

The Western allies strongly supported the creation of a federalist system, ratified in 1949. Though more decentralized than neighbouring Austria, the state of Bavaria refused to ratify the basic law as a protest for even more decentralization. Separatism never gained a significant following, though the Bavaria Party, which included both separatists and advocates of extreme federalism, won around 20 per cent of the regional vote in the state in the first federal elections. In the new republic, federal states were given significant authority in education and culture and were represented within a new Bundesrat that bore substantially more power than the Reichsrat of the Weimar Republic. Article 30 of the new basic law reserved all rights not given to the federal government to the regional states.

The allies directed the new republic to redraw its regional state borders, which the occupiers had provisionally drawn. Many regionalists viewed this as a unique opportunity to forge regional states drawn descriptively according to regional identities. While the federal map would never be redrawn, attempts to envision the project proved revealing. The provision of the constitution which included regional belonging among the factors to be considered in redrawing the map triggered the establishment of a large parliamentary-scholarly apparatus to discover where such spaces lied. The project revealed fundamental disparateness in popular imaginings of regional community. A host of factors could inform territorial imaginings of region, including dialect borders, geographic features, ritual traditions, confession, tribe, orientation to urban centres or past territorial states, but none created universally shared cognitive maps of region. This phenomenon parallels both Kabatek and Hopkin's observations that dialect spaces and ecotypes of folkloric practices both deeply influenced regional identities but often did not neatly correspond to borders of imagined regional belonging.[89] In contrast to nations, which underwent long and often violent histories to define their geographic contours, more highly divergent cognitive maps of region circulated underneath the surface.

Federalist enthusiasm and notions of region as restraining nationalism were not universally shared, particularly by many expellees. As one Silesian argued in an expellee newspaper, West Germans were excessively focused on their own regions and should 'be German and not Bavarian or Hessian, or God knows what else'.[90] Loss of home based on national belonging, experience of expulsion and desire for recognition of their plight by maintaining national territorial claims all informed a more nation-affirming vision of region among many expellees. While expellee *Heimat* books were saturated with assertions of their region's Germanness, expellee political leaders emphasized their region's critical role in the nation and argued for greater national spirit among their fellow westerners.[91]

Though visions of a federalism of *Heimat* states never bore fruit, democratic regionalists had more success in reshaping regional identities. Vaguely defined ideas of 'democracy', 'Europeanness' and 'world-openness' as regional values emerged in discourses in a number of territories. Ideas of regional 'Europeanness' could particularly be seen in western border regions and maritime areas, which rapidly abandoned former nationalist regional narratives. In the Rhineland, the trope of the 'Watch on the Rhine' was nowhere to be found, while the Hanseatic cities, known as 'gates to the world', abandoned narratives of the gate as an exit point of German power. Evoking regional Roman and medieval histories, Rhenish regionalists emphasized their role as a 'world-open bridge' to Western Europe, while Hanseatic localists defined their local 'gates' as rooted in a 'Hanseatic world-openness' and international reconciliation. Badenese regionalists like Reinhold Schneider similarly argued that his region was an open 'hall on the Rhine' and gate to the West.[92]

Articulation of vague ideas of 'democracy' as an alleged regional value became prevalent by the late 1940s, reflected in ideas such as 'Badenese democracy', 'Cologne democracy', 'Swabian-Alemannic democracy' and 'Hanseatic democracy'. While Hanseatic citizens drew on their long histories as city republics, Cologner drew on histories going back to their medieval 'guild democracy'. Regional histories of the 1848 revolutions particularly became useful, evoked with alacrity among regionalists in Baden, Swabia and the Rhineland. Histories of regional anti-Prussian sentiment also proved instrumental, with Prussian militarism, rigidity and class hierarchies serving as a foil for new regional identities. Reinvention of regional traditions further offered a useful tool. Rhinelander, for example, advanced notions of Carnival as a regional democratic tradition and magnified historic practices of expressing anti-Prussian sentiment in the tradition.[93]

Articulations of democracy and Europeanness as alleged regional values were by no means without their pitfalls. For one, they aggravated failures to come to grips with the regional Nazi past. Though regionalists seldom argued directly that such values lessened guilt, the implication undoubtedly reinforced their appeal. Nor did they suddenly transform regionalists into adept practitioners or democracy, with many undemocratic continuities persisting in the early Federal Republic. At the same time, greater identification with democracy and European unification on a local and regional level did aid in disbanding the dangerous notion that democracy was a foreign body.

Contested revaluations

Leaving the world of rubble behind them, West Germans, Austrians and other West Europeans experienced tremendous economic growth, followed by a series of political, cultural and generational changes that would alter attitudes towards regionalism. In the short term, economic growth harmonized with regionalist desires, facilitating reconstruction and domestic nesting, while providing additional resources for regional cultural activities. Throughout this period, *Heimat* films also reached their height in West Germany and Austria, depicting the 'wholesome' rural life, often situated in mountainous bucolic landscapes. While historians have debated whether such films were anti-modern and escapist or about negotiation between modernity and rootedness, they often represented a generic regionalism that was less representative of popular interest in *Heimat*.[94] Popular desires for *Heimat* after the war were for places anything but generic, and, as one Lower Saxon *Heimat* enthusiast argued, film often misrepresented experience of *Heimat*.[95]

Over the long term, economic growth and reconstruction reduced both the fears of lost *Heimat* and compensatory needs for local communities which had fuelled regionalism. By the end of the 1950s, the *Heimat* concept also became increasingly intertwined in heated political debates over expellee claims to the former east. While emphasis on an expellee 'right to Heimat' seemed more reasonable in the early post-war years, passage of time, increased integration, the unlikelihood of return and desires for *rapproachment* with the east brought the *Heimat* concept increasingly into heated Cold War debates. These developments combined in the 1960s with generational changes that resulted in a cultural turn against regionalism.

A new youth generation differed from their parents in coming of age at a time of stability, more intact communities and absence of forced movement, with their perception of *Heimat* increasingly coloured by its use in rancorous expellee politics. They also reacted against their parents' generation preoccupation with local rootedness. As one author argued, she had been 'fattened up' with 'Heimat' and Swabian regionalism in her youth, leading her to grow tired of home and craving foreign places.[96] Many responded to expellee's political wielding of *Heimat* against *rapprochement* by appropriating histories of its misuse in Nazi propaganda. As the author Gabriele Wohmann wrote in the mid-1960s, reflecting on expellee rhetoric, 'Heimat Heimat Heimat' provoked sentimental recalcitrant impulses that do not allow peace without 'Heimat'. Displaying little knowledge of the concept's history, Wohmann claimed it had been on its death bed in the Weimar years until its great awakening under Nazism when, so she claimed, the range of compound words with *Heimat* had been formed.[97] The 1960s further saw the elimination of *Heimatkunde* as a school subject in most states, while anti-*Heimat* films and anti-*Heimat* literature emerged as artistic genres which depicted regional culture as largely backward, ruralist and regressive.

Regionalists societies by no means closed down in the 1960s, while the 1970s and 1980s saw contested regionalist revivals, with progressives playing a notable role. After a period of economic stagnation and disappointment over failed utopian visions of the 1960s, regionalism came to the fore as a means of protesting environmental destruction, centralization and technocratic remaking of cities and local landscapes.[98] Regionalism became a locus of new protest movements against centralized overhaul of cities that disregarded regionalist particularities and against environmental destruction of regional landscapes. The protests against the construction of a nuclear plant near the Badenese town of Wyhl illustrated the mobilization of both regional dialect and culture in protest against both environmental destruction and increasing feelings that citizens had become objects of centralized administration.

The growth of regionalism beginning in the mid-1970s hardly remained uncontested, with equation of *Heimat* with backwardness persisting. As the sociologist and scholar of regional culture Hermann Bausinger noted in 1979, when using the *Heimat* concept, one still had to watch over one's shoulder.[99] National reunification in the 1990s would bring new developments to the movement, witnessing both the awakening of regionalist sentiments in the former GDR and the formal recognition of Germany's eastern border. Given the passage of time, expellee cultural preservation, incapable of preserving regional cultures as 'lived' cultures, became increasingly limited to the realm of museums and cultural performances.

Throughout the latter half of the twentieth century and into the present, immigration became an ever-growing issue facing regionalists. Exclusionary forms of regionalism could easily be found, though more inclusively-minded regionalists advanced ideas of region that could embrace foreign immigrants. Some regionalist arguments for acceptance of immigrants drew on earlier narratives used to argue for embrace of expellees. As one Cologne localist argued in the early post-war years, their local natures were defined by their ability to embrace outsiders, stretching back to local integration of foreign artisans and Dutch refugees in centuries past, making expellee integration harmonious with local tradition.[100] Decades later, as Italian and Greek immigrants began moving to the region, a Rhenish regionalist at the annual *Heimat* day argued that the Rhineland had a long history of immigration, and further pointed to their Roman history, noting how influx from the Mediterranean historically enriched their regional culture.[101] Such arguments provided only conceptual tools to promote greater inclusion. More recently, examples of the second generation of immigrant families laying claim to the culture of regionalism can be seen in figures such as cabaret of Django Asül performed in lower Bavarian dialect or in the Bernese dialect comics of Semih Yavsaner. Embrace of immigration remains central to the future viability of regionalism, which itself could arguably be harnessed as an integrative tool.

Conclusion

The centrality of region to debates over German nationhood and the turbulence of twentieth-century Central European history both provide a rich basis through which to illustrate the diverse political, national and cultural framings of regionalism. Popularized during a period of rapid modernization and nation building, regionalism proved a useful asset in negotiating change and the relationship of region and nation. The attraction of different political groups to the movement continued into the Weimar years, which simultaneously saw the further growth of nationalist regionalism. Though quite marginal, separatist movements in the Weimar years remind us that the relationship of nation and region was, in theory, never set in stone. The rise of fascism displayed how National Socialism could appropriate regionalist language for propaganda, even if the regime displayed ambivalence towards the movement's inwardness.

Far from tainted in the aftermath of the war, regionalism emerged in the west as a useful asset, offering a site of flexible identity and federalist ideas of nation. Meanwhile, in the neighbouring GDR, the regionalist movement proved more muted under the control of the new regime which used *Heimat* selectively in state propaganda. By the 1960s, diverse forces resulted in a contested turn against regionalism in the west, followed by revivals in the 1970s and 1980s. In contemporary Germany, contested notions of *Heimat* as tainted have remained, as have progressive strains of regionalism – manifested at events like that of Rhenish dialect bands which came together before a group of 100,000 to sing in protest against violence against foreigners.[102] The future development of regionalism and its engagement with questions of immigration, globalization and raucous political developments remains to be seen.

Notes

1. '... nur noch Deutsche', *Vaterstädtische Blätter* 7, no. 12 (December 1956): 4.
2. Joost Augusteijn and Eric Storm, eds, *Region and State in Nineteenth-Century Europe: Nation-Building, Regional Identities and Separatism* (Basingstroke: Palgrave Macmillan, 2012); Philipp Ther and Holm Sundhaussen, eds, *Regionale Bewegungen und Regionalismen in europäischen Zwischenräumen seit der Mitte des 19. Jahrhunderts* (Marburg: Herder-Institut, 2003); and Peter Haslinger, ed., *Regionale und nationale Identitäten. Wechselwirkungen und Spannungsfelder im Zeitalter moderner Staatlichkeit* (Würzburg: Ergon, 2000).
3. Wilhelm Heinrich Riehl, *The Natural History of the German People*, trans. David Diephouse (Lewiston, NY: Edwin Mellen Press, 1990).
4. Mack Walker, *German Home Towns: Community, State and General Estate 1648–1871* (Ithaca, NY: Cornell University Press, 1971).
5. David Blackbourn and James Retallack, 'Introduction', in *Localism, Landscape, and the Ambiguities of Place: German-Speaking Central Europe, 1860–1930*, ed. David Blackbourn and James Retallack (Toronto: University of Toronto Press, 2007), 15–16.
6. Hermann Bausinger, 'Heimat in einer offenen Gesellschaft', in *Die Ohnmacht der Gefühle*, ed. Jochen Kelter (Weingarten: Drumlin, 1986), 93–94.
7. Nigel Reeves, 'Heimat aus der Ferne', in *Heimat im Wort*, ed. Rüdiger Görner (Munich: Iudicium, 1992), 72.
8. See the chapter by Hopkin.
9. See the chapter by Storm.
10. Hans-Ulrich Wehler, *Deutsche Gesellschaftsgeschichte: Von der 'Deutschen Doppelrevolution' bis zum Beginn des Ersten Weltkrieges*, volume 3 (Munich: Beck, 2008), 493–510.
11. Ibid., 512.
12. On industrialization and urbanization generating interest in regional culture, see Hermann Bausinger, *Folk Culture in a World of Technology*, trans. Elke Dettmer (Bloomington: Indiana University Press, 1990).
13. Eric Storm, *The Culture of Regionalism: Art, Architecture and International Exhibitions in France, Germany and Spain, 1890–1939* (Manchester: Manchester University Press, 2010).
14. See the chapter by Molina and Núñez Seixas.
15. Storm, *Culture of Regionalism*.
16. Jeremy DeWaal, 'The Reinvention of Tradition: Form, Meaning, and Local Identity in Modern Cologne Carnival', *Central European History* 46 (2013): 495–532.

17. Celia Applegate, *A Nation of Provincials: The German Idea of Heimat* (Berkeley: University of California Press, 1990), 62. See also Alon Confino, *The Nation as a Local Metaphor: Württemberg, Imperial Germany, and National Memory, 1871-1918* (Chapel Hill: University of North Carolina Press, 1997); and Eric Kurlander, 'The Landscapes of Liberalism: Particularism and Progressive Politics in Two Borderland Regions', in *Localism*, ed. Blackbourn and Retallack, 124-45.
18. William Rollins, *A Greener Vision of Home: Cultural Politics and Environmental Reform in the German Heimatschutz Movement, 1904-1918* (Ann Arbor: University of Michigan Press, 1997). See also the chapter by Meyer.
19. Karlheinz Rossbacher, *Heimatkunstbewegung und Heimatroman* (Stuttgart: Ernst Klett, 1977).
20. On the regional art movement throughout Europe, see Storm, *Culture of Regionalism*. On *Heimat* art and urban culture, see Jennifer Jenkins, *Provincial Modernity: Local Culture and Liberal Politics in Fin-de-Siècle Hamburg* (Ithaca, NY: Cornell University Press, 2003).
21. Maiken Umbach and Bernd-Rüdiger Hüppauf, eds, *Vernacular Modernism: Heimat, Globalization and the Built Environment* (Stanford, NY: Stanford University Press, 2005).
22. Hugo Jüngst, 'Los von Berlin', in *Heimat deine Heimat*, ed. Jürgen Liebing (Darmstadt: Luchterhand, 1982), 39.
23. On *Heimat* as a mediating point, see Applegate, *Nation of Provincials*. Alon Confino in a different approach argues for *Heimat* as a local metaphor of nation. See Confino, *Nation as a Local Metaphor*.
24. Stefano Cavazza 'Regionalism in Italy: A Critique', in *Region and State*, ed. Augusteijn and Storm, 69-89; Timothy Baycroft, 'National Diversity, Regionalism and Decentralism in France', in *Region and State*, ed. Augusteijn and Storm, 57-68; and Robert Colls, 'Gaelic and Northumbrian: Separatism and Regionalism in the United Kingdom, 1890-1920', in *Region and State*, ed. Augusteijn and Storm, 172-91. See also the chapter by Molina and Núñez Seixas.
25. Oliver Zimmer, *A Contested Nation: History, Memory and Nationalism in Switzerland, 1761-1891* (Cambridge: Cambridge University Press, 2003).
26. Peter Haslinger, 'How to Run a Multilingual Society: Statehood, Administration and Regional Dynamics in Austria-Hungary, 1867-1914', in *Region and State*, ed. Augusteijn and Storm, 111-28.
27. Zimmer, *A Contested Nation*.
28. Abigail Green, *Fatherlands: State-Building and Nationhood in Nineteenth-Century Germany* (Cambridge: Cambridge University Press, 2001); and Siegfried Weichlein, *Nation und Region: Integrationsprozesse im Bismarckreich* (Düsseldorf: Droste, 2004).
29. Confino, *Nation as a Local Metaphor*.
30. Andreas Schumann, *Heimat denken: Regionales Bewusstsein in der deutschsprachigen Literatur zwischen 1815 und 1914* (Cologne: Böhlau, 2002).
31. See the chapter by Bassin and Suslov.
32. See James Bjork, *Neither German nor Pole: Catholicism and National Indifference in a Central European Borderland* (Ann Arbor: University of Michigan Press, 2008).
33. Jeremy King, *Budweisers into Czechs and Germans: A Local History of Bohemian Politics, 1848-1948* (Princeton, NJ: Princeton University Press, 2005); and Peter Sahlins, *Boundaries: The Making of France and Spain in the Pyrenees* (Berkeley: University of California Press, 1989).
34. Daniel Mollenhauer, '"Aufgepfropftes Franzosentum auf deutschen Stamm": Der elsässische Volkscharakter in der deutschen Elsaß-Publizistik', in *Regionale und Nationale Identitäten*,

ed. Haslinger, 95–112; and Christopher Fischer, *Alsace to the Alsatians?: Visions and Divisions of Alsatian Regionalism, 1870–1939* (New York: Berghahn, 2010).

35. Pieter Judson, 'Tourismus, Nationalisierung der Landschaft und lokales Identitätsmanagement um die Jahrhundertwende: Böhmen, die Steiermark und Trentino/Südtirol' in *Regionale und Nationale Identitäten*, ed. Haslinger, 112–28.
36. Applegate, *Nation of Provincials*, 108–20.
37. Confino, *Nation as a Local Metaphor*, 165–69, 184–85 and 194–200.
38. Gerhard Schneider, 'Zur Mobilisierung der 'Heimatfront': Das Nageln sogenannter Kriegswahrzeichen im Ersten Weltkrieg', *Zeitschrift für Volkskunde* 95 (1999): 32–62.
39. Philipp Ther, 'Einleitung: Sprachliche, kulturelle und ethnische 'Zwischenräume' als Zugang zu einer transnationalen Geschichte Europas', in *Regionale Bewegungen*, ed. Ther and Sundhausen, xix.
40. Christiane Kohser-Spohn, 'Der Traum von gemeinsamen Europa. Autonomiebewegungen und Regionalismus im Elsaß, 1870–1970', in *Regionale Bewegungen*, ed. Ther and Sundhaussen, 89–111.
41. Winson Chu, *The German Minority in Interwar Poland* (Cambridge: Cambridge University Press, 2012).
42. Bundesarchiv, B 234/626, 'Patenschaften–Brücken zur alten Heimat: Mannheim erneuerte seine Patenschaft für das Memelland', *Badische Neueste Nachrichten* (14 August 1953).
43. Gerald Stourzh, *Vom Reich zur Republik. Studien zum Österreichbewusstsein im 20. Jahrhundert* (Vienna: Wiener Journal Zeitschriftenverlag, 1990).
44. Laurence Cole, 'The Construction of German Identity in Tirol, 1848–1945', in *Regionale Bewegungen*, ed. Ther and Sundhaussen, 20.
45. Eduard Spranger, 'Das Bildungswert der Heimatkunde' (1923), in Eduard Spranger, *Gesammelte Schriften II: Philosophische Pädagogik* (Heidelberg: Quelle & Meyer, 1975), 294–319.
46. Hugo Preuß, *Reich und Länder* (Berlin: Carl Heymanns, 1928), 21, 157; Celia Applegate, 'Democracy or Reaction?: The Political Implication of Localist Ideas in Wilhelmine and Weimar Germany', in *Elections, Mass Politics, and Social Change in Modern German*, ed. James Retallack and Larry Eugene Jones (Cambridge: Cambridge University Press, 1992), 247–66.
47. See Peter Haslinger, 'Nationalismus und Regionalismus: Konflikt oder Koexistenz?', in *Regionale Bewegungen*, ed. Ther and Sundhausen, 267–74.
48. Kurt Stavenhagen, *Heimat als Lebenssinn*, 2nd ed. (Göttingen: Vandenhoeck & Ruprecht, 1948), 49–50.
49. Celia Applegate, 'The Question of Heimat in the Weimar Republic', *New Formations* 17 (1992): 64–74.
50. Peter Fritzsche, 'Cities Forget, Nations Remember', in *Pain and Prosperity: Reconsidering Twentieth-Century German History*, ed. Paul Betts and Greg Eghigian (Stanford, CA: Stanford University Press, 2003), 35–59.
51. See Maiken Umbach and Claus-Christian Szejnmann, eds, *Heimat, Region, and Empire: Spatial Identities under National Socialism* (Basingstoke: Palgrave Macmillan, 2012); and Thomas Schaarschmidt, *Regionalkultur und Diktatur: Sächsische Heimatbewegung und Heimat-Propaganda im Dritten Reich und in der SBZ/DDR* (Cologne: Böhlau, 2004). See also Xosé M. Núñez Seixas and Maiken Umbach, 'Hijacked Heimats: National Appropriation of Local and Regional Identities in Germany and Spain, 1930–1945', *European Review of History* 15, no. 3 (2008): 295–316.

52. Lutz Raphael, 'Pluralities of National Socialist Ideology', in *Visions of Community in Nazi Germany: Social Engineering and Private Lives*, ed. Martina Steber and Bernhard Gotto (Oxford: Oxford University Press, 2014), 73–86.

53. On the need to shift from 'institutionally bound analysis' to culture in Nazi ideas of region, see Geoff Eley, 'Commentary: Thoughts on Nazism's Spatial Imaginary', in *Heimat, Region, and Empire*, ed. Szejnmann and Umbach, 252–67.

54. Dietrich Klagges, *Geschichtsunterricht als nationalpolitische Erziehung* (Frankfurt: Moritz Diesterweg, 1937), 165–67.

55. Julia Faehndrich, 'Entstehung und Aufstieg des Heimatbuchs', in *Das Heimatbuch: Geschichte, Methodik, Wirkung*, ed. Matthias Beer (Göttingen: V & R Unipress, 2010), 62–72.

56. See Martina Steber, 'Regions and National Socialist Ideology', in *Heimat, Region, and Empire*, ed. Szejnmann and Umbach, 25–42; and Catherine Epstein, 'Germanization in the Warthegau: Germans, Jews and Poles in the Making of a "German" Gau', in *Heimat, Region, and Empire*, ed. Szejnmann and Umbach, 93–111.

57. See the chapter by Núñez Seixas. See also Kay Dohnke, Norbert Hopster and Jan Wirrer, eds, *Niederdeutsch im Nationalsozialismus. Studien zur Rolle regionaler Kultur im Faschismus* (Hildesheim: Georg Olms, 1994).

58. Jeremy Noakes, 'Federalism in the Nazi State', in *German Federalism: Past, Present, Future*, ed. Maiken Umbach (Basingstroke: Palgrave Macmillan, 2002), 113–45; and Michael Kissener, 'Nationalsozialismus und Widerstand', in *Heimat: Konstanten und Wandel im 19./20. Jahrhundert*, ed. Katharina Weigand (Munich: Deutscher Alpenverein, 1997), 210–11.

59. These themes can be seen extensively from 1933 to the outbreak of the war in volumes 10–16 of the *Rheinische Blätter*.

60. Heinrich Lersch, *Rheinische Blätter* 19, no. 10 (October 1942): 295.

61. These themes were dominant from 1933 to 1939 in volumes 10–16. On the need of regionalists to make German will 'radiate' beyond the national border, see Robert Brandes, 'Der Kampfbund im Rheinland', *Rheinische Blätter* 10, no. 10 (October 1933): 909–12.

62. Oberstarbeitsführer Helff ed., *Grenzland Baden* (Karlsruhe: C. F. Müller, 1936), 28.

63. Adolf Hitler, 'Meine eigene Heimat', reprinted in Jürgen Liebig, ed., *Heimat deine Heimat. Ein Lesebuch* (Darmstadt: Luchterhand, 1982), 71–72.

64. Jakob Schaffner, 'Rings um die alemannische Kulturtagung', in *Alemannenland*, ed. Franz Kerber (Stuttgart: Engelhorn, 1937), 28–31.

65. See Applegate, *Nation of Provincials*, 197–227; and Storm, *Culture of Regionalism*, 261–82.

66. *Rheinische Blätter* volumes 17 to 20, published from 1940 to 1943. On the German-Flemish cultural festival, see volume 18, number 7.

67. See the chapter by Leerssen.

68. Alfred Delp, 'Heimat', in Alfred Delp, *Gesammelte Schriften. Band II: Philosophische Schriften*, ed. Roman Bleistein (Frankfurt: Knecht, 1983), 249–69.

69. On the example of the Soviet Union, see Lisa Kirschenbaum, '"Our City, Our Hearths, Our Families": Local Loyalties and Private Life in Soviet World War II Propaganda', *Slavic Review* 59, no. 4 (Winter 2008): 828–47.

70. Julie Torrie, *'For Their Own Good': Civilian Evacuations in Germany and France, 1939–1945* (New York: Berghahn, 2010).

71. Statistischen Amt der Stadt Köln, *Verwaltungsbericht der Stadt Köln, 1945/47* (Cologne: Stadt Köln, 1947), 54–55.

72. Max Brauer, 'Rede am 22. November 1946', in *Nüchternen Sinnes und Heissen Herzens: Reden und Ansprachen*, ed. Max Brauer (Hamburg: Auerdruck, 1956), 24–25; Otto Feger, *Konstanz: Aus der Vergangenheit einer alten Stadt* (Konstanz: Curt Weller, 1947), 11; and Celia Applegate, 'Senses of Place', in *The Oxford Handbook of Modern German History*, ed. Helmut Walser Smith (Oxford: Oxford University Press, 2011), 63.
73. Kurt Koszyk, 'Presse und Pressekonzentration in den 50er Jahren', in *Modernisierung im Wiederaufbau: die westdeutsche Gesellschaft der 50er Jahre*, ed. Axel Schildt and Arnold Sywottek (Bonn: J. H. W. Dietz, 1993), 441.
74. Applegate, *Nation of Provincials*, 228–46; and Jörg Arnold, *The Allied Air War and Urban Memory: The Legacy of Strategic Bombing in Germany* (Cambridge: Cambridge University Press, 2011).
75. Jeremy DeWaal, *Redemptive Geographies: Heimat and Democratization in West Germany, 1945–1990* (in preparation).
76. Untitled excerpts in *Alt und Neu-Köln* (1946), 2.
77. Jan Palmowski, *Inventing a Socialist Nation: Heimat and the Politics of Everyday Life in the GDR, 1945–1990* (Cambridge: Cambridge University Press, 2009); Schaarschmidt, *Regionalkultur*.
78. Reinhard Johler, 'Die Wissenschaft der Heimat', in *Heimat*, ed. Weigand, 91.
79. Stourzh, *Vom Reich zur Republik*, 58, 83.
80. Andrew Demshuk, 'Reinscribing Schlesien as Śląsk: Memory and Mythology in a Postwar German-Polish Borderland', *History & Memory* 24, no. 1 (Spring/Summer 2012): 39–86.
81. Bundesarchiv B 234, Nr. 634, BdV, Liste I: Bestehende west-ostdeutsche kommunale und Landespatenschaften (1961).
82. Yuliya Komska, *The Icon Curtain: The Cold War's Quiet Border* (Chicago, IL: University of Chicago Press, 2015).
83. Alon Confino, *Germany as a Culture of Remembrance: Promises and Limits of Writing History* (Chapel Hill: University of North Carolina Press, 2006).
84. Wolfgang Borchert, 'In Hamburg', in *Lieder und Sprüche auf Hamburg*, ed. Paul Neumann (Hamburg: Hans Christians, 1960), 77.
85. Leo Wohleb, 'Rede', 24 February 1946, in *Humanist und Politiker: Leo Wohleb*, ed. Paul Ludwig-Weinacht and Hans Maier (Heidelberg: Kerle, 1969), 171.
86. Bundesarchiv B 144, no. 253, Walter von Cube, 'Um die Selbständigkeit des Landes Baden', 1 July 1951, in Circulatory, 'Vom See bis des Maines Strand'.
87. Max Picard, *Hitler in uns Selbst* (Zürich: Eugen Rentsch, 1946), 262.
88. Otto Feger, *Schwäbisch-Alemannische Demokratie* (Konstanz: Curt Weller, 1946).
89. See the chapters of Hopkin and Kabatek.
90. Bundesarchiv B 234, No. 626, 'Polnische sorgen um die Oder-Neiße-Linie', *Ost-West-Kurier*, 22–28 October 1949.
91. Ulrike Frede, '"Unsere Heimat war deutsch!"', in *Heimatbuch*, ed. Beer, 179–202.
92. Heimatbund Badenerland, *Baden als Bundesland* (Waldkirch: Waldkircher, 1955), 28.
93. DeWaal, 'Reinvention of Tradition', 523–28.
94. Johannes von Moltke, *No Place Like Home: Locations of Heimat in German Cinema* (Berkeley: University of California Press, 2005).

95. Herbert Röhrig, 'Der Heimatgedanke in unserer Zeit', *Jahrbuch Deutscher Heimatbund* (1959): 29–32.
96. Margarete Hannsmann, untitled contribution, in *Literatur im Alemannischen Raum: Regionalismus und Dialekt*, ed. Jochen Kelter and Peter Salomon (Freiburg: Dreisam, 1978), 46–47.
97. Gabriele Wohmann, 'Wörter mit Temperatur', in *Gegen den Tod: Stimmen deutscher Schriftsteller gegen die Atombombe*, ed. Gudrun Ensslin (Stuttgart: Cordeliers, 1964), 104–6.
98. Wilfried von Bredow and Hans-Friedrich Foltin, *Zwiespältige Zufluchten: Zur Renaissance des Heimatgefühls* (Bonn: J. H. W. Dietz, 1981).
99. Hermann Bausinger, 'Heimat und Identität', in *Heimat und Identität: Probleme regionaler Kultur*, ed. Konrad Köstlin (Neumünster: Karl Wachholtz, 1980), 22.
100. Adam Wrede, 'Um die Erhaltung Kölner Eigenart', *Alt-Köln* 2, no. 3 (March 1948): 9–10.
101. Adolf Flecken, *Gestaltung der Heimat nach rheinischer Eigenart* (Neuss: GfB, 1966), 15–16.
102. AG Arsch huh, ed., *Arsch huh, Zäng ussenander! Gegen Rassismus und Neonazis* (Cologne: Kiepenheuer & Witsch, 1992).

Further reading

Applegate, Celia, *A Nation of Provincials: The German Idea of Heimat* (Berkeley: University of California Press, 1990).

Applegate, Celia, 'Senses of Place', in *The Oxford Handbook of Modern German History*, ed. Helmut Walser Smith (Oxford: Oxford University Press, 2011), 49–70.

Blackbourn, David, and James Retallack, eds, *Localism, Landscape, and the Ambiguities of Place: German-Speaking Central Europe, 1860–1930* (Toronto: University of Toronto Press, 2007).

Green, Abigail, *Fatherlands: State-Building and Nationhood in Nineteenth-Century Germany* (Cambridge: Cambridge University Press, 2001).

Palmowski, Jan, *Inventing a Socialist Nation: Heimat and the Politics of Everyday Life in the GDR, 1945–1990* (Cambridge: Cambridge University Press, 2009).

Rollins, William, *A Greener Vision of Home: Cultural Politics and Environmental Reform in the German Heimatschutz Movement, 1904–1918* (Ann Arbor: University of Michigan Press, 1997).

Umbach, Maiken, and Bernd-Rüdiger Hüppauf, eds, *Vernacular Modernism: Heimat, Globalization and the Built Environment* (Stanford, CA: Stanford University Press, 2005).

von Moltke, Johannes, *No Place Like Home: Locations of Heimat in German Cinema* (Berkeley: University of California Press, 2005).

CHAPTER 11
SCANDINAVIA: REGIONALISM IN THE SHADOW OF STRONG STATES
Peter Stadius

Introduction

Regionalism in Scandinavia, or the Nordic Region if we also include both Iceland and Finland, has to a certain extent its own forms, marked by strong states. If we understand regionalism from a traditional regional studies approach as the political battle and negotiation of regions for autonomy, increased influence in decision-making and ultimately the pursuit of independence, Scandinavia offers very little in this respect.[1] There is little evidence of regions operating autonomously according to the principles of subsidiarity, a principle largely absent in Nordic political culture since the state traditionally has not handed over much responsibility to other substate structures.[2] The strong state tradition in Scandinavia, dating back to the state-driven Reformation processes of the sixteenth century, has put effective boundaries to regionalism in a stricter sense. Regionalism connects mainly to policymaking within the nation states as a level of decision-making, or as cultural articulations and traditions connected to various spaces. However, there are several cases of border regions affected by geopolitical turmoil in the past, and there are even some Scandinavian examples of regionalist claims and voicings, both in political and cultural terms. The outcome of the Napoleonic Wars in particular had a visible impact on the regional-spatial dynamics of Scandinavia, producing some regionalist movements.

In this chapter, some central tendencies of regionalism in Scandinavia will be presented, with focus on the cultural and ideological construction of two types of regionalism: national heartland regions and transnational border regions. At the end of the chapter, the northern fringe of Fennoskandia will be analysed as a space for parallel and spatially overlapping regionalist strategies. The chapter is not a systematic presentation of all regionalist movements, and the reader will observe a certain inclination towards the eastern half of the Nordic region. The timeframe from 1890 to the present also, to some extent, limits the story to be told here. Some nation states emerged during the nineteenth century through nation-formation processes that include dynamics akin to regionalist development, according to the classical ABC theory of Miroslav Hroch concerning the birth of national movements in three stages from cultural historical interest among smaller groups to a consolidation of a sovereign nation state.[3] The birth of Norway (1905), Finland (1917) and Iceland (1944) as sovereign nation states can thus be characterized as regionalist processes in a broader Scandinavian setting.

Also, the development of four chronological stages of regional institutionalization, as defined by Anssi Paasi, will be tested against some of the cases presented. According to Paasi, these stages include a first assumption of a space, mainly referring to mid-nineteenth-century romantic essentialization. The second phase is the strategic naming of the region, while the third phase involves the establishment of institutions to mobilize both symbolic cultural capital and real political bargaining power. Finally, the fourth stage refers to a consolidation into a system of regions.[4]

Heartland regions as part of nation-building

In the late nineteenth century, a culturally oriented regionalism, supportive or at least non-conflictive with the centralized efforts to build nation states, became a general trend in Europe.[5] In Scandinavia one finds cases fulfilling this category, and special attention here will be given to the Swedish region of Dalecarlia and Karelia in Finland, both elevated to archetypic landscapes seen as cradles of national culture.[6] The former presents an interesting dynamic between traditional regionalism and the integration into a process of national modernization.

Dalecarlia, or *Dalarna* in Swedish, is the typical heartland region, and has stood as a symbol for national independence in Sweden. Dalecarlian men have traditionally been seen as prototypes of the free Swedish peasant, and vernacular heritage and folklore was in the late nineteenth century championed as the most authentic in its Swedishness. Artur Hazelius, the founder of the Skansen open-air museum in 1891 (regarded as the first museum of its type in the world) was highly influenced by Dalecarlian cultural heritage; the first two buildings to be removed and reassembled at Skansen in Stockholm were from the Dalarna region.[7] In the summer of 1872, Hazelius had spent a longer period in the region, observing and documenting local customs and artistic expressions, from songs to clothing and architecture. Industrial development in the region was an object of concern for him, and the idea of preserving the national peasant heritage became his lifelong project. He started collecting local artefacts, which were to form the basis for a Scandinavian ethnographic collection showcased in Stockholm. In 1897, during the General Art and Industrial Exposition, this collection was transferred to the new Nordic Museum, Nordiska Museet, a magnificent museum building next to Skansen.[8]

In nineteenth-century Swedish history writing, events connected to Dalecarlia became central. The Engelbrekt rebellion in 1434 against the first King of the Kalmar Union, Eric of Pomerania, was reinterpreted as a national freedom fight and a first sign of democratic involvement of yeomen peasants in local decision-making: the local nobleman Engelbrekt rose against the king with the help of his Dalecarlian yeomen army. Secondly, the strong desire for self-determination connected to the Dalcarlian men - referred to as *dalkarlar* or Dale churls - has functioned as a symbol for the role of peasants in national politics. The three rebellions of the Dale churls against King Gustav Vasa (King of Sweden between 1523 and 1556), originally exaggerated by the king's chroniclers in order to show the challenges the King faced to unite Sweden, have later served as evidence of a primordial democratic resistance against tyranny. In somewhat paradoxical terms, the Dale churls, as the essentially most Swedish peasants, and Dalarna, as the heartland region, have also served in memory culture to accentuate the bond between Gustav Vasa and the nation. In the 1830s, seven frescoes painted by Johan Gustav Sandberg were added to the Vasa Chapel in Uppsala Cathedral to surround the grave monument of Gustav Vasa. Two of them present scenes in Dalarna and the support of the Dale churls to the Swedish rebel king in the fight against the Danes.

The cult of Engelbrekt, the Dale churls and the heroic escapes of Gustav Vasa from the Danes was cemented in history paintings and schoolbooks. In 1914, a National Romantic-style church was completed in Stockholm and named after Engelbrekt, who also was honoured with a monument in the old town of the capital erected in 1916, where he is depicted as a Wilhelm Tellian figure stretching his crossbow. The tales connected to King Gusav Vasa have many proven connections with popular folk tales, and the number of huts he visited and beds he was assumed to have slept in increased steadily during the nineteenth century. Based on the chronicle of Peder Svart, a contemporary of the King, the tales were amended during later centuries and in 1914, the educator and author Anna Maria Roos published a popular book, 'The adventures of Gustav Vasa in Dalecarlia' (*Gustav Vasas äventyr i Dalarna*), inspiring schoolbooks and other popular national cultural history well up to after the Second World War. One heroic escape on skis has inspired the annual ski event Vasaloppet, established in 1922 and claiming to be the biggest ski event in the world today. The event's homepage states,

> Vasaloppet started in 1922, but really it is much older than that. The first Vasalopp was carried out as early as 1521 by Gustav Eriksson. During his flight from the Danish king, he stopped in Sälen and returned to Mora to lead the uprising against the occupation forces. Gustav Eriksson eventually united the realm and became Sweden's first king, better known under the name Gustav Vasa. In other words, Sälen is not only the starting point for the world's largest exercise race; it is also the starting point for the history of our entire country.[9]

The size and organization of the Danish 'occupation forces' back in the sixteenth century may be questionable, but, nonetheless, Dalecarlia's position as the Swedish heartland region and champion of independence is still part of the mindscape of national self-perception. Dalecarlia has over time achieved a position as the ideal Swedish region, all based on nationalist historical narratives and outright propaganda of rather unclear origin.[10] The peasant architecture of this region is generally considered the most authentic, and it was central in the creation of a Swedish National Romantic style around 1900.

Sweden entered a new era of modernity during the 1930s, with the emergence of a comprehensive national welfare state project driven by the Social Democratic Party, which came into power in 1932. This modernization project, also referred to as the People's Home, *folkhemmet*, made Sweden future- (and planning-) oriented as a nation. However, the persuasion and rooting of the new politics curiously had a connection to Dalecarlian regional traditions. In the summer of 1930, the Stockholm Exhibition of Swedish Arts and Crafts Industry would draw over a million visitors to the Swedish capital. This exhibition has been seen as the turning point between old and new in Swedish contemporary history, since the Swedish nation was literally marched into a new and modern mass society based on rational planning and industrial production.[11] All exhibition buildings were executed in a functionalist architectural style, and the mastermind architects behind the exhibition later published a radical pamphlet, *Acceptera*, in which they urged all Swedes to accept the new and modern lifestyle. The authors aimed to nationalize their radical avant-garde architecture, by referring to its connection with traditional Swedish peasant architecture. The best known traditional wooden building in the country, the Ornäs hut (*Ornässtugan*), was chosen as a point of reference and comparison to show the similarity between old and new.[12]

The Ornäs hut was a Dalecarlian shrine for the cult of Gustav Vasa and a central scene for his legends of bravery escaping the Danes. This unholy union between *Heimat* style and radical functionalism was used repeatedly in Sweden to nationalize and popularize the latter.[13] Another Dalecarlian symbol, the Dala horse, has preserved and expanded its leading role. This traditional wooden decoration object has often symbolized Sweden, and sometimes even entire Scandinavia, when branded internationally. The industrial production of this souvenir started during the 1930s and was introduced to an international audience in the World Fair in Paris (1937) and New York (1939), respectively, when Sweden presented itself as a modern and rational country offering a middle way between capitalism and communism (Figure 11.1). The use of premodern regional folk culture elements is an example of integrative regionalism, seeking to sustain historic identities and loyalties within a new national modernizing project.[14]

In Finland, the dynamics of regional and national cultural tradition is centred on the eastern border region Karelia. The region's condition as a heartland, as a strong and independent agent and even as a Finnish region altogether, can be contested. This does not, however, alter the fact that Karelia is the region that in the nineteenth century defined the purest of Finnishness and after the end of the Second World War became a lost region and object for a very strong memory culture. The cult of Karelia was introduced by the National Romantic movement during what has been referred to as the golden era of Finnish art: roughly the period 1885–1910. The national Finnish programme found its prehistoric cultural heritage in the mythology of the national epic Kalevala. The oral folk song tradition collected by Kalevala's creator Elias Lönnrot, and first published in 1835, was forged into a comprehensive system of mythological events, stories and personalities. It was an essentialist cultural separation of Finnishness from any Swedish and Scandinavian influence, at a time when old-Norse mythology was attributed to all the northern parts of Europe. During the entire nineteenth century, there was a dispute over the origins of the Kalevala material, since some claimed their western Finnish origins. Lönnrot explicitly named the first so-called Old Kalevala of 1835 as a collection of Karelian folk songs. The choice of Karelia as the heartland of Finnish culture and the major element in forging a national cultural consciousness had a strategic relevance in the quest for being accepted by Russian authorities.[15] It clearly contested any Swedish and Scandinavian traditions and connections and offered an

Scandinavia

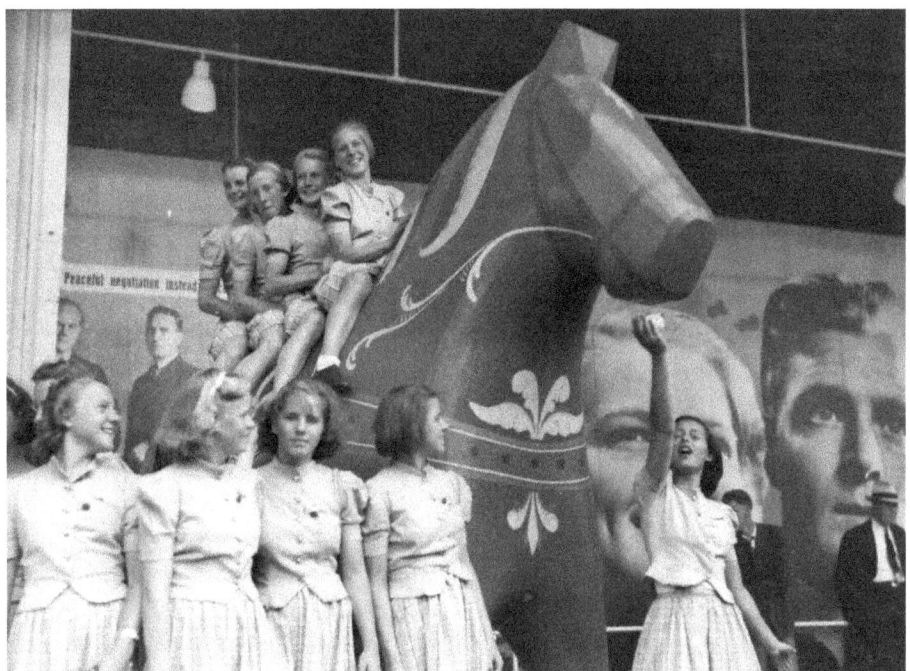

Figure 11.1 *A gigantic Dala horse welcoming the visitors at the Swedish pavilion at the New York World Fair 1939 (photographer unknown/Nordiska museet).*

eastward-oriented interpretation of Finnish culture, accentuating the affinity with other Fenno-Ugric language groups within the borders of the Russian Empire.[16]

As a region in itself, Karelia and its inhabitants never constituted a strong regional force of self-articulation, but it was rather the object of a cultural construction process largely steered from Helsinki. The term 'Karelianism', alluding to this national practice of self-exoticism on behalf of the academic and artistic elite, was coined as late as 1939 by Yrjö Hirn, professor of literary history at the University of Helsinki. He described it as the worship of the Karelian cultural heritage and the act of pilgrimage to the 'Karelian song lands' by artists and authors, which was at its height during the 1890s.[17] In 1893, a Karelian soiree was celebrated in Helsinki, involving the front figures of the national artistic movement. Jean Sibelius conducted parts from his Karelia Suite, and Akseli Gallen-Kallela had painted the backcloths with the help of the young architecture student Eliel Saarinen; authentic rune singers performed for an awed Helsinki audience. From that point, Karelia was the main point of reference for authentic Finnish culture in its purest and most ancient form.

The loss of most parts of Karelia, historically a border region, at the end of the Second World War to the Soviet Union sparked a collective phantom agony among Finns. The dream of returning Karelia, with its largest city Viipuri (Viborg/Vyborg) to Finland became a central part of a vivid cultural memory.[18] The interest in Karelia was expressed in cultural terms and as a private practice due to the difficult relationship with the Soviet Union during the Cold War. On the level of regional cooperation, the post-communist era has brought increased opportunities for travel and establishing contacts. However, one cannot speak about any self-driven conscious regional agency in a region parted by a border between the European Union and Russia. From a Finnish national point of view, Karelia is still as much ideography as it is geography.[19]

In the western parts of Scandinavia, regionalism as part of the nation-building project followed a similar path. During the period of nineteenth-century national awakening, specific regions provided for the ideal national landscape and the essence of purest national peasant culture. In Norway, National Romantic painters canonized the majestic Hardanger Fjord region in order to represent a national landscape par excellence. In a similar fashion, the inland region in southern Norway, Telemark, grew to be regarded as the most authentic and pristine sanctuary of Norwegian folk culture. These heartland regions functioned in the same fashion as the eastern Scandinavian examples discussed previously. However, the Norwegian sense for regions and their importance has a more pronounced level of consciousness in the Norwegian national self-conception. The promotors of the national programme sought to distance themselves from urban and Danish culture, which resulted, for instance, in the emergence of two different national languages, *Bokmål* and *Nynorsk*, officially approved in 1929 by the Norwegian parliament. The former is closer to the traditional Danish-influenced 'language of books', while the latter, the 'New Norwegian', is based on popular dialects. Ivar Aasen (1813–1896), the father of *Nynorsk*, called this language *Landsmål*, literally 'the language of the countryside'. His collection work around the country still stands today as a visible symbol of the positive recognition regional and rural culture enjoys in Norway, a recognition that has a strong sense of anti-elitism connected to it. It is common to hear the dialect spoken on Norwegian state television, while it is almost inexistent in the Finnish case. Another phenomenon, suggesting a conscious rootedness in premodern folk culture, is the increasing use of the folk costume *bunad* in Norway, visible in the celebrations of Constitution Day on 17 May each year. The increasing use of this national symbol is an act of performing a national identity and can, to a certain extent, be compared to the use of the kilt in Scotland and the dirndl in Bavaria. In a Nordic context, the usage of this Norwegian folk costume is popular far beyond folk dance groups, and the institutionalization of the folk costume surpasses that of other Scandinavian countries.[20]

The border regions

The cultural border regions present various forms of regionalist development in the Nordic case. Of the border regions, Karelia has already been presented as a national heartland, while it actually is a border region. Other historical border regions are southern Jutland on the German-Danish border, Scania and the Torne Valley. Some of these traditionally competitive regions question the authority of central power while actively promoting local history, heritage and culture. Other regions are so-called hyphenated regions, that is, transnational regions emerging around expectations of positive cross-border effects in an increasingly integrating Europe.[21]

Scania (Skåne) in southern Sweden, part of Denmark until 1658, is perhaps the Scandinavian region that could potentially qualify as a case of competitive regionalism. Since the 1860s, a local history consciousness had been cultivated within certain circles at Lund University, with historian Martin Weibull as the driving force. His work was continued by his two sons and other local patriots, contesting historical interpretation based on a centralized conception of Sweden. Different organizations, from early heritage associations to later grass-roots organizations and populist parties have continuously cultivated a Scanian regional identity; the protests against a Stockholm driven cultural levelling became a unifying figure of thought. A Scanian flag with a red cross on a yellow background and the heraldic symbol of a griffin's head is part of everyday regionalist practices in the region.

During the early decades of the twentieth century, local activists, such as David Assarsson, propagated the recognition of the region's medieval, pre-modern and pre-state history. Catholicism was highlighted as one instrument of differentiation from a Lutheran-conservative Swedish nation state.[22] As Fredrik Persson has shown, the Skåne regional patriotism developed partly as a popular critical counter-movement to a dominating Swedish historical interpretation and has some features in its early development that cohere with Hroch's theory of nation-building processes, but fails to reach the third and final stage of consolidation.[23] The cultivation of a Scanian cultural separatism has never been a serious political threat to Swedish national unity. The Scanian movement became increasingly conservative and in the 1990s even became associated with xenophobic, anti-immigration groups. The connection between a populist and right-wing discourse and a Scanian ethnohistorical regional identity to a certain extent marginalized the Scanian cause on a cultural level. The emergence of a parallel regional development, the Öresund (Øresund) region, consisting of both Sjælland in Denmark and Scania in Sweden, has in many ways diminished the appeal of the Scanian regional tradition, even if local regional traditions are still widely practiced, like within gastronomy.

The transition process from the intra-national Scania region to its incorporation into the transnational Öresund region has changed the outlook of regionalism in southern Sweden. The reconnection of the historical Danish region with the Öresund Bridge (2000) as the ultimate material and symbolic *pièce de résistance* has until now been one of the success stories in the new Europe of the regions. The Öresund Region is essentially a modern economy – and a mobility-driven integration process of redefining a border region as the central region it once was. The role as a hub for economic activity in Scandinavia gives the new transnational region an air of modern and dynamic urban development, meeting all the requirements for a Euroregion in a modern sense.[24] The visionary dream from the 1960s of a mega-region amalgamating the cities of Malmö and Copenhagen has, to a certain extent, become a reality.[25] The region is a typical example of what is referred to as a New Regionalism.[26] The present cultural construction mechanism of narrating Öresund is also in the making, portraying this region as a heartland region of entire Scandinavia in the mind of a global audience. The TV series *The Bridge*, a Danish-Swedish co-production, was first shown in 2011 and has since been broadcasted in around 100 countries globally. The external image of a cool, rational and wealthy, but still crime-ridden, Scandinavian welfare state is narrated through this new Euroregion.

The other potential Euroregion in Scandinavia is the Torne Valley Region, which historically evolved beside the Torne River separating Finland and Sweden. It is estimated that 7,000 Finnish speakers remained on the western side of the border together with 25,000 Swedish speakers and 500 Sámi speakers after the partition in 1809.[27] During the first half of the nineteenth century, the language policy of parochial life in this northern periphery remained fairly intact, meaning that Finnish would be used in religious sermons and religious literature would be available in Finnish, even on the Swedish side of the border. Intermarriages between Finnish speakers across the border remained frequent and the local culture has always defied the national border in cultural terms. However, during the nineteenth century, the idea of Finnish being a historical language of the country disappeared from the Swedish nationalist self-conception; a long period of language assimilation followed. When Sweden joined the European Union in 1995, it soon had to acknowledge this forgotten history. In 2000, a number of historical minority languages were granted official status in Sweden. Among them was Finnish, but also *Meänkieli*, which was the local language of the Torne Valley Finns and literally means 'our language'.

The assimilatory politics on the part of the Swedish government only had a limited effect, and in 1930, it was still estimated that 12,000 persons spoke only Finnish, which was 28 per cent of the region's population. This intensified throughout the 1950s, although the first small signs of change were beginning to be seen: the unconditional ban on speaking Finnish in school, even during breaks, was revoked in 1958. However, it would take some time before an articulated regionalism would be voiced. The particular Finnish language culture of the Torne Valley still possessed some constitutive elements in addition to the obvious language identity. One was the revivalist Laestadian movement: the Pietism movement's founder, Lars Levi Laestadius (1800-1861), spread his message in Lapland by preaching in Finnish. The other strong tradition is communism, or at least a long leftist political tradition based on the numerous low-yielding small farms and the mining communities; these were channels for putting radical thought into reality with regard to central authorities. The general circumstance of the Torne Valley Finns can be defined as a subaltern position in the Swedish modernization project, and the whole process of cultural self-articulation has been described as a process of empowerment and emancipation.[28]

The regionalist ideology defining the locally spoken Finnish dialect as a separate language has largely been connected to initiatives taken by local activist Bengt Pohjanen. He initiated the formalization of a regionalist programme with roots in the localist awareness of the 1970s, which was consolidated over the following two decades tying in the connection to the regionalist renaissance of the European Union during the 1990s. The categorical voicing of regionalist identity evolved around the construction and creation of the local dialect as a written language. Bengt Pohjanen published the first novel in *Meänkieli* in 1986, and his later production includes an opera libretto trilogy, poetry and a translation of the New Testament. *Meänkieli* has strong elements of Swedish loan words that are transcribed from oral pronunciation.[29] Children's literature in *Meänkieli* has been greatly developed, and academic efforts to document and conserve the local language began in the 1980s with the founding of the Swedish National Torne Valley Association (Svenska Tornedalens Riksförbund), producing the first dictionary in 1992 and a grammar four years later. Through these efforts, *Meänkieli* is now also a school subject in the region.

If we apply Paasi's theory of four stages of regional development, Meänmaa or the Torne Valley appears as weak in its third and institutional development. The official minority status has given birth to subnational symbols, such as a flag and an annual day of celebration on 15 July, both introduced in 2007. However, there is still diverging opinion on the true essence of *Meänkieli* as a separate language, and the region as such benefits economically in terms of mobility and tourism from the open border. However, a wider acceptance of it as a political and sociological creation out of Finnish language is becoming more present, and the question remains as to whether the cultural essentialist project of Meänmaa can reach further.

Following the theory of the institutionalization of regions developed by Paasi, the Åland Islands are closest to a model region. In 1921, the League of Nations decided that the Åland Islands between Finland and Sweden should be part of Finland. This was a controversial decision in the light of the Wilsonian doctrine of national self-determination. The islands had historically been an integral part of the Swedish core area in the North Baltic since medieval times. For strategic military reasons, Russia had insisted on the islands in 1809 at a time when the Swedish kingdom was in a state of weakness. Therefore, the entirely Swedish-speaking Åland became part of the Grand Duchy of Finland in 1812 when it was created by Alexander I. In this context, it was logical that it would remain part of Finland when the country declared its independence in 1917. However, just a week after the Finnish declaration of independence, local political activists led by Julius Sundblom started to collect signatures to endorse the incorporation of Åland into Sweden. A vast majority of the local population supported this Åland movement, whose aim was to hold a referendum. The petition was handed over to King Gustavus V of Sweden, and was vividly supported by the Swedish government.

The outbreak of the Finnish Civil War in late January 1918 provided an opportunity for Swedish military action. As a not entirely unselfish act, Sweden landed a small contingent of soldiers on Åland with the pretext of helping the white side. This created tensions with the Finnish government and would affect the relations between the countries well into the 1920s. This was the backdrop to the Åland part of the Paris Peace Treaty. A new address was promoted in 1920, with 95 per cent of the adult Åland population supporting a secession in favour of Sweden; the Åland Convention signed in Geneva in 1921 awarded Åland to Finland. However, Swedish was to be the only official language, and the island group became a demilitarized zone and was granted cultural autonomy. This is usually regarded as the only decision of the League of Nations still in vigour at present. On 9 June 1922, the local parliament *Landstinget* thus assembled for the first time.

The autonomy of Åland was reinforced with a new law in 1952, which also gave the 'Landscape', as it is referred to in contrast to the other counties of Finland, the right to use its own flag. In 1984, the first official stamps of Åland were issued. The right of domicile (*hembygdsrätt*, comparable to *Heimatsrecht*) statute was reinforced in 1952, stating that the right to own land and vote in municipal elections only belonged to native inhabitants, or to Finnish citizens having lived at least five years on the islands and showing good skills in the Swedish language.[30] The conscious local identity and memory culture was reinforced in a similar but more effective way than in Scania. In 1933, Matts Drejer was appointed landscape archaeologist with the strong support of Åland's leading political figure, Sundblom. Drejer, who, only after the appointment, had to acquire the formal academic archaeology training that he lacked, became a tireless advocate of an Åland-centred historical paradigm. He managed to document an impressive amount of local archaeological findings. As local historian, he made an important and enduring contribution to the formation of a strong regional identity.[31]

Åland, with 30,000 inhabitants today, is an economically stable autonomous region with a strong regional identity separating itself in terms of self-image both from Finland and Sweden. Åland negotiated its own favourable tax exemptions connected to ferry traffic while entering the European Union in a process separate from that of Finland. It also preserves its status as a non-military zone, and a Peace Research Institute on the main island contributes to this part of the islanders' self-identity and policy strategy.[32] The position of being a proper entity between Finland and Sweden has traditionally distanced the Åland population from identifying itself with the Swedish-speaking population on mainland Finland and their subnational identity project.

Parallel nation-building: Sweden–Finland

The Grand Duchy of Finland retained most of its laws from Swedish times, and Lutheranism remained the official faith. Finland also maintained Swedish as the administrative language of the state apparatus. Approximately 20 per cent of the population in Finland circa 1812 were Swedish speakers and dominated political and cultural life. During the last four decades of the nineteenth century, the political reforms and the nation-building project in Finland were tightly connected to the rise of the majority language of Finnish in all sectors of society. Political life developed much according to the language divisions and the Fennoman movement, whose objective was the emancipation of the Finnish language and culture, soon provoked the creation of a 'Svecoman' counter-movement that was built upon similar nationalistic ideas.

This Svecoman movement has traditionally been divided into two early fractions: the cultural Svecomans and the rural Svecomans. The former viewed themselves as representatives of the Scandinavian and European legal tradition and consisted mainly of the urban and upper-class academic elite. Their main goal was to preserve a strong Swedish language dimension of the Finnish nation-building project, which during the entire nineteenth century would not articulate any serious claims for national independence from the Russian Empire. The latter worked for a separate National Romantic movement within Finland, with a focus on rural Swedish-speaking population. This distinction between two fractions should not be taken too literally and is mainly a self-denomination within the movement in the early years.[33] However, not all Swedish speakers in Finland would adhere to this identity construction, and the labour movement has its own strong tradition of Swedish language organization.

In 1885, the Swedish Literature Society was founded as a counterweight to the founding of the Finnish Literature Society back in 1831. The self-recognition of a minority position became a growing factor during the decades to come; parliamentary reform in 1905 signified perhaps the most decisive political shift. The four-estate diet was replaced by a unicameral diet with universal suffrage for both men and women. The mainly Swedish-speaking nobility now lost its hegemonic position in politics, which urged a new approach within the Svecoman movement and in 1906, the Swedish People's Party (Svenska Folkpartiet) was founded. The addition of 'People' in the name is significant and symbolizes the imperative of unifying all Swedish speakers in one political party. The first party programme concentrated exclusively on the language question, deliberately omitting any broader social programme for fear of internal divisions. Simultaneous with these events, the adjective Finland-Swede (*finlandsvensk*) was introduced, denominating a subnational reference of belonging.

The outcome of the Finnish Civil War in 1918, with the bourgeois white side prevailing over the reds, secured a favourable position of the Swedish language as part of a legalist and Western-oriented national self-conception. Furthermore, the consolidation of an independent Finland strengthened the Finnish language and brought with increasing confrontation between the two language groups during the 1920s and 1930s. This increased the feeling of insecurity and diminished future prospects for a flourishing Swedish language minority culture in a national setting. All this had many forms of cultural, social and political expression. Concerns were voiced over Swedish-speaking families selling their farmsteads to Finnish speakers when emigrating westwards to Sweden and America.[34] Questions concerning both the eugenic quality and quantity of the coming generations of Finland-Swedes were also addressed and acted upon in forms of positive eugenic measures. In 1921, *Folkhälsan* ('Public Health' in Swedish), a private organization, was founded. Its main task was to promote popular education concerning health issues and reproduction. During its early years, it would battle eugenic degeneration among the rural Swedish-speaking population by initiating racial-biological research projects among them. A prize for mothers who gave birth to at least four healthy Swedish-speaking children was established for a shorter period.[35]

One main problem of the Finland-Swedish movement, perhaps more important than any early division of strategy, was the fact that it did not possess a unified territory. The two main Swedish-speaking areas were separated. The southern area and Ostrobothnia in the north-west are not connected geographically. The Swedish movement has managed to bridge this on an institutional level by establishing a multitude of institutions ranging from universities to sports associations according to a principle of creating Swedish-language organizations parallel to Finnish-language counterparts. But still the dilemma of creating an autonomous territory presented a problem impossible to solve.

The aims to form a separate territorial unit remained at a rhetorical level, establishing the territorial concept of *Svensk-Finland* (Sweden–Finland), today mainly written as *Svenskfinland*. Subnational symbols were created, such as a flag, and a day of Swedishness celebrated on 6 November. The leitmotifs of the Sweden–Finnish cultural self-expression are mainly connected to rural coastal life: fishing, seafaring, maritime life and the landscape offered by the North-Baltic archipelago with small pine trees striving to grow in unfavourable conditions constitutes an identity discourse intended to create distance from group from the Fennonman-defined lake district Finland (Figure 11.2).[36]

Swedish-language regionalism has up until the present relied on strong institutions (ranging from universities to schools, newspapers, public service radio and TV, a Lutheran state church diocese, a Swedish language garrison, strong publishing houses, sports and cultural organizations[37]) and obviously also on strong legal rights, which is partly the result of its favourable socio-economic position in Finnish society, suggesting the classification of Sweden–Finland as a competitor region. However, this categorization is problematic, as Swedishness is also understood as constituting a crucial and integrated part of the Republic, and both Finnish and Swedish are official languages. Swedish is not officially a minority language, though only 5.5 per cent are registered as Swedish speakers. This group constitutes a minority in sociological terms. A total of thirty-three municipalities on mainland Finland is defined as bilingual. The regionalist identity of the Finland-Swedes has always been practiced in a dialogue of both separatist tension and patriotic sense of belonging to the grander patria of Finland. After the consolidation of the Republic of Finland, the Swedish regionalist movement has never challenged national unity, but rather promoted its own cause within the national structure.

The northern fringe and regionalism

The northernmost parts of Norway, Sweden and Finland, also geographically referred to as northern Fennoscandia, is an interesting European case concerning regionalist development. The number of overlapping claims and projects of regional reconceptualization, also including the north-western most part of Russia, has been considerable during the period 1890–2000. The Torne Valley, or the Meänmaa, case has already been dealt with as a historical transnational region. This region is part of several other regional denominations, such as Lappland, Norrland, North Calotte and Sápmi. The competing regional projects in the Scandinavian northernmost fringe reflect the different interests projected on the region from within and without.

The overlapping and confusion concerning this area are manifold. In the 1890s, the term Nord-Norge (Northern Norway) was launched among so-called Northlander migrants in the capital Kristiania (from 1924, Oslo). The initiative was an attempt

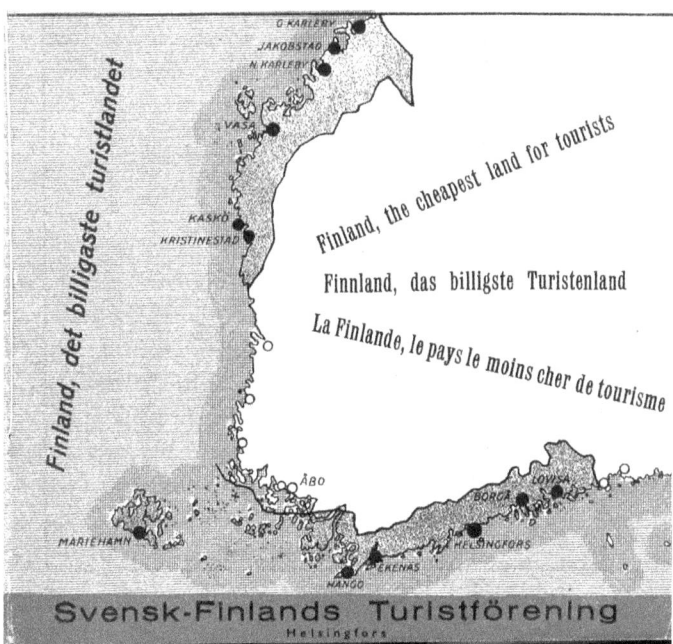

Figure 11.2 *A tourist brochure from 1937 promoting Svensk-Finland for an international audience. Åland is included here, but generally the Ålanders themselves would be ambiguous about considering themselves part of* Svenskfinland.

to launch a development oriented and modern spatial conception of Norway's northern parts. It contested both the terms of Finnmark and Hålogaland; the latter was the current historic denomination of the northernmost part of Norway. Its use was reintroduced culturally as part of National Romantic revival around 1900.[38] Hålagoland embodied the rich traditions of Viking Age and Old-Norse culture, and for many, it was the cradle of this heritage; the denomination Finnmark is a broader term also used in Sweden since the eighteenth century. In Norway, however, it also implied a subaltern position to the notions of Nord-Norge and Hålogaland, since it alluded to the Finnish ethnic settlement of the region; still today, Finnmark is the name of the northern and easternmost county in Norway. The term Northern Norway, however, was increasingly used during the first half of the twentieth century for magazines, institutions and associations.

By the 1950s, Nord-Norge was an integral part of the vocabulary of state-level regional policy.[39] As a name, it represented the national and state driven modernization project and its connectedness to the local societal elite; this process bears great similarity to the introduction of the term Norrland in Sweden. As Sverker Sörlin has shown, Norrland was introduced in the late 1880s to designate the new northern frontier and land of the future for a Sweden steadily marching forward on a path of industrialization and prosperity. As a regional concept, its focus is on the natural resources in the form of mining prospects and hydropower as an asset for national growth.[40] Norrland was introduced as a counter-concept to Lappland or Lappmarken, symbolizing an appropriation of a remote and exotic region in the name of national progress.

On a transnational level, several strategic regional concepts coexist. The term The North Calotte – Nordkalotten – was introduced in the 1960s during an increased and successful Nordic cooperation period and became an integral part of Nordic cooperation vocabulary in the 1970s.[41] The Fenno-Scandian area north of the Polar Circle thus became an established regional denomination, alluding to the close and unproblematic cooperation between the Nordic neighbours. As a regional concept, it is also future- and development-oriented, since it is often connected to economic and social questions.[42] Recently, the term North Calotte seems to vanish at the same pace as the reginal denomination the Barents Region is conquering ground; this is a spatial reconception of the northernmost border region between Norway and Russia introduced in 1993.[43] This was the start of an increasing activity to root this regional concept including writing its history: the core narrative is that of an age-old, peaceful and functioning trade between Russian Pomor traders of the Kola and Archangelsk coastal lands, and inhabitants of the Norwegian part of the Arctic Ocean shore. Recently, the Barents Region seems to have expanded in size, probably as a sign of the intensified interest for achieving favourable positions in the Arctic region, with its potential natural sources and a new eastern sea route to Asia. The recent main contribution to writing the history of this region appeared in 2015 under the title *The Barents Region: A Transnational History of Subarctic Northern Europe*. The subtitle is telling, since it suggests an extension of the Pomor trade area to a wider Arctic and international scene. As the term North Calotte has vanished from the context of transnational policy, a new regional denomination for future-oriented development aspirations connecting the local and national political elite seems to have taken its place.

However, perhaps the most important regionalist claim for the northernmost areas of Fenno-Scandia is Sápmi, the land of the Sami, the European Union's only indigenous people. The renaming of Lappland and 'Lapps' to Sápmi and Sami, is part of a long process during the twentieth century. The early Lappophilia, exercised by leading academic institutions in the capital cities, gave way to a Sapmi awareness and action during the 1960s. The assimilation and development policies concerning primary education paradoxically contributed to this. It connected local youth to each other and to the radical new left ideas of the late 1960s. Veli-Pekka Lehtola, the leading Sápmi historian in Finland, has referred to this as a boarding school generation, who formulated an overarching idea and strategy for the entire Sami population and region.[44] One visible sign of this new radical empowerment, reaching national media and attracting environmentalist activists, was the strong protest action against the building of a hydropower plant in Alta, Norway, in 1979; this is held to have been the political turning point for the Sámi.[45] Today, the Kautokeino uprising in 1852, a violent revolt against representatives of central administration in this Norwegian Sámi town, is also often referred to as an early sign of independent collective action. The battle against external exoticization and recognition is constantly gaining ground; institutional developments are also ongoing. In 1956, the Nordic Sámi Council was established as an umbrella organization for all Sámi-related non-governmental organizations. In the 1990s, the denomination 'Nordic' was dropped, when Russian organizations also joined in. The establishment of national Sámi parliaments took place later and only in 2000 was a transnational Sami Council created as an umbrella organization for the official national Sámi parliaments established. Since 1986, Sápmi has had its own flag, well established in Scandinavia today alongside the five national flags and those of Åland Islands, Greenland and the Faroe Islands. Sápmi is today on its way to establishing itself as one of the regions in Europe. However, political power and institutional self-articulation remains politically weak, even if the regionalist advancements have been considerable.

Conclusion

Regionalist movements in Scandinavia since the late nineteenth century are manifold. Cultural heartland regionalism as part of nation-building processes are present. Furthermore, the outcome of the Napoleonic Wars in Scandinavia resulted in new territorial partitions and borders, which created the conditions for later regionalist movements. In the light of recent regionalist development and hopes invested in a regionalist revival in Europe, there are two obvious cases in Scandinavia that follow this development: Scania in the south and the Torne Valley in the north. These two regions have experienced a reconnection of historical units and a re-enforcement of geographical proximity enabled by Nordic cooperation, the European Union and infrastructure investments.

Strong political and cultural regionalism has traditionally not been seen as vital and significant in a way that would challenge the nation state. Regionalist articulations have almost exclusively been articulated within a national paradigm, or in the cases where they have been challenging the nation state, they have been politically weak. However, there is a certain myopia in regard to the image of the nation state as a historical unit and supra-regional Nordic identity as a uniting factor in the region. Regionalism has played a key role, perhaps more than is recognized, and several regionalist movement are in line with similar European examples. The dominating paradigm is the agency of the strong Nordic nation states, and seeing regionalism as slightly different from nay European examples. At the beginning of this study, it was queried whether there was there specific regionalism in Scandinavia. This regionalism would be loyal to nation states, and no clear transformations of these loyalties can be detected. This claim is not entirely accurate, at least not in cultural terms, and Scandinavia offers cases of strong regional development on all fronts, but also emerging regions, such as Sápmi, that might evolve into strong separatist regionalism in the near future.

Notes

1. Dag Hunstad, 'Historikeren som regionbygger? Et fagkritisk perspektiv på fire landsdelshistoriske verk', *Historisk tidsskrift* 91, no. 2 (2012): 44.
2. Henrik Stenius, 'The Good Life is a Life of Conformity: The Impact of Lutheran Tradition on Nordic Political Culture', in *The Cultural Construction of Norden*, ed. Øystein Sørensen and Bo Stråth (Oslo-Stockholm-Copenhagen-Oxford-Boston: Scandinavian University Press, 1997), 171.
3. Miroslav Hroch, *Social Preconditions of National Revival in Europe: A Comparative Analysis of the Social Composition of Patriotic Groups Among the Smaller European Nations* (New York: Colombia University Press 1985).
4. Anssi Paasi, 'The Institutionalization of Regions: A Theoretical Framework for Understanding the Emergence of Regions and the Constitution of Regional Identity', *Fennia* 164 (1986): 105–46.
5. Joost Augusteijn and Eric Storm, 'Introduction: Region and State', in *Region and State in Nineteeth-Century Europe. Nation-Building, Reginal Identities and Separatism*, ed. Joost Augusteijn and Eric Storm (Basingstoke: Palgrave Macmillan, 2012), 1.
6. Susanne Österlund-Pötzsch, 'Walking Nordic: Performing Space, Place and Identity', in *Performing Nordic Heritage. Everyday Practices and Institutional Culture*, ed. Peter Aronsson and Lizette Gradén (Farnham: Ashgate, 2013), 30.
7. Edward P. Alexander, *Museum Masters: Their Museums and Their Influence* (Nashville: Altamira Press, 1983), 250.
8. Magdalena Hillström, 'Sweden versus *Norden* in the Nordiska Museet', in *Performing Nordic Heritage. Everyday Practices and Institutional Culture*, ed. Peter Aronsson and Lizette Gradén (Farnham: Ashgate, 2013), 49–55.

9. http://www.vasaloppet.se/en/about-us/history/, last access on 1 February 2017.
10. Ulf Sporrong, 'The Province of Dalecarlia (Dalarna): Heartland or Anomaly?', in *Nordic Landscapes: Region and Belonging on the Northern Edge of Europe*, ed. Michael Jones and Kenneth R. Olwig (Minneapolis-London: Minnesota University Press, 2008), 193.
11. Göran Therborn, *Klasstrukturen i Sverige 1930–1980: Arbete, kapital, stat och patriarkat* (Lund: Zenith, 1981), 25.
12. Gunnar Asplund, Wolter Gahn, Sven Markelius, Gregor Paulsson et al., *Acceptera* (Stockholm: Liber, 1931), 144.
13. Carl Marklund and Peter Stadius, 'Acceptance and Conformity: Merging Modernity with Nationalism in the Stockholm Exhibition in 1930', *Culture Unbound* 2, no. 5 (2010): 630.
14. Michael Keating, 'Contesting European Regions', *Regional Studies* 51, no. 1 (2017): 13.
15. Matti Klinge, *The Finnish Tradition. Essays on Structures and Identities in the North of Europe* (Helsinki: SHS, 1993), 165.
16. Matti Klinge, *A European University. The University of Helsinki 1640–2010* (Helsinki: University of Helsinki 2010), 326–27.
17. Yrjö Hirn, *Lärt folk och landsstrykare i det finska Finlands kulturliv* (Helsingfors: Holger Shilds förlag 1939), 205.
18. Maunu Häyrynen, 'A Kaleidoscopic Nation: The Finnish National Landscape Imagery', in *Nordic Landscapes: Region and Belonging on the Northern Edge of Europe*, ed. Michael Jones and Kenneth R. Olwig (Minneapolis-London: Minnesota University Press, 2008), 500.
19. Rainer Knapas, *Landet som var. Karelska kulturbilder* (Helsingfors: Schilds & Söderströms, 2015), 7.
20. Margun Bjørnholt, 'Hvorfor er folkedrakt så viktigt i Norge og marginalt i nabolandene?', *Nordic Journal of Cultural Policy* 8, no. 2 (2005): 11–13.
21. Celia Applegate, 'A Europe of Regions: Reflections on the Historiography of Sub-National Places in Modern Times', *American Historical Review* 104, no. 4 (1999): 1164.
22. Fredrik Persson, *Skåne, den farliga halvön: Historia, indentitet och ideologi 1865–2000* (Lund: Sekel, 2008), 81.
23. Persson, *Skåne, den farliga halvön*, 126.
24. Magnus Jerneck, 'Nordic Politics Viewed in a Changing Territorial Perspective', in *Local and Regional Governance in Europe: Evidence from Nordic Regions*, ed. Janerik Gidlund and Magnus Jerneck (Cheltenham; Northampton, MA: Edgar Elgar, 2000), 24.
25. Anna Wieslander, 'Att bygga Öresundsregionen: Från 1960-talets utvecklingsoptimism till 1960-talets lapptäcksregionalism', in *Öresundsregionen – visioner och verklighet*, ed. Sven Tägil (Lund 1997), 78–79.
26. Hundstad, 'Historikeren som regionbygger?', 45.
27. Jouni Korkiasaari and Kari Tarkiainen, *Suomalaiset Ruotsissa* (Turku: Siirtolaisinstituutti, 2000), 116.
28. Leena Huss and Erling Wande, 'Orastava emansipaatio? Tornionlaaksolaisten ja ruotsinsuomalaisten kielipoliittisesta kehityksestä', in *Kahden puolen Pohjanlahtea II*, ed. Marianne Junila and Charles Westin (Helsinki: SKS, 2007), 265.
29. See also the chapter by Kabatek.
30. Rhodri C. Williams, 'Excluding to Protect: Land Rights and Minority Protection in International Law', in *Den åländska hembygdsrätten*, ed. Sia Spiliopoulou Åkermark (Mariehamn: Ålands lagting & Ålands fredsinstitut, 2007), 93–95.

31. Henrik Meinander, *Nationalstaten: Finlands svenskhet 1922–2015* (Helsingfors: SLS, 2016), 197.
32. Nils Storå, 'Landscape, Territory, Autonomy, and Regional Identity: The Åland Islands in a Cultural Perspective', in *Nordic Landscapes: Region and Belonging on the Northern Edge of Europe*, ed. Michael Jones and Kenneth R. Olwig (Minneapolis-London: Minnesota University Press, 2008), 451.
33. Henry Rask, 'Finland och Sverige – finskt och svenskt', in *Finlands svenska litteraturhistoria I*, ed. Johan Wrede (Helsingfors: SLS, 1999), 18–25.
34. Max Engman, 'Emigrationspolitik i utvandrarlandet Finland', in *Mångkulturalitet, migration och minoriteter i Finland under tre sekler*, ed. Mats Wickström and Charlotta Wolff (Helsingfors: SLS, 2015), 68.
35. Markku Mattila, '"Det får ej finnas dåliga svenskar i detta land!" Rasbiologi och rashygien som vetenskapliga vapen i språkstridens Finland', in *Mångkulturalitet, migration och minoriteter i Finland under tre sekler*, ed. Mats Wickström and Charlotta Wolff (Helsingfors: SLS, 2015), 295.
36. Anssi Paasi, 'Finnish Landscape as Social Practice: Mapping Identity and Scale', in *Nordic Landscapes: Region and Belonging on the Northern Edge of Europe*, ed. Michael Jones and Kenneth R. Olwig (Minneapolis-London: Minnesota University Press, 2008), 520.
37. Henrik Meinander, *Nationalstaten: Finlands svenskhet 1922–2015* (Helsingfors: SLS, 2016), 221–78.
38. Einar Niemi, 'Regionalism in the North: The Creation of "North Norway"', *Acta Borealia* 10, no. 2 (1993): 40.
39. Niemi, 'Regionalism in the North', 42.
40. Sverker Sörlin, *Framtidslandet. Debatten om Norrland och naturresurserna under det industriella genombrottet* (Stockholm: Carlsson, 1988), 262–72.
41. *Nordisk rådets verksamhet 1971–1986: Översikt över rådets rekommendationer och yttringar* (Göteborg: Nordiska rådet, 1988), 333.
42. Maria Lähteenmäki, 'Foreword', in *The North Calotte: Perspectives on the Histories and Cultures of Northernmost Europe*, ed. Maria Lähteenmäki and Päivi Pihlaja (Helsinki: University of Helsinki, 2005).
43. Lars Elenius, 'Introduction', in *The Barents Region: A Transnational History of Subarctic Northern Europe*, ed. Lars Elenius et al. (Oslo: Pax, 2015), 18.
44. Veli-Pekka Lehtola, '". . . inte som någon nådegåva utan för att samerna årligen har förtjänat det". Samer som politiska aktörer i det efterkrigstida Finland', in *Mångkulturalitet, migration och minoriteter i Finland under tre sekler*, ed. Mats Wickström and Charlotta Wolff (Helsingfors: SLS, 2015), 277.
45. Elenius et al., 'The Barents Region', 395.

Further reading

Aronsson, Peter, and Lizette Gradén, *Performing Nordic Heritage: Everyday Practices and Instiutional Culture* (Farnham: Ashgate, 2013).
Elenius, Lars, Hallvard Tjelmeland, Maria Lähteenmäki, Alexey Golubev et al., eds, *The Barents Region: A Transnational History of Subarctic Northern Europe* (Oslo: Pax, 2015).

Gidlund, Janerik, and Magnus Jerneck, eds, *Local and Regional Governance in Europe: Evidence from Nordic Regions* (Cheltenham; Northampton, MA: Edgar Elgar, 2000).

Jones, Michael, and Kenneth R. Olwig, eds, *Nordic Landscapes: Region and Belonging on the Northern Edge of Europe* (Minneapolis; London: University of Minnesota Press, 2008).

Lähteenmäki, Maria, and Päivi Maria Pihlaja, eds, *Perspectives on the Histories and Cultures of Northernmost Europe* (Helsinki: University of Helsinki, 2005).

Skov, Lise, ed., *Berg Encyclopedia of World Dress and Fashion. West Europe* (Oxford: Berg, 2011).

CHAPTER 12
REGIONALISM IN THE LOW COUNTRIES
Joep Leerssen

Background

Depending on how the term is defined, regionalism affected the Low Countries either very strongly or very weakly; its impact was also markedly different in Belgium, the Netherlands and Luxembourg. Though small in size, the very densely inhabited, and linguistically diverse, Low Countries present a culturally and politically very complex aspect, with numerous terminological pitfalls; a brief outline is therefore in order, also to disambiguate the categories used in the following pages (Figure 12.1). At the outset it should be clarified that 'Netherlandic' covers different areas in its political or linguistic application. Politically, it describes the Kingdom of the Netherlands, colloquially called (after its heartland) 'Holland', with the colloquial adjectival form 'Dutch'. Linguistically, the language spoken, not only in the Netherlands but also in the northern half of Belgium, is also called 'Netherlandic'. The Netherlandic-speaking northern half of Belgium is colloquially called (after its heartland) 'Flanders', and the Netherlandic language as used in Flanders is usually called 'Flemish'. As such, it is usually often juxtaposed with its twin sister 'Dutch' (the Netherlandic language as used in the Netherlands) and opposed to Belgium's other main language, French (much as Flanders as a linguistically defined region is often juxtaposed with the country's French-speaking – 'Walloon' – southern half). Even more complicating dialect finesses will be introduced further on to the extent that they influenced regionalism.

The Low Countries cover the present-day Benelux countries; the name reflects the usage in the late-medieval Duchy of Burgundy referring to the *pays d'en bas* as opposed to the duchy's heartland Bourgogne. The territories in question were always uneasily distinguished from the French kingdom on the one hand and the German empire on the other, sharing cultural overlaps and uneasily fluctuating claims and borders with both. The Burgundian Netherlands were always bilingual, with the Dukes of Burgundy (like their predecessors, the Dukes of Brabant) conducting their administrative business in both Netherlandic and French, depending on the locality in question. Some cities, being the administrative centres of different language communities, maintained a diglossic administration. Territorially, the linguistic frontier has shifted little since the Middle Ages, with the exception of the city of Brussels (whose mass population became predominantly francophone as the municipality swelled in the course of nineteenth-century urbanization).

The religious wars of the Early Modern period created a strong divide between the northern and southern Netherlands, as the Reformation was suppressed in the southern

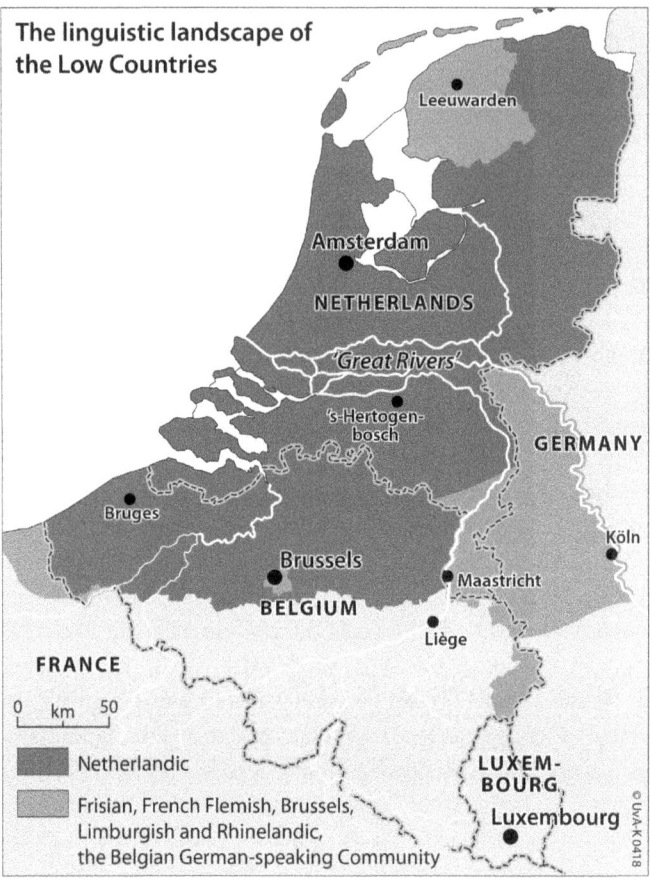

Figure 12.1 *The linguistic landscape of the Low Countries (© J.Th. Leerssen).*

provinces but proved successful in the north. The northern, Protestant provinces, after a long rebellion against Spanish-Habsburg rule, gained independence between 1564 and 1648 as the Republic of the United Provinces, while the south remained under Catholic Habsburg rule, first as the Spanish then as the Austrian Netherlands. Both halves were characterized by a decentralized political system perpetuating (as in the case of Switzerland) a premodern, 'feudal' division into lordships and free cities. The united 'Provinces' of the Dutch Republic were the perpetuation of feudal counties, duchies and lordships, and the Austrian Netherlands likewise maintained their ancient seigneurial distinctions. Real power was vested in the cities: Ghent, Antwerp and Brussels in the south; and Amsterdam, Groningen and others in the north. City privileges were broken in the south but stayed strong in the north.

Out of this strongly decentralized and historically heterogeneous complex, a monarchical unitary state was created in 1815, which, besides the erstwhile United Provinces and the Austrian Netherlands, also included Luxembourg (turned into Grand

Duchy by Napoleon), the former Prince-Bishopric of Liège and some smaller Free Imperial fiefdoms of the Ancien Régime. Unsurprisingly, the new state proved to be unsustainable. Its deep-seated heterogeneity was fatally mismanaged, largely owing to the insensitive policies of the government, which considered the new united kingdom simply as an enlarged successor state to the Dutch Republic. The revolutionary year 1830 led to a secession of the southern half from the northern-based government; out of which emerged a reduced Kingdom of the Netherlands, a new kingdom called Belgium and two subsidiary territories which were placed in different degrees of personal union with the monarch of the Netherlands: the Grand Duchy of Luxembourg and the Duchy of Limburg. The new states, Belgium and the Netherlands, were very uneasily demarcated. The border was straddled by provinces rendered hybrid and peripheral by the new frontier now running through them.

Luxembourg as a Grand Duchy (in personal union with the Netherlandic Crown) ceded part of its territory to Belgium, where it became a Province of Luxembourg.

Between the Netherlandic province of Zeeland and the Belgian province of Flanders was a buffer zone called 'Zeelandish Flanders', left to the Netherlands with the express aim of controlling access to the Belgian port of Antwerp.

The province of Limburg was split between a western Belgian half and an eastern half (the aforementioned 'Duchy of Limburg', under the Netherlandic Crown) running south as far as Maastricht, with the express aim of cutting Belgian off from the German hinterland.

Between Limburg and Zeelandish Flanders, the Belgian province of Brabant abutted the Netherlandic province of 'North Brabant'.

Despite these very uneasy territorial demarcations, both states born out of the 1830 secession would cultivate a strong national identity. And it is against this background (nineteenth-century state-building on the unassimilated wreckage of ancien regime localisms) that we should situate the rise of regionalism in the Low Countries.

The present chapter will survey some cases of regionalism in the post-1830s Low Countries. Between them, they present a variegated palette of different modalities that regionalism can take, from a mild *petite patrie* cultural particularism to an incipient stage of secessionist nationalism. Between them, the cases also represent an interesting example of multiscalar interaction, in that they interacted with each other and with nation-building processes in a complex variety of ways. The driving centrifugal forces that opposed regions to the states' nation-building processes were different in the Netherlands and in Belgium. In the Netherlands, the main intra-national division was religious; in Belgium, it was the language. Two regions stood apart from these borderline disputes: Friesland (with which the following survey will open) and Luxembourg (which will provide a coda).

Friesland: Provincial particularism as subsidiary Netherlandism

The federal past of the United Provinces meant that a sense of subsidiary diversity was firmly established in the Netherlands' self-awareness. Culturally, this expressed itself above all in a foregrounded interest in the country's regional styles of traditional peasant dress. From the late eighteenth century onwards, the depiction of these regional dress types had been popular for prints and engravings.[1] This subsidiary provincialism was especially heightened in the case of Friesland. Its participation in the United Provinces had always had a particularist tinge because the Stadholdership of Friesland had been vested in a different branch of the Orange-Nassau family than that of the other United Provinces. This heteronomy[2] tied in with a historical myth that the ethnic Frisians had maintained their tribal democracy more staunchly and successfully against monarchical and feudal encroachment.

In the nineteenth century, two cultural aspects intensified this Frisian particularism: one was the new prominence of Frisian in the new Germanic philology, the other the erosion of the tribal myth of the Batavian Republic. As to the former, the recognition gained ground that Frisian took up a separate position from the other continental West Germanic languages,[3] and that, with its similarities to Anglo-Saxon, its taxonomical position was that of a fully fledged language rather than a mere dialect – a distinction which is moot and imponderable at the 'etic', formal-descriptive level, but highly relevant at the 'emic' level of social experience.[4] Concurrently, the early modern Dutch ancestry myth of the ancient Batavians was replaced by an ethnolinguistic root system deriving the population of the Netherlands from three Germanic tribes: Franks, Saxons and Frisians[5] – with Grimm celebrating the Frisians (alongside the Hessians) as one of the tribes still inhabiting the region where they had been located, centuries before the Great Migrations, by Tacitus. This cultural particularism was intensified in a backlash response to the traumatic fact that the province had lost its own university, in Franeker: it was abolished by Napoleon in 1811, provoking the foundation of a number of learned societies intensely aware of and cultivating their Frisian-provincial roots and culture. As a result of all this, the Frisians by 1890 had become a sort of special hyper-Dutchmen, distinct from the national average, different in some respect, but yet not opposed to it, and representing its purported characteristics in a more intense and concentrated way – comparable to the position of Tyrol in Austria, Yorkshire in England or Andalusia in Spain.

After the death of the unhinged misanthropist Willem III in 1892, the Netherlands belatedly developed a form of imperial patriotism or *Reichspatriotismus* (or what in Denmark was known as *Kongekærlighed*), in which the monarchy was glorified as a benevolent subsumption of all regional and cultural diversities within the realm, and the monarch was glorified as a paternal figure charismatically uniting the unmediated and spontaneous affection and cultural peculiarities of all his/her subjects. Such 'Monarchical Patriotism' emerges between George IV donning a Highland kilt on his 1822 Edinburgh visit and the Austro-Hungarian *Kronprinzenwerk* of 1886 and often works in tandem with a controlled regionalism which, while tolerated and even symbolically encouraged in its cultural manifestations, is harnessed to the monarchy and prevented from developing autonomist or secessionist ambitions. In the Netherlands, monarchical patriotism focused on the figure of the young girl-queen Wilhelmina who, after ascending the throne in 1892, undertook a charm offensive across the country to atone for the vast unpopularity of her late father. The moody and irascible widower Willem III had seen both his sons predecease him, opening the prospect of an actual extinction of the house of Orange-Nassau, involving in all likelihood an amalgamation of the Netherlands into a coalescing Germany. The succession was only assured in the person of Wilhelmina, born from a second marriage contracted late in life. In any event, Wilhelmina was barred from the male-only succession to the Great Duchy of Luxembourg, so that after Willem III's death that small fiefdom became an independent sovereign state (1892).

The fervent celebrations around Wilhelmina's coming of age and ascent to the throne were intensified, therefore, with a solicitude concerning the very viability of the Netherlands. The monarchical patriotism that focused on her girlish charm, poise and vulnerability strongly played into the idea of a subsidiary regional/provincial diversity (almost as if to stress the shared non-Germanness of all these diverse Provinces) and tended to foreground Friesland as the country's most salient regional subtype. Photographs and prints of Wilhelmina in Frisian traditional dress gained great popularity. The echo of George IV in Highland kilt, or of the Hohenzollern or Wittelsbach princes in the regional costumes of their new South-east European kingdoms of Romania and Greece, is obvious to the modern historian. In addition, the regional dress diversity of the Netherlands was now cultivated as an expression of the country's specific character – the Volendam costume having gained international fame thanks to the tourist trade, which offered popular day trips to Volendam from Amsterdam.[6] Traditional dress pageants were held under national auspices as the country caught the tide of international ethnographic interest in rustic culture. Ethnographers once again looked to Friesland as the country's most authentic, characteristic and archaic region, with the town of Hindeloopen as an international showcase for premodern housing styles on the north-European seaboard.[7] Frisian popular culture such as finding the first lapwing's egg of the year, pole-vaulting across canals (*fierljeppen*), ice-skating races between the Eleven Frisian Towns (the *Elftedentocht*, institutionalized into a mass sporting event in the course of the twentieth century) or traditional sailing-boat races on the province's lakes (*Skûtsjesîlen*) came to attract great numbers of tourists from the other parts of the Netherlands.

While a Frisian cultural imaginaire played a salient role in the palette of Dutch regional diversity, and it was almost a commonplace to acknowledge that 'Frisian is a language, not just a dialect', the Dutch palette was equally appreciative of other less salient regional variants: the 'Saxon' north-east of the country (mainly the provinces of Groningen and Drenthe), the Isles of Zeeland and the coastal fishing villages of the Zuiderzee. Dutch *costumbrismo* was celebrated in the flourishing genre of the streekroman or rustic novel, of which the most pronounced representative was the work of Anne de Vries, with a non-Frisian setting. Anne de Vries cooperated with the ethographer P. J. Meertens to edit a series of 'Netherlandic folk characters', *De Nederlandse volkskarakters*, a series of vignettes of Dutch national character as differentiated by region (1938). Friesland was only one of the many types, which also included representatives of the other parts of the country and even 'the Amsterdam Jew' (indeed, the Meertens-De Vries collection deliberately set out to distance Netherlandic ethnography of the overtly racist ethnography that was shaping up in Germany at the time). Here, as well as in the open-air folk museum that was set up in Arnhem in 1918, Frisian cultural particularism was merely a *primus inter pares* in the subsidiary diversity of an overriding Dutchness.

Friesland was, then, a cherished object of Netherlands regionalism; but what agency did Frisians themselves take to translate this symbolic cultural position into one of greater recognition or autonomy? What transition was there (if any) from provincialism into a regionalist or even subnationalist movement?[8] A number of cultural associations founded in the nineteenth century developed a more activist mobilization in the twentieth century, beginning with the Young Frisian Community (Jongfryske Mienskip), founded in 1915, which organized summer camps and brought out a periodical; its founder, Douwe Kalma, wrote a history of Friesland in 1934 and translated some Shakespeare plays into the language. It is in these circles (rebaptized as the 'Community for Frisian National Development', Mienskip for Fryske Folksûntjowing) that increased self-government for the Frisian Province was suggested in 1930. At the same time, there were interregional contacts with Frisian associations based in Northern Germany and Denmark (Aurich and the Frisian Islands), leading to the establishment of a Frisian Council (Fryske Rie), also in 1930.[9]

The Nazi ideology was, given its fetish for Germanic racial purity, well disposed to Frisians and their culture, and attempted to harness the movement to its own aims. There had been some manifestations of fascism in Friesland, and a small Fryske Folkspartij was active between 1938 and 1941; more insidious was the Saxo-Frisia organization, which tried to reframe Frisian regionalism into a *völkisch*-Germanic mode under Ahnenerbe auspices – an organization dependent on the SS, which took care of heritage issues. Some Frisian cultural leaders bought into the Nazis' sympathetic policies towards Frisian culture during the German occupation, while others (notably those of a communist or robustly Christian persuasion) actively resisted.[10] In the post-war years, the associational life which had carried Frisian regionalism heretofore, dwindled, although institutions such as the Frisian Academy or Fryske Akademy (established in 1937) continued to consolidate a sense of regional specificity, even for writers and intellectuals who worked in a more individualist or anti-traditionalist mode. A telling shift is the recent development, since the mid-1990s, of the avant-garde Oerol festival on the Frisian island of Terschelling, which has a global outreach. As such, it complements the more traditionalist pan-Frisian Friesen-droapen (Frisian encounter) organized by the Fryske Rie on Helgoland, which features traditional dress and folk dances. The Fryske Rie had been re-activated in 1952 and even issued a 'Frisian Manifesto' in 1955.

A federative Council of the Frisian Movement (Ried fan de Fryske Beweging), uniting various activist groups including the subsisting Jongfryske Mienskip, was established in 1945. The political vindication of Frisian regionalism was provoked from an unexpected quarter when some members of the Netherlands judiciary evinced, in the post-war climate, a supercilious intolerance to the public use of the Frisian language. The use of colloquial Frisian names for milk and buttermilk (in lieu of the legally official Dutch terms) was met in 1948 with judicial sanctions; this provoked widespread anger and escalating unrest. From the mid-1950s, the use of Frisian in court rooms was officially allowed. Later legislation covered the usage of Frisian in education and public governance, giving the language full legal status in the province as a subsidiary alongside Dutch. Use on the local radio and, later, television broadcast followed suit. Since then, Frisian regionalism has been an uncontentious presence in the Netherlands political and cultural landscape, and its manifestations have once again subsided into the field of culture.

The Netherlands' Catholic periphery: Brabant, Limburg

The post-1830 Netherlands differed from the old Republic of the United Provinces in that it included two large provinces 'south of the great rivers' (i.e. Meuse and Rhine) which were almost totally Roman Catholic: North Brabant and the Duchy of Limburg. A good deal of this territory had been under the military and administrative rule of the The Hague government even during the Ancien Régime, but only as centrally administered tax provinces without representation in the Estates General; now they were fully fledged provinces in a centralized modern nation state, and their demographic weight strengthened the not-inconsiderable Catholic minority 'north of the rivers' so as to effect an almost-parity nationwide between Protestants and Catholics. This shift in balance occurred just as the Roman Catholic Church was developing its ultramontane policies. As Catholics became more assertive in what traditionally was a state predicated on Protestantism, Netherlandic politics were dominated for most of the period 1845–1970 by deep confessional antagonism. It went beyond party-political enmity and quarrels over educational control and affected all aspects of the public sphere. From media to leisure clubs and socio-economic choices (trade unions, insurance companies and, most importantly, education), parallel organizational structures locked each confession into its own hermetically sealed ambience, a process known as 'pillarization'. (A third, secular 'pillar' was that of the liberals and social democrats.)

In Brabant and Limburg, these confessional politics reinforced a long-standing grievance at having been disenfranchised subjects of an unsympathetic and unrepresentative regime. In Brabant, this went no further than a general *ressentiment de province* sometimes evinced in periodicals such as *Brabantia nostra*. This mouthpiece ran from 1935 until 1951, juxtaposing the marginalized position of the present-day province with the Burgundian medieval greatness of the ancient Duchy of Brabant. Its driving force were students around the Catholic Teachers' Training College in Tilburg (forerunner of the present-day Tilburg University). Its conservative religious regionalism lost appeal in the post-war years.[11]

Things were slightly more sharp-edged in Limburg. It had been included in the Netherlands against its will (the population having participated in the Belgian secession of 1830), as a bargaining chip, and the fact that as a duchy it sent delegates to the German Confederation was exploited in 1848 when disaffected Limburg delegates in the Frankfurt Parliament demanded secession from the Netherlands – a brief crisis on the Schleswig-Holstein model, but inconsequential as events turned out. As a province and duchy, Limburg had perhaps as many points of particularism as Friesland vis-à-vis the rest of the Netherlands. And it was only very belatedly that it merged into the centralization processes that turned the Netherlands into a unitary state in the course of the nineteenth century – connections with roads and railway networks, the presence of national political parties in local elections and so on.[12] The process was only concluded under the pressure of the First World War, which saw the hermetic closure of the borders between the neutral Netherlands with neighbouring Belgium and Germany; this also enclosed Limburg finally and definitively into the Dutch economy. The burgeoning coalmining industry and a brusque, hotly resisted Belgian annexation attempt in 1919 did the rest. Even so, Limburg developed a very strong sense of regional particularism thanks to its very strong diocesan-Catholic identity, which, in the pillarized country and the climate of ultramontanism, translated into a strong Limburgish internalism in matters of education and sociability. In addition, the hilly Limburg landscape with its medieval cities and castles, strongly different from the rest of the country, created an intense tourist industry and an exoticizing *imaginaire* about how different Limburg was, which in turn was internalized by the provincials themselves. This cultural exoticism remained even after the religious irritant lost its force from the 1960s on, as the Netherlands as a whole secularized rapidly in those decades.[13]

As in the case of Friesland, Limburg expressed mere provincialism rather than full-blown political regionalism, and regional cultural associations and periodicals were content to highlight localisms as subsidiary elements within the Netherlandic spectrum. A more anti-Netherlandic (or at least anti-Protestant) group, the Limburgsche Liga, showed signs of incipient radicalization in the early 1920s. One parallel between the Limburgsche Liga and the Brabantia Nostra group was a shared grievance: both were irked by the fact that industrialization and modernization (the electrical industries in Eindhoven, the mining industries in Limburg) brought an influx of technically trained personnel from 'north of the rivers', often Protestants, speaking a noticeably northern variant of the Dutch language with a tell-tale 'hard G', and ill-assimilated into the local social structures which they were called to administer or lead. These were resented as a quasi-colonial alien 'cadre' superimposed on the provinces' native populations. The colonial phraseology was raised by the sarcastic self-appellation *wingewesten* by Brabant and Limburg intellectuals such as Gerard Knuvelder, later a prominent literary historian.[14] As the case of Knuvelder illustrates, young southern Catholic intellectuals moved from ultramontanism towards corporatism after 1930. A movement towards Christian personalism (Jacques Maritain's more liberal alternative to corporatism) was also noticeable, but rarer.

The Limburgsche Liga remained marginal and was soon absorbed into more mainstream organizations like the dialect organization Veldeke, founded in 1926. Collaboration with the Nazi occupiers was minimal; while a good number of protest votes had in the early 1930s gone to the country's fascist Nationaal-Socialistische Beweging (NSB) movement, this trend was quickly reversed by stern admonitions from the Church authorities. Regional activism revived when the province's economic mainstay, the coal-mining industry, was phased out in the late 1960s, while, in the framework of European cooperation, the international borders with the neighbouring areas of Belgium and Germany became more porous. Politically, the area's interests were vindicated within the existing framework of the national party-political and governance structure, so that, after the waning of the grip of confessional politics, the main expression of Limburg regionalism was cultural. A dialect revival started in the 1980s which in 1997 led to the recognition of Limburgish as a regional language. Significantly, this linguistic emancipation was achieved at the intra-national Netherlandic level thanks to a supranational momentum: against national indifference, Limburg activists successfully invoked the Charter for Regional and Minority Languages that had been adopted by the European Council in 1992. As in the case of Friesland, Limburg regionalism is more heteronomist than autonomist, more directed against Dutch cultural centralism than towards a political empowerment of the province. The situation in Belgium was much more antagonistic.

From regionalism to nationalism: The Flemish movement

Established in 1830, the new kingdom of Belgium reacted against earlier Netherlandic supremacism by leaning in a strongly pro-French direction, while stressing its 'Burgundian' (Brabant-Flemish) rather that French historical roots. Flemish artists and intellectuals (mainly in the urban centres of Ghent and Antwerp) initially followed this trend in a pan-Belgian honeymoon period, which saw the new country's identity as linguistically French but rooted in a bicultural (Flemish/Brabantine and Liégeois) past. Soon, however, the hegemony of the French language became irksome and Flemish language rights (first cultural/symbolical, then social) were vindicated in the new Belgian state. This 'Flemish movement' is among the best-documented national movements of Europe and exhibits a mobilization and radicalization pattern typical of many such movements.[15] After an initial period of Flemish cultural consciousness-raising within the bilingual, French-dominated Belgian frame, cultural recognition and social rights were demanded with increasing urgency in the years 1840–1880, especially the right to address the Belgian administrative and judicial authorities in Flemish. At the same time, educational and literacy initiatives sought to raise the status of Flemish (often the object of francophones' denigration as a mere patois) by establishing a standardized orthography and, later, eradicating localisms and Gallicisms in favour of a 'pure' (*algemeen beschaafd*) usage.

In practice, this meant a convergence of linguistic standards with those in the Netherlands – something which, in a country recently seceded from that northern neighbour, was less than obvious. While linguistic activists from an urban-bourgeois, liberal background had traditionally had been more pro-Netherlandic, the more Catholic ones (traditionally concentrated in rural West Flanders, where the local dialects differed most markedly) felt reservations about the imposition of Northern linguistic standards. Their reaction is known as 'particularism'. It was felt that, much as Afrikaans was in these decades moving from being a mere patois towards acknowledged linguistic independence, so too Flemish could develop a written and literary standard that would stand alongside the northern, Protestant one. This west Flemish particularism found an important literary champion in the late nineteenth century in the priest-poet Guido Gezelle, but eventually declined in favour of a common Netherlandic standard.

The social assertion of Flemish language rights in the Belgian public sphere had been gathering pace when the country was invaded in August 1914 by the German Empire. A tiny corner of West Flanders remained unoccupied and formed part of the Western Front and its hinterland. It is here that the Flemish movement radicalized into full-blown separatism; a major irritant was that most officers belonged to the francophone elite, while Flemish speakers were over-represented in the rank and file. Their casualties were seen as a blood sacrifice which could only be rewarded with full linguistic recognition; failing that, the Belgian state lost its claims to Flemish loyalty. Meanwhile, in occupied Flanders, Flemish loyalty was seduced by the German-occupying forces, who, playing on notions of ethnic Germanic familiarity and a shared antagonism against Frenchness, gave preferential treatment to Flemish demands and even established a Flemish-speaking university in Ghent, a claim long unheeded by the national government. After 1918, those who had fallen for the German siren call were considered traitors to the fatherland by the Belgian authorities and were exposed to severe repression – a pattern repeated, with even greater intensity, in the Second World War.

The politicization of the Flemish movement in the interwar years took on a marked ethnonationalist and fascist character. Uniform-bearing, banner-waving, nationality-asserting movements of various hues along the reactionary-to-fascist spectrum arose; pan-European as this trend was, it also manifested itself in the French-speaking parts of the country (e.g. the Rex movement under Léon Degrelle); but more markedly so in Flanders, where the fascist-style movements profiled themselves as the logical, radicalized continuation of a long-standing cultural linguistic emancipation struggle. Although both Flemish fascists (organized in the Vlaams Nationaal Verbond, VNV) and Dutch ones (organized in the Nationaal-Socialistische Bond, NSB) proclaimed their adherence to a greater-Netherlandic unity, in practice there was little cooperation between the two. The greater-Netherlandic ideal was never taken seriously by the Nazi occupiers and was a non-starter in any case since Belgium and the Netherlands were under separate Nazi regimes: the Netherlands as an SS-controlled *Reichskommissariat*, Belgium (including Flanders) as a Wehrmacht-controlled military administration.

The entanglement of the Flemish movement with Nazi collaboration went much further than in the Netherlands and Wallonia, where fascist-style movements were more marginal to the political spectrum and could not claim to be the inheritors of a broad, long-standing national movement. As a result, the Flemish movement was deeply discredited after 1945 and, indeed, for a generation or two, continued to harbour the resentments and disappointments, or at least the embarrassment, of their collaborationist elders of the mid-century. In communitarian Belgian debates, anti-Flemish attacks from the francophone side of the divide still habitually impute, overtly or in 'dogwhistle' mode, ethnonationalist and post-fascist motives, while for its part the Flemish movement as a whole has been less than successful in generating a credible left-wing progressive agenda, in shedding its ingrained ethnoterritorial rhetoric in favour of language rights as a matter of social equity, and continues to gravitate to the conservative end of the political spectrum. The main successor party to the Flemish Movement after 1944 was the Volksunie, founded in 1954; it dissolved when a far-right component split off in 1978 as Flemisch Bloc or Vlaams Blok (now renamed Vlaams Belang), and a conservative component in 2001 as New Flemish Alliance (Nieuw-Vlaamse Alliantie), leaving its very few liberal-progressive members to join with the Green Party in 2009.

Meanwhile, the mainstream Flemish demands had become a cross-party issue, supported also by the powerful Christian Democrats, and have been almost fully met as Belgium is now increasingly a federal state with far-reaching autonomy for its Flemish and francophone halves. An administrative frontier along linguistic lines was established in 1962 amid some acrimony, involving, as it did, the transfer of some localities from one half of Belgium to the other and leaving orphaned minorities on both sides. What is more, the intractable bilingualism of the capital Brussels and its expanding suburbs posed, and continues to pose, a major political irritant. Most importantly, however, the establishment of the linguistic frontier meant that in matters of language, *ius sanguinis* (the 'personality principle') was changed into *ius soli* (the 'territoriality principle'); whereas previously, all Belgian citizens had had the right (at least theoretically) to use the language of their choice anywhere in the kingdom (which in practice tended to perpetuate French-language hegemony), language rights were now territorialized so that each half of Belgium had its own linguistic regime, with some minor rural areas (besides, of course, Brussels) subject to compromise exceptions. All official communications in Flanders take place in Netherlandic, while Wallonia only uses French.

A special case is that of the German-speaking areas on the country's eastern border (which has fluctuated in the course and aftermath of the world wars). *Heimat* movements in the first half of the century were an extension of similar developments within Germany proper, felt the lure of their cultural kin east of the border and after 1945 pursued their language rights as part of the Walloon Province of Liège. That process was very complex, since the Liégeois-German borderlands overlap with the Liégeois-Limburgish borderlands (which were transferred to Flanders in 1962); frictions or regionalist mobilization were placated after the creation of the Linguistic Frontier 1962; local autonomy was established in 1973 with a Council of the German-speaking community (Rat der deutschsprachigen Gemeinschaft). This *microcosmos* of linguistic-regional relations in Belgium shows all the signs of a curious multiscalarity: German-language regionalism originally formed part of a Great German national movement, then got squeezed between the competing nation-building processes of two neighbouring states, developed a brief internationalist stance (one locality declaring itself, around 1900 officially Esperanto-speaking) and got embroiled in the conflicting loyalties of two world wars with shifting annexations and reannexations. By now, ironically, the German-speaking communities count as the last 'true Belgians' since they have most to lose from a Flemish-Walloon disintegration of the country.

Frictions between Flanders and the francophone community are now largely fiscal and governance-related, except when the situation of Brussels and its suburbs and satellite towns crops up. Here, the right for francophone Belgian citizens to speak their own language is often tantamount to the right not to have to use or understand Flemish, which, since the suburbs are located in what is technically Flemish territory, continues to set *ius sanguinis* and *ius soli* against each other. On the whole, however, this is an irritant in national politics rather than a mobilizing platform for regionalism. The traditional major parties (Christian Democrats, Social democrats, Liberals) are sharply divided into Flemish and Walloon sibling organizations, which take sharply opposing sides when the matter of communitarian rights and claims comes up – the Liberal Party maintaining a more firmly pan-Belgian stance.

From nationalism to regionalism: The Walloon movement

The francophone side of the Belgian argument is a *ius soli* / *ius sanguinis* hybrid, in that it is sometimes defined territorially ('Wallonia', the French-speaking provinces in the south of the country) and sometimes linguistically (the French-speaking citizens of Belgium). This linguistic *communauté française* includes, besides the Walloon provinces, also Brussels and its adjacent areas, which are located as an enclave in (Flemish) Brabant.[16] Historically, Walloon Belgium was concentrated in the erstwhile prince-bishopric of Liège with its major, industrialized capital and in the provinces of Namur and Hainault with their municipal centres and mining industry. The official language in these territories had always been French, with an underlying set of local dialects. The Liège dialect especially had gained some currency in working-class and bourgeois city culture. In the course of the nineteenth century, these dialects began to use the self-appellation *Wallon*, from the Flemish *waals* meaning, generically, 'a foreign language'. This self-articulation occurred after the mid-nineteenth century, as the Flemish movement was crystallizing: *Wallon* came to designate the language or territories where Belgium showed its true identity in being neither Netherlandic, nor part of France (for all that standard French was the standard language both of France and of Belgium).

For most of the twentieth century, the Walloon movement has positioned itself as the patriotically minded defence of Belgium's true, francophone nature against Flemish ethnolinguistic encroachments. That was the rhetoric of Jules Destrée's 1912 Walloon manifesto, the notorious open letter to King Albert asserting that among the King's subjects there were no actual Belgians, only Fleming and Walloons – and proceeding to address the King in a communal, complicit first-person plural 'we' while denouncing the Flemish vindications as an alien 'them'.[17] This discourse was amplified after 1918, and again after 1945, as the Flemish movement (and, by extension, any vindication of Flemish linguistic rights in the Belgian state) had become tainted, in both world wars, with *incivisme*, that is, the betrayal of civic duties by siding with those who would destroy the country's integrity. By contrast, the Walloon movement would (with some selective amnesia) proclaim 'anti-Nazi resistance and anti-Fascism' as one of its four foundational principles alongside language, territory and culture.[18] Prior to the establishment of the Linguistic Frontier in 1962, the Walloon movement concentrated on attacking and discountenancing Flemish demands and maintaining French-language primacy in Belgium; increasingly, after 1962, it has retrenched into a defence of the remaining francophone 'rump' of Belgium (Wallonia and the Brussels district) against what it considers the encroaching secessionism of Flanders. Some Walloonists would want to maintain the integrity of Belgium as a state and within that state ensure the consolidation of the rights of the French-language community; some accede to the notion of a breakup and to ensure a viable French-language successor state after a Flemish secession. A small but not inconsiderable portion, the so-called *rattachistes*, would in that scenario favour unification with France.

Seen in this light, the Walloon movement is a type of Belgian 'rump nationalism', rather than a regional movement. It does carry within itself some regionalist and culturalist aspects, however, which date back to its nineteenth-century Liégeois origins and which manifest themselves in a problematic relationship between the movement's Brussels and Liégeois 'wings'. In 2009, a group of Liégeois-focused Walloonist intellectuals stated that 'Wallonia must secure all competences that relate to its symbolic image, its culture'. Their *Livre Blanc pour la Wallonie*[19] was the group's third manifesto after the tellingly-titled *Manifeste pour une culture wallonne* (1984) and *Pour une Wallonie maîtresse de sa culture, de son éducation et de sa recherche* (2004). A Walloon renaissance would not materialize, so it was argued, if Wallonia lacked a cultural project alongside its economic and political project; thus, a cultural consciousness-raising and a more regionalist tinge was given to what had throughout the century positioned itself as sociopolitical movement.

This move constantly had to placate fears that such a regionalist Wallonism would abandon its linguistic solidarity ties with the francophone Brussels population. In the party-political landscape, this is reflected in the more Brussels-centred Front des francophones (FDF), whose roots go back, by way of a Democratic Front of Brussels Francophones (established in the 1960s, following the establishment of the linguistic frontier), to a Ligue contre la flamandisation de Bruxelles that was active in the 1930s. The main Walloonist party, the Rassemblement Wallon, was active between 1968 and 1985, and in that period saw frequent electoral alliances with the Brussels FDF, but also a shift from federalism to autonomism and even *rattachisme*. That shift took place as its electoral base dwindled: increasingly, the francophone wings of Belgium's mainstream parties (especially the Socialist Party) have taken Walloon regional interests into their programmes, and its small successor organizations do not have the same importance in the party-political landscape as the Flemish nationalist parties do on the other side of the Linguistic Frontier.

Regionalism into sovereignty: Luxembourg

During what Miroslav Hroch would label a culturalist 'phase A' in the second half of the nineteenth century,[20] the Walloon movement exercised a remarkable influence on what we may call the Luxembourg ethnogenesis. At the time, the Grand Duchy was still in a personal union with the Dutch king, but its intellectuals by and large had pro-Belgian sympathies, or else strong ties with the adjacent Prussian Rhineland. A localist regionalist movement unwittingly prepared the ground, intellectually, culturally and institutionally, to what in 1892 would become a separate statelet, almost as a dynastic accident: the only child of the King/Grand Duke Willem III, Wilhelmina, though she could ascend the throne of the Netherlands, was prevented from doing so in the Luxembourg succession because of a ban on female succession. A distant relative from the Nassau dynasty became the grand duke of what was almost an operetta state. That state merged neither with Belgium nor with Germany because it could fall back, not only on an international balance-of-power policy, but also on cultural *lieux de mémoire* which had been cultivated by regionalist associations in the preceding century. These early beginnings of a Luxembourg 'cultivation of culture' mirror provincial trends which were cropping in many other peripheral parts of the Low Countries, which, without necessarily developing regionalist ambitions, evinced a strongly local-historical and local-cultural interest – much as in the French *petite patrie* trend or the German *Heimatbewegung*.

However, although those names for localist trends suggest a certain countryside rusticity, it should be stressed that the basis for the Netherlandic and Luxembourgh variants was located in the provincial cities and their middle-class sociability. In Luxembourg as in other cities, there was an amateur association for local history and archaeology; this society started to move its collections into a museum and sported a periodical; it occasionally also showed an interest in the local dialect and used it in a half-comic, carnivalesque way for literary purposes: all that is a pattern of cultural conviviality which we also encounter in provincial cities like Maastricht (in Limburg), Leeuwarden (in Friesland), Liège (in Wallonia) or Bruges (in West Flanders).[21] In Luxembourg, however, such initiatives and institutions would unexpectedly, after 1892, prove to be protonational rather than local-regional, and provide the basis for cultural state-building.

Most of the formative developments and culturalist lifelines run their course prior to 1892 and are thus outside the time-scope of this volume; but they were in place in 1892 and still give present-day Luxembourg its sense of national identity.[22] Among the regionalist vindications of the statelet's separate identity and character as neither French nor German, the most important cultural markers were the evocation of the Grand Duchy's medieval glory days and the language. Used repeatedly to bolster a sense of intransigent anti-German independence, Lëtzebuergesch (Luxembourgish, since 1982 an official language of the Grand Duchy) had been fostered by the regionalism that proliferated in the nineteenth-century southern Netherlands. The first poems in the Luxembourg dialect were written by men whose career took them into independent post-1830 Belgium. Anton Meyer (1801–1857), author of *E Schréck op de Lëtzebuerger Parnassus* (1829, 'A step onto the Luxembourg Parnassus') ultimately was appointed professor at the University of Liège, where he was inspired by the thriving Walloon dialect culture there; Jacques Diedenhoven (1809–1866), author of *De Bittgank no Conter* ('The Pilgrimage to Contern'), became an officer in the Belgian army. Michel Lentz (1820–1893) studied in Brussels, Edmond de La Fontaine (1823–1891) in Liège and Heidelberg. Such figures were part of an emigration, between 1830 and 1839, of anti-Orangist intellectuals from Luxembourg and Limburg (areas that unwillingly remained under Dutch rule) to Belgium, where they encountered the post-1840 revival of Walloon (especially Liégeois) dialect literature.[23]

As the Grand Duchy moved towards modernization, it did so with an increasing reliance on its cultural peculiarities. Tellingly, the opening of the railway connection with Germany was celebrated in a spirit of cosmopolitan modernity together with an affirmation that the national identity be maintained unchanged: Michael Lentz's poem/chanson *Der Feierwon* (The fiery waggon) of 1859 has in its refrain the line 'We want to stay who we are' ('Kommt hier aus Frankräich, Belgie, Preisen, / Mir wellen iech ons Hémecht weisen, / Frot dir no alle Säiten hin, /Mir welle bleiwe wat mir sin').[24] That was written before the Luxembourg Crisis of 1867 demonstrated Luxembourg's geopolitical exposure between the German and French spheres of influence. As Germany between 1914 and 1945 repeatedly occupied the country with annexationist intent, the phrase 'we want to remain what we are' (informally often changed to 'we do not want to be Germans') became first the unofficial, then the official, motto of the Grand Duchy.

The need to assert separateness may also explain why the regionalist movements on the eastern borders of the Low Countries have on the whole made little connection or common cause with each other. Not only do they lack a common regional language; from the *Nedersaksisch* area of Groningen by way of Limburg and the Belgian Eastern Cantons to Luxembourg, their relative relations with neighbouring Germany and with the national centre were in each case too dissimilar to establish a common basis. Only Limburg and Luxembourg have in recent decades developed some tentative contacts, bolstered to some extent by the establishment of a European Euroregion for the Meuse-Rhine area. There is also cooperation in small-scale cross-border tourism in the area, which 'brands' itself by referring to the common ancestral figure of Charlemagne and to ancient territories antedating the rise of the nation states.[25]

Conclusion

Despite their small size, the Low Countries present a complex palette of varieties of regionalism. These follow on the whole the historical lordships from which the post-Napoleonic Kingdom of the Netherlands of 1815, and its Benelux successor states post-1839, were assembled – although one of the most robust forms of regionalism is based in a province, Limburg, that had no territorial or governmental cohesion whatsoever pre-1815. Indeed all the regionalist movements surveyed here took shape in reaction to the centralism of the modern state, in varying degrees of intensity and antagonism, and drew on the urban sociability, municipally based, of bourgeois elites in provincial cities. The Flemish movement evolved towards outright nationalism; Luxembourg had a national identity thrust upon itself through dynastic and geopolitical happenstance; the Walloon movement is a 'rump Belgian' successor to what was anti-Netherlandic Belgian nationalism and what is now an intra-Belgian regionalism. Elsewhere, localisms generated local-interest societies which in peripheral cities (Leeuwarden, Bruges, Maastricht) could mobilize a subsidiary or particularist sense of regional identity.

To complicate matters even further, these various localisms, regionalisms and nationalisms also extended into a macroregional, transnational level of cultural geography. Dutch nationalists and Flemish separatists made common cause in what s known as the 'Greater Netherlandic' (Groot-Nederlands, or Diets) movement; nostalgic yearning for a return to the Burgundian Netherlands of the High Middle Ages are united in what they call a pan-Netherlandic (Heel-Nederlands), and in the course of the later nineteenth century, one wing of the Flemish movement proposed an alliance with the Low-German (*plattdeutsch*)-speaking areas of Northern Germany.[26] Generally speaking, these were fringe movements carried by a small number of cranks, but during wartime occupations and at other moments of political instability, these cranks obtained considerable political traction in the public debate, in a tradition reaching from the SS Ahnenerbe to certain neo-Nazi elements in contemporary ethnopopulism.

Thus the history of nationalisms and regionalisms in the Low Countries exemplifies a multiscalar dynamics where, from the municipal to the macroregional, various levels of aggregation coexist and interact. The various regional and national movements of the Low Countries were and are, not just local, individual manifestations of a standard centre-periphery dynamics: one movement inspired or provoked others. Therefore, they ought to be studied as such, transregionally and, indeed, transnationally, and in a multiscalar optics, capable of seeing the connections between the local, the national and the transnational.

What is more, these 'movements' of political regionalism or subnationalism are invariably the political intensification of a more persistent cultivation process of cultural particularism, drawing on a stock-in-trade of mnemonic and cultural markers which set the region apart from the larger whole. To see their emergence purely in terms of a political or social response theory elides the fact that all of these movements, without exception, gained their convincing and mobilizing power as the result of a nineteenth century process of a 'cultivation of culture',[27] usually around cultural markers like language, history and popular traditions. The most powerful self-asserting arguments in all regions of the Low Countries were without exception made available by nineteenth-century culture-building.

Notes

1. Evelien Koolhaas-Grosfeld, *De ontdekking van de Nederlander in boeken en prenten rond 1800* (Zutphen: Walburg, 2010).

2. Joep Leerssen, 'Medieval Heteronomy, Modern Nationalism: Language Assertion between Liège and Maastricht, 14th–20th century', *Revue belge d'histoire contemporaine* 34, no. 4 (2004): 581–93. See also Oscar Breukers and Anteun Janse, eds, *Negen eeuwen Friesland-Holland: Geschiedenis van een haat-liefde-verhouding* (Zutphen: Walburg, 1999).

3. Generally Philippus Breuker, *Opkomst en bloei van het Friese nationalisme* (Leeuwarden: Wijdemeer, 2016); and http://ernie.uva.nl/viewer.p/21/56/filter/91-140110.

4. Ward Goodenough, 'Describing a Culture', in *Description and Comparison in Cultural Anthropology* (Cambridge: Cambridge University Press, 1970), 104–19. See also the chapter by Kabatek.

5. Marnix Beyen, 'A Contested Trinity: The Rise and Fall of the Franks, the Frisians and the Saxons in Historical Consciousness of the Netherlands since 1850', *European History Quarterly* 30, no. 4 (2000): 493–532.
6. Dolly Verhoeven, ed., *Klederdracht en kleedgedrag: Het kostuum Harer Majesteits onderdanen 1898–1998* (Nijmegen: SUN, 1998).
7. Ad de Jong, *De dirigenten van de herinnering: Musealisering en nationalisering van de volkscultuur van Nederland, 1815–1940* (Nijmegen/Arnhem: SUN/Nederlands Openluchtmuseum, 2001).
8. Generally, Goffe Jensma, 'The Consequences of Transport by Steam: Dutch Nationalism and Frisian Regionalism in the Nineteenth Century', in *Region and State in Nineteenth-Century Europe: Nation-Building, Regional Identities and Separatism*, ed. Joost Augusteijn and Eric Storm (Basingstoke: Palgrave Macmillan, 2012), 229–45; Sjoerd van der Schaaf, *Skiednis fan de Fryske Biweging* (Ljouwert/Leeuwarden: De Tille, 1977); and online at dbnl.org.
9. Thomas Steensen, 'Zur Entstehung und Entwicklung interfriesischer Beziehungen', in *Handbuch des Friesischen*, ed. Host-Haider Munske (Tübingen: Niemeyer, 2001), 698–703.
10. Gjalt R. Zondergeld, *De Friese beweging in het tijdvak der beide wereldoorlogen* (Leeuwarden: De Tille, 1978).
11. J. L. G. van Oudheusden, 'Brabantia Nostra: Een gewestelijke beweging voor fierheid en "schoner" leven, 1935–1951' (Ph.D. dissertation, Kath. Universiteit Nijmegen, 1992); and A. J. A. Bijsterveld, ' "Zóó is Brabant": Noord-Brabant als casus van dynamisch regionalisme in Europa', in *Het nieuwste Brabant*, ed. Wim van de Donk et al. ('s-Hertogenbosch: Lecturis, 2014), 552–70.
12. Hans Knippenberg and Ben de Pater, *De eenwording van Nederland. Schaalvergroting en integratie sinds 1800* (Nijmegen: SUN, 2011, 7th ed.).
13. Joep Leerssen, 'De Limburgse identiteit', in *Limburg: Een geschiedenis*, vol. 3, ed. Paul Tummers et al. (Maastricht: LGOG, 2015), 303–22.
14. Gerard P. M. Knuvelder, *Vanuit wingewesten. Een sociografie van het zuiden* (Hilversum: Brand, 1930).
15. Generally, Reginald de Schryver, ed., *Nieuwe Encyclopedie van de Vlaamse Beweging* (3 vols. Tielt: Lannoo, 1998); and http://ernie.uva.nl/viewer.p/21/56/filter/91-140108.
16. I neglect, for the present argument, the remaining vestiges of a francophone bourgeoisie in the Flemish cities of Gent and Antwerp; they are the traces of an arrested and reversed process of nineteenth-century frenchification with a certain cultural presence but little political impact.
17. The full text is online at http://ernie.uva.nl/viewer.p/21/54/object/351-188082.
18. Thus in the Wikipedia article on 'Mouvement wallonne', which reflects a broad consensus: the movement's 'Fondements' are rubricated as 'Langue française', 'Wallonie', Identité wallonne' and 'Résistance et anti-fascisme'. Generally, http://romanticnationalism.net/viewer.p/21/56/filter/91-140142.
19. *Livre Blanc pour la Wallonie*, May 2009, online at http://www.larevuetoudi.org/fr/story/1-culture-et-citoyenneté-en-wallonie. Generally, Maarten Van Ginderachter and Joep Leerssen, 'Denied ethnicism: on the Walloon movement in Belgium', *Nations and Nationalism* 18, no. 2 (2012): 230–46; and the *Encyclopédie du Mouvement Wallon*, online at http://www.wallonie-en-ligne.net/Encyclopedie/index.htm.
20. Miroslav Hroch, *Social Preconditions of National Revival in Europe: A Comparative Analysis of the Social Composition of Patriotic Groups among the Smaller European Nations* (Cambridge: Cambridge University Press, 1985).

21. Tymen Peverelli, 'Kerken en kanonnen: Stedelijk verleden en historische genootschappen in Maastricht, 1853–1914', *De Negentiende Eeuw* 39, no. 2 (2015): 118–40.
22. The volume of *Lieux de mémoire au Luxembourg/Erinnerungsorte in Luxemburg* (ed. Sonia Kmec et al., Luxembourg: Saint-Paul, 2008) lists language, *heimat* songs and the various historical and cultural myths, tropes and icons that are canonical for the country's mnemonic community and sense of identity. Generally, http://ernie.uva.nl/viewer.p/21/56/filter/91-140121.
23. Cf. Lou Spronck, 'De Maastrichtse dialectliteratuur vóór 1840', in *Miscellanea Trajectensia: Bijdragen tot de geschiedenis van Maastricht* (Maastricht: Limburgs Geschied-en Oudheidkundig Genootschap, 1962), 435–96; and Lou Spronck, 'De Bittgank no Conter & De Percessie van Scherpenheuvel, twee negentiende-eeuwse satires in de streektaal', *Veldeke Jaarboek* (2010): 21–49. On Walloon dialect literature, see, besides the relevant entries in the *Encyclopédie du Mouvement Wallon*, Daniel Droixhe, 'Les lettres dialectales: Le théâtre wallon', in *La Wallonnie: Le pays et les hommes (Lettres – arts – culture)* vol. 2 (Bruxelles: La renaissance du livre, 1976), 481–96.
24. 'Come hither from France, Belgium and Prussia, we want to show you our homeland, be cheerful towards all sides, we want to remain what we are.' http://ernie.uva.nl/viewer.p/21/54/object/351-230472.
25. Almut Kriele, *Das ist ungeheuer bunt hier! Die Euregio Maas-Rhein nutzt die Chancen ihrer Vielfalt. Grenzüberschreitende Zusammenarbeit in der Euregio Maas-Rhein* (Aachen: Skaer, 2005); and Johanna Kamermans, *Euregio Carolus Magnus. Grenzen im Fluss. Wissenswertes, Historisches, Kurioses rund um das Städtedreieck Maastricht – Aachen – Lüttich* (Aachen: Verlag Mainz, 2004).
26. Piet Blaas, 'Gerretson en Geyl: De doolhof der Grootnederlandse gedachte', *Tijdschrift voor geschiedenis* 97 (1984): 37–51; Joep Leerssen, *De bronnen van het vaderland: Taal, literatuur en de afbakening van Nederland, 1806–1892* (Nijmegen: Vantilt, 2011); and Bruno de Wever, 'Groot-Nederland als utopie en mythe', *Bijdragen tot de eigentijdse geschiedenis* 3 (1997): 163–80.
27. Joep Leerssen, 'Nationalism and the Cultivation of Culture', *Nations and Nationalism* 12, no. 4 (2006): 559–78.

Furher reading

Breuker, Philippus, *Opkomst en bloei van het Friese nationalisme, 1840–1875* (Leeuwarden: Wijdemeer, 2016).

Delforge, Paul, Philippe Destatte and Micheline Libon, eds, *Encyclopédie du Mouvement Wallon*, 4 vols. (Namur: Institut Jules Destrée, 2000–2010; online at Encyclopedie/index.htm).

Jensma, Goffe, 'The Consequences of Transport by Steam: Dutch Nationalism and Frisian Regionalism in the Nineteenth Century', in *Region and State in Nineteenth-Century Europe: Nation-Building, Regional Identities and Separatism*, ed. Joost Augusteijn and Eric Storm (Basingstoke: Palgrave Macmillan, 2012), 229–45.

Leerssen, Joep, *De bronnen van het vaderland: Taal, literatuur en de afbakening van Nederland, 1806–1892* (Nijmegen: Vantilt, 2011).

Péporté, Pit, Sonja Kmec, Benoît Majerus and Michel Margue, *Inventing Luxembourg: Representations of the Past, Space and Language from the Nineteenth to the Twenty-First Century* (Leiden: Brill, 2010).

Schaaf, Sjoerd van der, *Skiednis fan de Fryske Biweging* (Ljouwert/Leeuwarden: De Tille, 1977).
Schryver, Reginald, ed., *Nieuwe Encyclopedie van de Vlaamse Beweging*, 3 vols. (Tielt: Lannoo, 1998).
Tummers, Paul et al., eds, *Limburg: Een geschiedenis*, 3 vols. (Maastricht: Limburgs Geschied- en Oudheidkundig Genootschap, 2015).
van Ginderachter, Maarten, and Joep Leerssen, 'Denied Ethnicism: On the Walloon Movement in Belgium', *Nations and Nationalism* 18, no. 2 (2012): 230–46.

CHAPTER 13
REGIONALISM IN SOUTH-WESTERN EUROPE: FRANCE, SPAIN, ITALY AND PORTUGAL

Xosé M. Núñez Seixas and Fernando Molina

This chapter explores the expression of regional identity and regionalism in four South-Western European states: Portugal, Spain, France and Italy. It will give particular attention to the region-building process resulting from constant negotiation and interdependence between region and nation.[1] In the process, classic paradigms, such as that of Eugen Weber – which argued that a national project moulded in purportedly civic values eroded the local sphere – will be revised.[2] State-led nationalism has also influenced how regions have been historiographically conceptualized from a methodological point of view. In France, the regional sphere has often been overwhelmed and obscured by the national in a historiography committed to a republican narrative, while 'peripheral' historiographies in Spain and even Italy have tended to regard any manifestation of regionalism as precursory to the later emergence of substate nationalisms.[3] Inverting the mirror for this narrative suggested that the existence of regionalism was in fact an expression of state failure to nationalize its citizens.[4]

The region is regarded here as another sphere in which spatial identity can be represented, brought to fruition by liberal modernity and subject to dispute among a variety of actors. This debate also relates to terminology: both region and regionalism are ambiguous concepts that have become politically polysemic over time.[5] The region in France conjures up terms such as *pays* (county), *department* or *région*, which are often subsumed into the concept of the *petite patrie*. In Spain, the region encompasses the local, the *comarca* (county), the province, the *terruño* (native land), *país* or *región*. In Italy – the country of 100 cities – the region (*regione*) has played only a minor role in the dynamics of self-definition by the population, which tend to favour the *paese* (county), the province and particularly the town or *città*.[6] In Portugal, the region scarcely figured as a space of belonging, except in northern areas. Instead, the parishes and municipalities (*autarquias*) comprising the local sphere were regarded as primary areas of social allegiance.

Regionalism in all these countries often had no historical region to claim and thus referred to local, provincial or administrative spheres of territorial belonging. Subnational units often had blurred borders in political discourse. Thus, regionalism must be viewed not 'as a political force, but as a political idiom', which functions as a collection of icons and slogans that provide diverse groups with cultural and political arguments.[7] Common to all these groups is the subnational territorialization of political and cultural demands to ensure some form of collective recognition of the singularity of territorial units, even as mass nationalization fostered increasing homogenization of the state territory.

Regional identity was swiftly adopted by writers, journalists and other 'nation-makers', who sought to craft the region as a stable and homogeneous community. This notion became intertwined with the idea of the nation as an organic sum of territories and localities, which entailed a geometry of diverse allegiances. While in some cases and time periods this arsenal of subordinated narratives may have supported political claims for decentralization and constituted the basis for political regionalism, in other cases the narratives remained pre-political and became complementary expressions of either state-led or *regionalized* nationalism. Regionalized nationalism existed almost everywhere and decisively contributed to the consolidation of state-led nationalism. Political regionalism may or may not evolve towards substate nationalism; however, it usually coexists within a single state or even within regional borders with regionalized (state-led) nationalism, and, thus, they condition each other.

Picturesque ruralism and fin-de-siècle regionalism

Regions were institutionalized around the time of the 'crisis of liberal reason' that accompanied peak nationalization of the masses between 1890 and 1914.[8] Regionalism at that time was led by middle-class liberal professionals, clerks and intellectuals who believed that the most representative sectors of the nation were peasants, farmers and artisans – in other words, those who incarnated the folk values that were being threatened by urban modernization. This strategy also encouraged national identity to take stronger root among the rural populations. A new generation of middle-class actors, who had already internalized nationhood as a banal identity, crafted regional identities that would act as intermediary spheres between the invoked folk identity and abstract national identity. Once the national narrative was established, it had to be propagated. The Italian experience provides a good example. There, a new generation of regionalist intellectuals and politicians who had come of age after unification set out to disseminate a more organic national identity, one capable of 'creating Italians'. Italians could only truly be made by fostering their primary sentiments of spatial identification, which could then be linked to an Italian national narrative.

The increasing interaction and hybridization of cultural revivalism and political regionalism resulted in the territorialization of political and social claims. These followed parallel but interrelated trajectories and sometimes argued for the emergence of an alternate substate nationalist narrative that competed with state nationalism: as some historians argued that the Basques were the authentic Spaniards while stressing their difference with those from other regions, in the end, those arguments could also endorse the opposite view, that the Basques were not Spanish at all.[9] To take this step, regionalists had to define their territory as a subject of sovereignty and craft an autonomous narrative that broke with any dependence or subordination to the wider nation-state narrative.

Mixed stages and differing interpretations of the imagined territory could also coexist simultaneously within the same regionalist movement.

The emergence of the 'regional issue' in Southern European cultural and political debates enhanced the complexity of state-building and nation-building processes, calling into question the narrative offered by modernization theory. This shows how modern nation-building went hand in hand with region-building, and the Spanish case displays this paradox. Nonetheless, cultural region-building carried out by the state or by civil society was not always accompanied by political or administrative decentralization.[10] Something similar can be seen in Italy, where the unification process and its *lacunae* – mainly the economic imbalance between the north and the south – gave rise to the emergence of a 'regional debate' that took many forms in southern Italy and Sardinia.[11] In contrast, no 'regional debates' emerged on the Portuguese mainland, though claims for decentralization sporadically arose in its insular periphery, particularly the Azores. These claims coexisted with certain cultural expressions that sought a common identity for the entire archipelago.[12]

Continental European region-building processes presented a diversity of inflections in each nation state. The French paradox resulted from the long-term erosion of local traditions, combined with the cultural reinvention of regions aimed at facilitating the imagination of the republican nation.[13] The Italian paradox grew out of the combination of late political unification and the lack of state resources to fully implement the agenda of Risorgimento nationalism, which led to the need for mediation and negotiation with local and regional elites.[14] The Spanish paradox is complex. The liberal state was respectful of the cultural identity of the 'historical' regions inherited from the Ancien Régime but divided them into new provinces. Local elites maintained former territorial allegiances, and the state was never strong enough to definitively replace them with new ones. However, the traditional territorial model enjoyed widespread acceptance among political elites of diverse inclinations; so traditionalists, democrats and republicans all 'regionalized' their political cultures. In Portugal, national identity was moulded by its imperial dimension and there was almost no political concurrence among the regions.[15]

These paradoxes highlight the enormous diversity of regionalist expressions in territories and national settings. In fact, only a few common patterns can be identified. One of these was the concept of the region as a 'nationalizing device' that mediated national identity, enriching its inner plurality and meanings while also questioning some aspects of them.[16] As a result, the actors who constructed national identity often used similar narratives to promote regional identity also. During the Third Republic, the *petite patrie* was introduced to French schoolchildren as their 'primary love', the motherland. Meanwhile, the nation, the homeland, was presented as their adult love for the mother and the father.[17] Rural aesthetics and icons associated with the region gave it a perennial quality as sanctuaries and Catholic sites of memory were rediscovered and became central elements of the 'imagined territory' for Catholics opposed to state secularization. The invention of folklore ran parallel to this idealization of rural life.[18] These, along with the exaltation of picturesque landscapes and mores accompanied the role of religion in representations of the region. Meanwhile, republican and democratic variants of regionalism idealized the local sphere as the main repository of ancestral democratic traditions and offered the sense that 'pride of place' was the first step in experiencing love for the nation.[19]

Modalities of south-western European regionalisms

Different modalities of region-building can be found in all four countries. In the French case, mass nationalization was accompanied by a revivalist discourse that venerated the peasantry as custodian of the continuity of the nation. A set of actors (literary societies, musical choirs, etc.) promoted new symbols and ceremonies by exalting the historical glories of the regions as organic components of national identity.[20] Ethnocultural revivalism, sometimes imbued with political claims, overlapped with the intensification of mass nationalization in Southern Europe after 1890. This interacted with new phenomena, such as the emergence of tourism, which contributed to the 'rediscovery' of the region by making it an object of desire for modern mass consumption. The region attracted attention for reasons ranging from the codification of regional gastronomy to the preservation of medieval architecture and heritage.[21] With the development of tourism in France in the 1890s, some regions were 'reinvented' and given renewed iconography. In Italy, tourism also fostered the re-enactment of medieval and renaissance urban traditions – such as the *palio* in Siena – as well as local folklore and gastronomy.[22] The Spanish case presents similarities, from the early influence of the Court summer residences that forged the image of the northern coastal cities of San Sebastián and Santander to neo-romantic travel literature and the first attempts to attract tourists to Castilian cities as sites of medieval heritage.[23]

Diverse actors implemented and consumed revivalist policies. Some involved local associations and institutions committed to the survival or elaboration of subnational identity, either as a form of preserving heritage and tradition or as a political claim for decentralization that later adopted regionalist and/or substate nationalist vocabulary (Fédération Régionaliste Française, Félibrige, Union Régionaliste Bretonne, Sociedad Euskalerria, Centre Català, Lliga de Catalunya, Asociación Regionalista Gallega, Irmandades da Fala, etc.). Others were statewide political parties – from Italian Christian Democrats and *Action* parties to certain republican currents – that incorporated the claim for (administrative, political or federal) decentralization into their agenda. Similarly, regional and local branches of republican and democratic parties in the cultural peripheries employed decentralization rhetoric and insisted upon regional devolution. Such interactions can be observed from Sicily to southern France and the Azores.

Regionalism in Southern Europe often supported national identities shared by very diverse political projects, from the left to the right, which aimed at challenging the central government. In France, this meant that regionalism vanished from the political agenda once the political opposition came to power. In Spain and Italy, it reinforced the political identity of anti-establishment currents that increasingly identified themselves with decentralization to counter the corruption of the central government. Such narratives linked the capital to power, corruption and cosmopolitanism but equated the local and the regional with tradition, national virtues and authenticity. The left tended to associate the capital with political corruption and capitalist dominance, while the Catholic right often regarded the city as epicentre of disrupting cosmopolitanism. The idea of the local as the repository of the virtues that would stimulate national regeneration from below was common to all political persuasions.

During the first third of the twentieth century, regionalism in France became a political and cultural label that encompassed a range of ideas, from exaltation of the local by the *sociétés savantes* to rejection of state centralism and the very notion of the French nation by Alsatian and Corsican ethnonationalists. Accordingly, the meaning ascribed to the term became increasingly vague. Regionalism was associated with activities such as trade fairs, the promotion of rural aesthetics in architecture and painting and the advancement of political proposals committed to administrative decentralization.[24] Republican-oriented cultural regionalism was transmitted through the institutional agency of the state, particularly through primary education. A dense network of locally based associations, from erudite *sociétés savantes* to local museums and antiquarians, also fostered this revivalist creed. Through public sculptures, commemorations and the arts, the 'local pedagogy' of the nation also manifested itself and enriched the narrative of French identity from below.[25]

In Spain, republicanism, from its very inception, had also embraced the idea of local liberties and regional decentralization as a necessary step towards achieving a representative government. While national history was regarded as a struggle between 'authentic' Spanish pride and exotic centralism imposed by foreign dynasties, the local was the beloved and privileged sphere for implementing democratic government. However, during the short-lived First Spanish Republic (1873–1874), a basic dichotomy emerged between Jacobean republicans, who regarded a strong national state as a necessary precondition to societal transformation, and federal republicans, who radicalized previous tenets of radical liberalism. The Bourbon restoration of 1874 signalled the return to a centralist state model based on the provinces, though sympathetic to regionalist revivalism.

However, following the 1898 crisis (in which Spain lost its last overseas colonies), radicalization of ethnoterritorial demands among regionalist groupings in Catalonia, the Basque Country and later in Galicia forced every territorial discourse in Spain to position itself in relation to the regional question and thereby become embroiled in a double dynamic of imitation and reaction. This manifested itself in two ways. First, old-style regions persisted as identity constructs among the supporters of Ancien Régime ideas. The Carlists were a prime example of this: for them, traditional territorial privileges expressed what Spain was before the arrival of 'foreign' liberalism. Second, it also allowed some groups to bypass the liberal model of a centralized nation state. Republican federalists, for example, adopted regionalist tenets to reinforce a Proudhonian view of society and state, which included organic-historicist claims for every region.

From its foundation in 1900, the Fédération Régionaliste Française, led by Jean Charles-Brun, had defined the agenda of political regionalism in France. This was also affected by the radicalization of some Breton and Occitan groupings with aims now based on purely romantic, ethnonational demands. However, the weak character of these movements until 1914 limited their capacity to determine the evolution of regionalism across France.[26] This displayed that the national context within which each regional movement emerged was also decisive. Thus, Basque, Catalan and Flemish cultural and political regionalisms in France followed very different paths from those of their 'brethren' on the other side of the border.[27] They scarcely surpassed the stage of regionalized nationalisms in the 1930s, while their counterparts in Spain and Belgium had been defining themselves as full-fledged nationalist movements since the final years of the nineteenth century. Similarly, peripheral nation-building projects were also confronted in their own imagined territory with the emergence of 'regionalized nationalisms', which raised the flag of local and provincial identity as a political instrument to oppose separatism. Navarrese and Valencian regionalisms in Spain are good examples of this.[28]

With less intensity than in Italy and Portugal, interaction between the local and the regional also fostered the emergence of an ambivalent representation of certain urban identities. These were invoked as sites of modernization, even though they were rooted in ancient and medieval history. While socially rooted urban identities, such as that of Bilbao, often competed with the region, the regional sphere of belonging also absorbed others: Barcelona, for example, was subsumed into Catalan identity.[29] This tension connected subnational identities with political debates. The liberal left (Marxists, anarchists) focused its political discourse on local and municipal identity, while conservatives and traditionalists tended to associate counties, provinces and historical regions with rural life and tradition. However, the regions never vanished from the political repertoire of the left: federal republicans often equated the political empowerment of 'historical regions' with a return to Spain's most authentic democratic past.

Parallel to this regionalization of popular culture, the new trend of Spanish nationalism in the wake of the 1898 crisis included expansion of the reform movement (*regeneracionismo*), which committed itself to modernizing the country from below. It saw the revitalization of the local and the regional as an appropriate instrument for recovering Spain's historic essence. Reformers were flanked by a new generation of writers and intellectuals who looked towards Castile as the ethnic and historic repository of Spain's positive values. The Castilian language thus became a main ethnic marker of the nation as liberals, republicans and fascists alike increasingly regarded Castile as the ethnic core of Spain. Nineteenth-century stereotypes persisted alongside this, insisting on regional icons such as the Aragonese male peasant (*majo*) as symbols of Spanishness, which were expressed in film and other forms of art.[30] Similarly, rural life in the Basque Country or Northern Castile was depicted as authentic and patriotic, in contrast to the corrupting effect of the big cities. An analogous process occurred in Portugal, where the Catholic right idealized the northern Minho region. The urban identities of Porto and Lisbon became the supreme sites of republican representations of the nation alongside the imperial imaginary, before and after the proclamation of the Republic (1910). As in France, however, regional icons were often created from a centralized organization. Portugal's Propaganda Society, founded in 1906, assumed this task; it managed the diffusion of regional icons and contributed to regional architecture especially with the invention of a model Portuguese 'farmhouse'.[31]

Italian state-building until 1914 was marked by institutional weakness. Thus, the central state always looked for local and regional mediators among the local elites. This helped reinforce local (and regional) identities as intermediate spheres between the national and the local. It reshaped regional stereotypes, particularly in areas such as southern Italy and Sardinia. In the search for authentic tradition, revivalist cultural associations and local writers turned to picturesque icons, folklore, gastronomy and dialects. However, the cities continued to forge the most powerful link between the individual and the nation, and urban identities decisively shaped the image of modern national identity.[32]

Revivalism also brought with it new expressions of territorial(ized) demands. An example of this was the emergence of the 'southern question' (*questione meridionale*), developed by intellectuals and politicians in the early twentieth century. These individuals were accompanied by a portion of the Sardinian elite. They presented the 'insular question' as the major pending territorial question of Italian unification, which was only obscured by irredentism.[33] Another variant consisted of territorializing political criticism of the liberal state in the pre-war years: in contrast with corrupt national politics, urban identity and local government were idealized and presented as the real repositories of civic values linked directly to the tenets of the Risorgimento and the golden age of the early Modern Renaissance.[34]

1914–1945: Regionalism turns (partially) to the right

Mass nationalization was accompanied by ideological polarization and cultural wars between Catholics and secularists. This peaked after the First World War, with the subsequent impact of the Soviet revolution and rise of Fascism. The new configuration also affected regionalism. Political Catholicism in France, Portugal, Spain and Italy continued to see regional identity as a device for combatting state secularism and (from 1917 on) the threat of social revolution. Its views on the local sphere thus became radicalized as the site where tradition and social order coalesced.[35] This seemed to give a definitive impulse to homogeneous nation-building processes in France, Portugal and Italy. The implosion of the multi-ethnic empires in East-Central Europe and the triumph of the nationality principle in 1918–1919 also contributed to regionalist radicalization. With the diffusion of national self-determination doctrines, some political regionalisms became full-fledged nationalisms, including those of Brittany, Galicia and Corsica. However, the experience of war was also crucial for the ethnic mobilization of war veterans in Sardinia. They formed the main social base of the new Sardinian political regionalism that led to the foundation of the Partido Sardo d'Azione.[36]

In France, radical republicanism and the left increasingly regarded the local as the source of reactionary politics. However, the historical experiences of the Breton movement, the Félibrige movement in the Midi, and the even weaker North Catalan movement challenge this view. Cultural and political regionalism was compatible with Catholic militancy and republican nation-building. Reactionary Catholics and republicans, and even some Proudhonian federalists and socialists coexisted within the same organizations.[37] Certainly, Catholic conservatives stressed local and regional symbols in their political propaganda, as an instrument to oppose republican secularization. Local priests became ardent supporters of folk cultures. The former *félibrige* Charles Maurras challenged republican nationalism – much as Maurice Barrès had – and called for a pre-liberal concept of national identity. Regionalism appeared as a central element in the Action Française narrative of a 'true France' made up of many local cultures.[38]

The discussion surrounding authentic national essence and its expression in the regional sphere became radicalized in the 1930s. Folklore gained credence as an academic discipline – increasingly dominated by scholars close to political Catholicism – and became one more battlefield in the fight to define the 'true' France. The Vichy new state largely relied on their findings to build a new public image of French identity and spread it through public and cultural performances and exhibitions that placed regionalism as the cornerstone for the survival of the nation. This regionalism also served as a common umbrella for fascists, traditionalists and conservative republicans, with the collaboration of some moderate *brétonnants* and political regionalists from Roussillon and Occitania. The Musée des Arts et Traditions Populaires, founded several years before, became the most visible symbol of this para-fascist appropriation of cultural regionalism, even though its director, Georges H. Rivière, was a left-wing Resistance activist.[39] A similar phenomenon occurred in Salazar's Portugal from the 1930s on, where the pre-war Catholic concept of the local continued to associate rural life with the national essence and tradition with peasant culture. Folklore was thus promoted as a companion to imperial mystique in mass performances, political rallies and exhibitions, such as the one devoted to the Colonial Empire in 1940. A prize was even established to praise the nation's 'most Portuguese village', and the winners mostly came from the Northern region, where Catholic traditions were preserved best.[40]

Along with Catholicism, a form of vaguely defined cultural regionalism also became a symbolic container for the message of the 'true Spain'. New sanctuaries from Covadonga (Asturias) to Begoña (Biscay) became veritable icons of regional identity and were held up as repositories of the nation's virtues.[41] This shaped a repertoire of symbols that also fuelled the new national Catholicism and from the 1920s on gave the anti-liberal right a common label. Spain, according to the late nineteenth-century historian Marcelino Menéndez Pelayo, was a mosaic of different landscapes and cultures united by a common monarchy and the Catholic faith. Within this image, the regions were, as the Carlist leader Juan Vázquez de Mella stated years later, the natural 'tributaries' that fell into a common river of Spanish national identity. The advent of the Primo de Rivera dictatorship in September 1923 was greeted with cautious optimism by moderate nationalists and many regionalists throughout Spain, including Catalans. Primo de Rivera's priority was to restore social order, but he generally seemed to prefer promoting decentralization. Shortly after he seized power, however, the army pushed for greater centralization. Public use of regional languages was restricted, Catalonia's limited home rule (introduced in 1914) was abolished and any alleged sign of separatism was fiercely opposed.

Nevertheless, the regime envisioned some degree of decentralization and expressed it by strengthening the autonomy of the municipalities and reinforcing the administrative functions of the provinces. This was the purpose of José Calvo Sotelo's administrative reforms in 1924 and 1925 (the 'Provincial Statute' and the 'Local Statute'), which were never actually translated into political practice. Primo de Rivera thus faced the basic dilemma of reconciling Spanish traditionalist scepticism regarding the provinces with the need to reinforce the provincial administrations that would implement the 'modernizing' policies initiated in 1924/1925, without resurrecting the threat of separatism. The apparent solution was a reconceptualization of the province that would dissociate it from nineteenth-century liberalism and ascribe to it many 'objective' qualities – from natural characteristics to ethnic markers – that had previously been associated with the region. Festivals and contests representing provincial folklore were staged in Madrid, and parades of provincial representatives displaying local costumes and symbols accompanied popular demonstrations of support for the dictator.[42] This strategy seemed the only viable alternative to granting political power to the regions, which would have provided a political platform for Catalan and Basque 'separatists'.

The Second Spanish Republic (1931–1936) put localism and regionalism back on the political agenda. In April 1931, pressure from Catalan republican nationalists forced the provisional government to adopt a quasi-federal structure for the Republic, beginning with the re-establishment of Catalan self-government. The Constitution of 1931 outlined a decentralized system under which Catalan, Basque and Galician nationalists ensured that their home-rule projects were passed by referendum prior to the outbreak of the Civil War in July 1936. This had mixed effects in other parts of Spain, which expressed varying degrees of imitation and rejection. Local and regional republicans, and even some conservatives and anti-republicans, supported greater regional autonomy as an opportunity to democratize their political spaces and demand symmetrical treatment to ensure that no special privileges were given to certain territories. Claiming home rule for Castile, Aragon, Valencia or the Canary Islands seemed the best way to render the Republic more democratic and link all Spanish regions to a common destiny. By the same token, local and provincial demarcations lost political value in the eyes of republicans and anti-republicans alike, who dreamed of making regional identities a refuge for tradition. Consequently, after the outbreak of the Civil War, both republican and insurgent camps were eager to use regional identities as frames of territorial identification and political mobilization.[43]

As in Vichy France, regionalism was an element of the legitimizing discourse of the Francoist dictatorship. Yet, competition between full-fledged peripheral nationalisms in some territories determined the regime's restrictive approach, which only allowed regional identities that were devoid of any political component. The diverse political factions that competed for hegemony (fascists, Carlists, Catholic monarchists) argued over the cultural and political limits of a return to 'healthy' regionalism. Fascists and members of the military who shared a martial and disciplined view of the nation also advocated full homogenization. They regarded local diversity as harmless but saw regional identity as potentially dangerous for national integrity.[44]

State-sponsored cultural policies presented local culture as the core of national tradition, with its Catholic essence. Francoist discourse also stressed the role of Castile as the ethnic core of the nation, though other 'historic regions' such as Aragon, Asturias, Valencia and Navarre – which transmitted the memory of the ancient medieval kingdoms – were exalted as intermediate spheres of the nation. Thus, limited ethnic polycentrism was a feature of regime discourse, which intensified in the 1950s.[45] Internal diversity in Francoist nationalism concerning the regional question had considerable impact on later developments during the transition to democracy in the late 1970s. This factor also contributes to explain the emergence of a decentralized structure after 1978.

In Italy, fascism seized power much earlier, giving the regime more time to define its regional policy. From the very first moment, the new fascist state willingly fostered cultural regionalism and urban identity, while repudiating any political content in these discourses. In Sardinia, the regime negotiated with Sardinian regionalists and allowed the emergence of 'Sardo-Fascism', a cultural hybridization with Sardinian myths and icons that emphasized the Mediterranean imperial dimension of Italian fascism.[46] Schoolchildren learned the history and folklore of their region, while municipalities seeking to draw tourists to Italy devoted greater effort to preserving their cultural heritage and re-enacting medieval traditions. State-sponsored local associations promoted local folklore and a limited literary cultivation of dialects. This coexisted with the harsh homogenization imposed on the border regions of South Tyrol and Gorizia, where German and Slavic cultures were systematically targeted as potential threats to national unity. Partly as a result of this coexistence of diverse ethnoterritorial dimensions, the regime adopted an anti-regionalist stance at the beginning of the 1930s. The public use of dialects and languages other than Italian was banned, and a more uniform national narrative was imposed in schools. This accompanied the adoption of state imperialism as the 'highest stage' of the national project inherited from the *Risorgimento*.[47]

In all four fascist or pseudo-fascist states, regionalism became institutionalized through revivalist practices and diglossic treatment of regional languages and dialects. Local cultures were linked to both the survival of tradition and a primordialist and (in the Spanish, French and Portuguese cases) Catholic concept of the nation. The institutionalization of folklore and its inclusion within authoritarian nation-building policies accompanied standardization and internal homogenization: regional landscapes, costumes and songs were crafted and diversity reduced to an identifiable number of easily consumable archetypes. Eventually, the local was fully integrated into national(ist) narratives, most of which had inherited their discursive and iconic patterns from nineteenth-century nation-building, where it was often presented as a continuation of liberal and especially Catholic and traditionalist variants.

Post-war regionalism: Decentralization and democratization

After 1945, mainstream Western European public opinion intrinsically associated both political regionalism and substate nationalism with ethnic tenets, potentially exclusive politics and para-fascist inclinations. This seriously affected the development of regionalism in France and Italy, while Salazar's Portugal continued to foster revivalist policies as an integral part of its traditionalist agenda. In Franco's Spain, the regime displayed a steady and increasing tolerance towards regionalist and localist cultural expressions, though all forms of political regionalism were banned.

However, there were some exceptions to this general picture. In the Spanish context, political regionalism was increasingly linked to left-wing and anti-fascist thinking, thanks to the prestige acquired by peripheral nationalists in exile. Beginning in the 1950s, ethnonationalists also led anti-Francoist agitation in the Spanish periphery. Similarly, Sardinian regionalists who returned from exile and adopted an anti-fascist bias were able to rebuild the Partito Sardo d'Azione. It became a fully legitimized political actor in post-war Sardinian politics.

In Western Europe, the reinvention of state nationalisms through the anti-fascist consensus legitimizing national reconstruction meant strengthening the identity of nation-states and marginalizing the 'regional question'. France thus maintained its traditional centralist structure, which was not substantially altered until the socialist president François Mitterrand came to power in the early 1980s. Breton, Occitan and Basque regionalist and nationalist claims in France languished amid huge difficulties and the Alsatian movement vanished after 1945. In the 1980s, increasing pressure on the French state from the Corsican nationalist movement, along with the modest resurgence of the Basque and Breton movements, put decentralization back on the table and paved the way for limited political regionalization provided by the Defferre Law of 1984. Nonetheless, regional councils and meso-territorial institutions (located between local and national dimensions) still play only a minor role in French politics and society.[48]

In Italy, the regional question evolved differently. After the difficult transition to the new Republic, accompanied by unprecedented territorial tension in Sicily (due to the emergence of a fiercely anti-communist separatist movement supported by local elites and the mafia),[49] an asymmetric, decentralized structure was established by the 1948 Constitution. This entailed the creation of several regions 'with special status' (Aosta, South Tyrol-Trentino, Sardinia and Sicily), to which Venezia-Giulia was added in 1964. In the 1980s and 1990s, 'regional councils' became more widespread and some administrative devolution to the regions occurred, but it scarcely resembled 'home-rule all round'.

The claims of the ethnic minorities of the Italian border regions, particularly from the French-speaking minority in the Aosta Valley and the German-speaking population of

South Tyrol, were now efficiently channelled through consolidated ethnic parties with bargaining capacity in Rome. However, economic tensions between the industrialized north and the less-developed southern regions, which were highly dependent on subsidies and capital transfers from the state, led to new territorial splits in the mid-1980s, particularly in the northern regions. Elements of ethnoterritorial mobilization were evident in the origins of the Liga Veneta and several Lombard groupings, though their main impulse came from the adoption of a more pragmatic, catch-all strategy by the Lega Nord in the early 1990s. This program merged a federalist agenda and ethnonationalist rhetoric with populist, far-right tenets containing xenophobic ingredients, making newly defined Padania a strong region within the Italian state.[50]

The 1950s and especially the 1960s saw new developments in the field of regionalism. First, with the spread of the 'principle of subsidiarity' and the decentralizing impulse of economic geography, many political leaders and intellectuals insisted on the need to bring administration closer to the citizens and create meso-territorial entities as ideal spaces for managing economic development and social policy. Even in centralist France, this helped secure a place for decentralization on the political agenda. A second element was the reappropriation of regionalism by left-wing groups. The influence of liberation movements from Africa and Asia on some intellectuals of the French periphery, such as Robert Lafont, led them to reframe regionalism as the 'internal decolonization' of Western Europe. Liberation of the 'proletarian' regions within the European nation states could constitute a first step towards world revolution. Dozens of left-leaning regionalist groups emerged in the wake of the student protests of May 1968, and ethnonationalist movements from Galicia to Corsica felt the effects of this 'wave'. A third element was the influence of the European integration process and the diffusion of the new concept of a 'Europe of the regions', beginning in the 1970s. According to this, decentralization from below and the strengthening of supra-state powers in Brussels from above would eventually lead to a definitive crisis of the nation state.[51]

Portugal and Spain returned to democracy between 1974 and 1978, further encouraging the re-emergence of political regionalism. The Carnation Revolution and subsequent period of political instability in Portugal brought a resurgence of regionalist claims in the Atlantic islands, particularly the Azores, where a radical separatist movement was refounded. The 1976 constitution gave Madeira and the Azores a special statute of autonomy, which solved the problem. However, the metropolitan core of Portugal became increasingly centralizing and most citizens rejected attempts at decentralization from above. The image of a rural country was replaced by the urban dynamism of the big coastal cities of Porto and Lisbon.[52]

In Spain, the process ran a very different course. Catalan, Basque and Galician nationalist movements had been key players in the opposition to the Franco regime. Thus, decentralization became a central issue during the Spanish transition. The constitution of 1978 provided the political solution to the national question by combining the concept of Spain as a single political nation with the granting of autonomy statutes to all regions. The State of the Autonomous Communities was initially conceived as a decentralized structure composed of seventeen regions (autonomous communities), which reframed the existing provinces. They were neither uniform nor equal in size, population or economic weight.

As a result of political agreement between the various political actors that intervened in shaping the constitution that brought Spanish democracy into being, a decentralized state structure was extended to the entire Spanish territory. Basque and Catalan nationalists pressed for self-government within the framework of a multinational state. This claim was unacceptable to the right-wing parties, which would tolerate nothing more than mild administrative decentralization. In theory, the left advocated a federal solution. In the end, the right to achieve autonomy was extended to all regions, though different routes to home rule were established. The quickest and greatest degree of decentralization was accorded to the three 'historical nationalities'. Sovereignty was held by the Spanish state, which in turn transferred broad powers to the autonomous communities and strengthened them with legislative and executive powers in many areas (i.e. agriculture and fishing, transport, culture and education, public health, tourism, commerce, etc.).

The decentralized Spanish state also became a laboratory for emerging new regional identities. New administrations created new political opportunity-structures that were open to the regional elites. This dynamic also led to the proliferation of regionalist parties in many of the newly created regions during the 1980s and 1990s. Some of them fostered a 'regional identity' and the final goal of achieving an autonomy statute by imitating tactics developed by Catalan and Basque peripheral nationalists. Nonetheless, they never claimed self-determination. This led to 'multiple ethnoterritorial concurrence',[53] which made the evolution of the regional question in Spain much more complex by the end of the twentieth century. Concessions to the 'ethnonationalist peripheries' always had to be settled within a decentralized system, and tensions between asymmetry and symmetry emerged between the 'historical nationalities' – Catalonia, the Basque Country and (to some extent) Galicia – and the rest of the regions.

Notes

1. See Maiken Umbach, 'Nation and Region', in *What Is a Nation? Europe 1789–1914*, ed. Timothy Baycroft and Mark Hewitson (Oxford: Oxford University Press, 2006), 63–80; Andreas Fahrmeir and H. S. Jones, 'Space and Belonging in Modern Europe: Citizenship(s) in Localities, Regions, and States', *European Review of History/Revue Européenne d'Histoire* 15, no. 3 (2008), 243–53.
2. Eugen Weber, *Peasants into Frenchmen. The Modernization of Rural France, 1871–1914* (Stanford: Stanford University Press, 1976); Miguel Cabo and Fernando Molina, 'The Long and Winding Road of Nationalization: Eugen Weber's *Peasants into Frenchmen* in Modern European History (1976–2006)', *European History Quarterly* 39, no. 2 (2009), 264–86.
3. See Xosé M. Núñez Seixas, 'Reflections on the Model of Miroslav Hroch and Historical Research on Western European Ethnonationalism', in *Historische Nationsforschung im geteilten Europa, 1945–1989*, ed. Pavel Kolár and Milos Rezník (Cologne: SH Verlag, 2012), 103–17.

4. Ferran Archilés, 'Melancólico bucle. Narrativas de la nación fracasada e historiografía española contemporánea', in *Estudios sobre nacionalismo y nación en la España contemporánea*, ed. Ismael Saz and Ferran Archilés (Valencia: PUV, 2011), 245–330.
5. Xosé M. Núñez Seixas, 'Historiographical Approaches to Sub-National Identities in Europe: A Reappraisal and Some Suggestions', in *Region and State in Nineteenth-Century Europe. Nation-Building, Regional Identities and Separatism,* ed. Joost Augusteijn and Eric Storm (Basingstoke: Palgrave Macmillan, 2012), 13–35.
6. Rolf Petri, 'Heimat/Piccole patrie. Nation und Region im deutschen und im italienischen Sprachraum', *Geschichte und Region/Storia e Regione* 12 (2003): 191–212.
7. Umbach, 'Nation and Region', 80.
8. Eric Storm, 'The Birth of Regionalism and the Crisis of Reason: France, Germany and Spain', in *Region and State*, ed. Augusteijn and Storm, 36–54.
9. See Jon Juaristi, *El linaje de Aitor: La invención de la tradición vasca* (Madrid: Taurus, 1998); and Fernando Molina, *La tierra del martirio español. El País Vasco y España en el siglo del nacionalismo* (Madrid: CEPC, 2005).
10. Xosé M. Núñez Seixas, 'The Region as Essence of the Fatherland: Regionalist Variants of Spanish Nationalism (1840–1936)', *European History Quarterly* 31, no. 4 (2001), 483–518; and Ferran Archilés, ' "Hacer región es hacer patria". La región en el imaginario de la nación española de la Restauración', *Ayer* 64 (2006): 121–47.
11. See Carl Levy, ed., *Italian Regionalism: History, Identity and Politics* (Oxford; Washington, DC: Berg, 1996).
12. Carlos Cordeiro, *Insularidade e continentalidade. Os Açores e as contradições da Regeneraçâo (1851–1870)* (Coimbra: Minerva, 1992); and Carlos Cordeiro, *Nacionalismo, regionalismo e autoritarismo nos Açores durante a Iª República* (Lisbon: Salamandra, 1999).
13. Anne-Marie Thiesse, 'Centralismo estatal y nacionalismo regionalizado. Las paradojas del caso francés', *Ayer* 64 (2006): 33–64.
14. Stefano Cavazza, 'El culto de la pequeña patria en Italia, entre centralización y nacionalismo. De la época liberal al fascismo', *Ayer* 64 (2006): 95–119.
15. Nuno Monteiro and António Costa Pinto, 'Cultural Myths and Portuguese National Identity', in *Contemporary Portugal: Politics, Society and Culture*, ed. António Costa Pinto (Boulder CO: Social Science Monographs, 2003), 55–72.
16. Ferran Archilés and Manuel Martí, 'La construcció de la regió com a mecanisme nacionalitzador i la tesi de la dèbil nacionalització espanyola', *Afers* 48 (2004): 265–308.
17. Jean-François Chanet, *L'école républicaine et les petites patries* (Paris: Aubier, 1996).
18. Caroline Ford, *Creating the Nation in Provincial France: Religion and Political Identity in Brittany* (Princeton, NJ: Princeton University Press, 1993); Tim Baycroft and David Hopkin, eds, *Folklore and Nationalism in Europe During the Long Nineteenth Century* (Leiden: Brill, 2012).
19. Stéphane Gerson, *The Pride of Place: Local Memories and Political Culture in Nineteenth-Century France* (Ithaca, NY: Cornell University Press, 2003).
20. John Hutchinson, *Nations as Zones of Conflict* (London: Sage, 2005), 58–59; and Joep Leerssen, 'Nationalism and the Cultivation of Culture', *Nations and Nationalism* 12, no. 4 (2006): 559–78.
21. Eric Storm, 'Regionalism in History, 1890–1945: The Cultural Approach', *European History Quarterly* 33, no. 2 (2003), 251–65.

22. Stefano Cavazza, *Piccole Patrie. Feste popolari tra regione e nazione durante il fascismo* (Bologna: Il Mulino, 2003), 171–244.

23. See Eric Storm, 'A More Spanish Spain: The Influence of Tourism on the National Heritage', in *Metaphors of Spain: Representations of Spanish National Identity in the Twentieth Century*, ed. Javier Moreno-Luzón and Xosé M. Núñez Seixas (New York/Oxford: Berghahn, 2017), 239–59.

24. Reinhard Sparwasser, *Zentralismus, Dezentralisation, Regionalismus und Föderalismus in Frankreich: eine institutionen-, theorien- und ideengeschichtliche Darstellung* (Berlin: Duncker & Humblot, 1986).

25. Anne-Marie Thiesse, *Ils apprenaient la France. L'exaltation des régions dans le discours patriotique* (Paris: Editions de la MSH. 1997); Gerson, *The Pride of Place*, 102–39; and Francesca Zantedeschi, 'The Antiquarians of the Nation: Archaeologists and Philologists in Nineteenth-Century Roussillon' (Ph.D. thesis, Pompeu Fabra University, Barcelona, 2016).

26. See Julian Wright, *The Regionalist Movement in France, 1890–1914: Jean Charles-Brun and French Political Thought* (Oxford: Clarendon Press, 2003); and Timothy Baycroft, 'National Diversity, Regionalism and Decentralism in France', in *Region and State*, ed. Augusteijn and Storm, 57–68.

27. James E. Jacob, *Hills of Conflict. Basque Nationalism in France* (Reno: University of Nevada Press, 1994); Nicolas Berjoan, *L'identité du Roussillon: Penser un pays catalan à l'âge des nations, 1780–2000* (Canet: Trabucaire, 2014); and Timothy Baycroft, *Culture, Identity, and Nationalism. French Flanders in the Nineteenth and Twentieth Centuries* (London: Royal Historical Society/Boydell Press, 2004).

28. See Angel García-Sanz, Iñaki Iriarte López and Fernando Mikelarena, *Historia del navarrismo (1841–1936). Sus relaciones con el vasquismo* (Pamplona: UPNA, 2002); Iñaki Iriarte, *Tramas de identidad. Literatura y regionalismo en Navarra (1870–1960)* (Madrid: Biblioteca Nueva, 2000); and Alfons Cucó, *El valencianisme polític, 1874–1939* (Catarroja: Afers, 1999).

29. Jon Juaristi, *El chimbo expiatorio (La invención de la tradición bilbaína, 1876–1939)*, 2nd ed. (Madrid: Espasa, 1999); and Stéphane Michonneau, *Barcelone, mémoire et identité, 1830–1930* (Rennes: PUR, 2007).

30. Marta García Carrión, *Por un cine patrio: Cultura cinematográfica y nacionalismo español (1926–1936)* (Valencia: PUV, 2013).

31. António Medeiros, *A moda do Minho. Um ensaio antropológico* (Lisbon: Colibri, 2004); and Daniel Melo, 'Regionalismo, sociedad civil y Estado en el Portugal del siglo XX', *Hispania Nova* 7 (2007), available at: http://hispanianova.rediris.es/7/articulos/7a012.pdf.

32. Ilaria Porciani, 'Lokale Identität – nationale Identität. Die Konstruktion einer doppelten Zugehörigkeit', in *Zentralismus und Föderalismus im 19. und 20. Jahrhundert. Deutschland und Italien im Vergleich*, ed. Oliver Janz, Pierangelo Schiera and Hannes Siegrist (Berlin: Duncker & Humblot, 2010), 103–36; and Stefano Cavazza, 'Regionalism in Italy: A Critique', in *Region and State*, ed. Augusteijn and Storm, 69–89.

33. Martin Clark, 'Sardinia: Cheese and Modernization', in *Italian Regionalism*, ed. Levy, 81–106.

34. Cavazza, *Piccole Patrie,* 19–22.

35. Joseba Louzao, 'Catholicism versus Laicism: Culture Wars and the Making of Catholic National Identity in Spain, 1898–1931', *European History Quarterly* 43, no. 4 (2013), 657–80.

36. Salvatore Cubeddu, *Sardisti. Viaggio nel Partito Sardo d'Azione tra cronaca e storia. Volume I (1918–1948)* (Sassari: Edes, 1992).

37. Francesca Zantedeschi, *Une langue en quête d'une nation: la Société pour l'Étude des Langues Romanes et la langue d'oc (1869–1890)* (n.p.: Institut d'Estudis Occitans, 2013);

and Philippe Martel, *Les Félibres et leur temps. Renaissance d'oc et opinion (1850–1914)* (Bordeaux: PUB, 2010).

38. Hermann Lebovics, *True France. The Wars over Cultural Identity, 1900–1945* (Ithaca, NY: Cornell University Press, 1992), 143–44.

39. Sudhir Hazareesingh, *Political Traditions in Modern France* (Oxford: Oxford University Press, 1994), 143–44; and Christian Faure, *Le projet culturel de Vichy. Folklore et révolution nationale, 1940–1944* (Paris: CNRS, 1989).

40. Daniel Melo, *Salazarismo e cultura popular (1933–1958)* (Lisbon: Imprensa de Ciências Sociais, 2001).

41. Carolyn Boyd, 'The Second Battle of Covadonga: The Politics of Commemoration in Modern Spain', *History & Memory* 14, nos. 1–2 (2002): 37–64; and Francisco J. Ramon Solans, *La Virgen del Pilar dice…Usos políticos y nacionales de un culto mariano en la España contemporánea* (Zaragoza: PUZ, 2014).

42. Alejandro Quiroga, *Making Spaniards. Primo de Rivera and the Nationalization of the Masses* (Basingstoke: Palgrave Macmillan, 2007).

43. Xosé M. Núñez Seixas, *¡Fuera el invasor! Nacionalismos y movilización bélica durante la guerra civil española, 1936–1939* (Madrid: Marcial Pons, 2006), 291–319.

44. Xosé M. Núñez Seixas, 'La región y lo local en el primer franquismo', in *Imaginarios y representaciones de España durante el franquismo*, ed. Stéphane Michonneau and Xosé M. Núñez Seixas (Madrid: Casa de Velázquez, 2014), 127–54.

45. See Andrea Geniola, 'El nacionalismo regionalizado y la región franquista: dogma universal, particularismo espiritual, erudición folklórica (1939–1959)', in *Naciones y Estado. La cuestión española*, ed. Ferran Archilés and Ismael Saz (Valencia: PUV, 2014), 189–224; as well as some details in Gustavo Alares, *Políticas del pasado en la España franquista (1939–1964)* (Madrid: Marcial Pons, 2017).

46. Salvatore Cubeddu, ed., *Il Sardofascismo* (Cagliari: Fondazione Sardinia, 1997).

47. See Sandro Fontana, ed., *Il fascismo e le autonomie locali* (Bologna: Il Mulino, 1976).

48. See Yves Mény, *Centralisation et décentralisation dans le débat politique français (1945–1969)* (Paris: Pichon/Duran-Auzias,1974).

49. See Giuseppe C. Marino, *Storia del separatismo siciliano* (Rome: Riuniti, 1979).

50. Daniele Petrosino, 'Is It Possible to Invent Ethnic Identity? Some Reflections on Ethnic and Territorial Politics in Italy', in *Nationalism in Europe: Past and Present*, ed. Justo G. Beramendi, Ramón Máiz and Xosé M. Núñez (Santiago de Compostela: USC, 1994), vol. 2, 609–44; and Stelio Mangiameli, ed., *Italian Regionalism: Between Unitary Traditions and Federal Processes* (Cham: Springer International, 2014).

51. See Xosé M. Núñez Seixas, *Movimientos nacionalistas en Europa. Siglo XX* (Madrid: Síntesis, 2004), 265–377.

52. Maria I. Joâo (1996), 'Identidade e autonomia', *Ler História* 31 (1996), 103–31.

53. See Luis Moreno, *The Federalization of Spain* (London: Routledge, 2001).

Further reading

Augusteijn, Joost, and Eric Storm, eds, *Region and State in 19th Century Europe: Nation-Building, Regional Identities and Separatism* (Basingstoke: Palgrave Macmillan, 2012).

Baycroft, Timothy, *Culture, Identity, and Nationalism: French Flanders in the Nineteenth and Twentieth Centuries* (London: Royal Historical Society/Boydell Press, 2004).

Levy, Carl, ed., *Italian Regionalism: History, Identity and Politics* (Oxford/Washington: Berg, 1996).

Monteiro, Nuno, and António Costa Pinto, 'Cultural Myths and Portuguese National Identity', in *Contemporary Portugal: Politics, Society and Culture*, ed. António Costa Pinto (Boulder, CO: Social Science Monographs, 2003), 55–72.

Núñez Seixas, Xosé M., 'The Region as Essence of the Fatherland: Regionalist Variants of Spanish Nationalism (1840–1936)', *European History Quarterly* 31, no. 4 (2001): 483–518.

Storm, Eric, *The Culture of Regionalism. Art, Architecture and International Exhibitions in France, Germany and Spain, 1890–1939* (Manchester: Manchester University Press, 2010).

Wright, Julian, *The Regionalist Movement in France, 1890–1914: Jean Charles-Brun and French Political Thought* (Oxford: Clarendon Press, 2003).

CHAPTER 14
BORDERLANDS, PROVINCES, REGIONALISMS AND CULTURE IN EAST-CENTRAL EUROPE
Irina Livezeanu and Petru Negură

Regional identities may be more enduring than national ones in East-Central Europe, where regions, regional identities and regionalist movements have attracted renewed interest, spurred by the historiographic flowering that ensued after 1989 as much as by the search for a useable past.[1] The end of the Soviet bloc, the Yugoslav wars, the Velvet divorce between Czechs and Slovaks and separatist conflicts in the former Soviet Union, as well as the eastern expansion of the European Union have stimulated this interest. European Union architecture seems to welcome a 'Europe of Regions'.[2] The search in former communist lands for a less tainted past has wandered through centuries-old imperial borderlands such as Transylvania, Bukovina, Slovakia, Silesia or Banat, where the lack of linguistic homogeneity and frequently shifting boundaries favoured political compromise and mutual tolerance. Nation-centred narratives have failed to account for hybrid identities of some populations in East-Central Europe, particularly those in cosmopolitan cities and frontier zones.[3] Regions construed as transitional spaces (*Zwischenräume*), as well as small nations have been ignored by national histories, but they can be rescued by region-focused scholarship.[4]

Regional identities often derive from shared histories punctuated by diplomatic and military ruptures. Modern European states generally came into existence through the fusion of pre-modern entities, such as voivodeships, principalities or duchies, and regional toponyms bear the signs. 'Banat', for example, a province now split between Hungary, Romania and Serbia, derives from the Hungarian term for royal governor, 'ban'.[5] As such polities were absorbed into larger states, their afterlives unfolded as regionalism.

In this chapter, we focus mainly on cultural regionalisms in modern Romania and contemporary Moldova, with comparisons to other parts of East-Central Europe. The modern Romanian state came about from the 'little union' of the Wallachian and Moldavian Principalities, Ottoman vassals, into a state called 'the United Principalities'.[6] The first regionalism in modern Romania emerged from the merger of Moldavia and Wallachia, which had had separate, though parallel rulers, histories and memories, and populations that spoke different, if mutually intelligible, dialects. In the run-up to the 1859 union, Moldavia's political elites were divided. Some favoured union but only in a confederation guaranteeing each part a measure of autonomy. Moldavians feared that with Bucharest becoming the capital of the new state, Iași, the capital of Moldavia, would lose clout.[7] The unification and subsequent centralization caused Moldavia to lose institutions, prestige, revenue and commerce. The Military Academy was moved to Bucharest, while the status of the recently founded Iași University was put in doubt. The Supreme Court might have been placed, in a compensatory gesture, in Iași, but it was not. Centralism vanquished Moldavian particularism.[8]

The Balkan Wars and the First World War saw the further, almost imperial, enlargement of the Romanian Kingdom. The 'Old Kingdom', as the smaller Romania came to be known in the postwar context, expanded into Southern Dobrudja in 1913. In 1918, Bessarabia, Transylvania, Banat and Bukovina were added. State builders throughout East-Central Europe, where states were stitched together after the First World War from fragments of pre-war empires faced regionalist challenges, every bit as difficult to overcome as irredentist minority nationalisms with which the former were sometimes intertwined.[9] Centralization was the practice of choice for newly forged nation states after 1918.

Czechoslovakia, for instance, incorporated Czech and Slovak lands that had been part of both halves of the Austro-Hungarian Monarchy. A full range of Czech cultural institutions and publications had flourished in Bohemia and Moravia in the nineteenth century, and Czech became an official language in 1880. Czechs gained confidence and social advancement in a prosperous economy driven by industrial development and the 'national revival' movement.[10] Slovakia, on the other hand, part of the Hungarian Kingdom, had a largely agrarian economy, high rates of illiteracy and few Slovak cultural institutions, leading many Slovaks to 'Magyarize' as they climbed the social ladder. While some Czech nationalists, including Thomas Masaryk, the future president of Czechoslovakia, favoured collaboration with Slovaks, others preferred to pursue Czech rights to Germanized territories; to Slovaks a similar strategy of historical rights would have meant resignation to the 'Magyar embrace'.[11] In 1918, Czechs and Slovaks joined in a new Czechoslovak state. Masaryk was keen on claiming a nine-million-strong Czechoslovak nation as against the three-million German minority, but many Slovaks grew disappointed with the centralist formula of the First Republic. The first taste of Slovak autonomy came amid the trauma of Czechoslovak dismemberment by the Nazis after the Munich agreement in 1938. Secession followed in 1939 as Bohemia and Moravia became a Nazi protectorate. Similarly, after the Warsaw Pact invasion of Czechoslovakia in 1968, Slovaks obtained federalism, which had eluded them. Slovakia broke away after the 1989 revolution first obtaining the hyphen in Czecho-Slovakia, then drafting a Slovak constitution and declaring sovereignty. The Czecho-Slovak federation thus ended on 1 January 1993.[12]

In Romania, a new wave of centralization began with the hasty dismissal in April 1920 of the transitional regional bodies that had formed in Bessarabia, Bukovina and Transylvania amid the revolutionary upheaval at the end of the Great War.[13] A tactic used by centralizers was the reordering of regional divisions within a state. In Romania, for example, the 1938 administrative law eliminated on paper the province of Bukovina, amalgamating into the new 'Suceava Region', Bessarabian, Bukovinian and Old Kingdom districts, in an effort to scramble local networks and erase regionalism. But the new regions thus created 'were stillborn' as they lacked cohesion and tradition. Moreover, while fighting regionalism, the Romanian government also fuelled it, by continuing to celebrate each year the 'reunification' of Bukovina, Transylvania and Bessarabia with the Old Kingdom. Even officially issued postage stamps featured the old regions. The state thus repeatedly reintroduced the old regions into public space and memory.[14]

Transylvania

A medieval fief conquered by the Hungarian Crown, Transylvania became an autonomous principality in the sixteenth century. It remained quasi-independent while Crown territories to the west came under direct Ottoman or Habsburg control. To the south-west, the Banat of Temesvár also came under Ottoman rule. From the 1690s, Transylvania and then Banat reverted to Habsburg control. In the eighteenth century, colonists from the Holy Roman Empire settled in Banat and came to be known as Banat Swabians.[15] Banat and Transylvania were reunited with Hungary briefly during the 1848 revolution and then decisively in 1867. The end of the First World War brought Transylvania and part of Banat into Greater Romania.[16]

Until the end of the eighteenth century, Transylvania belonged constitutionally to three privileged nations, Hungarians, Saxons and Szeklers. Romanian speakers were not represented politically. Ethnicity in Transylvania was extraordinarily complex.[17] During the nineteenth century, Hungarian and Saxon publications, literary and learned societies, theaters, libraries and museums were joined by Romanian periodicals and cultural societies. In the second half of the century, an intellectual transition occurred from a concentration on regional 'fatherland studies' (*Landeskunde* for the Saxons, *honismeret* for the Hungarians) to nationalized histories or geographies of on one's nation. Hungarian, Romanian and Saxon cultural elites increasingly focused beyond the region's borders, to academic institutions and discussions taking place in Pest, Bucharest and German cultural centres.[18]

When Transylvania joined Romania in 1918, the Romanianization of the university was accomplished with utmost speed. The nationalization of culture in the region at all levels, begun the previous century under Hungarian auspices, continued and intensified but now under the Romanian state.[19] And yet, as elsewhere in Europe, the interwar decades saw not only the triumphalism of one nationality over others but also the emergence of local, regional solidarities and imaginaries. Transylvanism rejected all nationalisms in favour of the veneration of sovereign Transylvania's own past and specific civilization and of the belief in a 'Transylvanian psyche' shared among the region's various populations. The authentic Transylvanian soul and history were first topoi for Hungarians and Saxons – both relegated after 1918 to minority status in Greater Romania.[20] Between 1918 and 1923, when a unitarist Romanian constitution was adopted, many Hungarians hoped for self-government and cooperation with local Germans and Romanians.[21] Like the Romanians in Bessarabia, Transylvanians had intended to negotiate for a set of conditions to preserve some autonomy.[22] Self-consciously Central European, and somewhat proud of the Habsburg legacy, some

Transylvanian Romanians felt superior to Romanians from south of the Carpathians who were now setting the political rules. On 1 December 1918 at the solemn gathering at Alba Iulia where the union with Romania was proclaimed, Romanians from Transylvania demanded provisional autonomy, a regional parliament, and respect for minority rights. *Consiliul Dirigent* (the Directing Council), the provisional regional government, was tasked with integrating Transylvania with the other Romanian provinces. The Romanian premier who signed the Minority Protection Treaty in Paris, the Transylvanian Alexandru Vaida-Voievod, was dismissed before passing legislation to uphold regional autonomy.[23]

With politics seeming bleak after these early measures, cultural and literary Transylvanism blossomed among minority populations. Hungarian intellectuals envisaged literature as no mere pastime but 'the main pillar of our national life [. . .] the only means of defense and promoter [. . .] of our national language, culture [. . .] [and] national consciousness'.[24] Cultural regionalism could serve the purpose of declaring Transylvania's distinctiveness vis-à-vis Budapest, while also defending Transylvanian Hungarians' interests as a national minority against Romania's 'nationalizing [. . .] cultural politics'.[25] The prevailing narrative of national conflict between Magyars and Romanians during these decades ignores the fact that some Transylvanian Magyars preferred Transylvania, even under the new circumstances. While many Hungarians from the region emigrated to Hungary beginning in 1920, some found their way back, homesick and somewhat disillusioned. Among them was the novelist Miklós Bánffy, a member of the pre-war Parliament, the director of the Budapest Opera and National Theater until 1918 and the foreign minister of Hungary in 1921–1922.[26] In 1926, he turned to cultural work in his native land. Returning to Transylvania, he became active in the Helikon, a salon that organized yearly gatherings for writers, poets and journalists and literary evenings in honor of Saxon writers that some Romanians also attended. Helikon was intertwined with the publishing house Erdélyi Szépmíves Céh (the Transylvanian Artists' Guild) inaugurated in 1924, and the periodical *Erdélyi Helikon* (1928–1944). Both published authors belonging to Helikon and promised 'pure literariness, Europeanness, and Transylvanianism'.[27] Transylvania was represented as 'a distinct entity with its own history, even more advanced, more liberal and more cosmopolitan than [. . .] [core Hungary]', although the Helikonists were not all liberals. Conservatives distanced themselves from the 'modernism of "decadent" Budapest'; others saw themselves as a 'spiritual orchestra above politics'.[28]

Bánffy owned an imposing castle sometimes referred to as the 'Versailles of Transylvania' in Bonțida/Bonchida near Cluj/Kolozsvár/Klausenburg, and he had 'good connections' with the Romanian royal court. He served as a patron to the Transylvanists, helped the Céh publish without government obstruction and distributed their limited-edition volumes to subscribers.[29] While the situation for Hungarian writers in Greater Romania was not rosy, the new international borders that isolated them from Hungary allowed them to become known to Transylvanian readers, who had focused until then on the Budapest literary scene. The Budapest establishment disapproved of a Transylvanian Magyar literature rife with regional themes.[30]

Transylvanism held a specific interpretation of local culture, articulated in Károly Kós's *Transylvania: An Outline of Its Cultural History*, first published in 1929 by Erdélyi Szépmíves Céh as *'Erdély' Kultúr történeti vázlat*.[31] Born in Temesvár/Timişoara, Kós studied engineering and architecture in Budapest; his career encompassed architecture and art, as well as writing and editing in Budapest and in Transylvania.[32] In 1921, together with Árpád Paál and István Zágoni, Kós penned a pamphlet, *The Voice That Cries: Toward the Magyars in Transylvania, Banat, the Criş Rivers Region, and Maramureş*. It urged the Hungarians of Transylvania to struggle for autonomy but to do so as Transylvanians. While Old Hungary had ceased to exist, Transylvania was still alive; Transylvanian Magyars should remember that they had behind them a thousand years of 'our own Transylvanian consciousness, with our own culture and dignity'.[33] However, in 1929, Kós produced a very different kind of text: a cultural history of Transylvania illustrated with sixty linocuts, to demonstrate the existence of a distinct regional culture.[34] His account avoided the standard squabbles between Hungarian and Romanian nationalists. In the modern period, Transylvania consisted of Hungarians-Szeklers, Saxons and Romanians, according to Kós.[35] He showed that the ethnic communities in Transylvania blended during their long shared history generating 'a common Transylvanian matrix', different from Hungarian culture in Hungary, Romanian culture in the Old Kingdom and German culture in Germany. Each retained its 'racial characteristics' while also developing 'a common Transylvanian identity'. The architectural monuments pictured in the book's linocuts illustrated the blending of Romanian, Saxon and Hungarian Transylvanian styles.[36]

Saxon and Romanian intellectuals also came to the table of Transylvanism. German Saxons had inhabited the Königsboden (crownlands) in Southern Transylvania since the twelfth century. During the Dualist period, they and the Romanians experienced Magyarization, the memory of which, as well as hopes for democratic rule after 1918, predisposed Saxons to collaboration with Bucharest. For the younger generation of Saxons, alliances with other German speakers in Romania and with other ethnic groups, and thus regionalism, became an option only now.[37]

Klingsor, a review of the young generation of Saxon literati, was edited by Heinrich Zillich, who had studied political science in Berlin. The publication represented the best writers in the community but also included Hungarian and Romanian writers. *Klingsor* was linked to an artistic salon, a concert bureau and the publishing house Deutsche Buchgilde, which published fine collectors' editions, much like the Erdélyi Szépmives Céh did for the Helikon circle.[38] To get a sense of the Saxons' take on Transylvanism, a citation from a 1926 *Klingsor* article by the Saxon writer Egon Hajek is exemplary. He described Transylvania as 'a territorial unit with its own atmosphere, its own living conditions, its air, its spirit, its language. [. . .] True, a Transylvanian language does not exist in terms of sounds that penetrate our ears as articulated, ordered word patterns, but rather as a spiritual center [. . .] For the Transylvanian soul [has become] a historical actuality of which all who live on this soil have a part'.[39] Indeed, much of the fiction by *Klingsor* and *Erdélyi Helikon* writers explored the relationships among the region's ethnic groups.[40]

Transylvanism thrived on mutual familiarity and exchanges among the region's literati. Translations, special issues of periodicals filled by literature written in the 'others" regional languages, and wine-fueled evenings of readings and discussions drove cultural intercourse until the mid-1930s. *Klingsor, Erdélyi Helikon,* and *Pásztortűz* alongside the Romanian magazine *Gândirea*, which began in Cluj before moving to Bucharest, all published translations and dedicated special issues to 'foreign' regional literature. Poets translated each other's poetry, and literary debates and book reviews crossed language barriers – proving that Transylvanian letters existed and were appreciated across such divides. The Romanian poet and philosopher Lucian Blaga, who taught philosophy at the University in Cluj after a diplomatic career, was friendly with Transylvanians writing in Hungarian and German, and translated the Hungarian poet Endre Ady. Blaga's own poems were rendered into Hungarian and German and published in *Erdélyi Helikon* and in *Klingsor*. Similarly, the Romanian Liviu Rebreanu began his career in Hungarian periodicals, and his novels broached Transylvanian themes, while Octavian Goga, another Romanian Transylvanian poet and politician was friends with Ady, and translated Imre Madách's Hungarian play *The Tragedy of Man* into Romanian. Hungarian literary reviews published 'Saxon issues' and German reviews reciprocated. Hungarian-Saxon banquets and cultural gatherings took place and some Romanians also participated.[41]

By the mid-1930s, however, relationships became strained as radical nationalism, racism and revisionism gained ground and the established diplomatic order began to unravel. *Klingsor*'s editor embraced Nazism and portrayed anti-Nazi views as stemming from Jewish influence. A 'Festschrift' on *Klingsor*'s tenth anniversary in 1934 served as an opportunity to welcome the 'rebirth of the whole (German) volk'. Hungarians felt betrayed although, occasionally, very rarely, their works might still be reviewed sympathetically in *Klingsor*. The Transylvanist consensus frayed, but gradually. In 1933, the periodical *Erdélyi Fiatalok* (Transylvanian Youth), founded three years earlier, voiced a commitment to '"Transylvanian realities" and to a third way of development that was neither capitalist nor socialist'. Moreover, *Erdélyi Fiatalok* collaborated with the Bucharest school of sociology. Some Romanian publications continued as late as 1935 to mediate between Romanian and Hungarian writers.[42] But also in 1935, Heinrich Zillich departed to Germany where he would become a general staff officer in the Wehrmacht. Some Hungarian authors in Transylvania also developed Nazi sympathies even if most opposed Saxon Nazism.[43] Meanwhile, in December 1937, the Transylvanian poet Octavian Goga became the prime minister of the first openly anti-Semitic Romanian government. He had never been a true Transylvanist, but his policies now threatened some of Romania's minorities, including the Jews of Transylvania.[44] In September 1939, the Second World War began; a year later, the Axis Powers' Second Vienna Arbitration granted Northern Transylvania to Hungary. Both Hungary and Romania became Axis allies, each fighting the war largely in order to secure Transylvania's territory. This militarized polarization spelled the end of transcultural regionalism.

One refuge of Transylvanism remained in leftist circles and publications such as the Hungarian magazine *Korunk* (Our Age) which ran from 1926 to 1940 (then from 1957 to 1989, and in a third series from 1990 to the present). Its first editor, László Dienes, felt that 'to be a true Transylvanian meant to be a true European'. Another early editor, Gábor Gaál, also contributed to *Erdélyi Helikon*, although he eventually took the publication in a communist direction. Cosmopolitanism has been one of *Korunk*'s strong suits through most of its life. During its communist incarnation, it served as a bridge between Romanian and Hungarian intellectuals and even had some Romanian collaborators. Its most recent editor has described *Korunk* as 'an amalgam of Europeanness and Transylvanianism'.[45]

Banat

The region of Banat, included with Transylvania in the interwar period, has its own peculiarities. It was divided after the First World War between the Kingdom of Serbs, Croats and Slovenes and Greater Romania, with a 'minute wedge' reverting to Hungary. In the 1930s, young Swabians in Romania and Yugoslavia joined Nazi-influenced renewal movements. They forged a new identity as Germans together with the Saxons, and many were recruited into the *Schutzstaffel* (SS) during the war.[46] Germans then suffered after the war's end. Somewhere between 70,000 and 97,762 able-bodied ethnic Germans from Romania, and perhaps 20,000 from Yugoslavia were deported to Soviet forced labour camps between 1944 and 1949, when survivors were allowed to return home. Germans who avoided deportation also lost their property and their civil and political rights even before the collectivization of agriculture. In Tito's Yugoslavia, many Swabians were executed or interned.[47]

Regional solidarities were ruptured during the war. But the communist period brought new regionalisms. In Romania, the Szekler area in eastern Transylvania was designated the Hungarian Autonomous Region receiving 'Soviet-style territorial autonomy' with a full range of Hungarian cultural institutions, including higher education between 1946 and 1959.[48] This was a far cry from interwar Transylvanism as the intercultural dimension was mostly missing. Regional traces also emerged in Banat. In response to the demographic and social engineering of the communists who expropriated and collectivized property, uprooted locals, and resettled workers and party activists from outside the region in Banat, ethnic differences among local Romanians, Hungarians, Germans and Serbs declined, allowing for a regional 'we' versus 'them' identity to emerge. Present already in the interwar period, it had disappeared during the war. Banaters now again imagined themselves as bearers of a Central European civilization and the newcomers as denizens of the uncivilized Balkans, dogmatic communists, and unreconstructed nationalists. Locals were proud of their Habsburg past and of the architecture of Timișoara, imagined as the 'little Vienna'.[49]

During communism, the Banat milieu with its Central European identity produced much of Romania's oppositional culture. The *Aktionsguppe Banat*, with which the future Nobel Prize-winning writer Herta Müller was involved, began as a literary and political student circle in Timișoara in 1972, its members mainly rural Swabians reading Western literature in German and writing as a 'collective author'. They identified as 'ethnic Germans in communist Romania' but also 'as people from the marginal Banat region in the German-speaking space'. They revolted against their parents' Nazified past, which had become an unmentionable open secret. Although contemporary German literature and the New Left influenced them, these Banat Swabians identified primarily as East Europeans marked by communism. The group, however, was decidedly Marxist, reclaiming words like 'action' and 'commitment' which had been emptied of meaning by their propagandistic overuse in communist Romania.[50]

Another dissident Romanian literary group in Timişoara authored collectively a post-modernist novel that combined Habsburg history, ethnography and fiction and articulated a sense of a Central European past and hopes for a future of democratic activism. While the novel was written in 1988, it was published after the 1989 revolution, which also – significantly – began in Timişoara, with a demonstration of interethnic solidarity in defense of Reformed Hungarian pastor, László Tőkés.[51]

Nationalism and regionalism in Bessarabia and Transnistria

Regionalism in Bessarabia was an epiphenomenon of state- and nation-building efforts. The tsarist, Romanian and Soviet authorities all created the region, which, unlike Transylvania, Bohemia and Moravia, and other 'historical' regions in East-Central Europe, had not existed before its Russian annexation in 1812. Similarly, Transnistria emerged as a region in 1924 when the Soviets established the Moldovan Autonomous Soviet Socialist Republic. Like Bukovina, Southern Dobrudja, Galicia and the Sudetenland, Bessarabia and Transnistria were by-products of geopolitical games and border changes.

Cultural elites in Bessarabia and Transnistria articulated regionalist claims based on an identity created by imperial or national structures outside the regions. The models around which local populations were organized were also generally conceived elsewhere. Yet at times, local elites acted with remarkable agency in negotiating with distant authorities attempting to absorb their regions. Here we examine how regionalism was formulated in tsarist Bessarabia from 1812 to 1917, in Romanian Bessarabia from 1918 to 1940, in the Moldovan Autonomous Soviet Socialist Republic established in 1924 in Transnistria, in the Moldavian Soviet Socialist Republic from 1944 to 1991 and, finally, in the independent Republic of Moldova after 1991.

After the Russian annexation in 1812, Bessarabia became the staging ground for state-building and modernizing policies. In the nineteenth century, native elites were sparse and somewhat indistinct, having fallen prey to Russification. The countryside, where schools were few and illiteracy widespread, was less Russified before the introduction of mass schooling.[52] By 1906, the tsarist administration had opened over 1,000 elementary schools, a majority of which had Russian as the language of instruction, unlike schools in the Austrian Monarchy that employed a variety of local languages.[53] Among Russia's western provinces, Bessarabia had the weakest national movement, in part because of its small Romanian-speaking elite, much of which was Russified, politically inactive or in exile.[54] Some prominent intellectuals took refuge in Romania, where they contributed to conceptualizing the 'Bessarabian question' and helped integrate Bessarabia into a Romanian symbolic geography, rather than organizing locally.⁵⁵

A Moldovan movement emerged in Bessarabia, during the 1905 Russian Revolution, among intellectuals and students attending Russian universities. Moldovans borrowed their hybrid nationalist and socialist vision from non-Russians hailing from other imperial provinces. Local peasants were to be emancipated both as nationally oppressed and as a dominated social group. But the peasants did not respond to the revolutionaries. Thus, the periodicals they launched – *Basarabia* in 1906 and *Viața Basarabiei* (Bessarabia's Life) in 1907 – closed for lack of audience, as well as due to tsarist repression.⁵⁶

The First World War and the Russian Revolution led to Bessarabia's separation from the disintegrating Russian Empire. In November 1917, local soldiers called for autonomy within a democratizing Russian state. Soon, the Moldovan Democratic Republic declared independence. In April 1918, Sfatul Țării (the National Parliament) voted to join neighbouring Romania, stipulating conditions for the region's internal self-government. The Bessarabians were forced to abandon even this trace of autonomy as Romanian delegates insisted on projecting complete national unity to the Great Powers deciding the fate of Europe's – and Romania's – international boundaries at the Paris Peace Conference of 1919–1920.⁵⁷ It was the international conjuncture of war, collapse of the Russian Empire and its army, Ukrainian claims to Bessarabia and the presence of Romanian troops that determined the region's hurried unification with Romania in 1918, rather than the dreams and demands of local agitators and politicians.⁵⁸

While Bessarabia became part of Greater Romania, neighbouring Transnistria, across the Dniester River, an area inhabited by Romanian speakers among others, was 'inherited' by the Bolshevik state together with Eastern Ukraine. In 1924, Transnistria became home to the Moldovan Autonomous Soviet Socialist Republic. The Soviets needed it in order to encourage Bessarabian irredentism and for fomenting revolution in the region, just as Soviet Ukraine served to export revolution to Polish Galicia and the Karelian Soviet Autonomous Republic to attract Finnish (Northern) Karelia into the Soviet Union.⁵⁹

In Bessarabia and Transnistria, Romanian and Soviet administrations pursued ambitious modernizing and nationalizing projects to distance these provinces radically from their Russian and Tsarist pasts. In both Bessarabia and Transnistria, new national elites were to be trained in growing networks of educational institutions, and locals were the targets of literacy, educational and economic campaigns. Yet, in Romanian Bessarabia, just as in Soviet Transnistria, the 'people' generally remained passive objects of these high modernist projects dubbed 'cultural offensives' or 'cultural revolutions'. Local peasants, notables, ethnic minorities, teachers and institutional players often exercised agency through passive resistance.⁶⁰

In the interwar period, the relationship between Bessarabian intellectuals' educational training and their political and national agendas appears paradoxical. Although the older generation born in the Bessarabian Guberniia of the Russian Empire had attended Russian universities, they became Romanian nationalists and 'unionists' advocating for unification with Romania. After the Great Union in 1918, they were known as *generația unirii* (the pro-union generation). By contrast, younger Bessarabian writers and journalists, educated in post-unification Romanian schools and universities, identified as fierce regionalists in the 1930s. While not exactly questioning the unification, their slogans expressed dissatisfaction and an indisputable regionalism: 'More autonomy for Bessarabia!' 'Bessarabia for the Bessarabians!' and 'Integration, not assimilation!'[61] Yet, on some issues the two generations were not far apart. In 1924, a group of senators and deputies from Bessarabia – including the famous unionists Pan Halippa, Constantin Stere and Ion Buzdugan – addressed a petition to Romania's King Ferdinand, dubbed the Unifier, in which they denounced the lack of civil liberties and autonomous institutions and the systematic abuses to which locals were subjected (Bessarabia was placed under a state of emergency after 1918, as its status remained disputed between Romania and the Soviet Union).[62] Stipulations for Bessarabian autonomy that Sfatul Țării had presented to Romania prior to unification were part of the petition.[63] Clearly, the frustrations with the Romanian state that young regionalists articulated in the 1930s had been anticipated by their senior colleagues in 1918 and 1924.

The periodical *Viața Basarabiei* (Bessarabia's Life), the main cultural monthly in 1930s' Bessarabia, provides an example of intergenerational intellectual and literary collaboration. It began as a venue for the older generation, men such as Pan Halippa and Teodor Păduraru, but gradually its discourse shifted from a *Landespatriotismus*-style cultural regionalism, compatible with the nationalist agenda of the Romanian authorities, to a more radical, self-conscious regionalism assumed by the younger editors Nicolai Costenco and Vasile Luțcan, who proudly called themselves 'Regionalists'. This increasingly assertive stance in the 1930s represented a reaction against a Bucharest-centred, and centralist, national politics. The younger generation's regionalism readied them for accepting Soviet communism and the creation of the Moldovan Soviet Socialist Republic. Many of them chose to remain in Bessarabia, thus in the Soviet Union, after 1940, when Romania had to cede Bessarabia and Northern Bukovina to the USSR.[64]

From the creation of the Moldovan Autonomous Soviet Socialist Republic in 1924 until the late Stalin era, and even up to the collapse of the Soviet Union in 1991, Soviet authorities entrusted Soviet Moldovan 'creative intellectuals' with the production of a literary language and a local cultural heritage distinct from the Romanian, thereby legitimating Soviet claims to the existence of an authentic and separate Moldovan 'socialist nation'.[65] The Soviet Moldovan national project was designed and implemented rapidly so as to enable Moldova to 'catch up' to nations – including Soviet ones – more advanced in national construction.[66] Moldovan writers, scholars and artists undertook a large-scale linguistic, literary, cultural and national enterprise, under state and party supervision.

Both in the Moldovan Autonomous Soviet Socialist Republic (1924–1940) and, later, in the Moldovan Soviet Socialist Republic (1940–1991), local authorities and intellectuals splintered into antagonistic camps according to their political capital and their position on the national language. In the 1930s, Moldova's administrative and cultural institutions became battlegrounds between so-called *Moldovanists* and *Romanianists*. The *Moldovanists* advocated for a stand-alone 'Moldovan' language, in a clear-cut rupture with literary Romanian norms. The *Romanianists*, on the other hand, favoured a literary 'Moldovan' language identical in almost every way with Romania's written and spoken language, except for the use of the Cyrillic alphabet, which remained the only marker of the 'Moldovan' language, distinct from its Romanian *Doppelgänger*. In Romania, the Cyrillic alphabet had been replaced by Latin in the mid-nineteenth century. These struggles brought frequent reversals in linguistic policies, each built on the ruins of a previous official 'Moldovan' grammar and spelling. During the Stalinist era both Moldovanists and Romanianists were repressed in turn, and many were killed during the Great Purges of 1937–1938.[67]

However, the Moldovanist–Romanianist divide survived further territorial changes. In accord with the secret clauses of the Nazi–Soviet Pact of August 1939, in June 1940 Soviet troops occupied north-eastern Romania: Bessarabia, Northern Bukovina and the Herța district. A Moldovan Soviet Socialist Republic that incorporated central Bessarabia and a part of the Autonomous Republic founded in 1924 on Transnistrian territory was declared on 2 August, with the other seized territories ceded to Soviet Ukraine.[68] The Soviet Moldovan literary establishment was thus enlarged with writers and journalists who had lived in Romania since 1918. While this iteration of the Republic lasted only a year until Romanian and German troops overran it during Operation Barbarossa, after 1944, the Moldovan Soviet Socialist Republic was reborn, setting the stage for a fierce cultural war between Transnistrian writers, critics and scholars and the Bessarabian 'newcomers'. They struggled over power, literary language and cultural heritage. The Bessarabians won. Riding the wave of the post-Stalinist thaw, they imposed a version of the 'Moldovan' literary language that was close to standard Romanian, even as they claimed classic nineteenth-century Romanian writers from right-bank Moldova, such as Vasile Alecsandri and Mihai Eminescu, as 'Moldovan'. Those who wanted the elevation of the local dialect to the status of the national Moldovan language and a clear-cut break with the Romanian literary and cultural patrimony lost out. The one concession made, again, to the Moldovanists was the Cyrillic alphabet, which remained the symbol of a separate 'Moldovan' language.[69]

Starting in the mid-1950s, behind the façade of a 'Moldovan' language and literature written in the Cyrillic alphabet, the Soviet Socialist Republic of Moldova saw the quiet 'Romanianization' of its language and high culture. Bessarabian intellectuals educated in interwar Romania executed this policy with support from high-ranking writers and scholars from the Soviet Writers' Union and the Academy of Sciences in Moscow. At the same time, policies implemented starting in 1924 by the Moldovanists in the Moldovan Autonomous Soviet Socialist Republic to make Moldovan distinct from Romanian also had profound effects.[70] Thus, in 2018, a majority of the Romanian-speaking population in the Republic of Moldova define themselves and call their language 'Moldovan', whereas an important segment of the Romanian-speaking intellectual elite favours a Romanian identity.

The Soviet thaw gave Moldovan intellectuals a brief taste of freedom. But in 1959 the local Communist Party denounced 'nationalist' tendencies among the intelligentsia and the 'Romanianization' of Moldovan culture, and began to promote Russification.

The Moldovan language ceased to be a compulsory subject in the Republic's schools, and Romanian cultural events were banished from public space, retreating to private venues. This allowed writers, paradoxically, the freedom to escape from the official, Soviet-imposed discourse that they were nevertheless forced to use in their published works.[71] These Moldovan writers and artists were sometimes accused by Transnistrian colleagues of exhibiting Moldovan nationalist tendencies when their works celebrated the Moldovan homeland without the requisite mention of the great Soviet fatherland. However, in a further paradox, Muscovite writers and dignitaries defended the 'nationalists'. For example, after Ion Druță's play *Casa Mare* ('the Sitting Room') was criticized by the Party Central Committee, he moved to Moscow, where he acquired a certain reputation. Writers like Druță exemplify the ambiguity of the nation-building project promoted by Soviet authorities in the non-Russian republics. On the one hand, Moldovan-language education, the press and cultural institutions nurtured Moldovan patriotism (although Moldovan identity was systematically differentiated from the Romanian). On the other hand, writers who produced works dedicated to Moldova and its people had also, without fail, to pay homage to the great Soviet fatherland. When Soviet authorities considered that expressions of local patriotism were too intense and Soviet patriotism muted, they reprimanded the 'nationalists'.[72]

The liberalization of the Soviet Union in the 1980s provided fertile ground for 'national rebirth' in Moldova, as in other Soviet republics. Writers, most of all, and other intellectuals were in the vanguard of the movement in Moldova's capital, Chișinău.[73] Street demonstrations and other kinds of pressure brought about linguistic and political concessions that climaxed in Moldova's declaration of independence on 27 August 1991. Success, however, concealed a Moldovan society riven by ethnolinguistic and ideological cleavages, and communities that harboured distinct geopolitical preferences. Only some residents saw their future in an independent Moldova. In a poll conducted in January 1991 on a representative sample of 1,133 citizens of Moldova, to the question, 'How do you see the future of Moldova?', 43 per cent of respondents answered 'in the Soviet Union', 42 per cent, in an independent state, and 3 per cent, within Romania. If Romanian speakers favoured independence, other ethnic groups preferred that Moldova remain in the Soviet Union.[74] Between 60 and 70 per cent of local Russians, Ukrainians, Bulgarians and Gagauz feared imminent ethnic conflict. In regions heavily populated by Russian speakers, such as Transnistria, where Romanian speakers represented only around 35 per cent of the total, these fears were even more pronounced.[75] Shortly after the August 1989 adoption of the law making Moldovan/Romanian the state language, Transnistria became the site of massive protests. Moldova's declaration of sovereignty a year later further escalated tensions in Transnistria and in the southern area populated by Gagauz and Bulgarians. Armed conflict broke out in March 1992, resulting in around 1,000 victims and thousands of refugees on both sides of the Dniester. Transnistrian and Russian Federation authorities supported the armed rebels, responding to popular sentiment. Recent studies have shown as well that in March–June 1992 Moldovan authorities also acted with intransigence and brutality in Transnistria, where an unofficial and internationally unrecognized state was established in November 1991 and in the south where the Gagauz obtained autonomy in 1994. The irony is that the nations that fought for independence from the Soviet Union have not always known how to handle regionalist claims within their newly independent polities.[76]

Following the 'Euromaidan' protests in Kiev in 2014, Russia's annexation of Crimea and Putin's support of the separatists in Donbas, identity issues and geopolitical controversies intensified in Moldova. The Ukrainian crisis exemplified the failure of a centralized and nationalizing state to federalize a divided society right next door to Moldova.[77] For the last twenty-five years, a pro-Romanian nationalism has been promoted in state schools through the teaching of a primordialist 'History of the Romanians'. Periodically, public spaces become symbolic battlegrounds between spontaneous expressions of 'banal' nationalism.[78] St. George's ribbons are displayed on car bumpers by Russophiles to symbolize the victory of the Soviet Union – and, by extension, Russia – against Nazism in 1941–1945, while Romanian tricolour ribbons are sported by Romanian nationalists.

Despite such popular expressions of nationalism, Romanian-speaking and Russian-speaking ethnolinguistic communities in Moldova have managed to coexist quite harmoniously in everyday life and have shared public spaces just as Romanians and Hungarians have in Transylvania.[79] However, such linguistically based communities can also represent 'two solitudes', their members living in different social environments, studying in separate educational institutions and watching TV channels produced in different tongues and filled with dissimilar cultural references – this is also the case with other multilingual societies such as Belgium or Switzerland.[80] Romanian speakers and Russophones in Moldova do not feel that they are involved in a state-building project together, overseen by a state capable of producing solidarity and social cohesion.

Conclusion

Not only in Moldova but also in Romania and elsewhere in East-Central Europe, 'regionalism' resurfaced in new ways after the fall of communism. Radical and ethnicized regionalisms splintered Yugoslavia and Czechoslovakia into smaller nation-states. Slovak regionalism had evolved since 1918 towards a national movement seeking independence, which it obtained in full in 1993. In part in response to European Union requirements for regional development, Romanians have contemplated regional devolution. The Hungarian speakers of Eastern Transylvania, in what was once the Hungarian Autonomous Region and where Hungarians form a majority, have a strong interest in autonomy. This, however, is unpopular with the Romanian majority in the country, and particularly with the Romanian minority in that region.[81] Polarizing ethnic nationalism within historic regions now haunts and may scuttle projects for the European Union-prescribed regional devolution.[82] But political scientists have also noted the long shadow of imperial legacies in the contemporary political culture of Romania's regions despite the intervening influence of the communist order. For example, Gabriel Bădescu and Paul Sum have found that 'trust in other ethnicities, efficacy and trust in NGOs are [. . .] higher among Transylvanians [than the rest of Romania's population]'.[83]

In areas where the ethnic landscape has been flattened by the Holocaust and the emigration of surviving Jews, Germans, and other minorities but where regionalism connotes memories of multi-ethnic pluralism and cosmopolitanism, such vague remembrances are being put to use. For example, in north-eastern Romania, the Suceava County Council and hospitality industry (Suceava county is part of the former Habsburg Bukovina crownland) currently boast about Suceava's Habsburg heritage. Tourist guidebooks differentiate the county from surrounding Moldova through 'the myth of a multi-cultural, German-speaking world, peopled by the so-called *homo bucovinensis*'.[84] We have largely ignored Bukovina in this chapter, a province now divided between Ukraine and Romania, for lack of space. But Bukovina's regional afterlife is ceaseless and abundant as the Suceava County tour books attest. Post-war literature written in German, Hebrew and Romanian by celebrated authors, born and raised in Bukovina, and for whom their birthplace plays a significant part in their oeuvre, is another marker of the region's robust and prolific afterlife. Simply listing some of their names calls to mind Bukovina's key role as a matrix of primordial multiculturalism in the contemporary imagination: Paul Celan (1920–1970), Gregor von Rezzori (1914–1998), Aharon Appelfeld (1932–2018) and Norman Manea (b. 1936).

Notes

1. See Irina Livezeanu and Árpád von Klimo, 'Introduction', in *The Routledge History of East Central Europe since 1700* (London: Routledge, 2017), 1–26; and the Regionalism thematic issue of *Ethnologia Balkanica* 11 (2007), esp. Ulf Brunnbauer, 'Editorial', 5–6; Pamela Ballinger, 'Beyond the "New" Regional Question? Regions, Territoriality, and the Space of Anthropology in Southeastern Europe', esp. 59, 60, 62–63; and Christian Giordano, 'Ethnic vs. Cosmopolitan Regionalism?', 51.

2. Sven Tägil, 'Editor's Preface', in *Regions in Central Europe: The Legacy of History*, ed. Sven Tägil (West Lafayette, IN: Purdue University Press, 1999), xii. See also the Introduction by Núñez Seixas and Storm.

3. Philipp Ther, 'Sprachliche, kulturelle und ethnische "Zwischenräume" als Zugang zu einer transnationalen Geschichte Europas', in *Regionale Bewegungen und Regionalismen in europäischen Zwischenräumen seit der Mitte des 19. Jahrhunderts*, ed. Philipp Ther and Holm Sundhaussen (Marburg: Herder-Institut, 2003), x; Tara Zahra, *Kidnapped Souls: National Indifference and the Battle for Children in the Bohemian Lands, 1900–1948* (Ithaca, NY: Cornell University Press, 2008); Jeremy King, *Budweisers into Czechs and Germans: A Local History of Bohemian Politics, 1848–1948* (Princeton, NJ: Princeton University Press, 2002); Pieter Judson, *Guardians of the Nation: Activists on the Language Frontiers of Imperial Austria* (Cambridge, MA: Harvard University Press, 2006); and Pieter Judson, *The Habsburg Empire: A New History* (Cambridge, MA: Belknap Press of Harvard University Press, 2016).

4. Ther, 'Sprachliche', xi; and Celia Applegate, 'A Europe of Regions: Reflections on the Historiography of Sub-National Places in Modern Times', *American Historical Review* 104, no. 4 (1999), 1158–59.

5. John Fine, 'The Medieval and Ottoman Roots of Modern Bosnian Society', in *The Muslims of Bosnia-Herzegovina: Their Historic Development from the Middle Ages to the Dissolution of Yugoslavia*, ed. Mark Pinson (Cambridge, MA: Harvard Center for Middle Eastern Studies,

1996), 11; Judy Batt, 'Reinventing Banat', *Regional & Federal Studies* 12, no. 2 (2002): 180; and Irina Marin, *Contested Frontiers in the Balkans: Ottoman, Habsburg and Communist Rivalries in Eastern Europe* (London: I. B. Tauris, 2012), 4, 19, 71–72, 80–81.

6. Charles Jelavich and Barbara Jelavich, *The Establishment of the Balkan National States, 1804-1920* (Seattle: University of Washington Press, 1955), 116, 178.

7. Adrian Cioflâncă, 'Naționalism și parohialism în competiție: Note pe marginea dezbaterilor politice privind unirea Principatelor Române', in *Vârstele unirii: De la conștiința etnică la unitate națională*, ed. Dumitru Ivănescu, Cătălin Turliuc and Florin Cântec (Iași: Fundația Academică A.D. Xenopol, 2001), 109–34.

8. T. W. Riker, *The Making of Modern Romania: A Study of an International Problem, 1856-1866* (London: Oxford University Press, 1931), 347, 502–504; Cioflâncă, 'Naționalism și parohialism', 124; and D. Berlescu, 'Universitatea din Iași de la 1860 pînă ls 1918', in *Universitatea 'Al. I. Cuza' Iași, Contribuții la istoria dezvoltării Universității din Iași, 1860-1960* (Bucharest: n. ed., 1960), 117–22.

9. Irina Livezeanu, *Cultural Politics in Greater Romania: Regionalism, Nation Building, and Ethnic Struggle, 1918-1930* (Ithaca, NY: Cornell University Press, 2000) (rev. ed.).

10. Carol Skalnik Leff, *National Conflict in Czechoslovakia: The Making and Remaking of a State, 1918-1987* (Princeton, NJ: Princeton University Press, 1988), 11–17, 26.

11. Ibid., 18–34, 36–37, here 34.

12. Ibid., 38–41; 133–40, 163–65, 173–77.

13. Livezeanu, *Cultural Politics*, 23, 42, 132–34.

14. See Philippe Blasen, 'Suceava Region, Upper Land, Greater Bukovina or Just Bukovina? Carol II's Administrative Reform in North-Eastern Romania (1938 – 1940)', *Anuarul Institutului de Istorie 'A. D. Xenopol'* 52 (2015): 279–86.

15. Marin, *Contested Frontiers*, 4–81, 144–45.

16. Peter Sugar, 'The Principality of Transylvania', in *A History of Hungary* (Bloomington: Indiana University Press, 1994), 121–137; and Livezeanu, *Cultural Politics*, 129–30.

17. Sorin Mitu, 'Regional Identities from Transylvania in the "Longue Durée"', in *Entangled Identities: Regionalism, Society, Ethnicity, Confession and Gender in Transylvania (18th–19th Century)* (Cluj-Napoca: Argonaut, 2014), 10–21; Katherine Verdery, *Transylvanian Villagers: Three Centuries of Political, Economic, and Ethnic Change* (Berkeley: University of California Press, 1983), 83–84; and Jonathan Kwan, 'Transylvanian Saxon Politics, Hungarian State Building and the Case of the Allgemeiner Deutscher Schulverein (1881–82)', *English Historical Review* 127, no. 526 (2012): 47.

18. Borbála Zsuzsanna Török, *Exploring Transylvania: Geographies of Knowledge and Entangled Histories in a Multiethnic Province, 1790-1918* (Leiden: Brill, 2016), 136–64; Tanya Dunlap, 'Astra and the Appeal of the Nation: Power and Autonomy in Late-Nineteenth-Century Transylvania', *Austrian History Yearbook* 34 (2003): 2125–46; and John Neubauer, 'Conflicts and Cooperation between the Romanian, Hungarian, and Saxon Literary Elites, 1850–1945', in *Cultural Dimensions of Elite Formation in Transylvania (1770–1950)*, ed. Victor Kárády and Borbála Zsuzsanna Török (Cluj-Napoca: EDRC Foundation, 2008), 161–62.

19. Livezeanu, *Cultural Politics*, 129–87, 219–24.

20. Zsuzsanna Török, 'Transylvanism: A Politics of Wise Balance? Minority Regionalism in Interwar Romania (1918-1940)', in *Regionale Bewegungen,* ed. Ther and Sundhaussen, 132; and László Kürti, *The Remote Borderland: Transylvania in the Hungarian Imagination* (Albany: State University of New York Press, 2001), 28.

21. Rachel Renz Mattair, 'Looking to Themselves: The Tension between Self-Reliance, Regionalism, and Support of Greater Romania within the Saxon Community in Transylvania 1918–1935' (MA thesis, Central European University, 2012), 68.
22. Gabor Egry, 'Crowding Out: Experiences of Difference, Discourses of Identity and Political Mobilization in Interwar Transylvania', *Studia Universitas Cibiniensis Series Historica*, no. 9 (2012), 210–11.
23. Egry, 'Crowding Out', 211–13, 217; Florian Kührer-Wielach, 'The Transylvanian Promise: Political Mobilization, Unfulfilled Hope and the Rise of Authoritarianism in Interwar Romania', *European Review of History* 23, no. 4 (2016): 580–94 (particularly, 582–84); Török, 'Transylvanism', 130–33; and Livezeanu, *Cultural Politics*, 22.
24. Erdélyi Szépmíves Céh, Cluj, 1926. Cited in Török, 'Transylvanism', 135.
25. Török, 'Transylvanism', 130.
26. Holly Case, *Between States: The Transylvanian Question and the European Idea during World War II* (Stanford, CA: Stanford University Press, 2009), 27; Ion Chinezu, 'Literatura maghiară și cea germană în Ardeal', in *Pagini de critică* (Bucharest: Editura pentru literatură, 1969), 286; Neubauer, 'Conflicts and Cooperation', 164; and Liviu Malița, 'Transilvanismul în presa culturală românească dintre cele două războaie', *Studia Universitatis Babes-Bolyai, Historia* 55, no. 1/2 (December 2010): 21–40.
27. Zoltán Szász, 'Bánffy Miklós erdélyi Magyar Története', *Korunk*, no. 8 (2015): 64, 68; Török, 'Transylvanism', 128, 135; Györgyi Kusztos, 'A Model of Unifying Innovation and Reproduction – Miklós Bánffy and "Transylvanism"', *Trans: Internet-Zeitschrift Kulturwissenschaften* 16 (August 2006), available at: http://www.inst.at/trans/16Nr/09_5/kusztos16.htm; István Nemeskürty, 'Károly Kós's Transylvania', in *Transylvania: An Outline of Its Cultural History* (Budapest: Szépirodalmi Könivkiadó, 1989), iii; Chinezu, 'Literatura maghiară', 285; Neubauer, 'Conflicts and Cooperation', 176; Malița, 'Transilvanismul', 38–39; and Zsuzsa Frisnyak, 'Az "Erdélyi-üzlet" működése Magyarországon: Az Erdélyi Szépmíves Céh', *Századok* 126 (1992): 173–201, here 173.
28. Török, 'Transylvanism', 134–36; and Malița, 'Transilvanismul', 22.
29. Nemeskürty, 'Károly Kós', iii; Kusztos, 'A Model'; Emanuela Grama, 'Searching for Heritage, Building Politics: Architecture, Archaeology, and Imageries of Social Order in Romania (1947–2007)' (Ph.D. diss., University of Michigan, 2010), 238, 344–353; and Török, 'Transylvanism', 135.
30. Török, 'Transylvanism', 133, 135; and Malița, 'Transilvanismul', 27.
31. Károly Kós, *Transylvania: An Outline of Its Cultural History* (Budapest: Szepirodalmia, 1989), translated by Lorna Dunbar of the original 1934 edition.
32. Nemeskürty, 'Károly Kós', i–ii; Lucian Năstasă and Levente Salat, eds, *Maghiarii din Romania și etica minoritară (1920–1940)* (Cluj: Ethnocultural Diversity Resource Center, 2003), 50.
33. 'Glasul care strigă: Către maghiarimea din Ardeal, Banat, Ținutul Crișurilor și Maramureș!' in Năstasă and Salat, *Maghiarii din Romania*, 45–51, here 48.
34. Nemeskürty, 'Károly Kós', ii–iii.
35. Ibid., 86–87.
36. Ibid., 109–11; and Malița, 'Transilvanismul', 22.
37. John Swanson, 'The Second World War and Its Aftermath: Ethnic German Communities in the East', in *The Germans and the East*, ed. Charles Ingrao and Franz Szabo (West Lafayette: Purdue University Press, 2008), 351; and Renz Mattair, 'Looking to Themselves', 31, 46–47, 80.

38. Chinezu, 'Literatura maghiară', 287–88; and Neubauer, 'Conflicts and Cooperation', 173.
39. Egon Hajek, 'Vom Siebenbürgischen Menschen', *Klingsor* 3 (January–December 1926): 138–39, cited in Renz Mattair, 'Looking to Themselves', 75.
40. Chinezu, 'Literatura maghiară', 288; and Neubauer, 'Conflicts and Cooperation', 169–71.
41. Irina Livezeanu, 'Generational Politics and the Philosophy of Culture: Lucian Blaga between Tradition and Modernism', *Austrian History Yearbook* 33 (2002): 207–37; and Neubauer, 'Conflicts and Cooperation', 159–72, 175–77.
42. Keith Hitchins, 'Erdélyi Fiatalok: The Hungarian Village and Hungarian Identity in Transylvania in the 1930s', *Hungarian Studies* 21, nos 1–2 (June 2007): 85–99, here 88; and Neubauer, 'Conflicts and Cooperation', 180–81.
43. Neubauer, 'Conflicts and Cooperation', 177–78.
44. Dov Lungu, 'The French and British Attitudes towards the Goga-Cuza Government in Romania, December 1937–February 1938', *Canadian Slavonic Papers/Revue Canadienne des Slavistes* 30, no. 3 (September 1988): 324–38.
45. Mária Botházi, '*Korunk* 1926–2016: The Emblematic Intellectual Workshop of Transylvania', *Journal of Media Research – Revista de studii media* 9, no. 2 (2016): 79–91, here 90; and Levente Székedi, 'Discursul De Reabilitare a Sociologiei în Revista "Korunk" (1957–1964)', *Revista Română de Sociologie* 28, nos 1–2 (2017): 41.
46. Marin, *Contested Frontiers*, 105–9, 111, 120, 122, 139; and Swanson, 352–54.
47. Marin, *Contested Frontiers*, 142–45; and János Kristóf Murádin, 'The Deportation of Germans from Romania to the Soviet Union in 1944–1945', *Acta Universitatis Sapientiae, European and Regional Studies* 7, no. 1 (2015): 42–46.
48. Case, *Between States*; Stefano Bottoni, 'National Projects, Regional Identities, Everyday Compromises: Szeklerland in Greater Romania (1919–1940)', *Hungarian Historical Review* no. 2 (2013): 503–4; Stefano Bottoni, 'The Creation of the Hungarian Autonomous Region in Romania (1952): Premises and Consequences', *Regio: Minorities, Politics, Society – English Edition* 1 (2003): 71, 89, 93; and Lucian Năstasă, 'Avatarurile unei Universități Maghiare la Cluj', *Analele Universității din București. Seria Științe Politice* 1 (2014): 81–83, 85–96.
49. Liviu Chelcea, 'Regionalismul bănățean înainte și după communism: transformări sociale, relații entice și memorie istorică', *Altera* 5, no. 10 (1999): 39–53.
50. Cristina Petrescu, 'Aktionsgruppe Banat Reconstructs Its Past, I: Personal Memories and Collective Identity', *Arhivele Totalitarismului* 1–2 (2015): 180–93, here 183.
51. Chelcea, 'Regionalismul bănățean'; and Adriana Babeți, Mircea Mihăieș and Mircea Nedelciu, *Femeia în roșu* (Bucharest: Ed. Cartea Românească, 1990).
52. Ludmila Coadă, *Zemstva Basarabiei. Aspecte istorico-juridice* (Chișinău: Ed. Pontos, 2009), 92–102; and Nikolai Troinitskii, ed., *Pervaia vseobschaia perepis' naseleniia Rossiiskoi Imperii 1897 g. III. Bessarabskaia Guberniia* (St. Petersburg: Izdanie Tsentral'nogo Statisticheskogo Komiteta Ministerstva Vnutrennikh Del, 1905), 12–23, 42–65.
53. See Ben Eklof, *Russian Peasant Schools: Officialdom, Village Culture, and Popular Pedagogy, 1861–1914* (Berkeley: University of California Press, 1986), 283–307; and Coadă, *Zemstva*, 79–104.
54. Theodore Weeks, *Nation and State in Late Imperial Russia: Nationalism and Russification on the Western Frontier, 1863–1914* (DeKalb: Northern Illinois University Press, 1996); Gheorghe Negru, *Țarismul și mișcarea națională a românilor din Basarabia* (Chișinău: Prut Internațional, 2000), 44–57; and Andrei Cușco and Oleg Grom, 'Natsional'nyi vopros nakanune Pervoi Mirovoi Voiny', in *Bessarabiia*, ed. Cușco, Taki and Grom, 333–46.

55. Andrei Cușco, *A Contested Borderland. Competing Russian and Romanian Visions of Bessarabia in the Second Half of the 19th and Early 20th Century* (Budapest: CEU Press, 2017), 31–62.
56. Cușco, *Contested*, 214; Charles King, *The Moldovans: Romania, Russia, and the Politics of Culture* (Stanford, CA: Hoover Institution Press, 1999), 11–35.
57. Livezeanu, *Cultural Politics*, 97–98; and Svetlana Suveică, 'The Bessarabians "between" the Russians and the Romanians: The Case of the Peasant Party Deputy Vladimir V. Tiganko (1917–1919)', in *Politics and Peasants in Interwar Romania: Perceptions, Mentalities, Propaganda*, ed. Sorin Radu and Oliver Jens Schmitt (Newcastle upon Tyne: Cambridge Scholars Publishing, 2017), 232–50.
58. Ștefan Ciobanu, *Unirea Basarabiei. Studiu și documente cu privire la mișcarea națională din Basarabiei în anii 1917–1918* (Chișinău: Universitas, [1929] 1993), 13–71; Onisifor Ghibu, *De la Basarabia rusească la Basarabia românească. Analiza unui proces istoric, însoțit de 185 documente* (Cluj: n. ed, 1926), 181; Gheorghe Cojocaru, *Sfatul Țării: itinerar* (Chișinău: Civitas, 1998); and Svetlana Suveică, 'Between the Empire and the Nation-State: Metamorphoses of the Bessarabian Elite (1918)', *Euxeinos: Governance and Culture in the Black Sea Region* 15/16 (2014): 34–45.
59. Charles King, 'The Ambivalence of Authenticity, or How the Moldovan Language Was Made', *Slavic Review* 58, no. 1 (Spring 1999), 117–42; King, *The Moldovans*, 51–57; Elena Negru, *Politica etnoculturală în RASS Moldovenească (1924–1940)* (Chișinău: Prut Internațional, 2003), 3–23; Terry Martin, *The Affirmative Action Empire: Nations and Nationalism in the Soviet Union 1923–1939* (Ithaca, NY: Cornell University Press, 2001); Petru Negură, *Ni héros, ni traîtres. Les écrivains moldaves face au pouvoir soviétique sous Staline* (Paris: L'Harmattan, 2009), 47–66; and Paul Austin, 'Soviet Karelian: The Language that Failed', *Slavic Review* 51, no. 1 (Spring 1992): 19.
60. Livezeanu, *Cultural Politics*, 29–48, 100–12, 116–20; Cătălina Mihalache, *Copilărie, familie, școală: politici educaționale și receptări sociale* (Iași: Ed. Universității 'Al. I. Cuza', 2016), 255–66; Negru, *Politica etnoculturală*, 71–83; and King, *The Moldovans*, 76–77.
61. Cited in Negură, *Ni héros*, 97–107.
62. 'Memoriul unui grup de senatori și deputați aleși din Basarabia în Parlamentul României, printre care și P. Halippa, I. Buzdugan, C. Stere, adresat Regelui, prin care se aduce la cunoștință situația jalnică a basarabenilor, 1924', National Archives of Romania, Fund 'Pantelimon Halippa', file 116, 1–9.
63. Ghibu, *From Russian Bessarabia*, 156–81; and Suveică, 'The Bessarabians "between" the Russians and the Romanians', *passim*.
64. Negură, *Ni héros*, 112. See also Anne-Marie Thiesse, *Écrire la France. Le mouvement littéraire régionaliste de langue française en France entre la Belle Époque et la Libération* (Paris, PUF, 1991); Xosé M. Núñez, 'Historiographical Approaches to Sub-National Identities in Europe: A Reappraisal and Some Suggestions', in *Region and State in Nineteenth-Century Europe Nation-Building, Regional Identities and Separatism*, ed. Joost Augusteijn and Eric Storm (Basingstoke: Palgrave Macmillan, 2012), 19.
65. Negură, *Ni héros*, 47–66.
66. Yuri Slezkine, 'The USSR as a Communal Apartment, or How a Socialist State Promoted Ethnic Particularism', *Slavic Review* 53, no. 2 (Summer 1994): 414–52; and Rogers Brubaker, *Nationalism Reframed: Nationalism and the National Question in the New Europe* (Cambridge: Cambridge University Press, 1996), 23–54.
67. Negură, *Ni héros*, 173–80; and Igor Cașu, *Dușmanul de clasă. Represiuni politice, violență și rezistență în R(A)SSM* (Chișinău: Cartier, 2014), 95–107.

68. George Ciorănescu, *Bessarabia: Disputed Land between East and West* (Bucharest: Editura Fundației Culturale Române, 1993), 127–28.
69. King, *The Moldovans*, 106–12; and Negură, *Ni héros*, 331–44.
70. King, *The Moldovans*, 106–12; and Negură, *Ni héros,* 227–353.
71. Igor Cașu, '*Politica națională*' *în Moldova sovietică, 1944–1989* (Chișinău: Cardidact, 2000), 82–102, 103–14.
72. Negură, *Ni héros*, 321–52. See also Brubaker, *Nationalism Reframed*, 23–54; and David Brandenberger, *National Bolshevism: Stalinist Mass Culture and the Formation of Modern Russian National Identity, 1931–1956* (Cambridge, MA: Harvard University Press, 2002).
73. Irina Livezeanu, 'Moldavia, 1917–1990: Nationalism and Internationalism Then and Now', *Armenian Review* 43, nos 1–2 (1990): 153.
74. Petru Negură, 'The Republic of Moldova's Transition. Between a Failed Communism and an Un-commenced Capitalism?', *Studia Politica: Romanian Political Science Review* 16, no. 4 (2016), 541–68.
75. Negură, 'The Republic', 544.
76. King, *The Moldovans*, 178–208; Octavian Racu, 'Tragedia de la Bender/Tighina și sfîrșitul războiului de pe Nistru', *Platzforma. Revista de critică socială*, 19/06/2017, http://www.platzforma.md/tragedia-de-la-bender-tighina-si-sfirsitul-razboiului-de-pe-nistru/, last access on 13 August 2017; and Rebecca Chamberlain-Creangă and Lyndon Allin, 'Acquiring Assets, Debts, and Citizens: Russia and the Microfoundations of Transnistria's Stalemated Conflict', *Demokratizatsiya* 18, no. 4 (Fall 2010): 329–45.
77. See Timm Beichelt and Susan Worshech, eds, *Transnational Ukraine?: Networks and Ties that Influence(d) Contemporary Ukraine* (Stuttgart: Ibidem, 2017), esp. Nikolai Mitrokhyn's and Mikhail Minakov's contributions.
78. Michael Billig, *Banal Nationalism* (London: Sage, 1995).
79. Rogers Brubaker, Margit Feischmidt, Jon Fox and Liana Grancea, *Nationalist Politics and Everyday Ethnicity in a Transylvanian Town* (Princeton, NJ: Princeton University Press, 2006).
80. Hugh MacLennan, *Two Solitudes* (Toronto: MacMillan, 1945).
81. József Benedek and Hunor Bajtalan, 'Recent Regionalization Discourses and Projects in Romania with Special Focus on the Székelyland', *Transylvanian Review of Administrative Sciences* 11, no. 44 (2015): 23–41.
82. Academician Dinu Giurescu, 'Despre coincidențe – regiunile de dezvoltare sau de destrămare', *Ardealul nostru*, 22 March 2011, https://ardealul.blogspot.com/2011/04/academician-dinu-giurescu-despre.html, last access on 1 January 2018.
83. See, e.g., Gabriel Bădescu and Paul Sum, 'Historical Legacies, Social Capital and Civil Society: Comparing Romania on a Regional Level', *Europe-Asia Studies* 57, no. 1 (January 2005): 117–33.
84. Onoriu Colăcel, 'Regional Identification in Present Day Romania: The Case Study of Suceava County', *Messages, Sages and Ages* 2, no. 1 (2015): 7–16.

Further reading

Cușco, Andrei, *A Contested Borderland. Competing Russian and Romanian Visions of Bessarabia in the Second Half of the 19th and Early 20th Century* (Budapest: CEU Press, 2017).

King, Charles, *The Moldovans: Romania, Russia, and the Politics of Culture* (Stanford: Hoover Institution Press, 1999).
Kührer-Wielach, Florian, *Siebenbürgen ohne Siebenbürger: zentralstaatliche Integration und politischer Regionalismus nach dem Ersten Weltkrieg* (Munich: Oldenburg, 2014).
Livezeanu, Irina, *Cultural Politics in Greater Romania: Regionalism, Nation Building, and Ethnic Struggle, 1918–1930*, rev. ed. (Ithaca, NY: Cornell University Press, 2000).
Martin, Terry, *The Affirmative Action Empire: Nations and Nationalism in the Soviet Union 1923–1939* (Ithaca, NY: Cornell University Press, 2001).
Negură, Petru, *Ni héros, ni traîtres. Les écrivains moldaves face au pouvoir soviétique sous Staline* (Paris: L'Harmattan, 2009).
Slezkine, Yuri, 'The USSR as a Communal Apartment, or How a Socialist State Promoted Ethnic Particularism', *Slavic Review* 53, no. 2 (Summer 1994).
Ther, Philipp, and Holm Sundhaussen, eds, *Regionale Bewegungen und Regionalismen in europäischen Zwischenräumen seit der Mitte des 19. Jahrhunderts* (Marburg: Herder-Institut, 2003).

CHAPTER 15
REGIONALISM IN RUSSIA
Mark Bassin and Mikhail Suslov

Introduction

Strategies of branding today's Russia are based on the language of superlatives. Russia has the largest territory in the world; it is the most populous country in Europe, the most diverse in ethnic terms, hosting some 190 indigenous nationalities, and it has the largest number – eighty-five – of federal subjects. One more might be added on top of all these: Russia arguably has the least well-developed tradition of regionalism for a country of its proportions. The paradoxical interplay between forces, which have the potential of making Russia a hotbed of regionalism in Europe, and counter-forces which effectively prevent this from happening, is in the focus of this chapter.

Across all of modern history, Russia has existed as a culturally heterogeneous, multi-ethnic empire.[1] In its extraordinary attempt to control and govern this disparate conglomerate of peoples, cultures and faiths, the central government developed special sensibilities and ruthless cruelty towards any outbreaks of separatism. Moscow and then St Petersburg were at pains to wipe out the feudal traditions of centuries of independent and often glorious regional powers – the Great Dutchies of Riazan or Tver, for example, or the land of Great Novgorod – all of which had at one time competed with Moscow for political ascendance in the Russian land. Today, these territories represent typical Russian provincial backwaters featuring not even a vague shadow of bygone proud autonomy.

Yet, at times of weakening of the central power, regional identities could quickly resurface, as happened most recently after the fall of the Soviet Union in the 1990s. In 1994, Blair Ruble, the then director of the Kennan Institute in Washington, DC, and a seasoned Russia-watcher, observed that Moscow would soon resemble Rome, becoming a symbol of national unity but in fact a very weak centre in a country of powerful regions.[2] While Ruble's foresight was rather less than prophetic – indeed, nothing could be further from his prognosis than today's Russia – he nonetheless accurately captured the political realities of the 1990s. At the time, Russia's regions assumed 60 per cent of state power,[3] and although this has been lost today, they remain resilient and undoubtedly possess the intellectual and material resources to come to the fore again, if and when Moscow stumbles.

There has always been a regionalist agenda of sorts in the policies of the central government; indeed, a certain degree of (meticulously controlled) regional autonomy was seen as necessary for the purposes of managing a country, which at the apex of its expansionism covered some 23 million square kilometres. Thus, the central leadership, especially when it was strong and self-confident, has been engaged in constant drawing and redrawing regional boundaries, dispensing and re-dispensing power at the regional level, creating and recreating regional elites. The interplay of regionalist policies from above and regionalist identities, growing from below, is intricate – and complicated by the fact that 'regionalism from below' is not necessarily 'indigenous' or localized in this particular region. All too often, regional identities were culturally and politically promoted by intellectuals, residing in the capitals or even abroad. More often than not, the central government's regionalist projects disoriented and disarmed regionalism from below. The recent administrative reform, which introduced 'federal districts' in 2000, was promulgated precisely to this end.

The 'big picture' of Russian regionalism is further complicated by the fact that, by virtue of the country's imperial character and multinational population, regionalist sentiment broke down into two distinct categories: non-Russian ethnic versus ethnic Russian regionalisms. To be sure, the line separating these two has never been cast in iron. Both forms have often tried to play the ethnic card by representing their identities as at least partially contingent upon some sort of ethnic or linguistic specificity of the regional population, such as the Cossacks, *pomory*, *sibiriaks*, *novorossy*, and so on. At the same time, in the case of Ukraine, an identity once considered to be a regional variant of 'Great Russia' eventually developed into a fully fledged national vision.

Regionalism in Russia exists in various ideological landscapes. It initially emerged as a distinct political concept in the first quarter of the nineteenth century in the milieu of the Decembrists: nobles who mounted a radical democratic protest against autocracy and the lawlessness of the regime in the 1820s. Later on, regionalist ideas persisted in the movement of Siberian *oblastnichestvo* (from the word *oblast'* or region) and in the ideological soil of the Russian Populists (*narodniki*). The latter were inspired by a mixture of socialist views and Slavophile back-to-the-land sympathies towards the Russian peasants and their imagined authentic lifestyle. At the turn of the twentieth century, regionalism was embraced both by the proponents of democratic, republican and federalist reforms as well as conservative critics of the Westernized central bureaucracy such as Sergei Sharapov, who saw the revitalization of regional autonomies as a way to reconnect with Russia's authentic self. This ideological ambiguity of regionalism persisted well into our days, when regionalist slogans accompany manifestations of anti-Putin protesters and radical nationalists alike. Thus, regionalism can be seen both as an instrument for boosting modernization as well as a means of protesting against it.

In this chapter, we aim to give a general account of the main tendencies of the development of regionalism and to discuss the interrelationship between local regional identity, regional ideology and centre-driven policies of regionalization. We begin with an historical overview of regionalist ideas and sentiments in Russia, and then move on to a more detailed examination of one specific case, namely regionalist sentiment in Siberia. The literature on these subjects is vast, but it is limited in important respects. Most historical studies focus on regionalism in its relations to nationalism, separatism and the main political ideologies of that time.[4] The brief heyday of Russian regionalism in the 1990s noted above stimulated considerable scholarship, mostly in the fields of political studies and economy. The fact that in this period regional governors were popularly elected created an entire industry of political consultancy (*polittekhnologiia*) which capitalized on branding regions, excavating and constructing regional identities. Many of these spin doctors became theorists and scholars of regionalism. A new discipline of *regionalistika* (regional studies), informed by geopolitical approaches, was proclaimed and introduced into university curricula for students of politics.[5] After the crackdown on the regionalist tendencies under President Putin, however, a number of retrospective studies by Russian as well as Western specialists contextualized the eruption of regionalism in the 1990s in the broader historical and international perspective, and provided an interpretation for the recentralization of power in the Putin era.[6]

Historical survey

As in other European countries, so in Russia the breakup of an ancient centralized state structure into a collection of feudal principalities provided the historically entrenched grid of regional differences. At various times, regional centres such as Novgorod, Kiev or Vladimir rose to prominence as the capital of the Russian lands. These cities – all founded in the ninth century – are far more ancient than Moscow, the earliest historical reference to which came only in 1147. Ancient Russia differed from Western countries, however, by virtue of the openness of its southern and eastern steppe border, which conditioned the exposure of the country over most of its history to its greatest external foe: the fearsome cavalries of the steppe nomads. From the eleventh century, the area which is now Russia first engaged in protracted military conflicts with the Kipchak peoples, then endured 250 years of domination by the Genghisid Golden Horde and continued to fight over the steppe frontier with the successors of the Mongols well until the end of the eighteenth century. This constant military threat produced a persistent thrust for national unity and the suppression of regional difference in the face of a powerful enemy. Russia's greatest epic poems, *The Tale of Igor's Campaign* and the *Lay of the Ruin of the Russian Land*, both emphatically identified the source Russia's military misfortunes in its struggles against the steppe nomads in the disunity and feuding (*usobitsy*) among the appanage princes. Down to the present day, Russia's leadership has effectively instrumentalized this call for unity and self-image of Russia as a besieged fortress.

The openness of the steppe had other effects on the formation of regional identities in Russia. While it is possible to see a rough correspondence between the demarcations of *oblasti* in Central Russia today and those of the medieval principalities that preceded them, the shifting location of the southern and eastern frontiers from the sixteenth to the nineteenth centuries led to the constant administrative reconfiguration of districts in this zone. This in turn meant that regional borders were entirely fluid, determined almost exclusively by questions of expediency and governability.[7] This top-down, imperial regionalism of sorts came in full sway under Tsar Peter I, who in 1708 carried out the first official regional subdivision of Russian territories. In order to facilitate the collection of taxes that could support his many military endeavours, he divided the country into eight vast *gubernias*, each under the control of a military officer, with very little regard on the traditional territorial divisions. The size of these territories was radically reduced in 1775 by Catherine II, who subdivided them into fifty *gubernias* (called *namestnichestva*) ruled by governors. For the most part, these territorial divisions retained their original form until the end of the tsarist rule.

There was one further consequence of Russia's open borders. After the centralized Muscovite state had established its dominance over the other appanage principalities, it embarked upon a determined policy of territorial expansion to the south and east. This was motivated in part by the pursuit of national security in the form of secure borders and in part by the irresistible allure of the natural resource wealth (largely furs) that lay beckoning in these large and sparsely populated regions. From this point on, the scale of Russian expansion was completely unprecedented. In the second half of the sixteenth and seventeenth centuries, Moscow conquered and incorporated Kazan, Astrakhan the West Siberian khanates, Eastern Siberia and Far East. In the eighteenth century, the empire absorbed territories near the Black Sea, Crimea, parts of Kazakhstan and Alaska. The conquest of Central Asia, the Caucasus and Far East was concluded in the nineteenth century. This imperial expansion produced a large number of ethnically non-Russian colonial regions, even if they were significantly populated by Russian settlers. Besides those Russian migrants, communities of the Cossacks on the south and south-east periphery of the country also tended to develop a frontier identity, often juxtaposed culturally and socially to the identity of the country's central regions.

The coffers of the central government quickly became dependent on the resource wealth extracted from these newly incorporated territories. The share of the fur trade in the structure of Russian export in the seventeenth century roughly corresponds to the revenues from exporting oil and gas in contemporary Russia (which, it may be noted, come from formerly colonial territories).[8] And as is the case today, this medieval 'resource curse' – overdependence on revenue generated by natural resource exports – meant that the Russian leadership was less interested in modernization, infrastructure reforms, developing an internal market and raising the living standards of the population. These two arguments, colonialism on the one hand and the 'resource curse' on the other, have always fed regionalist sentiments, especially in Siberia and the Urals.

With the development of the Russian public sphere in the nineteenth century, decentralization became an important component of political debate. The anti-hegemonic and democratic potential of decentralization was for the first time explored by the Decembrists. After the incorporation of Georgia in 1801, the annexation of Finland in 1809 and the Duchy of Warsaw in 1815, the imperial government faced the necessity of governing culturally advanced and nationally conscious peoples who had long traditions of autonomous political existence. As a result, Finland and Poland enjoyed rights of autonomy within the empire that were unprecedented in tsarist Russia. This naturally raised the question of decentralization as an empire-wide issue. It was discussed in the early 1820s in the constitutional project of Nikolai Novosil'tsev, one of the closest associates of Tsar Alexander I,[9] and was eagerly picked up by the Decembrists themselves. Nikita Murav'ev wrote a constitutional charter in 1822, which suggested transforming

Russia into a federation of sixteen states. He tried to base his administrative project on long-existing local identities in Russia's regions themselves, referring, for example, to Novgorod by its old name Velikii Novgorod (Great Novgorod) and stipulating that the regional government would be named after Novgorod's medieval *veche*.[10] On a more politically neutral note, the vision of Russia as an empire of scientifically differentiated regions was developed in early academic studies, which purported to find the 'natural', that is, geographical, climatic and economic foundations for the division of the country into regions. Studies by Konstantin Arsen'ev, Petr Semenov Tian-Shanskii, Vasilii Dokuchaev and others laid grounds for the Soviet academic discipline of *raionirovanie* (from the Russian word *raion* – 'region') or 'regionalization': the attempt to 'scientifically' construct regions of Russia.[11]

The ideology of the Slavophiles, inspired by a Romantic quest for national authenticity and criticism of the Westernized officialdom, gave a new impetus for regionalist projects. In the 1850s, a secret society – the Brotherhood of Saint Cyril and Methodius – in Kiev led by the Ukrainian historian Nikolai Kostomarov, emerged as an offshoot of Slavophilism and quickly developed towards Ukrainophilism, veneration of the Ukrainian past, praise of the Cossacks and dreams of the reinstatement of the Ukrainian autonomy. A university professor, Kostomarov developed a 'regionalist' history of Russia as a composite body of regions which had existed long before the rise of the centralized state and which essentially retained their territorial and ethnocultural particularities under the tsars. Driven by the romantic quest for an authentic 'soul' of the Russian nation, Kostomarov found it in the Northern democracies of the Appanage period.[12]

Sergei Sharapov, a neo-Slavophile journalist active at the turn of the twentieth century, moved in a similar direction, but his projects were inspired by conservative and authoritarian ideas. He envisaged the autonomy of provinces as a means of promoting pan-Slavism and the further expansion of the Empire. He argued that Russia should play the role of a sort of Slavic Prussia, with the mission of assembling a greater pan-Slavic Union on the model of the Prussian-led establishment of the German Empire. This new political entity should not be Russia writ large but rather a genuinely Slavic state, the members of which would enjoy formal equality. This would be possible, he argued, only when the Slavic peoples were not scared away from Russia by its despotic centralized government. Thus, Russia should lead by example and reorganize itself internally into a union of eighteen autonomous and self-governing provinces (*oblasti*).[13] In this manner, Sharapov envisaged decentralization within Russia as a way to extend the country's borders and oppose the bureaucratic attempts to westernize the country.

The turbulent years of revolution and civil war (1917–1922) led to fragmentation of Russia's imperial space, the secession of Finland, Poland and the Baltic Republics, and the short-lived independence of many non-ethnic Russian regional entities. Ethnically Russian regionalism, by contrast, was manifested relatively weakly in this period, despite the marked feebleness of the central authorities. By the early 1920s, the Bolshevik government had established control over most of the former Russian Empire, and the Soviet Union was organized as a federal 'union' consisting of two types of territorial-administrative units. On the one hand were the ethnically based regions – Soviet socialist republics (SSRs), autonomous SSRs, autonomous *okrugs* and so on – which notionally represented the formerly colonized peoples, and civil-administrative *oblasti* or districts on the other, which were not ethnically designated but whose population was largely ethnic Russian. A principal intention of this federal structure was to deliver Vladimir Lenin's pre-revolutionary promise of national self-determination for the former empire's colonized peoples, an intention further promoted by what Terry Martin has famously termed 'affirmative action' policies intended to support the consolidation and enfranchisement of non-Russian ethnic communities across the country.[14] This policy served not only to preserve the underdeveloped state of ethnic Russian regionalism, but in fact also strengthened processes of cultural and political homogenization of Russia proper, where bottom-up regional manifestations were exterminated with the same vigour as under the tsars.

But if grass-roots regionalist and nationalist sentiments were suppressed in this manner, the Soviet state boldly took the lead in implementing its own regionalist schemes within the federal structure. By 1938, two decades of constant reshuffling of regional borders had yielded a stable system of forty-one *oblasti* (roughly corresponding to the pre-revolutionary *gubernias*) and a few dozen ethnonational entities – the populations of which, it should be noted, were themselves highly multinational and frequently resembled a *matrioshka* doll of ethnonational territories nested in strict hierarchies of power and prerogative. Against this background, the large-scale industrialization and urbanization of the early Soviet decades – enacted on the principles of scientific *raionirovanie* – restructured the country's territory as a rationally functioning organism, in which each region was supposed to perform its own function in unison with others. The legacy of pre-revolutionary regional identities was further disrupted by a nation-wide program of renaming regions and cities after famous revolutionary leaders. Thus, Tver became Kalinin, Yekaterinburg – Sverdlovsk, Nizhniy Novgorod – Gorky, St Petersburg – Leningrad, and so on.

Regionalism after communism

Disintegration of the Soviet Union in 1991 brought all fifteen subjects of this federation into existence as independent nation states. Since this chapter focuses on ethnic Russian regionalism, from this moment on it follows the history of the largest Socialist republic, what is known today as the Russian Federation. The end of the Soviet Union gave a historical chance to regionalism in Russia. The evaporation of the national power in Moscow, on the one hand, and the slow process of establishing of the Russian republican administration, on the other, had the effect of relocating the centre of power into the regions. Already in 1990, Boris Yeltsin, the then chair of the Supreme Council of the Russian Soviet Socialist Republic, admonished regional leaders to 'take as much power as you can swallow'.[15] This initiated the so-called 'parade of sovereignties', when many Autonomous Soviet Socialist Republics (ASSRs) were redesignated as full 'republics' (i.e. first-order federal subjects) and adopted constitutions proclaiming their sovereignty.

In 1992, a Federative Treaty was signed between Moscow and several non-Russian republics, which established the contractual nature of the federation and distributed powers between central and regional levels. The Russian leadership saw this as a way to preserve state unity at a time when the centre was paralysed and the most powerful regions, such as the Sverdlovsk and the republics of Tatarstan, Bashkortostan and Iakutia, were on the verge of introducing their own currencies and formally seceding. With the adoption in 1993 of a federal constitution that defined the nature of the federation not as contractual but as constitutionally established from above, however, the special status granted to non-Russian republics within Russia was eclipsed and the central government gradually regained strength and confidence. The constitution stipulated that all subjects of federation, regardless whether they are ethnic republics or Russian *oblasti*, were formally equal. Regional constitutions were adjusted to the federal constitution, and any discussion of regional sovereignties and the rights of secession was cut off.

One of the most prominent regionalist projects of that period developed not out of legacy of medieval appanage regionalism in Russia's central provinces but rather on a periphery of the post-Soviet state. This was the idea of the Ural Republic, promoted by the governor of Yekaterinburg Eduard Rossel in 1993. This was a bottom-up, 'indigenous' regionalism which capitalized on age-old perceptions of Moscow as a colonial master.[16] Paradoxically, however, it also drew inspiration from the specifically Soviet vision of the Urals region as the industrial backbone of the state: a veritable 'metallurgical civilization' of the Urals, or 'Perm matrix', entirely distinct from agrarian and backward Russia.[17] Rossel's intention was to elevate the *oblast* to a position of a republic, in order to achieve greater economic autonomy in relations with Moscow. In 1992, a regional currency the 'Ural frank' began to be printed, and on 1 July 1993 the 'Great Ural Republic' was formally proclaimed by the council of the *oblast* and work began on the preparation of the constitution. Moscow's reaction was immediate and decisive: Rossel was removed from his position in November 1993 and all decisions related to the Ural Republic were annulled.

In 2000, newly elected president Vladimir Putin moved to relocated political power in the country back to the centre by grouping dozens of federal subjects into seven giant 'federal districts' headed by representatives appointed directly by the president himself. These centralizing policies enjoyed widespread support in public opinion, which saw them as a long awaited return to normalcy after the 'Time of Troubles' in the 1990s. Later on, Putin undertook other measures to combine regions, replace elected governors with presidential appointees and limit the power of the regional representatives in the upper chamber of the Russian parliament. If nothing else, a consistent policy of curbing regional autonomy could be called the mainstay of Putin's regime. In 2013, the State Duma adopted a new law making the propagation of separatism a criminal act with the penalty of up to five years in prison. Notoriously flexible definitions have turned this law into a weapon against any kinds of public debates on regionalism.

Despite these increasing political pressures from the center, regionalist sentiment continues to resonate across the country. The *pomory* are aboriginal residents of Russia's White Sea littoral in the far north, mostly descendants from Novgorod after it had been pillaged by the Moscow tsars. This small group of three thousand people claims that they are culturally, ethnically and linguistically different from the majority of Russians, as well as having a specific political ethos, and a legacy of the free-trading traditions of the republic of *Velikii Novgorod*. As part of the crackdown on the opposition following the election of Vladimir Putin in 2012, the state actively persecutes the *Pomor* leader Ivan Moiseev for extremism, and their formal territorial organization was abolished by order of the Ministry of Justice in 2012. On a similar note, regionalism in Karelia and Ingria (St Petersburg and Leningradskaia *oblast*) insists on ethnocultural difference from the center, similarly pointing to the imperialistic politics of the center, which crushed democratic traditions of these regions.[18] Elsewhere, regionalisms 'from below' intersect with national movements in ethnic republics. The specter of separatism in Chechnya, Tatarstan and Yakutia continues to haunt the Russian political leadership, although, in fact, non-Russian and Russian grass-roots regionalisms rarely reinforce one another. Consistently marginalized by the central authorities, neither plays any significant role in the political life of Russia today.

It is important to note, however, that the obsessive fear of separatism on the part of the central authorities does not prevent the Kremlin from seeking to foster separatist movements elsewhere in the former Soviet Union. The most notorious example is the project 'Novorossiia', an attempt undertaken in 2014 to carve out the Russian-speaking eastern part of Ukraine with the view of its subsequent incorporation into Russia. When the pro-Russian rebellion flared up in Donbas, the self-proclaimed People's Republics in Donetsk and Luhansk declared the creation of the regional confederation Novorossiia. Similar to other regionalist movements in Russia and in Europe, Novorossiia soon became seen through the prism of two metaphoric operations. First, it was viewed as a metonymy for Russia as a whole: its condensed and best part, which heralds the universal regeneration and salvation of the spirit of 'Russianness' worldwide. The very name 'Novorossiia' – New Russia – suggested the palingenetic idea of national revival. Moreover, Novorossiia was framed as a metaphor of the frontier, the warring outpost of Russia in its confrontation with the hostile West and the Ukrainian 'fascists' in particular. Clearly aligned with the conservative and hegemonic forces, Novorossiia was to a great extent a brainchild of Kremlin's spin doctors, rather than a grass-roots phenomenon. Regionalism in this case is deployed in the service of Russian territorial enlargement, a feature which resonates more clearly with the logic of Sergei Sharapov than that of Nikita Murav'ev. Similarly to Sharapov's vision of the federative pan-Slavic Union, the leaders of Novorossiia envisage it as a cornerstone for the new spatial entity, bigger than Russia – the 'Russian World'.

In an indication of the volatile nature of regionalist politics in Russia today, however, in May 2015, the Novorossiia confederation was abruptly and unceremoniously disbanded, barely one year after it had been established. For most analysts, this meant that the puppet republic no longer suited the plans of the Kremlin to freeze the conflict in Ukraine. But there were also internal reasons preventing the successful political construction of the region. One of these was the instability of its borders and, as a result, the sedimentation of conflicting historical legacies in this region – a situation that is repeated across Russia.

In fact, the territory controlled by the insurgents in the 2014 only tangentially coincided with the historical borders of the Novorossiia *gubernia* established by Catherine II in 1764 as a result of a series of conquests in the Northern Black Sea region. Indeed, the original name disappeared from the maps almost immediately, as its territory was split into several other *gubernias* in 1775. Thereafter, the designation 'Novorossiia' survived as an informal toponym of the vaguely delineated lands on the northern shore of the Black Sea and also as the name of the town Novorossiisk in Kuban and the university in Odessa.[19]

Siberia: Regionalism on the eastern frontier

As has already been noted, the relationship of Siberia to the Russian state was historically that of a resource colony.[20] It was as a reaction against this colonial status that a regionalist movement – *oblastnichestvo* – first took shape in the mid-nineteenth century. The immediate context was a powerful mood of national reform that swept across Russia in the 1850s and 1860s, the most momentous consequence of which would be the abolishment of serfdom in 1861. The governor general of Eastern Siberia, Nikolai Murav'ev, shared these reformist sentiments and indeed made his own significant contribution to the dynamic spirit of the day by securing Russia's annexation of the vast Amur and Ussuri river basins, on Siberia's remote south-eastern frontier, from the Chinese empire.[21] Murav'ev engaged with progressive thinkers such as Peter Kropotkin and Mikhail Bakunin, who were located in Siberia at the time, and is reputed to have discussed with them progressive schemes of imperial reform that featured the creation of an independent, democratic and federalized 'United States of Siberia'.

At the same time, a regional movement coalesced out of the activities of such young Russian-Siberian intellectuals as Afanasii Shchapov, Grigorii Potanin and Nikolai Iadrintsev. Denouncing the exploitative and oppressive nature of Siberia's relationship with the imperial centre, these self-identified Siberian *oblastniki* called for Siberian self-government, local economic development and the raising of cultural and educational standards.[22] They expressed strong solidarity with other parts of the Russian empire that were similarly subject to a colonial subjugation, and in 1863 – the year of an insurrection in Poland against Russian rule – they issued their own call for Siberia to separate from the Russian empire and become a fully independent democratic republic. In the event, however, the Polish insurrection was crushed, the reformist dynamism that had stirred the nation faded and the central government became increasingly intolerant of localist sentiment. By the end of the decade, many of the youthful *oblastniki* had spent time in prison.

In the years that followed, Siberian *oblastnichestvo* developed into a multifaceted political and social vision, supported, among other things, through the establishment of local newspapers, most significantly *Vostochnoe Obozrenie* (1882–1906). It was edited by Iadrintsev, who had emerged as a leading intellectual figure east of the Urals. In 1882, he published the landmark polemical study *Siberia as a Colony*, which remains today the most comprehensive presentation of the regionalist perspective.[23] Directly comparing Siberia to other extra-European colonies such as India or Brazil, Iadrintsev argued that its relationship with the Russian centre was by its very nature unequal and exploitative. The Russian metropole had exploited Siberia's natural resource wealth for centuries, and it was against the interests of the centre ever to allow the modernization, industrial development and enlightenment that Siberia so desperately needed.

Oblastnichestvo, by contrast, was committed precisely to a program of progressive regional development. Above all, this meant that the revenues generated by Siberian resources should remain in Siberia, where they could provide the basis for the extensive development of industry and commerce in the region. Siberia should be governed not by bureaucrats dispatched from Moscow, whose lack of knowledge about or concern with the localities they administered was matched only by their relentless determination for self-enrichment. It was the Siberians themselves who understood and cared about the true interests of the region's inhabitants – indigenous peoples as well as ethnic Russians – and it was they who should hold power. The goal was to create an educated civil society through public education, cultural development, the rule of law and secure establishment of civil rights.

In the view of the regionalists, Siberia represented a unique region and society, distinguished from other parts of the empire not only geographically but historically as well. The medieval institution of serfdom, which for centuries fundamentally shaped society in Russia's central zones, had not migrated east across the Urals and was virtually unknown in Siberia. This circumstance, the regionalists maintained, meant that Siberians were different than their Great Russian counterparts, more independent and free in thought and action – a circumstance indeed often remarked upon by travellers to the region. It was further argued that the social psychology of Siberians had rather more in common with colonist societies such as the United States or Australia than with European Russia.

Indeed, some *oblastniki* even believed that over the centuries Siberians had evolved into what was effectively a distinct ethnonation, or least a proto-ethnonation. Invoking the then popular scientific precepts of environmental determinism, Shchapov maintained that in the special geographical conditions of Siberia, a variety of different peoples had intermingled and blended, creating the rudiments of a new, ethnically distinctive 'national-regional type'.[24] This was the *sibiriaki*, who Iadrintsev maintained, differed as much from European Russians as from other peoples of north Asia. Yet, however compellingly Shchapov put the case for a distinct *sibiriak* nationality, it was not accepted by most regionalists. To the contrary, most *oblastniki* stressed the polyethnic heterogeneity of Siberia's population, which included dozens of European and Asiatic nationalities. Indeed, they argued that the defining regional characteristic of Siberia was precisely its nature as a harmonious and ethnically diverse community (a perception very similar, paradoxically, to that which many Russians entertained about their country as a whole).

The fact remained that regionalist sentiments appealed largely to the intellectual class based in Siberia's major urban centers. Significantly, they did not attract much support of the Siberia's non-Russian peoples – Buriats, Yakuts, Evenks, Tuvans, Khanti-Mansi and many others – who in the imperial period were busy developing nascent ethnonational identities of their own.²⁵ The *oblastniki* were thus largely of ethnic Russian background, and indeed for most of them there was no contradiction between their regionalist identification with a polyethnic Siberia and a clear sense of national connection with Russians across the empire. This sense of kinship was reciprocated by Russian nationalists in European Russia, who in the nineteenth century often pointed with pride to Siberia as a place where remoteness and lack of development had the effect of protecting its primordial Russian culture and customs against the forces of modernity better than anywhere else. In the main, Russian Siberians regarded themselves as a regional variant of the Great Russian nation, different from other parts of the country but inseparable nevertheless.²⁶

Although the menace of 'separatist Siberian nationalism' was regularly evoked by the central authorities keen to discredit demands for self-government, Siberian regionalism did not, for the most part, support the political separation of Siberia from the rest of Russia. To the contrary, the program of industrial development, political autonomy and cultural enlightenment was understood as an intrinsic part of a broader movement of reform and development that would revitalize the entire empire. While *oblastnichestvo* denounced the empire's neglect of Siberia, 'its predominantly Russian interests' were never in any doubt.²⁷ Ultimately, the regionalists believed that the transformation of Siberia could inspire the progressive renovation of the country as a whole. Siberia would secure its self-determination not through political independence but rather through the restructuring of Russia as a whole as a federal state – the models of the United States or Switzerland were particularly popular – that would guarantee each region the necessary degree of cultural and economic autonomy.²⁸

Siberia in the Soviet Union

Although the collapse of the central authorities in the years following 1917 provided unprecedented freedom for regionalist agitation across the country, the effect in Siberia was mitigated precisely by the ambivalences we have just noted. A Provisional Siberian Government was established in December 1917, and a comprehensive Declaration of the State Sovereignty of Siberia was promulgated in July of the following year. Local support for independence remained highly uneven, however, and many regionalists were positively alarmed by the chaos unleashed by the Bolsheviks and the threat it posed to the greater unity and endurance of the Russian state. Eventually, Siberia became a major scene of military operations during the Civil War. After the defeat of the counter-revolutionary White forces in late 1919, the fledgling Soviet government took full control, and all political traces of Siberian regionalism were eliminated.²⁹

In the ambitious plans of the Bolsheviks for industrialization and national development, Siberia occupied a central position, and the decades after the revolution saw massive efforts to develop the Siberian economy, population resources, urban infrastructure and public welfare. The stimulus for this activity came directly from the Soviet centre, and its broader purpose was not primarily the development and enlightenment of Siberia itself but rather the modernization of the country as a whole. Indeed, however unprecedented the dramatic Soviet reconstruction of Siberia may have been, it continued faithfully to reflect the traditional approach to Siberia described so well by Iadrintsev: a gigantic resource colony whose natural wealth should be exploited to serve the interests of the rest of the country.[30] A particularly important aspect of national development strategies that impacted directly on Siberia were the policies of the Soviet state regarding nationality issues. The promulgation of so-called 'affirmative action' policies, intended to promote the individual welfare and development of the country's non-Russian nationalities, logically undermined the regionalist vision of Siberia.[31] And although the Soviet Union did adopt the federalism long cherished by the *oblastniki* in the nineteenth century, we have seen that the Soviet version was based on the criterion of ethnoterritoriality, and thus could not in principle accommodate Siberia as a single cohesive polyethnic entity.

Despite all of this, the old *sibiriak* self-image persisted after the revolution, and the regionalist legacy continued to develop in the Soviet Union.[32] No longer permitted as a subject of political discourse or agitation, the articulation of a Siberian identity now became essentially a cultural project pursued by writers and poets. Through the work of such writers as Viacheslav Shishkov, the poet Ivan Molchanov-Sibirskii and many others, Siberian literature emerged already before the Second World War as a recognized category within Soviet *belles lettres*. Its visibility was enhanced significantly by the establishment of the literary journal *Sibirskie Ogni* in the 1920s, which brought the work of writers from across all of Siberia's regions and its many nationalities to the attention of the entire country. Their work, which played heavily on the themes of Siberia's ethnographic diversity, folk traditions and its unique, often ancient Russian dialects, served to further embellish the picture of Siberia as a unique region with its own special characteristics. Remarkably, the journal continues to publish down to the present day.[33] To be sure, over most of its existence this literature was careful not to allow politics in any way into its juxtaposition of Siberia to the Russian centre and rather restricted itself to faithfully rehearsing official themes – the virtues of Soviet development and the evils of the feudal-capitalist past – in a Siberian context. But nonetheless, operating within this spectrum of sanctioned Soviet values, it remained 'regionalist' by keeping alive and even embellishing a notion of Siberian distinctiveness and pride of place.[34]

The fidelity of Soviet Siberian literature to party-approved dogmas did eventually begin to break down, however, and at this point it assumed a national prominence of the highest order. This moment came in the post-Stalinist 1970s, when official controls on literature and art were loosed to allow for some debate and even criticism of the state. Perhaps the most important national literary development of this time was the emergence of the so-called *derevenchiki* or 'village writers' – a collection of writers from the Russian provinces and regional peripheries, whose works gained wide critical acclaim. Taking a critical stance towards the Marxist-inspired ethos of industrial development and modernization, these authors confronted their readers with painfully realistic descriptions from their home regions of the social dislocation, material poverty and environmental destruction to which these polices had led.

Many of the leading *derevenchik* authors – Sergei Zalygin, Viktor Astaf'ev, Vasilii Shukshin, Valentin Rasputin and others – came from Siberia. Their work clearly chronicles the devastation of the Soviet years, but at the same time the region also emerges as an enduring repository of the lost or almost-lost values of the Russian people: the communal traditions of village and family life, a strong moral code, deep religious faith, veneration of their forefathers and love of primordial nature. After decades of wanton plundering by a materialistic and corrupt officialdom, these novelists describe a 'deep' Siberia which has still not lost its essential authenticity and its commitment to enduring national values.[35]

Although the work of the Siberian *derevenchiki* achieved great national acclaim, however, its implications for Siberian regionalism remained stubbornly ambivalent. The positive image of Siberia as a distinctive region that emerges quite powerfully from their work was not directed exclusively to Siberians, and its appeal was not limited to them. To the contrary, it proved equally meaningful to all Russians across the country who shared the same criticism of the biases and excesses of Soviet Marxist officialdom. Ultimately, the *derevenchik* literature served to confirm the point made above that however different and special *sibiriaki* considered their native region to be, it still remained for them an organic and inalienable part of the larger entity that is Russia. As Rasputin declared in 1990, 'Being a Russian, I naturally concern myself first of all with the level of Russian consciousness and with the necessity for cultural and spiritual renaissance in Russia'.[36]

Post-Soviet Siberia

The late 1980s witnessed a surge of regionalist sentiment across the country. In Siberia, this resulted in the formation in 1990 of Sibirskoe Soglashenie, or 'Siberian Agreement': a broad coalition of local political leaders who joined together to promote the interests of industry, agriculture, and resource extraction in the region.[37] After the fall of the USSR, the program of radical economic reform adopted by the Russian Federation – so-called shock therapy – had a special impact on Siberia. Sibirskoe Soglashenie initially proved highly effective in consolidating its support in the region and also winning concessions from the Yeltsin government. Although regionalist sentiment was particularly exacerbated in this period, with some in Siberia openly demanding its 'decolonization' from the control of the central authorities,[38] the concerns of Sibiriskoe Soglashie echoed quite precisely the old *oblastnik* calls for greater autonomy *within* the Russian Federation and for a higher share of the revenue generated by Siberian resources to be reinvested back into the region.[39]

The success of Sibirskoe Soglashenie proved to be short-lived, however, and a new constitution adopted in 1993 put a break on devolutionary trends across the country. The political control of the Moscow over the regions was then significantly expanded after 2000, when president Vladimir Putin redrew the political-administrative map of the Russian Federation by combining dozens of federal subjects into seven so-called 'federal districts' represented by his own appointees. Unsurprisingly, these changes served to stimulate regionalist sentiments in Siberia, which continue to be expressed by the political and business leadership and also civic organizations, especially those concerned with environmental protection or cultural heritage. Sibirskoe Soglashenie is still in operation, and local politicians regularly exhort Siberians to 'recognize their special interests' and create a regional block of some sort to promote them.[40] In recent years, calls for Siberian self-determination, for the region to 'take back its land' and 'stop feeding Moscow [with Siberian resources]' have even been raised at public rallies.[41]

Along with the question of Siberia's political status within the Russian Federation, there has been a revival of the debate about the nature of Siberian identity. The term *sibiriak* remains a popular identity tag for the region's inhabitants – at least for ethnic Russians – but as before its specific meaning is highly contested.[42] There have been attempts to embellish the *sibiriak* image by identifying a distinctively Siberian language based on the Old Russian dialects whose influence can still be traced in parts of Siberia.[43] A more popular and inclusive vision of Siberian 'neo-regionalism' has been promoted for the last ten years or so by a broad assortment of intellectuals, artists and civic activists. They appeal to Siberians to develop an awareness of the region's unique character and its problematic relation to the Russian centre. Siberians are commonly referred to as a 'nation' (*natsiia*), but once again this is a nation that is polyethnic and multicultural and inclusive of all expressions of Siberian culture and traditions.

While neo-regionalism venerates the legacy of pre-revolutionary *oblastnichestvo*, its deeper dynamic is post-modern. It is focused not on the recovery and resurrection of a primordial past but rather on the construction of a future-oriented Siberian alternative to European Russia. In order to popularize this cause, the movement deploys such twenty-first-century devices as promoting an 'I am Siberian' commercial brand (adorning T-shirts, passport covers and other products)[44] or staging sensationalist political theatre, for example, an art exhibition in 2014 devoted to 'The United States of Siberia', replete with its own flag.[45]

Such publicity stunts do not escape the vigilance of the central authorities in Moscow, who are quick to denounce them as evidence of Siberian regionalism's treasonous determination to fragment the united Russian people through political separation.[46] To be sure, there are extremist elements who support such a program. In 2010, a clandestine group in Novosibirsk allegedly plotting to organize an insurrection and declare a sovereign Siberian state was uncovered by the authorities, and in the following year an activist tried to organize a public referendum on Siberia's independence, claiming that it would be supported by the United States and would result in Siberia becoming America's fifty-first state.[47] Indeed, even thoughtful *Sibiriaki* can describe self-determination in terms that sound very much like political independence.[48]

These tendencies are, however, in no way indicative of the mainstream of Siberian regionalism, which continues to reflect the original Russocentric orientation of nineteenth-century *oblastnichestvo* with remarkable fidelity. As always, the goal is not separation and political independence but rather a fundamental rearrangement of the terms of existing Russian federalism so that greater political and economic autonomy can be devolved to the federal subjects. The recent conflict in Ukraine and, in particular, the formal inclusion of a 'Republic of Crimea' within the federal structure of the Russian Federation in 2014, has given a renewed impetus to this demand. Siberians call not for independence but rather for similarly granting a united Siberia the same republic status.[49]

On the most basic level, the desire of Siberian regionalism for enhanced regional authority remains married to a profound sense of solidarity with Russia west of the Urals – a bias that carries over into the present day. The conservative Novosibirsk journal *Sibirskaia Gornitsa* was founded in the early 1990s to explore and celebrate Siberian history and culture, but it is clearly inspired by the values and ideals of Russian nationalist culture under Putin: its political and social conservatism, orthodox religiosity and its obvious xenophobia. Effectively, the journal seeks to 'regionalize' these all-Russian values by identifying their special manifestation in Siberia – a service valuable enough to win recognition from the conservative Moscow-based Russian Writers' Union as the country's best regional publication.[50] Much the same can be said of the thematic thrust of the novelist Valentin Rasputin's recent work.[51]

Other regionalists, at pains to condemn political separatism as a 'betrayal of the homeland' (*izmena Rodine*), insist on the necessity of the Siberia-Russia nexus by arguing that the former – with its vast geographical expanse, its natural resource wealth and unlimited potential for settlement and development – embodies a necessary complement to European Russia and a guarantor of its future.[52] As the Tyumen writer Anatolii Omel'chyk puts it, Russia simply needs Siberia, and the sooner this is realized, the sooner a genuinely fair accommodation can be reached. It is the expanses of Siberia that 'make the [Russian] Fatherland great', he declares; it is 'precisely Siberia that makes Russia unfathomable'.[53] 'Why can Tatarstan, Chechnya, and Crimea all be federal republics, but our region cannot be?' demands a *Sibiriak* blogger. 'In fact, this is all backwards: WE ARE RUSSIA, SIBERIA IS THE CENTER OF RUSSIA. WHATEVER IS BENEFICIAL FOR SIBERIANS IS BENEFICIAL FOR THE ENTIRE COUNTRY.'[54]

Conclusion

For four centuries, Russia under the tsars was a continental empire, whose modus vivendi consisted in never-ending territorial expansion and colonization of the neighbouring peoples as well as its own Russian population. The central government steadily sought to obliterate regional differences and undermine regional affinities across the territories under its control. But at the same time, in order to facilitate the political administration of the vast country, the state paradoxically embarked on its own top-down projects of territorial reorganization. In the nineteenth century, when the *intelligentsia* began to participate in political discussions, regionalism 'from below' was envisaged as an emancipatory idea, concomitant to the large-scale reformist projects that aimed to overhaul the entire empire and reconnect with the 'democratic' traditions of northern Russian medieval principalities. Today, this anti-colonial and republican thrust is seen in the regionalisms on the periphery of the historical Russian mainland, in Siberia, the Urals, 'Ingria', the land of *pomory* and so on. Regionalism was also embraced by the nineteenth-century Romantic tradition of Slavophilism, whose proponents accentuated regionalism's conservative aspects, such as 'back-to-land' ideas, strivings for national rebirth and for regaining the nation's lost authenticity by means of 'going local'. There is also a connection between conservative regionalism as an indigenous initiative and its state-sponsored instrumentalization for the purpose of further territorial enlargement. The example of Siberian regionalism suggests that perspectives for Russian regionalism are uncertain. Viewed with suspicion by the state authorities and suffering from the inability to harmonize Russian and non-Russian regionalist aspirations from below, Russian regionalism remains as ever a vision for the future rather than a story of successes achieved.

Notes

1. Andreas Kappeler, *Russland als Vielvölkerreich: Entstehung-Geschichte-Zerfall* (Frankfurt a. M.: Büchergilde Gutenberg, 1993); and Jane Burbank, Mark von Hagen and Anatolii Remnev, eds, *Russian Empire: Space, People, Power, 1700–1930* (Bloomington: Indiana University Press, 2007).
2. Bler Rubl [Blair Ruble], 'Institut Kennana i regional'naia Rossia', in *Zemstvo. Arkhiv provintsial'noi istorii Rossii* no. 3 (Penza, 1994), 35.
3. Estimated in Arbakhan Magomedov, *Misteriia regionalizma: Regional'nye praviashchie elity* (Moscow: MION, 2000), 9.
4. Andrei Dvoinev, *Otechestvennaia istoriografiia sibirskogo oblastnichestva*, Diss. kand. istor. nauk (Omsk, 2006); Natal'ia Ablazhei, *Sibirskoe oblastnichestvo v emigratsii* (Novosibirsk, 2003); and Mikhail Shilovskii, *Sibirskie oblastniki v obshchestvenno-politicheskov dvizhenii v kk. 50-60-kh gg. XIX veka* (Novosibirsk: Izd-vo Novosibirskogo un-ta, 1989).
5. See, inter alia, Sergei Shishov, *Ekonomicheskaia geographiia i regionalistika* (Moscow: Finstatinform, 1998); and Viktor Kovalev, *Politicheskaia regionalistika* (Syktyvkar: IPO SGU, 1999).
6. J. Paul Goode, *The Decline of Regionalism in Putin's Russia: Boundary Issues* (London/New York: Routledge, 2011); Graeme Gill, ed., *Politics in the Russian Regions* (Houndsmills: Palgrave Macmillan, 2007); and William Reisinger, ed., *Russia's Regions and Comparative Subnational Politics* (Abingdon: Routledge, 2013).
7. Michael Khodarkovsky, *Russia's Steppe Frontier: The Making of a Colonial Empire* (Bloomington: Indiana University Press, 2002), 47.
8. Alexander Etkind, *Internal Colonization: Russia's Imperial Experience* (Cambridge: Polity, 2011).
9. For the translation of the Novosil'tsev's project, see Mark Raeff, *Plans for Political Reform of Imperial Russia, 1730–1905* (Englewood Cliffs: Prentice-Hall, 1966), 110–20.
10. John LeDonne, 'Regionalism and Constitutional Reform 1819–1826', *Cahiers du monde russe* 44, no. 1 (2003).
11. Marina Loskutova, 'Regionalization, Imperial Legacy, and the Soviet Geographical Tradition', in *Empire De/Centered: New Spatial Histories of Russia and the Soviet Union*, ed. Sanna Turoma and M. Waldstein (Farnham: Ashgate, 2013).

12. Dimitri von Mohrenschildt, *Towards a United States of Russia: Plans and Projects of Federal Reconstruction of Russia in the 19th Century* (Rutherford: Associated University Presses, 1981), 40–85.
13. Mikhail Suslov, '"Slavophilism is True Liberalism": The Political Utopia of SF Sharapov (1855–1911)', *Russian History* 38, no. 2 (2011): 281–314.
14. Terry Martin, *The Affirmative Action Empire: Nastions and Nationalism in the Soviet Union, 1923–1939* (Ithaca, NY: Cornell University Press, 2001).
15. Quoted from Timothy Colton, *Yeltsin: A Life* (New York: BasicBooks, 2008). See also Jeronim Perovic, 'Regionalisation Trend in Russia: Between the Soviet Legacy and the Forces of Globalization', *Geopolitics* 9, no. 2 (2004): 342–77; Vladimir Gel'man and Ted Hopf, eds, *Tsentr i regional'nye identichnosti v Rossii* (St Petersburg: Evropeiskii Universitet, 2003); Andrei Makarychev, 'Russian Regions as International Actors', *Demokratizatsiya: The Journal of Post-Soviet Democratization* 7, no. 4 (1999): 501–26; and Vladimir Gel'man, 'Regime Transition, Uncertainty and Prospecdts for Democratisation: The Politics of Russia's Regions in a Comparative Perspective', *Europe-Asia Studies* 51, no. 6 (1999): 939–56.
16. See http://afterempire.info/2016/11/02/why-after-emp/.
17. Cf. the TV documentary film series 'Khrebet Rossii' ('Russia's Backbone') directed by Leonid Parfenov and Aleksei Ivanov in 2009. Available at: https://www.youtube.com/watch?v=T965iref3eI&list=PLQn6X4U2uxvYx5Nc4UQD1neHAYlpLttnr.
18. http://afterempire.info/2016/11/02/why-after-emp/. See also Mikhail Pozharskii, 'Sostoianie poluraspada: Stoit li boiat'sia razvala strany', 4 May 2017. Available at: http://afterempire.info/2017/05/04/poluraspad/; and Dmitrii Vitushkin, 'Dve Rusi', 19 May 2017. Available at: http://afterempire.info/2017/05/19/2-rus/. Cf. also the documentary film by Andrei Loshak about Novgorod, represented as Russia's lost alternative of democratic development (2014). Available at: https://tvrain.ru/lite/teleshow/puteshestvie_iz_peterburga_v_moskvu_osobyj_put/puteshestvie_iz_peterburga_v_moskvu_osobyj_put_film_andreja_loshaka_velikij_novgorod_serija_2-378741/.
19. Mikhail Suslov, 'The Production of "Novorossiya": A Territorial Brand in Public Debates', *Europe-Asia Studies* 69, no. 2 (2017): 202–21.
20. On the history of Siberia and its interactions with the Russian center, see Alan Wood, *Russia's Frozen Frontier: A History of Siberia and the Russian Far East 1581–1991* (London: Bloomsbury, 2011); Bruce W. Lincoln, *The Conquest of a Continent: Siberia and the Russians* (Ithaca, NY: Cornell University Press, 2007); Yuri Slezkine, *Arctic Mirrors. Russia and the Small Peoples of the North* (Ithaca, NY: Cornell University Press, 1994); Mark Bassin, 'Imperialer Raum/Nationaler Raum: Sibirien auf der kognitiven Landkarte Rußlands im 19. Jahrhundert', *Geschichte und Gesellschaft* 28, no. 3 (2002): 378–403; and Mark Bassin, 'Inventing Siberia: Visions of the Russian East in the Early 19th Century', *American Historical Review* 96, no. 3 (1991): 763–94.
21. Mark Bassin, *Imperial Visions. Nationalist Imagination and Geographical Expansion in the Russian Far East, 1840–1865* (Cambridge: Cambridge University Press, 1999).
22. David Rainbow, 'Siberian Patriots: Participatory Autocracy and the Cohesion of the Russian Imperial State, 1858–1920' (Ph.D. dissertation, New York University, 2013); and Stephen Watrous, 'The Regionalist Conception of Siberia, 1860 to 1920', in *Between Heaven and Hell: The Myth of Siberia in Russian Culture*, ed. Galya Diment and Yuri Slezkine (New York: St. Martin's Press, 1993), 113–32.
23. Nikokai Iadrintsev, *Sibir' Kak Koloniia: V Geograficheskom, Etnograficheskom I Istoricheskom Otnosheniia* (St Petersburg: M. M. Stasiulevich, 1882).

24. Thomas Marsden, *Afanasii Shchapov and the Significance of Religious Dissent in Imperial Russia, 1848–70* (New York: Columbia University Press, 2008); and Dimitri von Mohrenschildt, 'Shchapov: Exponent of Regionalism and the Federal School in Russian History', *Russian Review* 37, no. 4 (1978): 387–404.
25. Watrous, 'Regionalist Conception', 124–26; and Galya Diment, 'Valentin Rasputin and Siberian Nationalism', *World Literature Today* 67, no. 1 (1993): 69–73.
26. Watrous, 'Regionalist Conception', 117–19.
27. Diment, 'Valentin Rasputin and Siberian Nationalism', 72.
28. Victor L. Mote, *Siberia: Worlds Apart* (Boulder, CO: Westview Press, 1998), 65.
29. Jonathan D. Smele, *Civil War in Siberia: The Anti-Bolshevik Government of Admiral Kolchak, 1918–1920* (Cambridge: Cambridge University Press, 2006).
30. Fiona Hill and Clifford Gaddy, *The Siberian Curse. How Communist Planners Left Russia out in the Cold* (Washington, DC: Brookings Institution Press, 2003). See also the chapter by Smith-Peter.
31. Martin, *Affirmative Action Empire*.
32. Francine Hirsch, *Empire of Nations: Ethnographic Knowledge and the Making of the Soviet Union* (Ithaca, NY: Cornell University Press, 2004), 129.
33. Edith W. Clowes, 'Being a Sibiriak in Contemporary Siberia: Imagined Geography and Vocabularies of Identity in Regional Writing Culture', *Region: Regional Studies of Russia, Eastern Europe, and Central Asia* 2, no. 1 (2013): 47–67, 52.
34. Alexis Kathryn Gunderson, 'Regional Identity and the Development of a Siberian Literary Canon' (Ph.D. dissertation, University of Oregon, 2011).
35. K. V. Anisimov and A. I. Razuvalova, 'Dva veka – dve grani sibirskogo teksta: oblastniki vs 'derevenchiki'', *Vestnik Tomskogo Gosudarstvennogo Universiteta (Filologiia)* 1, no. 27 (2014): 75–98.
36. Quoted in Diment, 'Valentin Rasputin', 69.
37. James Hughes, 'Regionalism in Russia: The Rise and Fall of Siberian Agreement', *Europe-Asia Studies* 46, no. 7 (1994): 1133–61.
38. Hughes, 'Regionalism in Russia', 1147.
39. M. K. Bandman, 'Geopoliticheskoe polozhenie Sibiri posle raspada SSSR', *Izvestiia AN. Seriia Geograficheskaia* 3 (1994): 85–93.
40. Eduard Kriukov, 'Sibiriskii separatism…pod maskoi sibirskogo natsionalizm', *Krasnaia Vesna* (17 March 2013), http://rossaprimavera.ru/article/sibirskiy-separatizm-pod-maskoy-sibirskogo-nacionalizma, last access on 19 June 2017.
41. Vitalii Kamyshev, 'Uroki irkutskogo referenduma', http://www.igpi.ru/bibl/other_articl/1145953040.html, last access on 19 July 2017; and Vitalii Kamyshev, 'Khvatit' kormit' Moskvu', *Argument*, 4 August 2014, http://argumentua.com/stati/khvatit-kormit-moskvu, last access on 19 June 2017.
42. Roland Scharff, 'Sibirjak: Wiederbelebung eines Stereotyps?', *Osteuropa* 48, no. 2 (1998): A82–A88; N. V. Sverkulova, 'Fenomen Sibiriaka', *Sotsiologicheskie Issledovaniia* 8 (1996): 90–94; and Clowes, 'Being a Sibiriak in Contemporary Siberia'.
43. 'Sibirskii iazyk', https://traditio.wiki/Сибирский_язык, last access on 19 June 2017; and 'Sibirskaia vol'gota', www.volgota.com, last access on 19 June 2017.
44. E.g. http://en.imsiberian.com/ or https://www.56thparallel.com/im-siberian/, both last access on 19 June 2017.

45. Stanislav Zakharkin, 'What's in Store for the Siberian Movement?', *Eurozine* (11 June 2015). http://www.eurozine.com/whats-in-store-for-the-siberian-movement/, last access on 19 June 2017.
46. 'Sovremennoe sibirskoe oblastnichestvo', https://traditio.wiki/Современное_сибирское_областничество, last access on 19 June 2017; 'Chto takoe sibirskii natsionalizm I chem on grozit putinskoi Rossii', *Obozrevatel'* (28 July 2015), https://www.obozrevatel.com/abroad/45806-ugroza-separatistov-s-vostoka-matushki-rossii.htm, last access on 19 June 2017.
47. J. Paul Goode, 'Russia's Failed Federalization Marches and the Simulation of Regional Politics', *Russian Analytical Digest* 156 (5 December 2014): 12; and 'Chleny podpol'noi organizatsii gotovili vosstanie za nezavisimost' Sibiri', Kavkazcenter, 5 May 2010, http://www.kavkazcenter.com/russ/content/2010/05/05/72206.shtml last access on 19 June 2017.
48. 'Oblastnichestvo kak pozitsiia sibirskogo politika', *Sibirska vol'gota* (18 January 2006), http://www.volgota.com/lib/kulpozi.html, last access on 19 June 2017.
49. 'March for federalizing Siberia, August 17: Liveblog', *Euromaidan Press* (17 August 2014), http://euromaidanpress.com/2014/08/17/march-for-federalizing-siberia-august-17-liveblog/, last access on 19 June 2017.
50. 'Zhurnal "Sibirskaia Gornitsa"', *Literaturnaia karta g. Novosibirska*, http://infomania.ru/lit/view_lit?id=29, last access on 17 June 2017.
51. Clowes, 'Being a Sibiriak', 58; Sophia Kishkovsky, 'Valentin Rasputin, Russian Writer Who Led "Village Prose" Movement, Dies at 77', *New York Times* (19 March 2015), https://www.nytimes.com/2015/03/19/world/europe/valentin-rasputin-russian-writer-who-led-village-prose-movement-dies-at-77.html?_r=0, last access on 17 June 2017; and David Gillespie, 'From Rasputin to Putin and Back Again', http://dentisty.org/from-rasputin-to-putin-and-back-again-in-search-of-the-russian.html, last access on 17 June 2016.
52. Dmitrii Verkhoturov, 'Bor'ba s sibirskim separatizmm kak izmena Rodine', http://schriftsteller.livejournal.com/742135.html, last access on 17 June 2017.
53. Clowes, 'Being a Sibiriak', 60.
54. 'Baikalskaia respublika kak vykhod iz krizisa', http://liveangarsk.ru/blog/sprf/20151017/baikalskaya-res, last access on 17 June 2017.

Further reading

Bassin, Mark, 'Inventing Siberia: Visions of the Russian East in the Early 19th Century', *American Historical Review* 96, no. 3 (1991): 763–94.

Clowes, Edith W., 'Being a Sibiriak in Contemporary Siberia: Imagined Geography and Vocabularies of Identity in Regional Writing Culture', *Region: Regional Studies of Russia, Eastern Europe, and Central Asia* 2, no. 1 (2013): 47–67.

Diment, Galya, and Yuri Slezkine, eds, *Between Heaven and Hell: The Myth of Siberia in Russian Culture* (New York: St. Martin's Press, 1993).

Goode, J. Paul, *The Decline of Regionalism in Putin's Russia: Boundary Issues* (London and New York: Routledge, 2011).

Hughes, James, 'Regionalism in Russia: The Rise and Fall of Siberian Agreement', *Europe-Asia Studies* 46, no. 7 (1994): 1133–61.

Lincoln, W. Bruce, *The Conquest of a Continent: Siberia and the Russians* (Ithaca, NY: Cornell University Press, 2007).

Pereira, N. G. O., 'The Idea of Siberian Regionalism in Late Imperial and Revolutionary Russia', *Russian History* 20, no. 1/4 (1993): 163–78.

Petro, Nikolai, 'A Tale of Two Regions: Novgorod and Pskov as Models of Symbolic Development', *Journal of Socio-Economics* 35, no. 6 (2006): 946–58.

Rasputin, Valentin Grigorevich, *Siberia on Fire: Stories and Essays*. Translated by Gerald Mikkelson and Margaret Winchell (De Kalb: Northern Illinois University Press, 1989).

Rodger, Peter W., 'Contestation and Negotiation: Regionalism and the Politics of School Textbooks in Ukraine's Eastern Borderlands', *Nations and Nationalism* 12, no. 4 (2006): 681–97.

Slezkine, Yuri, *Arctic Mirrors. Russia and the Small Peoples of the North* (Ithaca, NY: Cornell University Press, 1994).

Stavrakis, Peter J., Joan DeBardeleben, Joseph Laurence Black and Jodi Koehn, *Beyond the Monolith: The Emergence of Regionalism in Post-Soviet Russia* (Washington, DC: Woodrow Wilson Center Press, 1997).

Suslov, Mikhail, 'The Production of "Novorossiya": A Territorial Brand in Public Debates', *Europe-Asia Studies* 69, no. 2 (2017): 202–21.

Von Mohrenschildt, Dimitri S., *Toward a United States of Russia: Plans and Projects of Federal Reconstruction of Russia in the Nineteenth Century* (Madison, NJ: Fairleigh Dickinson University Press, 1981).

CHAPTER 16
BALTIC AND POLISH REGIONALISM(S): CONCEPTS, DIMENSIONS AND TRAJECTORIES
Jörg Hackmann

Baltic and Polish regionalism(s)

Presenting regionalism on the southern rim of the Baltic encounters three major problems that require clarification before going into details of concepts, developments, actors and impact. First, one should speak of regionalisms in plural, as there are various diverging notions in spatial scope, which in addition reveal quite different trajectories. Second, focusing on substate regionalisms requires the inclusion of a perspective on the changing shape of state borders in Central and Eastern Europe in the twentieth century. This implies, thirdly, an examination of the changing semantics of 'Baltic' in the nineteenth and twentieth centuries as well as of the changing connotations of regional distinctions in Poland.

Discussions about regional identity, regionality and regionalism in the Baltic Sea area appeared like mushrooms after the rain, as one would say in Polish, since the mid-1980s, when the new thaw in the Soviet hemisphere allowed the ice of the Cold War to melt. The area then was discovered and mapped anew, first with reference to the powerful image of a new Hansa, which was seen as a supranational model and as one overcoming or bridging the borders between east, west and north. In that regard, region-building was seen first of all as a supranational (and often non-state) challenge, whereas regionalism as a subnational, ethnic or even separatist agenda was afforded less attention.[1] Debates about the Baltic area and, as a consequence, Baltic states and nations, were largely shaped by perceptions based on the whole Baltic littoral. Scholarly approaches to regionality had a strong theoretical background in discussions about the construction of regions and identities in Northern Europe.[2] In that perspective and in particular in contemporary debates, a regionalism referring to a supranational Baltic Sea area[3] has to be distinguished from regionalisms within state borders, with the latter first of all visible in Poland after 1989. The debates in Poland are, however, also shaped by transnational aspects, as they widely refer to the legacy of historical regions, which, in many cases, transcend current state borders.

For better orientation, a short overview on political history shall be provided here: Until the First World War, today's Baltic states were parts of the Tsarist Russian Empire, although they had different political status: Estonia and Latvia (without its eastern region Latgale) formed the three Baltic provinces of Estland, Livland and Kurland. From 1918 until the Soviet occupation in 1940, which resulted from the Ribbentrop-Molotov Pact, Estonia and Latvia were independent nation states with significant German and Russian national minorities. Apart from the German occupation during the Second World War from 1941 to 1944/1945, both countries remained republics of the Soviet Union until August 1991. The case of Lithuania was slightly different: its territory also was part of the Russian Empire, but was separated in various smaller provinces, which in particular after the defeat of the January uprising of 1863 on Polish and Lithuanian territories were heavily suppressed by the Tsarist authorities. Besides, parts of today's Lithuania on the Baltic littoral belonged to the Prussian state and after 1871 to the German Reich. In 1923, the northern part of this so-called 'Lithuania Minor', the Klaipėda region ('Memelland' in German), was occupied by the Lithuanian state, which had also emerged at the end of the First World War. The major territorial question of Lithuania, however, referred to its historical capital city, Vilnius (Wilno in Polish). In the aftermath of the war between Poland and Bolshevist Russia, it was occupied by Poland in October 1920 and then handed over to Lithuania by the Soviet Union in December 1939, after the Soviet occupation of Eastern Poland following the Ribbentrop-Molotov Pact. After 1945, the Lithuanian Soviet Republic comprised both the Vilnius and the Klaipėda regions.

The Polish case is even more complex: After the partitions of the Polish Republic of Nobles from 1772 to 1795, there was no Polish statehood beyond the borders of the partitioning empires of Habsburg, Prussia and Russia until November 1918. Polish elites made several – albeit unsuccessful – attempts to restore the Polish state during that period, and they largely consented that a future Polish state, if not restored within the borders of 1772, must at least include territories from all three empires. As a result of the First World War and the fights with Soviet Russia, the Second Polish Republic emerged with a new borderline in the East, whereas the western and northern boundaries at least partially followed the situation before 1772. The territorial shape of Poland was fundamentally altered once again as a result of the Nazi-Soviet cooperation in August 1939. The Soviet Union occupied the territories east of today's Poland's eastern border, and after the defeat of Nazi rule, Poland was extended westwards, incorporating parts of the former Prussian provinces of East Prussia, Pomerania and Silesia and the former Free City of Danzig. Against this background of non-existing statehood and shifting borders, in Poland (and similarly in Lithuania), regional distinctions within their state territories were largely seen as negative consequences of imperial rule, which should be dissolved by the new states.

This brief historical sketch may explain why the emergence of regionalisms and nationalisms during the nineteenth and partly even during the twentieth century went hand in hand and thus cannot be clearly separated from each other, as they refer to similar social processes. In the case of Poland, there is also a close connection between regionalism and discourses on the Polish nation before the restoration of Polish statehood in 1918. Since then, debates about regional identities or specific forms of regionality were positively or negatively judged according to their relation to the Polish nation. This pattern has been challenged after 1989, but it is still reactivated from time to time.

Regionalisms before the First World War

At the beginning of the post-Napoleonic era, the term 'Baltic' referred to the whole area of the *mare balticum* and was still largely synonymous with the European 'North'. Since the 1830s, however, a smaller regional perspective emerged with a focus on a part of the Baltic littoral under Tsarist rule, which subsequently turned into a specific Baltic (German) regionalism. In its centre were the three 'Ostseeprovinzen', although these Baltic provinces did not include St Petersburg and Finland but only the area with a specific sociopolitical structure of dominating German-speaking elites. In the mid-nineteenth century, these traditional elites felt that their social position was threatened by the politics of the Tsarist authorities regarding non-orthodox confessions and by language policies in the administration and schooling system as well as by unrest of Estonian and Latvian peasants against the predominantly German landed elites. The Germans in the Ostseeprovinzen now strongly underlined their regional privileges (going back to tsar Peter I and Catherine II) – and they did so in Germany to avoid Russian censorship.

This dispute between traditional privileges and the striving for administrative homogenization (based on the Russian language) reached its peak with the controversy between Iurii Samarin and Carl Schirren at the end of the 1860s. Whereas the Slavophile Samarin, who had served for several years in the Tsarist administration in Riga, in his book on the 'Russian Baltic coastal land',[4] warned of alleged German attempts to Germanize the Estonians and Latvians and argued for a closer integration of the region into Russia proper, Schirren (a professor of history at Dorpat University) stated that 'Livland is not a [Russian] guberniia [. . .]: it is a province with an own landed state'.[5] As a result of the harshness of this reply, he eventually had to leave Dorpat/Tartu and emigrated to Germany.

In the German public sphere, the privileges of the German-speaking elites were first of all addressed as an issue not only of the Tsarist provinces but of the whole German nation. Therefore, until the mid-1860s, German reactions to the claim of fully integrating the Baltic provinces under Russian rule can be regarded as part of German nationalism. With the foundation of the German Empire in 1871, however, and Bismarck's renunciation of including the Baltic Germans into it, German nationalism in the Russian Baltic provinces was replaced by a German Baltic regionalism. In cultural terms, this is reflected in the changes at the Baltic song festivals, where Ernst Moritz Arndt's popular 'Was ist des Deutschen Vaterland' disappeared from the official programmes after 1861 and was subsequently replaced by songs praising the Baltic *Heimat*. The new regionalism, which centred on the term *baltisch*, was not so much shaped by the traditional social, noble and urban elites but in particular by intellectuals (*literati* in the local discourse) like Schirren. Initially, Baltic regionalism was based on the assumption of German cultural hegemony and, therefore, included in a paternalistic perspective also the ethnic groups of Estonians and Latvians. This attitude changed, however, with the emerging national movements among these groups and the Russification of the school system since the 1880s.

The revolution of 1905 and new regulations on voluntary associations led to the formation of 'German societies' in the Baltic provinces, which defined themselves now in national terms and sought contacts to *alldeutsche* organizations, which were called upon to help their fellow nationals.[6] Nevertheless, expressions of an open German nationalism were limited by a widely felt loyalty towards the tsar. Thus, *Heimat* as a new term in this Baltic regionalism was shaped by the Baltic German notion of uniting the German speaking population in the provinces of Estland, Livland and Kurland focussing on the distinct German culture as well as the nature of the region.[7] Although this notion remained confined to the Baltic region, it found only little resonance among the Estonians and Latvians, who before the First World War thought of autonomy of their ethnic homelands. In that respect, there was no specific regionalism apart from their national movements. Here, one may also ask, whether the increasing presence of Russians in the region promoted a Russian regional identity within the Baltic provinces. Whereas in publications the connection with Russia proper was highlighted, forms of sociability show specific Baltic regional features.[8]

At this point, one has to look into the regional notions of the Estonians and Latvians. For them, their homeland was understood as national, and consequently there was no regional discourse apart from the national, as there were larger external ethnic communities only in the Tsarist capitals of St Petersburg and Moscow. Furthermore, Estonians and Latvians addressed the regional dimensions of the Baltic provinces as relics of the German domination of the region, which, in the eyes of their protagonists, should be overcome by the national movements. This became manifest at the song festivals in the region since the 1860s, as choral singing played an important role in the formation of the Latvian and Estonian movements with considerable influence from German (and in the case of Estonians also Finnish) singing traditions. These transfers were, however, subject to various internal disputes, which centred on the question whether to acknowledge cultural transfers between the different linguistic groups within the region or to claim the national movements as direct emanations of a Herderian *Volksgeist*.[9] These national foci together with the Baltic German use of the regional discourse may also explain why regional interferences received scarce attention from historians to date.[10]

The situation of the Lithuanians differed significantly for several reasons. The major divergence was the intensified Russification of the area after the defeat of the 1863 uprising. As a result, Tsarist authorities introduced a harsh policy of cultural and religious control of Lithuanian Tsarist subjects including the prohibition of publishing books in Lithuanian using the Latin alphabet.[11] Besides, the ethnic territory of the Lithuanians within the Tsarist Empire was regarded by the Polish public as 'lands taken away', a perspective which provoked conflicts after the First World War. The situation of the Lithuanians in Tsarist Russia gave special relevance to the formation of a Lithuanian regionalism in the northern parts of East Prussia as part of the German Reich.[12] In 'Lithuania Minor', there was a protestant Lithuanian population, whereas the Lithuanians in the Tsarist provinces were in their vast majority Catholics. The relevance of this Prussian regionalism resulted from its impact on Lithuanian society, not least due to the printing of journals and books in Lithuanian, which were then smuggled across the Russian border. What emerged here was a 'Baltic' and by the same time ethnic understanding of the Lithuanian nation, as in Jonas Basanavičius's newspaper *Auszra* (Dawn), first published in East Prussia in 1883. In contrast, the historical Polish notion of Lithuania, as expressed famously by the poet Adam Mickiewicz, who addressed Lithuania as his fatherland in the Polish language, lost its relevance for ethnic Lithuanians.

With regard to Prussia, two regionalisms that were more visible than the Lithuanian in East Prussia have to be addressed: among the 'Kashubs', a Slavic population west and north of Gdańsk/Danzig in today's Pomorze Gdańskie – historically West Prussia – a political movement first appeared in 1846, when Florjan Ceynowa, a student and promotor of Kashubian language, supported the Polish attempt of an uprising in Prussia. He was then put into prison and among those who were sentenced to death in the so-called 'Poles' Process' in Berlin-Moabit in 1847. After being freed during the revolution of 1848, he promoted a Kashubian regionalism, in close connection with the Polish national movement in Prussia. Ceynowa, however, distanced himself from the Polish nobility and focused on the peasant culture of the Kashubian population.[13] The movement grew in the following decades, predominantly under the influence of Polish intellectuals and writers discovering the region as a touristic one. In addition, a 'young-Kashubian' movement emerged after 1900, which strengthened the role of Kashubian as a literary language. Despite the dominating pro-Polish orientation of Kashubian regionalism, it drew also criticism from the Polish public, which claimed that the Kashubs were an integral part of the Polish nation.[14]

The second regional movement emerged among the Polish-speaking population of East Prussia. Here, one has to distinguish between the Catholic population of the region of Ermland (Warmia in Polish), and the Protestant population of Masuria (Masuren in German /Mazury in Polish). The latter region attained cultural and ethnical distinction in the mid-nineteenth century. Supporters of an own regional identity were first of all Protestant pastors and in the decades after 1863 also increasingly Polish intellectuals, who migrated to the region from Greater Poland with the intention to counteract Prussian Germanization politics and to build a Polish national identity among the Masurian population.[15] Similar processes of an expanding Polish identity occurred among the Slavic inhabitants in Upper Silesia. Here, however, the situation was shaped by the *Kulturkampf* of the Prussian administration with the Catholic Church and dynamic industrialization. Besides the politics of Germanization and Polish reactions as in the activities of the newspaper editor Karol Miarka or the politician Wojciech Korfanty, a large part of the Silesian population remained nationally indifferent.[16] Thus, one can hardly speak of a Silesian regionalism at that time, but rather of a persistence of local culture and regional linguistic varieties. In general, all these Slavic or Polish regionalisms cannot be separated from the general conflict of nationalities in Prussia, which shaped the period from the 1880s until the First World War.

This connection between regional features and a national Polish framework was especially close in the case of Podhale, the mountain region south of Cracow, which until 1918 was part of the Habsburg empire. The folk culture of the *Górale*, including clothes, music and architecture, was regarded as representing forms of authentic Polishness, and thus spread also among the urban elites and became an important element of Polish cultural life around 1900, for example, in Ignacy Paderewski's adaptations of folk music or the architecture of Kazimierz Dolny.

Regionalisms in the Baltics and Poland, 1918–1970

The fundamentally altered political landscape in East Central Europe after 1918 left little place for regional movements for several reasons. First, in the new states of Estonia, Latvia and Lithuania, the former ethnonational movements of Estonians, Latvians and Lithuanians now were transformed into titular nations. Second, all states in the area (except those that were part of Soviet Russia) were interested in linguistically and ethnically homogenizing their state populations, in that respect regional divergences were – particularly in Poland, but to a similar extent also in Lithuania – regarded as negative consequences of imperial rule. Therefore, the main political focus in all states was on national minorities, not on regional movements. In addition, in Estonia, the cultural autonomy of national minorities gave them the possibility to organize on a non-territorial basis. If there were elements of a German *Heimat* movement visible before 1914, as, for instance, in Estonia, it was concealed by the national question and hardly saw any continuation.

New regional aspects, however, can be noticed in border regions. In Estonia, this was the case with the 'Setu', an ethnic kin group of the Estonians largely of Orthodox confession, whose region around the town of Petseri / Pechory was included into the Estonian state with the treaty of Tartu in 1920. Similarly, the significantly larger region of Latgale, which did not belong to the Tsarist Baltic provinces, was added to Latvia. In contradistinction to the Baltic parts of Latvia, Latgale was largely Catholic and partly Orthodox, its ethnic composition was more diverse and a Latvian cultural movement had emerged only after 1900. Against this background, it was regarded by Latvians rather as a remote, undeveloped region. In Lithuania, Memelland / Lithuania Minor received new attention, in particular after it was occupied in 1923. As a result, the regional movement among the Germans in the region was overshadowed by the issue of (German) national identity in conflict with the Lithuanian state.[17] On the other hand, a Small Lithuanian regionalism was promoted by intellectuals as Wilhelm Storost-Vydūnas and Martynas Jankus; however, it remained contested by the politics of homogenization of the Lithuanian state.

In Poland, despite the aforementioned politics of overcoming the consequences of imperial rule, for instance, in infrastructure or the legal system, some regionalist tendencies may be noticed in border regions. The Kashubs now found themselves in the so-called 'corridor' of Poland to the Baltic; in the tensions between Poland and Germany, the Kashubian region received increasing attention in Poland. Against this background, highlighting the Polish framework of Kashubian identity was also supported by Kashubian intellectuals.[18] The most contested and combatted region became Upper Silesia, which was claimed by Germany and Poland after the First World War. Apart from such national claims on the region, there were also arguments of a Silesian autonomy used on both sides. On the one hand, a Silesian movement emerged which claimed Silesia for the Silesians, arguing, however, against a cession of the region to Poland.[19] The Polish state, on the other hand, was interested in strengthening a Polish-Silesian identity and granted autonomy to the region under its control already in 1920, before the border with Germany was drawn. Debates on Silesian regional identity continued after the settlement of the region in 1922; they focused first of all on providing arguments for German or Polish claims on Upper Silesia, and in this connection, the crucial question was whether the Silesian was to be regarded as an independent language or as Polish dialect.[20]

Due to the fact that the Masurian region after the plebiscite of 1920 remained part of the German Reich, it lost relevance for Polish debates on regionalism, whereas a specific German regionalism emerged in East Prussia after 1914.[21] One should, however, point at further regional issues in the eastern regions of interwar Poland (the so-called *kresy*): in the Belorussian regions, the term of *tutejsi* became popular, describing the national indifference of large parts of the population. The situation in Polish-Ukrainian regions in the south-east was different. There, demands of regional autonomy were connected to the Ukrainian national movement. The violent conflict that emerged between the Polish state and the Organization of Ukrainian Nationalists at the end of the 1920s decisively changed Polish politics towards national minorities, and it also shaped Polish politics in the region after 1945. In both cases, the interest of the government was to limit the influence of national minorities that were suspected of separatism.

The observation that regionalisms played only a limited role in the interwar period applies also or even more to the post-1945 era. On the territory of the three Baltic states, which were annexed by the Soviet Union in 1940, all regionalist tendencies disappeared or were banned. There are several reasons for this situation: first, the resettlement of the Baltic Germans, which was organized by Nazi Germany in 1939–1940, removed not only the people but also a major part of the region's traditions. Secondly, remaining regional groups like the Swedes in Estonia or the Poles in the Vilnius region were marginalized. Thirdly, the Soviet immigration of mostly Russian-speaking workers did not lead to regionalist tendencies, but the opposite: to increase political and social control by Moscow. Even if one regards the national song festivals of the Estonians and Latvians as expressions of regional cultures, their impact on preserving national or regional identities remained limited.[22]

The situation in Socialist Poland after the end of the Second World War was not favourable for any kind of regionalism either. The newly 'regained' former Prussian territories were claimed to be 'old Polish lands', whose Polish character had to be restored. In East Prussia and Upper Silesia, where parts of the previous population with German citizenship remained as so-called 'autochthones', they had to declare their Polishness and loyalty towards the new order. Regional distinctions of these areas were – similar to the situation after 1918 – regarded as unwanted relics of foreign rule. Furthermore, those Poles who were expelled or resettled from the Eastern Polish territories that after 1945 belonged to the Soviet Union could not publicly express their connection to their home regions.

In addition, the ethnic cleansing in south-eastern Poland during the 'Action Vistula' in 1947 effectively destroyed the regional societies of Lemkos and Ukrainians, and prevented a new regional formation of the Ukrainian minority in socialist Poland. In Silesia, regional tendencies were partly tolerated, as long as they underlined the Polish option of the Silesian population, whereas a fostering of German language was seen as a threat. The only group spared of homogenization were once again the Kashubs, who could connect to their regionalist traditions after the end of Stalinism. In 1964, they formed the 'Kashubian-Pomeranian Society', which also highlighted the regional aspect in its name. Nevertheless, regionality during socialist Poland remained largely limited to folklore and cultural activities.

New regionalisms in the Baltics and Poland since the 1970s

In the Baltic area, regionality returned as a supranational movement only within the late Soviet Union and received attention by exile communities and more visibly among international scholars. In their discussions on Baltic regionalism, 'Baltic' comprised the three Baltic Soviet republics. However, contrary to what one might expect at first glance, this was not primarily based on presenting the Baltic region as a Soviet *Pribaltika*,[23] but instead focused on their titular nations. From official Soviet perspective, this had a dangerous implication, as these discussions addressed issues of post-war Soviet immigration and memories of the pre-1940 states. There was, however, one more relevant aspect of the approach towards regionalism: until then, Baltic issues outside the Soviet republics had been discussed in national exile communities with a dividing line between the small nations on the one hand and the Baltic Germans (in West Germany) on the other. Now, however, scholars from the different groups met and developed a perspective that was not based on Soviet integration, but on distinct political, social, cultural patterns of the region and not least a consciousness of an individual historical identity.[24] Against critical remarks on the German origin of Baltic regionalism, the debates of those years show attempt to bridge former national divides and to include scholars from the Soviet republics. In the era of glasnost, these attempts found resonance in the Soviet Baltic republics and quickly turned political during the 'Singing Revolution'.[25]

In that context, regionalism was based first on parallel civic protests against ecological devastation, which focused on phosphorite open mining in north-eastern Estonia (called by Estonian activists the 'Phosphorite War') in 1987 and a hydroelectric power plant on the Daugava river near Daugavpils in Latvia in 1986–1987. The protests in the case of Latvia were launched by two writers, among them Dainis Īvāns, who later became a leader of the Latvian Popular Front, with an article in a literary journal. Success came rather unexpectedly, when the plans were stopped in 1987, although they had already been approved in Moscow.[26] In addition, these protests against environmental devastation were not only a criticism of technological projects but were also connected to the romantic idea of protecting the homeland as well as the ethnic nation, because those large Soviet industrial projects implied the immigration of (Russian-speaking) workers from all over the Soviet Union. This connection introduced national images and symbols into the form of protests. The focus on the national homeland also became a core issue of the movements for monument preservation. In Estonia, the focus was on a large number of castles, churches, manor houses and cemeteries, although many of these monuments would not fit into a narrow ethnonationalist reading of the Estonian nation. From its beginnings, the Estonian Heritage Society (Eesti Muinsuskaitse Selts), founded in December 1987, departed from an understanding of itself as a secret dissident organization but strove for official approval in order to act openly, although such activities as publicly displaying the Estonian pre-war flag in April 1988 remained illegal.

The second focus was on memory politics, first with regard to the secret protocol of the Molotov-Ribbentrop pact from 23 August 1939, which was silenced in official Soviet discourse. Commemorating the pact as a first step to the Soviet annexation in 1940 started in 1987 in Riga and Tallinn, and reached Vilnius with a demonstration of 150,000 to 200,000 people in August 1988. The commemoration of the pact's fiftieth anniversary took place as the 'Baltic way', a human chain between the three capitals, which involved between one and two million people out of a population of circa eight million. The statement issued by the organizers claimed a 'peaceful restoration of our statehood' and a strive for 'social security, civil rights, and economic progress to all peoples in the Baltic republics regardless of their nationality'.[27] This event marked the symbolic peak of the common endeavour of the Baltic social movements for political self-determination. On the occasion of the chain, a rock song was recorded addressing the common fate of the 'Baltic sister nations' and calling upon them in their three languages to awake.[28] This Baltic regional cooperation was based on the formation of 'Popular Fronts' among the three nations as informal mass organizations (Rahvarinne in Estonia, Tautas Fronte in Latvia) or simply Movement (Sąjūdis) in Lithuania. They emerged between April and October 1988 and initially stressed the support of perestroika, which was part of the movements' first names in Estonia and Lithuania. All three Popular Fronts served as umbrella organizations, where dissident intellectuals met with reform-oriented communists who tried to distance the republic party branches from the Communist Party of the Soviet Union.

Apart from the joint cooperation, the trajectories within the single republics differed at least slightly, as show the so-called 'calendar demonstrations' remembering the dates of Soviet-time deportations. In Latvia, the commemoration of the deportations of June 1941 was joined by some 5,000 people in 1987 and more than 100,000 one year later. In Estonia, a first demonstration took place on 23 August 1987 in the Hirve Park in Tallinn. Further demonstrations in early 1988 commemorated the 1920 Tartu peace treaty between Estonia and Soviet Russia and the declaration of independence of 1918. In Lithuania, many mass demonstrations took place from the summer of 1988; the demonstration on 23 August 1988 in Vingis Park in Vilnius included 150,000 to 200,000 people.

The Baltic framework of these single national movements became visible not only in similar cultural and social forms, such as rock concerts in addition to the 'calendar' events, but also in the creation of a common cultural narrative through collective singing as a feature of common protest in Juris Podnieks's documentary *Krustceļš/Homeland*. Released in 1990, it is a significant document of the political climate based on the stark contrast between peaceful singing in choirs and gatherings on the one hand and the military power of the Soviet army on the other.

After the last Soviet elections of March 1990, all three Republic Supreme Councils were dominated by the national movements. As a result, all three councils named new governments, which were now led by representatives of the Popular Fronts such as Edgar Savisaar in Estonia, Kazimiera Prunskienė in Lithuania and Ivars Godmanis in Latvia, and quickly issued declarations of independence with the restitution of national symbols. Lithuania was first on 11 March, then followed by Estonia and finally Latvia on 4 May. In Lithuania, the declaration claimed the beginning of full, *de facto* sovereignty and was answered by Moscow with economic sanctions and various activities of the army and special units. After this experience, the following declarations were rather indirect, claiming *de jure* independence and against the background of *de facto* occupation a transition period that should lead then to full independence.

A major distinction in these joint developments was the approach towards citizenship, which was closely connected to the Soviet-period immigration of so-called Russian-speaking persons, amounting to 35 per cent of circa 1.5 million in Estonia in 1989 and around 42 per cent of 2.7 million in Latvia. Whereas the national movements in Estonia and Latvia tried to exclude them from citizenship, in Lithuania a 'zero-option' was applied, which opened the possibility to almost all residents to gain Lithuanian citizenship.

The restoration of national independence following the failed coup in the Soviet Union in August 1991 changed the role of the tripartite Baltic regionalism from a substate phenomenon with in the Soviet Union towards a transnational phenomenon, which materialized on different levels, for instance, in common institutions as the parliamentary Baltic Assembly and a Baltic Council of Ministers, which were formed during the Singing Revolution and mirrored Nordic structures.

If one looks at new forms of substate regionalism, the major question is whether a Russian regionalism in the Baltics may be identified. This issue on the one hand reiterates the situation of the late nineteenth century, as addressed above. On the other hand, it cannot be separated from the issues of Soviet-time immigration and the withholding of citizenship in Estonia and Latvia. Tendencies towards a Russian regionalism or autonomy, as it was postulated for instance in north-eastern Estonia with Narva as its centre until 1993,[29] are understood by the Estonian public as a threat towards sovereignty. This leads to a dominance of the question of loyalty and national identity. In Latvia, the situation is somehow different, as there are signs of Latgalian regionalism, which is based on the Latvian-speaking population. Apart from that, a re-emergence of 'Baltiia' can be detected in Russian publications since the 1990s, which tends to depart from the Soviet claim of hegemony and might be compared to the Baltic German notions of the interwar period putting the region first.

In Lithuania, regionalist tendencies among the Polish population, which lives mainly in the Vilnius region, have largely since 1991 been discussed as endangering Lithuanian statehood, mainly referring to the Polish indifference towards the independence movement after the failed coup in August 1991. Thus, the issue is rather discussed under the heading of national minority rights. Different is the situation in Lithuania Minor, where traditions of a regionalism from the interwar period have been revived since the 1990s, with the decisive difference that the national conflict between Germans and Lithuanians has ceased to exist.

In Poland, the situation fundamentally changed after the end of socialism in 1989.[30] First, the Kashubian regionalism left its folklore niche and developed into a political one, which had a major impact not only on the Gdańsk region but also on liberal Polish politics as well as on regional politics of the European Union in the Baltic Sea area.[31] Secondly, a Silesian regionalism emerged besides the formation of a German minority in Poland, which has its major background in the region of Opole in the western part of Upper Silesia. Silesian regionalism is based on the assertion that Silesian is a Slavic language and not a Polish dialect. The linguist Tomasz Kamusella claims that the Silesians form a distinct ethnic group of 'Szlonzoks'.[32] In 1990, a movement for Silesian autonomy with reference to the interwar autonomy was formed as a political party. Since 1997, several attempts have been made to claim a specific Silesian nationality and to register it as a national minority. They were, however, blocked by Polish courts and the Polish Sejm, and neither did they receive support from European institutions.

The third field of regionalism in Poland is a new one, which finds its background in the multicultural traditions of the former German areas as well as in the Polish-Belorussian-Lithuanian overlap, which was also shaped by strong Jewish traditions. Among the major new actors have been the society Pogranicze (Borderland) in Sejny, which has its main focus on the Polish-Lithuanian borderland, and Borussia in Olsztyn in the territory of former East Prussia. Borussia in particular promoted a new approach towards an 'open regionalism'. Among the leading ideas is to shift previous debates on the *mała ojczyzna* (small homeland) from the private to the public sphere. Furthermore, the new regionalism does neither intend to promote a prettified picture of the East Prussian past nor to follow traditional national front lines nor to promote an alternative collective identity beyond the German or Polish ones. The name 'Borussia' was meant to be provocative in order to stimulate debates about the region's past, which should be stripped of its nationalist narratives and redefined with reference to its multicultural traditions. Open regionalism thus intends to overcome and to promote the acceptance of multiple and changing identities.[33] Borussia focuses on culture, literature and history, including heritage preservation and reconciliation through transnational youth projects. Besides, Borussia supports contacts between the national groups that lived or live in the region of former East Prussia: Germans, Lithuanians, Poles and Russians. With its focus on culture and publications, Borussia revives cultural regionalist traditions from the period before 1914, whereas a political regionalism – different from the Kashubian region or Upper Silesia – plays no role here.

Conclusion

Regionalisms in the area presented here oscillate between substate and supranational dimensions. This finding is not only based on the many changes of the political borders during the twentieth century but also on the diverging notions and trajectories of these regionalisms. Summarizing the features and developments on the Baltic littoral between Reval/Tallinn and Danzig/Gdańsk as well as in southern Poland, five aspects shall be highlighted: First, regionalisms discussed here were shaped by notions of distinct cultural landscapes, which show connections or parallels to discourses on *Heimat* in Germany, or by specific ethnic/linguistic areas. The latter aspect, secondly, put regionalisms either in contrast to the national movements of the non-German groups, or led to a self-understanding of being part of a larger national community. Thirdly, between 1918 and 1989, the development of regionalisms was – with only few exceptions – regarded with suspicion, as a source of separatism with a potential threat to state integrity. Fourthly, this situation changed fundamentally since the 1980s, when a new regionalism developed in the Baltic Soviet republics, which comprised the three nations under Soviet rule. References to the preservation of the cultural landscape as well as to the ethnic homeland had a major impact on the restoration of the independence of the Baltic states. In Poland, various regionalisms emerged after 1989 with political roots in dissent traditions during the socialist period. In that respect, uncovering the multilayered cultural traditions and building a civil society went hand in hand. The notion of 'open regionalism', which is strong in border regions of Poland and on those territories that were part of Germany before 1945, reveals various connections to the regionalisms and *Heimat* discourses before 1914, but combines it with new transnational perspectives. Besides the cultural dimensions visible here, fifthly, political dimensions have changed over recent years too, as particularly in Poland the administrative division into sixteen voivodeships implemented in 1999, and the establishment of border-transgressing Euroregions have intensified debates about regionalisms.

Notes

1. Pertti Joenniemi, ed., *Neo-nationalism or Regionality: The Restructuring of Political Space around the Baltic Rim* (Stockholm: NordREFO, 1997); Pertti Joenniemi and Ole Waever, 'Regionalization around the Baltic Rim: Notions on Baltic Sea Politics', in *Co-operation in the Baltic Sea Area: The Second Parliamentary Conference on Co-operation in the Baltic Sea Area*, ed. The Nordic Council (Nord, Stockholm: The Nordic Council, 1992), 118–56; and Hilde Dominique Engelen, 'Die Konstruktion der Ostseeregion: Akteure, mentale Landkarten, und ihr Einfluss auf die Entstehung einer Region', in *Die Ordnung des Raums. Mentale Karten in der Ostseeregion*, ed. Norbert Götz, Jörg Hackmann and Jan Hecker-Stampehl (The Baltic Sea Region: Nordic Dimensions – European Perspectives, 6) (Berlin: Berliner Wissenschaftsverlag, 2006), 61–90.
2. Anssi Paasi, *Territories, Boundaries, and Consciousness: The Changing Geographies of the Finnish-Russian Border* (Chichester: Wiley, 1996); see also Iver B. Neumann, 'A Region-Building Approach to Northern Europe', *Review of International Studies* 20, no. 1 (1994): 53–74.

3. Jörg Hackmann, 'Wo liegt das "Baltikum"? Entstehung, Verwendung und Semantik des Begriffs seit dem 19. Jahrhundert', in *Das Baltikum als Konstrukt (18.-19. Jahrhundert): Von einer Kolonialwahrnehmung zu einem nationalen Diskurs*, ed. Anne Sommerlat-Michas (Würzburg: Königshausen & Neumann, 2015), 23–43; and Pärtel Piirimäe, 'The Baltic', in *European Regions and Boundaries: A Conceptual History*, ed. Diana Mishkova and Balázs Trencsényi (New York; Oxford: Berghahn, 2017), 57–78.

4. Jurii Samarin, *Okrainy Rossii. Seriia 1: Russkoe Baltiiskoe pomor'e* (Prague 1868); and Edward C. Thaden, 'Samarin's "Okrainy Rossii" and Official Policy in the Baltic Provinces', *Russian Review* 33 (1974): 405–15.

5. Carl Schirren, *Livländische Antwort an Herrn Juri Samarin* (Leipzig: Duncker & Humblot, 1869), 115.

6. Alfred Geiser, *Die russische Revolution und das baltische Deutschtum* (Munich: Lehmann, 1906); for details, see Jörg Hackmann, 'Nationalisierung als Strategie gesellschaftlichen Obenbleibens? Die Deutschen Vereine in den Ostseeprovinzen Russlands', in *Schutzvereine in Ostmitteleuropa. Vereinswesen, Sprachenkonflikte und Dynamiken nationaler Mobilisierung 1860–1939*, ed. Peter Haslinger (Marburg: Herder-Institut, 2009), 53–78.

7. See, e.g., the journal *Heimatstimmen. Ein baltisches Jahrbuch* and on the Baltic German *Heimat* discourse, Jaan Undusk, 'Umweltphilosophie und Naturdenken im baltischen Raum. Zur Einführung und Irritation', in *Umweltphilosophie und Landschaftsdenken im baltischen Kulturraum*, ed. Liina Lukas et al. (Tallinn: Underi ja Tuglase Kirjanduskeskus, 2011), 15–21.

8. Karsten Brüggemann, 'Ein Russe in Riga: Evgraf Vasil'evič Češichin (1824–1888) als Journalist und Historiker im Dienst des Imperiums', in *Geisteswissenschaften und Publizistik im Baltikum des 19. und frühen 20. Jahrhunderts. Baltische Biographische Forschungen*, ed. Norbert Angermann, Wilhelm Lenz and Konrad Maier (Berlin: LIT, 2011), 157–92.

9. Jörg Hackmann, 'Sängerfeste in den russländischen Ostseeprovinzen vor 1914: Symbolische Ordnungen zwischen kulturellen Verflechtungen und Abgrenzungen', *Forschungen zur baltischen Geschichte* 12 (2017): 131–61; and Jörg Hackmann, *Geselligkeit in Nordosteuropa* (Wiesbaden: Harrasowitz, 2019, forthcoming).

10. Ea Jansen, *Eestlane muutuvas ajas. Seisusühiskonnast kodanikuühiskonda* (Tartu: Eesti Ajalooarhiiv, 2007), see the summary, 463–506; Jörg Hackmann, 'Narrating the Building of a Small Nation: Divergence and Convergence in the Historiography of the Estonian "National Awakening", 1868–2005', in *Nationalizing the Past: Historians as Nation Builders in Modern Europe*, ed. Stefan Berger and Chris Lorenz (Basingstoke: Palgrave Macmillan, 2010), 170–91.

11. Darius Staliūnas, *Making Russians: Meaning and Practice of Russification in Lithuania and Belarus after 1863* (Amsterdam: Rodopi, 2007).

12. Robert Traba, ed., *Selbstbewusstsein und Modernisierung. Soziokultureller Wandel in Preussisch-Litauen vor und nach dem Ersten Weltkrieg (Einzelveröffentlichungen des Deutschen Historischen Instituts Warschau, 3)* (Osnabrück: Fibre, 2000).

13. Ferdinand Neureiter, *Geschichte der kaschubischen Literatur. Versuch einer zusammenfassenden Darstellung* (Munich: Sagner, 1991); and Cezary Obracht-Prondzyński and Tomasz Wicherkiewicz, eds, *The Kashubs: Past and Present* (Bern; New York: Peter Lang, 2011).

14. Roman Wapinski, *Polska i małe ojczyzny Polaków: z dziejów kształtowania się świadomości narodowej w XIX i XX wieku do wybuchu II wojny światowej* (Wrocław: Ossolineum, 1994), 120–23.

15. Andreas Kossert, *Masuren: Ostpreußens vergessener Süden* (Berlin: Siedler, 2001); and Robert Traba, *Niemcy–Warmiacy–Polacy 1871–1914. Z dziejów niemieckiego ruchu katolickiego i*

stosunków polsko-niemieckich w Prusach (Olsztyn: Osrodek Badan Naukowych, Wspólnota Kulturowa 'Borussia', 1994).

16. James E. Bjork, *Neither German nor Pole. Catholicism and National Indifference in a Central European Borderland* (Ann Arbor: University of Michigan Press, 2008); and Kai Struve and Philipp Ther, eds, *Die Grenzen der Nationen: Identitätenwandel in Oberschlesien in der Neuzeit* (Marburg: Herder-Institut, 2002).

17. Vasilijus Safronovas, *Kampf um Identität. Die ideologische Auseinandersetzung in Memel/Klaipėda im 20. Jahrhundert* (Wiesbaden: Harrassowitz, 2015).

18. Józef Borzyszkowski, *Aleksander Majkowski 1876-1938. Biografia historyczna* (Gdańsk, Wejherowo: Instytut Kaszubski w Gdansku, 2002).

19. Tomasz Kamusella, 'Language and the Construction of Identity in Upper Silesia during the Long Nineteenth Century', in *Die Grenzen der Nationen*, ed. Struve and Ther, 45-70 (63-65); see also Kai Struve, ed., *Oberschlesien nach dem Ersten Weltkrieg: Studien zu einem nationalen Konflikt und seiner Erinnerung* (Marburg: Herder-Institut, 2003).

20. Tomasz Kamusella, 'Silesian in the Nineteenth and Twentieth Centuries: A Language Caught in the Net of Conflicting Nationalisms, Politics, and Identities', *Nationalities Papers* 39, no. 5 (2011): 769-89.

21. Robert Traba, *Ostpreußen-die Konstruktion einer deutschen Provinz. Eine Studie zur regionalen und nationalen Identität 1914-1933* (Osnabrück: Fibre, 2010).

22. Guntis Šmidchens, *The Power of Song: Nonviolent National Culture in the Baltic Singing Revolution* (Seattle; London: University of Washington Press, 2014), 135-59.

23. Dietrich André Loeber, 'Towards Baltic Regional Identity', *Journal of Baltic Studies* 18, no. 2 (1987): 115-24 (116-19).

24. Dietrich A. Loeber, V. Stanley Vardys and Laurence P. A. Kitching, eds, *Regional Identity under Soviet Rule. The Case of the Baltic States* (Hackettstown, NJ: AABS, 1990); and Gert von Pistohlkors, 'Regionalismus als Konzept der baltischen Geschichte. Überlegungen zum Stand der Geschichtsschreibung über die Baltischen Provinzen Rußlands im 19. Jahrhundert', *Journal of Baltic Studies* 15 (1984): 98-118.

25. Karsten Brüggemann, '"One Day We Will Win Anyway": The Singing Revolution in the Soviet Baltic Republics', in *The Revolutions of 1989. A Handbook*, ed. Wolfgang Mueller, Michael Gehler and Arnold Suppan (Wien: Österreichische Akademie der Wissenschaften, 2015), 221-46; and Anatol Lieven, *The Baltic Revolution: Estonia, Latvia, Lithuania and the Path to Independence* (New Haven, CT: Yale University Press, 1994).

26. Robert Welling Smurr, *Perceptions of Nature, Expressions of Nation: An Environmental History of Estonia* (Seattle: University of Washington, 2002); and Nīls R. Muižnieks, 'The Daugavpils Hydro Station and "Glasnost" in Latvia', *Journal of Baltic Studies* 18, no. 1 (1987), 63-70. See also the chapter by Meyer.

27. Quoted following Rein Taagepera, 'Estonia's Road to Independence', *Problems of Communism* 38, no. 6 (1989): 11-26 (21).

28. Šmidchens, *The Power of Song*, 249-50.

29. David J. Smith, 'Narva Region within the Estonian Republic: From Autonomism to Accommodation?', *Regional & Federal Studies* 12, no. 2 (2002): 89-110.

30. See as an overview: Robert Traba, 'Regionalismus in Polen: Die Quellen des Phänomens und sein neues Gesicht nach 1989', in *Regionale Bewegungen und Regionalismen in europäischen Zwischenräumen seit der Mitte des 19. Jahrhunderts*, ed. Philipp Ther and Holm Sundhaussen (Marburg: Herder-Institut, 2003), 275-83.

31. Cezary Obracht-Prondzyński, 'Dilemmas of Modern Kashubian Identity and Culture', in *The Kashubs: Past and Present*, 179–226.
32. Kamusella, 'Language and the Construction of Identity', 63–69.
33. Traba, 'Regionalismus in Polen', 279–81; and Robert Traba, *Kraina tysiąca granic: szkice o historii i pamięci* (Olsztyn: Borussia, 2003b), 223–30.

Further reading

Davies, Norman, *God's Playground: a History of Poland*, 2 vols (Oxford: Clarendon Press, 1989).
Götz, Norbert, Jörg Hackmann, Jan Hecker-Stampehl, eds, *Die Ordnung des Raums. Mentale Karten in der Ostseeregion* (Berlin: Berliner Wissenschaftsverlag, 2006).
Joenniemi, Pertti, ed., *Neo-nationalism or Regionality: The Restructuring of Political Space around the Baltic Rim* (Stockholm: NordREFO, 1997).
Kasekamp, Andres, *A History of the Baltic States* (Basingstoke; New York: Palgrave Macmillan, 2010).
Kirby, David, *The Baltic World 1772–1993: Europe's Northern Periphery in an Age of Change* (London: Longman, 1995).
Loeber, Dietrich A., V. Stanley Vardys and Laurence P. A. Kitching, eds, *Regional Identity under Soviet Rule: The Case of the Baltic States* (Hackettstown, NJ: AABS, 1990).
Plakans, Andrejs, *A Concise History of the Baltic States* (Cambridge, New York: Cambridge University Press, 2011).
Porter-Szűcs, Brian, *Poland in the Modern World: Beyond Martyrdom* (Chichester: Wiley-Blackwell, 2014).
Safronovas, Vasilijus, *Kampf um Identität: Die ideologische Auseinandersetzung in Memel/Klaipėda im 20. Jahrhundert* (Wiesbaden: Harrassowitz, 2015).
Traba, Robert, 'Regionalismus in Polen: Die Quellen des Phänomens und sein neues Gesicht nach 1989', in *Regionale Bewegungen und Regionalismen in europäischen Zwischenräumen seit der Mitte des 19. Jahrhunderts*, ed. Philipp Ther and Holm Sundhaussen (Marburg: Herder-Institut, 2003), 275–83.

CHAPTER 17
REGIONALISM IN SOUTH-EASTERN EUROPE
Tchavdar Marinov

South-eastern Europe/Balkans and regionalism: Introductory remarks

Every discussion of the problems of political and cultural regionalism in South-eastern Europe inevitably faces the problem of the very definition of this area as well as of its counterpart, the Balkans. Since the nineteenth century, various definitions of 'Turkey of Europe', Balkans, South-eastern Europe, Südost and so on have delimited different macro-regional entities. Mappings proposed by Western/Central European, Russian/Soviet or 'local' scholars have been putting together territories that remained Ottoman well until different moments in the nineteenth and the early twentieth centuries with others that never belonged to the Ottoman Empire, or ceased to belong long ago.[1] Here, we are inevitably simplifying the picture with our preference for the concept of South-eastern Europe. While the Balkans are traditionally seen as the area of the Ottoman legacy in Europe, South-eastern Europe has the advantage to be a more neutral concept covering a larger area, where Ottoman legacy gives way to other cultural imprints: Habsburg, Venetian and so on.

Against this background, the choice of cases in the present chapter is certainly debatable. Moreover, it must be taken into account that political and cultural regionalism in this part of Europe has been rarely discussed.[2] The chapter will present an overview of the construction and evolution of regionalism since the late nineteenth century, primarily within the South-east European Slav-speaking countries minus Slovenia – that is, in Bulgaria, the Republic of Macedonia, Serbia, Montenegro, Bosnia-Herzegovina and Croatia. The cases of Greece (plus Cyprus) and of Romania (plus Moldova) are taken into account, although to a lesser extent, for the sake of comparison. Slovenia is not examined here. This is not only because of its rather Central European and Mediterranean character (the same pattern of belonging also being claimed by Croatia). Although the country has certain regional variety in being composed of former Austrian crownlands or parts thereof (Carniola, Carinthia, Styria, Coastland, which is part of Istria, as well as the formerly Hungarian Prekmurje), these never developed important grass-roots regionalisms. Nevertheless, forms of cultural (and, in particular, of literary) regionalism certainly exist in the Slovenian context as well.[3] Similarly, Albania is not included in the present overview despite its regional variety – in reality, historically richer than the much-discussed division into Tosk-speaking South and Gheg North. No regionalist movements have marked the history of modern Albania and, as a whole, the ethnic Albanian movements in other Balkan countries and the present state-building of Kosovo do not question the attributes of Albanian identity in favour of another, local/

regional belonging. Again, exceptions to the rule do exist, in particular in the case of Kosovo, where a weekly newspaper written in the local Gheg idiom challenged a salient feature of modern Albanian identity: the single standard language that is based on the southern Tosk dialect. The editors of the newspaper dedicated special attention to the particularities of a Kosovar identity within the Albanian ethnonational context.[4] Turkey is also excluded from the chapter. Its case is certainly complex given the huge regional socio-economic and cultural discrepancies and even ethnic differences between the west/northwest and the southeast of the country or between the Thracian, Aegean and Mediterranean territories and the Anatolian interior. Yet, despite the existence of diverse political and other identities and the importance of national and confessional movements, it is unlikely that any of these could be included in the rubric of regionalism. As a whole, publications on 'regionalism in Turkey' focus on practices of administrative decentralization, economic issues and on the political role of Turkey in macro-regional entities (the Balkans and the Middle East, the Turkic-speaking world, etc.).[5]

The second main problem that the discussion of regionalism in South-eastern Europe necessarily faces is related, of course, to its very definition.[6] Here, we are concerned primarily with substate identities and projects: these are regional insofar as they are located somewhere between the micro/local/municipal level and the nation-state level – sometimes also in parts of two or more nation states. Concerning their relationship to the latter, regionalisms could be also diverse. They may be inclusive and supplementary to the nation state and to the dominant national identity: in South-eastern Europe as well, many forms of regional imagination, with their narratives and symbols, do not challenge mainstream nationalism and even seek to consolidate it through an emphasis on its regional variety and 'richness'. Regional identities could thus be rather folkloristic, related to the peculiarities of a certain dialect, musical traditions or to a pretended local mental character, or even to a specific cuisine. In many cases, it may be far-fetched to speak of regionalism insofar as this concept entails a certain ideology. In South-eastern Europe as elsewhere, there are strongly marked local identities that never developed into regionalist cultural or political claims. However, regionalisms could be also exclusive and competing with national projects. Thus, they could be *stricto sensu* territorial political projects with certain cultural contents, legitimizing narratives and symbols. As such, they may not differ much from forms of nationalism and their definition as regionalisms could be correct only from the point of view of the nation state.

Conversely, the characterization of these agendas as regional may be perceived as offensive by their supporters. From this point of view, it is utterly difficult to establish a clear distinction between exclusive regionalisms and movements representing, within a certain substate region, the national(ist) cause of another nation state: for instance, Albanian nationalism in the former Serbian province of Kosovo, Serbian nationalism in the Republika Srpska in Bosnia or Greek nationalism in Albania's Northern Epirus. Here, our choice is to exclude such cases from the present overview insofar as they do not display any important particularities that might distinguish these from the cross-border 'mainstream' nationalism they represent. This choice might seem to be too restrictive: in the case of Western Europe, the notion of regionalism is often used for all kinds of substate identity projects and movements. Applied to the context of South-eastern Europe or the Balkans however, such an approach would render the discussion exceedingly long. Traditionally, the area has had the negative reputation of being a hotbed of nationalist movements and conflicts, expressed in clichés such as the 'powder keg of Europe'.[7] Without falling into the essentialism of such representations, we must admit that the great number of territorial controversies and claims in South-eastern Europe imposes necessarily a narrower reading of the concept of regionalism.

It should be emphasized that the relationship between supplementary ('cultural' or 'folkloristic') regionalisms, exclusive and politicized regional projects and fully emancipated nationalisms is complex, given that, historically, there were many cases of evolution and transition from one category to another. In some cases, forms of local patriotism ultimately evolved into distinct nationalism, although this was not necessarily a linear process. This is the reason for the inclusion of cases such as Macedonian or Montenegrin identity in the present overview – a choice that may be surprising at first. Indeed, Montenegro had its own statehood in the moment of the creation of modern Serbia – it was not and currently is not a substate project. However, our choice would look less odd if one more closely examines the history of these and similar identities – in particular, their previous entanglement with specific national identities and the sinuous way of their differentiation from the latter. Of course, this does not mean that national identities and ideologies of Macedonians, Montenegrins or Bosniaks are nowadays less legitimate than those of their neighbours. From a mainstream Bulgarian point of view, Macedonian nationalism is still reduced to a regional 'Macedonianism', but in the mid-nineteenth century the promoters of the incipient Bulgarian nationalism were themselves rejected by the Greek elites as 'Bulgarianists'.[8] A recent scholarly work on the construction of Albanian nationhood in the late nineteenth and the beginning of the twentieth century used in a perfectly legitimate way the term 'Albanianists' to denote the supporters of various inclusive or exclusive cultural and/or political forms of Albanian identity in that period.[9]

Taking into consideration the complexity of South-east European identities, in this contribution I attempt to tackle the phenomenon of regionalism in its various articulations vis-à-vis nationalism. Firstly, south Slavic national contexts marked by strong substate regionalist movements are presented. They are followed by cases of Slavic identities that, a century ago, would have been largely perceived as regional traditions and movements within a larger national context but that evolved into separate national identities. Finally, the specific cases of regionalism in the Romanian and Greek contexts will be presented.

Croatia: Dalmatian and Istrian regionalisms

Unlike most other cases in South-eastern Europe, Croatia has a long tradition of regionalist political thought and movements. Nowadays, its four main parts – Croatia Proper, Slavonia, Dalmatia and Istria – as well as some smaller areas (such as Međimurje and Baranja) retain a strong sense of regional identity based on a distinct historical development. While Croatia Proper (centred on the capital city of Zagreb) and Slavonia have been traditionally under Habsburg and Hungarian domination, the coastal territories of Dalmatia and Istria have a marked Venetian legacy. Although, in the nineteenth century, after a brief French domination, the two Adriatic regions were also annexed to the Habsburg Empire, they became part of Cisleithania – unlike Croatia and Slavonia. The latter were trying to promote their own identity against campaigns of Magyarization (and of Germanization) and a Croatian national 'Revival' advanced well on their territories. At the same time, in its different forms (initially as 'Illyrianism', followed by Yugoslavism and rivalling ethnocentric projects),[10] Croatian nationalism lagged behind in Dalmatia and Istria where it was opposed by the local Italian-speaking élites. It was also to a large extent impeded by the existence of a specific 'Dalmatianism'. Until the 1880s, Dalmatianism was the prevalent political ideology in the Adriatic region. It was articulated by a number of local intellectuals, journalists and politicians such as Niccolò Tommaseo and Stipan Ivičević. As a whole, they were educated and socialized in the Italian language and culture but also endorsed the Slavic majority and cultural tradition in Dalmatia. In their view, Dalmatia had a special historical mission of mediation between the Italian West and the Slavic East that they formulated in various ways: from enlightening the Slavic population through the Italian culture to the transformation of Dalmatia into the centre of a pan-Slavic cultural revival.[11] Politically, Dalmatianism opposed the unification of Dalmatia with Croatia-Slavonia that was otherwise the constant goal of Croatian nationalists; instead, it advocated the particular interests of Dalmatian Italians and Slavs and claimed even the particularity of a '(Slavo-)Dalmatian nation'. Nevertheless, the political agenda of Dalmatianism was progressively undermined by the Croatian national movement and, at the beginning of the twentieth century, the Autonomist Party, which represented Dalmatianist ideology, gradually lost support and came to be dominated by Italian irredentists. Italian nationalism remained strong in Istria and in the Dalmatian city of Zadar, while a regionalist movement existed also in the city of Fiume (Rijeka), belonging to Hungary. A specific case was the city of Dubrovnik. Annexed to Dalmatia by the Habsburgs, it had its own identity based on a separate tradition of statehood (the Ragusan Republic). Croatian nationalism had to face not only this local identity there but also the fact that part of the citizens had embraced Serbian-Catholic nationhood.[12]

Despite the plethora of regional and national identities, after the First World War, Dalmatia lost its autonomy as most of it became part of the first Yugoslavian state and in the wake of and during the Second World War it was part of Croatia. Following the war, within the second, socialist and federative Yugoslavian state, nearly the whole of Dalmatia and – for the first time – most of Istria as well as Rijeka (both hitherto Italian) became part of Croatia, after the expulsion of almost the entire local Italian population. The Croatian national homogenization process notwithstanding, Dalmatian and Istrian regionalisms resurfaced in a political form in the beginning of the 1990s, with the breakup of Yugoslavia and the proclamation of Croatia's independence (Figure 17.1).

Both movements had to face the unfavourable conditions of the war in Croatia and Bosnia as well as the nationalist rule of President Franjo Tuđman. This was the period when the Serbs in Croatia carved out part of the country (including part of Dalmatia) as the so-called Republic of Serbian Krajina – presumably a continuation of a long tradition of Serbian autonomy within the Habsburg Military Frontier. Against this background, accusations of undermining national unity were levelled against regionalist parties and also led to the banning of some of them.

Dalmatian regionalism was represented by parties such as Dalmatian Action that aimed to (re-)establish the region's autonomy within the borders of the historic crown land.[13] Yet, despite its notable historical precedent, the movement was largely unsuccessful and not only because it was explicitly opposed by the government. The party's programme oscillated between various definitions of Dalmatian identity: supranational (advocating the solidarity of all ethnonational communities within the region) and quasi-national (seeing Dalmatians as a particular community with unclear articulation regarding Croatian nationhood). However, it failed to represent the interests of most of the Dalmatians; moreover, the pro-Italian aspects of its interpretation of history only provoked a nationalist counter-reaction. As a result, there is currently no important political mobilization for the autonomy of Dalmatia.

By contrast, Istrian regionalism, chiefly represented by the Istrian Democratic Assembly, has been far more successful – to a large extent because it embraced the rhetoric of other European pro-European Union regionalisms.[14] Its programme calls for the protection of Istria's economic interests and multicultural character. Similarly, the party promotes a historical narrative idealizing a tradition of multi-ethnic tolerance and coexistence (*convivenza*) in Istria (see figure 17.1). Since 1992, it has consistently won a majority of the Istrian vote in local and state elections and has even participated in national governmental coalitions twice. As a result, in 2003, the party managed to push through a special Statute of the Istria County, which officialized bilingualism (Croatian-Italian) in the entire county. Thus, Istria, which, unlike Dalmatia, constitutes one single county in the current administrative division of Croatia, obtained a quasi-autonomous status, especially in the field of language and education.

Serbia and Vojvodinian regionalism

Established in the early nineteenth century, modern Serbia initially remained relatively homogenous. Indeed, there were minor regional cultural and dialectal differences: particularly those of the south-eastern area around the town of Niš (which joined Serbia in 1878) were emphasized by the turn of the twentieth century in works by the writers Stevan Sremac and Borisav Stanković. After the Balkan Wars (1912–1913) and the First World War, Serbia annexed more territory and ultimately became the centre of the Kingdom of Yugoslavia, which soon turned into a hotbed of diverse regionalist and nationalist movements. Through the interwar period, the situation was especially problematic in 'Old Serbia' or 'Southern Serbia' – a top-down imposed regional designation of Macedonia, Kosovo and the *sanjak* (a former Ottoman administrative unit) of Novi Pazar. These were territories where Serbs actually were a minority.

Figure 17.1 *Campaign poster of the Istrian Democratic Assembly from 2016. The message in Croatian says, 'Istria is economically the most developed region in Croatia. Istria is strong. Let's fight to make her stronger! #decentralization'. Note also the slogan in Italian to the right. Source:* http://www.ids-ddi.com/site_media/media/ISTRA-JE-JAKA-GOSPODARSTVO-plakat.jpg *(last access on 18 October 2017).*

The second, socialist Yugoslavian state tried to offer new solutions to the existing national questions but again only to those of Slavic nations. Yet, in recompense, Serbia was the only constitutive republic to include autonomous regions with important non-Slavic populations: Kosovo (and Metohija) and Vojvodina. In the post-Yugoslav period, the existing national and regional identities in these two regions evolved politically in two characteristic ways. In Kosovo, which declared its independence in 2008, Serbia faced a secessionist movement led by representatives of the local Albanian majority. The case of the northern region of Vojvodina is significantly different.

Traditionally a multi-ethnic area with a Serbian plurality/majority but including significant numbers of Hungarians, Germans (until the Second World War), Croats, Slovaks, Romanians and other populations, Vojvodina had a short-lived autonomous status within the Habsburg Empire. However, it should be emphasized that the present-day region does not match the territory of the officially recognized 'Voivodeship of Serbia and Banat of Temeschwar' (1848–1860). The latter covered also the present Romanian part of the region of Banat while it excluded the southern periphery of Vojvodina today, which belonged to the Habsburg Military Frontier. Indeed, Vojvodina is largely a twentieth-century invention as the present region covers three historical provinces or parts thereof (Syrmia, Bačka and Banat). Vojvodina obtained its definitive mapping and own administrative identity only after the Second World War, within socialist Yugoslavia.

The 1974 Yugoslav Constitution enhanced its self-rule (as well as the one of Kosovo) and, as a result, its autonomous powers became nearly equal to those of the Yugoslav federative republics. Although a certain Vojvodinian regionalism had existed already during the interwar period, it became a popular self-identification and political force only after the breakup of Yugoslavia. This happened to a large extent as a reaction to the authoritarian regime of the Serbian President Slobodan Milošević who, in the 1990s, almost completely suppressed the autonomy of the region. Since 2000, Vojvodina regained some of its autonomous powers but not entirely those from the socialist period.

The resulting regionalist movement enjoys support across different ethnic communities, including Serbs – hence its main characteristics: it is not an ethnic-based regionalism and it does not aspire to territorial secession from Serbia.[15] A number of political parties, among which the most important one is the League of Social Democrats of Vojvodina led by Nenad Čanak, advocate greater autonomy for the region. For a certain period, even the creation of a Republic of Vojvodina within a federalized Serbia was proclaimed as a political goal – a slogan that was never abandoned by some of Vojvodina's regionalists.

The result of these battles is the 2008 Statute of the Autonomous Province of Vojvodina, which is the region's most authoritative legal document. It refers to the equality of all local ethnic communities and the use of six official languages. Although no particular historiography of Vojvodina emerged, historical narratives and symbols legitimizing regionalism, including (un)official flags, are common. In general, these emphasize the multiethnic character of Vojvodina, the precedents of autonomy under the Habsburgs and the Central European cultural pattern of the region that presumably distinguishes it from the 'Ottoman' Serbia proper. At the same time, Vojvodina is often exalted as the cradle of the Serbian Enlightenment and national movement in the eighteenth to nineteenth centuries – hence the historical relations to Serbia are by no means rejected. Nevertheless, it is certainly difficult to foresee the future development of Vojvodinian regionalism. In October 2017, the League of Social Democrats of Vojvodina expressed its support for the Catalan independence referendum; Catalan flags and graffiti reading 'Vojvodina=Catalonia' appeared in the city of Novi Sad, the region's capital.

From local patriotism to nationalism: Montenegro and Bosnia-Herzegovina

While Vojvodinian regionalism is a rather recent phenomenon, lacking a proper tradition of statehood and is (still) not exclusive vis-à-vis Serbian nationhood, the latter has maintained a longer and more ambiguous relationship to another identity: the Montenegrin. In the nineteenth century, Montenegro had a particular cultural and political character based on its tradition of self-rule, clan structure and statehood. All this notwithstanding, its rulers and political figures, such as the famous poet and Prince-Bishop Petar II Petrović Njegoš, imagined Montenegro as a Serbian land and even as a possible centre of the unification of all Serbs. Despite all forms of local patriotism, 'Serbdom' and 'Montenegritude' coexisted in various political orientations and projects that evolved within Montenegro until the First World War.[16]

In the aftermath of war, Montenegrin particularism arose as a result of the deposition of the Montenegrin King Nikola and the absorption of the country into the new Kingdom of Serbs, Croats and Slovenes/Yugoslavia dominated by the Serbian dynasty.

Two political camps crystallized: the Whites, proponents of the unilateral unification with Serbia, and the Greens, who insisted on a 'fair' solution on conditions of equality that would preserve Montenegro's historical 'dignity'. While during the first half of the 1920s, Montenegro was in a state of a civil war between adherents of the two camps, even the Greens did not necessarily reject the Serbian identity of Montenegrins. Progressively, Montenegrin particularism evolved into more moderate demands of regional autonomy and federalization of Yugoslavia. At the same time, the Yugoslav communists espoused the most radical solution, seeing Montenegrins as a separate Slavic nationality.

After the Second World War, socialist Yugoslavia favoured to a certain extent the emancipation of this nationality: Montenegro became a republic and the Montenegrins were officially considered as one of Yugoslavia's six constituent nations. Since the 1990s, especially after the proclamation of the country's independence in 2006, Montenegro's authorities espoused Montenegrin nationalism. The Constitution of 2007 proclaimed the Montenegrin language as official; while there were some attempts to differentiate it from Serbian, according to the last census (as of 2017), the speakers of Serbian as native tongue remain more numerous. A considerable part of the population of Montenegro also continues to declare its national identity as Serbian.[17]

The case of Bosnia and Herzegovina demonstrates in another way the polyvalent relationship between regionalism and nationhood. In the early modern period, Bosnia retained a considerable sense of particular Bosnian identity, which was widespread among all local confessional communities: Catholics, Orthodox Christians and Muslims. By contrast, Herzegovina, the southern region with which Bosnia has traditionally been associated, never developed politically important forms of particularism. To a large extent, Bosnian and Herzegovinian identities were shaped by the Ottoman administrative division which, in this particular case, tended to perpetuate traditions of pre-Ottoman statehood: Bosnia traditionally formed a separate grand administrative unit (*eyalet/vilayet*) within the Empire. During the nineteenth century, the Bosnian(-Herzegovinian) sense of belonging was challenged by the gradual adoption of Serbian nationalism by the local Orthodox Christians and of Croatian nationalism by the Catholics. As a result, for the two communities, the names 'Bosnian' (also in its form *Bošnjak* = *Bosniak*) and 'Herzegovinian' were transformed into regional appellations of Serbian or the Croatian nationhood.[18]

Different was the case for the local Muslims who were progressively compelled to choose among different identity options, especially after Bosnia-Herzegovina was occupied by Austria-Hungary in 1878. The Bosniak identity of local Muslim intellectuals and political leaders such as Savfet-beg Bašagić was particularly fostered by the new regime: the Austrian-Hungarian administration endorsed the ideology of 'Bosniakhood' (*Bošnjaštvo*) as a way of consolidating the different confessional communities and to keep them away from irredentist agendas. Opposed by the Serbs and the Croats, Bosniak particularism lost official support after the First World War, when the area became part of Yugoslavia; during the Second World War, the region was annexed by the fascist Independent State of Croatia.

Bosnia-Herzegovina again became a distinct entity after the war: it formed one of the six constituent republics in socialist Yugoslavia, although the Bosnian Muslims were initially not categorized as a separate Slavic nation (*narod*) within the socialist federation. In the 1960s, the national equality of Bosnian Muslims started to be discussed by the communist party and state authorities and, as a result, in 1971, they were recognized as a constituent Muslim nation of Yugoslavia.[19] Nevertheless, for representatives of the Bosnian Muslim leadership and intelligentsia, this remained a compromise as local Muslims gradually adopted the identity of Bosniaks as national. It was only after the break-up of Yugoslavia and the proclamation of the country's independence that Bosniak identity finally replaced the 'Muslim nationhood'. Yet, this passage was made possible by the fact that Bosnia-Herzegovina was largely perceived within the Muslim community as homeland of Muslims and the two identities had become interchangeable. In addition, since the 1990s, the version of the former Serbo-Croatian language spoken in Bosnia has been normalized as a separate Bosnian language.

Bosniak identity is therefore an example of how an initially regional identity shared by different cultural communities was ultimately appropriated by one of them – by the one which was not able to identify with already existing nationalisms – and later on serving for the construction of a particular nationhood. Moreover, the adoption of a Bosniak identity did not only affect the Muslim population of Bosnia-Herzegovina but also other Slavic Muslim communities within former Yugoslavia. This is particularly the case of the Muslims in the adjacent region of Sandžak, the former Ottoman *sanjak* of Novi Pazar, divided between Serbia and Montenegro. In the 1990s, regional autonomy was advocated by political actors such as the Party of Democratic Action and the Sandžak Democratic Party.[20] Yet, it failed to mobilize greater support outside the local Muslim/Bosniak community and, gradually, the demands for territorial autonomy were dropped by both parties.

Bulgaria and the Macedonian identity

In the Bulgarian context, there has been no regionalist imagery developed and, to an even lesser extent, particular regionalist claims and movements. Regional (sub)divisions do exist, such as the territorial 'holy trinity' of Bulgarian nationalism: the regions of Moesia (i.e. northern Bulgaria, or simply 'Bulgaria' as it used to be called in the nineteenth century), Thrace and the much-disputed Macedonia. Territorial controversies with Balkan neighbours also contributed to the symbolic construction of regions, such as Dobrudja (disputed with Romania). As a whole, these territories never constituted particular administrative units and never acquired specific identities. When the interwar period saw the formation of particular Thracian and Dobrudjan movements, these promoted the objectives of Bulgarian irredentism in the neighbouring countries.

The case of Macedonia, however, was different – specifically, the case of its Orthodox Christian Slavic population. In the late Ottoman period, Macedonia was inhabited by a number of Christian (Slavs, Greeks, Vlachs) and Muslim populations (Turks, Muslim Albanians and Slavs, etc., as well as by Jews who were the largest community in Salonika, the region's largest city). The region was progressively transformed into a battleground of cultural, ecclesiastic and, finally, armed political movements. Since the mid-nineteenth century, the formation of a local Slavic intelligentsia challenged the domination of the Patriarchate of Constantinople and of the (pro-)Greek élites among the Macedonian Orthodox Christians. In general, these intellectuals defined their native language and ethnonational belonging as 'Bulgarian', but they also adopted a certain Macedonian regional identity. From the outset, this identity was incited particularly by the definitive standardization of the Bulgarian language on the basis of the Eastern Bulgarian dialects – a process that marginalized the Macedonian Slavic dialects.[21]

The emergence of the 'Macedonian question' after 1878 largely politicized this identity. While newly established Bulgaria, but also Greece and Serbia, claimed Macedonian territories that were still under Ottoman domination, diverse agendas crystallized within the first Macedonian political organizations, among which the most important one was the Internal Macedonian Revolutionary Organization.[22] Until the Balkan Wars that put an end to the Ottoman domination in Macedonia, various factions within the organization favoured different scenarios for the future of Macedonia, from the direct unification of the whole region with Bulgaria to the creation of an 'autonomous Macedonia' as a first step towards the establishment of a future Balkan Federation. In general, its political documents insisted on the supranational character of the organization: the statutes granted the right of membership to all 'unsatisfied elements', both in Macedonia and in the vilayet of Adrianople in Thrace, regardless of their ethnicity. This was the meaning of the slogan 'Macedonia for the Macedonians' promoted by the organization. However, Macedonian Slavic revolutionaries, such as the famous Goce Delčev, continued to employ the standard Bulgarian language in their writings. Moreover, their publications defined the majority of Macedonia's population as 'Bulgarian', while in reality the Orthodox Christian Slavic population remained divided into pro-Greek, pro-Bulgarian and, to a lesser extent, pro-Serbian segments. By contrast, several figures such as Krste Misirkov – who were active outside of the revolutionary movement – promoted the existence of a distinct Macedonian Slavic nationhood.[23]

The specific political setting after the First World War led to a transformation of the political programmes and identity patterns in Macedonia. The notion of Macedonian 'autonomy' clearly acquired the meaning of independence, while the region was divided between three Balkan states: Greece, Yugoslavia and Bulgaria. Gradually, leftist circles within the Macedonian movement embraced not only an independentist agenda but also the idea of a separate Macedonian Slavic nationhood. The Balkan communist parties also supported the Macedonian national emancipation that evolved in particular in Yugoslav Macedonia.[24] The definitive emancipation happened during the Second World War, when the local communist and democratic resistance opposed the Bulgarian occupation. In 1944–1945, the leaders of this movement established a Macedonian republic within the new, socialist Yugoslavia. It was up to the latter to homogenize the Macedonian nation and to build its institutions, standardize its language and construct its historical narrative.

Furthermore, individuals and groups inside Bulgaria also adopted a Macedonian national identity. After the fall of the communist regime in the country, they tried to establish political parties such as OMO Ilinden, which were systematically banned by

Bulgarian authorities. As a result, Macedonian nationalism remained marginal inside Bulgaria and it is nowadays much less visible than in the 1990s.

Regionalism in the Romanian and Greek contexts

The cases of Romanian and of Greek-speaking areas, respectively, present a number of interesting points of comparison with the Slav-speaking part of South-eastern Europe. Romania was founded in 1859 as a union of two principalities, Wallachia and Moldavia, each with its own historical traditions, while both initially vassal to the Ottoman Empire. Following the First World War, Romania incorporated from the defunct Austro-Hungarian monarchy a third large region – Transylvania – along with most of Banat and other smaller historical provinces. These were co-inhabited by a Romanian majority and by socially dominant Hungarian and German communities, as well as by Jews and others. The national homogenization of these territories presented a special challenge to the interwar 'Greater Romania'; indeed, it was finalized during the communist era under the leadership of Nicolae Ceaușescu.[25]

While, from the outset, the national capital Bucharest was asymmetrically located in the southern Wallachian plain, different regionalist attitudes and trends evolved in the Transylvanian and Moldavian territories. In the latter, the Moldavian identity did not immediately cede its place to Romanian nationhood well into the nineteenth century, even though Moldavian intellectuals insisted on the common origin and language of their compatriots and the inhabitants of Wallachia.[26] Moldavian identity remained even more vital in the eastern part of the region (Bessarabia), which was part of the Russian Empire between the early nineteenth century and the First World War. Annexed by the Soviet Union as a result of the Second World War, Bessarabia formed a Moldavian Soviet republic with a separate Moldavian nationhood and language – the latter being almost identical with standard Romanian but written in Cyrillic. Since the proclamation of its independence in 1991, the Republic of Moldova has witnessed a series of political struggles concerning the proper definition of its language (henceforth written in Latin characters) and ethnic majority: Moldavian or Romanian.

By contrast, Transylvanian nationhood never appeared, although particular forms of Transylvanian cultural regionalism do exist. In general, these recall the pattern of regionalism characterizing Serbia's Vojvodina: the formerly Habsburg Transylvania is often imagined as culturally superior to the rest of Romania (former Ottoman vassal regions); it is considered both as a region endowed with a unique tradition of multi-ethnic coexistence and as the intellectual hearth of Romanian nationalism.[27] Nevertheless, from a political point of view, these regionalist claims are considerably less developed than the similar ones in Vojvodina.

The case of modern Greece is different. Since its establishment in the 1830s, Greece has pursued a homogenizing policy aiming to suppress a number of local, regional and even ethnic identities. Indeed, regional variety has always existed with all the stereotypes dividing Peloponnesians and Roumeliots (inhabitants of Central Greece), north and south, and so on. Apart from the important Albanian – and Vlach-speaking – populations in Greece, there were even linguistic differences between Greek-speakers within and without Greece, with communities such as the Tsakonians in the Peloponnese. A certain sense of cultural superiority characterizes places such as the formerly Venetian (and also French and British) Ionian Islands and local patriotism is widespread in areas such as Crete: in the nineteenth and early twentieth centuries, these islands also had their moments of limited statehood. Cretan identity has been also, to a large extent, constructed by modern Greek art and literature owing to writers such as Nikos Kazantzakis. Numerous cultural associations of refugee communities coming from the so-called 'lost homelands' – territories that remained outside Greece, in particular, in Turkey (e.g. the Pontic Greeks) – also developed certain forms of regionalist imagery.

However, all these regional identities evolved as complementary to Greek national identity, and therefore regionalism never became a political challenge to modern Greek nationalism.[28] The emphasis on regional variety remained, to a large extent, limited to the field of folklore studies – the so-called laographia. The lack of a regionalist 'threat' may also explain the fact that, unlike the Balkan countries, the administrative division of Greece has been based traditionally on historical regions – although, in many cases, on 'revived' regions from the Antiquity that do not necessarily correspond to modern identities.

Nevertheless, the official 'homogeneity' of modern Greece faced certain challenges in the northern parts of the country. A special concern was the (initially considerable) Slav-speaking population in the Greek region of Macedonia. The fact that, in the interwar period, the Communist Party of Greece supported the Comintern policy of creating a Macedonian republic was heavily used by mainstream parties to discredit the communists as pro-Slavic 'traitors'. Even more problematic was the readoption by the communists of the slogan of self-determination for the Macedonian Slavs during the Greek Civil War (1946–1949) and the massive participation of these in the struggle on the side of communists. As a result, the Macedonian question remained a sensitive topic in contemporary Greece, and not only in its strained relations with the former Yugoslav Republic of Macedonia, which proclaimed its independence in 1991. Inside Greece, a small political party (the Rainbow) also claims to represent the local 'ethnic Macedonians', and the questions regarding the status of the Muslim community in Thrace and the alleged Turkish influence in the region are equally sensitive.[29]

In spite of such ethnic minority agendas, Greek nationalism kept its paramount prestige and homogenizing potential not only in Greece but also in the case of Cyprus where a contending political ideology – Cypriotism – has been advocating the particular interests of the island and promoting a supranational solidarity of Cypriots of different ethnic origins.[30] While political particularism also has had a certain impact on historiography, where different narratives – Helleno-centric and Cypriotist – compete at a grass-roots level, the idea that Greek and Turkish Cypriots possess common features that distinguish them from the mainland Greeks and Turks retains certain credibility among members of the two communities.

Conclusion

As the present overview suggests, regionalist imagination in South-eastern Europe displays a great diversity of characteristics that vary from one region/country to another. As a whole, the northern/north-western periphery of South-eastern Europe seems to be closer to forms of cultural and political regionalism of a Central European type: while Croatia inherited several crownlands of the Habsburg monarchy with their own identities and symbolism, Romania was constructed on the basis of principalities, each one with a separate historical development. These have developed a strong sense of regional identity based on this legacy. At first glance, it may seem that the notion of regionalism is less obvious in the Balkan context – that of the Ottoman legacy in Europe – since the Ottoman pattern of governance was never based on a feudal system territorialized in units such as duchies or counties. Hence, Balkan countries such as Serbia, Bulgaria or Albania lack more or less established traditions of statehood and forms of historical symbolism that are different to those of the modern and strongly homogenizing nationalisms of the nineteenth and twentieth centuries. Nevertheless, the former Ottoman Balkans are characterized by various regional identities and forms of political regionalism. These confirm a banal fact: the presence of 'real' historical precedents is only an optional premise of modern regionalism. Regionalist imagination is shaped by diverse political contexts, social antagonisms and cultural interactions and it tends to invent mappings, traditions and symbols even there where these have never existed.

In some cases, Ottoman administrative divisions helped the symbolic construction of territorial boundaries claimed by contemporary regionalisms and nationalisms: for example, in the case of Bosnia-Herzegovina or the Sandžak, or the eastern and southern boundaries of 'geographical Macedonia', which conspicuously follow those of late Ottoman *vilayets*. The dramatic process of disintegration of the Ottoman and the Habsburg Empires and the formation of nation states in South-eastern Europe suppressed an indefinite number of regional particularities and (often negative) stereotypes among people that were later deemed to be members of the 'same' nation. Yet, in other cases, identities that seemed to be nothing more than forms of local/regional patriotism (Macedonian, Bosniak, Montenegrin) evolved into separate national identities. In these cases, one should also take into account the impact of leftist concepts of nationhood as well as of state socialism in South-eastern Europe. In the first decades of the twentieth century, socialists and communists promoted internationalist solutions to nationalist controversies existing in problematic regions such as Macedonia. Ironically, in this manner they contributed greatly to the development of new national ideologies. The legacy of the second, socialist Yugoslavia with its complex federative structure is particularly important as well for the understanding of the evolution of South-east European regionalist and nationalist agendas. Moreover, patterned on the Soviet model, ethnography and folklore studies were actively developed during state socialism and they, to a certain extent, promoted regionalist imagery.

Sometimes, existing traditions and smaller historical provinces were assembled into bigger units and thus served for the creation of new imagery; in particular, this is the case of Vojvodina – to a large extent a creation of socialist Yugoslavia. In this and other cases (such as Istria or Transylvania), the presence of cultural legacy and traditions considered to be superior to those of the majority of fellow countrymen and/or of stronger economic development generated regionalist trends despite the initial enthusiasm of the unification with the 'mother country'. Indeed, leading nationalist activists, societies and projects of national unification often originated in provinces that later tended to orientalize most of 'their' country as backward and 'uncultured'. Nowadays, this pattern of orientalism is blended together with European Union principles of subsidiarity and liberal multiculturalism in the development of new regionalist movements that draw on the rhetoric of decentralization and 'Europe of the regions'.

Notes

1. Roumen Daskalov, Diana Mishkova, Tchavdar Marinov and Alexander Vezenkov, eds, *Entangled Histories of the Balkans, Vol. 4: Concepts, Approaches, and (Self-)Representations* (Leiden; Boston, MA: Brill, 2017), 1–256.
2. Klaus Roth and Ulf Brunnbauer, eds, *Region, Regional Identity and Regionalism in Southeastern Europe: Part 1*, Ethnologia Balkanica 11 (Berlin: LIT Verlag, 2007); and Klaus Roth and Vesna Vučinić-Nešković, eds, *Region, Regional Identity and Regionalism in Southeastern Europe: Part 2* = Ethnologia Balkanica 12 (2009) (Berlin: LIT Verlag, 2009).
3. Miran Hladnik, 'Regionalism in Slovene Rural Prose', *Slovene Studies* 13, no. 2 (1991): 143–53.
4. Migjen Kelmendi and Arlinda Desku, eds, *Who Is Kosovar? Kosovar Identity: A Debate* (Prishtina: Java Multimedia, 2005).
5. Kyle Evered, 'Regionalism in the Middle East and the Case of Turkey', *Geographical Review* 95, no. 3 (2005): 463–77.
6. See the introduction by Núñez Seixas and Storm.
7. Maria Todorova, *Imagining the Balkans* (New York; Oxford: Oxford University Press, 1997).
8. Vasilis Gounaris, *Ta Valkania ton Ellinon. Apo to Diafotismo eos ton A' Pankosmio Polemo* (Thessaloniki: Epikentro, 2007), 260, 276–77.
9. Nathalie Clayer, *Aux origines du nationalisme albanais: la naissance d'une nation majoritairement musulmane en Europe* (Paris: Karthala, 2007).
10. See Dejan Djokić, ed., *Yugoslavism: Histories of a Failed Idea, 1918–1992* (London: Hurst, 2003).
11. Dominique Reill, 'A Mission of Mediation: Dalmatia's Multi-National Regionalism from the 1830s–60s', in *Different Paths to the Nation: Regional and National Identities in Central Europe and Italy, 1830–70*, ed. Laurence Cole (Basingstoke: Palgrave Macmillan, 2007), 16–36; and Dominique Reill, *Nationalists Who Feared the Nation: Adriatic Multi-Nationalism in Habsburg Dalmatia, Trieste and Venice* (Stanford, CA: Stanford University Press, 2012).
12. Ivo Banac, 'The Confessional "Rule" and the Dubrovnik Exception: The Origins of the "Serb-Catholic" Circle in Nineteenth-Century Dalmatia', *Slavic Review* 42, no. 3 (1983): 448–74.
13. Dejan Stjepanović, 'Regions and Territorial Autonomy in Southeastern Europe', in *Political Autonomy and Divided Societies: Imagining Democratic Alternatives in Complex Settings*, ed.

Alain-G. Gagnon and Michael Keating (Basingstoke: Palgrave Macmillan, 2012), 185–99; Dejan Stjepanović, 'Territoriality and Citizenship: Membership and Sub-State Polities in Post-Yugoslav Space' CITSEE Working Paper Series, no. 22 (Edinburgh: CITSEE, 2012), 19–22; and Dejan Stjepanović, *Multiethnic Regionalisms in Southeastern Europe: Statehood Alternatives* (Basingstoke: Palgrave Macmillan, 2017).

14. See Stjepanović, *Multiethnic Regionalism*; John Ashbrook, *Buying and Selling the Istrian Goat: Istrian Regionalism, Croatian Nationalism, and EU Enlargement* (Brussels: Peter Lang, 2008); and Pamela Ballinger, 'Multiculturalism against the State: Lessons from Istria', in *Understanding Multiculturalism. The Habsburg Central European Experience*, ed. Johannes Feichtinger and Gary Cohen (New York; Oxford: Berghahn, 2014), 101–21.

15. Stjepanović, *Multethnic Regionalism*; see also Vassilis Petsinis, 'The Serbs and Vojvodina. Ethnic Identity within a Multiethnic Region' (Ph.D. thesis, University of Birmingham, 2005); and Jovana Saračević, 'Vojvodinian Regional Identity: A Social Fact or a Modern Construct?' (MA thesis, Central European University, 2012).

16. Ivo Banac, *The National Question in Yugoslavia: Origins, History, Politics* (Ithaca, NY: Cornell University Press, 1984), 270–91.

17. Nearly 30 per cent, according to the data of the 2011 census, http://monstat.org/cg/page.php?id=534&pageid=322, last access on 2 May 2017.

18. See Banac, *The National Question*, 359–76.

19. On Bosnia in Socialist Yugoslavia, see Noel Malcolm, *Bosnia: A Short History* (London: Pan Books, 2002), 193–212.

20. See Stjepanović, 'Territoriality and Citizenship', 19–20; and Marija Todorović, 'The Emergence of the Bosniak Identity Politics in Sandžak in the 1990s' (MA thesis, Central European University, 2012), http://www.etd.ceu.hu/2012/todorovic_marija.pdf, last access on 2 May 2017.

21. Victor Friedman, 'The Modern Macedonian Standard Language and Its Relation to Modern Macedonian Identity', in *The Macedonian Question: Culture, Historiography, Politics*, ed. Victor Roudometof (Boulder, CO: East European Monographs, 2000), 173–201.

22. On different national movements in late Ottoman Macedonia: Vemund Aarbakke, *Ethnic Rivalry and the Quest for Macedonia, 1870–1913* (Boulder, CO: East European Monographs, 2003).

23. On the development of a separate Macedonian identity and its entanglement with the neighboring Balkan national ideologies, see Tchavdar Marinov, 'Famous Macedonia, the Land of Alexander: Macedonian Identity at the Crossroads of Greek, Bulgarian and Serbian Nationalism', in *Entangled Histories of the Balkans, Vol. 1: National Ideologies and Language Policies*, ed. Roumen Daskalov and Tchavdar Marinov (Leiden; Boston, MA: Brill, 2013), 273–330.

24. Banac, *The National Question*, 307–27.

25. See Irina Livezeanu, *Politics in Greater Romania: Regionalism, Nation Building, and Ethnic Struggle, 1918–1930* (Ithaca, NY; London: Cornell University Press, 1995); and Katherine Verdery, *National Ideology under Socialism: Identity and Cultural Politics in Ceaușescu's Romania* (Berkeley; Oxford: University of California Press, 1991); as well as Livezeanu and Negura in the present volume.

26. Lucian Boia, *History and Myth in Romanian Consciousness* (Budapest: CEU Press, 2001), 130. See also the chapter by Livezeanu and Negura.

27. See Boia, *History and Myth*, 12–14.

28. See Dimitris Tziovas, 'Heteroglossia and the Defeat of Regionalism in Greece', *Kambos: Cambridge Papers in Modern Greek* 2 (1994): 95–120.
29. Michael Herzfeld, *Ours Once More: Folklore, Ideology, and the Making of Modern Greece* (New York: Pella, 1986).
30. On the Macedonian question in Greece, see Victor Roudometof, *Collective Memory, National Identity, and Ethnic Conflict: Greece, Bulgaria, and the Macedonian Question* (Westport, CT: Praeger, 2002).

Further reading

Ashbrook, John, *Buying and Selling the Istrian Goat: Istrian Regionalism, Croatian Nationalism, and EU Enlargement* (Brussels: Peter Lang, 2008).
Banac, Ivo, *The National Question in Yugoslavia: Origins, History, Politics* (Ithaca, NY: Cornell University Press, 1984).
Livezeanu, Irina, *Politics in Greater Romania: Regionalism, Nation Building, and Ethnic Struggle, 1918–1930* (Ithaca, NY; London: Cornell University Press, 1995).
Marinov, Tchavdar, 'Famous Macedonia, the Land of Alexander: Macedonian Identity at the Crossroads of Greek, Bulgarian and Serbian Nationalism', in *Entangled Histories of the Balkans, Vol. 1: National Ideologies and Language Policies*, ed. Roumen Daskalov and Tchavdar Marinov (Leiden; Boston, MA: Brill, 2013), 273–330.
Reill, Dominique, *Nationalists Who Feared the Nation: Adriatic Multi-Nationalism in Habsburg Dalmatia, Trieste and Venice* (Stanford, CA: Stanford University Press, 2012).
Roth, Klaus, and Ulf Brunnbauer, eds, *Region, Regional Identity and Regionalism in South-eastern Europe: Part 1*, Ethnologia Balkanica, no. 11 (Berlin: Lit Verlag, 2007).
Roth, Klaus, and Vesna Vučinić-Nešković, eds, *Region, Regional Identity and Regionalism in South-eastern Europe: Part 2*, Ethnologia Balkanica, no. 12 (Berlin: LIT Verlag, 2009).
Stjepanović, Dejan, *Multiethnic Regionalisms in Southeastern Europe: Statehood Alternatives* (Basingstoke: Palgrave Macmillan, 2017).
Stjepanović, Dejan, 'Territoriality and Citizenship: Membership and Sub-State Polities in Post-Yugoslav Space', CITSEE Working Paper Series, no. 22 (Edinburgh: CITSEE, 2012).
Tziovas, Dimitris, 'Heteroglossia and the Defeat of Regionalism in Greece', *Kambos: Cambridge Papers in Modern Greek* 2 (1994), 95–120.

CHAPTER 18
THE EMERGENCE OF CONJOINED NATIONALISMS AND REGIONALISMS IN THE BRITISH ISLES
James Kennedy

The Brexit referendum in June 2016 laid bare the national and regional diversity across the United Kingdom of Great Britain and Northern Ireland. While overall there was a narrow vote to leave the European Union, that vote was uneven, a reflection of quite distinct political cultures: in Scotland, Northern Ireland and London, there were majorities to remain, while in Wales and across outlying regions of England, majorities voted to leave. In a meaningful sense, then, the vote could be read as a verdict on the state of the British union as much as the European Union.

This chapter charts the ebb and flow of national and regional identities across the British Isles more widely and relates these to political developments from the late nineteenth century. The central focus is on the minority nations of Scotland, Ireland and Wales, rather than the majority nation, England, and its regions. It places a particular emphasis on changes in political rule in Scotland, Ireland and Wales. In doing so, my argument shares much with those that stress the importance of the modern state in explaining the emergence of nationalism and regionalism.[1] In the process of modernization the state became an active agent in the everyday lives of those it ruled, taxed and conscripted. This often resulted in a politics of popular representation, in which demands for political voice were couched in the language of nationalism or regionalism.[2] The state faced a crisis of legitimacy as a result, and again it was nationalism that presented a political solution, providing the state with the 'ideological glue' to bind rulers and ruled.[3] It was, in effect, the transition from indirect rule to direct rule in the modern era which explains much about the strength of political nationalism and regionalism generally,[4] and, as this chapter will argue, across the British Isles. Indeed, the tension between the exercise of direct and indirect rule constitutes its central theme.

I depart somewhat from others in this volume in making a distinction between nationalism and regionalism. In part, this is simply a reflection of the way in which 'nation' has been employed in the British Isles to denote its chief component parts: Scotland, England, Ireland and, latterly, Wales. While it is certainly the case that Britain was constituted as a nation, it was 'forged' on top of these pre-existing, though not fully developed, nations.[5] However, there is also an analytic necessity to distinguish it from regionalism. I define nationalism as 'a political project that seeks an arrangement in which the status of the nation is politically and/or culturally enhanced'.[6] This deliberately ambiguous definition allows for both political and cultural forms of nationalism, but most importantly it does not entail that political independence is the ultimate goal; rather, other forms of political/cultural autonomy may suffice. In contrast, regionalism seeks to maintain or elevate, either politically or culturally, the standing of a regional entity *within* a nation, as a distinct but subcomponent of a larger nation; it does not claim a national status.

This chapter draws extensively and innovatively on recent historical scholarship on the nations and regions of the British Isles and places it within a wider theorization on nationalism and regionalism. It employs a comparative sociological framing in examining the relationships among state, nation and region by emphasizing the contrasts as much as the similarities among these nations and regions. The chapter first offers some immediate context by establishing the political means by which the minority nations were incorporated and accommodated within what became the United Kingdom state. It then traces the emergence of political nationalism from the late nineteenth century, initially in the demand for home rule and then in the patterns of devolution, both legislative and administrative, that followed. These settlements came under very considerable strain: violent conflict in Northern Ireland and the peaceful demand for Scottish and Welsh parliaments. Devolved legislatures were established in the 1990s. English regionalism was a feature through this era but only gained a degree of political prominence in this last moment. The conclusion reflects on the relationship among nationalism, regionalism and the state.

Unions

Britain is a modern state, founded in 1707, the result of the Treaty of Union between Scotland and England. It is perhaps best understood as a composite state, in which the minority nations of Scotland, Ireland and Wales were differentially incorporated and accommodated within an existing and long-standing English state. Notably, while the Scottish union of 1707 and the later Irish union of 1801 were portrayed as unions of parliaments, in practice they effectively incorporated the Scottish and Irish legislatures within those of England and Great Britain, respectively.[7]

England achieved statehood much earlier than its continental competitors. It was marked by a high degree of administrative and cultural uniformity: English was the established dominant language. It was the strength of the English state which had made possible the invasions of its neighbours in the Middle Ages and the incorporation of Scotland and Ireland in the modern era. Indeed, the long history of English statehood meant that much of the distinctiveness of regional cultures, such as Cornwall's, had been eroded over centuries. Famously, Dolly Pentreath, who died in 1777, was the last native Cornish speaker.[8] However, in regions that maintained administrative regional autonomy, and a political status formally outside the state, the retention of cultural distinctiveness was longer lasting. The Crown Dependencies of the Isle of Man and the Bailiwicks of Jersey and Guernsey (including the islands of Alderney and Sark) were acquired by the English state in 1399 and 1259, respectively. There, distinct languages,

Manx and distinctive forms of Norman French in the Channel Islands predominated until the nineteenth century.

It is also worth emphasizing that England was an empire with considerable overseas possessions in the Americas, Africa and Asia. Its imperial status may well have had implications for the expression of Englishness. That is, like other imperial nations such as Russia, the imperial project took precedence over everyday expressions of nationalism; indeed, it may be that in the interests of unity, majority English nationalism was suppressed.[9] However, there is another view of the relationship of the nation to the empire.[10] The degree to which 'Britain' and 'England' were used interchangeably suggests that there was little suppression; rather, Britain (with due recognition of Scottish and Irish national distinctiveness) was England writ large. What is true, of course, is that England was not politically articulated; in this sense it was 'central and invisible'.[11]

Scotland shared a monarch with England as a result of the 1603 Union of Crowns. However, in the 1707 treaty, a unified state was sought. In that patrician bargain, Scottish elites gave up legislative sovereignty for economic stability and crucially access to England's imperial trade. Despite this, its civil society, founded on the trinity of church (the Presbyterian Church of Scotland), education and law, together with a distinct system of local government, was largely unaffected and retained considerable autonomy. Scotland was in Tom Nairn's phrase a 'decapitated national state' retaining institutions normally associated with statehood.[12] These institutions as well as a growing number of charities and associations effectively governed Scottish society through the eighteenth and much of the nineteenth centuries. The British state concerned itself with issues of war and peace, trade and not least the running of what by the end of the nineteenth century was a vast Empire. Therefore, domestic issues such as education and rudimentary health and welfare remained local concerns governed in Scotland by an array of distinctly Scottish, often religious organizations. And these institutions governed what was a regionally diverse nation.

British national identity, which followed the 1707 union, emerged often entwined with Scottish, Irish and Welsh identities, but at other times was antithetical to these identities, and especially to Catholic Irish identity. Interestingly, at least initially, it was a popular identity which minority national and regional elites, excluded social classes and women gravitated towards, in part as a means of making claims for entry to the polity.[13] But more generally, British national identity, which grew through the eighteenth century, was built on the success of war, initially with France. In Linda Colley's memorable phrase,

> [Britain] was an invention forged above all by war. Time and time again, war with France brought Britons, whether they hailed from Wales or Scotland or England, into confrontation with an obviously hostile Other and encouraged them to define themselves collectively against it.[14]

Empire and the opportunities for trade that it provided was another factor. And Scots were quick to take advantage of their self-styled position as 'partners' in Empire. For example, within ten years of Union, Scots were disproportionately involved in the East

India Company.[15] What underlay the uniting force of both war and empire was shared Protestantism, shared among Protestants of various denominations across the British Isles; the failure to effectively accommodate Irish Catholics was a serious deficiency,[16] as will be discussed below.

Ireland was formally brought within the British state through the union of 1801, thereby creating the United Kingdom of Great Britain and Ireland. Union meant the abolition of the Irish Parliament in 1798, and Ireland, through its representatives, was given direct representation at Westminster. Some of the same factors lay behind the union of 1801 as the union of 1707. Indeed, the union with Scotland had provided its architects with a model. And a key part of this model was the degree to which Scottish Presbyterianism in the guise of the established Church of Scotland was effectively co-opted through a separate act of parliament, which protected its status and its organization. The intention was that a similar measure could be afforded to the majority religion in Ireland – Catholicism – thus potentially bringing considerable support for union.[17] The failure to do so was to have a particularly detrimental effect on the apprehension of union by Ireland's majority population.

In any case, union was not the erosion of Irish autonomy since the Irish Parliament was, in effect, under British control through the Viceroy, who manipulated parliament through his extensive network of patronage and held ultimate power.[18] And crucially, the Catholic majority were excluded from this parliament as both voters and candidates. The tragedy was that the new union did little to accommodate Catholicism; indeed, it appeared only to augment the standing of the Protestant Ascendancy in Ireland: Protestants were assured that their privileges were secure, not least in uniting the Anglican Church of Ireland with the Church of England. It was overwhelmingly individuals from the Ascendancy that held the important offices: the Irish Office, the Chief Secretary for Ireland and the Lord Lieutenant.[19] This was a missed opportunity that would have very serious repercussions.

Deep religious division marked Ireland. There existed a 'cultural division of labour'.[20] Crudely, landowners of English extraction belonged to the Anglican Church of Ireland while the peasantry were Catholic, and in the north of Ireland there was a further complication with the existence of a considerable population of largely Scottish extraction who were Presbyterian and who formed both the business and industrial working class in the nineteenth century. Catholics and Presbyterians found common cause in the radical United Irishmen led by Wolf Tone in the 1780s and 1790s, inspired by the American and French Revolutions. Both experienced exclusion from the political and economic privileges afforded to those from the established Church of Ireland. However, industrialization provided Presbyterians with new material advantage.

Ireland lacked Scotland's civil society. Religion was the determining factor. Protestants, for example, were unwilling to join with Catholics in forming a National Board of Education in the 1830s.[21] This meant that the British state was denied civil society partners with which to share political rule. As a result, it employed 'despotic power' rather than 'infrastructural power': it ruled over society rather than through it in agreement with intermediate groupings.[22] The result was, in effect, a quasi-colonial form of administration. So, politically, Scotland was ruled through a largely non-interventionist state in London. Its political managers, those who ingratiated themselves among London political elites such as Henry Dundas, were Scottish. Ireland lacked Scotland's civil society, meaning that the British state was more interventionist and that its rule was often securitized. Its rulers were from the Ascendency and England, based in Dublin Castle.[23]

Long-denied Catholic emancipation was finally enacted in 1829, the result of a very considerable mobilization. It allowed over the course of the nineteenth century for the emergence of a Catholic middle class. This was a nationally minded class, which provided the personnel, certainly at the lower rungs, for government administration, but at the same time found its mobility through the Empire thwarted by Irish Protestants and Britons.[24] Yet, the famine of 1845–1852, which devastated the Irish population, killing a million people with a further million emigrating, was borne overwhelmingly by the Catholic population. The cause was the failure of the potato crop on which the Irish peasantry was dependent. The British state took responsibility for famine relief, with the result that its failings, which were considerable, were borne by it rather than intermediate Irish organizations.

Wales was the most politically integrated of the three minority nations. Its integration within the English state dates from the sixteenth century. While the English conquest of Wales was concluded in 1282, it was not until 1536 that Wales was formally incorporated within England. Complete integration was sought. English law replaced Welsh law and Wales was given direct representation at the Westminster parliament. The acts which, implemented these changes, have since been referred to as the Acts of 'Union', though this is not how they were understood at the time. They were simply a means of ensuring that Welsh political practices followed English norms. Rather, this was a term first used in 1901, but misleadingly giving, as Davies suggests, the impression that they were on a par with the unions of 1707 and 1801. They were not.[25]

Indeed, Welsh national status was in question until the late nineteenth century. In the contemporary popular imagination, Britain was thought of as constituting just three nations: Scotland, England and Ireland. Aside from religious institutions, Welsh political institutions were formed only through the late nineteenth century, acquiring a university, library and museum, and a national team in that most popular of sports in Wales: rugby.[26] As a result, it secured some of the institutional trappings of nation, though most would be acquired in the twentieth century. At the same time, and formally from 1746, administratively and legally Wales constituted a single jurisdiction with England, defined simply as 'England and Wales'. In other words, all laws passed in England applied in Wales.

These were strikingly different unions, and these differences, and indeed their deficiencies to a large degree, explain the contrasting character of the substate nationalisms that would emerge through the nineteenth century. The incorporation of Scotland and Ireland also had an impact on England. It gave rise to anxieties about *Englishness*, especially among those who resented the advantages secured by 'Celtic careerists' in London and across the Empire. And this is precisely the point; these anxieties were expressed through nationalism rather than regionalism.[27] English regionalism, certainly in its political form, is a more recent development.

Home rule

Ireland was central to British politics in the late nineteenth and early twentieth centuries. Rural discontent and the demand for land reform lay behind much of the support for Irish Home Rule and its champion, the Irish Parliamentary Party (IPP) led by the charismatic Anglo-Irish Protestant Charles Stewart Parnell.[28] The Irish Question took centre stage in British politics in 1886. British Prime Minister William Gladstone's support for Irish home rule was, in part, a result of the IPP holding the balance of power in the House of Commons. Gladstone's conversion split his Liberal Party, with the formation of the breakaway Liberal Unionist Party. In the end, the home rule bill failed to pass, and Parnell was later politically weakened when revelation of a long-term affair became public. The more unassuming John Redmond replaced Parnell in pressing the demand for Irish home rule.[29]

Irish home rule was once again on the British political agenda in the 1900s. Liberal governments were committed to home rule, and again it was reliance on IPP votes at Westminster that placed it centre stage. And again a home rule crisis followed the introduction of a Home Rule Bill in 1912. This time armed militias, the Irish Volunteers and the Ulster Volunteers, were formed on either side of the sectarian divide. Prominent UK Conservative politicians, who could not countenance Protestants being ruled by Catholics, were once again vocal in their support of Ulster. Despite this, the Home Rule Act was passed by parliament in 1914, but the outbreak of the First World War prevented its implementation.

Might the enactment of Irish home rule have been sufficient to meet majority opinion and diffuse more radical demands? Perhaps. Instead, British miscalculation provided an opportunity for advanced nationalists. The political failure to enact home rule in Ireland in the 1880s and 1890s resulted in a turn towards an introspective, cultural nationalism, one that drew on and had remarkable similarities with contemporaneous national movements in east central Europe.[30] This was an ethnic nationalism which romanticized Ireland's Celtic past, its Gaelic language, still the majority language across western Ireland or Gaeltacht, and promoted a cult of sacrifice. The poet Padraig Pearce through his Gaelic League championed this direction. There was little space for Irish Protestants or Ulster Unionists in this nationalism.[31] Irish nationalists were also rethinking the relationship with Britain and its empire. Arthur Griffith, later president of Sinn Féin, was inspired by how Hungary had achieved dual-nationality status within the Habsburg Empire.[32] This was wholly unrealistic. However, it does highlight that Ireland, certainly Catholic Ireland, enjoyed a very different relationship to Empire than that enjoyed by Scotland.

The poet W. B. Yeats was swept up in the new nationalism, but as an Irish Protestant, remained outside it. His ambivalence was summed up in his line 'a terrible beauty is born' describing the events of Easter 1916 during which 'advanced' nationalists, including Pearce and James Connolly, seized key buildings in Dublin including the General Post Office. After a week of fighting it was defeated. It was the British government's response to 1916 that was pivotal: by deciding to execute the leaders of the rebellion, and arresting thousands of nationalists, the British authorities effectively turned an unpopular episode – certainly on the streets of Dublin – into a celebrated event and its leaders into martyrs. Sinn Féin replaced the IPP in the general election of 1918, winning in a landslide. An effective war broke out the following year after Sinn Féin established itself as an Irish parliament (Dáil Éireann) and proclaimed Irish independence from Britain. The Irish Republican Army (IRA) became the armed defender of the proclaimed republic.

The Anglo-Irish Agreement of 1921 temporarily brought hostilities to an end, and the Partition of Ireland was the result. Northern Ireland was created as a separate entity, the result of the Government of Ireland Act, and opted not to join the Irish Free State, as the new dominion was to be called. The precise terms of secession from the United Kingdom divided nationalists. A civil war ensued between supporters of the Treaty, including Michael Collins, and those that opposed it, led by Eamon De Valera. The anti-Treaty side was defeated.[33] Treaty opponents reconstituted themselves as a political party, Fianna Fáil, and under De Valera's leadership, it became Ireland's dominant party, responsible for establishing Ireland as a republic in 1948.

The story in Scotland contrasted markedly. A distinctive Scottish culture firmly embedded within Britain was created through the nineteenth century. The Scottish novelist and staunch unionist Walter Scott was especially important. In novels such as *Waverley* (1814), he depicted a romantic Scotland, but one firmly planted in the past. Scotland's past was also celebrated in the erection of monuments to William Wallace, hero of the Wars of Independence in the thirteenth and fourteenth centuries. At the same time, the wearing of tartan became de rigueur, not least by British monarchs from George IV onwards, and by Scottish regiments within the British military, which marched to the drone of the once outlawed bagpipes. Moreover, the Scottish Highlands and the Balmoral estate afforded Queen Victoria a summer getaway. Britishness had a Scottish hue. These developments constituted 'unionist nationalism', a nationalism in which the celebration of Scottish distinctiveness was understood as strengthening rather than weakening the union.[34] Thus, symbols that might have been in conflict with or indeed inimical to British rule, were celebrated as making possible Scotland's distinct contribution, and equal place, within the union. This curious nationalism took a political form through the mid-nineteenth century National Association for the Vindication of Scottish Rights, which arose in opposition to United Kingdom centralization on the belief that it would diminish Scotland's status as an equal partner in the union. It sought to preserve the status and autonomy of those Scottish local elites who governed Scotland through its powerful local government and the boards and charities of civil society.[35]

However, towards the late nineteenth century, these local institutions proved increasingly ineffective at meeting the demands of a majority urban and industrial population. Nationalists in this period sought to harness state power through the creation of a Scottish Home Rule parliament, that is, legislative devolution through the establishment of a substate parliament within the United Kingdom. Ireland was influential here. The demand for Irish home rule led to calls for federalism or, in the parlance of the day, 'home rule all round', in which each of the constituent nations of the United Kingdom would have a parliament responsible for domestic affairs. In the 1880s, it was the cross-party Scottish Home Rule Association, set up in 1886, that pressed the case; while in the early twentieth century, it was the Young Scots' Society, an independent organization composed largely of Liberal Party members, the dominant party in Scotland.[36] Arguments were based on the need for a more efficient and democratic government. There was frustration at the limited time available to debate and legislate for Scotland at Westminster and the resulting legislative backlog, and at that substandard legislation that was passed: legislation had either not been properly scrutinized or it had been devised for England and Wales, without considering Scottish particularities. And at the same time, the increasingly powerful government-appointed boards, which oversaw key aspects of Scottish society and economy, were unaccountable.[37]

While these successive campaigns for home rule were ultimately unsuccessful, they did have the effect of ensuring considerable administrative devolution, whereby distinct Scottish institutions would administer British policy. Indeed, it was from these moments that administrative devolution was gradually implemented. The Scottish Office and the Scottish Education Department were both established in the 1880s and headquartered in London before moving to Edinburgh in 1939. These departments were overseen by the Scottish Secretary, a position which was (re-)created in 1885. The Scottish Secretary became a Secretary of State in 1926 and acquired full cabinet rank.

Ireland was also influential on Welsh nationalism. Cymru Fydd ('The Wales to be'), too, was founded in 1886 in support of Welsh self-government and directed initially at Welsh exiles in England.[38] David Lloyd George, the charismatic future UK prime minister, became its driving force as it organized across Wales, holding public meetings as it sought the support of the institutions of the Welsh Liberal Party. However, Welsh nationalism was also significantly entwined with religion. Nonconformist Methodism was a powerful force through the nineteenth and early twentieth centuries. Its chapels grew remarkably; by 1851, there were 2,813. Nonconformity was especially popular in the industrial areas of Wales, and by catering to its flock in Welsh it took on the semblance of a distinctively Welsh institution.[39] Its influence was apparent in support for temperance and the disestablishment of the Church of England in Wales, as articulated by Lloyd George and the Liberal Party. However, as disestablishment faded as an issue in the interwar years, so too did the demand for home rule.

There was also the parallel development of cultural nationalism focused on the Welsh language. It is estimated that two-thirds of the Welsh population spoke Welsh in the 1840s. Importantly, by the 1860s, Welsh was an established literary language with publications, including the Bible, that were profitable and had a considerable circulation. Other non-historic European nations, such as the Slovenes or Slovaks, could only look on in envy at the widespread interest in the Welsh language and culture which culminated in the establishment of the National Eisteddfod or festival in 1861 and the thousands it attracted. By the 1880s, and as a result of lobbying, Welsh made an appearance on the schools' curriculum.[40]

Ironically, it was the Great Western Railway, the instrument of industrialization, which brought the 'Cornish revival' to Cornwall. English romanticists had initiated interest in Cornish history and its Celtic culture, which culminated in the Cornish language revival in 1904. Though no longer a living language, there were echoes of the language in place names and surnames. These activists eschewed the term 'nationalist', preferring 'autonomist' or 'regionalist'. Wales was an inspiration for these revivalists, an activism again bound up with Nonconformism and Liberal politics.[41]

Indeed, there was a more general interest in English folklore among the late Victorian middle class. The Folklore Society was established in 1878 to document and explore folk customs and music. It was also at this time that Morris dancing, a step dance in which its participants wear bell pads on their shins, became the focus of revivalists. While its generic form has become synonymous with English national folk culture, its practice contained quite distinct regional variants: 'Cotswold Morris', 'North West Morris', 'Border Morris' from counties bordering Wales, and a style from the north-east in which swords were used. More widely, a cultural regionalism was conveyed in nineteenth-century English novels, perhaps most especially in Thomas Hardy's depiction of 'Wessex', a region largely of his own creation that included many of the counties of southwest England, and captured best in *Tess of the d'Urbervilles* (1891) and *Far from the Madding Crowd* (1874). In the first half of the nineteenth century, the Brontë sisters had depicted Yorkshire through novels such as *Jane Eyre* (1847) and *Wuthering Heights* (1847).

British Isles substate nationalisms and, to a lesser extent, regionalisms, experienced a 'liberal moment' at the turn of the twentieth century: the IPP, the Young Scots' Society and Cymru Fydd all offered nationalisms that were embedded in the language of liberalism. Ecclesiastical politics was also a feature of these parties and movements: Presbyterians in Scotland and Methodists in Wales (and Nonconformists in Cornwall) were exercised by campaigns to disestablish the Anglican Church of England. However, Catholicism's subservient position in Ireland was more existential. In other words, while the demand for home rule across the British Isles might appear rhetorically similar it was embedded in contrasting contexts each with quite different stimuli.

Devolution[42]

The failure to enact Irish home rule and 'home rule all round' more generally had two consequences: Irish independence and a mixture of UK devolutions. Northern Ireland acquired legislative devolution, while Scotland, and to a lesser extent Wales, secured administrative devolution. Legislative devolution was enacted for Scotland and Wales, and a new devolved settlement for Northern Ireland in the 1990s.

Indirect and direct rule has characterized the governance of Northern Ireland. There is particular irony that Ulster Protestants, who had vehemently opposed Irish home rule, became the recipients themselves of a 'home rule assembly' at Stormont, which spanned the years 1921 to 1972. Political Protestant hegemony in the north was maintained through the Stormont assembly. Those in power ensured their hegemony through significant abuse of that power: gerrymandering of political boundaries and in the distribution of social services, notably public housing. Inspired by the black Civil Rights movement in the United States, a similar movement sought equality for the Catholic population. The Stormont assembly was suspended and direct rule from London took its place.

The British military was deployed in 1969, initially to protect the Catholic community, but lost support through its clumsy and insensitive action. The newly formed provisional IRA sought to establish itself as the protector of the Catholic community and to wage an 'armed struggle'. This effectively launched a period referred to as 'the troubles', which resulted in some 3,000 deaths and a total of some 50,000 casualties. State reaction often exacerbated the violence, not least since the emphasis on security policy had the effect of entrenching rather than marginalizing the perpetrators of violence.[43]

The Good Friday Agreement signed in 1998 signalled an end to the scale of violence that marked the troubles. This was a consociational, power-sharing agreement founded on the participation of all the main parties. The contrast with the ill-fated Sunningdale Agreement of 1973 could not have been starker. That agreement was unable to secure the support of popular Unionism: in 1974, the leader of the Ulster Unionist Party, Brian Faulkner, was abandoned by his party; and a general strike by Protestant workers sealed its fate. The Good Friday Agreement faced no similar mobilization. Crucially, it was underpinned by an all-Ireland referendum. Voters in Northern Ireland and the Republic of Ireland approved it, with voters in the south agreeing to remove the Republic's constitutional claim to the six counties of Northern Ireland.

And the Agreement was innovative in its introduction of federal elements: east-west ties were formalized through the British-Irish Council, a body which includes the UK and Irish governments, the United Kingdom's devolved governments (Scotland, Wales and Northern Ireland) and its dependencies (Jersey, Guernsey and the Isle of Man); nationalists were appeased through the creation of the North/South Ministerial Council which fosters cooperation across key policy areas, for example, agriculture in the north and south of Ireland.[44] In this way, the Democratic Unionist Party, an initial opponent of the agreement, became an important participant providing three First Ministers with Sinn Féin's Martin McGuiness as Deputy First Minister.

A direct cultural consequence of the Good Friday Agreement has been not only official recognition of Irish Gaelic, a long-held republican demand, but also the elevation of the Ulster Scots dialect as an official language. In part, this was an attempt to ensure parity between the two communities; but it was also a way to manage Ulster Protestants' 'ethnic reversal',[45] the way in which this previously dominant majority experienced a decline or reversal in its status.

The European Union played an important role in this settlement by placing the relationship between southern and Northern Ireland within a wider arena, crucially providing for the free movement of goods, services and people between the two jurisdictions. Northern Ireland's vote by 56 per cent to remain in the European Union should be seen in this context, a cross-community vote as much in favour of the continuation of the Good Friday Agreement as remaining in the European Union. The UK government is committed to ensuring a 'soft border' is retained post-Brexit between Northern Ireland and the Republic.

In the interwar, Scottish nationalism took a cultural turn. The Scottish literary renaissance that emerged, offered a corrective to the 'Caledonian *antisyzygy*', in which Scottish novels were held to embody two contradictory traits, for example, in Robert Louis Stevenson's *Kidnapped*, in which the main protagonists embodied divisions between rational/romantic, Lowland/Highland and urban/rural. The renaissance included the poets Hugh MacDiarmid and Edwin Morgan and novelists Lewis Grassic Gibbon and Neil Gunn; each drew on a distinct regional experience, for example, Grassic Gibbon's depiction of Kincardineshire, but their reception was national. MacDiarmid was notable in his attempt to develop a distinct Scots literary language, 'lallans'. The period was also marked by the formation of parties dedicated to self-government: the National Party of Scotland in 1928, succeeded by the Scottish National Party (SNP) in 1934.[46]

The First World War revealed just how formidable state power had become. Under conditions of total war it had proved adept at mobilizing the civilian population and industry for war. For socialists this suggested possibilities for state-led social reform.[47] The Labour party in Scotland, which had become the main champion of home rule following the 'strange death' of the Liberal party, oriented itself increasingly to control of the British state and less towards the achievement of Scottish home rule, a founding aim of the Scottish Labour Party.

Tom Johnston exemplified this. Johnson, a Labour politician and MP, had been a prominent supporter of Scottish home rule during the 1920s' incarnation of the Scottish Home Rule Association. In 1941, he was appointed wartime secretary of state for Scotland and used the power of the office to undertake a series of initiatives, securing industry and employment in Scotland, inaugurating a health service and developing hydroelectricity in the Highlands with the establishment of the North of Scotland Hydro-Electric Board. Perhaps the most successful of Scottish secretaries, he exercised the powers of the office as a 'benign dictator'.[48] His tenure suggested that politics had become to a considerable extent the 'administration of things'. That is, while ultimate power resided in London, Scottish institutions constituted a 'Scottish political system' with substantial administrative autonomy and the possibility of producing policy initiatives.[49]

The creation of a UK-wide welfare state and its much-venerated National Health Service (NHS) can be understood as the last genuinely popular British national project. It was policies which sought to roll back the state's role in welfare, broadly understood, that would be the greatest spur to Scottish nationalism in the 1980s. The state's role in another arena, regional planning, may also have had the unintended consequence of spurring an initial rise of political nationalism in Scotland in the 1960s and 1970s. By labelling Scotland a problem in need of social and economic regeneration, it played into the hands of those who argued that Britain was failing Scotland.[50] The discovery of North

Sea Oil off the coast of Scotland provided the SNP with the means to make the case that an independent Scotland would not only be economically viable but also economically prosperous. 'It's Scotland's Oil' was the campaign slogan in the 1974 general elections. The SNP achieved it highest representation at Westminster in those elections: increasing representation from seven MPs in February to eleven in October. However, the failure of the 1978 referendum on Scottish devolution (which was narrowly won but had failed to secure 40 per cent of the electorate, a condition inserted in the Bill), together with the recriminations that followed, meant that the SNP entered a period of demobilization.

In the 1980s, the home rule movement was revitalized by Margaret Thatcher's UK Conservative governments. These governments were dedicated to reducing and reforming the public sector – a sector on which Scotland was disproportionately dependent. The Conservatives' declining electoral fortunes in Scotland meant that these policies were experienced as an imposition, that the Conservative government lacked a democratic mandate. The implementation of the Poll Tax in 1988, a local government tax, one year ahead of the rest of the United Kingom appeared to epitomize this. These policies brought many state employed professionals – those employed in education, the NHS and local government – to support home rule; in other words, precisely those whose position and status were undermined by Conservative policies.[51]

Immediately prior to the restart of the home rule campaign, in the 1980s, Scottish culture flourished in novels, poetry, journalism and popular music. Whether on the written page or on the airwaves, these writers (James Kelman, Alasdair Gray, William McIlvaney, Liz Lochhead), broadcasters (Kirsty Wark and James Naughtie) and musicians (The Proclaimers) wrote, spoke and sang with Scottish accents. Gaelic, spoken by between 1 and 2 per cent of the Scottish population and regionally concentrated in the inner and outer Hebridean islands, enjoyed something of a renaissance, too, in the poetry of Sorley Maclean, and in the folk rock of Runrig. It ushered in a period of cultural confidence. In the 1990s, the SNP made much of Mel Gibson's Hollywood-produced *Braveheart* (1995), but it was Irvine Welsh's gritty *Trainspotting* (1996) novel, film and poster that spoke to and of the new urban Scotland.

The SNP enjoyed some success in the late 1980s, most spectacularly at the Glasgow Govan by-election in 1988. This spurred on the creation the Scottish Constitutional Convention, set up in 1989, which brought together political parties (but not the SNP or the Conservatives), the churches, trades unions and members of the business community, key elements of Scottish civil society, in other words, to debate devolution. The Convention agreed to what became the blueprint for the present Scottish Parliament in 1995. However, there was concern outside the central belt that devolution would simply mean trading one remote capital city for another. This was especially true in the northern isles of Orkney and Shetland, the latter geographically closer to Norway, which continue to exhibit remnants of Norse culture, in dialect, in place names and most spectacularly in the *Up Helly Aa* winter festival in Shetland. It is marked by a torchlit procession, which culminates in setting fire to a replica Viking longship. In its current form it dates from the 1880s. This cultural regionalism has also taken a political form: the Orkney and Shetland Movement contested the 1987 general election on a platform to achieve devolution for the islands, it did so with the support of the SNP, though its candidate secured only 14 per cent of the islands' vote.

The landslide election of the UK Labour government in 1997 paved the way for the introduction of legislative devolution. A referendum held the same year produced 74 per cent support for the establishment of a Scottish parliament, while 63 per cent agreed that the parliament should have tax varying powers. Much was expected of the Scottish Parliament and its early governments. Yet, despite some notable policy innovations and departures from UK policies, such as the abolition of tuition fees and the introduction of free personal care for the elderly, these Labour-Liberal Democrat coalition governments disappointed. Circumstance contributed: the sudden death of Scotland's first First Minister, Donald Dewar, succeeded by the hesitant Henry McLeish, in turn replaced by the dull but competent Jack McConnell. In 2007, the SNP was elected as a minority government. It immediately set about raising the national profile of the Scottish administration: 'Scottish Government' replaced 'Scottish Executive'. It established itself as a popular administration: the abolition of road tolls and NHS prescription charges contributed to this.

The devolution settlement had been designed explicitly to prevent any one party from achieving a majority of seats. In 2011, the SNP achieved the remarkable feat of becoming a majority government, and was thus able to initiate its manifesto commitment to hold a referendum on Scottish independence. The ground rules for the referendum were agreed between the Scottish and British governments – the so-called 'Edinburgh Agreement': the date, the question, eligibility to vote (the voting age was lowered to 16) and its legality (as a reserved power the UK constitution was devolved for this occasion) were all agreed. This contrasts markedly from the Spanish government's refusal to countenance, let alone agree to, a legally recognized Catalan independence referendum. The British government's insistence that only independence be placed as an option on the ballot paper was perhaps a miscalculation, because the absence of an alternative option, including the most popular 'devo max' or maximal devolution, meant that independence was the only option for those in favour of constitutional change.[52]

The 'No' side won the Scottish independence referendum, held on 18 September 2014, by 55 per cent to 45 per cent. The 'Yes' campaign, through its grass-roots mobilization, had significantly increased support for independence from its 27 per cent level at the start of the campaign. The SNP enjoyed significant post-referendum support, effectively translating support for independence into support for the SNP. In 2015, it won all but three constituencies in Scotland in the UK General Election. In 2016, it was re-elected as the Scottish Government, although as a minority government, failing to achieve an overall majority by two seats. And yet, with the inclusion of Green MSPs, a majority of MSPs in the Scottish parliament remain in favour of independence.

Further powers have accrued to the Scottish Parliament since its establishment. The Smith Commission was set up in the wake of the independence referendum following a 'vow' made by UK party leaders that more powers would be devolved in the event of a 'No' vote. The Commission's most important recommendations concerned finance and welfare namely income tax and social security. Both were previously 'reserved matters'.

These recommendations formed the Scotland Act 2016, and built on the previous Calman Commission and the Scotland Act 2012.

The 2016 European Union referendum placed independence, or at least the prospect of a second referendum or 'IndyRef2', on the agenda. While the overall UK result was 51.9 per cent in favour of leaving the European Union, in Scotland 62 per cent voted to remain. The decline in SNP support at the 2017 UK general election has placed this in doubt.

The protection of the Welsh language, making it the official language of Wales was a key mobilizing factor for Welsh nationalism in the interwar. It was this, rather than self-government, that was the overriding concern of Plaid Cymru (the Party of Wales) established in 1925. And to some extent this association with the Welsh language has historically restricted its appeal from the Welsh-speaking heartlands of the rural north and the market town of Aberystwyth[53] to the non-Welsh-speaking industrial valleys of the south. However, the increased popularity of Plaid post-devolution has narrowed this regional divide in its support somewhat.

Efforts to prevent, and indeed reverse, the decline of the Welsh language have had considerable success. Census data suggests that around one fifth is able to speak Welsh (20.51 per cent in 2001 and 19 per cent in 2011). Though the percentage for those with some Welsh language skill is higher. In 1993, Welsh was given the same status as English where this was 'practicable and expedient'. Both Welsh and English medium schools have played an important role, Welsh has become a core part of the curriculum. Of particular note is that while there has been a decline in the traditional northern heartlands, the numbers with some knowledge of Welsh has grown considerably in the south and Cardiff. The establishment of a dedicated Welsh language television channel, S4C, has played a role, generating popular and critically successful programmes such as the noir-thriller *Y Gwyll/Hinterland* (2013–2016).[54]

While Welsh administrative devolution followed a similar pattern to Scotland, it was considerably less developed and established much later. A Minister of Welsh Affairs was created in 1951 and was upgraded to Secretary of State for Wales only in 1964; in the same year the Welsh Office was established, following a period in which distinctly Welsh administrative bodies had developed. Its competencies were gradually extended.[55] However, the Welsh Office had considerably less administrative latitude than its Scottish counterpart. England and Wales continued to constitute a single legal jurisdiction.

Wales, like Scotland, experienced deindustrialization under Margaret Thatcher's Conservative government, and, like Scotland, the movement in favour of devolution gained momentum, though never to the same extent.[56] Those in favour frequently invoked Scotland, with the implication that what was good for Scotland was good for Wales. Yet, this tended to paper over very real differences in the pattern of campaigning and support for a Welsh Assembly. The election of the Labour government in 1997 offered the prospect of devolution for Wales. During that year's devolution referendum campaign, both Plaid Cymru and the Welsh Labour Party made much of the Scottish connection. Indeed, the referendum took place one week after the Scottish referendum in order to benefit from a momentum created by a positive vote in Scotland. Yet, the result of that referendum was close, with just over 50 per cent voting yes.

The National Assembly for Wales possessed considerably fewer powers than those of the Scottish Parliament. Crucially, it lacked legislative power: it could only recommend to the Westminster parliament legislation that it wished to enact. And it did not possess the power to increase or lower general taxation, the result was that the initial years of the National Assembly were dominated by discussion about the powers that the Welsh Assembly should have. Since then the Assembly, like the Scottish Parliament, has acquired additional powers, notably through the 2006 Government of Wales Act and through a 2011 referendum, which was won by 63 per cent, giving the Welsh Assembly the power to pass laws within its competencies without the need for Westminster's agreement.

The impact of devolution has been considerable. Perhaps most consequentially, Wales now has a distinct system of education, extricated from the one it shared with England and allowing it to better address its priorities.[57] And Plaid Cymru has established itself as a political force in Welsh politics, with appeal beyond its traditional electoral base in the north. In 2007, it became a coalition partner with Labour in the Welsh government. Yet, to a remarkable extent, and despite the growth in importance of Welsh political institutions and in the powers of the Welsh Assembly, Welsh voting patterns differed little from those of England in their support for United Kingdom Independence Party (UKIP) and 'Leave' in the European Union referendum.

English working-class regional culture grew in prominence in the late 1950s and 1960s as a critical response to the social mores of the time but also to BBC-sponsored 'received pronunciation', or standard southern English, which conveyed a sense of class and regional privilege. Kitchen sink realist dramas for theatre, television and film, such as *Saturday Night and Sunday Morning* (1960), and their leading male actors Albert Finney and Michael Cain, offered an alternative social reality. The rise of popular music, most especially The Beatles, made a significant contribution in placing northern regional English accents at the centre of British cultural life. Cultural regionalism continued through the 1970s and 1980s in the plays of the Yorkshire writer and playwright, Alan Bennett, the Liverpool playwright, Alan Bleasdale, especially his *Boys from the Black Stuff* (1982) and in the television series, *Auf Wiedersehen Pet* (1983–1984, 1986).

Cornish regionalism shared in the 'Celtic revival' of the 1960s, taking inspiration from Wales and Scotland. Its political impact was modest, however: founded in 1951, Mebyon Kernow's electoral breakthrough came in 1967 when it secured a seat on Cornwall's County Council. It has maintained local representation since then, and has campaigned for a Cornish Assembly and against Cornwall's incorporation within a large south-west region, with the creation of a generic 'Devonwall' in which Cornwall's distinctiveness is lost. Indeed, there is a sense in which Cornish culture is indeed more secure, not least in the widespread use of the Saint Piran flag and Celtic symbols to represent Cornwall.[58]

In the 1990s, as devolution was being rolled out by the Labour government, it was the north-east of England that was the primary candidate to have an elected English regional assembly. It was here that there appeared the most notable enthusiasm. Regional activists pointed to the benefits that Scotland, on its northern border, was enjoying. But they failed to convince: a regional assembly was overwhelmingly rejected by 77.9 per cent in a 2004 referendum. Only London proved popular, with an elected assembly and mayor established in 2000, and endorsed in a 1998 referendum by 72 per cent. The nine administrative regions that had been set up in 1994 in line with the European Union's development of a Committee of the Regions continued to exercise coordinating functions.

'Combined authorities', composed of several local councils with directly elected mayors and often based on 'city regions', have proved a more popular locus of devolution. Although an English region, London provided the model. Mayoral elections took place in May 2017 for the new combined authorities in Greater Manchester, Sheffield, Liverpool, West Midlands and Tees Valley. Interestingly, Cornwall has been able to secure a devolution agreement as county, and without the need to combine with other counties or to have an elected mayor. Much of the focus of this initiative, however, has been to stimulate the northern English economy, to create a 'Northern Powerhouse', and address England's 'bottom-heavy' character, in which the South dominates economically, politically and culturally.[59] The proposed high-speed rail line (HS2) to improve the connection time between London and Birmingham and then Manchester and Leeds is part of this.

English regionalism was one response to Scottish, Welsh and Northern Irish devolution, the other was English nationalism and the suggestion that England, too, should have a parliament of its own. Devolution has had the effect of decoupling England from Britain. That is, polling data has suggested the growth of a distinct English national identity. The diffusion of the flag of St George at English sporting occasions rather than the Union flag is just one manifestation of this. Conservative Party Euroscepticism and the rise and success of the UKIP were articulations of a certain English nationalism.[60]

Within hours of the 2014 Scottish independence vote being declared, the UK PM David Cameron announced not only more powers for Scotland but also support to enable English MPs to legislate on domestic policies unencumbered by Scottish MPs. This became known as English Votes for English Laws (EVEL). This has proved controversial because it effectively suggests a 'dual mandate' English Parliament composed of UK MPs representing English constituencies. It is a debate that continues.

Devolution has been a feature of UK politics through the twentieth and twenty-first centuries, first administrative and then legislative. And while Northern Ireland had a prior experience, the devolution of powers to national and regional units is novel, and has ushered in a new national and regional politics.

Conclusion

Michael Mann contends that the existence of 'regional administration' is a better predictor of the emergence of nationalism (and regionalism) than the possession of distinct cultural attributes.[61] The British Isles offers empirical support and suggests a more complicated relationship with direct and indirect rule. Scotland and Ireland, through their respective unions, retained distinct but very different institutions and political systems. Indeed, the manner in which rule was exercised differed considerably. Indirect rule characterized rule through Dublin Castle, and again through Stormont, but in its practises failed to accommodate the Irish Catholic population. Nationalism was the response, in both pacific and violent forms. While Westminster formally employed direct rule in Scotland, in practice, Scotland enjoyed considerable autonomy; rule was indirect through civil society and then, to a degree, through administrative devolution.[62] As a result, nationalism was somewhat sporadic, a response to moments in which Scottish autonomy was undermined.

England and Wales constituted a single jurisdictional unit, the result of long-established processes of political incorporation. Welsh and English regional institutional distinctiveness is historically more recent as a result. Indeed, Welsh nationalism and Cornish regionalism were initially culturally oriented with concerns about language foremost; political concerns followed later. Other English regions, such as Yorkshire or Northumberland and the North East of England, celebrated cultural regionalism from brass bands to the 'Geordie shore', but these have largely not taken an explicitly political form. The advent of distinct regional institutions may provide the opportunity for a political regionalism to develop. English nationalism rather than English regionalisms has proven to be a more potent political force.

The unions that held the British Isles archipelago within a single state were quite distinct. Each was marked by a distinct pattern of political rule, which differently sought the accommodation, incorporation or integration of minority nations and regions. Crudely, political nationalism and regionalism is reflective of the success or otherwise of these processes. It is these patterns that dictate the development and strength of nationalism and regionalism.

In response to these patterns of political development, nationalists and regionalists looked sideways towards continental Europe for inspiration but also for instruction on how to secure cultural safeguards or political autonomy. Yet, it was the wider British imperial world and its self-governing Dominions, Canada and Australia that provided the most immediate source of inspiration for home rulers and independentists alike. In the late twentieth century, the European Union replaced the British Empire as the transnational entity through which national aspirations might be accommodated.[63] In the 1990s, the SNP set its objective to secure 'Independence in Europe'. The European Union offered the possibility that Scotland could be independent within a community of states that included similarly sized nations such as Denmark and the Republic of Ireland. For Welsh nationalists, it was the looser Europe of the Regions that inspired, in which autonomy rather than sovereignty was the objective. The later institutionalization of European regions through the European Union's Committee of the Regions, in part, laid behind UK government plans to regionalize England. Moreover, the European Union provided a framework within which a new relationship could be developed among the Republic of Ireland, the United Kingdom and Northern Ireland. And negatively, the European Union, or rather its depiction, provided the 'other' against which post-devolution English nationalism mobilized.

But importantly, the main source of inspiration was nearer still, and lay within the confines of the British state. That is, nationalisms and regionalisms across the British Isles were conjoined. They provided each other with models to be emulated. The campaign for Irish home rule spurred on similar campaigns in Scotland and Wales. Through the twentieth century, Scotland has provided the motor for constitutional change. This 'quasi-nation state', and its demands for national recognition, had a knock-on effect on Wales, not just in the realm of culture and sport, and the right to be represented in international sporting competitions.[64] It allowed Welsh representatives to argue that as a nation, Wales should enjoy similar institutional distinctiveness. English regionalism, too, is a result. But so, too, is debate on an English parliament. The British Isles in this sense offers an instance of conjoined nationalisms and regionalisms.

Notes

1. Cf. John Breuilly, *Nationalism and the State* (Chicago, IL: University of Chicago Press, 1994); Michael Hechter, *Containing Nationalism* (Oxford: Oxford University Press, 2000); and Michael Mann, 'A Political Theory of Nationalism and Its Excesses', in *Notions of Nationalism*, ed. Sukumar Periwal (Budapest: Central European University Press, 1995).
2. Mann, 'A Political Theory of Nationalism'.
3. Breuilly, *Nationalism and the State*.
4. Hechter, *Containing Nationalism*.
5. I follow Michael Mann in acknowledging the role that the Reformation in the sixteenth century and the development of the early modern state and commerce in the seventeenth century played in the 'proto-national' emergence of nations. Mann, 'A Political Theory of Nationalism'.
6. James Kennedy, *Liberal Nationalisms: Empire, State and Civil Society in Scotland and Quebec* (Montreal: McGill-Queen's University Press, 2013), 16.
7. Alvin Jackson, *The Two Unions: Ireland, Scotland and the Survival of the United Kingdom, 1707-2007* (Oxford: Oxford University Press, 2012), 108.
8. Linda Colley, *Acts of Union and Disunion* (London: Profile Books, 2014), 57–60.
9. Krishan Kumar, *The Making of English National Identity* (Cambridge: Cambridge University Press, 2003).
10. Liliana Riga, *The Bolsheviks and the Russian Empire* (Cambridge: Cambridge University Press, 2012).
11. Rogers Brubaker, *Nationalism Reframed* (Cambridge: Cambridge University Press, 1996).
12. Tom Nairn, *The Break-Up of Britain* (London: Verso, rev. ed., 1981), 129.
13. Linda Colley, *Britons: Forging the Nation, 1707–1837* (London: Pimlico, 1992).
14. Colley, *Britons*, 5.
15. Kennedy, *Liberal Nationalisms*, 33–34.
16. Colley, *Britons*.
17. Jackson, *The Two Unions*, 109–11.
18. Lindsay Paterson, *The Autonomy of Modern Scotland* (Edinburgh: Edinburgh University Press, 1994), 74–79.

19. Jackson, *The Two Unions*, 111, 114.
20. Michael Hechter, *Internal Colonialism: The Celtic Fringe in British National Development* (London: Routledge, 1975).
21. Paterson, *The Autonomy of Modern Scotland*, 77.
22. Michael Mann, *States, War and Capitalism* (London: Blackwell, 1988), chapter 1.
23. Jackson, *The Two Unions*, 113–14.
24. Jackson, *The Two Unions*, 209, 214; cf. John Hutchinson, *The Dynamics of Cultural Nationalism: Gaelic Revival and the Creation of the Irish Nation State* (London: Allen & Unwin, 1987).
25. John Davies, *A History of Wales* (London: Penguin, 2007), 225–32.
26. Davies, *A History of Wales*, 387.
27. Colley, *Acts of Union and Disunion*, 57–60.
28. R. F. Foster, *Modern Ireland, 1600–1972* (London: Penguin, 1988), 405; cf. Thomas Bartlett, *Ireland: A History* (Cambridge: Cambridge University Press, 2010).
29. Foster, *Modern Ireland*, 400–28.
30. Hutchinson, *The Dynamics of Cultural Nationalism*.
31. Foster, *Modern Ireland*, chapter 18.
32. Foster, *Modern Ireland*, 457.
33. Bill Kissane, *The Politics of the Irish Civil War* (Oxford: Oxford University Press, 2005).
34. Graeme Morton, *Unionist Nationalism: Governing Urban Scotland, 1830–1860* (East Linton: Tuckwell, 1999).
35. Morton, *Unionist-Nationalism*.
36. Kennedy, *Liberal Nationalisms*.
37. Kennedy, *Liberal Nationalisms*, chapter 5.
38. Davies, *A History of Wales*, 441–42, 452–55.
39. Davies, *A History of Wales*, 349–50.
40. Davies, *A History of Wales*, 374, 404–5, 443.
41. Bernard Deacon, Dick Cole and Garry Tregida, *Mebyon Kernow and Cornish Nationalism* (Cardiff: Welsh Academic Press, 2003), 2, 7, 9, 14–15, 19–20.
42. I make a distinction between the use of 'home rule' in the previous section, and 'devolution' in this. While these terms are largely interchangeable, I want to distinguish between the bottom-up movement for home rule and the forms of devolution, administrative and legislative implemented by the state in an occasionally top-down fashion.
43. Brendan O'Duffy, 'Containment or Regulation? The British Approach to Ethnic Conflict in Northern Ireland', in *The Politics of Ethnic Conflict Regulation*, ed. John McGarry and Brendan O'Leary (London: Routledge, 1993).
44. Brendan O'Leary, 'The Belfast Agreement and the British-Irish Agreement', in *The Architecture of Democracy*, ed. Andrew Reynolds (Oxford: Oxford University Press, 2002), 293–356.
45. Liliana Riga and James Kennedy, 'Tolerant Majorities, Loyal Minorities and "Ethnic Reversals": Constructing Minority Rights at Versailles 1919', *Nations and Nationalism* 15, no. 3 (2009): 461–82.
46. Richard Finlay, *Independent and Free: Scottish Politics and the Origins of the Scottish National Party 1918–1945* (Edinburgh: John Donald, 1994).

47. Michael Mann, 'Sources of Variation of Working Class Movements in Twentieth Century Europe', *New Left Review* I, no. 212 (1995): 25.
48. T. H. Devine, *The Scottish Nation: A Modern History* (London: Penguin, 1999), 551–52.
49. James G. Kellas, *The Scottish Political System* (Cambridge: Cambridge University Press, 4th ed., 1984).
50. Breuilly, *Nationalism and the State*, 324–25.
51. Jonathan Hearn, 'Identity, Class and Civil Society', *Nations and Nationalism* 8, no. 1 (2002): 15–30.
52. For an examination of issues that arose during the referendum campaign, cf. Michael Keating ed., *Debating Scotland: Issues of Independence and Union in the 2014 Referendum* (Oxford: Oxford University Press, 2017).
53. Rhys Jones and Carwyn Fowler, eds, *Placing the Nation: Aberystwyth and the Reproduction of Welsh Nationalism* (Chicago, IL: Chicago University Press, 2008).
54. Davies, *A History of Wales*, 697, 699–704.
55. Davies, *A History of Wales*, 640–41.
56. Cf. Richard Finlay, 'Thatcherism, Unionism and Nationalism: A Comparative Study of Scotland and Wales', in *Making Thatcher's Britain*, ed. Ben Jackson and Robert Saunders (Cambridge: Cambridge University Press, 2012).
57. Davies, *A History of Wales*, 705.
58. Deacon et al., *Mebyon Kernow*, 51–52, 85–87, 107, 118, 115.
59. Colley, *Acts of Union and Disunion*, 62.
60. Ailsa Henderson, Charlie Jeffery, Daniel Wincott and Richard Wyn Jones, 'How Brexit Was Made in England', *British Journal of Politics and International Relations* 19, no. 4 (2017): 631–46; Ailsa Henderson, Charlie Jeffery, Robert Liñiera, Roger Scully and Daniel Wincott, 'England, Englishness and Brexit', *Political Quarterly* 87, no. 2 (2016): 187–99; cf. Arthur Aughey, *The Politics of Englishness* (Manchester: Manchester University Press, 2007); and Ben Wellings, *English Nationalism and Euroscepticism: Losing the Peace* (Bern: Peter Lang, 2012).
61. Mann, 'A Political Theory of Nationalism', 49–50.
62. Paterson, *The Autonomy of Modern Scotland*.
63. István Deák makes a similar claim for the space vacated by the Habsburg Empire. Cf. *Beyond Nationalism: A Social and Political History of the Habsburg Officer Corps, 1848-1914* (Oxford: Oxford University Press, 1990).
64. Davies, *A History of Wales*, 708.

Further reading

Bartlett, Thomas, ed., *The Cambridge History of Ireland. Volume 4: 1880 to the Present* (Cambridge: Cambridge University Press, 2018).
Deacon, Russell, Alison Denton and Robert Southall, *The Government and Politics of Wales* (Edinburgh: Edinburgh University Press, 2018).
Kenny, Michael, *The Politics of English Nationhood* (Oxford: Oxford University Press, 2014).
McCrone, David, *The New Sociology of Scotland* (London: Sage, 2017).

CHAPTER 19
CONCLUSION: OVERCOMING METHODOLOGICAL REGIONALISM
Xosé M. Núñez Seixas and Eric Storm

The objective of *Regionalism in Modern Europe* is not merely to summarize the findings of a large number of existing case studies. Because of its comparative approach, it also aims to produce fundamental new insights. However, there are also limitations: throughout the chapters of this volume, it has become clear that many aspects of regionalism have barely been researched and that there are large differences in the various research traditions, for instance, between Western Europe, where regions are embedded within long-established nation states, and East-Central Europe, where most nation states are of a much more recent date. Moreover, there are also clear differences between the empirical case-study tradition of historians focusing particularly on the period before 1945 and the much more comparative field of political science dealing with the Europe of the regions during more recent decades. Nevertheless, we will present some tentative conclusions from the various thematic and geographical chapters contained in the volume. We will also add some reflections on the current state of the art and make suggestions for further research.

Regionalism in Europe: Some long-term trends

Not all regions and mesoterritorial units have a strong identity. There seem to be some structural factors that can at least partially explain why certain regions have a strong collective identity and whether regional movements have gained much appeal. These factors are age, linguistic peculiarities, the level of autonomy and the presence of characteristic highlights. However, most of these factors have little predictive value.

Many regions on the Old Continent go back to subdivisions from the feudal era, such as duchies, counties, margraviates, and so on. In some parts of the continent and its islands – such as Great Britain – these ancient territories were never dissolved and remained integrated into an imperial polity; in others they were replaced during or after the French Revolution by a more rational system or provinces or departments, which are more uniform and generally of a similar size. In the parts of Europe that had belonged to the Ottoman or Russian Empire, these feudal territories did not exist or had disappeared a long time ago. However, longevity does not automatically imply that a territorial identity is very pronounced. Sometimes, memories of independent statehood from the past, such as is the case in Scotland, Bohemia or Bavaria, can lead to strong regional identities and even to pleas for national self-determination. In other cases, territories with a long history, such as for instance the Dutch province of Gelderland (which coincides more or less with the ancient duchy of Gelre) or the English county of Bedfordshire, have a rather nondescript identity.

Ethnic and linguistic differences can be an important factor as well. The *Landespatriotismus* that regardless of ethnic or cultural background had stimulated feelings of loyalty to Land and Kaiser in the Austrian Empire largely disappeared in East-Central Europe after 1918. Moreover, in this part of Europe there were many ethnically mixed regions without a clear majority, so it would have been difficult to demarcate specific linguistically unified minority regions as was the case in some parts of Western Europe. On the other hand, strong centralized states such as the Third Republic quite easily assimilated those parts of France where dialects or languages were spoken that belonged to the same language family as French, such as Occitan, Catalan or Piedmontese dialects. This was done consciously by promoting the French language in school and in the contacts with the administration, but also happened almost automatically as a consequence of the rise of new mass media such as the popular press, radio and, later, television. The Flemish- and Basque-speaking parts – where distance languages (*Abstandsprachen*) were used – were probably too small to resist the advance of the French language. This was easier in Brittany, which was substantially larger; moreover, Breton was not spoken in a neighbouring country (like Flemish or German) and was therefore less suspect. Thus, the presence of a different language did not always offer a motive to create a strong regionalist movement with political claims. However, in many other cases it led to the creation of a strong regional movement, which often spilled over into nationalism – Wales, Flanders, Brittany, Catalonia, the Basque Country, Galicia, Sardinia, South Tyrol, Macedonia and Kosovo are just a few cases that come to mind. Recently, some regions where many different languages are spoken, such as Vojvodina or Transylvania, are presenting this as their defining quality.

A significant positive factor seems to be the level of autonomy. In centralized countries like France, most departments do not have a large budget for or much interest in trying to create a strong identity in order to legitimize themselves amongst the population. The German Länder or the Spanish Autonomous Communities, on the other hand, are responsible for education and culture and, in general, subsidize projects lavishly, or even take the initiative to strengthen the specific cultural identity of the region.

There are also regions that without necessarily having their own language and culture have a very strong and recognizable identity. This is particularly the case with rural areas where ancient traditions supposedly were still alive and which often were presented as a kind of national heartland. This was, for instance, the case with Karelia in Finland, Dalarna in Sweden, Tyrol in Austria, the Pustzas in Hungary and Andalusia in Spain. In general, they were also chosen in such a way as to clearly distinguish the country from its neighbours. Thus, Telemark, with its mountains and fjords was definitely not Swedish, while the Highlands distinguished Scotland from the low rolling countryside of its southern neighbour. Other regions received a pronounced identity because they were claimed by various rivalling nationalist movements: Alsace, Wallonia, Northern Ireland, Upper Silesia, Bosnia, Macedonia and (with some nuances) Transylvania.

Some regions are well known because they are associated with specific agricultural products (generally alcoholic beverages such as wine or whisky): Burgundy, La Rioja or Scotland. Industrial areas, like Lancaster or the Ruhr-area, can also have a very strong brand, although nowadays they are largely based on past glories. Other regions are famous for their artistic treasures (Tuscany, Provence), folklore (Andalusia, Bavaria, Tyrol) or natural beauty (Riviera, Highlands), while some are celebrated because of their fictional literary heroes (Transylvania, La Mancha, Gascoigne). Areas that do not have broadly recognized, specific highlights tend to have a weak regional identity, both internally and externally, and the same is true for strongly urbanized or large metropolitan areas. This, for instance, is the case in Île de France, the London metropolitan area, the Autonomous Community of Madrid, the Western parts of the Netherlands, or in Italy, where urban identities seem to have largely prevailed over regional ones, particularly in the north and centre of the country.

Chronology is also of utmost importance, since the character and expressions of regionalism changed profoundly over time. Although some awareness of regional differences did already exist, clearly demarcated regional identities were only created towards the end of the nineteenth century. Regionalism, like nationalism, is therefore a product of modernity, and whereas Ernest Gellner linked the rise of nationalism to the transition from agricultural to industrial society, one could argue that regionalism is the product of the second industrial revolution of the late nineteenth century. New secondary railways, improved communications and the creation of more uniform markets made it possible and commercially attractive to market products as coming from a specific region. However, one could also argue that it was maybe not so much the technological revolution but the rise of consumer society that led producers to diversify their products. Towards the end of the nineteenth century, entrepreneurs in the tourism and agribusiness industries began to emphasize the exceptional and unique qualities of their homeland in order to stand out among the rest.

Cultural trends were crucial as well. Already during the Romantic era, the countryside began to be perceived as the national heartland, where the authentic traditions and customs of the nation were still largely intact. Towards the end of the nineteenth century, there was a new interest in the authentic culture of the countryside, although its *Volksgeist* was no longer seen as representing the nation as a whole; many activists and intellectuals now argued that each region had its particular landscape, folklore and values. Regional highlights, such as historical monuments, typical landscapes, vernacular constructions and artisanal products, had to be salvaged and protected and should even inform contemporary culture, which became manifest in the new vogue for arts and crafts, neo-vernacular architecture and regional literature.

In addition to technological, economic and cultural factors, geopolitics played a major role as well; for example, the collapse of the Russian, Austro-Hungarian, Ottoman and German Empires at the end of the First World War offered a clear window of opportunity for political entrepreneurs.[1] Territories which were seen so far as multiethnic regions, such as Lithuania, Latvia and Estonia became independent nation states, while Bohemia, Moravia and Slovakia formed the new state of Czechoslovakia. Ukraine briefly became a nation state and Finland and Ireland – although already considered nations thanks to the previous development of strong nationalist movements – became independent. However, the indirect endorsement to the principle of national self-determination given by Allied propaganda during the First World War, as well as by President Woodrow Wilson's Fourteen Points and the parallel appeal to national liberation by the revolutionary Bolsheviks, had even wider effects. Thus, the population of the Finnish Åland Islands requested to be reintegrated into Sweden, Belgium claimed Zeelandic Flanders and Limburg from the Netherlands, while some Swabian regionalists dreamt of creating a greater Swabian nation state that included Württemberg, Bavarian Swabia, parts of Switzerland and Austria and even the Alsace.[2] At the same time, regionalist movements in Brittany, Occitania, Corsica, Wales, Galicia and (to some extent) Sardinia became fully fledged nationalist movements.

During the interwar period, both fascists and communists appropriated the flowering regional movements to their own ends. Any form of political regionalism – let alone demands for autonomy – were out of the question, but fascists and communist regimes strongly stimulated cultural forms of regionalism, particularly folkloric dresses (primarily for women who supposedly were more strongly connected to the soil and traditions of the homeland), dances and songs. Especially in the beginning, regional cultural and natural heritage received recognition and was protected by creating national parks, local museums and preserving ancient monuments. This positive attitude was sometimes even extended to dialects and regional languages. Over time, efficiency and new forms of (urban) mass culture became more important and national unity and imperial expansion prevailed over regional peculiarities.

In democratic countries, regional planning and regional development plans were initiated in the 1920s and 1930s, although the best-known example can be found in the United States: the Tennessee Valley Authority, which was part of Franklin D. Roosevelt's New Deal. Cultural regionalism was often stimulated by local authorities, while political regionalism was generally seen as problem. Regional autonomy was not something that many constitutional democracies were eager to grant.

The end of the Second World War in 1945 was a genuine turning point. Because of its association with the crimes of Nazi Germany, exalted nationalism and essentialist interpretations of regional identities had become suspect. The Cold War petrified the borders of the new post-war settlement and, therefore, secessionist tendencies were out of the question, both in East and West. In addition, many regionalist movements and minority nationalists – from Brittany and Flanders to Ukraine and Croatia – had collaborated with the Nazis, but even where this had not been the case, pleas for regional autonomy were anathema. Only a few movements, such as Basques, Galicians and Catalans in Spain, as well as Sardinians in Italy, had aligned themselves with anti-fascism.[3] Everybody understood that strong nation states were needed to ward off the threat from the enemy on the other side of the Iron Curtain. Regionalism, therefore, largely disappeared from the political sphere. However, as the case of Germany has made clear, regionalism was still very much alive in the private and cultural domain. The number of regionalist associations increased rapidly and regional movies, television series and novels reached a large audience. The often quite nostalgic identification with the homeland had a reassuring effect after decades of political, social and economic turmoil.

In the 1960s, a new generation began to criticize this state of affairs. The process of decolonization in the Third World made those who sympathized with the national liberation movements in the non-Western world turn their attention to 'oppressed minorities', or what the Occitan regionalist Robert Lafont defined as 'internal colonies', at home.[4] The thaw also lessened the pressure of the Cold War and created space for demands for more autonomy, at least in the West. In the East, beginning with the 'Croatian Spring' of 1968, demands for enlarged self-government for ethnic minorities and regions also emerged. The new emphasis on authenticity and inner feelings of the youth movement, on the one hand, discredited the artificial 'folklorism' of the traditional regionalist associations while, on the other hand, stimulating new interest in more 'genuine' folk culture. At the same time, more people became engaged in specific endeavours to protect the environment and cultural heritage of their own (immediate) surroundings. Shortly afterwards, in 1972, the European Economic Community developed a plan for cross-border cooperation in the form of Euroregions, of which there are currently about eighty. Three years later, it also created the European Regional Development Fund, thus implicitly stimulating a more active economic and administrative role of the regions in member states. In order to attract investors and tourists, regions also began to actively promote and brand their regions in the international market: both cultural and political regionalism therefore made a strong comeback during this period.

The fall of the Berlin Wall in 1989 provided another window of opportunity. The ethnic identity of many national or regional groups had been recognized under communism, and many of them even had their own only nominally independent soviet republic. This clearly prepared the way for many of these groups or republics to use the moment and become an independent nation state. This happened with the Baltic states, Ukraine, Georgia and others after the dissolution of the Soviet Union in 1991. The split of Czechoslovakia into two new nation states also occurred peacefully, while the breakup of Yugoslavia led to a number of violent conflicts. In 2004 and 2007, many former communist countries in East-Central Europe became members of the European Union and therefore had to set up more autonomous regional administrations.

The end of the Cold War also led to increased activities of regionalist movements in the West. After several rounds of decentralization, Belgium became a federal state in 1993. The Lega Nord was founded in 1991 in order to plead for more autonomy for Padania, a newly invented region in the rich northern part of Italy. Although the end of the traditional nation state was predicted by many analysts who saw in the consolidation of the European Union a new paradigm of coexistence of stronger supranational institutions with enforced regional and local administrations,[5] in fact by the first decade of the new century, nation states continued to play a crucial role in European politics and governance, while the project of the 'Europe of regions' seemed to have collapsed. The

Eastern enlargement of the European Union, with microstates like Cyprus, Estonia or Malta also entering the club, had a paradoxical effect on some West European regional/national movements: only the achievement of a state of their own would make it possible for them to have a voice in the European Union.[6]

The apparent weakening of the nation states because of neo-liberal reforms, the growing importance of supranational institutions such as the European Union and of transnational financial currents, seemed to have strengthened the appeal of identity politics. Although this also affected issues of gender, sexuality and race, another consequence was the increased interest in regional and substate identities. Many now argue that regional identities have to be protected against the levelling influences of global modernity; some even see the presence of immigrants as a threat to existing collective identities. On the other hand, immigrants also actively make use of regional identities to blend into their new national environment, for instance, by adopting a dialect, a language or other regional identity markers. Regional and subnational identities are increasingly civic and less ethnic, and may also function as a first step to integrate immigrants and refugees into European societies.

Localism, regionalism, nationalism and imperialism

However, regionalism did not develop in isolation. It constantly interacted with localism, nationalism and imperialism. And this has various consequences, also for these adjacent fields. A first striking aspect is the shifting and sometimes divergent use of key concepts such as 'region' and 'regionalism', as well as 'local' and 'localism'. Is region-building similar to regionalism? Should we distinguish between different layers of identity-building and territorial loyalty? Or should we instead accept that the limits between those layers are extremely diffuse, and hence their forms of identification are also blurred? Region and regionalism, as well as localism, have meant different things at different times in different countries.

The emphasis on regions as a form of mesoterritorial identity has tended to marginalize the emergence, consolidation and evolution of other forms of identification. Among them we may especially note two cases. The first is the increasingly important role played by cities as places of memory, as objects of identification and as generators of very specific forms of intermediate identity that link the nation to buildings, architecture and urban planning as a specific form of conquering space and nature.[7] The second is the more ambiguous place occupied by supralocal entities that vary in importance throughout Europe, but which mediate between the regional level (the imagined community that is not inherently sovereign) and the local sphere (the living spaces of daily life where physical interaction and mutual knowledge is possible). These are the *Kreis* in Germany, the *contrée* in France, the *paese* or *paesino* in Italy and the *comarca* in Spain.[8] Regions were often given priority because they were 'big' enough to generate a culture, a network of institutions involved in their maintenance and/or defence, a political claim or a historical narrative. Cities may also generate a narrative of their own. However, the local emerges as the place where the narratives of the nation receive concrete names, shapes and figures, where a particular hero incarnates the virtues of the nation. The 'intermediate' spheres between the living space of experience and the first imagined sphere of the region have barely been researched.

In fact, different concepts and images about what a region is, its limits and its definition may compete within a given mesoterritorial entity. New departments, provinces, *oblasts* and the like have also generated mechanisms of social identification and collected support from local elites. Although many local intellectuals and civil servants looked to past territorial demarcations as their term of reference, many others did not. Instead, they played the card of province-making, or of promoting 'pride in the place'. These actors often mixed and merged the *regional* imagery with the particular *local* one. The 'invention' of a *bilbaíno* tradition in the Basque town of Bilbao since the mid-nineteenth century illustrates all these ambiguities: local identity emphasized the Spanishness and liberal character of the town as opposed to the Basque-speaking and Catholic countryside, and at the same time elaborated a peculiar Basqueness exclusive to the town.[9]

The study of the region is generally marked by an insistence upon ideological genealogy: the forms of mesoterritorial identification are interesting to historians as long as they contain *in nuce* the elements that can later be codified into the cornerstones of a national narrative by nation-builders. In other words, the region is sometimes seen as a miniature of the nation that would emerge later: thus, any vindication of the Basque *fueros* or territorial rights in the eighteenth and early nineteenth centuries was regarded by later historians of Basque nationalism as a forerunner of later claims for nationhood. In the process, historians become captives of the nationalist narrative trap: accepting in a more or less teleological way the hierarchy of loyalties imposed by nationalism as the logical one, without necessarily considering how contingent these hierarchies may have been. The scarce available attempts at a comparative view of the role of region-building in two or more nation states arrive at important conclusions: it is problematic to maintain that a *pattern* of *normality* has ever existed in the relationships between the nation, the state and the region (and/or other subnational identities).[10]

Moreover, focusing on the dynamics of region-building and local identity has also meant studying state and/or substate nationalism from below. National consciousness was a multidirectional process; it can flow from the bottom up, through the dynamics generated by civil society. This helps to create spheres of everyday experience that contribute to the shaping of a *national culture* in a broader sense. From this angle, region-builders were often nation-builders: they linked the abstract narrative of the nation (from above) to more concrete forms of everyday experience (from below).[11] Related to this, we may advance the hypothesis that the diverse processes of territorial identity-building were not necessarily mutually exclusive or mutually complementary. The challenge is to find out the precise form of interaction that these identifications of 'changing geometry at different scales' may have had in each particular case and time. This leads us to question some broadly accepted (or at least commonly assumed) generalizations, such as the implicit association between democracy and federalism/regionalism on the one hand and between dictatorship and localism on the other. Yet there have been diverse conservative, and even traditionalist, Ancien Régime-type federalist proposals such as the 'organic federalism' put forth by French and Spanish conservative intellectuals in the nineteenth and early twentieth centuries. Even fascist dictatorships occasionally incorporated some form of regional demand or decentralization within their cultural and political practices.[12] Localism was also instilled in people by radical Republicans, who made communes and municipalities their preferred sphere of political agitation and imagined it as the privileged place where authentic grass-roots democracy could be built.

How do different layers of territorial identification and loyalties interact at the micro level, or even the personal level? There is some agreement on the need to distinguish multiple (or 'nested') identities from hybrid identities, such as German-Turkish or British-Pakistani. While double, multiple and shared identities can be understood as layers around a core, hybrid identities are harder to grasp, their lines of demarcation are diffuse and their hierarchy is unclear; they are more of a collage, an eclectic combining or even a fusion of traits. The buffer zones of shared identities can also relate to other types of non-territorial identification, such as religion or gender, and the hierarchies between those identities may vary. Nationhood may be confused with sentiments of local identity; provincial identification may overlap with regional/mesoterritorial identity. The transition moves us from the concept of national identities as a crucible or melting pot – to use a classic definition from immigration studies – where all elements combine into a new, singular identity with a precise shape, to a more flexible 'salad bowl' concept: the components remain identifiable but can flavour each other and combine to make the distinct flavour of the salad as a whole. Alon Confino has rightly suggested that individuals see the world through a multiplicity of experiences and social representations, and the challenge for historians consists in being able to grasp them.[13]

The region and the local sphere should be treated as nested identities and understood within the framework of European overseas expansion and empire formation. Empires have contributed to the consolidation of European nation states. They also provided a way to integrate different spheres of identification, by offering ways of combining subnational territorial allegiances that could also claim to be alternative national identities (from Scotland to Catalonia and Ukraine) within a broader imperial worldview, where more flexible models for integrating diverse territories had a better chance of being framed. Such models varied from overseas to continental empires, with diverging effects on the 'regional integration' of the territories in the imperial core.[14] However, a question still to be definitively answered is whether 'integration' and centralization in the imperial core was really necessary, rather than a more general tendency towards a varied geometry of relationships among different territories, regions, localities and ethnic groups around a monarchic or imperial 'centre'. Here, the example of Spain's imperial crisis of 1898, which led to gradual regional 'disintegration', could be compared to those of Britain, Belgium and France, where the overseas empire tended to integrate different ethnic groups and territories within the national project (or at least within a shared project). Another point of comparison were the continental empires, where substate nationalisms competed with other versions of territorial identity (regional, supraethnic) that were usually considered more compatible with imperial loyalty.[15] The relationship of the regions with the European Union would follow some astonishingly similar dynamics, since Brussels and the EU institutions have been sometimes considered as a form of 'informal empire' whose rule over the regions reminded that of imperial centres in the past.[16]

Conclusion

To conclude, it can be argued that region-building processes in Europe have involved historical dynamics somewhat similar to nation-building processes. The tendency has been to build regional identity upon arguments (history, tradition, the people's will) similar to those incorporated or defended by elites in pursuit of their own political or other interests. The theoretical difference between the region and the nation, and therefore between regionalism and nationalism, must be found in the notion of *present-day* collective sovereignty, which is exclusively ascribed to the nation. Thus, the difference does not necessarily lie in the principles of collective identification with a territory, since the mechanisms of nation and region-building may be quite similar. The differences must be sought in the *outcome* of these building processes, particularly in the presence or absence of a territorial foundation of sovereignty. This may also be a result of historical contingency, which is directly linked to the breakdown of multinational empires before and after the First World War, and again after 1989. The border changes sanctioned by international politics contributed to the legitimization of some of them as 'natural'. However, the identity-building processes before and after those changes were not necessarily different in nature, but rather in outcome.[17]

There are several European cases that illustrate how these dynamics may converge or diverge over time, but they remain deeply interrelated due to their similar historical origins. Although not all forms of regionalism, localism or ethno-territorial vindication have actually led to the emergence of a new substate nationalism, it is hard to find a nationalist movement that has not emerged from a previously existing form of collective identity or *ethno-territorial* mobilization. The egg did not always produce a chicken, but it is rare for a chicken not to have come from an egg: a complex relationship between regionalism and substate nationalism emerges, especially within a single political system or at the frontiers of a single state (or empire). Concurrent ethno-territorial movements within the borders of a single political entity introduce more intricate dynamics that may turn 'cultural regionalism' into political regionalisms and even contribute to the emergence of new minority nationalisms. The history of multinational empires reveals concurrent, local, 'pre-modern' identities based on different forms of *Landespatriotismus* and ethnonationalism. These translate into a fight between the perceived relics of old-fashioned imperial rule based on dynastic loyalty and religious belief, and the new 'modernity' based on the principle of nationality, as became evident before the outbreak of the First World War.[18]

While regionalism or mesoterritorial political mobilization did not imply an inherent contradiction or opposition to nation-building, in some cases it threw decisive elements of ideological and cultural friction into the mesoterritorial political arena, which may have resulted in the development of a distinct peripheral nationalism. In other words, region-building may be, but is not always in conflict with nation-building: it depends on the precise and particular articulation of both processes, each with their own social interests and cultural worldviews, as well as their interaction with political and social movements that would 'territorialize' their projects and aims. Once again, this is more the outcome of historical contingency than the necessary result of a set of given social, cultural or ethnic preconditions. Historical research on subnational identities definitively supports methodological constructivism.

Last but not least, this is a book on regions and regionalism *in* Europe. But some of its findings could perhaps also provide inspiration for similar research on regional movements and identities elsewhere in the world. First of all, it is striking that methodological regionalism is dominant here as well: comparative studies are largely lacking and generally there are no references to classical monographs on regionalism elsewhere in the world. Most studies are dedicated to 'unhappy' regions, such as Kashmir and Assam in India, Patagonia in Argentina or the South in the United States.[19] While in India and Africa the focus is very much on ethnic and religious cleavages, in the Americas there are already various studies on more political forms of regionalism.[20] The construction of regional identities has also been thematized for various high profile regions, such as the tourist island of Bali in Indonesia, the coffee region of Cauca in Colombia and New England and New Mexico in the United States.[21] The field of regionalism studies would highly profit from a global comparison, which underlines the differences and similarities between European regionalisms and those of other parts of the world. This challenge will hopefully be taken up by others.

Notes

1. Andreas Wimmer, *Waves of War: Nationalism, State Formation, and Ethnic Exclusion in the Modern World* (Cambridge: Cambridge University Press, 2013), 106–7.
2. Martina Stieber, *Ethnische Gewissheiten. Die Ordnung des Regionalen im bayerischen Schwaben vom Kaiserreich bis zum NS-Regime* (Göttingen: Vandenhoeck & Ruprecht, 2010), 193–221.
3. Xosé M. Núñez Seixas, 'Unholy Alliances? Nationalist Exiles, Minorities and Antifascism in Interwar Europe', *Contemporary European History* 25, no. 4 (2016): 597–617.
4. See Joel Belliveau and Tudi Kernalegenn, eds, *La vague nationale des années 1968: Une comparaison internationale* (Ottawa: Presses de l'Université d'Ottawa, 2018, forthcoming).
5. Kenichi Ohmae, *The End of the Nation State: The Rise of Regional Economies* (New York: The Free Press, 1996); and Kenichi Ohmae, 'The Rise of the Region State', *Foreign Affairs* 72, no. 2 (1993): 72–85.

6. Emmanuel Dalle Mulle, *The Nationalism of the Rich: Discourses and Strategies of Separatist Parties in Catalonia, Flanders, Northern Italy and Scotland* (London: Routledge, 2018).
7. Maiken Umbach, 'A Tale of Second Cities: Autonomy, Culture and the Law in Hamburg and Barcelona in the Long Nineteenth Century', *American Historical Review* 110 (2005): 659–92; Maiken Umbach, *German Cities and Bourgeois Modernism, 1890–1924* (Oxford: Oxford University Press, 2009); Jennifer Jenkins, *Provincial Modernity: Local Culture and Local Politics in Fin-de-Siècle Hamburg* (Ithaca, NY: Cornell University Press, 2003); and Oliver Zimmer, *Remaking the Rhythms of Life: German Communities in the Age of the Nation-State* (Oxford: Oxford University Press, 2013). For a global perspective, see Saskia Stassen, *Cities in a World Economy* (Thousand Oaks, CA: Pine Forge Press, 2011).
8. Xabier Ferreira, *La comarca en la historia. Una aproximación a la reciente historia jurídica de la comarca* (Santiago de Compostela: Universidade de Santiago de Compostela, 2000).
9. Jon Juaristi, *El chimbo expiatorio. La invención de la tradición bilbaína, 1876–1939* (Madrid: Espasa, 1999).
10. Julian Wright and Christopher Clark, 'Regionalism and the State in France and Prussia', *European Review of History/Revue Européenne d'Histoire* 15 (2008): 277–93; and Roberto Ruffilli, *La questione regionale dall'Unificazione alla dittatura (1862–1942)* (Milan: Giuffrè, 1971).
11. Anne-Marie Thiesse, *Ils apprenaient la France. L'exaltation des régions dans le discours patriotique* (Paris: Maison des Sciences de l'Homme, 1997); Anne-Marie Thiesse, *Écrire la France. Le mouvement littéraire régionaliste de langue française entre la Belle Époque et la Libération* (Paris: Presses Universitaire de France, 1991); Jean-François Chanet, *L'École républicaine et les petites patries* (Paris: Aubier, 1996); and Maarten Van Ginderachter and Marnix Beyen, eds, *Nationhood from Below: Europe in the Long Nineteenth Century* (Basingstoke: Palgrave Macmillan, 2012).
12. Stefano Cavazza, *Piccole patrie. Feste popolari tra regione e nazione durante il fascismo* (Bologna: Il Mulino, 2003).
13. Alon Confino, 'Lo local, una esencia de toda nación', *Ayer* 64 (2006): 19–31.
14. Stefan Berger and Alexei Miller, 'Nation-Building and Regional Integration, c. 1880–1914: The Role of Empires', *European Review of History/ Revue Europeenne d'Histoire* 15 (2008): 317–30; as well as Stefan Berger and Alexei Miller, eds, *Nationalizing Empires* (Budapest: Central European University Press, 2015).
15. See Peter Haslinger, *Nation und Territorium im tschechischen politischen Diskurs 1880–1938* (Munich: Oldenbourg, 2010), 4–34; Hans-Christian Maner, ed., *Grenzregionen der Habsburgermonarchie im 18. und 19. Jahrhundert: Ihre Bedeutung und Funktion aus der Perspektive Wiens* (Münster: LIT Verlag, 2005); and Alexei Miller, 'Between Local and Inter-Imperial: Russian Imperial History in Search of Scope and Paradigm', *Kritika: Explorations in Russian and Eurasian History* 5 (2004): 7–26.
16. Warwick Armstrong and James Anderson, eds, *Geopolitics of European Union Enlargement: A Fortress Empire?* (London; New York: Routledge, 2007); and Jan Zielonka, *Europe as Empire: The Nature of the Enlarged European Union* (Oxford: Oxford University Press, 2006).
17. Ralf Petri and Michael G. Müller, eds, *Die Nationalisierung von Grenzen. Zur Konstruktion nationaler Identität in sprachlich gemischten Grenzregionen* (Marburg a. Lahn: Herder-Institut, 2002); David Laven and Timothy Baycroft, 'Border Regions and Identity', *European Review of History/Revue Européenne d'Histoire* 15 (2008): 255–75; Hein Hoebink, ed., *Europäische Geschichtsschreibung und europäische Regionen: Historiographische Konzepte diesseits und jenseits der niederländisch-deutschen/nordrhein-westfälischen Grenze* (Münster: Waxmann,

2008); Caitlin E. Murdock, *Changing Places: Society, Culture, and Territory in the Saxon-Bohemian Borderlands, 1870–1946* (Ann Arbor: University of Michigan Press, 2010); and Omer Bartov and Eric D. Weitz, eds, *Shatterzone of Empires: Coexistence and Violence in the German, Habsburg, Russian and Ottoman Borderlands* (Bloomington: Indiana University Press, 2013).

18. Pieter M. Judson, *The Habsburg Empire: A New History* (Cambridge: Belknap, 2016).

19. Sanjib Baruah, *India against Itself: Assam and the Politics of Nationality* (Philadelphia: University of Pennsylvania Press, 1999); Chitralekha Zutshi, *Languages of Belonging: Islam, Regional Identity, and the Making of Kashmir* (London: C. Hurst, 2004); Susana Bandieri, *Historia de la Patagonia* (Buenos Aires: Sudamericana, 2005); and Martyn Bone, Brian Ward and William A. Link, eds, *Creating and Consuming the American South* (Gainesville: University Press of Florida, 2015).

20. Sumathi Ramaswamy, *Passions of the Tongue: Language Devotion in Tamil India, 1891–1970* (Berkeley: University of California Press, 1997); Yasmin Saikia, *Fragmented Memories: Struggling to be Tai-Ahom in India* (Durham: Duke University Press, 2004); and Robert L. Dorman, *Revolt of the Provinces: The Regionalist Movement in America, 1920–1945* (Chapel Hill: University of North Carolina Press, 1993). See also Ricardo Pérez Montfort, *Expresiones populares y estereotipos culturales en México, siglos XIX y XX* (Mexico City: CIESAS, 2007).

21. Michel Picard, *Bali: Cultural Tourism and Touristic Culture* (translated from French; Singapore: Archipelago, 1996); Nancy P. Appelbaum, *Muddied Waters: Race, Region, and Local History in Colombia, 1846–1948* (Durham: Duke University Press, 2003); Dona Brown, *Inventing New England: Regional Tourism in the Nineteenth Century* (Washington, DC: Smithsonian Institution, 1995); and Chris Wilson, *The Myth of Santa Fe: Creating a Modern Regional Tradition* (Alburquerque: University of New Mexico Press, 1997).

INDEX

Aasen, Ivar 198
Abrams, Daniel M. 36
Abruzzi 90
Abruzzo national park 71
Abstand languages 30–1, 344
Academy of Sciences (Moscow) 137, 261
acculturation 37
Ady, Endre 256
Afanasyev, Alexander 44
Africa 36, 93, 123, 244, 325, 352
agriculture 83, 85, 88, 92–4, 137, 141, 245, 257, 283, 332
Åland Islands 15, 201, 202, 205, 206–7, 346
Alava 123
Alba Iulia 254
Albania 138, 307–9, 312, 318–19
Albanian language 12, 30, 318
Alecsandri, Vasile 261
Alexander I 201, 274
Alicante 2
Allemannian 76
Alps 70–2
Alto Adige *see* South Tyrol
Alsace 51, 75–6, 153, 156, 174–5, 179, 243, 345–6
Alsatian movement 237, 243
Amsterdam 104, 111, 214, 217
Ancien Régime 10, 27, 153, 215, 219, 235, 237, 250
Andalusia 45, 51–2, 103, 113, 128, 216, 344
Anderson, Benedict 151
Andorra 1–2
Annales de Bretagne 53
anti-colonialism 12, 56, 285
Anttonen, Pertti 49
Antwerp 214–15, 221
Aosta Valley 51, 156, 159, 243
Appelfeld, Aharon 264
Applegate, Celia 173–4, 180
Aragon 34, 110, 124–5, 241–2
Archangelsk 49, 206
Arctic North 15, 206
Arezzo 104
Aribau, Bonaventura 29
Arnaudin, Félix 52
Arndt, Ernst-Moritz 174, 294
Arnold, Jörg 180
Arsen'ev, Konstantin 275
Asia 93, 206, 244, 280, 325

Central 274
East 102
North 280
Assarsson, David 199
Asturian dialect 125
Asturias 30, 126, 240, 242
Asül, Django 37, 186
Aubin, Hermann 124
Ausbau language 28, 30–1
Australia 91, 280, 339
Austria 15, 73, 84, 124, 169–70, 174–6, 179, 181, 183–5, 216, 344, 346
Austria-Hungary *see* Austro-Hungarian empire
autonomous communities (Spain) 1–2, 158, 244–5, 344
autonomism 3, 225
autonomy, administrative 3, 8, 12, 59, 155–7, 235–7, 239, 243, 245, 260, 272–3, 311–12, 324, 330–1, 333, 336, 339
  cultural 201, 296, 324
  political 1, 5, 7, 9, 14, 16, 17–18, 31, 50, 121, 140–1, 157, 161, 163, 183, 193, 202, 218, 223, 241, 244–5, 251–5, 257, 259–60, 263, 271, 274–5, 277, 281, 275, 294, 297, 300–1, 310–11, 313–16, 324–6, 329, 339, 343–4, 346–7, 350
Auvergne 53–4, 57
Azores 16, 52, 235–6, 244

Baden 75–6, 179, 182, 184–5
Bakunin, Mikhail 279
Balearic Islands 1–2
Balkan Wars 252, 311, 316
Balkans 17, 32, 105, 257, 307–9, 319
Baltic area 11, 143, 201, 204, 291–7
  provinces 144, 275, 293–4, 296;
  sea 73, 102, 291
  states 17, 30, 32, 137, 146, 293, 297, 301, 347
Banat 17, 101, 251–3, 255, 257–8, 312, 317
Banat Swabians 253, 257
Bánffy, Miklós 254
Barcelona 1, 35, 48, 111, 238
Barents Region 206
Barrès, Maurice 240
Barsebäck 76
Barzaz Breiz 52
Basanavičius, Jonas 295
Basic Organizations of Associated Labour 143

Index

Basque Country 16, 33, 35, 45, 51, 121, 126, 154, 159–60, 234, 237, 346
Basque language 12, 30–1, 35, 344, 349
Basque nationalism 3, 5, 131, 157, 159, 241, 243–5, 346
Bausinger, Hermann 186
Bautzen 127
Bavaria 15, 28, 30, 33, 37, 65, 73–4, 113, 119, 121, 158, 160, 173, 183, 186, 198, 343, 345–6
Bayonne 88
BBC (British Broadcast Corporation) 48, 337
Beauquier, Charles 52
Begoña, Sanctuary of 240
Belgium 1, 16–17, 36, 45, 47, 51, 69, 84–5, 91, 156, 160, 179, 213, 215, 220–6, 238, 263, 346–7, 350
Benelux 154, 213, 227
Benidorm 108
Bennet, Alan 337
Bessarabia 17, 252–3, 258–60, 317
Berlin 14, 102–3, 111, 121, 178, 255, 295, 347
Bilbao 111, 238, 349
Bilingualism 1, 35, 37, 204, 213, 221, 223, 311
Biscay 123, 240
Blackbourn, David 172
Black Forest 102
Bladé, Jean-François 45
Blaga, Lucian 256
Bleasdale, Alan 337
Bled Agreement 138
Bohemia 32, 100–1, 174, 252, 258, 343, 346
Bolsheviks 135–8, 259, 275, 281, 292, 346
Bosnia-Herzegovina 18, 307–10, 313–15, 319, 345
Brabant 16, 213, 215, 219–21, 224
Braga, Teófilo 52
Brazil 83, 280
Breton language 3, 12, 30, 34, 46, 52–3, 55, 344
Breton movement 3, 153, 236, 238–40, 243
Brezhnev, Leonid 140, 142, 144
Brillat-Savarin, Jean-Anthelme 88
Britain *see* Great Britain
British Isles 11, 18, 91, 323–5, 331, 338–40
Brittany 3, 5, 34, 46, 51–3, 55, 58, 60, 72, 100, 104, 113, 153, 156, 344, 346
Brokdorf 76
Brönte sisters 331
Brussels 92, 107, 156, 160, 213–14, 223–6, 244, 351
Bucharest 17, 101, 251–3, 255–6, 260, 317
Bukovina 251–3, 258, 260–1, 264
Bulgaria 18, 102, 138–40, 262, 307, 309, 315–17, 319
Bunad 198
Burgundy 84, 213, 219, 221, 345
Buzdugan, Ion 260

Cadic, François 56
Calabria 90
Calatrava, Santiago 111
California 92
Calvo Sotelo, José 241
Cameron, David 338
Canada 339
Čanak, Nenad 313
Canary Islands 123, 159, 241
Cape Colony 88
Cardiff 336
Carlists 119, 123, 237, 240, 242
Carniola 32, 307
Castellón 2
Castile 45, 121, 124, 238, 241
Castilian *see* Spanish
Catalan language 2, 12, 28–31, 34–5, 344, 346
Catalan nationalism 1–2, 5, 9, 100, 121, 131, 157, 159, 238, 241, 244–5, 313, 335
Catalonia 1–2, 7, 15–16, 33, 37, 48, 51, 123–4, 151, 154, 159–60, 163, 237, 241, 245, 313, 344, 350
Cathleen Ní Houlihan 48–9
Catherine II 274, 279, 293
Cattaneo, Carlo 10, 154
Cauca 352
Ceaușescu, Nicolae 317
Celan, Paul 264
Cévennes 74
Ceynowa, Florjan 295
Champfleury, Jules 48
Channel Islands 325
Charles-Brun, Jean 3, 153, 238
Chechnya 278, 285
Chicago 101, 103
Chisinau 17
Choleau, Jean 53
Christian Social Union (CSU) 65–6, 158, 160
Cisleithania 31, 310
Civil society 73, 145, 235, 280, 302, 325–7, 329, 334, 339, 349
class conflict 51
Closson, Ernest 48
Cluj/ Koloszsvár/ Klausenburg 254, 256
Cold War 10, 36, 72, 95, 107, 129, 170, 185, 198, 291, 346–7
collectivization 94, 138–9, 257
Collins, Michael 329
Cologne 93, 180
Colombia 352
colonialism 17, 237, 247, 274
Communist Parties 10, 32, 56, 135, 138–9, 142–5, 162, 257, 261, 299, 314–16, 318–19, 346
communist regimes 13, 17, 94, 108, 138, 143–6, 151, 154, 169, 251, 257, 263, 317
composite monarchy 10, 18, 119
 state 275, 324

356

Index

Connolly, James 329
conservatism 285
consumption society 89–90
　mass 44, 51, 84, 91–2, 94, 236
Conwentz, Hugo 70–1
Copenhagen 105, 110, 162, 199
Cork 48
Cornish language 34, 324, 332
Cornish movement 337, 339
Cornwall 324, 331, 337–8
Corsica 158–9, 163, 239, 344, 346
Corsican nationalism 159, 163, 237, 243
Cosquin, Emmanuel 45–7
Costenco, Nicolai 260
Côtes-du-Nord 46
Cotswolds 72
Council of Europe 34
Covadonga, sanctuary of 126, 240
Cracow 295
Crimea 88, 92, 107, 263, 274, 285
Croatia 18, 69, 74, 101, 135, 143, 307, 309–11, 314, 319, 346–47
Cuisine 84–9, 308
　regional 54, 84, 85–6, 89–92, 94
cultural claims 3, 109
　heritage 2, 12, 14, 50, 68, 70, 84, 99, 109–22, 172, 178, 194, 196–7, 242, 260–1, 284, 347
　marker 154, 158, 226, 228
　regionalism 2, 8–9, 16–18, 32, 119, 122, 128, 135, 153, 169, 208, 237, 240, 242, 251, 254, 260, 301, 307, 317, 331, 334, 337, 339, 346, 351
cultural renaissance 28–9, 225, 334
Cyprus 92, 307, 318, 348
Czech language 71, 252
Czech movement 3, 9
Czechoslovakia 11, 14, 30, 32, 36, 70–2, 74, 95, 101, 135, 138, 141–2, 252, 263, 346–7

Dalecarlia 15, 101, 103, 194–6
Dalmatia 18, 309–11
Delarue, Paul 45
De Valera, Éamon 329
decentralization; territorial 8–9, 14, 16, 52, 54, 110, 139, 141–2, 153, 157–9, 161, 161, 163, 174, 180–1, 234, 235–37, 241, 243–5, 274–5, 320, 347, 350
　administrative 3, 151, 235, 237, 245, 308
　economic 14, 138, 146
　political 8–9, 16, 155, 214, 235
Decembrists 272, 274
decolonization 10, 16, 244, 283, 347
Delčev, Goce 316
democratization 33, 89, 131, 173, 183, 243
Denmark 16, 44, 89, 110, 199, 216, 218, 339
Destrée, Jules 224

devolution 14, 18, 122, 163, 236, 243, 263, 286, 324, 330–1, 334–9
Dewar, Donald 335
dialect 8, 12, 14, 27, 30–1, 33, 35–8, 47, 49, 52, 58, 76, 120, 122–3, 125, 127, 129, 152–3, 170–3, 180, 183, 185–7, 198, 200, 213, 216–17, 220–1, 224, 226, 239, 242, 251, 261, 282, 284, 297, 301, 208, 311, 316, 332, 334, 344, 346, 348
Diedenhoven, Jacques 226
Dienes, László 256
Diglossia 29
Diputación (Provincial Council) 123
Dobrudja 315
　Southern Dobrudja 252, 258
Dokuchaev, Vasilii 275
Drejer, Matts 202
Dresden 102, 173
Druță, Ion 262
Dual monarchy 15, 101, 109
Dubcek, Alexander 141–2
Dublin 44, 327, 329, 337
Dubrovnik 310
Duhamel, Maurice 53, 55
Dundas, Henry 327

ecology 13, 38, 66–7, 75, 110
economic stagnation 14, 142, 144, 185
ecotype 47, 50, 183
Edam 89
education 1, 6, 12, 27, 34, 37, 50, 129, 174, 183, 203, 207, 218–21, 225, 237, 245, 257, 259, 262–3, 279–80, 311, 325–6, 330, 334, 337, 344
　mass 27
Elmdon 58
Eminescu, Mihai 261
empire; Austro-Hungarian 5, 7, 15, 18, 31–2, 69–71, 76, 170, 174–5, 216, 252, 292, 295, 310–14, 317, 319, 328, 345
　German 17, 124, 173–5, 213, 222, 275, 293, 345
　Ottoman 5, 18, 253, 307, 314–17, 319, 343, 345
　Roman 120
　Russian 7, 17, 71, 197, 203, 258–9, 274–5, 279, 291–4, 317, 343
　Venetian 18, 307, 310, 318
England 18, 51, 56, 72, 84, 86, 90, 101, 216, 323–7, 330–1, 336–9
Englishness 51, 91, 325, 327
enlightenment 28, 99, 313, 280–2
Ermland (Warmia) 295
Estonia 12, 17, 43, 55, 146, 291–4, 296–300, 346, 348
Estonian language 30
Estonian movement 55, 297–8, 300
ethnicity 2, 4, 120, 176, 253, 316
Ethnie 8
ethnology 43, 48, 101

357

Index

ethnonationalism 4, 9, 121, 125–6, 152, 157, 162, 222, 237–8, 243–5, 276, 280–1, 296, 299, 308, 311, 316, 351
Eurasia 46
Euromaidan 263
European Bureau for Lesser Used Languages 12, 34
European Economic Community 93, 110, 347
European Union 1, 10, 13, 18, 34, 76, 83, 93, 95, 110, 151, 154, 161–2, 164, 198, 200, 202, 207–8, 251, 263, 301, 311, 320, 323, 332–3, 336–9, 347–8, 351
Euroregion 347
Extremadura 45, 126

Falange 120–1, 123–6, 129
Faroe Islands 207
Fascism 11, 14, 119, 122–3, 130–1, 186, 218, 239, 242
   Italian Fascism 14, 71, 104, 107, 120, 122, 125, 131
   Portuguese Fascism *see* Salazarism
   Spanish Fascism *see* Falange
Fatherland 15, 1001, 103, 174, 222, 253, 262, 285, 295
Faulkner, Brian 332
Fauriel, Claude 44
Federal Republic of Germany (FRG) *see* West Germany
federalism 9–10, 14, 17, 52, 121, 132, 153–4, 160, 163, 169–70, 174, 176, 178, 180–4, 186, 225, 237, 240, 244, 252, 272, 282, 285, 330, 349–50
Fédération Régionaliste de Bretagne 53
Fédération Régionaliste Française 3, 52
Feger, Otto 183
Fennoskandia 193, 204
Ferrari, Giuseppe 154
Fessenheim 75–6
Fianna Fáil 329
Fichte, Johann-Gottlieb 27
Finland 1, 12, 15, 43, 49, 103, 193–4, 196–7, 200–4, 207, 274–5, 293, 344, 346
   Finland Swedes 203–4
Fishman, Joshua 33
Fjord, Hardanger 110, 198
Flanders 7, 33, 45–7, 51, 53, 156, 160, 213, 215, 221–3, 225–6, 344, 346
Flemish (Dutch) language 163, 221–4, 344
Flemish movement 9, 16, 157, 163, 221–5, 227–8, 238
Florence 43, 100, 104
Formentera 76
Foster, Norman 111
France 1, 5, 10, 14, 16, 34, 34, 36, 45, 47–8, 50–3, 57, 69–70, 73–6, 83–4, 88, 90–4, 100, 105, 108, 110, 120–1, 128, 130, 153–4, 156, 158–9, 163, 174, 224–5, 233, 236–41, 243–4, 325, 344–5, 348, 350
Franche-Comté 52
Franco, Francisco 14, 120–1, 123–4, 241–4
Francoism 32, 119–30
Freiburg im Breisgau 75
French language 1–2, 11, 25, 27, 30, 33, 45, 47, 53, 55, 91, 175, 213, 221–5, 243, 343
French revolution 11, 26–7, 31, 326, 343
Friesland/Frisia 215–18, 221, 226
Frisian language 32, 179, 216–18
Frisian movement 102, 179, 216–19
Fritz, Jean-Marie 87
Fueros 123, 349

Gaelic language 29, 48–9, 328, 33
Gaelic League 49, 328
Gaeltacht 48–9, 328
Gagauz 262–3
Galicia (Eastern Europe) 32, 101, 258–9
Galicia (Iberian peninsula) 16, 28–9, 45, 51, 121, 159, 163, 237, 239, 241, 244–5, 344, 346
Galician language 2, 31
Galician nationalism 5, 121, 241, 244, 346
Gallen-Kallela, Akseli 197
Garibaldi, Giuseppe 51
Gau 119, 122, 130, 178
Gaughan, Dick 56
Gdansk 143, 301
Gezelle, Guido 221
Gehry, Frank 111
Gellner, Ernest 345
German Democratic Republic (GDR) *see* East Germany
German Reich *see* German empire
Germany 1, 6, 32, 45, 65–6, 69–70, 73–5, 84, 90, 95, 107–8, 110, 119–23, 125, 127–8, 129, 131, 135, 138, 144, 153, 158–9, 169–72, 174–6, 178–9, 182–3, 185–7, 217–18, 220, 223, 226–8, 255–6, 293, 296–8, 302, 346–8
   East Germany 36, 73, 138, 181, 186–7
   West Germany 108, 154, 160
Ghent 214, 221–2
Gibbon, Grassic 333
Gladstone, William 328
globalization 11–13, 25, 28, 33, 38, 83–4, 93, 187
Godmanis, Ivars 300
Goga, Octavian 256
Good Friday agreement 18, 332–3
Gorbachev, Mikhail
Gorizia 120, 122, 242
Gorky, Maxim 137
Gouda 89
Government of Wales Act 1998
Gran Paradiso park 71

358

Index

Gray, Alasdair 334
Great Blasket 49
Great Britain 18, 36, 44–5, 48, 51, 56, 69, 83, 108, 110, 138, 153, 159, 163, 174, 323–4, 337–9, 343, 350
Greece 18, 88, 94, 153, 217, 307, 316–18
Griffin, Roger 123
Griffith, Arthur 328
Grimm, Jakob; Wilhelm
Groningen 214, 217, 227
Guardamar 1
Guernica 127
Guernsey 324, 332
Guipúzcoa 123
Gunn, Neil 333

Habsburg 124, 175, 214, 253, 257–8, 264
  empire *see* Austro-Hungarian empire
Hainaut 46
Hajek, Egon 255
Halippa, Pan 260
Hamann, Johann-Georg 27
Hamburg 74, 104, 182
Hansen, Emil Christian 86
Hardy, Thomas 331
Harel, Marie 92
Haslinger, Peter 32
Hazelius, Artur 103, 194
Heimat 4, 6, 8, 15, 69, 71–3, 95, 121, 124–6, 130–1, 154, 169–70, 172–87, 196, 202, 223, 226, 293, 296, 302
  Heimatkunde 15, 176, 178, 185
Helikon 254–7
Helsinki 44, 197
Herder, Johann-Gottfried 27, 43–4, 47
heritage 2, 12, 14, 49–50, 68, 70, 84, 93, 95, 99–104, 109–11, 113, 120, 122, 125, 153–4, 172, 178, 194, 196–9, 206, 218, 236, 242, 260–1, 264, 299, 301, 346–7
Herpin, Eugène 58
Hersart de la Villemarqué, Henri 52
Hindeloopen 49, 102, 217
Hirn, Yrjö 197
Hitler, Adolf 14, 120–2, 125, 128, 178–9
Holland 84, 111, 213
Holocaust 264
Home Rule 9, 18, 123, 241, 243, 245, 324, 328, 330–1, 333–4, 339–40
Hooke, Robert 86
Horthy dictatorship 107
Hroch, Miroslav 193, 199, 255
Humboldt, Wilhelm von 27
Hungarian Autonomous Region (Transilvania) 257, 263
Hungarian language 102, 252, 254–6, 310

Hungary 310
Hüppauf, Bernd 173
Hyde, Douglass 49, 51, 55

Iadrintsev, Nikolai 279–80, 282
Iași 251–2
Ibsen, Henrik 49
identity; collective 4, 6, 11, 151, 161, 301, 343, 348, 351
  concentric 5, 8, 10, 152
  linguistic 11, 25–6, 34, 37–8
  local 5–6, 10, 16, 29–30, 33, 153–4, 202, 275, 308, 310, 349–50
  national 2–3, 5–6, 10, 33, 70, 91, 111, 121, 152–3, 156, 164, 175–6, 180–1, 198, 215, 226–7, 234–6, 239–40, 281, 295–6, 300, 308–10, 314, 316, 318–19, 325, 337, 348, 350
  regional 2–3, 5–7, 11, 13–15, 17–18, 26, 28, 31, 33, 34, 38, 57–9, 65–6, 70, 73–4, 76, 99–100, 103, 110–11, 113, 120–2, 125, 127, 129, 131, 136, 154, 156, 170, 173–5, 180–1, 183–4, 199, 202, 227, 233–5, 239–42, 245, 251, 271, 271–3, 276, 291–2, 294–5, 297, 308, 310, 312, 315–16, 318–19, 323, 343, 345–6, 348, 351–2
  subnational 2, 6–7, 10–11, 119, 202, 236, 238, 348–9, 352
  territorial 2–3, 6, 8, 99, 153–3, 158, 241, 343, 348–51
imperialism 19, 57, 123, 242, 348
Independence 1, 7, 9, 17, 33–4, 49, 121–2, 146, 156, 159, 193–95, 201, 203, 214, 221, 226, 259, 262–3, 275, 281, 284–5, 299–302, 310, 312–18, 324, 329, 331, 335–39
India 46, 102, 280, 352
Industrial Revolution 89, 100, 345
Ingria 278, 286
Ireland 17, 30, 32, 48–9, 72, 84, 109, 111, 153, 163, 323, 326–32, 338–9, 346
  Northern 17, 34, 159, 323–4, 328, 330–3, 338–9, 345
Irish Free State 49, 329
Irish Republican Army (IRA) 329, 331
Iron Curtain 36, 73–4, 131, 185, 346
Isle de Saint-Cast 46, 57–8
Isle of Man 324, 332
Istria 17, 307, 309–11, 320
Italian Unification 51, 102, 239
Italy 8, 15–16, 45, 50–1, 68, 70–1, 74, 88, 90, 94, 100, 104, 107, 110, 119–22, 125, 129, 131, 154, 156, 158–60, 174, 176, 233, 235–6, 238–9, 242–3, 345–8
  Northern Italy 15, 164
  Southern Italy 90, 239
Ivičević, Stipan 310
Īvāns, Dainis 298

359

Index

Jacobins 11, 26, 33, 153, 237
Jahn, Ulrich 103
Jersey 324, 332
Johnson, Tom 333
Juncker, Jean-Claude 1
Jüngst, Hugo 173
Jutland 48, 198

Kalevala 49, 196
Kamusella, Tomasz 301
Karelia 12, 15, 49, 103, 194, 196–8, 259, 278, 344
Kashubs 17, 295–6, 298, 301
Kazantzakis, Nikos 318
Kelman, James 334
Khrushchev, Nikita 136, 140, 144
Kiev 17, 263, 273, 275
Kietzdeutsch 12
King Albert 274
King Carol I 101
King Eric of Pomerania 194
King Ferdinand of Romania 260
King George IV 216–17, 329
King Gustav Vasa 101, 194–6
King Gustavus V 201
King Louis XVI 88
King Nikola 313
King Willem III 216–17, 226
Klaipėda (Memelland) 292
Kloss, Peter 30
Knirim, Joseph 92
Knuvelder, Gerard 220
Korfanty, Wojciech 295
Kosovo 307–8, 311–12, 344
Kostomarov, Nikolai 275
Kraus, Peter A. 27
Kristiania *see* Oslo
Kropotkin, Peter 279
Kurdistan 1
Kurland 291, 294

Lady Augusta Gregory 48
Laestadius, Lars Levi
Lafont, Robert 244, 347
Lambrechts, Lambrecht 46
Lampe, John 141
Landespatriotismus 7, 260, 344, 351
landscape 4, 8, 13, 43, 65–70, 72–7, 104, 107, 109–10, 120, 122, 125–9, 131, 170, 172, 176, 180, 185, 194, 198, 202, 204, 214, 219–20, 235, 240, 242, 345
language; national 12, 30, 36–318, 129, 198, 254, 260
  regional 12, 14, 25, 27, 30–8, 129, 221, 227, 241–2, 256, 346
  policy 32, 129, 200, 293
  standardization 12, 28, 221, 316

vernacular 13, 28, 43, 49, 87, 119
Languedoc 110
Lapland 101, 200
Larzac 75
Latin America 88
Latgale 291, 296
Latvia 17, 107, 146, 291–4, 296–300, 346
Le Berre, Léon 53
Le Braz, Anatole 52–3
Le Diberder, Yves 53, 55
League of Nations 175, 201
Leeuwarden / Ljouwert 102, 226–7
Le Goffic, Charles 53
Lega Nord see Northern League
Lehtola, Veli-Pekka 207
Leiden 11, 19, 89
Leningrad *see* Saint Petersburg
Lenin 137, 143–4, 276
Lentz, Michael 226–7
liberalism 131, 237, 241, 331
Libiez, Albert 46
Limburg 16, 46, 215, 219–21, 226–27, 346
Lithuania 17, 146, 292, 294–6, 299–301, 346
Liverpool 337–8
Livland 291, 293–4
Lloyd-George, David 330
localism 17, 19, 120–1, 131, 140, 160, 215, 220–1, 227, 241, 348, 350–1
Lochhead, Liz 334
Loire valley 51, 57
Lombardy 163
London 18, 44–5, 56, 100–1, 111, 323, 327, 330, 332–3, 338, 345
Lönnrot, Elias 49, 196
Löns, Hermann 173
Lorraine 45, 47, 51–2, 54, 58, 175
Low Countries 11, 16, 179, 213–15, 225, 227
Lübeck 169
Luțcan, Vasile 260
Luxembourg 1, 16, 105, 179, 213–15, 217, 225–7
Luxembourgish language 1, 226
Lviv / Lemberg 102
Lyon 57

Maastricht 215, 226–7
Maastricht Treaty 161
MacDiarmid, Hugh 333
Macedonia 18, 101, 139, 307, 309, 311, 315–19, 344–5
Machado Álvarez, Antonio 47, 51–2
Macpherson, James 43
Madách, Imre 256
Madeira 244
Madrid 92–3, 121, 159, 241, 345

Index

Mahendran, Kest 37
Malmö 110, 199
Malta 348
Manchester 338
Manea, Norman 263
Manias, Chris 48
Mann, Michael 338
Martin, Terry 276
Martynas, Jankus 296
Marxism 12, 27
Masaryk, Thomas G. 252
Masuria 295, 297
Maurras, Charles 240
McGuiness, Martin 332
McIlvaney, William 334
McLeish, Henry 335
Mebyon Kernow 337
Mediterranean region 13, 87, 186
  coast 13, 108, 111, 113
Meertens, Pieter J. 47, 217
Mein Kampf 121
Memelland 175, 292, 296
Menéndez-Pelayo, Marcelino 240
Meuse 46, 219, 227
Meyer, Anton 226
Mezzogiorno see Southern Italy
Miarka, Karol 295
Mickiewicz, Adam 295
middle-class 76, 102, 226, 234
Middle East 87, 308
Migration 28, 36, 46, 89, 163, 172, 186–7, 199, 216, 226, 264, 297–8, 300, 350
Milan 88
Mill, John Stuart 27
Millet, Jean-François 100
Millien, Achille 53
Milošević, Slobodan 145
Misirkov, Krste 316
Moe, Jørgen 44
Moesia 315
Moiseev, Ivan 278
Moldavia 251–2
Moldova 16–17, 251, 258–63, 307, 317
  Moldovan Autonomous Soviet Socialist Republic 258–60
  Moldovan Soviet Socialist Republic 260
Moldovan language 260–2
Moldovan movement 259
Monmouthshire 36
Montenegro 18, 307, 309, 313–15
Montiers-sur-Saulx 46
Moravia 101, 252, 258, 346
Morgan, Edwin 333
Moscow 17, 139–40, 261–2, 271, 273–4, 276–8, 280, 283–5, 294, 297–8, 300

Mother tongue 1, 11–12, 26, 29, 32, 35, 52
Müller, Herta 257
multilingualism 31, 263
Munich agreement 252
municipality 16, 121–3, 204, 213, 233, 241–2, 350
Münster 48, 108
Mura'vev, Nikita 274, 278
Mussolini, Benito 14, 71, 107, 120, 122, 125

Nairn, Tom 325
Naples 88
nation-building 2–6, 38, 50–1, 58, 100, 170, 172, 176, 194, 198–9, 202–3, 207, 215, 223, 235, 238–9, 242–3, 258, 262, 349, 351–2
national narrative 8–10, 48, 50, 58, 90–92, 123–5, 181, 184, 186, 195, 206, 233–5, 237, 240, 242, 251, 254, 300–1, 308, 311, 313, 316, 318, 348–9
National Socialism 45, 72, 95, 119, 125, 127, 130, 178, 185–6, 218, 256, 263, 346
nationalism; minority 4–5, 252, 323–5, 327, 339, 346, 351
  regionalized 8, 123, 234, 238
  state 131, 151, 155, 161, 163, 181, 234, 243
  substate 3–5, 9–10, 119–20, 130, 151, 159, 233–4, 236, 243, 327, 331, 349, 351
nature conservation 67, 74–75, 77
Naughtie, James 334
Navarre 123, 242
Nazi Germany 72, 87, 95, 107, 119, 122, 125, 127, 131, 138, 169, 177–9, 297, 346
Netherlands 16, 36, 49, 86, 102, 104, 179, 213–24, 226–8, 345–6
New Economic Mechanism (NEM) 142
New England 352
New Mexico 352
New World 27
Nigra, Costantino 45, 51
Nizhniy Novgorod 276
Nordic Region 193
Normandy 105
North America 88
Northern League 8, 159, 244, 347
Norway 15, 44, 49, 85, 89, 103, 193, 198, 204, 206–7, 334
Novgorod 271, 273, 275
Novorossiia 278–9
Novosil'tsev, Nikolai 274
Núñez Seixas, Xosé M. 178
Nuremberg 102, 108

Oblast 136, 272–3, 275–81, 283, 349
Occitan language 156, 344
Occitan movement 238, 240, 243, 347
Occitania 128, 240, 346
O'Kennedy, Molly 49

361

Index

Omel'chyk, Anatolii 285
Öresund 16, 110, 199
Orhid 110
Orkney 334
Oslo 44, 204
Ostrobothnia 203

Páal, Árpád 255
Paasi, Anssi 194, 201
Pǎduraru, Teodor 260
Padania 8, 158, 244, 347
Pallas, Peter Simon 88
Paradores de Turismo 105
Paris 12, 44, 49, 55–7, 69, 75, 102–3, 111, 196, 201, 254, 259
Parnell, Charles S. 328
particularism 12, 25–7, 33, 121, 215–16, 218–21, 228, 252, 313–14, 318
Passerini. Luisa 109
Pasteur, Louis 86
Patagonia 352
Patrimony 12, 83, 93–4, 100–1, 109, 113, 261
patriotism 7, 52, 54–5, 199, 216–17, 260, 262, 309, 313, 318–19, 344, 351
Pearce, Pádraig 328–9
Peig Sayers 49
Pentreath, Dolly 324
Persson, Fredrik 199
Petrović Njegoš, Petar II 313
Petseri 296
Picard, Max 182
Piedmont 51, 120
Pieniny national park 72
Pieters, Theophiel 46
Pinck, Louis 52
Pinon, Roger 46
Pirin Macedonia 139
Plaid Cymru 159, 336–7
Plantadis, Johannès 53–5
Plitvice 69, 74
Podnieks, Juris 300
Pohjanen, Bengt 200
Poland 14, 17, 72, 95, 103–4, 108, 135, 138–9, 141, 143, 145, 162, 175, 274–5, 279, 291–8, 301–2
Polish language 47, 127, 181, 291, 295–6
Pollution 13, 15, 67–8, 74
Pomerania 108, 194, 292, 298
Portugal 2, 8–9, 14, 16, 83–4, 94, 107, 120–1, 128, 130, 153, 233, 235, 238–40, 243–4
Postmodernism 2, 38, 110
Potanin, Grigorii 279
Pousadas 105
Prague 71, 101, 103, 111
Prague Spring 141
Preuß, Hugo 176

Primo de Rivera, José Antonio 121
Primo de Rivera, Miguel 32, 240–1
Provence 153, 345
Province 2, 10, 16–17, 45–6, 48–9, 52, 58, 73, 88, 120, 123, 126, 130, 137, 173, 214–21, 2234, 227, 233, 235, 237, 241, 245, 251–2, 254, 258–9, 264, 275, 277, 282, 291–4, 296, 308, 312–13, 317, 320, 343–4, 349
Provincialism 216, 218, 220
Prunskienė, Kazimiera 300
Prussia 70, 108, 121, 174–5, 177, 225, 275, 292
   East Prussia 17, 73–4, 127, 294–5, 297, 301
Puszta 103
Putin, Vladimir 262, 272–3, 277–8, 283, 285
Pyrenees 1

Quebec 1, 47
Queen Victoria 329
Queen Wilhelmina 216

Raphael, Lutz 177
Rasputin, Valentin 283, 285
Rebreanu, Liviu 256
Reed, John 137
Regeneracionismo 237–8
region, concept of 2–10, 103, 151, 309
region-building 4–6, 16, 154, 233, 235–6, 291, 348–9, 351–2
Regional council 139–40, 243
   government 1, 74, 159, 254, 273, 275
   movement 2, 7, 12, 15, 18, 32–3, 91, 109, 158, 160, 225, 238, 279, 295–6, 343–4, 346–7, 352
   particularism 48, 220, 319
regionalism; cultural 2, 8–9, 16–18, 32, 119, 122, 128, 135, 153, 169, 208, 237, 240, 242, 251, 254, 256, 260, 301, 307, 317, 331, 334, 337, 339, 346, 351
   political 2, 8, 15, 51–2, 72, 128, 136, 153, 179, 220, 228, 234, 238–40, 243–4, 301, 319, 339, 346–7, 351
regionalization 15, 131, 151–2, 155, 157–8, 160, 162–4, 238, 243, 272, 275
religion 8, 16, 43, 46, 50, 52, 57, 85, 124, 126, 129, 200, 213, 215, 219–20, 235, 283, 285, 294, 325–7, 330, 350–2
Renaixença 28–9
renaissance 99, 104, 236, 239
Republicanism 237, 240
Retallack, James 172
Revolt of the regions 11
Rexurdimento 29
Rhine 75, 174, 184, 219, 237
Rhinelands 69, 173–5, 179, 184, 186, 225
Riehl, Wilhelm-Heinrich 170, 172
Riga 293, 299

362

Risorgimento 122–3, 154, 235, 239, 242
Rivière, Georges H. 240
Rodina 8
Romania 16, 18–19, 101, 119, 138, 144–5, 217, 251–64, 307, 309, 312, 315–17, 319
    Old Kingdom of 252–3, 255
    Greater Romania 253–4, 257, 259, 317
Romanian language 32
Romanticism 12–13, 15, 26–7, 43–4, 45, 49, 68, 100, 112, 121, 131, 172–3, 194–6, 198, 203, 206, 238, 275, 286, 298, 328–9, 331, 333, 345
Rome 71, 100, 102, 120, 244, 271
Roos, Anna Maria 195
Roquefort 75, 93
Rosenberg, Alfred 122
Rossel, Eduard 277
Roussillon 1–2, 128, 240
Ruble, Blair 271
Rudorff, Ernst 69
Ruhr 110, 176, 345
Rural areas 13, 100, 111, 223, 344
    rurality 57, 107
Russia 11, 17, 49, 70, 85, 87, 95, 104, 135, 139–40, 144, 174, 196, 198, 201, 204, 206, 258–60, 263, 271–85, 291, 293–4, 296, 299, 325
    Russian Soviet Federated Socialist Republic 140, 146
Russian language 30, 32, 263, 278, 293, 297–8, 300
Russification 32, 258, 261, 293–4

Saarinen, Eliel 197
Saarland 175, 178
Sadoul, Charles 53
Saint-Étienne 57
Saint Petersburg 276, 278, 293–4
Sainte-Menehould 88
Salazarism 14, 120–1, 128, 130, 240, 243
Samarin, Iurii 293
Santander 236
San Sebastián 236
Sápmi 207
Sardinia 16, 120, 131, 156, 159, 235, 239, 242, 244
Sardinian movement 4, 9, 33, 122, 130, 154, 246
Saussure, Ferdinand de 25
Savisaar, Edgar 300
Saxons (Transylvania) 111, 253–7
Saxony 105
Scandinavia 11, 15, 102, 153, 193–4, 196, 198–9, 202, 204, 207–8
Scania 15–16, 198–9, 202, 207
Schirren, Carl 293
Schlegel, August 27
Schlegel, Wilhelm 27
Schneider, Reinhold 184
Schultze-Naumburg, Paul 173

Schumacher, Fritz 104
Scotland 1, 15, 18, 72, 100, 109, 151, 154, 157, 159, 163, 198, 323–40, 343–5, 350
    Highlands 48–72, 216–17, 329, 333, 344–5
Scott, Walter 329
Scottish nationalism 151, 159, 163, 326–8, 333–6, 339
Sébillot, Paul 45
Secession 9, 17, 163–4, 201, 215–16, 219, 225, 252, 275, 277, 312–13, 329, 346
Seehofer, Horst 65
Seignobos, Charles 3
Sejny 301
self-government 8–9, 137, 156–7, 160, 163–4, 218, 241, 245, 253, 275, 281, 330, 333, 336, 339, 347
Semenov Tian-Shanskii, Petr 275
Serbia 143, 145, 251, 307–17, 319
Serbian language 30
Serres, Olivier de 87
Seville 103–4
Sharapov, Sergei 272, 275, 278
Shchapov, Afanasi 279–80
Sheffield 338
Shetland 334
Sibelius, Jean 197
Siberia 17, 136, 146, 272, 274, 279–86
Sicily 51, 90, 120, 156, 159, 236, 243
Silesia 101, 251, 292, 297–8, 301
    Upper Silesia 17, 175–6, 295–7, 345
Sinn Féin 328, 332
Sjælland 110, 199
Skåne 110, 199
Slavonia 309–10
Slovak language 252
Slovakia 71, 73, 77, 141, 251–2, 330, 346
Slovenia 70, 74, 145–6, 307
Smith, Anthony D. 8
Social Democrats 6, 169, 195, 219, 224, 313
socialism 139, 141, 301, 319
Socialist Revolutionaries 136
sociolect 27
solidarity (union) 143, 145
Sörlin, Sverker 206
South Africa 88
South America 84, 93
sovereignty 1, 5, 8–9, 44, 70, 151, 157, 225, 234, 245, 252, 263, 276–7, 281, 300, 325, 339, 348, 351
Soviet Union 6, 14, 17, 32, 36, 95, 107, 135, 137–8, 140, 142–4, 146, 181, 197–8, 251, 259–63, 271, 275–6, 278, 281–2, 292, 297–300, 317, 348
    republics 14, 262
Soviet Writers' Union 261
Spain 1, 3, 9–10, 16, 30, 32, 51, 83, 94, 100, 107–8, 110, 119–21, 123–6, 128, 130–1, 154, 156, 159,

Index

163, 216, 233, 236–41, 243–5, 344, 346, 348, 350
Spanish language 30, 119, 121, 129, 238
Sremac, Stevan 311
Stalin, Josef 6, 14, 17, 32, 95, 136–9, 144, 260–1, 298
Stanković, Borisav 311
state centralism 3, 17, 69, 153–4, 162, 221, 227, 237, 252
statehood 32, 162, 292, 299, 301, 309–10, 313–14, 318–19, 323–5, 343
Stavenhagen, Kurt 176
Stelvio national park 71
Stere, Constantin 260
Stevenson, Robert Louis 333
Stockholm 103, 194–5, 199
Storost-Vydunas, Wilhelm 296
Strogatz, Steven H. 36
Stuttgart 75
subsidiarity principle 193, 244, 320
Suceava 252, 264
Sudetenland 181, 258
Sundblom, Julius 201–2
Svart, Peder 195
Swabia 125, 174, 185, 346
Switzerland 15, 37, 44, 69, 71–2, 83–4, 89, 105, 169–70, 174, 176, 179, 214, 263, 281, 346
Synge, John M. 48
Szeklers 253, 255

Taldir-Jaffrenou, François 53
Tallinn 299, 302
Tatarstan 277–8, 285
Tatra mountains national park 70, 72, 74, 104
Tees Valley 338
Telemark 15, 103, 198, 344
Temesvár/Timisoara 253, 255, 257
Teruel 127
Thatcher, Margaret 334, 336
Thiesse, Anne-Marie 8
Third Reich *see* Nazi Germany
Thoms, William 43
Tito (Josip Broz) 14, 138–9, 143, 145, 257
Tommaseo, Niccolò 310
Tone, Wolf 326
Top, Stefaan 45
Torne Valley 15, 198, 200–1, 204, 207
Torremolinos 108
tradition(s); invented
traditionalism 52
Transleithania 31
Transnistria 17, 258–9, 261–2
Transylvania 17–18, 32, 49, 101, 110–11, 251–8, 263, 317, 320, 344–5

Treaty; of Versailles 177
 of Madrid 83
Trentino-Alto Adige 156, 159, 243
Trewerin 35
Triglav 74
Trotsky, Leon 136
Trubeck, Amy 91
Tuđman, Franjo 310
Tunisia 83
Turin 88
Turkey 36, 101, 307–8, 318
Tuscany 88, 113, 345
Tver province 137, 271, 276
Tyrol 216, 344–5
 South Tyrol 71, 77, 113, 120, 122, 131, 154, 156, 159, 163, 243–4, 344

Ukraine 135, 140, 259, 261, 264, 272, 278, 285, 346–47, 350
Ulmanis regime 107
Ulster *see* Northern Ireland
Umbach, Maiken 173
UNESCO 34, 69, 109
Unionist nationalism 259–60, 328–9, 332
Union of Soviet Socialist Republics *see* Soviet Union
Union Régionaliste Brétonne 52
United Kingdom *see* Great Britain
United Principalities 251
United States of America 89, 136, 138, 284, 332, 346, 352
Universal Declaration of Linguistic Rights 12, 34

Vaida-Voievod, Alexandru 254
Valencia (province) 2
Valencia (region) 2, 241–2
Valencian dialect 2, 129
Vallée, François 53
Van Leeuwenhoekkou, Antoni 86
Vázquez de Mella, Juan 240
Veneto 163
Venezia-Giulia 243
Vichy France 14, 120–1, 128, 130, 240–1
Vienna 101, 181, 256
Vienna Arbitration (Second) 256
Viipuri/Viborg/Vyborg 197
Vilnius/Wilno 292, 297, 299, 301
Vimoutiers 92
Vineyards 85, 87–8, 92
Vojvodina 18, 312–13, 317, 320, 344
Volksgeist 104, 107, 294, 345
Volksgeschichte 123–4
Volkslieder 43–4
von Gaal, Georg 44

Index

von Rezzori, Gregor 264
von Sydow, Carl 47
Voralberg 101, 176
Voskuil, J. J. 47

Wallace, William 329
Wales 18, 35–6, 48, 110, 157, 159, 163, 323–5, 327, 330–2, 336–7, 339–40, 344, 346
Wallachia 251, 317
Wallonia 16, 156, 213, 224–5
Walloon dialect 216
Walloon movement 9, 16, 224–5
Wark, Kirsty 334
Warsaw 108, 139, 274
Warsaw Pact 135, 252
Weber, Eugen 3, 233
Weibull, Martin 199
Weimar Constitution 32
Weimar Republic 15, 121–2, 130, 175–8, 185–6
Welfare state 18, 99, 160, 195, 200, 281–2, 325, 333
Welsh language 12, 18, 30, 34–6, 330–1
Welsh nationalism 18, 330, 336–40
Wendish 127
West Midlands 338
Wilson, Woodrow 346
Wine 13, 83, 86–8, 92–3, 256, 345
Wohmann, Gabriele 185

Word War First 5, 12, 17, 30–1, 55, 66, 68, 70–1, 85, 91, 95, 105, 153–4, 175, 220, 239, 252–3, 257, 259, 291–6, 310–11, 313–14, 316–17, 328, 333, 345–6, 351
  Second 10, 12, 15, 28, 33, 50, 55–7, 72, 85, 87, 94–5, 107, 111, 113, 135, 138, 152–7, 161, 163–4, 195–7, 222, 256, 282, 292, 297, 310, 312, 314, 316–17, 346
Worker's councils 14, 135, 137, 139–43, 145
working class 56, 68, 107, 135, 137, 139, 141, 143, 145, 224, 257, 299, 326, 332, 337
Wyhl 75–6, 185

Yeats, William Butler 48, 51, 55, 328
Yekaterinburg 276–7
Yeltsin, Boris 146, 273, 283
Yorkshire 18, 91, 216, 331, 336, 339
Yugoslavia 11, 14, 36, 47, 108, 110, 135, 138–9, 141–6, 257, 263, 310–16, 319–20, 347

Zágoni, István 255
Zagreb 310
Zaunert, Paul 45
Zeeland 215, 217, 346
Zillich, Heinrich 255–6
Zuiderzee 49, 217